D1796897

ICCA
CONGRESS SERIES NO. 11

INTERNATIONAL ARBITRATION CONFERENCE
LONDON, 12-15 MAY 2002

KLUWER LAW INTERNATIONAL
The Hague/London/New York

INTERNATIONAL COUNCIL
FOR COMMERCIAL ARBITRATION

INTERNATIONAL COMMERCIAL ARBITRATION:

IMPORTANT CONTEMPORARY QUESTIONS

GENERAL EDITOR: ALBERT JAN VAN DEN BERG

with the assistance of the
International Bureau of the
Permanent Court of Arbitration
The Hague

A C.I.P. Catalogue record for this book is available from the Library of Congress.

ISBN 90-411-2219-2

Published by Kluwer Law International,
P.O. Box 85889, 2508 CN The Hague, The Netherlands.
sales@kluwerlaw.com
http://www.kluwerlaw.com

Sold and distributed in North, Central and South America
by Aspen Publishers, Inc.
7201 McKinney Circle, Frederick, MD 21704, USA

Sold and distributed in all other countries
by Turpin Distribution Services Limited,
Blackhorse Road, Letchworth, Herts,
SG6 1HN, United Kingdom

Printed on acid-free paper

Preface

ICCA Congress Series No. 11 comprises the proceedings of the ICCA London Congress 2002 hosted by the Chartered Institute of Arbitrators on 12-15 May 2002. A warm word of thanks and congratulations goes to the Chartered Institute for the outstanding organization of this well-attended Congress, in particular, for opening to the participants the magnificent London venues of the Great Hall of the Royal Court of Justice, the Inner Temple, the British Museum and the Guildhall.

The Congress departed from the earlier format of simultaneous Working Groups and assembled more than 500 participants to hear about and discuss important contemporary questions in international commercial arbitration. The Congress opened with an innovation, a Debate on the proposition: "The parties, not the arbitrators, control the arbitration" chaired by Henri Alvarez. For the motion were Professors Hans Smit and Gabrielle Kaufmann-Kohler and against the motion were Lord Mustill and Sally Fitzgerald. A brief account of the debate can be found in the wonderfully humorous summary of the proceedings in Johnny Veeder's "Postscript" at the end of this volume (pp. 471-480). The remainder of the program focused on Contemporary Questions, following a more traditional panel format. The first topic was the current work of UNCITRAL on three timely issues, the requirement of a written form for an arbitration agreement, interim measures of protection and the model law on conciliation, all three sessions chaired by Jernej Sekolec, Secretary of UNCITRAL. The third issue was framed in terms of a question: "Do we need a model law of conciliation?" and it has been answered affirmatively by UNCITRAL which, shortly after the Congress, on 28 June 2002, approved the Model Law on International Commercial Conciliation. The text of the Model Law is appended to the article by Dr. Shavit Matias on this subject (pp. 288-299). This was followed by panels on "aspects of illegality in the formation and performance of contracts and in the conduct of arbitration" and "the detection of forgery and fraud". These panels were chaired by Jan Paulsson, and Julian Lew led the discussion. The Congress then moved on to "the psychological aspects of dispute resolution", chaired by Cecil Abraham, followed by "arbitration under investment treaties", chaired by Nigel Blackaby.

Another new aspect of this Congress was the call for papers and we would like to thank Cecil O.D. Branson, Q.C., Christopher R. Drahozal and Christoph Liebscher for their contributions which we have included in this volume (pp. 163-178, pp. 179-189 and pp. 300-313, respectively).

Looking ahead, the next ICCA Conference will be held in Beijing, China, on 16-18 May 2004, organized by the China International Economic Trade Arbitration Commission (CIETAC). Updated information on the Conference, as it becomes available, will be posted on the ICCA website at www.icca-arbitration.com with a link to CIETAC.

I would also like to express my continuing appreciation to the International Bureau of the Permanent Court of Arbitration in providing invaluable assistance to the ICCA publications and to thank the Secretary-General, Mr. Tjaco T. van den Hout, not only for making the facilities of the PCA available to ICCA, but also for agreeing to address us at this ICCA Congress (pp. 11-15).

The compilation and editing of this volume have been carried out by Dssa. Silvia

Borelli, Ms. Heather Kurzbauer, Ms. Alice Siegel and Mr. Theodore Mercredi, all under the able supervision of Ms. Judy Freedberg as managing editor. I would like to thank them all, as without each of their unique contributions, the editing of this volume would not be possible.

Prof. Albert Jan van den Berg
General Editor

TABLE OF CONTENTS

Welcome Address: Karen Gough
President, Chartered Institute of Arbitrators

My Lords, distinguished guests, ladies and gentlemen. On behalf of the Chartered Institute of Arbitrators it is my very great pleasure and a privilege to welcome you to London for the XVIth biannual ICCA Congress. I have spent many hours thinking about what it is I wanted to say to you this evening. I have looked at many quotations and books of wit and wisdom concerning dispute resolution, law and justice and wondered why I should find it so difficult to decide on a suitable address.

By way of example of my difficulty, and for your amusement, I found a quotation that was attributed to John Adams (the second President of the United States), who is said to have commented, "I have come to the conclusion that one useless man is called a disgrace, two such men are called a law firm, and three or more become a Congress!" In the context of what I was seeking to achieve here this evening, by way of a welcome to such an eminent gathering, that quote was, as we would say here in London, not "helpful"– and of course, as a lawyer, I could not help but note that even 200 and more years ago, there was even then, a strong desire to shoot the lawyers! However, in the last day or two the real reason for my difficulty has come to me. It is not necessary for me to search for authoritative words of divine wisdom or understanding to underpin my greeting to you all.

My message this evening is very, very simple and very clear. It is with great pride that the Chartered Institute of Arbitrators accepted the task of hosting this XVIth ICCA Congress in 2002. ICCA more than any other international non-governmental organization has led the intellectual debate concerning the development of modern techniques for the resolution of international commercial disputes. The Chartered Institute of Arbitrators, while based in London, is also an international non-governmental organization – which has led the world in the promotion of dispute resolution through its education and training programmes. What we have therefore, here in London in 2002, is a unique collaboration between two remarkable organizations dedicated to the same strategic objectives.

And what makes this occasion even more special is each of you. You the participants, who have gone to the time, trouble and expense, to journey to London from sixty different countries throughout the world to participate in this Congress. The topics for debate in 2002 reflect the concerns of the business community which we serve – through the provision of our diverse services in connection with the resolution of their disputes – either through international commercial arbitration, or other forms of dispute resolution

It was Plato who said, "no law or ordinance is mightier than understanding". At this Congress, we propose to consider important contemporary questions affecting international commercial arbitration and to ask ourselves whether indeed, as currently proposed by the working group constituted by UNCITRAL, the world needs a Model Law on Conciliation. Our task is to show the users of our services that we have not congregated here to engage in a festival of self-congratulation which has neither impact nor relevance to their businesses or the disputes which they need us to work with them to resolve.

While the questions may be contemporary, the issues for the business community are not new. How do we, in the twenty-first century, afford the business community processes for the resolution of their disputes that are at the same time, fair, expeditious, simple and cost effective? If, over the course of the next three days, we can improve our overall understanding of these issues and we can come to some conclusions that assist in the achievement of this overriding objective, we will have had a successful congress.

The challenge is to ensure that international commercial arbitration and ADR do not become like the Killy-Loo bird. The Killy-Loo bird is a creature which insisted on flying backwards because it did not care where it was going but it was mightily interested in where it had been!

So with this simple message, I welcome each and every one of you to this great debate. My hope is that you enjoy the stimulus of the challenging speeches and arguments and that you will, as ever, meet new and interesting people, make new friends and renew old friendships in the course of your stay here in London. And finally, since all work and no play is known to make Jack and Jill incredibly dull people – don't forget to enjoy yourselves! On behalf of the Chartered Institute of Arbitrators, I welcome you all.

Welcome Address Opening Ceremony: Fali S. Nariman
President, International Council for Commercial Arbitration

My Lords, Excellencies, ladies and gentlemen, I am happy to welcome you all to the 16th ICCA Congress held in the great metropolis of the commercial world. The only reason British commercial law continues to enjoy regard and respect in countries abroad is because of the quality of its judges, their sensitivity to legitimate commercial needs and their receptiveness to new legal instruments and concepts fashioned to serve those needs. As an American professor once told Lord Wilberforce, "The elegance, the style, and analytical powers of the British Judges have survived the decline of the British Empire." And we are privileged to have heard this evening two of the most outstanding judges of our time. By their presence and their words they have not only honoured ICCA, they have done more: They have given international commercial arbitration the recognition it richly deserves.

Commercial arbitration has moved significantly in the direction of becoming an aspect of public law. Private dispute resolution is no longer a private matter, it is one that affects the public good. International commercial arbitration exists not because it is cheap, nor because it is always necessarily quicker than court procedures, but often simply because there is no other choice.

Nearly ten years ago at the centenary celebration of the LCIA in London, Judge Howard Holtzmann and Judge Stephen Schwebel (who are with us here at this Congress) had suggested the creation of a new international court that would take the place of municipal courts in resolving disparities concerning the enforceability of international arbitral awards. But, these learned friends were tilting at windmills and like Don Quixote in "The Man of La Mancha", they were dreaming "the impossible dream"!

Ten years on we are still a distant dream away from an International Arbitration Court. In an imperfect international world then, where there is no universally applicable law, and no international forum for enforcement of foreign awards, arbitrators have to do their best. And England is fortunate in having judges who help along arbitrators who do their best.

I have often wondered about the utility of a President of an organization like ICCA: it only meets once in two years in what we call a "Conference", and then every four years in what we call a "Congress". There is of course legal justification for the office of President of ICCA, a body cannot be seen to function without a head. So, once in four years when we hold a congress, we change the head. I have been more fortunate than some of my predecessors because after the ICCA Congress in Vienna, when I first assumed this office, they just forgot to change the head at the Congress in Paris four years later. Thus, I have had two terms as President.

To have gone on for a third term is just not given to ordinary mortals. There is that delightful story about the swearing-in of an extraordinary personality, Franklin Roosevelt, as President of the United States for the third time. Chief Justice Charles Hughes who administered the oath of office later confided in a friend that he had an impish desire to break the solemnity of the occasion by telling the President, "Frank, don't you think this is getting a trifle monotonous?"

3

I will spare you a recitation of what I did during my two terms as President – not so much out of fear as to what someone else might complain I did not do, but more because of what a former Chief Justice of the New York State Court of Appeals told his audience some years ago when inaugurating a function of the International Bar Association in New York. He told us when he was first appointed Chief Justice of that hallowed Court he proudly showed his wife the room of Justice Benjamin Cardozo, his most illustrious predecessor in office. And he said to his wife in reverent tones, "See, this is Cardozo's room, this is where, I will sit." And his wife replied, not very reverently: "Yes, and after fifty years and five more Chief Justices it will still be Cardozo's room!"

Alas I could not show my wife any room when I was first elected ICCA President, simply because ICCA has no office; in fact it has no place of abode. It is an amorphous organization that materializes from out of nowhere at each conference and at each congress and so it has been for nearly fifty long years.

This morning's London Times carried in one of its supplements, a fascinating article about the great Picasso-Matisse Exhibition at the Tate Modern. The writer said of Matisse that he had "the ability to do nothing much, slowly". It is an unflattering but not accurate description of the work of ICCA. As someone said at our Council meeting this morning we are not "missionaries of arbitration" but a body that has from the beginning set itself the task of "disseminating the culture of arbitration". I do like to think that the culture of arbitration has gone forward a little during my two terms of office.

But I must frankly say that just as some countries get along *because* of what their governments do, and a few pull through *despite* what their governments do, so it has been with ICCA for these eight long years. ICCA, you see, is a self-propelled organization and gets along quite splendidly without much effort on the part of its President. This is of course because of ICCA's flagships, its publications: the *Yearbook* and the *Handbook*. They are our badge of fame. They were the indefatigable brain child of Pieter Sanders, our Honorary President, the father of the New York Convention who is here with us and whom I am delighted to welcome. The *Yearbook* has been carried to new heights by its General Editor Albert Jan van den Berg and the *Handbook* likewise by Jan Paulsson. For some years now the fact that the publications continue to be compiled is due to the single-minded devotion of Judy Freedberg, Managing Editor. She and her colleagues have kept the good ships afloat and they all continue to bring great credit to ICCA.

If it is known at all, ICCA then is known because of its *Yearbook* and *Handbook*. It is also known because of the glittering tycoons of arbitration that we manage to assemble at our gathering every two years in different parts of the world aided and advised almost always by sponsors. The sponsor of this, the 16th London Congress, is the prestigious Chartered Institute of Arbitrators much older than ICCA, of First World War vintage and still growing from strength to strength.

I said that ICCA works on the self-perpetuating principle, but this is somewhat of an exaggeration. It only appears to do so principally because of its unobtrusive but extraordinarily efficient, Secretary-General, my dear friend and comrade in arms, Ulf Franke, who is the factotum in charge of its entire administration.

Some of our colleagues here and abroad have questioned the utility of ICCA conferences of the type that we keep staging. "What does one learn from such a conference?" the more studious are accustomed to ask. The not-so-studious look for detailed information on free tickets and free social events! About the first, there is that touching story of a Master of Zen Buddhism who invited one of his students over to his house for afternoon tea. They talked for a while and then the time came for tea. The teacher poured the tea into the student's cup. Even after the cup was full, he continued to pour. The cup overflowed and the tea spilled out onto the floor. Finally, the student said, "Master you must stop pouring, the tea is overflowing from the cup." And the teacher wisely replied, "That's very observant of you. And the same is true with you. If you are to receive any of my teachings, *you must first empty out what you have in your mental cup.*"

I like to think that each one of us attends every ICCA conference and congress with our respective mental cups full to the brim. Some of us leave such conferences with the chastening thought that what we knew was not *all* there is to know. Some others leave these conferences having acquired the ability to unlearn what they thought they knew. "Emptying, and then filling the mental cup", that in the end is why we hold Conferences and Congresses.

There is another organization – a truly international one – that functions out of this great city. Recently it also celebrated its fortieth birthday as ICCA did not long ago. It is called Amnesty International (Amnesty). The story of the forty years of Amnesty has been compiled in a book, *Like Water on Stone.* I read a review of this book in The Economist. It said that Amnesty had made mistakes, some terrible mistakes in the past, but, and I quote, "Like water dripping on the stone, it is slowly changing the world." I like to think of ICCA in the same way – except that we cannot be accused of making mistakes, since we don't do too much. Perhaps we can be faulted for not doing more. But all in all, ICCA too is like water dripping on the stone, the edifice in stone of international arbitration and slowly but hopefully changing the arbitral world. With these few words, I once again welcome you all to this XVIth ICCA Congress.

Opening Address: Fali S. Nariman
President, International Council for Commercial Arbitration

Last month in an international newspaper there was a cartoon showing the Dove of Peace at a job centre, the bird looking disheveled and out of sorts. The Dove of Peace tells the man in charge at the job centre, "I need a career change. I'm getting nowhere in my current job." And the man in charge says, "Why not try *arbitration?*" And that is precisely what we are all going to explore today and tomorrow and till lunch on Wednesday.

The arbitral world is changing – at hell-neck speed as Lord Woolf reminded us last evening. For those of you who are as old as I am, my advice is *think young*. Don't behave like that old man, who had lived a long time. He was asked on his ninetieth birthday, "Have you seen many changes in your life?" and his response was, "Yes, and I was against every one of them!"

I have been often asked the question, "How do I become a good arbitrator?" There are two answers to this: first a serious one, and then the not-so-serious. The serious one goes back in time. Long, long ago, it was the Buddha who prescribed, with prescient wisdom, five principles that must be observed by a wise ruler when resolving disputes amongst his subjects. This is how they have been recorded in a book on the *Teaching of Buddhish*.[1]

> "First, examine the truthfulness of the facts presented; second, ascertain that they fall within his jurisdiction; third, enter into the mind of the parties to the disputes so that the judgment to be rendered be a just one; fourth, pronounce the verdict with kindness, not harshness; and fifth, judge with sympathy."

The modern-day international arbitrator, whether he hails from the East or the West, whether his cultural background be from the First World or the Third World, cannot go wrong if he follows these five principles laid down more than 2,000 years ago. And now, the not-so-serious, almost flippant answer. When God made the world he heard cries of protest. First came the moon with her complaint, "You have made the sun shine brighter than me and reduced me to second fiddle in the firmament." And the good Lord said, "O.K., I will make the tides flow to your command and lovers to sing praises of you and poets to write poetry about you." Exit moon satisfied.

Then came Switzerland, with a strong protest, "You have given us snow and mountains but no sea. You have surrounded us by land masses all round. We have no identity, no status." And the good Lord said, "O.K., I will make you a tourist paradise. In your country you will make watches and have peace conferences and you will never be at war." Exit Switzerland satisfied.

Then there entered groups of quarrelsome guys, most of them in black coats. They complained to God that they had no fixed place of abode, "We have no status, we have

---

1. Published by the Buddhist Promotions Foundations (Bukhyo Dendo Kyokai) 3-14 Shiba, 4 Chome Minato-ku, Tokyo, Japan.

no identity", they complained. And God said, "I will give you status, I will give you identity – I will make each one of you international arbitrators!"

One piece of advice to speakers who are not listed in the programme. If you feel compelled to make a comment or ask a question, always recall what the President of the Spanish Association of Arbitrators told a gathering such as this at the ICCA Congress in Hamburg in 1982: "If what is good is brief – it is twice as good."

And now a last bit of advice, to chairpersons at our sessions. We keep learning from other cultures. For instance, a question that has perplexed us for generations has been resolved by an ancient culture emanating from the African continent. How to pry long-worded speakers away from the podium without breaking their fingers? The answer is simple and effective. Speakers can speak as long as they like so long as they do so standing *on one foot*; when doing this, if the other foot falls, so does the curtain and the bell must ring. My other foot is about to fall and it is time to close.

Tribute to Sir Michael Kerr

Fali S. Nariman[*]

This is, I believe, the first conference held about International Commercial Arbitration anywhere in the world, since Sir Michael Kerr died. And it is but appropriate that we commence today's proceedings by paying tribute to a fine judge, a great arbitrator and a noble human being. He was, as you all know, a father figure of international arbitration, the founder and first President of the London Court of International Arbitration. My wife and I have had the privilege to know Michael and Diana Kerr for many years.

Just a month before he passed away, a Japanese corporation consulted me through their attorneys in New Delhi as to whether an international arbitral award rendered by Sir Michael Kerr as an umpire in a dispute between a Japanese corporation and an Indian corporation under our old arbitration law was a valid award. The award had been set aside by two judges of the Bombay High Court for an error of law. I opined, it was and advised an appeal to the Supreme Court. Strangely, the very day I got the news of Michael's death, the appeal came up on board for admission in the highest Court and it did not take much argument to convince the judges that the Bombay High Court was wrong and Michael Kerr was right. The admission of this appeal gave me great personal solace and satisfaction: it was difficult to fault Michael Kerr on an interpretation of law or on appreciation of facts. But even when he occasionally erred, he was noble, upright and gracious.

In the millennium issue of the London Times, 1 January 2000, William Rees-Mogg, a regular contributor, gave his memories of the century that went before. He described a visit to Hong Kong and dinner with the Pattens at Government House. Rees-Mogg took a taxi back to his hotel and the Chinese taxi driver made the following comment about the last representative of the Queen in Hong Kong:

"He was a *good* governor even when he was wrong."

This is an appropriate epitaph for any international figure – including Sir Michael Kerr whose death we mourn. A great old oak has fallen and the forest of international arbitration will not be the same, not for a very long time. May his soul rest in peace.

I would ask you all to rise and pay tribute for a couple of minutes to the memory of Sir Michael Kerr.

---

[*] President, International Council for Commercial Arbitration.

Luncheon Address: The Influence of International Commercial Arbitration on the Permanent Court of Arbitration

*Tjaco T. van den Hout**

I am honored to have the opportunity to address you as the final speaker at this enriching event.

When you represent an old institution, as I do, an historical aside seems an appropriate beginning to a speech and passing in front of Christie's auction house the other day supplied me with one. Seeing Christie's reminded me of a recent auction of a Fabergé egg. I believe it was called the "Winter Egg". It appeared to be covered in frost and glistening with ice crystals.

Sadly for me, the bidding went a few thousand times beyond what I had budgeted for my daughter's Easter present, but I could not help but notice the numerous parallels between the egg and my institution: the Permanent Court of Arbitration (PCA). Both are a century old, both have elegant outward appearances (one encrusted in diamonds, one housed in the Peace Palace), and both are subjects of interest in international commerce: one as a luxury commodity and one as a service provider in dispute resolution.

The closest parallel, however, is that each owes its existence to a Russian Czar. We all know that Czar Nicholas II commissioned Easter eggs from the French jeweler Fabergé, but fewer of you may know that it was in fact the same Czar who called the First Hague Peace Conference of 1899 where the convention founding the PCA was signed. At the time, the hope was that this first global mechanism for dispute resolution would put an end to military conflict between States.

In view of twentieth-century history, I can only say that the Czar failed miserably in this respect.

But arbitration, the main mechanism proposed to States by the PCA, is a tool for pragmatists. The twentieth century was to a large extent, however, a time of ideologues and nationalists. The PCA was therefore ahead of its time: it proposed an efficient mechanism for dispute resolution in an era when the governments of too many countries still subscribed to the "might makes right" school of international relations.

In contrast, international business leaders have often been the most pragmatic players on the international scene, seeking efficient resolution of their disputes without indulging in national chauvinism. This would explain why the international business community has, since the early days of the PCA, called upon the institution to step beyond its original treaty mandate in inter-State disputes and begin providing services in international commercial disputes.

The PCA declined to venture beyond inter-State disputes until 1935. In that year, the PCA was requested to put its services at the disposal of an arbitral tribunal constituted to resolve a contract dispute between the Chinese government and an American

---

*   Secretary-General, Permanent Court of Arbitration, The Hague.

company, Radio Corporation of America. In order to do so, the Secretary-General sought and received the approval of the PCA's Administrative Council, composed of representatives of all of the parties to the PCA's founding conventions.

Based on this precedent and the increasing interaction between States and non-State parties, the PCA promulgated its Rules for Arbitration and Conciliation for Settlement of International Disputes Between Two Parties of Which Only One Is a State in 1962. Although 1935 and 1962 were critical moments in the history of the PCA, it was UNCITRAL's adoption of Arbitration Rules in 1976 that brought the greatest demand for PCA services from the commercial arbitration world.

These ad hoc rules were meant to allow proceedings to be conducted without the involvement of an arbitration institution, but some mechanism was needed to safeguard the constitution of the arbitral tribunal. The drafters of the UNCITRAL Rules solved this problem by means of a designated "appointing authority" which may appoint arbitrators when parties fail to act or decide challenges against arbitrators. If the parties do not agree, or have not previously agreed, on the designation of an appointing authority, the Rules provide that either of the parties may request the Secretary-General of the PCA to select the appointing authority. This small role under the UNCITRAL Rules has resulted in consistent involvement of the PCA in international commercial arbitration between non-State parties.

Ironically, the first request to the Secretary-General for the designation of an appointing authority emanated not from a commercial arbitration tribunal, but from the Iran-US Claims Tribunal, established by the 1981 Algiers Accords with the assistance of the International Bureau of the PCA. In the ensuing years, the PCA witnessed the expansion of global commerce through the increase in the number of requests submitted to the Secretary-General under the UNCITRAL Rules. In recent years this number amounted to an average of one every two weeks, which is double the number of requests received ten years ago. The parties to these arbitrations originate in all regions of the world, as do the institutions that are ultimately designated as appointing authorities. The Secretary-General's visibility in performing this function has also led, with increasing frequency, to his being directly designated by parties as the appointing authority.

These UNCITRAL matters also appear to be increasing in terms of the complexity of the cases and the contentiousness of the parties. In recent months, the International Bureau has dealt with multi-party cases, objections to PCA authority to act, challenges, and consolidations. We have also felt the growth in investment treaty arbitration that was discussed earlier today. Last year, the PCA became registrar in an UNCITRAL matter under the Czech-Netherlands bilateral investment treaty. NAFTA too has presented the International Bureau with an interesting case that I cannot say more about at present, and PCA arbitration under Art. 27 of the Energy Charter Treaty may be drawing near. I predict that the complex and cumbersome nature of the proceedings in many of these investment treaty matters will cause more ad hoc tribunals to seek the administrative support of the PCA in coming years.

As the President of ICCA, Fali Nariman, stated in his message of welcome at this Congress, that the main challenge in the continuous evolution of commercial arbitration is "keeping up". One way the PCA has kept up with changes and increasing outside demands is through an increase in the staff of its International Bureau to twenty people, made up of thirteen lawyers from various jurisdictions and seven paralegal, administrative, and editorial staff. Among other sources, the Bureau stays abreast of developments in arbitration through ICCA itself, which, pursuant to our 1989 cooperation agreement, provides the PCA with information concerning arbitration institutions, experts, procedures and activities in various parts of the world; this cooperation was expanded in 1996 to include the editorial functions of the ICCA publications. Perhaps until today, for some of you, the ICCA *Yearbook* and its managing editor, Judy Freedberg, acting under the guidance of the General Editor Albert Jan van den Berg, have been your only contact with the PCA. The PCA also has editorial responsibility for the arbitration database disseminated on CD-ROM by Kluwer Law International and for Kluwer periodicals such as Journal of International Arbitration and World Trade and Arbitration Materials. The most exciting development in this area is the Kluwer web portal, which should be coming online virtually as I speak. This portal will offer a subscription service containing Kluwer and ICCA materials as well as a reporting service providing regular updates on court decisions, new legislation, new rules and other arbitration events. The PCA has provided both editorial and technical support in this venture and will have a continuing responsibility in advising on the development of this service.

All of this "keeping up" with the commercial arbitration world has not led the PCA to abandon its original mission as an intergovernmental institution and a forum for State-State disputes, or prevented it from considering new initiatives in such areas as environmental arbitration, or the arbitration of mass claims.

First, maintaining its role in dispute resolution between States remains the primary focus of the PCA, and the ever-increasing prominence of the United Nations (UN) does not make the task easy.

As you know, the PCA is not an organ of the UN, but rather an independent international organization with its own State membership, currently totaling ninety-seven States. Pursuant to Art. 4 of the Statute of the International Court of Justice (ICJ), however, the ICJ judges are elected by the UN General Assembly and Security Council from a list of candidates nominated by the national groups of the Permanent Court of Arbitration. This direct reference to the PCA in the ICJ Statute, which is part of the UN Charter, makes the PCA the only existing institution, other than the UN itself, mentioned by name in the Charter.

This special relationship was further strengthened when, in 1993, the General Assembly of the United Nations granted permanent observer status to the PCA, allowing it to participate in its work and thus facilitating collaboration between the two institutions. The PCA will be represented at the UNCITRAL meeting to be held in New York next month where one of yesterday's topics "Do we need a model law on conciliation?" will be further debated.

Although States have access to other such dispute resolution fora as the ICJ, several of the PCA's recent or current arbitrations have involved State parties exclusively, including the Eritrea/Yemen arbitration, the Eritrea/Ethiopia Boundary Commission, the France/Netherlands Rhine Pollution arbitration, as well as the Ireland/UK arbitrations regarding the marine environment of the northeast Atlantic. The procedural flexibility of the PCA and the ability of States to participate in the selection of arbitrators have been cited as reasons for the continuing appeal of arbitration in disputes between

States. The PCA has also sought to improve State access to arbitration through its Financial Assistance Fund created in 1994. The Fund is designed to help qualifying States meet the costs of international arbitration and has made four grants of assistance in recent years.

Environmental arbitration is one of the PCA's new initiatives. In June of last year, the PCA Administrative Council adopted Optional Rules for Arbitration of Disputes Relating to Natural Resources and/or the Environment.[1] The establishment of a separate panel of arbitrators specialized in this field and of a panel of scientific experts as foreseen in these Rules is currently underway. Environmental dispute resolution is an area where I firmly believe the PCA has a role to play. Presently there is no unified forum to which States, intergovernmental organizations, non-governmental organizations, corporations or private parties have recourse when seeking resolution of controversies concerning environmental protection, and conservation of natural resources. More than half of the instances where the International Bureau provided information to States concerning arbitration last year displayed a need for consideration of issues in these fields.

The example of a cyanide spill in Romania, which poisoned a river flowing through other countries in the Carpathian Basin, underscores the point that lack of adequate recourse can only lead to both increased frustration for those who have suffered damages and strained relations between polluter States and polluted States. The International Bureau expects the Rules will be included primarily in the dispute resolution clauses of international conventions and treaties relating to environmental protection and conservation because they provide structure and guidelines currently unavailable elsewhere. Already, these Rules are being considered as a dispute resolution mechanism for an emissions trading scheme being developed in connection with the Climate Control Convention and the Kyoto Protocol.

Another PCA initiative is in the area of mass claims. Recent years have seen the establishment of a number of tribunals and systems for settling large numbers of claims from historic events and diplomatic crises. These have included systems created to resolve claims resulting from events related to the Islamic Revolution in Iran, from damages suffered as a result of the Gulf War, from property losses in Bosnia-Herzegovina, claims by victims of Nazi persecution related to dormant bank accounts in Switzerland, insurance, slave labor and looted assets. The PCA has established a Steering Committee on Mass Claims, chaired by Judge Howard Holtzmann and composed of individuals who have been active in two or more of the mass claims processes currently operational.

The Steering Committee is producing comprehensive guidelines for setting up new systems to settle mass claims and expects to publish its work later this year. The expertise of the Committee has already been put to use in the constitution of the Eritrea-Ethiopia Claims Commission which is mandated to decide claims between the two governments or by nationals of one country against the government of the other arising out of the recent war between the two countries. The deadline for the submission of claims was December 2000 and the Commission expects to finish its work

---

1. Available online at www.pca-cpa.org.

within three years.

To sum up, while working to maintain its traditional role in disputes between States and making forays into other areas of international arbitration such as mass claims and the environment, the PCA has been inexorably drawn into the international commercial arbitration universe. This experience has enriched our institution, and I believe that our unique history has also provided something special to commercial arbitration. This symbiotic relationship shall continue and be intensified by the technological changes that are bringing the services and expertise of arbitrators, lawyers and institutions even closer together and more accessible to one another. The PCA is caught up in and adapting to a changing environment; we are studying how digital communication is becoming the foundation of a new "state-of-the-art" in dispute resolution. This allows us to overcome limitations of physical growth and continue to evolve in ways not always externally visible.

Some of the biggest changes are nearly invisible. I read just last week that technology-driven change has brought about the phenomenon of hyperagile thumbs among the youth of Japan. According to this article, "childhoods spent furiously thumbing hand-held computer games", and "young adulthoods spent thumbing e-mail messages on cell phone key pads", have made thumbs bigger and more muscular. I'm not sure what intensive thumb use bodes for arbitration, but I suspect that this Japanese "thumb generation" and its counterparts in India, China and around the world will leave a new imprint on our arbitration world.

Contemporary Questions

The Requirement of a Written Form
For an Arbitration Agreement:
When "Written" Means "Oral"

*Toby Landau**

---

* M.A.; B.C.L (Oxford); LL.M. (Harvard); FCIArb; Barrister-at-Law (Essex Court Chambers, London); also member of the New York State Bar and Northern Ireland Bar.

I.   INTRODUCTION

In what is a fast expanding corpus of literature on international commercial arbitration, there is already a substantial amount of writing on "writing". Whilst national laws and international conventions have long imposed a written form requirement for arbitration agreements, there is an increasing disparity among different systems as to how "writing" should be defined, and an increasing dislocation between legislative requirements and actual business practices. Just as the 1677 Statute of Frauds in England was designed to combat false claims by imposing a writing requirement, and yet itself became a means to evade genuine transactions,[1] so too the writing requirement for arbitration agreements is in danger of defeating the very process it is designed to secure. As recent cases demonstrate, it is a curious feature of international commercial arbitration that the formal validity of the very cornerstone of the whole process – the arbitration agreement – remains the subject of significant uncertainty.

One obvious aspect of the problem is the advent of technologies beyond the imagination of the drafters of 1958, and indeed those of 1985. In particular, the impact of "e-commerce" has been dramatic, and has put a strain on many legislative conceptions of the written form. Commerce over the Internet is expected to reach as much as € 7.64 trillion[2] in 2004,[3] worldwide, having reached € 214 billion in 2000. According to one study, since 1992 the number of computers with access to the Internet worldwide has increased from an estimated 1.3 million,[4] to 625 million in 2001.[5]

However, the problem with the form requirement runs deeper than evolving technologies. When subjected to scrutiny, the form requirement as currently expressed appears to cut across business practices that were widespread even before 1958. To this end, the requirement of a written form reflects a conception of arbitration and particular policy considerations that are no longer tenable, and that have long since been irreconcilable with many other doctrines in this field.

The debate on this topic has been galvanized by a series of well-known papers,[6] that

---

1. See Sect. IV below.
2. I.e., a thousand billion.
3. Forecast by Forrester Research, reported in Matthew R. SANDERS, "Global eCommerce Approaches Hypergrowth", 18 April 2000, available at: www.forrester.com/ER/Research/ Brief/Excerpt/0,1317,9229,00.html. This estimate includes both business-to-business (B2B) and business-to-consumer (B2C) transactions, although B2B transactions account for more than four-fifths of all transactions conducted online. See OECD *Business-To-Consumer E-commerce Statistics* 14 (March 2001) available at: www.oecd.org. These references have been taken from a note by Avril D. HAINES, entitled "The Impact of the Internet on the Judgments Project: Thoughts for the Future", prepared in connection with The Hague Judgments Convention negotiations.
4. U.S. GOVERNMENT WORKING GROUP ON ELECTRONIC COMMERCE, *Towards Digital eQuality*, 2nd Annual Report, 1999.
5. "Computer Industry Almanac", Press Release of July 2001, at: www.c-i-a.com/200107cu.html, again as cited by Avril D. HAINES, *op. cit.*, fn. 3.
6. See, in particular, HERRMANN, "The Arbitration Agreement as the Foundation of Arbitration and Its Recognition by the Courts" in *International Arbitration in a Changing World*, ICCA Congress Series no. 6 (1993) (hereinafter *ICCA Congress Series no. 6*) p. 41; KAPLAN, "Is the Need for Writing as Expressed in the New York Convention and the Model Law Out of Step with Commercial

in turn have generated negotiations within UNCITRAL on the possible modification of the UNCITRAL Model Law on International Commercial Arbitration of 1985 (the Model Law) and the United Nations Convention on the Recognition and Enforcement of Foreign Arbitral Awards of 1958 (the New York Convention). In relation to the Model Law, these negotiations have proceeded relatively happily, with good prospects of a palatable result. So far as the New York Convention is concerned, however, there is no current consensus, and every new proposal for compromise appears to betray a deeper difference in understanding.

It is the New York Convention, therefore, that is the focus of this paper.

II.   STRUCTURE OF THIS PAPER

Sect. III of this paper analyzes the problem, focussing on the underlying policies that have given rise to the current form requirement and reciting select war stories.

Sect. IV advances two fundamental but inconsistent propositions:

1. That the requirement of a written form for arbitration agreements is no longer defensible as a matter of logic or policy.
2. That the New York Convention should not be amended.

Sect. V addresses the range of possible solutions, and proposes a means of reconciling the inconsistency.

III.   THE CURRENT REQUIREMENT AND THE CURRENT PROBLEM

1.   The Justifications for a Written Form Requirement

It is difficult to analyze the current form requirement without a thorough scrutiny of its genesis. And yet, it is often simply assumed that the requirement is the product of a coherent policy, common to all legal systems that insist upon "writing". In fact, when examined carefully, a number of quite different policy considerations are discernible. As will be seen in Sect. IV, each particular rationale gives rise to a different form requirement. It is therefore vital to untangle each thread.

The various justifications for a written form may be grouped into two key categories, as follows:

Category One: Proving Initial Consent
The right of access to a court is generally considered a fundamental right of every citizen in a civilized state. It features in most constitutions, whether written or unwritten, and

---

Practice?", The 1995 Goff Lecture, 12 Arb Int'l (1996) p. 27; HERRMANN, "Does the World Need Additional Uniform Legislation on Arbitration?", The 1998 Freshfields Lecture, 15 Arb Int'l (1999) (hereinafter "Freshfields Lecture") p. 211.

is embodied in most if not all human rights conventions. Hence, for example, Art. 6 of the European Convention on Human Rights (ECHR).[7] This, of course, is not an absolute right, since, within defined limits, parties are generally free to contract for arbitration and thereby exclude themselves from a court. However, the exclusion of a court is treated as a serious step, and states therefore have an interest, as part of the public administration of justice, to ensure that any such agreement reflects a genuine consent. One way of policing the exclusion of access to a court is to insist that the arbitration agreement be in writing. This is the most commonly cited justification for the form requirement, which has often been seen as all the more important in international, as opposed to domestic, arbitration. As observed by Mann:

> "If the arbitration agreement is signed by only one party and if the other is alleged to have tacitly assented to it great difficulties are likely to arise.... An English party who has not signed anything would be exposed to foreign arbitration proceedings and to the enforcement here of a foreign award. This is a major legislative decision which the New York Convention did not require and which is open to much abuse. The converse case ... is equally serious: let us assume that ... parties entered in [a foreign state] into a contract of sale of goods. This they can do orally. But it does not follow that the foreign party has entered into an arbitration agreement, must arbitrate in London and must allow the award to be enforced in [the foreign state]. These again are grave matters of legal policy. The New York Convention did not require Parliament to take a position on them. Is it likely that it did so voluntarily and, in the absence of reciprocity, went far beyond anything contemplated by the Convention?"[8]

In fact, this justification has several different, but related aspects:

— "Cautionary" Function: The requirement of writing has a "cautionary" function, in that it distinguishes the conclusion of an arbitration agreement from other types of transaction, thereby alerting the parties to the special significance of the agreement. In turn, this is designed to provoke proper consideration before initial consent to the agreement is given.

It is for this reason that many legislatures impose form requirements in respect of other types of transactions which are regarded as especially significant (whether to the contracting parties themselves or to the wider community). Hence the requirement in many systems that contracts for the transfer of interests in land, or that testamentary

---

7. Art. 6 ECHR (Right to a fair trial) reads:

"1. In the determination of his civil rights and obligations or of any criminal charge against him, everyone is entitled to a fair and public hearing within a reasonable time by an independent and impartial tribunal established by law...."

8. F.A. MANN, "An 'Agreement in Writing' to Arbitrate", 3 Arb Int'l (1987) p. 171, criticizing the English Court of Appeal decision in *Zambia Steel v. Clark and Eaton* [1986] 2 Lloyd's Rep 225.

wills, be concluded in writing or be signed and witnessed.[9]

– "Evidential" Function: Writing has an obvious "evidential" function: it facilitates the resolution of a dispute as to whether or not an arbitration agreement was actually consented to and concluded. Given the significance of the rights that are thereby excluded, there has been a perceived need to be able to prove a party's consent to arbitration with particular certainty.

In this regard, it is interesting to note the growing jurisprudence from the European Court of Human Rights in Strasbourg on the issue of "waiver" of human rights. Arbitration as it is generally practiced in modern international trade is inconsistent with various elements of Art. 6 of the ECH. For example, it normally involves the denial of access to a national court, a private hearing, and a private judgment. This conflict has been resolved by the Strasbourg court by way of a developing doctrine of waiver. It is often said that the existence of a writing requirement significantly assists – and may sometimes be critical – in proving a clear and unequivocal waiver.

– "Channeling" Function: The imposition of a writing requirement has a "channeling" function, in that it allows for certain types of agreement to be singled out as special legal mechanisms with particular attributes. Equally, it requires that particular transactions take a prescribed form, in order to attract specific legal consequences or characteristics. In this way, parties have to take a deliberate decision to invoke the particular legal device, knowing of the consequences of such a choice. For this reason, in many systems, testamentary wills require writing, signatures and witnesses, thereby distinguishing them from other types of transaction, and elevating them into a specific device. In England, the requirement of writing in Sect. 5 of the Arbitration Act 1996 constitutes, in part, a "scope" provision; if an agreement is in writing, the 1996 Act will apply, with all its legal consequences; if an agreement is not in writing, it will still have some limited existence in English law, but outside of the regime of the 1996 Act.

Category Two: Proving the Terms of the Agreement
Aside from considerations concerning initial consent, the written form requirement has also been justified on the basis of overall certainty within the arbitral process itself. In other words, once parties have consented to arbitration, there is an interest in ensuring that the type of arbitration, and the terms of the process, are clear and susceptible of proof. Again, this justification comprises several different elements:

– Certainty within the Arbitral Process: It is generally thought that there is a premium

---

9. See, e.g., in England: Sects. 52 and 53 of the Law of Property Act 1925 (writing requirement for conveyances, as well as the creation and disposition of interests in land), and Sect. 9 of the Wills Act 1837, as substituted by Sect. 17 of the Administration of Justice Act 1982 (writing, signature and witness requirements for testamentary trusts).

in having a clear and certain arbitration agreement, in order to avoid breakdowns in the arbitral process itself. An agreement in writing is considered more certain than an oral agreement, where every aspect of the arbitral process might be in doubt.

— Minimizing Disputes in Court: As a related concern, writing is seen as a means of minimizing disputes before courts in relation to arbitration – an obviously important function, given that arbitration is designed to exclude national courts. As well as disputes concerning the parties' initial consent to arbitration (covered by Category One, above), writing is seen as a means of avoiding or narrowing disputes as to the particular type or nature or attributes of the arbitration in question.

— Facilitating Recognition and Enforcement: The greater the degree of certainty as to the form and nature of arbitration (i.e., the precise terms of the arbitration agreement), the less the scope there may be for challenges to the process at the stage of recognition and enforcement. Thus, forcing parties to meet requirements of form at the outset has the longer term advantage of securing an effective arbitral award. This was a specific policy behind Sect. 5 of the English Arbitration Act 1996, which gave rise to a requirement that *every* agreement made in relation to the arbitral process – not just the arbitration agreement itself – be in writing.[10]

Both Category One and Category Two justifications may explain the procedural requirement that a party seeking recognition and enforcement of an award produce an original of the arbitration agreement or a duly certified copy thereof (e.g., Art. IV of the New York Convention). This allows a court – that may well be located far from the arbitral seat – to satisfy itself, at least prima facie, that the arbitration award is the product of an agreed arbitration. Equally, it provides evidence as to the terms of the agreement, which will be especially important in ensuring that the award is consonant with the agreement (and that no ground for refusal in Art. V is established). This is particularly important where the application for recognition and enforcement proceeds in the absence of the respondent party. If there was no requirement of a written arbitration agreement, the task of an enforcing court might be made that much harder.

In evaluating the current form requirement, as well as any new solution, each of these individual rationales must be tested. Sects. IV and V below therefore revert to this analysis.

---

10. See the DEPARTMENTAL ADVISORY COMMITTEE (DAC), *Report on the Arbitration Bill 1996* of February 1996:

> "35. ... we have also made [other agreements] subject to a 'writing' requirement. Had we not done so, we could envisage disputes over whether, for example, something the parties had agreed to during the conduct of the arbitration amounted to a variation of the arbitration agreement and required writing, or could be characterized as something else. By introducing some formality with respect to all agreements, the possibility of subsequent disputes (e.g., at the enforcement stage) is greatly diminished. Indeed it seemed to us that with the extremely broad definition we have given to writing, the advantages of requiring some record of what was agreed with regard to any aspect of an arbitration outweighed the disadvantages of requiring a specific form for an effective agreement."

2.   The Model Law and the New York Convention

The contemporary debate on the written form requirement is focused on the New York Convention and the Model Law, since it is these documents which lie at the centre of the modern arbitration landscape, and which represent the latest (multilateral) expressions of the policies outlined above.

The New York Convention: Art. II of the New York Convention provides as follows:

> "1. Each Contracting State shall recognize an agreement in writing under which the parties undertake to submit to arbitration all or any differences which have arisen or which may arise between them in respect of a defined legal relationship, whether contractual or not, concerning a subject matter capable of settlement by arbitration.
>
> 2. The term 'agreement in writing' shall include an arbitral clause in a contract or an arbitration agreement, signed by the parties or contained in an exchange of letters or telegrams.
>
> 3. The court of a Contracting State, when seized of an action in a matter in respect of which the parties have made an agreement within the meaning of this article, shall, at the request of one of the parties, refer the parties to arbitration, unless it finds that the said agreement is null and void, inoperative or incapable of being performed."

Art. IV provides (in relevant part) as follows:

> "1. To obtain the recognition and enforcement mentioned in the preceding article, the party applying for recognition and enforcement shall, at the time of application, supply:
> (a) The duly authenticated original award or a duly certified copy thereof;
> (b) The original agreement referred to in Article II or a duly certified copy thereof.
> ...."

The Model Law: Art. 7 of the Model Law provides as follows:

> *"Article 7 Definition and form of arbitration agreement*
> (1) 'Arbitration agreement' is an agreement by the parties to submit to arbitration all or certain disputes which have arisen or which may arise between them in respect of a defined legal relationship, whether contractual or not. An arbitration agreement may be in the form of an arbitration clause in a contract or in the form of a separate agreement.
>
> (2) The arbitration agreement shall be in writing. An agreement is in writing if it is contained in a document signed by the parties or in an exchange of letters, telex, telegrams or other means of telecommunication which provide a record of the agreement, or in an exchange of statements of claim and defence in which the existence of an agreement is alleged by one party and

not denied by another. The reference in a contract to a document containing an arbitration clause constitutes an arbitration agreement provided that the contract is in writing and the reference is such as to make that clause part of the contract."

A footnote to the official text explains that this provision is intended to set maximum standards only, such that it would not be "contrary to the harmonization to be achieved by the model law if a State retained even less onerous conditions".

Art. 35 provides (in relevant part) as follows:

> "*Art. 35. Recognition and enforcement*
>
> ....
>
> (2) The party relying on an award or applying for its enforcement shall supply the duly authenticated original award or a duly certified copy thereof, and the original arbitration agreement referred to in Article 7 or a duly certified copy thereof...."

The legislative history of both instruments has already been the subject of exhaustive analysis elsewhere,[11] and is not rehearsed here. For present purposes, it is sufficient to note that Art. II(2) of the New York Convention was intentionally limited, so as to exclude cases involving acceptance by performance, conduct or tacit acceptance. Further, Art. 7(2), whilst in some respects broader, was drafted within the constraints of Art. II(2) of the Convention, in an attempt to ensure that national laws did not produce arbitral awards that are unenforceable under the Convention. As such, the current difficulties with both instruments derive from certain relatively hasty decisions that were taken in 1958.

3.   Two Key Problems

At their core, both Art. II(1) of the New York Convention and Art. 7(2) of the Model Law contain the same two requirements of form: an arbitration agreement must either be (1) signed by both parties, or (2) contained in an exchange of documents.

There is an increasing consensus that these two requirements fail to take account of a wide range of commercial activity. In some respects, modern technology has simply outgrown each of the texts. The problem, however, runs far deeper than this, since there are very simple and very old contract practices that have never been contemplated by either of these requirements of form.

Thus, the framing of Art. II(1) of the Convention and Art. 7(2) of the Model Law raises two different issues:

---

11. For the New York Convention, see, e.g., van den BERG, *The New York Arbitration Convention of 1958* (Kluwer 1981); DI PIETRO and PLATTE, *Enforcement of International Arbitration Awards* (Cameron May 2001); KAPLAN, *op. cit.*, fn. 6, p. 27. For the Model Law, see, e.g., HOLTZMANN and NEUHAUS, *Guide to the UNCITRAL Model Law on International Commercial Arbitration* (Kluwer 1989); BINDER, *International Commercial Arbitration in UNCITRAL Model Law Jurisdictions* (Sweet & Maxwell 2000); BROCHES, *Commentary on the UNCITRAL Model Law on International Commercial Arbitration* (Kluwer 1990).

— the definition of "writing" itself, and the extent to which it might include new forms of communication;

— the extent to which the requirement of "exchange" is inconsistent with commercial practices.

Each is assessed in turn.

a.   The definition of "writing"
In the years since 1985, there have been extraordinary advances in modern technology. In the years since 1958, when the language was of letters and telegrams, there are aspects of the modern commercial landscape which are simply unrecognizable. With the advent of electronic commerce, and new forms of generating and recording communications, many legislative texts that refer to writing have been subject to strain. The strain will only increase, as we face a future when magnetic, electronic and optical communications may well appear antiquated.

It would seem that the use of new methods of communication in concluding arbitration agreements should not pose any difficulty for Art. 7(2) of the Model Law, since this expressly validates the use of any means of telecommunication "which provides a record of the agreement" — wording which would cover most common uses of electronic mail or electronic data interchange (EDI) messaging.

However, given its different wording, this analysis is not available for Art. II(2) of the New York Convention. This article identifies exchanges of "letters or telegrams", but makes no reference to any other forms of communication. In practice, this particular aspect of Art. II(2) does not appear to have given rise to many difficulties, since most modern courts accept that the references to "letters" and "telegrams" must be interpreted in the light of developing technology. Indeed, a "functional equivalence" approach, as adopted by UNCITRAL in its Model Law on Electronic Commerce, appears to have received widespread support on this issue. This approach tests modern means of communication and storage of information against the functional characteristics of paper-based concepts such as "writing", "signature" and "original".[12] Hence, it has been held that telexes should be assimilated with telegrams.[13] The same approach is likely with respect to facsimiles, and other similar forms of communication.

Having said this, "functional equivalence" has yet to be universally accepted in this context. One court at least has already refused the recognition and enforcement of an award on the basis (albeit in part) that an exchange of E-mail messages does not satisfy

---

12. For a thorough description of the "functional equivalence" approach, see UNCITRAL's *Guide to Enactment of the UNCITRAL Model Law on Electronic Commerce* (1996) pp. 15-18.

13. See, e.g., *Bomar Oil NV v. ETAP*, Court of Appeal, Paris, 20 January 1987, Rev.Arb. (1987) p. 482; *G.S.A. v. T. Ltd*, Swiss Federal Supreme Court, 12 January 1989, ICCA *Yearbook Commercial Arbitration* XV (1990) (hereinafter *Yearbook*) p. 509; *Dimitros Varverakis v. Compañis de Navigacion Artico SA*, Court of First Instance, Savona (Italy), 26 March 1981, *Yearbook* X (1985) p. 455; Austrian Supreme Court, 2 May 1972, *Yearbook* X (1985) p. 417; *Carbomin SA v. Ekton Corp*, Court of Appeal, Geneva, 1987, *Yearbook* XII (1987) p. 502; *Tracomin SA v. Sudan Oil Seeds Co*, Swiss Federal Supreme Court, 1987, *Yearbook* XII (1987) p. 511; *Addullah M Fahem v. Mareb Yemen Insurance* [1992] 2 Lloyd's Rep 738.

the "writing" requirement of Art. II(2) of the Convention. In a decision of the Hålogaland Court of Appeal (Norway) of 16 August 1999,[14] it was held that a contract for the fixture of a vessel that was concluded by an exchange of E-mails by reference to the GENCON charter party did not give rise to an arbitration agreement "in writing" for the purposes of the New York Convention. The Court was shown eleven E-mail transcripts that had been exchanged between brokers, and a draft copy of the GENCON charter which had not been signed. The Court concluded that this evidence failed to meet the "basic requirements of legal protection set up by the Convention" and, therefore, that an arbitral award that had been rendered in London pursuant to the contract could not be enforced in Norway.

b.   The requirement of "exchange"
The second issue is far more problematic. Aside from particular types of "writing", a critical issue arises from the combination of the "form", and the way in which the arbitration agreement is actually concluded. Both the New York Convention and the Model Law use the expression "exchange of letters or telegrams" (or words to this effect). This formulation requires a written offer of a contract containing an arbitration clause, or of an arbitration agreement itself, as well as a written acceptance. As such, the requirement excludes a wide range of situations, as follows:[15]

i.   Written offers accepted by performance, conduct, tacitly or orally
Both the requirements of "signature" and "exchange" necessarily exclude any contract that has been set out in a written text or offer, but has been accepted in some way other than in writing – for example orally, by performance, by conduct or tacitly. Hence, the following commonplace situation is not covered: Goods are sent by a seller to a buyer, together with a purchase confirmation which sets out terms and conditions, including an arbitration clause. The goods are accepted and payment is made by the buyer, but the purchase confirmation is neither signed nor returned to the seller.

Acceptance by conduct or performance is obviously an extremely common phenomenon, with widespread modern variants, for example, the loading of computer software from a disk or CD-Rom. This frequently entails the conclusion of a licence agreement, which will be in writing and will often contain an arbitration clause. The acceptance occurs by breaking a seal on the disk container, or often by clicking an "I Agree" button on an initial screen. There is no signature, and there is no "exchange".

Cases in this category may well involve a purely oral acceptance of a written offer, in the absence of any performance or conduct on the part of the offeree. For example, a seller may make a written offer to a buyer, which the buyer accepts orally. The buyer may then refuse to perform the contract. The seller may have an action for the buyer's default, which he may wish to pursue in arbitration. Equally, the seller might commence

---

14. Stockholm Arbitration Report, vol. 2 (1999) p.121 (with observations by Gunnar NERDRUM).
15. See U.N. Doc. A/CN.9/WG.II/WP.108/Add.1, para. 12, for the list of fact situations which have formed the basis for UNCITRAL's current deliberations on this issue.

a court action, and the buyer might seek to enforce the arbitration agreement.[16]

ii.   Oral offer accepted in writing

Just as a written offer might be accepted by conduct or orally, so too an oral offer might be accepted in writing. If, for example, a seller makes an oral offer to a buyer, including provision for arbitration, and if the buyer accepts the offer in a letter, this will not satisfy the requirements of "signature" or "exchange".[17]

iii.   Incorporation by reference

In international trade, it is common for parties to rely upon pre-existing documents, such as standard industry forms or prior agreements, rather than setting out each and every term of their agreement in one document. Consequently, many contracts contain a reference to another document or text, with the intention of incorporating all or some of its terms. Whether or not a reference in one contract to text in another document constitutes an effective incorporation is a question of consent and the formation of contracts, and therefore a question for the substantive governing law.

However, incorporation by reference also raises issues of form, and these are frequently confused with issues of substance. As will be seen, whilst arbitration agreements might satisfy a substantive test of "consent" under a governing law, they may still be defeated by the "writing" requirement. Many courts elide the two issues, and rely upon Art. II(2) of the New York Convention in holding that the incorporation was inadequate to demonstrate consent.

To this end, in the context of its provisions on the meaning of "writing", the Model Law provides in Art. 7(2) that:

> ".... The reference in a contract to a document containing an arbitration clause constitutes an arbitration agreement provided that the contract is in writing and the reference is such as to make that clause part of the contract."

Further, the problem of incorporation by reference has been specifically addressed in many modern national laws. See, e.g., Sect. 6 of the English Arbitration Act 1996;[18]

---

16. As will be seen later, this particular scenario could be characterized as a contract that has been concluded orally, which incorporates by reference a written text. However, as a matter of analysis, this is a distinction without any real difference.

17. The other permutations of oral offer and oral acceptance, or oral offer and acceptance by conduct or performance, are obviously not covered, since they involve situations with no text at all.

18. Sect. 6(2) of the English Arbitration Act 1996:

"The reference in an agreement to a written form of arbitration clause or to a document containing an arbitration clause constitutes an arbitration agreement if the reference is such as to make that clause part of the agreement."

This provision (which does not form part of the definition of writing in Sect. 5) refers one back to a large body of case law on this issue. See, e.g., MERKIN, *Arbitration Law* (LLP loose-leaf) Sects. 4.19-4.32.

Sect. 1031(3) of the German Code of Civil Procedure (ZPO); Art. 1021 of the Netherlands Code of Civil Procedure; Art. 83(2)(2) of the Italian Code of Civil Procedure (Law No. 25 of 5 January 1994); Art. 10(3) of the Egyptian Law No. 27 of 1994 and Art. 1423 of the Mexican Commercial Code (Decree of 22 July 1993).

Unlike the Model Law, the New York Convention contains no provision dealing specifically with arbitration clauses incorporated by reference. Two different issues arise under this general heading:

- For the purposes of Art. II(2) of the Convention, what words of incorporation are required to satisfy the form requirement?
- For the purposes of both Art. II(2) of the Convention and Art. 7(2) of the Model Law, which of the many scenarios involving incorporation by reference are covered?

Required Words of Incorporation:
On one view, words of incorporation could only satisfy the form requirement in Art. II(2) of the Convention if the parties have specifically referred to the arbitration agreement contained in the second document.[19] This is at odds with the requirements of many national laws. Some courts have taken a liberal view of this issue, and enforced arbitration agreements contained in documents to which only a general reference has been made. Others, however, have adopted a restrictive position, thereby defeating the arbitration clauses in question.[20]

Different Scenarios:
The incorporation of a written text may occur in a number of different situations, and as each situation is analyzed, it becomes increasingly difficult to distinguish "written" from "oral" arrangements. What is clear, however, is that neither Art. II(2) of the Convention nor Art. 7(2) of the Model Law covers every possible scenario:

Written Offer/Written Acceptance: A written offer may make a reference to, and incorporate, a written arbitration clause or arbitration terms contained in another document. This offer may be accepted in writing (or, of course, embodied in one signed document). There are numerous examples of this, such as references in sale contracts to standard industry forms or the standard terms and conditions of one party; cross-references between construction contracts and sub-contracts, and so on. In fact, the list of examples could be extended ad infinitum. This is the simplest situation which is clearly covered by Art. 7(2) of the Model Law. Whether or not it is covered by Art. II(2) of the New York Convention is open to doubt, and may depend upon the precise words of incorporation that have been used.

---

19. See van den BERG, *op. cit.*, fn. 11, from p. 217.
20. See the extensive citations in Emmanuel GAILLARD and John SAVAGE, eds., *Fouchard, Gaillard Goldman on International Commercial Arbitration* (Kluwer 1999) (hereinafater *Fouchard Gaillard Goldman*) Sect. 494, fns. 155 and 156. See also the references to the *Bomar Oil* case later in this paper.

Written Offer/Oral or Tacit Acceptance: The written offer (which contains a reference to another text) could be accepted orally, by conduct, performance or tacitly. This is frequently the position with Bills of Lading, which are rarely signed by both parties, and rarely "exchanged". Bills of Lading often incorporate provisions contained in a related charterparty, including the arbitration clause. Other very common examples are sales contracts which are concluded on the basis of standard industry forms, where there is neither signature nor "exchange". This would include a large number of international commodity transactions which are concluded on the basis of GAFTA standard forms, including GAFTA Form 125, containing the GAFTA arbitration terms. Again, the acceptance could be oral, without any performance or conduct, for example, where a buyer agrees orally to purchase goods, but then fails to take delivery of them. It is unclear whether this situation is covered by Art. 7(2) of the Model Law, or Art. II(2) of the New York Convention.

Oral Offer/Written Acceptance: The offer (which contains a reference to another text) could be oral, not written. For example, a seller may offer goods for sale to a buyer by telephone. The offer may make reference to GAFTA Form 125. The buyer may accept the offer by a fax or recap telex. On one view, this is another example of an incorporation by reference. On another view, this is no different from the situation described in the second category above (oral offer accepted in writing). Again, it is unclear whether this is covered by Art. 7(2) of the Model Law, or Art. II(2) of the New York Convention.

Oral Offer/Oral or Tacit Acceptance: The oral offer (which contains a reference to a text) could be accepted orally or by performance or conduct. Whilst this might seem as the most extreme example – and the furthest from the traditional conception of a written form, it is also extremely common in practice: for example, the oft-quoted salvage situation, in which a vessel in distress is assisted by another vessel. It is common practice for such salvage operations to be conducted pursuant to an agreement incorporating the Lloyds Open Form (LOF), which is a standard industry set of terms and conditions, including an arbitration clause. Due to the exigencies of the situation, salvage contracts are regularly concluded by VHF radio, in other words by an oral offer, and an oral acceptance, by reference to the LOF form. There are, in fact, many other examples which also fall into this category. For example, a commodities trade concluded by telephone, by reference to a GAFTA form. On some analyses of Art. 7(2) of the Model Law and Art. II(2) of the New York Convention, this situation is not covered.

Problems involving incorporation by reference may manifest themselves in a variety of ways beyond the simple scenario of a substantive contract containing a reference to another document. Hence, a series of contracts may have been entered into between the same parties in a course of dealing, where previous contracts have included valid arbitration agreements but the contract in question has not been evidenced by a signed writing or there has been no exchange of writings for the contract. Equally, a contract might contain a validly concluded arbitration clause, but an addendum or extension of the contract, or a settlement agreement relating to the contract might not. Again, these are situations in which consent to arbitration might be found as a matter of substance, and yet where the issue of form might still defeat the process.

iv.   Documents neither signed nor exchanged

There are certain types of contract that will rarely satisfy the requirements of "signature" or "exchange", as a matter of trade practice. Most notably perhaps in this category are Bills of Lading. There are, broadly, two types of bills: liner bills and the Bills of Lading issued under charterparties. A liner Bill of Lading, which is usually issued by the carrier to the shipper (who may be the contractual counterpart of the carrier, or simply the person responsible for shipping the cargo), usually contains an arbitration agreement, often printed on its reverse side. A bill issued under a charterparty, in contrast, will usually refer to the clauses of the latter document. Both forms of bill are rarely signed by the shipper, or indeed any of the subsequent holders. Equally, in the absence of any relevant written booking confirmation or a liner booking note which refers to the arbitration clause, there is no obvious "exchange" that might be recognized by Art. II(2) of the Convention, or Art. 7(2) of the Model Law.[21]

The problem of Bills of Lading has been noted for some time, and indeed was the subject of discussion at the time the Model Law was finalized. During the preparation of the Model Law, a draft proposal was made by the Norwegian Government that Art. 7 include the following provision:

> "If a bill of lading or another document, signed by only one of the parties, gives sufficient evidence of a contract, an arbitration clause in the document, or a reference in the document to another document containing an arbitration clause, shall be considered to be an agreement in writing."[22]

This proposal found a certain amount of favour amongst delegates at the eighteenth session of the Commission in 1985[23] (at which the Model Law was finalized), but was ultimately not adopted.[24]

The difficulty with Bills of Lading will be further compounded in years to come with the increased use of electronic transportation documents and EDI in this field.[25]

---

21. See TRAPPE, "The Arbitration Clause in a Bill of Lading LMCLQ", (1999) p. 337.

22. U.N. Doc. A/CN.9/263 (Analytical Compilation of Comments by Governments and International Organizations on the Draft Text of a Model Law on International Commercial Arbitration) comments on Art. 7(5) (Norway), reproduced in the *UNCITRAL Yearbook*, vol. XVI (1985) part two, I.A.

23. Summary records of UNCITRAL for meetings devoted to the preparation of the UNCITRAL Model Law, 311th meeting, reproduced in *op. cit.* fn. 22, part three, II.

24. The failure of Art. 7(2) to address Bills of Lading was one of many specific points emphasized in the DAC Report of 1989, also referred to as the "Mustill Report", which recommended against the adoption of the Model Law in England and Wales. See *A Report on the UNCITRAL Model Law on International Commercial Arbitration* (HMSO 1989) ISBN 0 11 514692 X, pp. 23 and 52 ("[Art 7] could leave most Bills of Lading, many brokers' contract notes and other important categories of contracts outside the scope of the Model Law.").

25. See DALHUISEN, *International Commercial, Financial and Trade Law* (Hart 2000) Chap. 2.3 ("The Dematerialisation of Documents of Title and Negotiable Instruments....").

v.   Negotiable instruments

In addition to Bills of Lading, there are many other instruments which are negotiable, in the sense that they may give rise to rights or obligations with respect to non-signing third parties (such as subsequent holders or endorsees), who were not party to the original agreement. In so far as these instruments contain arbitration clauses, there is an obvious difficulty in satisfying the written form requirement with respect to a subsequent holder.

vi.   Intermediaries and companies

Similarly, the requirements of "signature" or "exchange" may exclude certain contracts concluded through intermediaries. For example, a broker may issue a text evidencing that which the parties have agreed upon (including an arbitration clause), in circumstances where there has been no direct written communications between the parties. This will be a written text, but there will have been no signature and no "exchange".

Other situations which are akin to this, and similarly outwith Art. II(2) of the New York Convention and Art. 7(2) of the Model Law, concern arbitration agreements that are contained in the articles of association or statutes of companies. Again, these are generally unsigned by shareholders, and rarely the subject of any "exchange". Under most modern systems, they are, however, recognized as valid and binding agreements, notwithstanding the lack of signature and "exchange".[26]

vii.   Other mechanisms

As a matter of substantive law, there are many other mechanisms which have been recognized across different legal systems, as having the effect of rendering a third person or entity a party to an arbitration agreement. For example:

- universal transfers of assets, including successions; mergers; de-mergers; and acquisitions of companies;
- specific transfers of assets, including transfers of contract; assignments of receivables or debts; novation; subrogation; contracts for the benefit of third parties and stipulations in favour of a third party (*stipulation pour autrui*);
- multiple party situations involving groups of contracts or groups of companies (doctrines such as the infamous "group of companies");
- doctrines of estoppel, whereby third persons have been prevented from evading the effect of an arbitration clause.

Again, these appear to be situations outwith the requirements in Art. II(2) of the

---

26. See, e.g., Austrian Supreme Court (OGH) 25 January 1995, 3 Ob 543/94; cf. *Powell Duffryn plc v. Petereit* (C-214/89) [1992] ECR I 1745, in which the ECJ held that a jurisdiction clause in a company's articles of association was binding on its shareholders. The requirement of writing was deemed satisfied by the fact that the statutes were invariably in writing, irrespective of how the shares were acquired, provided that the statutes were lodged at a place which was accessible to shareholders, or were kept in a public register.

Convention and Art. 7(2) of the Model Law. In each case, an entity may be held subject to an arbitration clause as a matter of substance, notwithstanding the lack of any signature or "exchange", as a matter of form.

4. Select "War Stories"

It is sometimes suggested that the problems associated with the written form requirement are overstated, and that few, if any, difficulties are actually experienced in practice. This is not so. There are in fact many examples of arbitration agreements and awards that have been defeated by reason of a failure to satisfy a written form requirement.

The nature of the form requirement is such that it presents a potential threat to the arbitral process at every stage. In particular:

— in the context of an application for a stay or a motion to compel arbitration, it may be argued that the arbitration agreement is null and void (e.g., pursuant to Art. 8(1) of the Model Law, or Art. II(3) of the New York Convention);
— a question as to the formal validity of an arbitration clause might impede the initial appointment of an arbitrator;
— in the course of arbitral proceedings, it may be raised as a ground for contesting the tribunal's jurisdiction (e.g., pursuant to Art. 16(2) of the Model Law);
— at the conclusion of the arbitral process, it may be deployed as a ground for setting aside an award (e.g., pursuant to Art. 34(2)(a)(i) of the Model Law);
— at the stage of seeking recognition and enforcement, it might be raised:
  1. pursuant to Art. IV(1)(*b*) of the New York Convention (requirement to produce the original arbitration agreement or a duly certified copy of it); or
  2. pursuant to Art. V(1)(*a*), as a ground for resisting recognition and enforcement of the award.

The defeat of reasonable commercial expectations on account of the written form requirement is evidenced by a series of recent cases in some of the jurisdictions of the United States. These involve commonplace examples of tacit acceptance, and each case warrants consideration.

In *Kahn Lucas Lancaster Inc. v. Lark International Ltd.* (1999)[27] the United States Court of Appeals, 2d Circuit, construed Art. II(2) of the Convention in the context of a motion to compel arbitration.

a. Kahn Lucas

The Facts: Lark, a Hong Kong corporation, acted as a purchasing agent for businesses seeking to buy and import clothing manufactured in Asia. Kahn Lucas, a New York corporation, was engaged in the resale of imported clothing to major retailers.

Since 1988, the two companies had enjoyed an ongoing business relationship. The parties' dealings were structured as follows. Kahn Lucas would place a purchase order

---

27. 186 F.3d 210 (2d Cir. 1999).

with Lark for clothes. Lark would forward this purchase order to manufacturers in Asia, and arrange for its completion. The manufacturers would issue to Kahn Lucas a seller's invoice for payment, once the ordered goods were completed. Lark would then issue a separate invoice for its commission (a percentage of the amount charged by the manufacturer). Kahn Lucas paid both of these invoices through draw-downs on an existing letter of credit, on which Lark was the named beneficiary. Lark would then remit payment to the manufacturer.

The dispute in this case arose from two purchase orders which Kahn Lucas issued in early 1995 for children's garments manufactured in the Philippines. These purchase orders stated that the garments were "ordered from" Lark, they listed Lark as the seller, and were signed by Kahn Lucas. They were not signed by Lark.

The purchase orders indicated that they contained a number of additional terms printed on the reverse side, and were made conditional upon the seller's acceptance of those terms. These terms included an arbitration agreement providing for arbitration in New York under the Federal Arbitration Act. Lark accepted the purchase orders without objection.

In July 1995, the manufacturers issued final invoices relating to the ordered garments, and Lark issued its commission invoice. Thereafter, on the basis of allegedly defective goods and failed deliveries, Kahn Lucas refused to release funds to Lark to pay either invoice.

Kahn Lucas commenced proceedings against Lark in the US District Court for the Southern District of New York, invoking diversity jurisdiction, and alleging breach of contract, breach of warranty, negligence and breach of fiduciary duty. Lark responded with a motion to dismiss for lack of personal jurisdiction. Kahn Lucas (at the Court's instance) then brought a motion to compel arbitration, pursuant to the Federal Arbitration Act (9 U.S.C. Sect. 206). It also filed a demand for arbitration with the American Arbitration Association.

The Motion to Compel Arbitration: Lark opposed this motion, on the basis that the purchase orders were directed at the manufacturers, not Lark, and (relevantly for present purposes) that the arbitration clauses relied upon were unenforceable, since Lark had not signed the purchase orders in which they were contained.

First Instance Judgment: In an Opinion and Order of 6 August 1997, the District Court granted Kahn Lucas' motion to compel arbitration.[28] On the issue of written form, the court referred to *Sphere Drake Ins. PLC v. Marine Towing, Inc.* (1994)[29] in which a 5th Circuit court, with limited analysis, had divided Art. II(2) of the New York Convention into two portions (effectively deleting a comma). In this way, the court felt able to divorce the words "signed by the parties or contained in an exchange of letters or telegrams" from the words "an arbitral clause in a contract". Hence, on this construction, Art. II(2) consists of two separate regimes, one concerning "an arbitral

---

28. *Kahn Lucas Lancaster, Inc. v. Lark International Ltd.,* No 95 CIV. 10506, 1997 WL 458785 at *8 (S.D.N.Y. 11 August 1997).
29. 16 F.3d 666, 669 (5th Cir. 1994).

clause in a contract" and the other "an arbitration agreement (a) signed by the parties or (b) contained in an exchange of letters or telegrams".

Relying upon this analysis, the District Court in *Kahn Lucas* held that although Lark had not signed the purchase orders, these orders represented an "arbitral clause in a contract", and as such were not caught by the requirements of signature or exchange. In reaching this conclusion, the court declined to follow *Sen Mar, Inc. v. Tiger Petroleum Corp.*, a Southern District of New York decision of 1991 in which it had been held that "An arbitration clause is enforceable only if it is found in a signed writing or an exchange of letters."[30]

Court of Appeals Judgment: In a very carefully reasoned judgment dated 29 July 1999, Justices Walker, McLaughlin and Parker held that the definition of "agreement in writing" in Art. II(2) of the New York Convention requires that such an agreement, whether it is an arbitration agreement or an arbitral clause in a contract, be signed by the parties or contained in a series of letters or telegrams. In the premises, the arbitration clauses here were not enforceable under the Convention, and Kahn Lucas' motion to compel arbitration failed.[31]

b.   Lo v. Aetna

The reasoning in this case has been applied subsequently in a number of other cases. On 29 March 2000, for example, in *Lo v. Aetna International*, 2000 WL 565465 (US District Court, District of Connecticut), an arbitration agreement was held ineffective on the basis that it failed to satisfy the writing requirement in Art. II(2).[32]

c.   Chloe Z Fishing

One month later, on 29 April 2000, in *Chloe Z Fishing Co., Inc. v. Odyssey Re (London) Ltd.*,[33] the US District Court, Southern District of California again affirmed the reasoning in *Kahn Lucas*. The court noted that Art. II(2) of the Convention has never been interpreted by the US Supreme Court, and that a difference of approach existed as between the Second Circuit (*Kahn Lucas*) and the Fifth Circuit (*Sphere Drake*). The Court preferred the analysis in *Kahn Lucas*, holding that both an arbitral clause and an agreement in writing must be found either in a signed writing or in an exchange of letters or telegrams under the Convention.

However, in this case the Court went on to hold that the requirements had been met with respect to the arbitration agreement in question (contained in a marine insurance broker's slip), by way of a liberal interpretation of the requirement of "exchange", as

---

30. *Sen Mar. Inc. v. Tiger Petroleum Corp.*, 774 F.Supp. 879 (S.D.N.Y. 1991), where it was held that an arbitral clause in a contract was invalid under the Convention, on the basis that the arbitration clause appeared in a telex that was not signed, and to which an objection had been made.

31. The reasoning in this case is discussed further in Sect. V below.

32. For an earlier decision on similar lines, see also *Ronald Borsack, AKA Ron Bell v. Chalk & Vermillion Fine Arts Ltd.* (S.D.N.Y. 7 August 1997) *Yearbook* XXVIII (1998) p. 1035.

33. 109 F.Supp.2d 1236 (2000).

well as a liberal interpretation of the words "letters or telegrams".[34] This case is discussed further in Sect. V below.

d.   Bothell and Bothell

Less than one month later, in *Bothell and Bothell v. Hitachi Zosen Corp.* (19 May 2000)[35] the US District Court, Western District of Washington, denied a motion to stay legal proceedings on the basis of a very restricted interpretation of "exchange".

The plaintiff had entered into an agreement for the manufacture of specialized equipment for use by the defendants. The plaintiff relied upon an oral agreement between the parties, which had been confirmed in a subsequent letter. Conversely, the defendants relied upon three separate purchase orders which they claimed were sent to the plaintiff and constituted the operative agreement. Each of these purchase orders contained a reference to "General Terms and Conditions", being a separate attachment containing, inter alia, an ICC arbitration clause. The plaintiff admitted that it had received the purchase orders, but without the "General Terms and Conditions" attached.

The plaintiff commenced proceedings in court for breach of contract, which was met by a motion by the defendant for a stay of legal proceedings, pending the completion of an arbitration, pursuant to 9 U.S.C. Sect. 3.

One of the grounds for resisting this motion was an argument that the ICC arbitration agreement failed the written form requirement in Art. II(2) of the Convention. The plaintiff argued that there were no documents signed by all parties that contained either the arbitration clause or a reference to the arbitration clause, and that there was no "exchange". The defendants argued that there is no requirement that an arbitration clause be part of a single paper signed by all parties. A series of documents incorporating

----

34. The Court took into account evidence that "London arbitration clauses are ubiquitous in the London marine insurance market, and a competent and diligent London broker would be familiar with all important terms of the insurance contract, obviously including arbitration clauses." It then construed the parties' conduct in accordance with English law, rather than federal law, since the events in question occurred in London, holding that the relevant conduct constituted an "exchange of letters or telegrams" for the purposes of Art. II(2) of the Convention. As is customary practice in the London insurance market, the assured plaintiffs were represented by brokers, who, each year, submitted the assureds' request for a quotation to the defendants by means of a "slip" (a document detailing the required terms and policy type). Following negotiations for coverage based on the defendants' standard form, the defendants effected the policies by affixing their stamp on the broker's slip and endorsing it with, among other things, the word "Bound", the date and the relevant policy number. The standard form, which was referred to in the "Conditions" section of the slip in turn contained London arbitration clauses. As a final step, the defendants issued Certificates of Insurance to the assureds' brokers to confirm the terms of the insurance. The brokers' slips and the defendants' certificates of insurance were held to constitute "letters or telegrams" (as these words had to be interpreted as including "... other forms of written communications regularly utilized to conduct commerce in the various signatory nations ..."), and their existence was held to satisfy the requirement of "exchange". The fact that the arbitration clause was not "contained" in either document was of no moment, given that there was a valid incorporation of the arbitration clauses by reference. Accordingly, the motion to compel arbitration and to stay the court proceedings was granted.

35. 97 F.Supp.2d 1048 (2000).

an agreement to arbitrate is sufficient, and the facts here were within the phrase "an exchange of letters or telegrams".

Perhaps surprisingly, the court (District Judge Burgess) disagreed. Upon a review of the relevant documents, the court concluded that the arbitration clause was not unequivocally incorporated in any "series of documents" exchanged between the parties. Rather, the "series of documents" merely contained a vague reference (i.e., "General Terms and Conditions for Purchasing") which, on its face, did not in any way implicate arbitration. In the court's view:

> "... in a series of documents, where the words used to refer to a proposed arbitration agreement are so vague as to be meaningless and no further explanation is provided, either by attachment, discussion or otherwise, the totality of the documents exchanged between the parties does not constitute a valid 'arbitration agreement' under the Convention". [36]

Accordingly, the motion to compel arbitration was denied.

On one view, this is really a case concerning substantive rules on incorporation rather than the writing requirement, and may be seen as part of the well-known debate as to how an arbitration clause in one document may be incorporated into another document. However, on another view, this case is interesting in that it treated the incorporation question as a facet of Art. II(2). As such (and as has occurred in many other cases), the substantive issue was resolved by reference to the form requirement. The case also represents a far more limited interpretation of the "exchange" requirement, as compared to the *Chloe Z* decision above. [37]

e.   *XL Insurance*

The effects of the *Kahn Lucas* decision have also already been felt on the other side of the Atlantic. In *XL Insurance Ltd. v. Owens Corning*, [38] a dispute was brought before the English Commercial Court concerning a contract of insurance between XL (a Bermudan insurance company) and Owens Corning (OC) (a Delaware corporation). The contract was negotiated in Bermuda. OC began proceedings in the Superior Court of the State of Delaware against the insurers, seeking a declaration that they were liable to indemnify OC for certain Y2K costs. XL applied to the English Court for a so-called "anti-suit" injunction to restrain OC from proceeding in the Delaware courts, in light of a London arbitration clause in the contract. OC resisted the application on the principal ground that the policy containing the arbitration clause was governed by New York law, by which (on the authority of *Kahn Lucas*) the clause would be unenforceable, since it failed

---

36. *Ibid.*, at 1053.

37. A similar decision was reached by the English Court of Appeal in *Aughton Ltd v. M F Kent Services Ltd* (1991) 57 BLR 1, in which it was held that words of incorporation in one contract were inadequate to incorporate an arbitration clause contained in another contract. Again, this conclusion was based in part on the lack of an agreement "in writing". This decision has since been doubted in a number of English cases.

38. [2000] 2 Lloyd's Rep 500 (Toulson J).

the "signature" and "exchange" requirements. Toulson, J held that as a matter of substance (rather than form), there was no doubt that XL and OC had concluded a contract which contained a London arbitration clause. Further, by virtue of the parties' choice of London as the arbitral seat, and the application of the English Arbitration Act 1996, the formal validity of the arbitration agreement was governed by English law (Sect. 5 of the Act), not New York law or the Federal Arbitration Act. Accordingly, *Kahn Lucas* did not govern the matter. If it had, the arbitration agreement would have failed.

f.   *Hålogaland Court of Appeal*
This is not just an issue of US jurisprudence.[39] Over the years, there have been many instances in many different countries of arbitration agreements failing because of a written form requirement – in situations where the underlying contract has been concluded in the normal course of commerce. By way of (random) example:

– In a decision of 16 August 1999 (cited above)[40] the Hålogaland Court of Appeal (Norway) refused to recognize and enforce an arbitration award that had been rendered in London, on the basis that the arbitration agreement failed to satisfy the "writing" requirement in Art. II(2) of the Convention. This case concerned an agreement between two brokers to fix a vessel for the carriage of 3,500 m.t. of herring from Norway to the Ukraine. Negotiations for the fixture were conducted by E-mail (giving rise to eleven E-mail transcripts), by reference to the GENCON standard form of charter party (which was referred to in the exchanges). In something of an ominous concluding comment, in the last E-mail of the exchange, which confirmed acceptance of the last contested point, one broker wrote to the other:

> "Thanks for confirmation as well. Suppose it's first one of ours which have done via e-mail. Just imagine how much we saved on tlxs/faxes!!!"

The savings were short-term. A dispute arose between the parties, and was referred to arbitration in London. An award was rendered, and taken to Norway for enforcement. The Court of Appeal refused to enforce the award, holding that:

> "The requirements in Article IV b ... [and] Article II [of the Convention], relating to the form of the arbitral agreement, are justified by basic considerations for

---

39. It is to be noted, of course, that other US jurisdictions have adopted a far more liberal approach to this issue. Some courts have found "writing" in an exchange of telexes, some of which contained arbitration clauses to which the parties did not object (e.g., *Genesco Inc. v. T. Kakiuchi & Co.*, 815 F.2d 840, 846 (2d Cir. 1987); *Oriental Commercial & Shipping Co v. Rosseel*, 609 F.Supp. 75 (S.D.N.Y. 1985)). Other courts have upheld arbitration clauses contained in unsigned forms (e.g., *Beromun AG v. Societa Industriale Agricola "Tresse"*, 471 F.Supp. 1163 (S.D.N.Y. 1979)). Others have allowed tacit acceptance (e.g., *Filantro spa v. Chilewich Int'l Corp.*, 789 F.Supp. 1229; *Sphere Drake v. Marine Towing* (cited in *Kahn Lucas*)).
40. *Op. cit.*, fn. 14, p. 121.

legal protection. It should not be sufficient for enforcement that the arbitral award is valid according to the law of the country in question. Also the requirements of the Convention should be assessed to ensure they have been complied with. This assessment is to be done by the local enforcement authority, and it need not to coincide with the question of the competence of the arbitrator according to his domestic law.

In this case there is no express arbitral clause signed by the two parties.... The basic requirements of legal protection set up by the Convention, Article II, cfr, Article IV b, for recognition and enforcement are hereby not satisfied."

g.   Ozsoy Tarim Sanayi Ve Ticaret Ltd.

In *Ozsoy Tarim Sanayi Ve Ticaret Ltd. (Izmir) v. All Foods SA (Buenos Aires)*, a decision of 8 April 1999, the Supreme Court of Appeal of Turkey refused to enforce a GAFTA arbitration award, on the grounds that it failed the writing requirement in Art. II(2). A broker's fax sent to sellers had confirmed the salient points of a sale contract, stating inter alia "other usual conditions". A contract was subsequently posted to the sellers, and referred to GAFTA Forms 24, 86 and 125. Forms 24 and 86 are standard contracts for pulses and for shipment in full container loads. Form 125 contains the standard GAFTA London arbitration agreement. The contract in this case also specified "Arbitration: GAFTA London". The contract was signed by the sellers only. A dispute arose and was referred to London arbitration. The tribunal found that during the relevant period, it was usual for the buyers to trade on GAFTA terms, including GAFTA arbitration. An award was rendered in sellers' favour, and recognition and enforcement were then sought in the Turkish courts. The Turkish Supreme Court of Appeal reversed a first instance judgment, and held that since the writing requirement in Art. II(2) of the Convention had not been satisfied, the award could not be recognized or enforced.[41]

h.   Bomar

The French *Cour de cassation* has held that an arbitration agreement made by telephone, even if subsequently confirmed by one of the parties in a letter (but not confirmed in writing by the other one), does not give rise to a written agreement.[42]

Also in France, the issue of incorporation of an arbitration clause from another document gave rise to a well-known (and widely criticized) decision of the *Cour de cassation* in the *Bomar Oil* case.[43] In this case, ETAP sold crude oil to Bomar Oil, pursuant

---

41. See, similarly, the Hong Kong decision in *Small v. Goldroyce* [1994] 2 HKC 526, as noted by KAPLAN in his 1995 Goff Lecture, *op. cit.*, fn. 6, pp. 29-30. Hong Kong law has since changed on this issue.

42. *Sté. Brittania v. Sté. Jézéquel et Maury, Cour de cassation*, 15 July 1987, Rev.Arb. (1990) p. 627. In other decisions, however, some French courts have adopted a liberal stance. See, for example, *Sté. Abilio Rodriguez v. S. Vigelor, Cour d'appel*, Paris, 30 March 1990, Rev.Arb.(1990) p. 691, in which the Court had regard to trade usages in sales and purchases in upholding an arbitration agreement contained in a confirmation letter that had been issued by a broker.

43. *Cour de cassation*, 1e civ., 11 October 1989, *Bomar Oil N.V. v. Enterprise Tunisienne d'Activités Pétrolières (ETAP)*, Rev.Arb. (1987) p. 482; *Yearbook* XIII (1988) pp. 466, 469-470 (in English). See comment by Catherine KESSEDJIAN, 114 J.D.I. (1987) p. 934.

to a contract that was concluded by an exchange of telexes referring to the general conditions of ETAP's standard contract. These general conditions contained an ICC arbitration clause. A dispute arose between the parties, and arbitral proceedings were commenced by ETAP. Bomar Oil objected to the tribunal's jurisdiction, on the grounds that it had not agreed to the arbitration agreement that was said to have been incorporated by reference. The tribunal rejected this ground, and its award was then challenged in the French courts. Reversing the *Cour d'appel* of Paris, the *Cour de cassation* set aside the arbitration award, ruling that although the New York Convention did not exclude the adoption of an arbitration agreement incorporated by reference, Art. II of the Convention required:

> "that the existence of the clause be mentioned in the main contract, unless there exists between the parties a longstanding business relationship which insures that they are properly aware of the written conditions normally governing their commercial relationships".[44]

Whilst many national systems (including France) have now arrived at satisfactory solutions to the incorporation issue as a matter of substance, as pointed out above there remains a significant difficulty with Art. II(2) (and Art. IV) of the Convention on the question of form. As long as the form requirement lags behind substantive solutions in national law, there remains the risk that arbitration agreements and awards will still be defeated.

i.   Marc Rich
In *Marc Rich* (which spawned litigation in Italy, London and before the European Court of Justice), Marc Rich (a Swiss company) had concluded a contract for the sale of Iranian crude oil with Impianti (an Italian company). Subsequent to this, Marc Rich sent a further telex to Impianti including a clause providing that Italian law would apply and that disputes were to be referred to arbitration in London. That fax was not answered in writing. The English Court's view was that the arbitration agreement was binding.[45] The Italian Court's view was that the arbitration clause was not enforceable, in the

---

44. It is to be noted that the case came back to the *Cour de cassation* (*Cass 1e civ.*, 9 November 1993, *Bomar Oil N.V. v. ETAP*, Rev.Arb. (1994) p.108) and was the subject of a second decision in which the Court set out a substantive rule of international arbitration law, without any reference to the New York Convention, as follows:

"in the field of international arbitration, an arbitration clause, if not mentioned in the main contract, may be validly stipulated by written reference to a document which contains it, for instance general conditions or a standard contract, when the party against which the clause invoked was aware of the contents of this document at the moment of concluding the contract and when it has, albeit tacitly, accepted the incorporation of the document in the contract".

45. *Marc Rich & Co. AG v. Società Italiana Impianti* [1992] 1 Lloyd's Rep 342; *Yearbook* XVII (1992) p. 233.

absence of a written acceptance.[46]

j. James Allen

In an older decision in *James Allen (Ireland) Ltd. v. Marea Producten B.V. (Netherlands)* in 1984,[47] the Court of Appeal in The Hague held that the regular prior use of particular general conditions of trade (containing an arbitration clause) could not give rise to an enforceable arbitration agreement in a particular case where such general terms had not been specifically referred to. This is an interesting case, given that the parties had traded in corn for many years, making constant reference in at least twenty-five successive transactions to the London "Conditions of the Grain and Feed Trade Association" (GAFTA), which as is well known, contain an arbitration clause. In their twenty-sixth transaction, for some reason, they did not refer to these terms. A dispute arose, and was referred to GAFTA arbitration on the basis that the parties' continuous use evidenced consent. The ultimate award, however, was refused recognition and enforcement in The Hague, on the basis, inter alia, that "... the requirement of the 'agreement in writing' referred to in Arts. IV, para. 1 under *b* jo. II of the Convention forecloses the possibility to invoke such continuous use".

The number and range of examples, no doubt, could be expanded over many more pages. Whilst there may be an equal number or perhaps even more examples of cases in which a liberal approach has been applied to the written form requirement, the fact remains that this is an area of grave uncertainty. And as long as there is any uncertainty, there is need for a cure.

IV.   TWO INCONSISTENT PROPOSITIONS

Upon a proper analysis, the written form requirement is extremely difficult to justify at all, as a matter of policy as well as practice. Equally, however, there are a number of compelling reasons why the New York Convention should not be amended. These two propositions reflect important strands in the current UNCITRAL negotiations, and each is therefore examined in turn. The fact that the two propositions are inconsistent reflects the complexity of this topic. The inconsistency, however, also dictates a particular solution, which is explored in Sect. V.

1.   A Writing Requirement Is No Longer Defensible

There are a number of reasons why, in a world without Arts. II(2) and IV(2)(*b*) of the New York Convention, there would be no written form requirement at all. In particular:

---

46. Following the decision in *Universal Peace Shipping Enterprise SA v. Montedipe*, Italian Court of Cassation, 28 March 1991, no. 3362, *Yearbook* XVII (1992) p. 562.

47. *Yearbook* X (1985) p. 485.

- once tacit acceptance is included in the form requirement, there is a logical difficulty in excluding any other case, including pure oral agreements;
- there are flaws in the traditional justifications for writing in any event;
- the form requirement is inconsistent with other doctrines;
- the requirement is out of line with many national legislations;
- the requirement is out of line with that for choice of court clauses.

Each reason is addressed in turn.

a.   The problem of drawing a line
In the 1995 Goff Lecture,[48] Neil Kaplan QC set out an extremely compelling case for the inclusion in the definition of "writing" of cases involving written offers and tacit acceptance.

This suggested extension has received widespread approval, for the simple reason that it reflects one of the most common trade practices, and that if the form requirement cannot account for it, then this constitutes a significant failing in the arbitral system. Where a seller makes a written offer to a buyer, including an arbitration clause, and the buyer accepts by taking delivery of the goods, there is no policy reason that can justify the seller being able to sue for the price of goods, and yet escape the obligation to arbitrate contained in the same contract. This is, of course, not a new issue, as Neil Kaplan has pointed out. It was the subject of a failed proposal during the drafting of the Convention in 1958, and has been the subject of debate ever since.

However, the extension of the definition of "writing" in this way has several important consequences.

i.   A different rationale for "writing"
Cases involving non-written or tacit acceptance may be justified as satisfying a "writing" requirement on the basis that even though the offer is not accepted in writing, there will still exist some writing to evidence the arbitration agreement. In truth, this represents an important shift in the rationale for a written form. If one party's consent to arbitration is not in writing, then the Category One justifications for having a written form (as defined in Sect. III above) fall away. Writing is no longer being used to prove the initial consent to arbitration: it is not acting as a caution; it is not, of itself, evidence of actual consent, and it is not, of itself, acting as a "channeling" technique. Instead, the writing is really serving the Category Two functions identified above, which relate to the arbitration terms themselves, rather than the initial consent to those terms. Thus, if a party's consent to the written terms is to be proven, this will have to be done by way of evidence of performance or other acts constituting a tacit acceptance. There is nothing in the text itself that will prove consent by one party.

To this end, the extension of "writing" to cases of non-written acceptance reflects the same shift that has taken place in the context of choice of court clauses and the Brussels Regulation (as discussed in detail below). Whereas the Brussels Convention initially required parties' consent to a choice of court clause to be in writing, as well as the

---

48. *Op. cit.*, fn. 6.

clause itself being written, the Convention has since been modified, such that only the clause itself must be in writing – not the parties' consent to it.

If writing is then performing Category Two functions, rather than Category One functions, it becomes extremely difficult to draw a line between, on the one hand, cases involving written offers and tacit acceptance, and, on the other hand, all the other cases listed in Sect. III above, which are not obviously covered by Art. II(2) or Art. 7(2) at the moment, but which also involve a written text which can serve Category Two functions.

These other cases are now explored.

ii.   Oral offer and written acceptance

If a written offer tacitly accepted is to be included within the scope of "writing", it is difficult to exclude an oral offer (including arbitration terms) which is accepted in writing. In both cases, there exists a text which will evidence the terms of the arbitration, and will thereby serve the Category Two functions of writing. In both cases, the actual consent of one party to the written terms is not proven or evidenced by the writing itself, but will require other evidence. In both cases, it would seem unfair to allow one party to escape the arbitration clause, whilst still being free to enforce the contract.

iii.   Written offer and oral acceptance

If a written offer tacitly accepted is to be included within the scope of "writing", it is also difficult to exclude a written offer which is accepted orally, without any performance. A seller may send a written offer to a buyer, and include terms and conditions, including an arbitration clause. The buyer may telephone the seller and accept the offer, and order the goods. The seller may then manufacture the goods and despatch them to the buyer. If the buyer then refuses to take delivery, the seller may have an action on the contract. However, once again, it would appear that whilst the buyer may be liable for his default, he is free to escape arbitration. Equally, the seller may be able to sue for his loss, and yet ignore the arbitration agreement This is a curious result. It is true that the lack of performance by the buyer might make it harder to prove the buyer's consent. However, in such a case, the buyer's consent to the written terms will need to be proven in any event if the seller is to succeed in his claim, and like the previous cases, there still exists a writing which will serve the Category Two functions. Indeed, the task of proving the buyer's consent is no different from the task of proving an oral offer, where there is a written acceptance (i.e., the example above).

iv.   Incorporation by reference

Similarly, once one includes a written offer tacitly accepted within the definition of "writing", it is difficult to exclude the various examples of incorporation by reference. In Sect. III above, the following permutations were listed under this heading:

i.   Written Offer referring to another text/Written Acceptance
ii. Written Offer referring to another text/Oral or Tacit Acceptance
iii. Oral Offer referring to another text/Written Acceptance
iv. Oral Offer referring to another text/Oral or Tacit Acceptance

The first permutation poses no difficulty for present purposes.

Each of cases ii, iii and iv is no different from the initial case posited by Neil Kaplan (a written offer tacitly accepted), or from any of the other cases listed above (i.e., an oral offer accepted in writing; or a written offer accepted orally). In each case:

— the parties' contract is concluded by an offer and an acceptance, which are not entirely in writing;
— thus, the parties' actual consent to the arbitration clause is not in "writing";
— there exists a text of the arbitration clause which will satisfy the Category Two functions;
— something other than the writing itself will have to be relied upon to prove the parties' consent to arbitration.

As a matter of analysis, therefore, once one includes a non-written acceptance, there is no principled basis to include some of these examples, but exclude others.

Oral Offers and Oral Acceptances: The case of an oral offer and an oral acceptance which is made by reference to written terms warrants further analysis. As pointed out above, whilst this has been seen as the most controversial example, it also reflects an extremely common area of commercial activity – and arbitration practice (in particular salvage cases). There are, therefore, strong policy reasons to include such cases within the form requirement. As pointed out above, the salvage scenario is, in fact, analytically no different from any other "incorporation by reference" case or any other example of non-written acceptance. Equally, it is indistinguishable from a text produced by an intermediary (such as a broker). In each case, there is a text that satisfies the Category Two functions, and in each case evidence beyond the text itself will be required to prove initial consent.

The fact that this appears to strain the meaning of "writing" is only a reflection of the confusion between Category One and Category Two above. As long as "writing" refers to the text of the arbitration terms, rather than the parties' initial consent to those terms (again, as it now does in the context of choice of court clauses), there is no difficulty at all.

Hence, Sect. 5(3) of the English Arbitration Act 1996 provides as follows:

> "Where parties agree otherwise than in writing by reference to terms which are in writing, they make an agreement in writing."

This wording covers the salvage example, but also encapsulates the core principle that is common to, and underlies each of the examples above. In short, the salvage example is no different.

As will be seen below in this section, this analysis has now been adopted in the latest negotiations of the UNCITRAL Working Group, in the context of proposed modifications to Art. 7(2) of the Model Law. Art. 7(2) currently provides for "incorporation by reference" in the following terms:

> "The reference in a contract to a document containing an arbitration clause

constitutes an arbitration agreement provided that the contract is in writing and the reference is such as to make that clause part of the contract."

Recognizing that "incorporation by reference" is indistinguishable from many of the scenarios listed above, and seeking to cover all such scenarios, the latest draft produced by the UNCITRAL Working Group has transformed this wording into the following:

"For the avoidance of doubt, the reference in a contract or a separate arbitration agreement to a writing containing an arbitration clause constitutes an arbitration agreement in writing provided that the reference is such as to make that clause part of the contract or the separate arbitration agreement, notwithstanding that the contract or the separate arbitration agreement has been concluded orally, by conduct or by other means not in writing."[49]

Oral References to a "Text": If an oral offer (by reference to a written text) accepted orally or by conduct, is to be included within the definition of "writing", then it becomes extremely difficult to justify any written form requirement at all. This is so, because of the difficulty of drawing a line between the following examples:

i.   an oral offer by reference to LOF, and an oral acceptance or acceptance by conduct (the salvage example);
ii. an oral offer by reference to the ICC pamphlet containing the ICC arbitration rules, and an oral acceptance or acceptance by conduct;
iii. an oral offer to arbitrate in London under the English Arbitration Act 1996, and an oral acceptance or acceptance by conduct.

Again, in each case there is a text setting out the arbitration terms (i.e., the Category Two function), and in each case the parties' actual consent to arbitration will need to be proven by some other means than the writing itself. There is no distinction as a matter of logic between a form such as the LOF which contains an arbitration "clause", and the ICC Rules. Each is simply a text, which has no significance at all until it is proven that the text has been incorporated into the parties' agreement. The fact that the LOF terms may begin with words such as "The parties hereby agree that ..." makes no difference – if the parties have not in fact incorporated this into their agreement, this wording has no more magic than any other wording. So too, the English Arbitration Act 1996, in example iii, serves precisely the same function as the LOF in example i. It is a text setting out arbitration terms in much the same way as the ICC Rules.

Logic, at this stage, produces odd results. As a matter of English law, every arbitration has a seat, even if none is expressed in the agreement itself. Once the seat has been determined, this will normally give rise to an arbitration law, as in example iii

---

49. U.N. Doc. A/CN.9/WG.II/XXXVI/CRP.1/Add.2 (6 March 2002), para 5.

above. On this logic, an oral agreement to "arbitration", is an agreement in writing.[50]

v.   Conclusions on logic

Aside from logic, there may be an instinctive comfort with written offers and tacit acceptance, as compared with all the other examples listed above. However, the important point is to recognize the significance of the shift from a written acceptance to a non-written acceptance. Once that shift is made (just as it has been made in the context of choice of court clauses), "writing" performs a different function, and any line that is drawn between different cases then becomes arbitrary. On this view, the only logical position is to abandon the written form requirement overall.

b.   Doubts about justifications

Upon a closer look, the traditional justifications for the written form requirement, as set out in Sect. III above, are open to attack.

i.   Category One rationales

It is often observed that contracts of very high value are concluded orally every day. Transactions may involve multiple millions, and may have the potential of a devastating impact upon one or all of the parties involved. Equally, such transactions might have a serious effect upon the wider community. In the absence of a writing requirement, the law imposes no cautionary, evidential or channelling device on these arrangements. And yet, in a world in which international commercial arbitration has become a necessary and integral feature of international trade, and is now regulated by a network of modern laws and conventions, it is somewhat strange that an agreement to arbitration is still considered more significant than other contracts. In truth, the Category One functions all betray an outdated conception of arbitration, in which the process was seen as an inferior alternative to national courts, to be treated with caution, and closely policed. Times and conceptions have changed. As Gerold Herrmann has pointed out in his 1998 Freshfields Lecture:[51]

> "... in an international setting the thrust of an arbitration agreement is not the negative idea of excluding court jurisdiction ... rather, it is the positive idea of creating for an individual case something that does not currently exist, namely an international commercial court. As Yves Fortier QC once put it, international arbitration here is not an alternative, it has become, to a great extent, 'the only game in town'."

What may originally have been a protection, is now a means of defeating legitimate

---

50. It will be noted that whilst the latest UNCITRAL Working Group's draft covers virtually every case above (including salvage), the expression "a writing containing an arbitration clause" excludes the arguably absurd examples of an oral agreement referring to a national law, or an arbitral seat. As such, the provision achieves a satisfactory result.
51. HERRMANN, "Freshfields Lecture", *op. cit.*, fn. 6, p. 215. See also: HERRMANN, *ICCA Congress Series no. 6, op. cit.*, fn. 6, pp. 45-46.

commercial expectations, as the war stories in Sect. III reveal. It cannot be right that a party is allowed to enforce a contract, yet escape an arbitration provision that may have been an integral part of the same deal.

Further, each of the constituent elements within the Category One rationale does not easily withstand scrutiny. The *Cautionary* function ignores the many cases in which a party is held bound to an arbitration clause, without having signed a contract, or having had his or her mind focused upon the arbitration clause. Hence, for example, cases on assignment, succession, novation, subrogation, groups of companies and so on. Equally, "consent" is often something of a legal fiction in simpler cases, such as those involving the incorporation by reference of standard terms or forms. In many scenarios, it cannot really be said that the existence of a text has acted as a "caution".

The *Evidentiary* function is also questionable. The assumption that "writing" has a certain special quality over other forms of evidence has historical roots – which have little relevance today. In England, the special significance of writing goes back at least to the Statute of Frauds of 1677 – one of the more important statutes in the development of English law, the effects of which are still resonant in English law today. This statute introduced writing requirements for a range of transactions. Whilst many of these requirements have remained (albeit in modified form), the original reasons for the statute have not. Firstly, in seventeenth century England, when the statute was passed, there was a particular problem in controlling unruly or dishonest juries. The medieval method of controlling the jury by "writ of attaint" (removal of civil rights) had become obsolete; the practice of controlling it by fine or imprisonment had been declared illegal,[52] and the modern device of getting an order for a new trial, when the verdict was clearly against the weight of evidence, was in its infancy. Secondly, though a jury was generally guided by the evidence, it was at the time entitled to decide a case from its own knowledge of the facts. It was therefore a necessary precaution to make certain kinds of evidence necessary for the proof of certain transactions, since it placed a limitation upon the otherwise uncontrolled discretion of the jury. Further, the rules of procedure at this time were such that neither the parties to an action nor their husbands or wives, nor any persons who had any interest in the result of the litigation, were competent witnesses. These rules were capable of working grave injustice, since the courts were effectively deprived from getting information upon the facts at issue from those most likely to know them. The requirement of writing was perceived as a specific solution. Whilst this did not preclude the risk of forgery or perjury, it at least ensured that some evidence of the given transactions was submitted to the court, thereby rendering the prosecution of wholly baseless claims more difficult.[53]

Even during its currency, however, the Statute of Frauds was heavily criticized, on the basis that the insistence on writing was out of line with commercial practice, and was

---

52. *Bushell's* Case (1670) Vaughan's Rep 435.
53. See HOLDSWORTH, *A History of English Law*, vol. 6 (Sweet & Maxwell 1937) pp. 379-396. See also, WIGMORE, "A General Survey of the History of the Rules of Evidence" in *Selected Essays in Anglo-American Legal History*, vol. 2 (Little, Brown & Co. 1908).

therefore capable of being used as a means of escaping genuine transactions.[54]

In the intervening 300 or so years, times and practices have (thankfully) changed. Juries are less common, and where used less unruly; and rules of evidence and procedure have largely met the criticisms of previous centuries. "Writing" must now include a wide range of physical, magnetic, electronic, optical and other media. As a type of evidence, it may no longer be the most reliable, or necessarily probative. Equally, rules of evidence and procedure now allow for the careful assessment of many other types of evidence – hence most legal systems' increasing toleration of oral contracts.

In any event, even if "writing" has a special evidential value, the same observations as with the *Cautionary* function also apply: there are many situations today in which "writing" exists, and yet where the text itself says very little if anything about a party's actual consent.

As for the *Channelling* function, there has been a marked tendency to relax requirements of form in many other areas where traditionally writing had been used to differentiate certain legal mechanisms. One example, where writing has long had a stronghold, is English land law, and in particular the requirement in English law that a conveyance of land be effected by "deed". In English law, a "deed" is a document which meets a series of special form requirements, including a statement on its face that it is intended to be a deed, a signature, witnesses, and in some cases (before 1989) a seal (originally a red wax seal, but nowadays a red and embossed paper disc) As one leading author has observed:[55]

> "It is curious to reflect on the importance attached historically to the requirement that a deed be signed, sealed and delivered by the grantor. Conveyancing, magic and sorcery have never been wholly unconnected phenomena, as is made clear by the medieval ritual and symbolism which attended the 'feoffment with livery of seisin'.[56] It is an interesting feature of the social anthropology of land law that the

---

54. See Papers of the Juridical Society 289, cited by HOLDSWORTH, *op. cit.*, fn. 53, p. 390, fn. 2:

   "The chief objection to the statute, and the cause to which most of its difficulties may be traced, seems to lie in this, that the prescribed mode of transacting business is so far at variance with the natural mode, that there is always in practice a conflict between them.... The statute, in prescribing a general use of writing, is at variance with a natural law of social action. Hence it is very commonly disregarded and so operates as a positive danger instead of a safeguard.... If it comes to pass that men may act, almost habitually, in a manner which will bring on them the penalties of the law, or at least deprive them of its protection, and yet without any imputation of moral blame on the score of dishonesty or even of negligence, it surely affords a strong argument to show, that in such a case the law is in fault, and has attempted to guide the conduct of men in a wrong direction: and such seems to be the case with the Statute of Frauds."

55. GRAY, *Elements of Land Law* (Butterworths 1987) p. 223.

56. A solemn ceremony whereby the parties to a transfer of the interest entered upon the land conveyed, where the feoffer (grantor) in the presence of witnesses, delivered the seisin (feudal possession) to the feoffee (grantee) either by some symbolic act, such as handing him a twig or clod of earth, or by expressing appropriate words of alienation and leaving him in possession of

talismanic effect of a little red wafer is such as to confer upon certain transactions a legal efficacy which they would not otherwise possess.... In 1971 Lord Wilberforce, speaking extra-judicially in the House of Lords, castigated 'this medieval doctrine of the seal' and expressed the hope that 'we might have got rid of that mumbo-jumbo and aligned ourselves with most civilized countries'.[57] "

By the Law of Property (Miscellaneous Provisions) Act 1989, the requirements for a "deed" were very significantly relaxed.

ii.   Category Two rationales

The insistence upon writing in order to ensure certainty within the arbitral process, as well as minimizing disputes before national courts and facilitating the enforcement and recognition of awards, has merit in itself. However, it expresses an aspiration, which is simply absent in many arbitration agreements. Most national systems now make every effort to enforce arbitration agreements. This is so, even if the agreement itself is sketchy or badly drafted. In the realm of ad hoc agreements, arbitration clauses may well be brief and may well make no mention of any particular terms or conditions. In English law, an agreement that provides "Arbitration: London" is a valid arbitration agreement, as is a clause providing simply "arbitration". Indeed, in one well-known case, the English Court of Appeal granted a stay of legal proceedings on the basis of a contract which included the heading "Suitable arbitration clause", although nothing further had been inserted.[58]

As long as such agreements are enforceable (as they should be), it is difficult to justify a written form requirement on the basis that the writing will forestall disputes about the particular arbitration terms.

c.   *Dislocation with other doctrines*

As has already been observed, there are a number of doctrines that are applied in many different legal systems by which parties who have not signed the arbitration agreement, and have not been involved in any "exchange" as such, are held subject to and bound by an arbitration agreement. In effect, these are doctrines which treat entities as parties to an arbitration agreement – notwithstanding the fact that the written form requirement has not been satisfied. For example, doctrines concerning the universal transfers of assets, including successions; mergers, de-mergers and acquisitions of companies; specific transfers of assets, including transfers of contract; assignments of receivables or debts; novation; subrogation; contracts for the benefit of third parties and stipulations in favour of a third party (*stipulation pour autrui*) and multiple party situations involving

---

the land. For a description of this ceremony, see Rudyard KIPLING, *Puck of Pook's Hill* (London 1906) p. 12. For an historical account, see *Manton v. Parabolic Pty Ltd.* [1985] 2 NSWLR 361, 367A-368C. Feoffments were gradually replaced by deeds, and eventually abolished by the Law of Property Act 1925.

57. Parliamentary Debates, House of Lords, Official Report (1970-1971), Vol. 315, Col. 1213 (25 February 1971).

58. *Hobbs Padgett & Co. (Reinsurance) Ltd. v. J.C. Kirkland Ltd.* [1969] 2 Lloyd's Rep 547.

groups of contracts or groups of companies.

One particular growth area in some systems (notably in the United States) concerns the use of estoppel doctrines to bind entities to arbitration agreements. There are several prevailing theories of equitable estoppel in relation to arbitration agreements, all of which appear to have developed without regard to the written form requirement, and all of which appear to be inconsistent with it. Under one theory, a non-signatory to an arbitration clause can be compelled to arbitrate when the non-signatory knowingly exploits the agreement containing the arbitration clause. This is so, even though the arbitration agreement has never been signed by the entity in question. Under another theory, signatories can be bound to arbitrate with a non-signatory because of a "close relationship between the entities involved, as well as the relationship of the alleged wrongs to the non-signatory's obligations and duties in the contract ... and [the fact that] the claims were intimately founded in and intertwined with the underlying contractual obligations".[59]

Doctrines such as these undermine the basic policy justifications for the imposition of a written form requirement. If a non-signatory can be bound by an arbitration clause on the basis of equity, in the absence of any writing, it becomes a little difficult to see why in other instances writing is still insisted upon. One distinction might be that these cases concern the compelling of a party to arbitrate, rather than the proof of consent, yet the reasoning in many of these cases appears to proceed on the basis of a party's implied consent (albeit coupled with a perceived unconscionability if the party is then allowed to act inconsistently with such consent).

The dislocation between doctrines such as these and the form requirement has recently been recognized in England. The Contracts (Rights of Third Parties) Act 1999 introduced into English law for the first time a right of third parties to enforce contractual rights for their benefit. By Sect. 8 of that Act, where a third party enforces a benefit under a contract which is subject to a written arbitration agreement, the third party is treated as a party to the arbitration agreement for the purposes of Sect. 5 of the Arbitration Act 1996. In this way, the section ensures that the arrangement is treated as satisfying the written form requirement.[60]

Further, this is an issue that has been addressed in connection with choice of court clauses. In the context of the Brussels I Regulation, it is clear that a third party who succeeds to the rights of an original contracting party may rely upon, and is bound by, the clause which, in point of form, bound the original contracting party. Hence, in *Gerling v. il Tesoro*,[61] a third party beneficiary was held to be entitled to rely upon a clause inserted into a contract made for his benefit, and in *Tilly Russ*,[62] a third-party holder of a Bill of Lading was held to be bound by the clause which had bound the shipper, the original contracting party to whose legal position the third party had, under national law, succeeded. Once the original formal validity of the clause has been established as

---

59. See, e.g., *E.I. DuPont De Nemours and Co. v. Rhone Poulenc Fiber and Resin Intermediaries,* 269 F.3d 187 (3d Cir. 2001); *Thomson-CSF, S.A. v. American Arbitration Association*, 64 F.3d 773 (2d Cir. 1995).

60. See MERKIN, *Privity of Contract* (LLP 2000) Sects. 5.115-5.122.

61. [1983] E.C.R. 2503.

62. [1984] E.C.R. 2417.

between the original contracting parties, its effect upon third parties appears to be a matter for the national law of the court seised with the dispute (including its conflict of laws rules). In this way, the form requirement will not defeat the arrangement.

As will be seen below, this reasoning is consonant with the writing requirement in the Brussels I Regulation (given the very liberal nature of that requirement). Such reasoning, if applied to arbitration agreements, however, would be inconsistent with Art. II(2) of the New York Convention, and Art. 7(2) of the Model Law.

d.   National disparities

One of the suggested functions of Art. II(2) of the New York Convention, and the core function of Art. 7(2) of the Model Law, was to create harmonization between different systems on the question of the enforceability of arbitration agreements. The fact remains that such harmonization has simply not occurred.

Further, and more importantly, the requirements in Art. II(2) and Art. 7(2) are now out of step with the positions taken by many national legislatures, many of which now allow purely oral arbitration agreements. In so far as Art. II(2) or Art. 7(2) seek to reflect the needs of international commerce, they are now anachronistic.[63]

As long as there are disparities between national legislation and the New York Convention on this issue, there remains the risk that a solution in one system will simply result in the defeat of an arbitration agreement or an award, once the Convention is applied. Indeed, more liberal national standards may even engender business expectations, which may simply be thwarted by the Convention.

A thorough survey of national arbitration laws is obviously beyond the scope of this paper. The following is by way of illustration only.

i.   England and Wales

In England and Wales, an arbitration agreement is within the scope of the English arbitration legislation only if it satisfies a "writing" requirement. This has been so at least since the Arbitration Act of 1698.[64] The form requirement is now embodied in Sect. 5 of the Arbitration Act 1996.[65] During consultation on the Bill that became the 1996 Act,

---

63. In addition to disparities with national legislatures, there are also disparities between the New York Convention and the Model Law, and other international conventions. Compare, for example, Art. II(2) and Art. 7(2) with Art. 1(2) of the European Convention on International Commercial Arbitration (Geneva, 1961); Art. 1 of the Inter-American Convention on International Commercial Arbitration (Panama, 1975); Art. 25(I) of the Washington Convention (1961). Indeed, Art. 1(a) of the Geneva Convention of 1927 required that an arbitration agreement be valid "under the law applicable to it", imposing no other specific requirements of form.

64. See MERKIN, *op. cit.*, fn. 18, Sect. 2.5; *Walters v. Morgan* (1792) 2 Cox Eq 369; *Fleming v. Doig (Grimsby) Ltd* (1921) 38 RPC 57. Under the 1698 Act and succeeding legislation, the submission itself, and not merely the agreement to arbitrate, had to be in writing before it could be made a rule of the court: *Ansell v. Evans* (1796) TR 1.

65. See MERKIN, *op. cit.*, fn. 18, Sects. 2.5-2.11; MUSTILL and BOYD, *Commercial Arbitration – Companion to 2nd Edition*; *Russell on Arbitration*, 21st ed. (Sweet & Maxwell 1997) Sects. 2-030 to 2-044; VEEDER, "National Report England" in ICCA *International Handbook on Commercial Arbitration* (hereinafter *Handbook*) (Kluwer) Supplement 23, March 1997, pp. 15-16; LANDAU,

the UK Government received submissions that the writing requirement should be abandoned, since it no longer reflected commercial realities. The Departmental Advisory Committee on Arbitration Law (DAC), being the specialist committee that advised the Government on this legislation, concluded that the writing requirement should be retained. In its Report of February 1996, the DAC commented (in part) as follows:

> "31. Article 7 of the Model Law requires the arbitration agreement to be in writing. We have not followed the precise wording of this Article, for the reasons given in the Mustill Report (p. 52)[66] though we have incorporated much of that Article in the Bill.
> 32. The requirement for the arbitration agreement to be in writing is the position at present under Section 32 of the Arbitration Act 1950 and Section 7 of the Arbitration Act 1975. If an arbitration agreement is not in writing then it is not completely ineffective, since the common law recognizes such agreements and is saved by Clause 81(2)(a).
> 33. We remain of the view expressed in the Consultative Paper issued with the draft Clauses published in July 1995, that there should be a requirement for writing. An arbitration agreement has the important effect of contracting out of the right to go to the court, *i.e.* it deprives the parties of that basic right. To our minds an agreement of such importance should be in some written form. Furthermore the need for such form should help to reduce disputes as to whether or not an arbitration agreement was made and as to its terms."…

However, two factors reduce the significance of the requirement. Firstly, the actual definition of an "agreement in writing", and secondly, the recognition of purely oral agreements.

The Definition of an "Agreement in Writing": The definition of an "agreement in writing" in the 1996 Act reflects English common law, which has long included a far broader range of situations than those articulated in Art. II(2) of the Convention and Art. 7 of the Model Law. Hence, Sect. 5 of the 1996 Act provides as follows:

> "5-(1) The provisions of this Part apply only where the arbitration agreement is in writing, and any other agreement between the parties as to any matter is effective for the purposes of this Part only if in writing.
> The expressions 'agreement', 'agree' and 'agreed' shall be construed accordingly.
> (2) There is an agreement in writing –
> (a) if the agreement is made in writing (whether or not it is signed by the parties),

---

"The Effect of the New English Arbitration Act 1996 on Institutional Arbitration", 13 J.Int.Arb., p. 113 at pp. 121-123.

66. The DAC Report of 1989, *op. cit.*, fn. 24, which recommended that England & Wales should not adopt the UNCITRAL Model Law.

(b) if the agreement is made by exchange of communications in writing, or

(c) if the agreement is evidenced in writing.

(3) Where parties agree otherwise than in writing by reference to terms which are in writing, they make an agreement in writing.

(4) An agreement is evidenced in writing if an agreement made otherwise than in writing is recorded by one of the parties, or by a third party, with the authority of the parties to the agreement.

(5) An exchange of written submissions in arbitral or legal proceedings in which the existence of an agreement otherwise than in writing is alleged by one party against another party and not denied by the other party in his response constitutes as between those parties an agreement in writing to the effect alleged.

(6) References in this Part to anything being written or in writing include its being recorded by any means."

Sect. 5 confirms the established principle of English law that an agreement in writing is binding whether or not the parties have signed it, as long as an intention to be bound can be ascertained from the surrounding circumstances. In fact, the 1996 Act defines "writing" in the broadest possible terms, and in so doing, reflects the same shift that has taken place in relation to choice of court clauses within the Brussels I Regulation: there remains a requirement of writing, but it is the *terms* of the arbitration agreement that must be in writing, not the parties' *consent* to those terms. This is clear, in particular, from Sects. 5(2)(c), (3) and (4) of the Act. As such, writing performs the Category Two function – not the Category One function – outlined in Sect. III above.[67] Hence:

i. By Sect. 5(6), "writing" means "recorded by any means", which would include any media, whether ink, magnetic, electronic, optical, or methods still beyond our imagination. Equally, Sect. 5(2)(b) refers to an exchange of "communications", rather than stipulating precise methods or technologies.

ii. A partly oral and partly written agreement falls within the Act, given the breadth of Sect. 5(2)(a), as well as Sect. 5(2)(c) and the concept of "evidenced" in writing.

iii. Sect. 5(3) addresses the many types of agreement where the consent to written terms is concluded otherwise than in writing. This caters for oral contracts for the sale of goods which have incorporated standard commodity arbitration rules, salvage contracts, and all forms of acceptance by performance or conduct or tacit acceptance.[68] The DAC justified this provision in its February 1996 Report as follows:

---

67. As pointed out earlier, the Category Two function was specifically endorsed by the DAC (in substance, albeit not in name). See para. 35 of its February 1996 Report, which is quoted in fn. 10.

68. For the equivalent position at common law on tacit acceptance, see *Zambia Steel v. Clark and Eaton* [1986] 2 Lloyd's Rep 225. Shortly before the passing of the 1996 Act, it had been held in *Jardine Birske v. Cathedral Works Organisation (Chester) Ltd.* [1996] ADRLN 14, that an oral agreement to adopt standard form arbitration rules was not within the Arbitration Act 1950, on the basis that the oral agreement remained the vehicle for the agreement to arbitrate. This decision has been reversed by Sect. 5(3) of the 1996 Act.

"36. Sub-Section 5(3). This is designed to cover, amongst other things, extremely common situations such as salvage operations, where parties make an oral agreement which incorporates by reference the terms of a written form of agreement (e.g. Lloyd's Open Form), which contains an arbitration clause. Whilst greatly extending the definition of 'writing', the DAC is of the view that given the frequency and importance of such activity, it was essential that it be provided for in the Bill. The reference could be to a written agreement containing an arbitration clause, or to a set of written arbitration rules, or to an individual written arbitration agreement. This provision would also cover agreement by conduct. For example, party A may agree to buy from party B a quantity of goods on certain terms and conditions (which include an arbitration clause) which are set out in writing and sent to party B, with a request that he sign and return the order form. If, which is by no means uncommon, party B fails to sign the order form, or send any document in response to the order, but manufactures and delivers the goods in accordance with the contract to party A, who pays for them in accordance with the contract, this could constitute an agreement 'otherwise than in writing by reference to terms which are in writing…', and could therefore include an effective arbitration agreement. The provision therefore seeks to meet the criticisms that have been made of Article 7(2) of the Model Law in this regard (see e.g. the Sixth Goff Lecture, delivered by Neil Kaplan QC in Hong Kong in November 1995, (1996) 12 Arb. Int. 35). A written agreement made by reference to separate written terms would, of course, be caught by Clause 5(2)."

iv. Sect. 5(4), in line with Sect. 5(2)(b), allows for an agreement to be evidenced in writing, and in particular to be recorded by, amongst others, a third party with the authority of the parties to the agreement (e.g., an intermediary). Given that this third party could of course be the tribunal, the parties are free during a hearing to make whatever arrangements or changes to the agreed procedure they wish, as long as these are recorded by the tribunal. Clearly, this sub-section also has a wider effect, allowing for the recording of an oral agreement at any stage.

Purely Oral Arbitration Agreements: Secondly, purely oral arbitration agreements (i.e., the rare case in which there is no writing at all to meet any of the requirements of Sect. 5 of the 1996 Act) remain valid as a matter of English common law, albeit outside the scope of the arbitration legislation. Hence Sect. 81(1) of the 1996 Act provides that:

"81.–(1) Nothing in this Part shall be construed as excluding the operation of any rule of law consistent with the provisions of this Part, in particular, any rule of law as to—
…
(b) the effect of an oral arbitration agreement;…"

The actual viability of a purely oral arbitration agreement remains in doubt, however, given that it will benefit from none of the protections (and judicial restraints) embodied in the 1996 Act.

ii.   France

French law requires domestic arbitration agreements to be in writing. Art. 1443 of the New Code of Civil Procedure provides that:

> "[a]n arbitration clause is void unless it is set forth in writing in the main agreement or in a document to which that agreement refers".[69]

However, as pointed out in *Fouchard Gaillard Goldman*,[70] Title V of Book IV of the French New Code of Civil Procedure, which addresses international arbitration, contains no similar provision with respect to either the form or the proof of an arbitration agreement.[71] Most commentators have concluded that French international arbitration law contains no requirement of form.

The only doubt appears to be Art. 1499, which indirectly addresses the issue of form by stipulating (in the context of the recognition and enforcement of awards), that the existence of an award shall be established by submitting the original document "together with the arbitration agreement". Again as noted in *Fouchard Gaillard Goldman*,[72] it is unclear whether one can infer from this that there exists a written form requirement. Those authors argue that no such inference arises:

> "because this provision in fact merely requires that the plaintiff should put the court hearing the action for enforcement in a position to establish, prima facie, the existence of an arbitration agreement".[73]

Indeed, even if an arbitration is subject to French law, it seems that the form requirements of Arts. 1443 and 1449 apply to the extent that the parties have not made any other specific agreement. It follows that oral agreements to arbitrate are valid as a matter of French law. This is so even when the arbitration is subject to French law, since, according to *Fouchard Gaillard Goldman*, the mere fact that an arbitration agreement is in a form other than that prescribed in Art. 1443 is sufficient to establish the parties' intention to depart from the provisions of that Article.[74]

---

69. Art. 1449 imposes an evidential requirement for submission agreements.
70. Sect. 607 et seq.
71. See FOUCHARD, "L'arbitrage international en France après le décret du 12 mai 1981", 109 J.D.I (1982) p. 374 at p. 385; cf. GOLDMAN, "La nouvelle réglementation française de l'arbitrage international" in *The Art of Arbitration – Liber Amoricum Pieter Sanders*, p. 153 at p. 161.
72. Sect. 608.
73. See also (as cited in *Fouchard Gaillard Goldman*) BELLET and MEZGER, "L'arbitrage international dans le nouveau code de procédure civile", Rev Crit. DIP (1981) p. 611 at p. 622; AUDIT, "A National Codification of International Commercial Arbitration: The French Decree of May 12, 1981" in T. CARBONNEAU, ed., *Resolving Transnational Disputes Through Arbitration* (1984) p. 117 at p. 126; DERAINS and GOODMAN-EVERARD, "National Report France" in *Handbook*.
74. See the decision of the *Cour d'appel* of Paris of 19 February 1988 in *Firme Peter Biegi v. Brittania* (affirmed by the *Cour de cassation*, 18 February 1992) Rev.Arb. (1993) p. 103.

iii.   Switzerland

Art. 178 of the Federal Private International Law Act provides as follows:

> "1. As regards form, the arbitration agreement shall be valid if made in writing, by telegram, telex, telecopier or any other means of communication which permits it to be evidenced by a text...."

This rule has been described as an "independent substantive conflict rule",[75] which was made necessary by the strong international criticism of the previous Art. 6 of the Concordat, which, in conjunction with Art. 13 of the Swiss Code of Obligations, imported a requirement of signature. By contrast, Art. 178 allows for a writing in any form, whether or not signed, and imposes no requirement of "exchange".

iv.   Netherlands

Art. 1021 of the Arbitration Act 1986 provides as follows:

> "The arbitration agreement shall be proven by an instrument in writing. For this purpose an instrument in writing which provides for arbitration or refers to standard conditions providing for arbitration is sufficient, provided that this instrument is expressly or impliedly accepted by or on behalf of the other party."

The 1986 Act abolished the possibility which existed under the old Dutch Act that an arbitration agreement be concluded orally.[76] However, this formulation is very broad, and is obviously far broader than Art. II(2) and Art. 7(2).[77]

v.   Sweden

The 1999 Swedish Arbitration Act imposes no form requirements at all, it being established that an arbitration agreement may be concluded orally.[78] This has long been the position in Swedish law.[79]

vi.   New Zealand

Perhaps the clearest and most liberal provision is Sect. 7(1) of the New Zealand Arbitration Act 1996 (a Model Law jurisdiction). This expressly provides for arbitration agreements concluded orally, without any further provisions as to the exact form such

---

75. BLESSING in BERTI, ed., *International Arbitration in Switzerland* (Helbing & Lichtenhahn/Kluwer 2000) pp. 174-175.

76. SANDERS and van den BERG, *The Netherlands Arbitration Act 1986* (Kluwer 1987) p. 12.

77. See further LAZIĆ and MEIJER, "Netherlands" in WEIGAND, ed., *Practitioner's Handbook on International Arbitration* (Beck 2002) p. 892.

78. BERGER, "The Arbitration Agreement under the Swedish 1999 Arbitration Act and the German 1998 Arbitration Act", 17 Arb Int'l (2001) p. 389 at pp. 395-396.

79. See *Arbitration in Sweden* (Stockholm Chamber of Commerce 1984) p. 29.

an oral agreement might take, or the way in which it might be evidenced.[80]

These are further reasons to revisit – and arguably to abandon – the written form requirement.

e. Choice of court clauses

Amongst the vast tracts on the written form requirement in the context of arbitration clauses, there has been very little consideration of the equivalent form requirements for jurisdiction or choice of court clauses. This is perhaps surprising, given the obvious parallels between the two, and given the similar debates that have already taken place in that context.

In addressing choice of court clauses under the Brussels Convention 1968 and the Lugano Convention 1988, (and now the Brussels I Regulation)[81] the European Court of Justice (ECJ) has repeatedly stated that the purpose of the written form requirement is to establish "clearly and precisely" the existence of consensus between the parties upon the agreement on choice of court.[82] In the original version of the 1968 Convention, jurisdiction agreements had to be "in writing or evidenced in writing", and this requirement was strictly interpreted by the European Court of Justice,[83] as well as in the highest courts in the original Contracting States.[84] The requirement excluded the sending of standard printed conditions, unless the recipient signed a document which expressly referred to the conditions. Hence, in *Salotti v. RÜWA* (1976), it was held that a choice of court clause clearly printed on the reverse side of a contract did not satisfy the form requirement, and in *Segoura v. Bonakdarian* (1976), a confirmation in writing by one party that a sale was made upon general trading conditions (which contained a choice of court agreement) was held to be unenforceable.

The strictness of this test led to a widespread concern that the requirement was out of step with the needs of international commerce. In particular, it was noted that the use

---

80. See the discussion of this provision in the *New Zealand Law Commission Report No. 20: Arbitration* (October 1991) pp. 165-166.

81. Council Regulation (EC) No. 4/2001 on Jurisdiction and the Recognition and Enforcement of Judgments in Civil and Commercial Matters of 22 December 2000. This came into force on 1 March 2002, and is the successor to the 1968 Brussels Convention. The text of the Regulation (in English) can be found at: http://europa.eu.int/eur-lex/en/consleg/pdf/2001/en_2001R0044_do_001.pdf

82. *Salotti v. RÜWA* [1976] E.C.R. 1831; Case 25/76 *Galeries Segoura Sprl v. Bonakdarian* [1976] E.C.R. 1851; *Mainschiffahrts-Genossenschaft v. Les Gravières Rhénanes SARL* (20 February 1997).

83. See *Dicey and Morris on The Conflict of Laws*, 13th ed. (Sweet & Maxwell 2000) Sects. 12-098 to 12-105 (hereinafter *Dicey and Morris*); BRIGGS and REES, *Civil Jurisdiction and Judgments*, 3rd ed. (LLP 2002) Sects. 2.85 to 2.89; and, e.g., Case 24/76 *Salotti v. RÜWA*, *op. cit.*, fn. 82; Case 25/76 *Galeries Segoura Sprl v. Bonakdarian* [1976] *op. cit.*, fn. 82. Subsequent decisions reflected a liberalization, such as Case 71/83 *The Tilly Russ* [1984] E.C.R. 2417; [1985] Q.B. 931 (and the comment by NORTH, L.M.C.L.Q. (1985) p. 177) (analysis by the ECJ as to jurisdiction clauses in a Bill of Lading); *Credit Suisse Financial Products v. Soc Gen d'Entreprises* [1997] I.L.Pr.165 (CA) (signature on document referring to printed conditions containing jurisdiction agreement).

84. See *Dicey and Morris*, *op. cit.*, fn. 83, citing *Itier v. Soc. Genovesi*, French *Cour de cassation*, 1985, Digest I-17.1.2-B32; *Lejeune v. Soc. F.I.A.S.*, French *Cour de cassation*, 1989, Rev Cri (1990) p. 58.

of printed standard conditions and communications by telex and fax were widespread, and yet apparently outwith the form requirement. As a result, the 1978 Accession Convention added that the agreement could be in a form which accorded with practices in international trade or commerce of which the parties were or ought to have been aware.[85] This was then developed in the course of the Lugano Convention negotiations, and further changes were reflected in the 1989 Accession Convention.[86] As the text of the Convention has developed, the requirement of consensus has remained unchanged, but the formalities themselves have become "signposts towards the existence of a consensus",[87] rather than mandatory requirements. The crucial shift, for present purposes, has been from the initial position, which required both the jurisdiction clause and the assent or agreement to be in writing, to an acceptance that the form requirement may be satisfied if the clause is in writing, albeit the assent or agreement is not. In other words, the accepted position in this context has crossed the critical threshold identified in Sect. III(4) above, and writing now serves Category Two – not Category One – functions. However, the form requirement continues to be justified.

For a choice of court clause to satisfy the current form requirement in Art. 23(1) of the Brussels I Regulation (Sect. 7 *"Prorogation of jurisdiction"*), it must be:

> "(a) in writing or evidenced in writing, or
> (b) in a form which accords with practices which the parties have established between themselves, or
> (c) in international trade or commerce, in a form which accords with a usage of which the parties are or ought to have been aware and which in such trade or commerce is widely known to, and regularly observed by, parties to contracts of the type involved in the particular trade or commerce concerned...".[88]

Art. 23(2) of the Regulation provides that:

> "Any communication by electronic means which provides a durable record of the agreement shall be equivalent to 'writing'."

As matters now stand, the three requirements in Art. 23(1) are interpreted broadly. For example, in *Tilly Russ v. Nova*,[89] a clause printed on a Bill of Lading was regarded as within the form requirement because it represented written evidence of an orally agreed clause. In *Berghoefer GmbH v. ASA S.A.*,[90] the ECJ held that the formal requirements of what was Art. 17 of the Brussels Convention was satisfied where A and B concluded an express oral agreement on jurisdiction, and A wrote to B confirming the agreement, and

---

85. "Schlosser Report", para. 170.
86. P. JENARD and G. MÖLLER, "Report on the Convention on jurisdicton and the enforcement of civil and commercial matters done at Lugano on 16 September 1988", OJ 1990 C 189, para. 170.
87. See BRIGGS and REES, *op. cit.*, fn. 83.
88. This wording replicates Art. 17 of the 1968 Convention.
89. [1984] E.C.R. 2417.
90. Case 221/84 [1985] E.C.R. 2699.

B raised no objection within a reasonable time of receipt of the letter (but never signed the only written document). Whilst the basis of this decision has been thought to be the principle of good faith, or a kind of estoppel, the rule has no rigid limits, and it has been observed that "it may operate to subvert the formal requirement of writing wherever actual agreement is able to be clearly established by other means".[91]

Further, in *Powell Duffryn plc v. Petereit*,[92] the ECJ held that a jurisdiction clause in a company's articles of association was binding on its shareholders. The requirement of writing was deemed satisfied by the fact that the statutes were invariably in writing, irrespective of how the shares were acquired, provided that the statutes were lodged at a place which was accessible to shareholders, or were kept in a public register. Hence, it would seem to follow from this that a party will be bound by an arbitration clause simply because he had the means of knowledge of its existence. This is a far cry from a writing requirement. In truth, the Category One policy grounds identified in Sect. III above have by now completely fallen away in this context, since the initial assent may be proven by means that have nothing at all to do with writing. The Category Two policy grounds, however, are still operative, and are satisfied by the requirement that the clause itself be in some form of writing.

Clearly, the second and third elements in the Brussels form requirement (as set out above) encompass a wide range of other contract practices, well beyond the restrictions of a traditional written form requirement. Indeed, if a previous course of dealing can be demonstrated, it may be that no writing is required at all.

Under the auspices of The Hague Conference on Private International Law, work has been underway for a couple of years on a draft "Convention on Jurisdiction and Foreign Judgments in Civil and Commercial Matters", which is intended to be of worldwide application. Whilst negotiations have recently faltered, the existing draft texts remain instructive.

The Preliminary Draft of the Convention that was adopted by the Special Commission on 30 October 1999, in its Art. 4(2), required that choice of court clauses be entered into or confirmed:

"a) in writing;
   b) by any other means of communication which renders information accessible so as to be usable for subsequent reference;
   c) in accordance with a usage which is regularly observed by the parties;
   d) in accordance with a usage of which the parties were or ought to have been aware and which is regularly observed by parties to contracts of the same nature in the particular trade or commerce concerned".

In an official commentary by Peter Nygh and Fausto Pocar of August 2000,[93] it was noted that under this regime, whilst there must be agreement between the parties,

---

91. BRIGGS and REES, *op. cit.*, fn. 83.
92. Case C-214/89 [1992] E.C.R. I-1745.
93. "Preliminary Document No. 11 of August 2000", prepared for the Nineteenth Session of the Conference, June 2001 (hereinafter the "Nygh-Pocar Report").

consent to the arrangement need not be given explicitly by each party or be signed by that party ("[i]t suffices when it appears from the general circumstances that each party has agreed or can be taken to have agreed".[94]).

Following a Diplomatic Conference in June 2001, the requirements in Art. 4(2) were further refined in an Interim Text,[95] in order to include agreements entered into:

"a) in writing or by any other means of communication which renders information accessible so as to be usable for subsequent reference;

b) orally and confirmed in writing or by any other means of communication which renders information accessible so as to be usable for subsequent reference;

c) in accordance with a usage which is regularly observed by the parties;

d) in accordance with a usage of which the parties were or ought to have been aware and which is regularly observed by parties to contracts of the same nature in the particular trade or commerce concerned".

It has been made clear that these requirements set both a minimum and a maximum, thereby precluding the application of national law on this subject.[96]

The question then is whether there are any policy grounds for distinguishing between choice of court clauses and arbitration clauses. On one view, it might be said that a choice of court is less significant an arrangement than a choice of arbitration, since the right of access to a court is not thereby denied – it is simply changed. Equally, within the context of a regional convention such as the Brussels I Regulation, it is implicit that each of the contracting states has a reliable and trustworthy judicial system. However, on another view, there is no real difference between arbitration clauses and choice of court clauses. In terms of Category One justifications, the same form requirement should apply, since both have the potential of confining parties to ineffective as well as effective fora. If a party is to be excluded from his or her local courts, and forced to pursue rights in a far-off court, under a foreign procedural law, this is no less significant than being forced to arbitrate. The "mutual trust" justification that may hold good in geographically limited arrangements such as the Brussels I Regulation loses credibility in a worldwide arrangement such as the draft Hague Convention, and yet the form requirement in each is equivalent.

In terms of the Category Two justifications, there may conceivably be some difference, given that national courts constitute standing structures with readily identifiable procedural rules and characteristics. Arbitration, on the other hand, is far more nebulous, and might profit from a form requirement that provides at least some certainty. Whether this, of itself, justifies a stricter form requirement for arbitration agreements, however, is open to doubt.

---

94. *Ibid.*, p. 41.

95. The Interim Text is available on The Hague Conference's website, at www.hcch.net.

96. See the "Nygh-Pocar Report", *op. cit.*, fn. 93.

f.   Conclusions

There are compelling reasons to change or clarify the current form requirement. As a matter of logic, policy and practice, there is every reason to abandon the written form altogether.

There is then the problem of what, in practice, should be done.

2.   *The New York Convention Must Not Be Amended*

Having established a goal as a matter of policy, the question as to what action should be taken raises completely different considerations.

As far as Art. 7(2) of the Model Law is concerned, the matter is relatively straightforward. The Model Law is a legislative model. Whilst it undoubtedly has normative value, as an expression of an international consensus on arbitration law, it is only of direct effect when enacted by national legislatures. It follows that there is no particular difficulty in amending it, on the basis that the amended text might have a normative value in the interpretation of existing national laws which have been based upon it, and further that the amended version might be enacted by Model Law or other jurisdictions.

To this end, negotiations on Art. 7(2) in the UNCITRAL Working Group have reached a developed stage. The current working draft (as of March 2002) of a new Art. 7 is along the following lines:[97]

> "*Article 7 Definition and form of arbitration agreement*
>
> (1) 'Arbitration agreement' is an agreement by the parties to submit to arbitration all or certain disputes which have arisen or which may arise between them in respect of a defined legal relationship, whether contractual or not. An arbitration agreement may be in the form of an arbitration clause in a contract or in the form of a separate agreement.
>
> (2) The arbitration agreement shall be in writing. 'Writing' means any form, including without limitation a data message, that provides a record of the agreement or is otherwise accessible so as to be usable for subsequent reference.
>
> (3) 'Data message' means information generated, sent, received or stored by electronic, optical or similar means including, but not limited to, electronic data interchange (EDI), electronic mail, telegram, telex or telecopy.
>
> (4) Furthermore, an arbitration agreement is in writing if it is contained in an exchange of statements of claim and defence in which the existence of an agreement is alleged by one party and not denied by the other.
>
> (5) For the avoidance of doubt, the reference in a contract or a separate

---

97. This draft is an assimilation by this author of the formal draft as it stood after the 35th session of the UNCITRAL Working Group held in November 2001, together with the conclusions reached at the 36th session held in early March 2002. It is *not*, however, agreed wording produced by the UNCITRAL Secretariat, since, at the time of going to press, the next formal draft had yet to be produced.

arbitration agreement to a writing containing an arbitration clause constitutes an arbitration agreement in writing provided that the reference is such as to make that clause part of the contract or the separate arbitration agreement, notwithstanding that the contract or the separate arbitration agreement has been concluded orally, by conduct or by other means not in writing. In such a case, the writing containing the arbitration clause constitutes the arbitration agreement for purposes of article 35."[98]

This draft takes account of much of the analysis that has been set out above:

i.   Para. (1) and the first sentence of para. (2) remain unchanged. Hence there is still a written form requirement, and as such, there is still an essential coordination between the Model Law and the New York Convention. All that has changed is the actual definition of "writing".

ii. Paras. (2) and (3) broaden the definition of "writing" itself, so as to account for all conceivable – and, hopefully, yet to be dreamed – technologies. This addresses the first of the "two problems" noted in Sect. III above. The wording is non-exhaustive, and reflects Art. 6(1) of the UNCITRAL Model Law on Electronic Commerce, as well as Art. 7(2) of the UN Convention on Independent Guarantees and Stand-by Letters of Credit.

iii. Para. (5) solves the second of the "two problems" identified in Sect. III above, by accounting for virtually all common contract practices, including:

   – Written Offer / Oral or Tacit Acceptance
   – Oral Offer / Written Acceptance

and each of the "incorporation by reference" scenarios, including:

   – Written Offer referring to another text / Written Acceptance
   – Written Offer referring to another text / Oral or Tacit Acceptance
   – Oral Offer referring to another text / Written Acceptance
   – Oral Offer referring to another text / Oral or Tacit Acceptance.

   Thus, even the entirely oral agreement which incorporates a written text (i.e., the salvage situation) is covered. The fact that this solution has been built upon the previous "incorporation by reference" wording also reflects the analysis above (i.e., that the common underlying principle in each example is the incorporation of a text into an agreement that has not been concluded in writing).

iv. Whilst oral agreements by reference to written texts are included, the words "a writing containing an arbitration clause" in para. (5) exclude oral references to mere rule books (such as the ICC Rules) or a national law. As explained above, this is an arbitrary distinction as a mater of logic, yet has been considered more

---

98. See U.N. Doc. A/CN.9/WG.II/XXXVI/CRP.1/Add.1 to Add.5.

acceptable as a matter of instinct.

v. Para. 5 now uses "writing" for Category Two functions – not Category One, and is thereby in line with the approach to choice of court clauses.

vi. Para. 5 also seeks to solve the procedural problem of Art. 35 (equivalent to Art. IV of the New York Convention) as to what document is the "arbitration agreement" for the purposes of an application to enforce.

vii. The only areas that have not been addressed are the substantive law doctrines such as succession, assignment, estoppel, etc., since this was considered beyond the Working Group's proper remit.

The task, then, that remains, is to find a way of replicating these results in the New York Convention. Whilst these results are already achieved in those jurisdictions that apply liberal interpretations, they have yet to be applied in all Contracting States.

a.   Amendments, protocols and new conventions
In contrast to the Model Law, amending, modifying or clarifying Art. II(2) as well as Art. IV(1)(*b*) of the New York Convention is a far more complex matter. The New York Convention is an older instrument. It has become one of the most successful commercial conventions of all time, as well the very foundation for the international arbitration system. It is a living document, that has been signed and ratified all over the world, with now about 131 parties. As such, the ramifications of an amendment, a modification or a clarification are far-reaching.

To date, it has been suggested that Art. II(2) and Art. IV(1)(*b*) of the Convention might be the subject of a formal Protocol, on the basis that:

> "redrafting, or promoting uniform interpretation of article II(2) could only be achieved with the required level of authority through treaty provisions similar in nature to those of the New York Convention".[99]

Alternatively, it has been suggested that a new convention separate from the New York Convention be prepared to deal with those situations which arise outside the sphere of application of the New York Convention.[100] These proposals have been justified on the basis that:

> "the very success of the New York Convention and its establishment as a world standard should make it possible for UNCITRAL to undertake a limited overhaul of the text if such work was needed to adapt its provisions to changing business realities, and to maintain or restore its central status in the field of international commercial arbitration".[101]

Each of these suggested techniques comes to a similar result, and has a similar effect.

---

99. See *op. cit.*, fn. 15, para. 17, and U.N. Doc. A/54/17, paras. 344 and 347.
100. See U.N. Doc. A/54/17, para. 349.
101. *Op. cit.*, fn. 15, para. 17.

And each would result in a far worse position than if nothing were done at all. In short, any amendment of the New York Convention would severely – and possibly irreparably – damage the current system of international arbitration. This is so for a number of reasons.

b. *"Collateral damage"*

As has been pointed out above, and as is addressed in more detail in Sect. V below, the number of "war stories" or difficulties associated with the form requirement is matched by a significant number of jurisdictions and individual decisions where liberal interpretations of Art. II(2) and Art. IV(1)(*b*) have been adopted. For example, many national legislatures and courts have interpreted Art. II(2) as specifying a non-exhaustive list of examples, thereby allowing for other scenarios within the definition of writing. Others have interpreted Art. II(2) as imposing different form requirements for arbitration clauses contained in contracts and separate arbitration agreements. Others have applied a "functional equivalence" standard. Others still have found many other ways of interpreting the Convention, in order to safeguard commercial expectations.

The immediate difficulty with any amendment of the Convention is an unintended consequence: it would crystallize and confirm for all time the narrow interpretations of the Convention. By its very existence, the amendment would suggest that liberal interpretations are not otherwise tenable (since, otherwise, there would be no need for an amendment). In an instant, unless the amendment is signed and ratified by each of the 131 parties, all the existing liberal interpretations would be undermined, and the resultant position would be substantially worse than it is now.

c. *Floodgates*

The New York Convention is unique not only because of its global acceptance, but also because it has survived for over forty years without any amendments or protocols. As such, it has given rise to a relatively harmonized and uniform regime – or at least the means to work towards relative harmonization. This is not to say, however, that the Convention is without fault. In fact there are a large number of issues that could usefully be clarified in terms of its interpretation and application. For instance, there are serious questions as to the concept of "public policy" in Art. V(2)(*b*); there are differences internationally on the issue of "arbitrability" (Art. V(2)(*a*)); there are disparities in the application of each of the grounds in Art. V(1) for refusing the recognition and enforcement of an award; there are disagreements as to the meaning of the word "may" in the opening words of Art. V; there are debates as to the recognition and enforcement of awards that have been set aside at their seat; and so on. The list of issues could be extended far, and each issue could easily be a candidate for a Protocol. Indeed, a fair number of these issues have already arrived on UNCITRAL's list of topics for possible future work.

As long as the Convention has no protocols, the chances of any amendment are slim. Once there is one Protocol, there will be many more, and the current regime will be that much weaker as a result.

d. The threat of a patchwork

Even if there is only one Protocol, or perhaps two or three Protocols, it is extremely unlikely that all 131 Contracting States will all sign and ratify each Protocol at the same time, or over a short period of time, or indeed at all. Thus, the relative uniformity of the current system will necessarily degenerate into a patchwork of different regimes, thereby causing great uncertainty, out of all proportion to any unevenness in the current operation of the Convention.

There are many precedents for what might occur. For example, the Convention for the Unification of Certain Rules relating to International Carriage by Air 1929 (the Warsaw Convention) was amended by Protocols in 1955 and 1971 and four Additional Protocols in 1975. It was also supplemented by a Convention in 1961.[102] The 1971 Protocol and one of the four 1975 Additional Protocols have even now not yet entered into force. Moreover, the parties to the various amending and supplementing instruments vary; some states remain parties to just the Convention; some to the Convention and to one or more of the other instruments; and some to one or more of the other instruments only. This has resulted in the limits of liability of an airline to its passengers being dependent primarily on which treaty obligations have been accepted by the state concerned, instead of a uniform regime applying throughout international aviation, as was the objective of the Convention. Indeed, establishing which version of the Warsaw Convention applies in a particular case can be extremely difficult – especially for national courts, and, as with the New York Convention, it is national courts which have responsibility for enforcing the regime.

e. Practical consequences

Further, and as a matter of practical politics, it is suggested that a Protocol will effectively kill this project. The New York Convention was opened for signature in 1958, yet it has taken most countries many years to sign or to ratify. Indeed, a significant number have only become parties in the last ten years or so; some only in the last year. It cannot be expected that a Protocol or a new Convention will be accepted in a shorter time. Even if there is a political will (and of this there is no guarantee at all), any such project is at the mercy of legislative timetables, and, as law reform in recent years has taught us, in most countries there are many issues that take precedence over arbitration. Indeed, for some countries where regimes have changed since ratification, there may well be justifiable fears if a national legislature were to be called upon to revisit the Convention.

In short, a Protocol or a new Convention would be a project with no ascertainable end, and in the intervening years all that would have been achieved would be the demise of liberal interpretations, and a new uncertainty.

---

102. 137 LNTS 11; UKTS (1933) 11. For 1955, see UKTS (1967) 62; for 1961, see UKTS (1964) 23.

V.   POSSIBLE SOLUTIONS

1.   Introduction: Reconciling the Inconsistency

Amending the New York Convention is not the only way forward. There are a range of possible solutions that address the shortcomings of the written form requirement, and that exist within the confines of the current text. It is obviously important to assess each one.

As will be seen, whichever particular interpretation is considered viable, there is a well-established principle of public international law that would enable a clarification to be made of the Convention – without any amendment, or any indulgence by national legislatures, or any risk to the current regime.

2.   Reliance on National Law

It has been suggested that as long as national legislatures amend their own arbitration laws, in order to solve the difficulties with Art. II(2) of the Convention, there is no need for any change to the Convention itself, since courts applying the Convention will rely upon an arbitration agreement's governing law (i.e., the test of validity and the choice of law rule in Art. V(1)(a)). In short, if an arbitration agreement is valid under its own applicable law in respect of form, it is unlikely to be defeated by Art. II(2).

In so far as this is an argument aside from Art. VII of the Convention (which is discussed separately below), this is an unsafe way forward. The simple truth, as shown above, is that national courts do not always take this approach, and there are enough war stories to show that something more is needed. By way of one recent example only, in its decision of 16 August 1999, the Hålogaland Court of Appeal (Norway) emphasized that solutions in an applicable substantive law do not detract from the requirements of the Convention itself:

> "The requirements in Article IV b ... [and] Article II [of the Convention], relating to the form of the arbitral agreement, are justified by basic considerations for legal protection. It should not be sufficient for enforcement that the arbitral award is valid according to the law of the country in question. Also the requirements of the Convention should be assessed to ensure they have been complied with. This assessment is to be done by the local enforcement authority, and it need not to coincide with the question of the competence of the arbitrator according to his domestic law."[103]

Further, this approach provides no comfort at all in respect of Art. IV(1)(b) of the Convention. Further still, it does not really address the problem of form at the stage of the enforcement of the arbitration agreement (as distinct from enforcement of an

---

103. See, similarly, judgment of 21 March 1995 of the Swiss Federal Supreme Court, *Yearbook* XXII (1997) p. 800 ("the issue of [formal] validity is determined solely according to the Convention ...").

award).

3. Art. II(2) Revisited: the Meaning of "include"

The English language text of Art. II(2) of the Convention provides that:

> "The term 'agreement in writing' *shall include* ..." (emphasis added).

There is a division of views as to whether the definition of writing in this provision (i.e., signature or an exchange of letters or telegrams) is exhaustive, or whether it is simply illustrative. If it is not exhaustive, then the provision does not set a minimum standard, but instead allows for other, more expansive, forms of "writing". This issue turns upon the proper construction of the word "include" in the English-language version, and its counterparts in each of the other authoritative versions.

In its work on the English Arbitration Act 1996, the DAC addressed this issue, and concluded that the specific definition in Art. II(2) is *not* exhaustive, because of the use of the word "include". On the contrary, it allows other forms of "writing" – including more expansive forms. This conclusion was based upon a comparison of the different language texts, and it was on the basis of this that the 1996 Act included a very wide definition of writing. As explained by the DAC in its February 1996 Report:

> "Clause 5 Agreements to be in writing.
> (a) Arbitration Agreements.
> ....
> 34. We have, however, provided a very wide meaning to the words 'in writing'. Indeed this meaning is wider than that found in the Model Law, but in our view, is consonant with Article II.2 of the English text of the New York Convention. The non-exhaustive definition in the English text ('shall include') may differ in this respect from the French[104] and Spanish[105] texts, but the English text is equally authentic under Article XVI of the New York Convention itself, and also accords with the Russian authentic text ('*включает*'); see also the 1989 Report of the Swiss Institute of Comparative Law on Jurisdictional Problems in International Commercial Arbitration (by Adam Samuel), at pages 81 to 85. It seems to us that English Law as it stands more than justifies this wide meaning; see, for example, *Zambia Steel v. James Clark* [1986] 2 Lloyd's Rep. 225. In view of rapidly evolving methods of recording we have made clear that '*writing*' includes recording by any means...."[106]

Hence, the very broad definition of writing in Part I of the English Arbitration Act 1996 (Sect. 5) is cross-referenced in Part III of the Act (which enacts the New York

---

104. The French text reads: "*On entend par 'convention écrite'*...."

105. The Spanish text reads: "*La expresión 'acuerdo por escrito' denotará*...."

106. See, similarly, judgment of 16 December 1992 of the *Oberlandesgericht* (Court of Appeal) Cologne, *Yearbook* XXI (1996) p. 535.

Convention). Thus, Sect. 100(2) provides in part as follows:

> "(2) For the purposes of ... the provisions of this Part ...—
> (a) 'arbitration agreement' means an arbitration agreement in writing, and
> (b) ....
> 'agreement in writing' ... [has] the same meaning as in Part I."

It is to be assumed that each of the other national legislatures which have also enacted a more expansive definition of "writing" share this view.

However, the view is by no means universal. For example, in *Chloe Z Fishing Co., Inc. v. Odyssey Re (London) Ltd*. (United States District Court, Southern District of California, 26 April 2000)[107] the court concluded that Art. II(2) is a self-sufficient and exhaustive definition, reasoning that the phrase "shall include" does *not* indicate a non-exhaustive definition, but rather a mandatory requirement:

> "... it is equally plausible that the word 'shall' leaves courts with little discretion in defining an 'agreement in writing' and directs that each 'agreement in writing' *must* include the elements that follow. See e.g. *Hewitt v. Helms* 459 U.S. 460, 471, 103 S.Ct. 864, 74 L.Ed.2d 675 (1983) (noting that 'shall' and 'must' are virtually synonymous under traditional principles of statutory construction and are both words of 'an unmistakably mandatory character'), ... *Hicks v. Miranda* 422 U.S. 332, 352, 95 S.Ct 2281, 45 L.Ed.2d 223 (1975) (Burger, C.J., concurring) ('It is well settled that "shall" means "must"'). Therefore, consistent with the applicable cases, Article II section 2 does not outline the minimum but the mandatory requirement of what constitutes an 'agreement in writing' under the Convention."[108]

This analysis may be criticized on the basis that the judge focused on the word "shall", without any consideration of the word "include". In certain contexts the words "shall" and "must" are interchangeable. However, the focus of the phrase in Art. II(2) is the word "include", and it seems somewhat artificial to construe the word "shall" in isolation from the verb to which it relates. As a matter of English language, the word "include", in most of its modern usage, has a non-exhaustive quality.[109]

---

107. *Op. cit.*, fn. 33.
108. *Ibid.*, 1245-1246.
109. See *The Oxford English Dictionary, Complete Text* (OUP 1971): "to contain as a member of an aggregate, or a constituent part of a whole; to embrace as a sub-division or a section..." (e.g., Shakespeare, *Henry VI* (Part I), 1 ii (1591): "With Henry's death, the English Circle ends, Dispersed are the glories it included"); "to contain as a subordinate element, corollary, or secondary feature..." (e.g., Contemp. Rev XLIII, 47 (1883): "There is a love that includes friendship, as religion includes morality"); "to place in a class or category; to embrace in a general survey or description; to reckon in a calculation, mention in an enumeration ..." (e.g., Pol. Econ. I i (1848): "It is necessary to include in the idea of [Labour] all feelings of a disagreeable kind ... connected with the employment of one's thoughts, or muscles, or both, in a particular occupation.").

The court in *Chloe Z* heard expert evidence as to the position in England with respect to Art. II(2) of the Convention, but was evidently unmoved:

> "... even the undeniable fact that the highest Court and the leading experts in the United Kingdom have recognized that the English Arbitration Acts implementing the Convention broaden the definition of an 'agreement in writing' found in Article II section 2 of the Convention is of limited persuasive value.... Since there is no recognition by any court or expert in the United States that Chapter 2 of the FAA performs a similar broadening function as the English Arbitration Acts, the defendants at most direct this Court's attention to English law in construing these parties' expectations as to what constitutes an 'agreement in writing'.... [A]lthough cognizant that Congress's goal in implementing the Convention was to encourage uniformity with respect to the enforcement of foreign arbitration agreements and foreign arbitral awards, this Court must find that Article II of the Convention exhaustively defines what constitutes an 'agreement in writing' under Chapter 2 of the FAA despite defendants' argument to the contrary." [110]

This is an obvious candidate for a declaratory statement or an interpretative instrument.

4.   *Art. II(2) Revisited: Deleting a Comma*

There is another construction of Art. II(2) that has been advanced by some courts, in an attempt to expand its scope. This entails, in effect, the deletion or ignoring of the comma in the middle of Art. II(2), so that the requirements of "signature" and "exchange" apply only to "an arbitration agreement" (i.e., a self-contained arbitration agreement), but not to "an arbitral clause in a contract".

This was the analysis in *Sphere Drake Ins. PLC v. Marine Towing, Inc.* (1994)[111] as cited in Sect. III above. This interpretation, however, was thoroughly deconstructed by the Court of Appeals of the 2d Circuit in *Kahn Lucas* (also discussed in Sect. III above).

In dismissing the motion to compel arbitration in that case, the court first considered the principles of construction or interpretation that are applicable to the Convention. It was held that (as a matter of relevant US law) treaties are construed in much the same manner as statutes,[112] and that statutory construction is "a 'holistic endeavor' and must account for the statute's 'full text, language as well as punctuation, structure and subject matter'".[113] Thus, the obvious starting point for construing a treaty is its text; that the

---

110. *Op. cit.*, fn. 33, 1246.

111. *Op. cit.*, fn. 29.

112. Citing *United States v. Alvarez-Machain*, 504 U.S. 655, 663, 112 S.Ct. 2188, 119 L.Ed.2d 441 (1992), and *Sale v. Haitian Ctrs. Council, Inc.*, 509 U.S. 155, 177-83, 113 S.Ct. 2549, 125 L.Ed.2d 128 (1993).

113. Citing *United States Nat'l Bank v. Independent Ins. Agents of Am., Inc.*, 508 U.S. 439, 455, 113 S.Ct. 2173, 124 L.Ed.2d 402 (1993).

plain meaning of a text "will typically heed the commands of its punctuation";[114] and that the grammatical structure of a statute, specifically the placement of commas, mandates a specific construction.[115] The court then noted the desirability of adhering to an interpretation consistent with all of the official languages. That said, however, it was stated that some of the official languages provided more insight into the drafters' intentions than others.[116] English, French and Spanish were the working languages of the United Nations Conference on International Commercial Arbitration which drafted the Convention, and all records of Conference meetings were kept in these working languages.[117]

Applying these principles to the text of Art. II(2) of the Convention, the court's reasoning was as follows: The meaning of the expressions "arbitral clause in a contract" and "arbitration agreement", when used in conjunction with each other, are self-evident: the first refers to an arbitration provision contained in a larger agreement, whereas the second refers to a stand-alone contract to arbitrate (e.g., a submission agreement).

On a plain reading of the English-language version of the Convention, the comma immediately following "an arbitration agreement" serves to separate the series ("an arbitral clause in a contract or an arbitration agreement") from the modifying phrase ("signed by the parties or contained in an exchange of letters or telegrams"), suggesting that the modifying phrase is meant to apply to both elements in the series. Indeed, this comma can serve no other grammatical purpose. *Kahn Lucas'* reading of the text would render the comma "mere surplusage", which was a "construction frowned upon".

This conclusion finds support aside from mere punctuation. The French- and Spanish-language versions of the text (being the other working languages) also compel the conclusion that the requirements of signature and exchange apply to both an arbitral clause in a contract and an arbitration agreement. In both, the word for "signed" appears in the plural form ("*signes*" and "*firmados*" respectively), therefore applying to each of the two antecedents (each of which appears in the singular).

Of the non-working official-language versions, it was concluded that these do not offer clear-cut support for this interpretation, but equally do not weigh strongly against it: The Chinese-language version (like the English-language version) cannot utilize a uniquely plural form of the verb for "signed". Further, in the Chinese-language version, the modifier "signed" precedes, rather than follows, the objects it modifies. The Russian-language version uses the singular form of the verb "signed" (transliterated as "PODPECANOYE"), thereby arguably supporting *Kahn Lucas'* construction. However, it was felt that this was outweighed by the other language versions, particularly given the stated purpose of the Convention of unifying standards amongst signatory countries.

---

114. Citing *United States Nat'l Bank*, supra, 508 U.S. at 454, 113 S.Ct. 2173.
115. Citing *United States v. Ron Pair Enters. Inc.*, 489 U.S. 235, 241-242, 109 S.Ct. 1026, 103 L.Ed.2d 290 (1989).
116. Citing *Eastern Airlines, Inc v. Floyd*, 499 U.S. 530, 534, 111 S.Ct. 1489, 113 L.Ed.2d 569 (1991), where the language employed by drafters was considered in order to gain an insight into the intention of the parties.
117. *Rules of Procedure*, United Nations Conference on International Commercial Arbitration, E/Conf.26/5/Rev.1 (1958) – Rules 32 and 36.

To the extent the plain meanings of the non-English-language versions of the Convention do not resolve any ambiguity that exists in the English-language version, the legislative history of Art. II was said to put the matter to rest. The text of Art. II, as reported by the UN Conference's Working Group, reverses the terms "arbitration agreement" and "arbitration clause in a contract". The Working Group's text thus reads:

> "The expression 'agreement in writing' shall mean an arbitration agreement or an arbitration clause in a contract signed by the parties, or an exchange of letters or telegrams between those parties."

As the Court observed, this text obviously required that an arbitral clause be signed by the parties. This text was subject only to modification by the Drafting Committee for form, not substance.[118] Therefore, as pointed out by the Court:

> "unless the modifier 'signed' in the Convention applies to both antecedents, the Drafting Committee's editorial changes would amount to an unintended, and unauthorized, substantive amendment to article II, section 2".

There are, therefore, considerable difficulties with this approach.

5.   *Teleological Interpretation and the Model Law*

Another possible solution within the confines of the existing text of Art. II(2) is to promote a teleological interpretation, by reference to the proposed amended Art. 7 of the Model Law.[119] To an extent, this approach is already evident in the extension of Art. II(2) to encompass telexes and faxes. Indeed, the "Guide to Enactment for the Model Law on Electronic Commerce" was apparently drafted with the New York Convention and other international instruments in mind. Its para. 6 reads as follows:

> "... the Model Law [on Electronic Commerce] may be useful in certain cases as a tool for interpreting existing international conventions and other international instruments that create legal obstacles to the use of electronic commerce, for

---

118. "Consideration of the Draft New York Convention on the Recognition and Enforcement of Foreign Arbitral Awards", UN Conference on International Commercial Arbitration, U.N. ESCOR, E/Conf.26/L.59, Agenda Item 4, para. 2 (6 June 1958), and "Summary of the 23rd Meeting", UN Conference on International Commercial Arbitration, U.N. ESCOR, E/Conf.26/SR.23 at 4, 7 (12 September 1958).

119. E.g., the observations of the Swiss Federal Tribunal in *Compagnie de Navigation et Transports S.A. v. MSC (Mediterranean Shipping Company) S.A.*, 16 January 1995 (1st civil division):

> "Art. II(2) must be interpreted in the light of [the Model Law], whose authors wished to adapt the legal regime of the New York Convention to current needs, without modifying [the actual Convention]."

Excerpts in 13 ASA Bulletin (1995) pp. 503-511 (and in particular p. 508).

example by prescribing that certain documents or contractual clauses be made in written form. As between those States parties to such international instruments, the adoption of the Model Law [on Electronic Commerce] as a rule of interpretation might provide the means to recognize the use of electronic commerce and obviate the need to negotiate a protocol to the international instrument involved."

If the Model Law can be used to interpret types of "writing", it should also be capable of acting as a guide to types of contract practice, as reflected in the proposed new Art. 7. To the extent that this approach is not adopted by national courts of their own motion, this may require some form of agreement or declaration.

6.   *Art. VII of the Convention*

If the word "include" in Art. II(2) indicates an *exhaustive* criteria, the question arises as to whether national courts may apply their own more liberal laws (where these exist) under Art. VII(1) of the Convention, rather than the strict requirements of the Convention. This issue remains controversial, and turns on whether the Convention is seen as establishing a uniform regime, or simply aiming to facilitate the recognition and enforcement of awards.

Art. VII of the New York Convention provides (in relevant part) as follows:

"1. The provisions of the present Convention shall not ... deprive any interested party of any right he may have to avail himself of an arbitral award in the manner and to the extent allowed by the law or the treaties of the country where such award is sought to be relied upon...."

In France, this issue was addressed in the 1987 decision of the Paris *Cour d'appel* in *Bomar Oil*,[120] in which it was held that Art. II(2) of the Convention expressed a "substantive rule which must be applied in all cases". That decision was then reversed by the *Cour de cassation*, but this issue was not directly addressed. It is significant, however, that when the case later returned to the *Cour de cassation*, the court applied a substantive rule of international arbitration law, and made no reference to the test in Art. II(2) of the Convention.

These decisions have been analyzed in *Fouchard Gaillard Goldman*, who suggest that the approach of the Paris *Cour d'appel* was unsatisfactory. In their view, Art. VII(1) of the Convention makes clear that:

"... the Convention imposes only a certain degree of liberalism in the recognition and enforcement of awards, and each country can always choose a less restrictive approach on the basis of its national law or other international instruments. Thus in the *Bomar Oil* case, the New York Convention could have been excluded once

---

120. See text at fn. 44.

it had been shown that French law offered the parties more freedom." [121]

There are indeed instances in which national courts have looked to local legal regimes in preference to the New York Convention, in order to uphold an arbitration clause. For example, in a decision of the German Supreme Court (*Bundesgerichtshof*) of 25 May 1970, an unwritten arbitration agreement was upheld between an Austrian textile company and its German agent, not under the New York Convention, but rather under the then applicable German law which allowed such agreements between merchants in the framework of certain commercial transactions. [122]

If, indeed, Art. VII(1) allows the application of more liberal standards in national law to the question of the written form, there is then the question whether a party can rely on only part of the Convention, in seeking the recognition and enforcement of an award. In other words, will (e.g.) Arts. IV, V and VI of the Convention apply, where an award has been rendered pursuant to an arbitration agreement that meets the form requirements under a national law, but fails the requirements of Art. II(2)?

According to Professor van den Berg, [123] the New York Convention is a self-contained regime. It defines the situations to which it applies, and thereby singles out those cases which deserve protection (albeit without prejudice to other more favourable regimes under national law). Thus, on the question of writing, the Convention only seeks to protect agreements in writing (as defined) or awards made on the basis of such agreements. It would therefore be contrary to the intentions of the authors of the Convention if awards made on the basis of agreements which do not comply with its requirements were nevertheless to benefit from the Convention's regime. Further, there is a strong argument that Art. VII can only refer to arbitral awards, not arbitration agreements, since otherwise Art. II(2) could well be redundant. Further, if the Convention and national laws are to be blended, there is a risk that the current (and relative) uniformity in the operation of the Convention will be lost, as inconsistencies come to light.

As against this analysis, others have argued (and some courts have held) that the Convention contains nothing to prevent the use of some of its provisions in conjunction with other more liberal provisions in national law. [124] Art. VII imposes no restrictions on the application of more favourable rules. Hence, for example, the decision of a German court of appeal (prior to the new German law) which simultaneously applied the provisions of both the German New Code of Civil Procedure and the New York

---

121. *Fouchard Gaillard Goldman*, *op. cit.*, fn. 20, para. 614 (with extensive citations to case law on this issue).

122. *Bundesgerichtshof* (Supreme Court) 25 May 1970, *Yearbook* XI (1977) p. 237.

123. Van den BERG, *op. cit.*, fn. 11, p. 180 et. seq. See also van den BERG, "Enforcement of Annulled Awards?" in 9 ICC Bulletin of the International Court of Arbitration (1998) p. 15 at p. 18, and van den BERG, "The New York Convention: Its Intended Effects, Its Interpretation, Salient Problem Areas" in ASA Special Series No. 9 (1996) pp. 25-45 at p. 44.

124. See, e.g., *Fouchard Gaillard Goldman*, *op. cit.*, fn. 20, Sect. 615, citing E. LOQUIN, 117 J.D.I. (1990) p. 633 at p. 638.

Convention to the enforcement of a foreign award.[125] Further, it has been said that the Swiss Federal Tribunal has implicitly accepted a "fragmented application of two competing systems"[126] in its determination that in cases of competing treaty provisions on the recognition and enforcement of arbitral awards, precedence should be given to "the provision allowing or making easier such recognition and enforcement".[127]

As pointed out by Gerold Herrmann in his 1998 Freshfields lecture,[128] Art. VII of the Convention could allow reference to the substantive law of the arbitration agreement for the guiding principles on matters of form – just as Article V(1)(a) of the Convention refers to the governing law for matters of substance. It would be curious indeed if the solution for formal validity were more onerous than that for substantive validity.

Again, this issue could be clarified by a declaration or interpretative instrument.

7.   *Public International Law: a Forgotten Resource*

The sections above illustrate various interpretive techniques to expand the scope of the New York Convention, without any violence to the text itself. The last element in this analysis is how such interpretations might be entrenched, and made universal, without actually amending the Convention.

The solution is provided by public international law. It is perhaps because arbitration practitioners tend to be commercial lawyers that public international law as a resource is frequently forgotten. This is curious, since the New York Convention is after all an international instrument which falls to be interpreted in accordance with the rules of public international law – which are quite different from rules of interpretation in most private law systems.

As a matter of public international law, modifications, clarifications and even amendments of treaties and conventions do not need to be embodied in formal protocols, or amending conventions. Art. 31(3)(a) of the Vienna Convention provides that in interpreting treaties, there should be taken into account together with the context:

> "any subsequent agreement between the parties regarding the interpretation of the treaty or the application of its provisions".[129]

It is well established that a "subsequent agreement" for these purposes need not be a formal agreement signed by all participating parties. As will be seen, it frequently takes the form of an interpretive declaration, which may be embodied in an informal decision

---

125. *X v. Y*, *Oberlandesgericht* (Court of Appeal) Hamm, 2 November 1983, *Yearbook* XIV (1989) p. 629.

126. See *Fouchard Gaillard Goldman*, *op. cit.*, fn. 20, Sect. 271.

127. *Denysiana v. Jassica*, Swiss Federal Tribunal, 14 March 1984, *Yearbook* XI (1986) p. 538.

128. *Op. cit.*, fn. 6, p. 217.

129. As confirmed by the ICJ, this provision reflects customary international law: *Libya v. Chad,* ICJ Rep. (1994) p. 4 at para. 41.

or resolution.[130]

As Aust points out, in the context of Art. 31(3)(a) of the Vienna Convention:

"Given that the parties can agree later to modify the treaty, they can also subsequently agree on an authoritative interpretation of its terms, and this can amount, in effect, to an amendment. There is no need for a further treaty, since the paragraph refers deliberately to an 'agreement', not a treaty."[131]

In its Commentary on what became Art. 31(3)(a) of the Vienna Convention, the International Law Commission stated that:

"an agreement as to the interpretation of a provision reached after the conclusion of the treaty represents an authentic interpretation by the parties which must be read into the treaty for purposes of its interpretation".[132]

This passage was cited (apparently with approval) by the International Court of Justice in the *Kasikili/Seduku Island* case (1999).[133]

Daillier and Pellet comment on subsequent agreements on interpretation as follows:

"*il est admis que cet accord postérieur peut être tacite et résulter des pratiques concordantes des Etats quand ils appliquent le traité. Cette formule souple présente des avantages bien qu'elle soulève souvent des contestations. L'article 31, paragraphe 3, de la Convention de Vienne place d'ailleurs sur le même plan d'interprétation par voie d'accord et celle qui résulte de la pratique ultérieure des parties.*"[134]

Similarly, *Oppenheim's International Law*, vol. 1, Sect. 630, states:

"Authentic interpretation. The parties to a treaty often foresee many of the

---

130. There is a wealth of material on this topic. See, e.g., HORN, *Reservations and Interpretative Declarations to Multilateral Treaties* (North-Holland/TMC Asser Instituut 1988); YASSEEN, "L'interprétation des traités d'après la Convention de Vienne sur le Droit des Traités", 151 *Recueil des cours* (1976-III) p. 20; SINCLAIR, *The Vienna Convention on the Law of Treaties*, 2nd ed. (MUP 1984), Chapter 5 (Interpretation of Treaties) esp. pp.135-138 ("Subsequent agreements and subsequent practice"); McNAIR, *The Law of Treaties*, 2nd ed. (Oxford 1961) Chapter XXIV (Effect of Subsequent Practice of the Parties: Contemporaneous Practical Interpretation) esp. pp. 427-431("subsequent interpretative agreements"); KONTOU, *The Termination and Revision of Treaties in the Light of New Customary International Law* (Oxford 1994); AUST, *Modern Treaty Law and Practice* (Cambridge 2000) Chapter 13 (Interpretation); Chapter 15 (Amendment) esp. pp. 191-194 ("subsequent agreements and practice"); REUTER, *Introduction to the Law of Treaties*, 2nd ed. (Kegan Paul Int'l 1995) paras. 138-144; DAILLIER and PELLET, *Droit International Public*, 6th ed., p. 254; *Oppenheim's International Law*, 9th ed. (Longman 1996) pp. 1268-1269.
131. AUST, *op. cit.*, fn. 130, p. 191.
132. *Yearbook of the International Law Commission*, vol. II (1966) p. 221, para. 14.
133. ICJ Rep. (1999) 1, para. 49.
134. DAILLIER and PELLET, *op. cit.*, fn. 130, p. 254.

difficulties of interpretation likely to arise in its application, and in the treaty itself may define certain of the terms used. Or they may in some other way and before, during, or after the conclusion of the treaty, agree upon the interpretation of a term, either informally (and executing the treaty accordingly) or by a more formal procedure, as by an interpretative declaration or protocol or a supplementary treaty. Such authentic interpretations given by the parties override general rules of interpretation."[135, 136]

There are some early examples of the judicial recognition of subsequent interpretative declarations in the context of treaties. In *The Franciska*,[137] an English case of 1855, Dr. Lushington referred to "modern exposition" in seeking extraneous aid for the interpretation of a treaty. In analyzing this source, he identified two types as follows:

"First, an explanation solemnly agreed between the two States reconcilable with the terms of the articles. An interpretation of this kind, though it might not be quite in unison with my own opinion [i.e. as a judge], I should hold myself bound to accept. Secondly, an interpretation which the words of the article do not admit. Such an interpretation might be more properly called a substitute for the original meaning, but a substitute agreed to by both the contracting powers. Assuming this to happen, I must have the authority of the Government under which I sit that such an agreed interpretation has taken place. I should then receive it, not as a construction, but as an agreed settlement of a difficulty...."

There are, indeed, instances where a doubt as to the meaning of a treaty has arisen after its conclusion, and has been settled by a subsequent agreement between the parties, embodied in a simple exchange of notes. McNair cites as an example the Exchange of Notes between the Congo Free State and France, dated 22 and 29 April 1887 (as printed in HERTSLET, *Map of Africa by Treaty*, 3rd ed. (1909) pp. 567-568).[138] See also, and more recently, the 1996 Czech-UK Exchange of Notes regarding the interpretation of the Consular Convention 1975 "for the purpose of paragraph 3, Article 31 of the Vienna Convention on the Law of Treaties."[139]
Importantly for present purposes, and as noted by Aust, an "agreement" for the purposes of Art. 31(3)(a) of the Vienna Convention can take various forms:

"... including a decision adopted by a meeting of the parties, provided the purpose is clear".[140]

---

135. *Oppenheim's International Law*, op. cit., fn. 130, pp. 1268-1269.
136. See also the "1964 Report of the International Law Commission", op. cit., fn. 132, p. 53 at p. 62.
137. *Spinks' Ecc. and Ad. Cases* (1855), 113, 150; see McNAIR, op. cit., fn. 130, p. 428.
138. McNAIR, op. cit., fn. 130, p. 429.
139. UKTS (1997) 5.
140. AUST, op. cit., fn. 130, pp. 191-192.

The fact that "agreements" for the purposes of Art. 31(3)(a) of the Vienna Convention might be concluded "informally" is echoed by Oppenheim, supra. There is even some authority to suggest that an agreement on interpretation may be expressed in a dispute resolution procedure (Arbitral Award Made by the King of Spain on 23 December 1906 (*Honduras v. Nicaragua*);[141] Kasikili/Seduku Island (*Botswana v. Namibia*) 1999.[142]

There are a number of recent and relevant instances of interpretative or declaratory agreements that have been concluded pursuant to Art. 31(3)(a) of the Convention by way of decisions at meetings or by resolutions. For example:[143]

— The Convention on International Trade in Endangered Species 1973 (CITES) was effectively modified by a resolution of the Conference of the Parties in 1986, despite an amendment procedure having been built into the Convention.[144]
— In 1993, the states parties to the Treaty on Conventional Forces in Europe (CFE) 1990 concluded a "Document of the States Parties" which included an "understanding" as to how certain provisions of the CFE Treaty would be interpreted and applied, and which are in effect amendments to the Treaty.[145]
— The Treaty of Rome establishing the European Economic Community, as amended, refers to the "ECU" (European currency unit). When in 1995 the Member States decided to replace the ECU with the "Euro", instead of amending the Treaty – which would have involved a lengthy ratification procedure and parliamentary scrutiny – the heads of state and government of the Member States recorded in the "Conclusions" of their meeting in Madrid that:

> "The specific name Euro will be used instead of the generic term 'ECU' used in the Treaty to refer to the European currency unit. The Governments of the fifteen Member States have achieved the common agreement that this decision is the agreed and definitive interpretation of the relevant Treaty provisions."[146]

— Under the Ramsar Wetlands Convention 1971, as amended in 1982 to include an amendment clause, the acceptance of "two thirds of the Contracting Parties" is

---

141. 1960, ICJ Rep. 192, at 206-207.
142. 1999, ICJ Rep. 1, at 31.
143. These examples are taken from AUST, *op. cit.*, fn. 130, pp. 191-194. This topic is addressed in detail, given widespread doubts that have been expressed during the recent meetings of the UNCITRAL Working Group on Arbitration. In particular, many delegations have expressed the view that an amendment or interpretation by "agreement" or resolution would have no significance as a matter of International Law. As the analysis here shows, this is simply not so.
144. 999 UNTS 243;12 ILM (1973) p. 1085; UKTS (1976) 101; "Proceedings of the Sixth Meeting of the Conference of the Parties" (Doc. 6.19; Res.6.2.4).
145. UKTS (1994) 21. See also, UKTS (1993) 44 at pp. 97-108.
146. "Conclusions of the Madrid European Council 1995" (Bulletin of the EU, 12-1995, p. 10). AUST, *op. cit.*, fn. 130, cites a further example, as noted by D. HOWARTH, "The Compromise on Denmark", CML Rev (1994) p. 765.

needed for an amendment to come into force.[147] However, it was not clear if the phrase referred to the contracting parties at the time the amendment was adopted, or at any given moment. Therefore, at a conference of the parties in 1990 a resolution was adopted that it should be interpreted to refer to the time of adoption of the amendment.[148]

— Art. IX(1) of the Antarctic Treaty of 1959 provides for certain of the parties (known as "Consultative Parties") to *recommend* to their governments *measures* in furtherance of the principles and objectives of the Treaty. Art. IX(4) provides that the measures "shall become effective" when they have been "approved" by all of the Consultative Parties. Between 1961 and 1995, over 200 measures were recommended. However, until 1995 there had been a misunderstanding, and a consequent misapplication of Article IX(1). From the very beginning the Consultative Parties had adopted instruments termed "Recommendations", of which the majority (as described by Aust) were no more than exhortatory, ephemeral or procedural. Nevertheless, they were treated as measures subject to the full approval procedure of Art. IX(4). This unsatisfactory situation was corrected in 1995, when the Consultative Parties agreed that in the future they would recommend under Art. IX(1) only "Measures" properly so-called (i.e., intended to be legally binding), and that in the future other matters would be the subject of "decisions" or "resolutions", and would be effective on their adoption at the annual Antarctic Treaty Consultative Meeting (ATCM). This agreement was embodied in Decision 1 of the 1995 ATCM. The new arrangements were explained by the proposers to be an agreement for the purposes of Art. 31(3)(a) of the Vienna Convention.

— The time for the first election of judges of the International Tribunal for the Law of the Sea was specified in the UN Convention on the Law of the Sea 1982. However, this date turned out to be premature. Accordingly, the date was amended by a consensus decision of a meeting of the parties, the decision being recorded in the record of the meeting.[149]

Contrary to a number of views expressed in recent UNCITRAL negotiations, there is, therefore, no doubt that a declaratory or interpretative resolution has effect as a matter of international law, and is often used as an alternative to a formal amendment or new treaty – particularly in the context of multilateral treaties, and notably when lacunae need filling, or terms updating.[150]

A proposal: In its advisory opinion in the *Jaworzina* case, the Permanent Court of International Justice ruled as early as 1923 that:

"... it is an established principle that the right of giving an authoritative

---

147. 35 ILM (1996) p. 1188.
148. 996 UNTS 245 (No 14583); 11 ILM (1972) p. 963; UKTS (1976) 34. See BOWMAN, "The Multilateral Treaty Amendment Process - A Case Study", ICLQ (1995) p. 540 at p. 552.
149. SPLOS/3 of 28 February 1995.
150. Both these situations are noted by AUST, *op. cit.*, fn. 130, p. 193, as being particularly appropriate for the use of interpretative "agreements", rather than new treaties.

interpretation of a legal rule belongs solely to the person or body who has the power to modify or suppress it".[151]

Given the origins of the New York Convention, this would appear to be a proper function for either UNCITRAL itself, or the UN General Assembly, of which UNCITRAL is a sub-committee.

A reconciliation between the two inconsistent propositions in Sect. IV above would be achieved by a resolution of UNCITRAL or the General Assembly, approving and adopting an interpretative declaration on the New York Convention.

Such a declaration could embody any one or more of a number of interpretations, for example:

— that Art. II(2) is to be treated as a non-exhaustive definition;
— that Art. II(2) and Art. IV is to be interpreted in accordance with the new Art. 7 of the Model Law;
— that Art. VII is to be interpreted as allowing reliance on more favourable national laws on formalities, without excluding other Articles of the Convention.

In fact, any interpretation is feasible, as long as it commands a consensus. As the examples above demonstrate, the fact that the interpretation is seen by some as an amendment, does not change the force of the declaration as a matter of public international law.

Any such declaration must be phrased in terms of a clarification (e.g., "For the avoidance of doubt ..."), in order to avoid the "collateral damage" effect described in Sect. IV above (i.e., to preserve existing liberal interpretations).

VI.   CONCLUSION

The current written form requirement presents a tangible and significant problem in the world of international commercial arbitration. It is not sufficiently significant, however, to warrant tampering with the New York Convention.

It may be said that a resolution or declaration will never be as good as an amendment, and that whilst it may have some existence as a matter of public international law, whether or not it will influence the application of the New York Convention still depends upon the attitudes of national courts. This is perfectly true. Yet it is still a more advisable approach than an amendment. Even if national courts will require persuasion to follow an interpretive declaration, the international community will have expressed a powerful consensus, which, at the very least, will constitute a significant resource. Amendment is an easier option. But in the long term, it may mark the beginning of the decline of the New York Convention. As one distinguished member of the English House of Lords was said to have commented, many years ago, when the settled public order was threatened by popular demonstrations, campaigns and marches for social,

---

151. P.C.I.J. ser. B, No. 8, at 37.

economic and electoral change:

"Why all this call for reform? Aren't things bad enough already?"

The Scope and Enforceability of Provisional Measures in International Commercial Arbitration: A Survey of Jurisdictions, the Work of UNCITRAL and Proposals For Moving Forward

*Donald Francis Donovan**

I.   INTRODUCTION

Interim measures address an epistemological reality: considered decision making by human agents takes time. To state the obvious, if it were possible for a court or tribunal

---

*   Partner, Debevoise & Plimpton, New York; advisor to United States Delegation to UNCITRAL Working Group on Arbitration; Vice President of ICCA.

     The author gratefully acknowledges the assistance in the preparation of this paper of his Debevoise colleagues Natalie S. Klein and Jeffrey L. Loop.

to render judgment immediately upon becoming seized of a dispute, the question of interim measures would not arise. At the same time, the effectiveness of that judgment may depend upon the ability of the court or tribunal to act so that when it renders judgment, after having afforded the parties the procedural rights to which they are due, the circumstances of the dispute remain effectively as if the court had entered immediate judgment. That is the purpose of interim measures.[1]

The authority to issue interim measures derives from the same source as the authority to render the award: the parties' contractual consent to have their dispute resolved by the arbitral tribunal before which they are appearing. If the tribunal is to have the authority to resolve the dispute fully and effectively, it must have the authority to order interim measures to the extent necessary to preserve that authority. While the types of measures available may vary in their details, their basic thrust must be to facilitate later enforcement of an award.

The need for an arbitral tribunal's authority to issue interim measures does not settle questions of procedure, scope, and enforceability. If parties have agreed to resolve their disputes through an ad hoc arbitral tribunal, an immediate problem can be faced when interim measures of protection are needed prior to the constitution of the tribunal. In these situations, the parties may resort to national courts for these types of orders.[2] The use of national courts may also be preferred because of their ability to assist in the subsequent enforcement of the measures granted.[3] The vast majority of jurisdictions grant the parties permission to seek court-ordered interim measures as complementary to arbitral proceedings.[4]

Once an arbitral tribunal is constituted, the tribunal provides either the preferred or a readily available forum in which to seek interim measures. Most rules of arbitral procedure recognize a tribunal's authority to grant interim measures, but little detail is afforded on the types of measures that are permissible. In particular, the necessary standards for the grant of such measures are not always expressed, nor are they always uniformly defined. Further, while it may be in the interests of the parties to adhere to interim measures of protection, to be fully effective those measures must be susceptible

---

1. Unless otherwise specified in the text, the terms "provisional measures" and "interim measures" of protection are used here interchangeably.
2. The use of local courts for interim proceedings is anticipated under the UNCITRAL Model Law on International Commercial Arbitration (1985) (hereinafter UNCITRAL Model Law or Model Law). Art. 9 of the Model Law provides: "It is not incompatible with an arbitration agreement for a party to request, before or during arbitral proceedings, from a court an interim measure of protection and for a court to grant such measure." The London Court of International Arbitration Rules permit resort to state courts only prior to the constitution of the arbitral tribunal or in exceptional cases thereafter. See London Court of International Arbitration, Arbitration Rules (effective 1 January 1998) (hereinafter LCIA Rules) Art. 25(3).
3. "Some measures, such as attachments of property in the hands of third parties, involving the exercise of public authority, require by nature the intervention of domestic courts." Gregoire MARCHAC, "Interim Measures in International Commercial Arbitration Under the ICC, AAA, LCIA and UNCITRAL Rules", 10 Am. Rev. Int'l Arb. (1999) p. 123 at p. 133.
4. See, e.g., Peter BINDER, *International Commercial Arbitration in UNCITRAL Model Law Jurisdictions* (2000) p. 69. There is some confusion on this point in the United States. See text accompanying fn. 282 below.

of court enforcement. There is not yet a uniform approach to the enforcement of interim measures under the New York Convention,[5] however, and there remain questions of jurisdictional limitations. These issues reduce the effectiveness of interim measures ordered by arbitral tribunals and hence the effectiveness of arbitral tribunals generally.

The practice of international courts and tribunals, as well as that of national courts, in ordering interim measures reflects both common and differing standards utilized in determining whether these measures should be granted and what form they should take. National courts have also followed different paths in their decisions on whether to enforce the interim measures that are ordered in an international setting.

These divergences have led the United Nations Commission on International Trade Law (UNCITRAL or the Commission) to turn its attention to the possible harmonization of the scope of measures to be issued and their subsequent enforcement in national courts. The work of the Commission is continuing as efforts are undertaken to formulate suitable texts on these two problems that could be included in national legislation dealing with international arbitration. As an attempt to bring together the divergent practice in this area, any solution proposed must reflect the most typical approaches that promote the continued effectiveness of international commercial arbitration practice. It is the purpose of this article to set forth a background to the effort to devise a unified approach to the scope and enforcement of interim measures of protection in international commercial arbitration by surveying the practice of national and international fora, analyzing the work of UNCITRAL thus far, and then making specific proposals.

II.   RECENT WORK OF UNCITRAL ON PROVISIONAL MEASURES

The United Nations Commission on International Trade Law was established by the General Assembly in 1966.[6] The general mandate of UNCITRAL is to further the progressive harmonization and unification of international trade law. Among the topics that fall within the purview of the Commission in this regard is international commercial arbitration and conciliation.

One substantial project completed by the Commission for the harmonization of international commercial arbitration was the adoption of the UNCITRAL Arbitration Rules in 1976. These Rules provide a comprehensive set of procedural rules upon which parties may agree for the conduct of arbitral proceedings arising out of their commercial relationship. The UNCITRAL Arbitration Rules, sometimes slightly modified, have been adopted for use in both ad hoc and institutional arbitrations.

Another major undertaking of the Commission in this area has been the UNCITRAL Model Law on International Commercial Arbitration, which was adopted in 1985.[7] The

---

5. New York Convention on the Recognition and Enforcement of Foreign Arbitral Awards (hereinafter New York Convention) 10 June 1958, 21 U.S.T. 2517, 330 U.N.T.S. 3.
6. G.A. Res. 2205 (XXI) 17 December 1966.
7. G.A. Res. 40/72, 11 December 1985.

Model Law was formulated to assist states in revising and updating their national laws on arbitral procedure so as to account for the particular features and needs of international commercial arbitration.

In 1999, the Commission considered the desirability and feasibility of further developing the law of international commercial arbitration in light of experience with national enactments of the Model Law and the use of the UNCITRAL Arbitration Rules.[8] A Working Group on Arbitration, consisting of all members of the Commission, was established to address several priority topics: conciliation, the requirement of a written form for the arbitration agreement, the enforceability of interim measures of protection and the enforceability of an award that had been set aside in the state of origin.[9]

The Commission generally agreed that the question of enforceability of interim measures of protection ordered by arbitral tribunals had significant practical importance and that the uniform treatment of this issue through national legislation could contribute significantly to international commercial arbitration practice.[10] The initial drafts formulated for discussion in the Working Group were partially based on Art. 36 of the Model Law, which addresses the grounds for refusing recognition or enforcement of an arbitral award. The Working Group considered how these grounds could apply with respect to interim measures.

It was further agreed that a non-legislative text should also be prepared to address the scope of interim measures of protection that an arbitral tribunal might order and the accompanying procedural rules.[11] Guidelines or practice notes could discuss issues such as the types of interim measures that an arbitral tribunal might order; its discretion for ordering such measures; and the circumstances warranting the ordering of such measures.[12] To this end, the Working Group requested that the Secretariat of the Commission prepare a document analyzing the rules and practices regarding interim measures issued by arbitral tribunals with the elements for a future harmonized non-legislative text. The Working Group discussed this topic at its subsequent sessions by reference to a draft prepared by the Commission's Secretariat that was developed from

---

8. "Possible Future Work in the Area of International Commercial Arbitration", UNCITRAL, 32nd Sess., UN Doc. A/CN.9/460.

9. "Report of the United Nations Commission on International Trade Law on the work of its thirty-second session", U.N. GAOR, 54th Sess., Supp. No. 17, UN Doc. A/54/17, pp. 40-45.

10. "Report of the Secretary General, Settlement of Commercial Disputes – Possible uniform rules on certain issues concerning settlement of commercial disputes: conciliation, interim measures of protection, written form for arbitration agreement", UNCITRAL, 32nd Sess., UN Doc. A/CN.9/WG.II/WP.108 (20-31 March 2000) (hereinafter Working Paper 108) p. 19.

11. "Report of the Secretary-General, International Commercial Arbitration – Possible future work: court-ordered interim measures of protection in support of arbitration, scope of interim measures that may be issued by arbitral tribunals, validity of the agreement to arbitrate", UNCITRAL, 33d Sess., UN Doc. A/CN.9/WG.II/WP.111 (20 November-1 December 2000) para. 31.

12. *Ibid.*

Art. 17 of the Model Law.[13]

These two topics were still under the consideration of the Working Group at the conclusion of its thirty-sixth session, held in New York in March 2002, though by then the proposal as to authority and standards had developed into a proposal for a legislative text.

III.   PROVISIONAL MEASURES IN NATIONAL AND INTERNATIONAL FORA

As part of their judicial and arbitral processes, international and national courts and tribunals have routinely issued interim measures of protection. The authority to grant these measures is typically established in legislation or in the constitutive instruments of the institutions. Even where no express authority is granted, the importance of provisional measures has caused tribunals to assert their inherent authority to issue provisional measures as part of their judicial or arbitral functions. The standards to be applied in deciding whether such measures are to be granted and the scope of those measures have either been codified in the different jurisdictions or have evolved in the jurisprudence of the relevant court or tribunal.

This part first surveys the practice of national courts and international courts and tribunals in the issuance of provisional measures. This background then provides the context for an analysis of the work of UNCITRAL in assessing the standards for and scope of provisional measures in international commercial arbitration. This part concludes with a proposal of a model legislative provision addressing the standards for the issuance of interim measures of protection.

1.   Provisional Measures in National Courts of Selected Jurisdictions

The standards for granting judicial interim relief in national jurisdictions typically consist of two interrelated issues: the objective need for the relief (and the need for urgency) and the amount of proof the applicant has that the relief sought is warranted. The various codes and case law of each national system may articulate these requirements in diverse ways, but the touchstone for granting interim relief in most jurisdictions is a variation on a theme: "Has the applicant demonstrated sufficiently that a right has been infringed or threatened by the defendant, and is the relief sought (objectively) urgently necessary to protect that right before a full decision on the merits?" This section will examine this concept as evidenced by the provisional measures available in various national court systems.

---

13. Art. 17 of the UNCITRAL Model Law reads:

"Unless otherwise agreed by the parties, the arbitral tribunal may, at the request of a party, order any party to take such interim measure of protection as the arbitral tribunal may consider necessary in respect of the subject-matter of the dispute. The arbitral tribunal may require any party to provide appropriate security in connection with such measure."

a.   Australia

The Australian judicial system is a federal one, with the individual states having their own independent court systems.[14] The procedures for obtaining provisional measures such as injunctions or attachment vary between the states and territories, and the federal courts, but all are given broad powers to fashion interlocutory relief.[15] Nonetheless, the general outlines for obtaining interlocutory relief are common to all jurisdictions. It is also important to note that there are numerous state, territorial and commonwealth statutes that prescribe injunctive relief in particular kinds of cases.[16] The range of interlocutory relief is wide, including prohibitive injunctions, *Mareva*[17] injunctions, and *Anton Piller*[18] orders.[19] Both inter partes and ex parte orders may be issued, although the latter are limited to cases of "particular urgency".[20]

While the standards for various kinds of orders vary,[21] the general standard for the granting of injunctive relief requires the applicant to establish that "there is a serious

---

14. See Garry DOWNES, Q.C., "Australia" in Anthony COLEMAN, ed., *Encyclopedia of International Commercial Litigation*, vol. 1 (1991 & 2000 Cum. Supp.) (hereinafter *EICL*) for a brief overview of the Australian judicial system.

15. *Ibid.* See also Sect. 23 Federal Court of Australia Act 1976 (Commonwealth) ("The Court has power, in relation to matters in which it has jurisdiction, to make orders of such kinds, including interlocutory orders, and to issue, or direct the issue of, writs of such kinds, as the Court thinks appropriate."); *BMW Australia Ltd. v. Phileo Australia Ltd. & Anor.* (2000) V.S.C. 308 (noting "inherent power" of court to grant injunctions under Sect. 37(1) of the Supreme Court Act 1986 (Victoria)).

16. See, e.g., Sect. 315 Superannuation Industry (Supervision) Act 1993 (Commonwealth); Sect. 276 Duties Act 2000, (Victoria); Sect. 298U Workplace Relations Act 1996 (Commonwealth); Sect. 115(2) Copyright Act 1968 (Commonwealth); Sect. 126(a) Trade Marks Act 1995 (Commonwealth).

17. So called after the leading English case *Mareva Compañia Naviera S.A. v. Int'l Bulkcarriers S.A.* [1975] 2 Lloyd's Rep. 509 (C.A.). The English Court of Chancery, interpreting Sect. 45 of the Supreme Judicature Act of 1925 held that "if it appears that [a] debt is due and owing – and there is a danger that the debtor may dispose of his assets so as to defeat it before judgment – the Court has jurisdiction in a proper case to grant an interlocutory judgment so as to prevent [the debtor] disposing of those assets". *Ibid.* (Lord Denning, M.R.). Thus, a *Mareva* injunction is usually sought ex parte to freeze the assets of a defendant or potential defendant pending a final judgment on the merits.

18. So called after the English Court of Appeal case *Anton Piller K.G. v. Manufacturing Processes Ltd.* (1976) 1 Ch. 55, 62 (C.A. 1975). "[A]n *Anton Piller* order allows a plaintiff, or a counterclaiming defendant, to serve an order on a party that authorizes entry onto premises controlled by the party in order to search and seize certain documents and other evidence that may be used later in a lawsuit or trial." Kern ALEXANDER, "The *Mareva* Injunction and *Anton Piller* Order: The Nuclear Weapons of English Commercial Litigation", 11 Fla. J. Int'l L. (Fall 1997) p. 487 at p. 490.

19. DOWNES, *EICL*, *op. cit.*, fn. 14, Sect. B6.26 et seq.

20. *Ibid.* at Sect. B6.34. A court may even act without affidavit evidence in extremely urgent circumstances "on the condition that [an] affidavit is ... filed as soon as possible". *Ibid.* at Sect. B6.35.

21. For example, to obtain an *Anton Piller* order, the applicant must demonstrate that he has a very strong prima facie case; that the potential damage to him is "very serious"; and that the defendant likely has inculpatory documents, and there is a "reasonable probability" that he will destroy them before a full hearing. *Ibid.*, Sect. B6.37.

question to be tried".[22] However, in cases implicating the "public interest", the petitioner must demonstrate "probability, even a distinct probability of success, in order to obtain an interlocutory injunction".[23]

b. Chile

Under the Chilean *Código de Procedimiento Civil* (CCP), several types of "precautionary measures" (*medidas precautorias*) are available. These include: (1) orders to deposit with the court (*secuestro judicial*) personal property in dispute where the property is in danger of being lost or damaged; (2) the appointment of *interventores* to supervise real or personal property and to retain income from such property to avoid danger to the rights of a plaintiff; (3) the judicial seizure of the defendant's money or property as a guarantee against a future judgment when it appears that the defendant may conceal or dispose of those assets; and (4) an order prohibiting the defendant from acting or contracting with respect to the disputed property, or with respect to a defendant's property not in dispute, as a means of preserving the defendant's assets in anticipation of a judgment.[24] The central theme in the *medidas precautorias* is the need to safeguard the status quo until a final judgment can be obtained.

Applications for interim relief are subject to the summary procedures for *los incidentes* (incidental matters) of CCP Title IX, Art. 82 et seq.[25] Under these procedures,

---

22. *Australian Coarse Grain Pool Pty Ltd. v. Barley Marketing Board of Queensland* (1985) 157 C.L.R. 605; *Tableland Peanuts Pty Ltd. v. Peanut Marketing Board* (1984) 52 A.L.R. 651 at 653; *Epitoma Pty Ltd. v. Australasian Meat Industry Employees Union* (1984) 54 A.L.R. 730; *Castlemaine Tooheys Ltd. v. South Australia* (1986) 161 C.L.R. 148 at 153 (Mason A.C.J.). The Australian standard has as its basis the English House of Lords decision in *American Cyanamid v. Ethicon Ltd.* [1975] A.C. 396. See below fns. 35-36 and accompanying text.

23. *Castlemaine Tooheys, op. cit.*, fn. 22, p. 154.

24. Art. 290 CCP reads:

"*Para asegurar el resultado de la acción, puede el demandante en cualquier estado del juicio, aun cuando no esté contestada la demanda, pedir una o más de las siguientes medidas:*
1. *El secuestro de la cosa que es objeto de la demanda;*
2. *El nombramiento de uno o más interventores;*
3. *La retención de bienes determinados; y*
4. *La prohibición de celebrar actos o contratos sobre bienes determinados.*"

(In order to secure the result of the action, the plaintiff may, at any stage of the proceedings, and even if the complaint has not yet been answered, ask for one or more of the following reliefs:
1. The sequestration of the thing that is the subject of the complaint;
2. The appointment of one or more interveners;
3. The retention of certain assets; and
4. The prohibition to execute acts and agreements upon certain assets.) (Unofficial translation.)

25. Art. 302 CCP (directing courts to apply summary procedures for *los incidentes*). Generally speaking, the procedure applied to incidental matters will extend no longer than eleven days. Once application for interim relief is made, the defendant is notified and has three days to reply. If the court finds no factual dispute between the parties, it may decide on the application as a matter of law. However, if there is a factual dispute, the court will order a *término probatorio* – a

applications for interim relief are inter partes by default; however, Art. 302 provides for ex parte applications when there are "serious reasons" to do so.[26] If an ex parte application is granted, the relief ordered will expire if the affected party is not served within five days.

In order to prevail on a request for a *medida precautoria*, the applicant must produce evidence sufficient to raise a "serious presumption" that the right claimed is endangered, and she may be required to post security against any harm to the opposing party.[27] In "urgent and serious" cases, a court may dispense with the evidentiary requirement and issue orders implementing the relief sought. However, the applicant must provide security against damage to the opposing party and must produce the necessary evidence within ten days.[28]

c.   England and Wales
Most of the varieties of interim relief available in English and Welsh courts are outlined in Part 25 of the new Civil Procedure Rules (CPR).[29] Rule 25(1) enumerates the various

---

period of time for receiving evidence – which may not exceed eight days.

26. Art. 302 CCP then provides in pertinent part:

"Podrán, sin embargo, llevarse a efecto dichas medidas antes de notificarse a la persona contra quien se dictan, siempre que existan razones graves para ello y el tribunal así lo ordene.
   Transcurridos cinco días sin que la notificación se efectúe, quedarán sin valor las diligencias practicadas. El tribunal podrá ampliar este plazo por motivos fundados La notificación a que se refiere este artículo podrá hacerse por cédula, si el tribunal así lo ordena."

(Said relief may, however, be effected before notice is given to the person against whom it is ordered, as long as serious reasons exist for doing so and the court so orders.
   After five days without notifying the other party, the relief ordered shall have no force. The court may extend such term due to serious reasons....) (Unofficial translation.)

27. Art. 298 CCP. Art. 298 provides:

"Las medidas de que trata este Título se limitarán a los bienes necesarios para responder a los resultados del juicio, y para decretarlas deberá el demandante acompañar comprobantes que constituyan a lo menos presunción grave del derecho que se reclama. Podrá también el tribunal, cuando lo estime necesario y no tratándose de medidas expresamente autorizadas por la ley, exigir caución al actor para responder de los perjuicios que se originen."

(The relief referred to in this title shall be limited to the assets that are necessary guarantee the results of the lawsuit, and in order to be issued, the plaintiff shall provide evidence that constitutes at least a serious presumption of the right that it is claimed. The court may also, when it deems necessary and when dealing with relief not expressly authorized by statute, demand security from the plaintiff in order to guarantee any damage [to the defendant].) (Unofficial translation.)

28. Art. 299 CCP.
29. These Rules came into effect on 26 April 1999. Prior to this enactment, England and Wales did not have a procedural code for all their courts; most procedural issues were dealt with in instruments such as the Rules of the Supreme Court and the County Court Rules. The new CPR controls procedure in all cases before the High Courts (Queen's Bench, Chancery, Admiralty),

types of provisional measures a court may grant, including injunctions, interim declarations, orders for the seizure, inspection or sampling of property, orders for the disclosure of documents, "freezing" orders (*Mareva* injunctions),[30] search orders (*Anton Piller* orders),[31] and orders for interim payments, among others. The standard for obtaining such relief is set out in general in CPR Rule 25(2)(2)(b), which gives the court wide discretion in granting relief, stating that "the court may grant an interim remedy before a claim has been made only if – (i) the matter is urgent; or (ii) it is otherwise desirable to do so in the interests of justice...". Applications for such relief "must be supported by evidence, unless the court orders otherwise".[32] Where a court requires evidentiary support, Practice Direction 25, Interim Injunctions para. 3(1) directs that such support must consist of an affidavit to obtain certain types of orders (e.g., *Mareva*, *Anton Piller* orders), or at a minimum, witness statements. However, a court may in its discretion require the applicant to produce affidavits in support of an application for any kind of injunctive relief.[33]

Relief may be granted ex parte, but such applications are limited to cases of special urgency. As one commentator has noted:

> "[E]x parte orders should only be made in exceptional circumstances. The most obvious are where, (a) the situation is one of extreme urgency so that there is no time to warn the defendant, or (b) where the purpose of the injunction might be frustrated if the defendant were warned, or (c) where the defendant cannot be found."[34]

When considering whether to grant injunctive relief, a court must be satisfied that there is a "serious question to be tried", and if so, must consider the "balance of convenience" in granting the relief. This "standard" was announced by the House of Lords in *American Cyanamid v. Ethicon Ltd.*[35] There, Lord Diplock articulated the analysis that English courts should follow:

---

as well as the County Courts. See Anthony COLEMAN, J.Q.B., "England and Wales" in 1 *EICL, op. cit.*, fn. 14, Sect. A1.10.

30. See above fn. 17. In 1981, Parliament codified the *Mareva* injunction in Art. 37 of the Supreme Court Act of 1981; the 1999 CPR terms them "freezing injunctions" and provides extensive guidance for their issuance in Part 25 and Practice Direction 25, Injunctions para. 6(1) et seq. Rule 25 expressly authorizes *Mareva* injunctions against assets not located in the United Kingdom. Rule 25(1)(1)(f) CPR.

31. See above fn. 18. "Search orders", as the *Anton Piller* order is now officially known in England, were codified in Art. 7 of the Civil Procedure Act 1997 and are controlled by Part 25 and Practice Direction 25, Interim Injunctions para. 7(1) et seq.

32. Rule 25(3)(2) CPR.

33. Practice Direction 25, Interim Injunctions para. 3(2).

34. Kevin GARNETT, et al., *Copinger and Skone James on Copyright*, 14th ed. (Sweet & Maxwell 1999) Sect. 22-56.

35. (1975) A.C. 396. The *American Cyanamid* standard continues to apply to the new CPR. See, e.g., *Sainsbury's Supermarkets Ltd. v. British Airways Plc, Air Miles Travel Promotions Ltd.* 2002 WL 346967 (E.W.H.C. Ch.); *Michael Douglas & Catherine Zeta-Jones v. Hello! Ltd.* (2000) EWCA Civ. 353.

"The court no doubt must be satisfied that the claim is not frivolous or vexatious, in other words, that there is a serious question to be tried.... So unless the material available to the court at the hearing of the application for an interlocutory injunction fails to disclose that the plaintiff has any real prospect of succeeding in his claim for a permanent injunction at the trial, the court should go on to consider whether the balance of convenience lies in favour of granting or refusing the interlocutory relief that is sought."[36]

Lord Diplock elaborated on the *American Cyanamid* standard in *NWL Ltd. v. Woods (The Nawala) (No. 2)*[37] to address cases where the grant or denial of relief would effectively resolve the dispute as a practical matter. In these instances, the likelihood of the plaintiff's ultimate success on the merits becomes an integral factor in the "balancing of the convenience":

"Where ... the grant or refusal of the interlocutory injunction will have the practical effect of putting an end to the action because the harm that will have been already caused to the losing party by its grant or its refusal is complete and of a kind for which money cannot constitute any worthwhile recompense, the degree of likelihood that the plaintiff would have succeeded in establishing his right to an injunction if the action had gone to trial, is a factor to be brought into the balance by the Judge in weighing the risks that injustice may result from his deciding the application one way rather than the other."[38]

The CPR applies a different standard for the granting of an order to make "interim payments" before a final decision. To issue such an order before a final judgment, one of several conditions must be demonstrated by the applicant: the other party has admitted liability; "if the claim went to trial, the claimant would obtain judgment for a

---

36. *American Cyanamid, op. cit.*, fn. 35, pp. 407-408. Lord Diplock continued:

"[T]he governing principle is that the court should first consider whether, if the plaintiff were to succeed at the trial in establishing his right to a permanent injunction, he would be adequately compensated by an award of damages for the loss he would have sustained as a result of the defendant's continuing to do what was sought to be enjoined between the time of the application and the time of the trial.... If damages in the measure recoverable under such an undertaking would be an adequate remedy and the plaintiff would be in a financial position to pay them, there would be no reason upon this ground to refuse an interlocutory injunction.

It is where there is doubt as to the adequacy of the respective remedies in damages available to either party or to both, that the question of balance of convenience arises. It would be unwise to attempt even to list all the various matters which may need to be taken into consideration in deciding where the balance lies, let alone to suggest the relative weight to be attached to them. These will vary from case to case.

Where other factors appear to be evenly balanced it is a counsel of prudence to take such measures as are calculated to preserve the status quo...."

37. *NWL Ltd. v. Woods (The Nawala) (No. 2)* (1980) 1 Lloyd's Rep. 1, 10 (1979 HL).
38. *Ibid.*

substantial amount of money (other than costs) against the defendant ...";[39] or, in the case of a suit over land, evidence such that "the court is satisfied that, if the case went to trial, the defendant would be held liable (even if the claim for possession fails) to pay the claimant a sum of money for the defendant's occupation and use of the land...".[40]

d. France

Provisional relief in the French legal system is controlled by the provisions of the *Nouveau code de procédure civile* (NCPC). There are different procedures and mechanisms for ex parte and inter partes applications for relief.[41] Both are provisional in nature and are not res judicata as to the merits of the dispute.[42] Ex parte orders, or *ordonnances sur requête*, are available under expedited procedures under the NCPC and are most often used to attach the assets of a defendant or to seize allegedly infringing goods in anticipation of a later judgment.[43] The power of a judge in respect of an *ordonnance sur requête* is quite broad. For example, the *Président* of the *Tribunal de Grand Instance* is empowered to "decree such urgent directions where the circumstances so demand ...".[44] Similar broad power is given to the judges of the other tribunals, limited only by the scope of their jurisdiction.[45] The broadly worded standard for granting an ex parte *ordonnance sur requête* leaves French judges a certain degree of discretion to appreciate the circumstances of each case. Nonetheless, one commentator has noted that French courts

---

39. Rule 25(7)(1)(c) CPR.
40. Rule 25(7)(1)(d)(ii) CPR.
41. See generally Jan PAULSSON and Jean Dominique MONDOLINI, "France" in 1 *EICL*, *op. cit.*, note 14, Sect. A6.1 et seq.
42. See, e.g., Art. 484 NCPC, "*L'ordonnance de référé est une décision provisoire....*" (A summary interlocutory procedure order shall be a provisional order....); Art. 493 "*L'ordonnance sur requête est une décision provisoire....*" (An ex parte order shall be a provisional order....).
43. Nicholas ROSE, *Pre-Emptive Remedies in Europe* (1992) pp. 102-103. Indeed, the most significant *ordonnance* is the *saisie conservatoire*, or protective attachment. Stephen O'MALLEY and Alexander LAYTON, *European Civil Practice* (Sweet & Maxwell 1992) Sect. 50.58, p. 1269. The *saisie conservatoire* (conservative seizure) "is available in support of all civil and commercial claims for a money judgment, whether liquidated or not". *Ibid.*, Sect. 50.59, p. 1269. These attachments are addressed in various code provisions, depending on the *res* sought to be attached (real property is excluded). *Ibid.*
44. Art. 812 NCPC. Art. 812 provides:

"*Le président du tribunal est saisi par requête dans les cas spécifiés par la loi.*
Il peut également ordonner sur requête toutes mesures urgentes lorsque les circonstances exigent qu'elles ne soient pas prises contradictoirement...."

(The president of the court shall be seised by petition in the circumstances provided by law.
He may equally decree such urgent directions where the circumstances so demand that they are not dealt with by way of adversarial proceedings. Incidental petitions relating to a current proceeding shall be presented to the president of the court-room to which the matter has been allocated or to the judge seised of the same.)

45. See, e.g., Art. 851 NCPC (Judges of the *tribunaux d'instances*); Art. 875 NCPC ("*le président*" of the *tribunaux de commerce*); Art. 958 NCPC (*premier président* of the *cour d'appel*).

"place[] the greatest value on the utility of the measure [sought]".[46]

The more common provisional measure is the summary proceeding seeking an *ordonnance de référé*. The proceedings *en référé* are inter partes, although the court may grant enforcement of an order *sur minute*, meaning that it may be enforced before formal communication of the order to the opposing party.[47] The power of a court in granting an *ordonnance de référé* is, like the *ordonnance sur requête*, very broad. The president of a *tribunal de grande instance*, for example, is empowered "in all cases of urgency ... [to] order by way of summary interlocutory proceedings such directions regarding which no serious objections is raised...".[48] In cases that are not urgent but where the creditor's claim is not seriously objectionable, the court may also order provisional payment of all or part of the creditor's claim (the so-called *référé provision*).[49] Thus, the "standard" for granting an *ordonnance de référé* is an urgent need for the relief and the absence of a "serious dispute as to obligation".[50] In certain cases, there is a presumption of "urgency"[51] sufficient to overcome a "serious objection" and to relieve the applicant of the need to prove urgency specifically where there is a need "to prevent imminent damage or to stop a nuisance that is clearly illegal".[52]

e.   Germany

There are two varieties of provisional relief available in German courts: the *Arrest* (attachment or seizure) and the *einstweilige Verfügung* (preliminary injunction).[53] Both are available before the commencement of an action as well as during the course of a trial.[54] The procedure outlined in the *Zivilprozeßordnung* (ZPO) for these measures is expedited;

---

46. ROSE, *op. cit.*, fn. 43, p. 104.

47. Art. 489 NCPC.

48. Art. 808 NCPC ("*Dans tous les cas d'urgence, le président du tribunal de grande instance peut ordonner en référé toutes les mesures qui ne se heurtent à aucune contestation sérieuse ou que justifie l'existence d'un différend.*") (In all cases of urgency, the president of the *Tribunal de grande instance* may order by way of summary interlocutory proceedings such directions regarding which no serious objections is raised or which ought to be given by reason of a dispute.); see also Art. 872 NCPC (*tribunaux de commerce*) and Art. 956 NCPC (*cours d'appel*).

49. Art. 809(2) NCPC.

50. ROSE, *op. cit.*, fn. 43, p. 109. Note that the standard is not one of potential harm, although the articulation of "urgency" as the determinant must partake of the potential harm to have any meaning in the context of a dispute.

51. Put another way, there is a presumption of harm should the relief sought *not* be found to be urgently needed.

52. ROSE, *op. cit.*, fn. 43, p. 105; Art. 809 NCPC 809 (*tribunal de grande instance*), Art. 849 NCPC (*tribunal d'instance*), Art. 873 NCPC (*tribunal de commerce*). These provisions have been used to enjoin "attacks on personal reputation, unfair competition, false advertising, illegal lockouts, or construction works that create a nuisance". PAULSSON and MONDOLINI, 1 *EICL*, *op. cit.*, fn. 41, Sect. B3.5. There is in addition a third species of injunctive order, the *injonction de payer*, or provisional order to pay money. Art. 1271 NCPC. O'MALLEY and LAYTON, *op. cit.*, fn. 43, Sect. 51.62.

53. O'MALLEY and LAYTON, *op. cit.*, fn. 43, Sect. 51.5.58 et seq. These measures are addressed in Sects. 916-945 of the German Code of Civil Procedure, the ZPO.

54. ROSE, *op. cit.*, fn. 43, pp. 118-119.

no formal hearing is required, and the standard of proof is lessened to require only "satisfactory proof" of a claim and the need for the relief.[55]

The *Arrest* is available in cases involving claims for a sum of money, or where the claim is otherwise capable of a valuation the plaintiff may seek a *dinglicher Arrest* of any of the defendant's assets.[56] The application for an *Arrest* may be made ex parte, and there are provisions for seeking the relief outside of normal court hours in pressing circumstances.[57] A *dinglicher Arrest* may not be obtained absent special circumstances. The party seeking the *Arrest* must demonstrate, with a "sufficient degree of plausibility",[58] that "there is a risk that the defendant will so deal with his assets as to obstruct or defeat the enforcement"[59] of the final judgment. Thus, "if enforcement of the creditor's claim [would be] frustrated or made more substantially difficult" without the *Arrest*, special circumstances are said to exist.[60]

When an *Arrest* is not appropriate to the relief or determination to be sought in the case-in-chief, a party may seek a preliminary injunction or *einstweilige Verfügung*. The two broad categories of *einstweilige Verfügung* have been termed by an English commentator "preservation orders" and "determination orders".[61] A "preservation order" may be used in a variety of ways, such as to preserve evidence, abate damaging or nuisance behavior by the defendant, or to preserve the status quo by preventing alienation of an asset or to preserve a right to specific performance (where an *Arrest* is not justified).[62] In seeking a preservation order, the critical factor examined by a court is whether "the

---

55. *Ibid.*, citing Sects. 920(2), 921 and 937(2) ZPO.

56. Sect. 917 ZPO. Sect. 917 provides:

> "1. *Der dingliche Arrest findet statt, wenn zu besorgen ist, daß ohne dessen Verhängung die Vollstreckung des Urteils vereitelt oder wesentlich erschwert werden würde.*
>
> 2. *Als ein zureichender Arrestgrund ist es anzusehen, wenn das Urteil im Ausland vollstreckt werden müßte....*"

 See also O'MALLEY and LAYTON, *op. cit.*, fn. 43, at p. 1309, Sect. 51.59; ROSE, *op. cit.*, fn. 43, p. 118.

57. O'MALLEY and LAYTON, *op. cit.*, fn. 43, p. 1309, Sect. 51.59.

58. In German, *Glaubhaftmachung*. Michael H. CARL, "Germany" in 1 *EICL*, *op. cit.*, fn. 14, Sect. A8.3.

59. O'MALLEY and LAYTON, *op. cit.*, fn. 43, p. 1309, Sect. 51.59.

60. ROSE, *op. cit.*, fn. 43, p. 118. There is also a much harsher *Arrest*, the *persönlicher Arrest*, whereby a defendant may be imprisoned or otherwise restricted in his freedom until he deposits with the court the sum claimed. Sect. 918 ZPO. Sect. 918 provides: "*Der persönliche Sicherheitsarrest findet nur statt, wenn er erforderlich ist, um die gefährdete Zwangsvollstreckung in das Vermögen des Schuldners zu sichern.*" Under Sect. 933, the court may order seizure of the defendant's passport, or order him to report to a local constabulary. *Ibid.*, p. 118 (citing Sect. 933 ZPO). The personal *Arrest* is often used against foreign defendants in Germany, but is only applicable when the defendant is potentially personally liable for the claim, and a *dinglicher Arrest* would not suffice to protect the claimant's interests. O'MALLEY and LAYTON, *op. cit.*, fn. 43, p. 1309, Sect. 51.59; ROSE, *op. cit.*, fn. 43, p. 118.

61. ROSE, *op. cit.*, fn. 43, p. 119.

62. CARL, *op. cit.*, fn. 58, Sect. A8.1; ROSE, *op. cit.*, fn. 43, p. 119 (citing Sect. 935 ZPO (indicating use of *einstweilige Verfügung* to protect a right by a mandatory or prohibitive order)).

enforcement of [the plaintiff's] rights could be frustrated or made substantially more difficult" by failing to prevent a change in the status quo or to act otherwise.[63]

A "determination order" is used to determine provisionally the rights of the parties with respect to the underlying litigation.[64] This variation is used "to regulate a temporary situation with regard to a legal relationship in dispute".[65] The immediate resolution of the legal relationship must be "necessary" to obtain the order. "Necessity" has been said to mean that the order is "required to avert substantial detriment" to the party seeking the determination.[66] A determination order is conversely not "necessary" if the applicant fails to demonstrate the need for an immediate or urgent determination, or if she fails to demonstrate that the infringement of her rights is ongoing.[67]

f.   India

Judicial interim or interlocutory relief in India is addressed in Order XXXIX of the Indian Code of Civil Procedure.[68] Order XXXIX addresses primarily "conservatory" relief aimed at preventing waste or damage to property that is the subject of a dispute, alienation of that property, fraudulent conveyances, dispossession of the plaintiff, and the like. To obtain such relief, the applicant must prove "by affidavit or otherwise" that the property in dispute is "in danger" of being wasted or damaged, or that the defendant "threatens or intends" to take action against the property or plaintiff.[69] Both inter partes and ex parte applications are permitted, although "[e]x parte relief is the exception rather than the rule".[70] Orders are generally accompanied by an opinion setting out the court's reasoning in granting the relief and are subject to at least one immediate

---

63. ROSE, *ibid.*

64. *Ibid.* (citing Sect. 940 ZPO).

65. *Ibid.*

66. *Ibid.*

67. *Ibid.*

68. Bomi ZAIWALLA and Dinsoo ZAIWALLA, "India" in 1 *EICL*, *op. cit.*, fn. 14, Sects. A10.1-A10.2 Order XXXIX provides:

"1. Where in any suit it is proved by Affidavit or otherwise—
(a) that any property in dispute is in danger of being wasted, damaged or alienated by any party to the suit, or wrongfully sold in execution of a Decree, or
(b) that the Defendant threatens, or intends, to remove or dispose of his property with a view to (defrauding) his creditors,
(c) that the Defendant threatens to dispossess the Plaintiff or otherwise cause injury to the Plaintiff in relation to any property in dispute in the suit,
the Court may by Order grant a temporary injunction to restrain such act, or make such other order for the purpose of staying and preventing the wasting, damaging, alienation, sale, removal or disposition of the property or dispossession of the Plaintiff, or otherwise causing injury to the plaintiff in relation to any property in dispute in the suit as the Court thinks fit, until the disposal of the suit or until further Orders."

69. Indian Code of Civil Procedure Order XXXIX 1.

70. ZAIWALLA and ZAIWALLA, *op. cit.*, fn. 68, Sects. B1.22- B1.23.

appeal.[71] Failure to comply with such orders may result in judicial seizure of the property and/or civil detention of the party failing to comply for up to three months.[72]

In addition to the relief articulated in Order XXXIX, the Supreme Court of India has granted Indian courts broad powers to afford a litigant preliminary relief. As one observer noted, the court has held that Indian courts "ha[ve] inherent power to issue temporary injunctions in circumstances not yet covered by [statute] if the court is of the opinion that the interest [sic] of justice require".[73]

g. *Japan*

Provisional remedies in Japanese courts are controlled by the Code of Civil Provisional Remedies enacted in 1989.[74] There are two broad categories of provisional measures available in Japanese courts: provisional attachment (*kari-sashiosae*) and provisional disposition (*keisobutsu ni kansuru karishobun*).[75] Such interim measures are widely used, with some form of interim relief granted in over half the cases filed in the district courts, the primary courts of first instance.[76]

Provisional attachment is used when a creditor has a monetary claim (or one convertible to a monetary value) against an alleged debtor to secure future enforcement of a final judgment. A court may order provisional attachment only if the applicant has made out a prima facie case that failure to do so would make enforcement of a final judgment "impossible or extremely difficult".[77]

The majority of provisional dispositions fall into two categories: those designed to "preserve the property at issue", and those meant "to establish an interim legal relationship between the parties".[78] The first measure is used by parties whose claim against property is non-monetary, such as for specific performance in a contract relating to real estate.[79] In such a case, the court may order the defendant not to dispose of or otherwise alter the property so as to preserve the status quo until a final judgment is reached.[80]

Provisional dispositions aimed at establishing an interim legal relationship are similar to interlocutory injunctions. In these orders, the court will provisionally grant all or some of the relief requested by the plaintiff if it is demonstrated that it is necessary to

---

71. *Ibid.*

72. *Ibid.*, Sect. A10.3 (Indian Code of Civil Procedure citing Order XXXIX 2A).

73. *Ibid.*, Sect. A10.5.

74. See Supreme Court of Japan, "Outline of a Civil Trial in Japan", at www.courts.go.jp/english/procedure/index.htm (last visited 22 April 2002). The rules on interlocutory measures were enacted by the Law on Civil Interlocutory Measures, Law No. 91 of 1989. Ichiro KATO et al., "Japan" in 2 *EICL*, *op. cit.*, fn. 14, Sect. A5.27.

75. *Ibid.* The latter is more fully translated "provisional disposition in respect of the subject-matter in dispute". See also KATO et al., *op. cit.*, fn. 74, Sect. A5.27.

76. Hiroshi ODA, *Japanese Law*, 2nd ed. (1999) p. 400; KATO et al., *op. cit.*, fn. 74, Sect. A5.38.

77. ODA, *op. cit.*, fn. 76, p. 400; KATO et al., *op. cit.*, fn. 74, Sect. A5.28.

78. ODA, *op. cit.*, fn. 76, p. 400.

79. *Ibid.*

80. *Ibid.*, p. 401.

do so to "prevent imminent harm to the plaintiff".[81] Typical uses, as noted by two commentators, are to prevent publication of allegedly libelous matter,[82] or to prevent damage to an ongoing legal relationship such as employment.[83] A third type of interlocutory order is the order to make an immediate, provisional payment of money "in order to preserve an obligee from urgent danger".[84] These orders are known as *kari no chii o sadameru karishobun* ("provisional dispositions for the purpose of provisionally settling the state of affairs").[85]

In addition to attachment and provisional disposition, there is also a limited range of provisional measures relating to the preservation of evidence prior to trial. A party may ask the court to take steps to secure evidence (documentary, physical or witness statements), or to conduct judicial inspections of premises, records, or the like.[86] To prevail on such a request, the applicant must establish that there are "grounds to believe that without such action, the prospective use of the evidence would be difficult".[87]

h. People's Republic of China

The law in the PRC regarding injunctions and other preliminary relief is unclear.[88] However, the Civil Procedure Law (CPL) does contain provisions on "prior execution" (or "prior enforcement") of judgments.[89] Chapter IX of the CPL permits a court to enforce a judgment prior to a final decision, which is the closest the CPL comes to authorizing an injunctive remedy.[90] While, except as to attachment of property, Chapter IX is silent on whether a "prior execution" order can be had before filing of the underlying case, the Supreme People's Court, in its "Opinion on Several Questions Concerning Application of the Civil Procedure Law" (July 1992) appears to have held that non-preservation injunctive relief is not available prior to filing suit.[91] However, at least one Chinese judge has stated that "such relief is given by the courts in appropriate

---

81. *Ibid.*, p. 400; KATO, et al., *op. cit.*, fn. 74, Sect. A5.35.
82. Note, however, that the Japanese Supreme Court has curtailed the use of such measures in libel actions against the press, stating that as a general rule they should not be used, and requiring a showing of falsity, that the article will not promote the public interest, and the likelihood of irreparable damage to the plaintiff to render such an order valid. Judgment of the Supreme Court, 11 June 1986 (*Minshu* 40-4-872: Hoppō Journal case), cited in ODA, *op. cit.*, fn. 76, p. 401.
83. *Ibid.*, pp. 400-401; KATO, et al., *op. cit.*, fn. 74, Sect. A5.35.
84. Supreme Court of Japan, "Outline of a Civil Trial in Japan", *op. cit.*, fn. 74.
85. *Ibid.*
86. KATO et al., *op. cit.*, fn. 74, Sect. A5.39.
87. *Ibid.*
88. Helena KOLENDA, et al., "China" in 1 *EICL*, *op. cit.*, fn. 14, Sects. A9.69, A9.75.
89. The People's Republic of China CPL is translated at the University of Maryland Law School's "Chinalaw" website at www.qis.net/chinalaw/lawtran1.htm (last visited 22 April 2002) and calls the relief discussed in these provisions (Arts. 97-99) "prior execution". KOLENDA, et al. term the orders "prior enforcement". Helena KOLENDA, et al., *EICL*, *op. cit.*, fn. 88, Sects. A9.69, A9.75.
90. See KOLENDA, et al., *EICL*, *op. cit.*, fn. 88, at Sect. 9.75.
91. *Ibid.*

cases",[92] leaving open the possibility that Chinese jurisprudence recognizes that courts must have a degree of inherent authority to shape provisional remedies in the interests of justice.

Most of the provisions of Chapter IX deal with preservation proceedings involving property that is in dispute (termed "applications for custody of property")[93] permitting a court to "seal-up, distrain, freez[e] and [take] other measures provided by law" to preserve the property until final judgment.[94] The CPL expressly authorizes the preservative measures as both interlocutory remedies after filing, as well as a preliminary measure provided that the court believes that the applicant's "legitimate rights and interests may be damaged beyond remedy" without such action.[95]

Art. 97 of the CPL authorizes the People's Courts to issue orders of prior execution in cases of claims for "support or upbringing, pensions for the disabled and medical expenses ... labour remuneration ... [or] [o]ther urgent circumstances that require prior execution".[96] Before it may issue orders under Art. 97, a court must satisfy itself that "the rights and obligations between the litigants are clear and the applicant's livelihood or business operation would be seriously affected if no prior execution is enforced...."[97]

i.   Russian Federation

Application of judicial interim relief measures in Russia is stipulated in both civil procedure and *arbitrazh* procedure. *Arbitrazhnye sudy* or "arbitration courts" are not arbitral panels as understood in most jurisdictions; they rather represent a branch of state courts that hear commercial cases where both parties are either legal entities or state authorities (authorities of constituent entities of the Russian Federation).[98] Civil courts, known simply as *sudy* or "courts" have general jurisdiction in commercial matters only if one of the parties is a natural person.[99] The *tretyeiskie* courts are closest to the Western notion of an arbitral panel.[100]

General provisions on judicial interim relief measures are set forth in Arts. 133 to 140 of the Code of Civil Procedure[101] (CCP) and in Arts. 90 to 100 of the Code of *Arbitrazh* Procedure[102] (CAP). In addition to the above provisions of the CCP and CAP, some individual norms regulate the application of certain specific types of judicial

---

92. *Ibid.* (citing an unnamed Chinese judge).

93. See Arts. 92-96 CPL.

94. Art. 94 CPL.

95. Art. 93 CPL.

96. Art. 97(1)-(3) CPL.

97. Art. 98(1) CPL.

98. See Nikolai Georgievich ELISEEV and Jay DRATLER, Jr., "Russian Federation" in 2 *EICL*, *op. cit.*, fn. 14, Sect. A1.1.

99. *Ibid.*

100. *Ibid.*

101. *Grazdanskij Protsesualnyi Kodeks RSFSR* (11 June 1964) (CCP).

102. *Arbitrazhnyi Protsesualnyi Kodeks RF* (24 July 2002) (CAP). (From 1 September 2002, a new CAP was introduced pursuant to a Federal Law of 24 July 2002).

interim measures.[103]

An exhaustive list of judicial interim relief measures is stipulated in Art. 134 of the CCP and Art. 91 of the CAP. The list includes sequestration of property or cash of the defendant;[104] prohibiting the defendant from participation in certain activities;[105] prohibiting third parties from use of the disputed property or from undertaking any activities involving the disputed property; temporary prohibition on alienation of property (when release of such property from arrest is in dispute); and temporary prohibition on execution of a writ or ruling of the court envisaging set-off with respect to a certain bank account. The court may apply several judicial interim relief measures simultaneously or change the measure in the course of proceedings.

Russian courts are entitled to apply judicial interim relief measures, at the request of the plaintiff, at any stage of the proceeding. Moreover, in civil, but not in *arbitrazh*, proceedings the court may apply judicial interim relief measures sua sponte.[106] The only test used by the courts in application of such measures is the existence of a risk that the subsequent court ruling may be complicated or impossible to enforce if such measures are not taken. Judges have wide discretion in making such determinations.

Failure to comply with the order of the court regarding the judicial interim relief measures may lead to imposition of a fine.[107] (Note, however, that the new CAP and CCP do not envisage such a provision.) In addition, the violating party must compensate any damages caused to the other party as a result of its failure to comply with the court order (in accordance with Art. 134 CCP). If the court rejects the claim, the defendant may seek compensation of damages caused by application of judicial interim relief measures.[108] The defendant may also ask the court to apply measures, which would secure compensation of such damages when the court decides on application of the judicial interim relief measures.

---

103. For example, provisions on the sequestration of the funds of a credit organization are set forth in Information Letter No. 31 of the Presidium of the Supreme *Arbitrazh* Court of the Russian Federation dated 25 February 1998. Provisions on the seizure of property and cash are set forth in Resolution No. 13 of the Plenum of the Supreme *Arbitrazh* Court of the Russian Federation dated 31 October 1996 (para. 6), and in Letter No. 6 of the Supreme *Arbitrazh* Court of the Russian Federation dated 25 July 1996. Provisions on application of judicial interim relief measures with respect to cases involving copyright and associated rights are set forth in the Law of the Russian Federation on Copyright and Associated Rights dated 9 July 1993 (Art. 50).

104. Sequestration of property or cash of the defendant is the most frequently used judicial interim relief measure. The relevant claim, however, may not be satisfied by transferring the sequestered property to the claimant. The court may satisfy the claim levying execution on such property in accordance with special procedures.

105. Until recently, for example, the legality of such judicial interim relief measures as prohibiting a company from convening a meeting of its shareholders had been widely discussed. The Supreme *Arbitrazh* Court ruled that such measures contradict the Constitution of the Russian Federation. See Decision of the Plenum of the Supreme Court of the Russian Federation No. 12, dated 10 October 2001.

106. Art. 133 CCP.

107. In *arbitrazh* proceedings, a fine may be in the amount up to US$ 3205 (Art. 119 CAP); in civil proceedings – up to US$ 320 (Art. 134 CCP).

108. Art. 98 CAP; Art. 140 CCP.

j.   United States of America

The federal system of government in the United States results in multiple jurisdictions with similar but separate standards for the granting of provisional relief. This section will address the jurisdiction most likely to impact international litigants, the federal courts of the United States. Provisional relief in the federal system is largely a matter of case law, although some procedural aspects are controlled by Federal Rule of Civil Procedure 65. The relief available falls into two categories: preliminary injunctions, which may be had only through an inter partes hearing;[109] and temporary restraining orders, which may be obtained ex parte.[110]

Federal district courts, the courts of first instance in the federal system, have broad discretion to fashion preliminary injunctions.[111] However, these courts view such measures as "drastic"[112] that require a "clear showing"[113] of:

> "(a) irreparable harm and (b) either (1) likelihood of success on the merits or (2) sufficiently serious questions going to the merits to make them a fair ground for litigation and a balance of hardships tipping decidedly toward the party requesting the preliminary relief".[114]

This "test", articulated by the Court of Appeals for the Second Circuit (the federal appellate court for New York, Connecticut, and Vermont) contains two standards, both of which may justify a preliminary injunction. However, they are linked by the central requirement of irreparable harm. As the Second Circuit has noted, an applicant "may succeed if he shows irreparable harm plus a likelihood of success on the merits. [Or he] may succeed if he shows irreparable harm, plus sufficiently serious questions going to the merits to make them a fair ground for litigation and a balance of hardships tipping decidedly [in his favor]."[115] Thus, the touchstone for the granting of a preliminary injunction is the urgent need to avert "irreparable harm".[116]

---

109. Fed. R. Civ. P. 65(a)(1).

110. Fed. R. Civ. P. 65(b).

111. *Deckert v. Independence Shares Corp.*, 311 U.S. 282, 290 (1940).

112. Charles Alan WRIGHT, Arthur R. MILLER and Mary Kay KANE, 11A Fed. Prac. & Proc. Civ.2d 2948.7 (1995 and 2002 Supp.) (hereinafter WRIGHT and MILLER 2d).

113. *Berrigan v. Norton*, 451 F.2d 790, 793 (2d Cir. 1971). A higher standard of proof is required if the injunction would in effect provide "substantially all the relief sought" – the movant must then make a "substantial" showing of the likelihood of success on the merits. *Tom Doherty Assocs., Inc. v. Saban Entertainment, Inc.*, 60 F.3d 27, 33-34 (2d Cir. 1995); see also *Reynolds v. Giuliani*, 35 F.Supp.2d 331, 338 (S.D.N.Y. 1999).

114. *Sperry Intern. Trade, Inc. v. Government of Israel*, 670 F.2d 8, 11 (2d Cir. 1982) (citing *Jackson Dairy, Inc. v. H.P. Hood & Sons, Inc.*, 596 F.2d 70, 72 (2d Cir. 1979) (per curiam)).

115. *Ibid.*

116. "Irreparable harm is 'the single most important prerequisite for the issuance of a preliminary injunction'." *Reynolds, op. cit.*, fn. 113, at 339 (quoting *Bell & Howell: Mamiya Co. v. Masel Supply Co.*, 719 F.2d 42, 45 (2d Cir. 1983) (internal quotes omitted)). Moreover, "the moving party must first demonstrate that such injury is likely before the other requirements for the issuance of an injunction will be considered". *Reuters Ltd. v. United Press Int'l, Inc.*, 903 F.2d 904, 907 (2d

One authoritative treatise has observed that "irreparable harm" means more than mere speculative harm; rather "[o]nly when the threatened harm would impair the court's ability to grant an effective remedy is there really a need for preliminary relief".[117] Consequently,

> "if a trial on the merits can be conducted before the injury would occur there is no need for interlocutory relief. In a similar vein, a preliminary injunction usually will be denied if it appears that the applicant has an adequate alternate remedy in the form of money damages or other relief".[118]

The "irreparable harm" may be presently occurring and ongoing,[119] but it is not necessary for purposes of a preliminary injunction that it has happened, or is certain to happen.[120] Nonetheless, there must be a "presently existing actual threat" that it will occur.[121]

The United States Court of Appeals for the Second Circuit has also articulated a series of factors that courts should examine when determining whether to grant a preliminary injunction:

> "In determining whether preliminary injunctive relief should be granted, the primary factors to be considered are the possibility of ultimate success on the part of the party seeking the relief and danger of irreparable injury if such relief is withheld.... Other important considerations include the direction of the balance of hardship between the parties ... and whether the relief requested will adversely affect the public interest."[122]

Closely related to the preliminary injunction is the temporary restraining order or TRO. A TRO may be obtained ex parte, but is much more circumscribed than the preliminary injunction. TROs are granted only when "irreparable injury will occur before the hearing for a preliminary injunction ... can be held".[123] Rule 65 of the Federal Rules of Civil Procedure governs their use and requires that

> "(1) it clearly appear[s] from specific facts shown by affidavit or by the verified complaint that immediate and irreparable injury, loss, or damage will result to the applicant before the adverse party or that party's attorney can be heard in

---

Cir. 1990).

117. WRIGHT and MILLER 2d, *op. cit.*, fn. 112, Sect. 2948.1.

118. *Ibid.*

119. *New York Pathological & X-Ray Labs., Inc. v. INS*, 523 F.2d 79, 81 (2d Cir. 1975) ("Irreparable harm can be found where there is a continuing wrong which cannot be adequately redressed by final relief on the merits.").

120. WRIGHT and MILLER 2d, *op. cit.*, fn. 112, Sect. 2948.1.

121. *Ibid.*

122. *New York Pathological*, *op. cit.*, fn. 119, p. 81.

123. WRIGHT and MILLER 2d, *op. cit.*, fn. 112, Sect. 2951.

opposition, and (2) the applicant's attorney certif[y] to the court in writing the efforts, if any, which have been made to give the notice and the reasons supporting the claim that notice should not be required".

The central purpose of the TRO is to preserve the status quo or prevent ongoing harm until a hearing for a preliminary injunction may be held. In other words, it is an "emergency procedure" and not a substitute for a preliminary injunction.[124] Critical to the TRO is not only the need to proceed expeditiously, but also to do so without notifying the adverse party, such as in cases involving the threat of destruction, sale or removal of disputed property. In such situations, "[i]mmediate action is vital", for to give the other party notice of a pending injunction "could result in an inability to provide any relief at all".[125] As the reason for the granting of a TRO is, at bottom, the same as for a preliminary injunction (i.e., the need to avert irreparable harm), courts have extended the analysis used in preliminary injunction cases to applications for TROs.[126]

TROs are expressly limited in duration by Rule 65 to ten days, with the possibility to extend for an additional ten days for "good cause shown".[127]

The Federal Rules also mandate that the movant for either a TRO or a preliminary injunction post as security an amount the court deems necessary to indemnify the adverse party should the order later be found improper. Without such security, an order may not be obtained.[128]

2.   Provisional Measures in Ad Hoc International Commercial Arbitration

The issuance of provisional measures is virtually always anticipated in the rules governing the constitution and operation of ad hoc international tribunals.[129] The range of measures that these tribunals may grant and the circumstances under which they will do so are rarely specified in the rules themselves. Some arbitral tribunals have gradually

---

124. *Ibid.* (quoting "Developments in the Law – Injunctions", 78 Harv. L. Rev. (1965) p. 994 at p. 1060) ("The *ex parte* temporary restraining order is indispensable to the commencement of an action when it is the sole method of preserving a state of affairs in which the court can provide effective final relief."); *see also Pan Am. World Airways, Inc. v. Flight Engineers' Int'l Ass'n*, 306 F.2d 840, 842 (2d Cir. 1962) ("The purpose of a temporary restraining order is to preserve an existing situation in *status quo* until the court has an opportunity to pass upon the merits of the demand for a preliminary injunction.").

125. "Developments in the Law – Injunctions", *op. cit.*, fn. 124, p. 1060; see also Fed. R. Civ. P. 65(b) (requiring a showing that "immediate and irreparable injury, loss, or damage will result to the applicant before the adverse party or that party's attorney can be heard in opposition").

126. See, e.g., *Merrill Lynch, Pierce, Fenner & Smith, Inc. v. Bishop*, 839 F.Supp. 68, 70 (D. Me. 1993); *Nation Magazine v. United States Dep't of State*, 805 F.Supp. 68, 72 (D.D.C. 1992).

127. Fed. R. Civ. P. 65(c).

128. *Ibid.* ("No restraining order or preliminary injunction shall issue except upon the giving of security by the applicant, in such sum as the court deems proper, for the payment of such costs and damages as may be incurred or suffered by any party who is found to have been wrongfully enjoined or restrained.")

129. The dispute settlement panels constituted to resolve disputes in the World Trade Organization stand out as an exception to this general rule.

elaborated on these rules in their practice, and though arbitral awards are only randomly reported, some information about arbitral practice is available. These features are surveyed below with respect to the tribunals constituted under the UNCITRAL Arbitration Rules, international commercial arbitration institutions, the World Intellectual Property Organization, the International Centre for Settlement of Investment Disputes and the Permanent Court of Arbitration.

a.   The UNCITRAL Arbitration Rules
UNCITRAL adopted a set of Arbitration Rules in 1976 that could be included in international commercial contracts to provide a dispute settlement framework. These Rules have also been influential in the formulation of arbitration procedures in different arbitral institutions and have been adapted for use in international tribunals, such as the Permanent Court of Arbitration and the Iran-US Claims Tribunal. The latter tribunal has been instrumental in the interpretation and application of the Rules, including the provision granting the tribunal authority to take interim measures.

Art. 26 of the UNCITRAL Arbitration Rules specifically empowers a tribunal operating under its Rules to "take any interim measures it deems necessary in respect of the subject-matter of the dispute".[130] Art. 26 reads in its entirety:

> 1. At the request of either party, the arbitral tribunal may take any interim measures it deems necessary in respect of the subject-matter of the dispute, including measures for the conservation of the goods forming the subject-matter in dispute, such as ordering their deposit with a third person or the sale of perishable goods.
> 2. Such interim measures may be established in the form of an interim award. The arbitral tribunal shall be entitled to require security for the costs of such measures.
> 3. A request for interim measures addressed by any party to a judicial authority shall not be deemed incompatible with the agreement to arbitrate, or as a waiver of that agreement."

The *travaux préparatoires* indicate that the list of measures is exemplary in nature rather than exclusive, and other instances may well arise where interim measures could be appropriate.[131] This flexibility has, however, produced some doubt as to the precise scope of the measures that a tribunal may take. When faced with such uncertainty, the Iran-US Claims Tribunal opted to rely on its inherent powers under international law

---

130. Art. 26(1) UNCITRAL Arbitration Rules (1976).

131. Stewart Abercrombie BAKER and Mark David DAVIS, *The UNICTRAL Arbitration Rules in Practice: The Experience of the Iran-United States Claims Tribunal* (1992) p. 133. See also Jacomijn J. van HOF, *Commentary on the UNCITRAL Arbitration Rules: The Application by the Iran-U.S. Claims Tribunal* (1991) p. 175.

in addition to Art. 26.[132]

In considering requests for interim measures, the Iran-US Claims Tribunal has referred to several requirements for the issuance of measures under Art. 26. First, the Tribunal has considered whether it has prima facie jurisdiction to support an order for interim measures.[133] This requirement is in line with the jurisprudence of the International Court of Justice and, in accord with that jurisprudence, does not prejudge a final determination on jurisdiction. Second, interim measures will be ordered when "necessary", which encapsulates "the notions that the party requesting the measure is facing harm to rights it is pursuing in the arbitration and that the harm is so imminent that it cannot await the tribunal's final decision on the merits".[134] Third, the Tribunal may also consider the impact of interim measures of protection on the final award. Such measures will be withheld in the event that they would render the claim moot or otherwise prejudge the claim.[135]

Art. 26(2) enables interim measures to be established in the form of an interim award. This terminology is designed to enhance the possibility of enforcement before national courts. If a party elects to proceed directly to a national court in seeking interim measures, such a request is not incompatible with the agreement to arbitrate, nor does it constitute a waiver of that agreement.[136] The Iran-US Claims Tribunal has rarely referred to this last provision in its practice.[137] At most, the Tribunal has allowed national courts' orders of attachments of Iranian assets to stand pending its final decision.[138]

The arbitral tribunal taking interim measures under Art. 26 is further entitled to require security for the costs of such measures.[139] In the application of this provision, the Iran-US Claims Tribunal has only relied on this power to require the requesting party to defray the costs, if any, imposed by the interim protection on the other side.[140]

b.   *The Rules of the International Chamber of Commerce, the London Court of International Arbitration and the American Arbitration Association*

Arbitral tribunals constituted to decide commercial disputes may be authorized to issue orders or awards for interim measures by express agreement between the parties

---

132. "The Tribunal has an inherent right to issue such orders as may be necessary to conserve the respective rights of the Parties and to ensure this Tribunal's jurisdiction and authority are made fully effective." *E-Systems, Inc. v. Iran*, 2 Iran-U.S. C.R.T., p. 51 at p. 57 (1983) (Award No. ITM 13-388-FT).

133. See, e.g., *Ford Aerospace v. Air Force of Iran*, 6 Iran-U.S. C.R.T., p. 104, at pp. 108-109 (1984) (Award No. ITM 39-159-3); *Bendone-DeRossi International v. Iran*, 6 Iran-U.S. C.R.T., p. 130 at pp. 131-132 (1984) (Award No. ITM 40-375-1).

134. BAKER and DAVIS, *op. cit.*, fn. 131, p. 139. See also van HOF, *op. cit.*, fn. 131, p. 189.

135. See, e.g., *United Technologies International, Inc. v. Iran* (Dec. No. 53-114-3), 13 Iran-U.S. C.R.T. p. 254 (1986) (Dec. No. 53-114-3). See also van HOF, *op. cit.*, fn. 131, p. 191.

136. Art. 26(3) UNCITRAL Rules.

137. BAKER and DAVIS, *op. cit.*, fn. 131, p. 141.

138. *Ibid.*

139. Art. 26(2) UNCITRAL Rules.

140. BAKER and DAVIS, *op. cit.*, fn. 131, p. 143.

themselves, through the institutional rules under the auspices of which the tribunal is appointed, or through the inherent power of the tribunal in arbitral proceedings. The parties can also expressly exclude the grant of interim measures by the arbitration tribunal in their agreement and thus limit the authority of the tribunal in this regard.[141] The most common scenario is that the contract between the parties will stipulate what institutional rules will apply in the event of an arbitration. These major administering institutions, such as the International Chamber of Commerce (ICC), the London Court of International Arbitration (LCIA), and the American Arbitration Association (AAA), all grant power to the arbitral tribunals to award interim measures in certain situations.[142] Even without a specific grant of authority, there is strong support for the

---

141. For example, Art. 17 of the UNCITRAL Model Law, reads in relevant part:

"Unless otherwise agreed by the parties, the arbitral tribunal may, at the request of a party, order any party to take such interim measure of protection as the arbitral tribunal may consider necessary."

BINDER comments that the phrase "unless otherwise agreed by the parties" indicates that the provision is of a non-mandatory nature and the tribunal's power to issue an order for interim measures only applies if the parties have not agreed otherwise. Peter BINDER, *op. cit.*, fn. 4, p. 115.

142. Art. 23(1) of the ICC Rules of Arbitration (effective 1 January 1998) (hereinafter ICC Rules) reads:

"Unless the parties have otherwise agreed, as soon as the file has been transmitted to it, the Arbitral Tribunal may, at the request of a party, order any interim or conservatory measure it deems appropriate. The Arbitral Tribunal may make the granting of any such measure subject to appropriate security being furnished by the requesting party. Any such measure shall take the form of an order, giving reasons, or of an Award, as the Arbitral Tribunal considers appropriate."

The AAA International Arbitration Rules (effective 1 November 2001) (hereinafter AAA Rules) provides in Art. 21:

"1. At the request of any party, the tribunal may take whatever interim measures it deems necessary, including injunctive relief and measures for the protection or conservation of property.
2. Such interim measures may take the form of an interim award, and the tribunal may require security for the costs of such measures.
3. A request for interim measures addressed by a party to a judicial authority shall not be deemed incompatible with the agreement to arbitrate or a waiver of the right to arbitrate.
4. The tribunal may in its discretion apportion costs associated with applications for interim relief in any interim award or in the final award."

Art. 25(1) of the LCIA Rules states:

"The Arbitral Tribunal shall have the power, unless otherwise agreed by the parties in writing, on the application of any party:
(a) to order any respondent party to a claim or counterclaim to provide security for all or part of the amount in dispute, by way of deposit or bank guarantee or in any other manner and upon such terms as the Arbitral Tribunal considers appropriate. Such terms may include the provision by the claiming or counterclaiming party of a cross-indemnity, itself secured in such manner as

proposition that arbitrators have inherent authority reasonably implied from the agreement to arbitrate to make interim orders.[143]

The parties to an arbitration agreement may wish to seek a range of provisional measures in order to protect their interests in the pending dispute. The types of orders envisaged in the different sets of rules include injunctive relief;[144] security for the amount of money in dispute;[145] measures for the protection or conservation of property;[146] and interim relief that is available as relief under the final award.[147] Art. 23 of the ICC Rules simply provides that the tribunal may "order any interim or conservatory measure it deems appropriate".[148] The standards typically applied for an order of provisional measures include "urgency, imminent harm, prevention of aggravation, maintenance of status quo or likelihood of success on the merits".[149]

---

the Arbitral Tribunal considers appropriate, for any costs or losses incurred by such respondent in providing security. The amount of any costs and losses payable under such cross-indemnity may be determined by the Arbitral Tribunal in one or more awards;

(b) to order the preservation, storage, sale or other disposal of any property or thing under the control of any party and relating to the subject matter of the arbitration; and

(c) to order on a provisional basis, subject to final determination in an award, any relief which the Arbitral Tribunal would have power to grant in an award, including a provisional order for the payment of money or the disposition of property as between any parties."

143. For example, the court in *Charles Construction Company v. Derderian*, 586 N.E.2d 992, 995 (Mass. 1992) stated:

"It is reasonable to assume that parties, in agreeing to arbitration, implicitly intended that the arbitration not be fruitless and that interim orders to preserve the status quo or to make meaningful relief possible would be proper. In such a circumstance, the arbitrators' authority to act would reasonably be implied from the agreement to arbitrate itself."

See also Gary B. BORN, *International Commercial Arbitration: Commentary and Materials*, 2nd ed. (2001) pp. 933-934; W. Michael REISMAN, et al., *International Commercial Arbitration: Cases, Materials and Notes on the Resolution of International Business Disputes* (1997) p. 755; Donald Francis DONOVAN, "Powers of the Arbitrators to Issue Procedural Orders, Including Interim Measures of Protection", 10 ICC Int'l Ct. Arb. Bull. (Spring 1999) p. 57 at pp. 64-68. REISMAN, et al. posit:

"Insofar as the parties are concerned, however, it is logical that the arbitrator should have inherent jurisdiction to take all provisional measures appropriate to the dispute that he has been empowered ultimately to decide. Where the parties have agreed that the arbitrator may make a final and binding award on the merits of the dispute, they should accept his power to make interlocutory procedural orders required for the efficacy of the process and of the award."

Ibid.

144. Art. 21(1) AAA Rules.
145. Art. 25(1)(a) LCIA Rules.
146. Art. 21(1) AAA Rules; Art. 25(1)(b) LCIA Rules.
147. Art. 25(1)(c) LCIA Rules.
148. See Art. 23(1) ICC Rules.
149. MARCHAC, *op. cit.*, fn. 3, p. 129.

c.   The World Intellectual Property Organization

The World Intellectual Property Organization (WIPO) offers a mechanism through its Arbitration and Mediation Center for the resolution of international commercial disputes concerning technology, entertainment and other intellectual property issues between private parties. The WIPO Arbitration Rules set out the institutional framework and procedure for the resolution of intellectual property disputes through arbitration. For arbitral proceedings, as well as expedited arbitral proceedings, any party may seek interim measures of protection, such as "injunctions and measures for the conservation of goods which form part of the subject matter in dispute".[150] The scope of the measures are not limited to a protective nature but may extend to measures designed to create or modify a particular state of affairs.[151]

Under Art. 46, the arbitral tribunal may make the granting of the interim measures subject to an appropriate security from the requesting party. Unlike the AAA Rules and the UNCITRAL Rules, there is no limitation on the security covering only the costs of such measures, but the amount may extend to the potential damage that may result from a particular measure.[152] Such an order is in addition to an order that will be granted in exceptional circumstances to provide security to cover the claim or counterclaim.[153]

The WIPO Arbitration Rules further provide that measures and orders of the arbitral tribunal may take the form of an interim award. This stipulation is intended to facilitate the enforcement of provisional measures in national court.[154] Art. 46 of the Rules provides that a request for interim relief from a national court is not incompatible with the arbitration agreement, nor deemed to be a waiver of that agreement.

d.   The International Centre for Settlement of Investment Disputes

The International Centre for Settlement of Investment Disputes (ICSID) was established under the Convention on the Settlement of Investment Disputes between States and Nationals of Other States (frequently called the "ICSID Convention" or the "Washington Convention"). ICSID provides facilities for the conciliation and arbitration of disputes between member states and investors who qualify as nationals of other member states. The submission of a dispute to ICSID conciliation and arbitration is voluntary, but once the parties have consented to arbitration under the ICSID Convention, neither can unilaterally withdraw its consent. Furthermore, all states parties of ICSID, whether or not parties to the dispute, are required by the ICSID Convention to recognize and

---

150. Art. 46(a) WIPO Arbitration Rules.
151. Marc BLESSING, "The Conduct of Arbitral Proceedings Under the Rules of Arbitration Institutions; The WIPO Arbitration Rules in a Comparative Perspective: [Articles 37 to 47 of the WIPO Rules in a Comparative Perspective]" in *Conference on Rules for Institutional Arbitration and Mediation*, 20 January 1995, Geneva, Switzerland, para. 46.8.
152. By comparison, Art. 25(2) of the LCIA Rules grants the tribunal a general authority to ask for security for legal and other costs of any party.
153. Art. 46(b) WIPO Arbitration Rules.
154. Problems nonetheless remain because the New York Convention, which provides for the recognition and enforcement of arbitral awards, does not define arbitral awards to include interim awards, and many national laws provide for enforceability of final or partial awards, not interim awards. BLESSING, *op. cit.*, fn. 151, para. 46.11.

enforce ICSID arbitral awards.[155]

Art. 47 of the ICSID Convention permits the tribunal, if it considers that the circumstances so require, to recommend any provisional measures necessary to preserve the respective rights of either party. The authority for granting provisional measures is subject to exclusion or variation by the parties. The procedural framework for the operation of this article is then set out in Rule 39 of the ICSID Rules of Procedure for Arbitration Proceedings. In particular, a party may request provisional measures for the preservation of its rights at any time during the proceeding, or the tribunal may so recommend at its own initiative. The request must specify "the rights to be preserved, the measures the recommendation of which is requested, and the circumstances that require such measures".[156] The circumstances giving rise to a need for provisional measures must normally indicate necessity and urgency.[157] Neither Art. 47 nor Rule 39 specifies what measures may be granted by the tribunal, and the nature of the measures recommended therefore depends on the circumstances of the case and the rights to be protected.

Although the measures are only provisional in nature and are measures required as a matter of urgency, the tribunal may only recommend such measures after giving each party an opportunity to present its observations.[158] Denying the possibility of ex parte motions was intended to avoid surprises or unintentionally unfair dispositions.[159] The obvious drawback to this situation is that the parties may only seek provisional measures once the tribunal is constituted. This delay could well prove detrimental to the very interests that the requesting party is seeking to protect. Although a party may wish to seek provisional measures from a national court, Rule 39(5) only permits the parties to do so if they have stipulated in the agreement recording their consent that resort to such judicial authority is allowed.

Art. 47 and Rule 39 both refer to measures to be "recommended". Schreuer has noted that the *travaux préparatoires* of the ICSID Convention clearly indicate that a deliberate decision was made not to grant the tribunal the power to order binding provisional measures.[160] Compliance would nonetheless be expected in accordance with the general obligations imposed on parties not to frustrate the object of the proceedings or to aggravate or extend the dispute. Furthermore, the possibility would remain that the tribunal would take a party's compliance into account in its final award, which would be binding on the parties.[161] Orrego Vicuña has relied on these features, as well

---

155. See www.worldbank.org/icsid/about/about.htm (last visited 10 October 2002) (providing general information about ICSID's purpose and functions).

156. Rules 39(1) ICSID Rules of Procedure for Arbitration Proceedings (hereinafter ICSID Rules).

157. Christoph H. SCHREUER, *The ICSID Convention: A Commentary – A Commentary on the Convention on the Settlement of Investment Disputes between States and Nationals of Other States* (2001) p. 751.

158. Rule 39(4) ICSID Rules.

159. SCHREUER, *op. cit.*, fn. 157, p. 750.

160. *Ibid.*, p. 758.

161. During negotiations, the drafters considered the inclusion of a provision to this effect, but the proposal was ultimately rejected. Nonetheless, the Chairman, in an unopposed statement, said that the tribunal would normally take compliance into account in its final award even if this factor was not specifically addressed. See *ibid.*, p. 761 (citing other commentators and Note B. to ICSID

as a distinction between the binding effect of the awards and their actual enforcement, to conclude that "the legal effects of measures recommended are really not different from those of measures prescribed".[162] Indeed, an ICSID tribunal, chaired by Professor Orrego Vicuña, decided in 1999 that orders for provisional measures under Rule 39 were binding:

> "The Tribunal does not believe that the parties to the Convention meant to create a substantial difference in the effect of these two words [namely, 'recommend' and 'order']. The Tribunal's authority to rule on provisional measures is no less binding than that of a final award. Accordingly, for the purposes of this Order, the Tribunal deems the word 'recommend' to be of equivalent value as the word 'order'."[163]

Orrego Vicuña considers that the question of whether the measures are recommended or ordered does not have to bear on the question of enforcement.[164] Yet if decisions on provisional measures were not binding in nature, then a national court may be less inclined to enforce that measure. This problem of the binding effect of provisional measures recommendations is exacerbated by the fact that several of the cases addressing requests for provisional measures have been directed against action taken in national courts.[165]

e.   *The Permanent Court of Arbitration*

The Permanent Court of Arbitration (PCA) has adapted the UNCITRAL Arbitration Rules to cover a range of disputes depending on the identity of the parties – namely, disputes between states, disputes between two parties of which only one is a state, disputes involving states and an international organization, and disputes between international organizations and private parties.[166] The only alteration to the UNCITRAL Arbitration Rules relating to provisional measures is that the list of measures available to tribunals to preserve the respective rights of either party or in respect of the subject

---

Rule 39 of 1968).

162. Francisco ORREGO VICUÑA, "The Binding Nature of Procedural Orders in International Arbitration", 10 ICC Int'l Ct. Arb. Bull. (Spring 1999) p. 45.

163. *Emilio Agustín Maffezini v. Kingdom of Spain,* ICSID Case No. ARB/97/7, p. 9.

164. ORREGO VICUÑA, *op. cit.,* fn. 162.

165. See SCHREUER, *op. cit.,* fn. 157, pp. 753-757 (describing the measures sought in several, typically unreported, cases).

166. See "Permanent Court of Arbitration Optional Rules for Arbitrating Disputes Between Two States" (effective 20 October 1992); "Permanent Court of Arbitration Optional Rules for Arbitrating Disputes between Two Parties of Which Only One Is a State" (effective 6 July 1993); "Permanent Court of Arbitration Optional Rules for Arbitration Involving International Organizations and States" (effective 1 July 1996); "Permanent Court of Arbitration Optional Rules for Arbitration between International Organizations and Private Parties" (effective 1 July 1996). All of the Permanent Court's Rules are available at www.pca-cpa.org/BD/ (last visited 24 September 2002).

matter of the dispute,[167] is only included in the PCA Rules dealing with disputes between two parties of which only one is a state. Otherwise, no indication of the measures available to a tribunal is made.

The PCA has also adopted rules for arbitrating disputes relating to natural resources and the environment.[168] Unlike the other sets of PCA rules, these rules specifically provide that a tribunal operating under these rules may not issue interim measures at the request of any party without obtaining the views of all the parties.[169] Once these views are obtained, then the tribunal may "take any interim measures including provisional orders with respect to the subject matter of the dispute it deems necessary to preserve the rights of any party or to prevent serious harm to the environment falling within the subject matter of the dispute".[170]

3. Provisional Measures in Permanent International Courts and Tribunals

Issues relating to the scope of provisional measures, the standards to be met for their issuance, and their binding quality have all been raised before permanent international courts and tribunals as well. As states are most commonly parties before these courts and tribunals, and greater sensitivity thus emerges in respect of the consensual nature of the dispute settlement process, particular emphasis is placed on determinations of prima facie jurisdiction as a prerequisite to the granting of interim measures. This question may be linked to the standards the requesting party must meet for the court or tribunal to issue provisional measures. The traditional consideration accorded to state sovereignty has also led to doubts over whether the interim measures are legally binding or not. The discussion below considers these issues with respect to the regional human rights courts and commissions, the International Tribunal on the Law of the Sea (and other tribunals constituted under the United Nations Convention on the Law of the Sea), and, finally, the International Court of Justice.

a. Human rights courts and commissions

The availability of provisional measures in international proceedings as a means to protect and uphold human rights varies greatly in regional human rights courts and commissions. On a global level, provisional measures granted by the International Court of Justice have upheld individual human rights only in some instances, and usually as an indirect result of the Court's order rather than as its primary purpose. The constitutive instruments and practice of the regional human rights tribunals only provide for the use of provisional measures in limited circumstances. While the American Convention on Human Rights specifically empowers the Inter-American Court of Human Rights to adopt provisional measures, no such grant of authority was expressly included in the Council of Europe's European Convention on Human Rights and its subsequent

---

167. Art. 26 UNCITRAL Rules. See also text accompanying fn. 130.

168. See "Permanent Court of Arbitration Optional Rules for Arbitration of Disputes Relating to Natural Resources and/or the Environment" (effective 19 June 2001), *op. cit.*, fn. 166.

169. *Ibid.*, Art. 26(1).

170. *Ibid.*

Protocols. Instead, the European Commission of Human Rights and European Court of Human Rights have adopted rules of procedure to formalize a cooperative practice of applying provisional measures pending the resolution of a matter. The African Commission on Human and Peoples' Rights may recommend provisional measures prior to its final report on the communications received from states parties.

i. Inter-American Court of Human Rights

The Inter-American Court of Human Rights is the only regional human rights tribunal specifically empowered in its constitutive instrument to adopt provisional measures. In accordance with Art. 63(2) of the American Convention on Human Rights, the Court may order provisional measures either in matters already under its consideration "as it deems pertinent" or at the request of the Inter-American Commission on Human Rights for cases not yet submitted to the Court. If the Court is not sitting at the time a request for provisional measures is made, the President must convoke the Court immediately but may also act independently and "call upon the government concerned to adopt such urgent measures as may be necessary to ensure the effectiveness of any provisional measures subsequently ordered by the Court at its next session".[171] For cases already before the Court, provisional measures may be ordered, at the request of a party or proprio motu, at any stage of the proceeding.[172]

Although not expressly required by Art. 63, the Court's power to grant provisional measures is subject to its initial prima facie finding of jurisdiction.[173] Such a determination must be made both when the case is already submitted to the Court and when a request is made by the Inter-American Commission on Human Rights. In the latter situation, "the Court should have to ascertain merely whether the State against which they are sought has accepted the Court's jurisdiction".[174]

Art. 63(2) of the Convention empowers the Court to adopt provisional measures in "cases of extreme gravity and urgency, and when necessary to avoid irreparable damage to persons".[175] Upon examination of the scope of this provision, Buergenthal concludes:

> "The wording and the legislative history of the provision make clear that its sole purpose is to protect human beings against the loss of life or extreme physical or

---

171. Rules of Procedure of the Inter-American Court of Human Rights (effective 1997) Art. 25(4) at www1.umn.edu/humanrts/iachr/rule1-97.htm (last visited 14 October 2002).

172. Art. 25(1) Rules of Procedure of the Inter-American Court of Human Rights.

173. See Thomas BUERGENTHAL, "Interim Measures in the Inter-American Court of Human Rights" in Rudolf BERNHARDT, ed., *Interim Measures Indicated by International Courts* (1994) p. 69 at p. 71.

174. See *ibid.*, p. 75.

175. Art. 63(2) of the American Convention on Human Rights reads in full:

"In cases of extreme gravity and urgency, and when necessary to avoid irreparable damage to persons, the Court shall adopt such provisional measures as it deems pertinent in matters it has under consideration. With respect to a case not yet submitted to the Court, it may act at the request of the [Inter-American] Commission [on Human Rights]."

mental abuse when there is a very strong likelihood that they are in imminent danger and there exists a corresponding urgency for protective action."[176]

The Court has thus adopted provisional measures in cases involving disappearances, death penalty sentencing, imprisonment involving cruel and unusual punishment, and assassinations threatening the rights to life and personal integrity, as well as clear and imminent damage to freedom of expression.

The Convention stipulates, in the English text, that "a judgment of the Court shall be final and not subject to appeal",[177] and further requires states parties to comply with the "judgment of the Court".[178] This language can be distinguished from the equally authoritative Spanish, Portuguese, and French texts, which refer to "judgments" of the Court being final and not subject to appeal whereas states parties must comply with "decisions" of the Court.[179] The Spanish, Portuguese, and French texts support the conclusion that provisional measures orders are legally binding on the states to which they are directed.[180] Reference to a "decision" is more inclusive and embraces all decisions and orders of the Court, in addition to its "judgments", and could thus encompass orders for provisional measures.[181] The different terminology used in the English text is not explained through an examination of the *travaux préparatoires* of the Convention.[182]

Nonetheless, a teleological approach supports an argument that the provisional measures orders of the Court are binding. These measures are adopted under limited circumstances and are not simply intended to maintain the status quo, but are applied in situations to avoid "irreparable damage to persons". "Given this function and the fact that the Convention is a human rights treaty, it is difficult to support the proposition that Article 63(2) decisions should not be deemed to be legally binding."[183] This reasoning would comport with that of the International Court of Justice in the *LaGrand* case.[184]

ii.   European Court of Human Rights

Unlike the American Convention on Human Rights, the European Convention does not contain a provision allowing for the grant of provisional measures. Instead, a practice began, based on cooperation rather than legal obligation, whereby the Commission

---

176. See BUERGENTHAL, *op. cit.*, fn. 173, p. 77.

177. Art. 67 American Convention on Human Rights.

178. Art. 68(1) American Convention on Human Rights.

179. See BUERGENTHAL, *op. cit.*, fn. 173, p. 85.

180. *Ibid.*

181. *Ibid.*

182. *Ibid.,* pp. 85-86.

183. *Ibid.*, pp. 86-87. By contrast, the orders of the President do not have the same legal status because the Convention does not delegate the power of the Court to the President. See *ibid.*, pp. 87-88.

184. *LaGrand Case (F.R.G. v. U.S.)*, 2001 I.C.J. Rep. 104 (June 27); see below fns. 215-221 and accompanying text.

would request states to take no steps pending the examination of a particular application by the Commission.[185] This practice eventually led to the adoption of rules by both the Commission and the Court. Rule 36 of the Commission's Rules of Procedures provides:

> "The Commission, or when it is not in session, the President may indicate to the parties any interim measure the adoption of which seems desirable in the interest of the parties or the proper conduct of the proceedings before it."

The Court may similarly recommend interim measures to any party, including the applicant, "which it considers should be adopted".[186] No specific conditions of "irreparable damage" or "extreme urgency" must be met prior to the recommendation of measures by either the Commission or the Court. These factors nonetheless underpin the situations where measures have been recommended. Interim measures have predominantly been applied in cases involving the possibility of extradition or expulsion, and less frequently in instances to secure evidence or to protect health conditions.[187]

Questions have arisen as to whether the interim measures adopted are recommendations only and thus not legally binding on states. The obligation of states to adopt interim measures of protection was addressed by the Commission and the Court in the *Cruz Varas* case, with the former deciding a violation of the Convention had occurred and a slim majority of the latter determining that there had been no violation.[188] The Commission formulated the matter for decision as a question of whether Sweden, the respondent state, had violated Art. 25 of the European Convention, which requires states not to hinder the effective exercise of the right of individual petition. By deporting Mr. Cruz Varas, Sweden effectively rendered his right of petition ineffective and thus violated the Convention in failing to act in accordance with the Commission's order of interim measures of protection. The Commission's decision did not therefore explicitly state that recommendations for interim measures were legally binding on states but recast the question in terms of the provisions of the European Convention. The Court instead took the view that as no specific provision of the European Convention empowered the Commission to order interim measures, the language protecting the right of individual petition was being strained by reading into it an obligation to comply with interim measures orders. The tradition of compliance with the orders of interim measures was a matter of good-faith cooperation where reasonable and practicable rather than of legal obligation.

iii. African Commission on Human and Peoples' Rights
The African Commission on Human and Peoples' Rights, which was established under the African Charter on Human and Peoples' Rights, is authorized under its Rules of

---

185. Rudolf BERNHARDT, "Interim Measures of Protection under the European Convention of Human Rights" in *op. cit.*, fn. 173, p. 95 at pp. 97-98.
186. European Court of Human Rights, Rules of Court, (in effect October 2002) Rule 39, available at www.echr.coe.int/Eng/EDocs/RulesofCourt2002.htm (last visited 14 October 2002).
187. BERNHARDT, *op. cit.*, fn. 185, p. 99.
188. See *ibid.* at pp. 104-113 (discussing the two decisions, along with the relevant reasoning).

Procedure to "inform the State Party concerned of its views on the appropriateness of taking provisional measures".[189] Provisional measures may be appropriate to avoid irreparable damage to the alleged victim of the human rights violation.[190] A state party may be informed of the appropriateness of provisional measures before the African Commission makes its final views known to the Assembly of Heads of State and Government.

In addition to provisional measures for the protection of the victim, Rule 111 provides that the Commission "may indicate to the parties any interim measure, the adoption of which seems desirable in the interest of the parties or the proper conduct of the proceedings before it".[191] A distinction thus seems to be drawn between "provisional measures", which are designed to protect the victim, and "interim measures", which are directed to states parties and the proceedings.

The procedures undertaken by the Commission in response to communications from states parties are not binding on those states parties. The Commission submits a report stating the facts and its findings in respect of the communications.[192] It further has the option of including recommendations with the submitted report.[193] As the Commission is not required to make recommendations, and recommendations, of their nature, lack legally binding character, it is clear that the provisional or interim measures similarly lack binding character. Furthermore, the interim measures are authorized as "indications" to the states parties, and the provisional measures designed for the protection of the alleged victim from irreparable damage are cast simply as "views" of the Commission of which the state party is to be informed.

b.   *Courts and tribunals constituted under the United Nations Convention on the Law of the Sea*

The United Nations Convention on the Law of the Sea (UNCLOS or LOS Convention) incorporates a system of mandatory arbitration or adjudication for disputes arising out of the interpretation and application of the LOS Convention, with only limited exceptions. States have a choice of fora under UNCLOS, including resolution before the International Court of Justice, the International Tribunal on the Law of the Sea (ITLOS or Tribunal) and ad hoc arbitration.

Art. 290(1) of UNCLOS permits a court or tribunal with prima facie jurisdiction to prescribe provisional measures that are considered "appropriate under the circumstances to preserve the respective rights of the parties to the dispute or to prevent serious harm to the marine environment, pending the final decision". This formulation first requires a determination that the relevant court or tribunal has prima facie jurisdiction. This basic prerequisite prevents parties to a dispute from acting unilaterally to exert pressure for

---

189. Rules of Procedure of the African Commission on Human and Peoples' Rights, Rule 111(1) (1995).

190. *Ibid.*

191. Rule 111(2) Rules of Procedure of the African Commission on Human and Peoples' Rights.

192. Art. 52 African [Banjul] Charter on Human and Peoples' Rights (entered into force 21 October 1986).

193. Art. 53, African [Banjul] Charter on Human and Peoples' Rights.

provisional measures.[194] Equally, states may not prevent the prescription of provisional measures by a simple invocation of one of the exceptions to the compulsory resolution of a dispute.[195]

States may further try to resist an order of provisional measures on the basis that prima facie jurisdiction cannot exist where the applicant states have not exhausted their obligations to settle the dispute through non-mandatory means prior to resorting to compulsory and binding procedures. The tribunal took the view in *Southern Bluefin Tuna* that the requirements for invoking the compulsory procedures in the LOS Convention were satisfied when a state party unilaterally concluded that the possibilities of peaceful settlement through means other than adjudication or arbitration had been exhausted.[196]

In some instances, a determination of prima facie jurisdiction may depend on whether the dispute is one relating to the interpretation and application of UNCLOS or another international convention. In *Southern Bluefin Tuna*, the tribunal decided that the fact that a trilateral agreement applied between the parties did not exclude their right to invoke the provisions of the LOS Convention in regard to the conservation and management of southern bluefin tuna,[197] nor did it preclude recourse to the dispute resolution procedures of the LOS Convention.[198] A similar position was taken in the *MOX Plant Case*, where ITLOS considered that separate dispute settlement procedures before other international fora did not preclude a finding of prima facie jurisdiction, since these other proceedings were not specifically addressing the interpretation of UNCLOS.[199]

If the tribunal determines it has prima facie jurisdiction, the standard that must then be met is whether the measures are so required in order to preserve the rights of the parties or whether there is a need to prevent serious harm to the marine environment.[200] By virtue of Art. 89(5) of the tribunal's Rules, the tribunal "may prescribe measures

---

194. John King GAMBLE Jr., "The 1982 UN Convention on the Law of the Sea: Binding Dispute Settlement?", 9 B.U. Int'l L.J. (1991) p. 39 at p. 42.

195. See *The M/V "Saiga" (No. 2)*, Order on Provisional Measures (*St. Vincent v. Guinea*) (11 March 1998) paras. 27 and 30 at www.itlos.org/start2_en.html (last visited 1 November 2002) (noting that the respondent relied on an exception to jurisdiction under Art. 297(3) but relying on Art. 297(1) as a prima facie basis of jurisdiction).

196. *Southern Bluefin Tuna*, Requests for Provisional Measures (*N.Z. v. Japan; Austl. v. Japan*) (Order of 27 August 1999) paras. 60 and 61 at www.itlos.org/start2_en.html (last visited 1 November 2002).

197. *Ibid.*, para. 51.

198. *Ibid.*, para. 55. Shabtai Rosenne has argued that ITLOS should be careful not to overstep the limits of its jurisdiction under Art. 290(5) because the measures are not "incidental" to the whole case since it is to be resolved by a different tribunal but are "'proceedings' pure and simple". Shabtai ROSENNE, "The International Tribunal for the Law of the Sea: Survey for 1999", 15 Int'l J. Mar. & Coastal L. (2000) p. 443 at p. 472.

199. *MOX Plant (Ir. v. U.K.)* Request for Provisional Measures (Order of 3 December 2001) at www.itlos.org/start2_en.html, at para. 52.

200. The need for the prescription of provisional measures to prevent serious harm to the marine environment was considered by ITLOS in the *MOX Plant* case. The tribunal unanimously decided that the circumstances of the case (including the undertaking of the United Kingdom not to transport radioactive material through the Irish Sea in the near future) did not indicate sufficient urgency for the grant of an order pending the constitution of the arbitral tribunal.

different in whole or in part from those requested". Once prescribed, the order may be modified or revoked once the circumstances justifying their prescription have changed or cease to exist.[201]

Art. 290(5) allows ITLOS to prescribe provisional measures pending the constitution of an arbitral tribunal if it considers that the arbitral tribunal has prima facie jurisdiction and that the urgency of the situation so requires.[202] The standard of the "urgency of the situation" was considered in *Southern Bluefin Tuna*, where the applicants argued that such measures were necessary in light of Japan's adoption of an experimental fishing program by which it harvested more tuna than had been agreed under the 1993 Convention for the Conservation of Southern Bluefin Tuna. In response to Japan's argument that there was no urgency requiring the prescription of provisional measures, the tribunal stated: "[A]lthough the Tribunal cannot conclusively assess the scientific evidence presented by the parties, it finds that measures should be taken as a matter of urgency to preserve the rights of the parties and to avert further deterioration of the southern bluefin tuna stock."[203] No reference was made to the possibility of "irreparable harm" or "irreparable damage" as the reason for prescribing measures.[204] The tribunal granted Australia and New Zealand's request that Japan should be prohibited from continuing the experimental fishing program, but this measure was directed at all of the parties.

The tribunal is authorized to prescribe provisional measures, and these measures are binding on the parties to the dispute. The obligations of the parties are often reinforced procedurally through a requirement that the parties submit reports to ITLOS on the measures taken to ensure compliance. In addition to prescribing measures, ITLOS may also make recommendations to the parties.[205] Such recommendations provide useful guidance for the conduct of the parties without creating the burden of sanctions under international law if they are not followed.

c.   *The International Court of Justice*
The power of the International Court of Justice (ICJ or Court) to indicate provisional measures is set out in Art. 41(1) of its Statute:

---

201. Art. 290(2) UNCLOS.
202. A request under Art. 290(5) must indicate the urgency of the situation and the legal grounds upon which the arbitral tribunal to be constituted would have jurisdiction. Art. 89(4) ITLOS Rules of the Tribunal (21 September 2001).
203. *Southern Bluefin Tuna, op. cit.*, fn. 196, para. 80.
204. Judge Laing endorsed this approach in his separate opinion:

   "Instead of irreparability, the key to UNCLOS provisional measures is the discretionary element of appropriateness.... Along with appropriateness, the formulation of preservation of the respective rights of the parties underscores the discretionary nature of provisional measures."

   Southern Bluefin Tuna, op. cit., fn. 196, para. 4 (Separate Opinion of Judge Laing).
205. See, e.g., *M/V "Saiga" (No. 2), op. cit.*, fn. 195, para. 52(2), where the tribunal chose to recommend that the parties enter into provisional arrangements to ensure that there would be no aggravation of the dispute pending its final settlement.

"The Court shall have the power to indicate, if it considers that circumstances so require, any provisional measures which ought to be taken to preserve the respective rights of either party."

This provision was also included in the Statute of the Permanent Court of International Justice, the predecessor court of the ICJ.

As a precursor to the indication of provisional measures, the Court must first determine whether it has prima facie jurisdiction. Collins has described this requirement as satisfied "if the absence of jurisdiction is not manifest and if the instrument said by the claimant to confer jurisdiction on the Court prima facie does so".[206]

The Court's orders in the *Icelandic Fisheries* cases stated three of the principal elements to be satisfied for the indication of provisional measures in accordance with Art. 41 of the Court's Statute.[207] These elements have been implicitly affirmed in the subsequent decisions of the Court.[208] First, the measures indicated must be intended to preserve the respective rights of the parties. Second, irreparable prejudice should not be caused to disputed rights. A sense of urgency is tied in to this second requirement. In the *Great Belt* case, the Court stated that measures would be "justified if there is urgency in the sense that action prejudicial to the rights of either party is likely to be taken before such final decision is given."[209] Finally, the Court's judgment on the merits should not be anticipated through the indication of measures, but at the same time, the rights for which a state is seeking protection must address the subject matter of the rights in dispute in the case on the merits.

Whether provisional measures indicated by the International Court of Justice are binding on states had long been a disputed question. The binding nature of the ICJ's Orders of provisional measures had been much debated in academic literature,[210] but had not been squarely before the Court for resolution prior to Paraguay's request for provisional measures to protect the rights of its citizen in the *Case Concerning the Vienna Convention on Consular Relations*.[211] Paraguay argued in its Memorial on the merits that the

---

206. Lawrence COLLINS, "Provisional and Protective Measures in International Litigation" in *Essays in International Litigation and the Conflict of Laws* (1994) p. 174, reprinted from 234 *Receuil des Cours* (1992-III) (1993). This view is consistent with the approach set out by Judge Lauterpacht in the *Interhandel* case. See 1957 I.C.J. Rep. 105, at 118-119 (Oct. 24).

207. *Icelandic Fisheries Jurisdiction*, 1972 I.C.J. Rep. 16 (*U.K. v. Ice.*, para. 21; *F.R.G. v. Ice.*, para. 22). In that case, the Court considered requests for provisional measures from the Federal Republic of Germany and the United Kingdom in respect of Iceland's decision to extend its maritime jurisdiction to fifty miles from its baselines, thereby disrupting years of German and British fishing in the region.

208. See H.W.A. THIRLWAY, "The Indication of Provisional Measures by the International Court of Justice", in Rudolf BERNHARDT, ed., *op. cit.*, fn. 173, p. 1 at p. 6 (1994).

209. *Case Concerning the Passage Through the Great Belt (Fin. v. Den.)* 1991 I.C.J. Rep. 12, para. 23.

210. See, e.g., COLLINS, *op. cit.*, fn. 206, pp. 169-171; Hersch LAUTERPACHT, *The Development of International Law by the International Court* (1958) pp. 253-254.

211. *Case Concerning Vienna Convention on Consular Relations (Para. v. U.S.)* 1998 I.C.J. 248 (April 9). Collier and Lowe have noted that the question was potentially before the Court in the *Nuclear Tests* cases when France refused to comply with the Court's provisional measures order, but the ICJ did not address it in its subsequent judgment. See John COLLIER and Vaughan LOWE, *The*

United States had breached a binding order of the Court when it failed to take the steps necessary to stop the execution of Paraguay's national, Mr. Breard.[212] Paraguay contested the United States' argument that the provisional measures indicated by the ICJ were merely precatory:

> "Particularly when read in the context of the Statute of the Court, the terms employed, by their ordinary meaning, describe a binding order. The 'power to indicate' measures that 'ought to be taken' in order to 'preserve the respective rights' of the parties can only be understood to carry a corresponding obligation of the parties to comply. Moreover, the object and purpose of Article 41 is to preserve the rights of the parties pending a binding final judgment, and that of the Statute as a whole is to provide for the binding, judicial resolution of disputes. These objects and purposes would be utterly frustrated if the parties retained a right to act prior to the final judgment in a manner that the Court has indicated will prevent it from rendering an effective judgment. Finally, the binding character of provisional measures under Article 41 is confirmed by the general rule that parties to a judicial proceeding must refrain from any step that might prejudice the court's capacity to provide relief. Simply put, the United States' undisputed obligation under Article 94(1) of the United Nations Charter to abide by a judgment of this Court that a new trial be granted Mr. Breard, or the plea offer be reconveyed, cannot be squared with the United States' suggestion that, in the meantime, it was free decisively to destroy the Court's capacity to provide that relief."[213]

The Court did not have occasion to address this argument, as Paraguay discontinued its case.[214] But the controversy was decisively laid to rest in the *LaGrand* Case, decided in 2001.[215]

The *LaGrand* Case, which Germany brought against the United States, was based on nearly identical facts to the *Case Concerning the Vienna Convention on Consular Relations*. It concerned the consular rights of Karl and Walter LaGrand, German nationals who had grown up in the United States. In 1982, the two brothers were arrested, and eventually convicted and sentenced to death for murder, attempted murder, attempted armed robbery and kidnapping. The competent US authorities failed to provide the LaGrands with the information required under the Vienna Convention on Consular Relations, and further failed to inform the relevant German consular post of their arrest.

After pursuing various diplomatic and legal avenues in the United States, Germany sought an order for provisional measures from the ICJ on the day before Walter LaGrand was scheduled for execution in Arizona. The Court found that the

---

Settlement of Disputes in International Law: Institutions and Procedures (1999) p. 175, fn. 238.

212. Memorial of the Republic of Paraguay, para. 1.9 (9 October 1998) at www.icj-cij.org/icjwww/idocket/ipaus/ipausframe.htm.

213. *Ibid.*, para. 1.10.

214. See *Case Concerning the Vienna Convention on Consular Relations*, 1998 I.C.J. 426 (Nov. 10).

215. *LaGrand, op. cit.*, fn. 184.

circumstances of the case required it to indicate provisional measures requiring the United States to "take all measures at its disposal to ensure that Walter LaGrand is not executed pending the final decision of these proceedings".[216] The Court also indicated that the United States should inform the Court of the measures taken, which were to include transmitting the Court's Order to the Governor of Arizona, who had the power to grant a temporary reprieve in the execution of the sentence. In reliance on the order, Germany sought relief from the United States Supreme Court. The Solicitor General, on behalf of the United States, informed the Supreme Court that "an order of the International Court of Justice indicating provisional measures is not binding and does not furnish a basis for judicial relief". The Supreme Court denied relief,[217] and Walter LaGrand was executed that same day.

In the case on the merits, Germany sought a declaration that the United States had violated its international legal obligation to comply with the Court's Order on provisional measures. The United States maintained that it had complied with the Order but that, in any event, the Order did not create a binding legal obligation. In a landmark decision, the Court decided that its provisional measures orders did impose binding legal obligations on the parties.

In reaching this conclusion, the Court interpreted Art. 41 of its Statute as required under customary international law – namely, in good faith in accordance with the ordinary meaning to be given to its terms in their context and in the light of the treaty's object and purpose.[218] After noting a slight divergence between the equally authentic English and French texts, the Court stated that it had to adopt the meaning that best reconciled the texts in line with the objects and purposes of the treaty.[219] The Court described the object and purpose of its Statute and its intersection with Art. 41 as follows:

> "The context in which Article 41 has to be seen within the Statute is to prevent the Court from being hampered in the exercise of its functions because the respective rights of the parties to a dispute before the Court are not preserved. It follows from the object and purpose of the Statute, as well as from the terms of Article 41 when read in their context, that the power to indicate provisional measures entails that such measures should be binding, inasmuch as the power in question is based on the necessity, when the circumstances call for it, to safeguard, and to avoid prejudice to, the rights of the parties as determined by the final judgment of the Court. The contention that provisional measures indicated under Article 41 might not be binding would be contrary to the object and purpose of that Article."[220]

The Court further reasoned that measures designed to avoid aggravating or extending

---

216. *Ibid.*, para. 32.
217. *Federal Republic of Germany v. United States*, 526 U.S. 111 (1999).
218. *Ibid.,* para. 99.
219. *Ibid.*, para, 101.
220. *Ibid.*, para. 102.

disputes had been indicated in the past with the purpose of being implemented.[221] Finally, the Court noted that the preparatory work leading to the adoption of Art. 41 did not preclude the interpretation that orders for provisional measures are binding and imposed legal obligations on the parties to which the measures are indicated.

4.   *Trends in the Standards for and Scope of Provisional Measures Before National and International Courts and Tribunals*

The above survey indicates both the types of measures that are commonly issued as well as the standards that are usually applied in determining whether interim measures of protection are indeed warranted. National laws and judicial decisions express more frequently the specific types of provisional measures that are available to parties in dispute; international courts and tribunals have typically not specified what measures might be available to the parties, and in the instances where sorts of measures are included in the grant of power to the tribunal or court, the list is exemplary rather than exhaustive. Attention is focused more on what the provisional measures are intended to achieve than on the precise form of action to be ordered.

When determining whether interim measures should indeed be ordered, national courts have often focused on whether the actions of the party against whom the measures are being sought will prejudice or otherwise prevent the enforcement of the final award; this feature is closely related to the urgency of the situation requiring an immediate remedy to protect the requesting party. The need for a finding of urgency is particularly prevalent when courts are considering ex parte orders. If urgency is not a specified requirement for inter partes orders, it is so stipulated for ex parte measures; and when urgency is already a feature of orders of interim measures, a greater degree of urgency must then be shown for an ex parte measure. The jurisprudence of international courts and tribunals more commonly includes necessity and urgency as required standards in determining whether provisional measures should be indicated.

National courts may also refer to the merits of the dispute to the extent that there is acknowledgement that there is a serious question to be tried, particularly in common law countries. Such a finding will enable a national court to issue provisional measures if other requirements are met. The United States and some international commercial arbitral tribunals have gone one step further and sought to determine if the requesting party is likely to succeed on the merits, not just that there is a serious issue in dispute. The criterion of success on the merits is in direct contrast to the practice of international courts and tribunals, which only consider the merits of the case to the extent necessary to determine if prima facie jurisdiction exists.

In sum, the types of provisional measures of protection that may be awarded are quite diverse, and generally need not be specified in any instrument granting power to a court or tribunal, provided that the overall objective of not frustrating the enforcement of the final measures is satisfied. The urgency for the issuance of provisional measures may well relate to the central goal of preventing the defending party from acting to the detriment of the requesting party in respect of the dispute. Urgency is nonetheless a hallmark of

---

221. *Ibid.*, para. 103.

provisional measures. Finally, a divergence in criteria is evident in respect of the impact that the merits of the dispute may have on the order for provisional measures.

5.   A Model Law Provision for Provisional Measures in International Arbitration

The rules governing the issuance of provisional measures in national and international fora provide useful guidance for the work of UNCITRAL in formulating standards for international arbitral tribunals. UNCITRAL's deliberations have focused on the scope of interim measures of protection, the criteria to be met for the issuance of these measures, and the authority of arbitral tribunals to issue ex parte interim measures. The thirty-sixth session of the Working Group on Arbitration did not finally resolve these issues, but it crystallized the issues and competing positions. Consideration can thus be given to the final form of an appropriate text.

a.   The recent work of UNCITRAL
Consideration of the topic arose within UNCITRAL in light of the increasing demand for interim measures and the lack of clear standards as to the scope of interim measures and the conditions for their issuance.[222] The Working Group noted that a variety of formulations are found in laws that authorize an arbitral tribunal to order interim measures of protection. Some laws allow an arbitral tribunal a broad power; others specify what measures may be taken; while still others expressly limit the range of measures that an arbitral tribunal may order.[223] Discussion on this topic initially focused on the text of Art. 17 of the UNCITRAL Model Law, with an additional provision defining interim measures and allowing for the grant of ex parte interim measures.[224]

Following these initial discussions, the Secretariat to the Commission formulated a new proposal, which was then revised and elaborated on during the thirty-sixth session of the Commission, held in March 2002.[225] The Secretariat proposal, in line with Art. 17 of the UNCITRAL Model Law, empowered the arbitral tribunal to issue interim measures it considered necessary at the request of a party. During the discussions, the Working Group considered whether the interim measures had to be with respect to the subject matter of the dispute. By reference to the subject matter of the dispute, the measures could be understood as limited to those directly related to the assets under dispute.[226] The reference was not viewed as necessary because a restrictive

---

222. Working Paper 108, *op. cit.*, fn. 10, p. 24.

223. *Ibid.*

224. "Report of the Secretary-General, Settlement of Commercial Disputes – Preparation of uniform provisions on: written form for arbitration agreements, interim measures of protection, and conciliation", UNCITRAL, 34th Sess., UN Doc. A/CN.9/WG.II/WP.113 (21 May - 1 June 2001) (hereinafter Working Paper 113) p. 12.

225. See "Note by the Secretariat, Settlement of commercial disputes – Preparation of uniform provisions on interim measures of protection", UNCITRAL, 36th Sess., UN Doc. A/CN.9/WG.II/WP.119 (2002) (hereinafter Working Paper 119) at pp. 22-23.

226. "Report of the Working Group on Arbitration on the work of its thirty-sixth session" (New York, 4-8 March 2002) UNCITRAL, 36th Sess., UN Doc. A/CN.9/508, (17-28 June 2002) (hereinafter Working Group Report 508) p. 14.

interpretation would inappropriately limit the powers of the arbitral tribunal.[227]

The Working Group recognized the need to define the requirements that a requesting party must meet in order for the arbitral tribunal to issue interim measures. The three elements initially considered were: an urgent need for the measure applied for; a significant degree of harm resulting if the interim measure were not ordered; and a likelihood of the requesting party succeeding on the merits of the underlying case. Members of the Working Group took the view that the assessment of the degree of harm suffered by the applicant if the interim measure was not granted should be balanced against an evaluation of the harm suffered by the other party in the event the requested measure was granted.[228] Questions over assessing the degree of harm were also raised in the Working Group – with suggestions that a reference to "irreparable harm" may be more qualitative than the quantitative "significant degree of harm".[229] A matter left unresolved at the close of the session was whether the three elements should be alternative or cumulative requirements.

A further element that could be required for the issue of interim measures is that the arbitral tribunal may request a party to provide appropriate security in connection with such measures. The requirement to pay security may be directed at any party, and not just the party requesting the interim measures. The decision to require security rests within the discretion of the arbitral tribunal.[230] A certain flexibility is also accorded here to allow for the option of a party against whom the order is made submitting alternative forms of guarantees to avoid the interim measures otherwise being ordered.[231]

With respect to the scope of the measures that can be ordered, the Secretariat's proposal posited two variants to form part of an illustrative and non-exhaustive list. The first variant anticipated measures that would maintain (and restore) the status quo pending determination of the questions at issue; provide a preliminary means of securing assets out of which an award may be satisfied; or restrain conduct by a defendant to prevent current or imminent future harm. As a more general formulation, the second variant proposed measures to avoid or minimize prejudice or to facilitate later enforcement of an award. Preference in the Working Group was for the more descriptive list of the first variant. This list was broadened to refer to measures that would restore the status quo; to provide a means to secure or facilitate the enforcement of the award (rather than just securing the assets for possible satisfaction); and restrain as well as order conduct by any party to prevent imminent harm.[232] The Working Group also decided to add a provision that would allow for measures that were intended as a preliminary means of securing evidence.[233] These measures could all be granted at any

---

227. *Ibid.*, p. 15.

228. *Ibid.*

229. *Ibid.*

230. There was support for making security mandatory, but the prevailing view was that while it should be the norm, it should not be mandatory. "Working Group Report 508", *op. cit.*, fn. 226, p. 16.

231. *Ibid.*, p. 17.

232. *Ibid.*, pp. 18-19.

233. *Ibid.*, p. 19.

time prior to the issuance of the award.

The proposed powers of the arbitral tribunal for issuing interim measures of protection also extend to granting ex parte interim measures. As some resistance to this provision was expressed in the Working Group,[234] suggestions were made for limiting the possible abuse of ex parte interim measures. These proposals included a previous agreement for such measures, only allowing measures intended to maintain the status quo, and requiring the requesting party to reveal all circumstances (including those adverse to the applicant) relevant and material to the requirements for the granting of such measures.[235] A further suggestion was to limit or exclude the possibility of court enforcement of ex parte interim measures.[236] There was general agreement within the Working Group that a time limit for the duration of the measures should be imposed by the arbitral tribunal.

The Working Group considered that ex parte measures could be granted in two possible situations: first, without notice to the party against whom the measure is directed or, second, before the party against whom the measure is directed has had an opportunity to respond. Although the suggestion was made that these situations should be combined, no final decision was reached on this issue.[237]

The Working Group further discussed the requirements that must be met to warrant ex parte interim measures. In particular, the Secretariat proposal set forth that such measures would only be granted where:

(a) it is necessary to ensure that the measure is effective;
(b) the applicant for the measure provides appropriate security in connection with the measure;
(c) the applicant for the measure can demonstrate the urgent necessity of the measure; and
(d) [the measure would be supported by a preponderance of considerations of fairness.]

The prevailing view within the Working Group was that the conditions for granting ex parte interim measures should at least be the same as those required for inter partes interim measures.[238] To this end, a proposal was made that ex parte measures could be granted where the requirements for inter partes interim measures were met and where the arbitral tribunal determined that "it is necessary to proceed in such manner in order to ensure that the measure is effective".[239]

Once an interim measure is granted on an ex parte basis, the party against whom the measure is directed must be given notice of the measure and an opportunity to be heard at the earliest practicable time. The proposal added a qualification to these rights in favor

---

234. Concerns arose from the principles that all parties should have equal access to the arbitral tribunal and a full opportunity of presenting their case. *Ibid.*
235. *Ibid.*
236. *Ibid.*, p. 20.
237. *Ibid.*
238. *Ibid.*, p. 21.
239. *Ibid.*, pp. 21-22.

of the party against whom the measures are sought whereby the arbitral tribunal could proceed without notice if the tribunal determined that it was necessary to proceed in that manner in order to ensure that the measures would be effective.[240] The Working Group lacked sufficient time to consider this proposal.

Further procedural requirements envisaged under the Secretariat's proposal refer to the extension or modification of both ex parte and inter partes interim measures. An obligation is also placed on the requesting party to inform the arbitral tribunal of any substantial change of circumstances with respect to the requirements for the issuance of the interim measures. Lack of time prevented any discussion on these final provisions of the draft text.

b.   A proposal

The work of UNCITRAL and the practice of both national and international courts and tribunals highlight certain features that are essential to a model legislative text on the power of an arbitral tribunal to order interim measures of protection. The particular issues that must be addressed are the power to grant and the definition of the interim measures, the conditions to be met for their issuance, and the possibility of and, if authorized, conditions for the issuance of ex parte interim measures.

In light of the survey of national jurisdictions, international tribunals, and ad hoc arbitral tribunals undertaken earlier in this paper, and of the work thus far of the Working Group, it is submitted here that the text should read:

"*Power of arbitral tribunal to order interim measures*
(1) Unless otherwise agreed by the parties, the arbitral tribunal may, at the request of a party, order another party to take interim measures of protection.

(2) An interim measure of protection is any temporary measure, whether reflected in an interim award or otherwise, by which, at any time prior to the issuance of the award by which the dispute is finally decided, the arbitral tribunal orders a party to

(a) maintain or restore the status quo pending determination of the dispute, in order to ensure or facilitate the effectiveness of an eventual award;
(b) take action that would prevent, or refrain from taking action that would cause, current or imminent harm, in order to ensure or facilitate the effectiveness of an eventual award;
(c) provide security for the enforcement of an eventual award; or
(d) preserve evidence that may be relevant and material to the resolution of the dispute.

(3) The arbitral tribunal may order an interim measure of protection when the requesting party has demonstrated that

(a) irreparable harm will result if the measure is not ordered, and that harm

---

240. *Ibid.*

substantially outweighs the harm that will result to the party opposing the measure if the measure is granted; and

(b) there is a substantial possibility that the requesting party will succeed on the merits of the dispute.

(4)(a) The arbitral tribunal may grant an interim measure of protection without notice to the party against whom the measure is directed or before the party against whom the measure is directed has had an opportunity to respond when, in addition to meeting the requirements of paragraph (3), the requesting party demonstrates that it is necessary to proceed in that manner in order to ensure that the measure is effective.

(b) Any interim measure of protection ordered under this paragraph shall be effective for no more than twenty days, which period cannot be extended. This subparagraph shall not affect the authority of the arbitral tribunal to grant, confirm, extend, or modify an interim measure of protection under paragraph (1) after the party against whom the measure is directed has been given notice and an opportunity to be heard.

(c) Except to the extent that the arbitral tribunal has determined under paragraph (4)(a) that it is necessary to proceed without notice to the party against whom the interim measure of protection is directed in order to ensure that the measure is effective, that party shall be given notice of the measure and an opportunity to be heard at the earliest practicable time.

(d) [A party requesting an interim measure of protection under this paragraph shall have an obligation to inform the arbitral tribunal of all circumstances that the arbitral tribunal is likely to find relevant and material to its determination as to whether the requirements of this paragraph have been met.]

(5) The arbitral tribunal may require the requesting party to provide appropriate security as a condition to granting an interim measure of protection.

(6) The requesting party shall, from the time of the request onwards, inform the arbitral tribunal promptly of any material change in the circumstances on the basis of which the party sought or the arbitral tribunal granted the interim measure of protection.

(7) The arbitral tribunal may modify or terminate an interim measure of protection at any time."

i.   Paragraph (1): the tribunal's authority

If arbitral tribunals are to fulfill their function as competent and effective fora for the resolution of international disputes, they must have the authority to take steps to ensure that the proceedings they conduct will yield effective results. There is little or no dispute generally about the wisdom of granting arbitral tribunals authority to issue interim measures, and none within the Working Group. It is appropriate, therefore, to commence the section with the grant of authority.

The Secretariat draft initially included the qualification "in respect of the subject matter of the dispute". As noted above, there was concern that, notwithstanding its use in Art. 17 of the Model Law, that phrase might be misread to limit the tribunal's authority to order measures for the provision of security, as opposed to measures affecting the merits of the dispute. That concern should be remedied by the express inclusion of security measures in the definition of interim measures, but in any event the phrase was unnecessary and hence appropriately deleted.

The Working Group did not disturb the phrase "as the arbitral tribunal may consider necessary", which carried over from present Art. 17 of the Model Law. Given that the second subparagraph of the draft text now defines the ends of such measures and the third the conditions under which they might be ordered, the breadth of the phrase "as the arbitral tribunal may consider necessary" may be read as inconsistent with the subsequent paragraphs. The better reading would be to treat the phrase as clarified and limited by the subsequent provisions, but, it is submitted here, the cleanest solution would be to delete it.

ii.   Paragraph (2): scope and form
Scope. Having recognized the tribunal's authority, the section should proceed to define interim measures so as to define the scope of that authority. The Working Group agreed in the March session that that provision should immediately follow the grant of authority.

The UNCITRAL Working Group defined interim measures as "any temporary measure … ordered by the arbitral tribunal pending the issuance of the award by which the dispute is finally decided". There was further agreement in the Working Group on the inclusion of an illustrative and non-exhaustive list of measures in the definition provision. Time was spent during the March 2002 meeting on how the list of these measures should be formulated, but there was broad consensus that the list be non-exhaustive.

That view should be reconsidered. An arbitral tribunal ordering provisional measures of protection should be left with wide discretion in light of the applicable law to order measures that best fit the circumstances of the case provided those measures fulfill their basic goal of facilitating the later enforcement of the final decision. The wide range of measures granted by international tribunals and courts to respond to the particular circumstances of a given case reflects the need for flexibility.

Still, it is important that the purpose and effect of interim measures of protection be set out, because these interim measures, unlike other interim orders of an arbitral tribunal, are intended to be enforceable. The drafters should not shy away from defining the proper scope of such measures by setting forth their legitimate end; the tribunal's discretion would be hampered only if the article attempted to limit the permissible means.

It might be possible to set forth a single definition of the aim. For example, one could take the view that the fundamental aim of facilitating later enforcement, which features prominently in the decisions of national courts on the grant of provisional measures, underscores all of the examples currently included in the March text. Any order that requires a party to take temporary measures intended to facilitate the later enforcement of the final decision might be viewed as necessarily incorporating measures maintaining or restoring the status quo, securing assets for potential satisfaction of an award, and restraining or ordering conduct to prevent current or imminent future harm. Taking that view, the text could read simply: "An interim measure of protection is any temporary measure ordered by the arbitral tribunal at any time prior to the issuance of the award by which the dispute is finally decided that is intended to facilitate later enforcement of that award."

Here, however, there would be a risk that concision would come at the cost of clarity. Maintaining the status quo and preventing current or future harm are such familiar formulations of the purpose of provisional measures that they, too, should be included. Reference to the principle of effectiveness further clarifies the purpose. Because security measures do not address the merits of the dispute (hence the concern about including the phrase "with respect to the subject matter of the dispute" in the provision granting the authority), they warrant a specific reference. So, too, does the aim of preserving evidence, because that species of order could reasonably be thought of as procedural and thereby distinguished from either security measures or measures addressing the merits directly.

Hence, a text is here proposed that refers to measures to maintain the status quo or prevent harm in order to ensure the effectiveness of an eventual award, which are measures essentially providing preliminary relief on the merits; measures requiring security for an eventual award; and measures for the preservation of evidence. It is submitted that these aims exhaust the proper purposes of interim measures and hence that the list may be treated as exhaustive. It is also submitted that stating the proper aims of interim measures should in no way circumscribe the means by which a tribunal chooses to achieve those aims.

Form. The Working Group also debated whether the definition should include reference to the form in which the interim measures are issued. The denomination of interim measures as an "award" has been incorporated into arbitral rules and has typically been assessed as reflecting the binding nature of the award or its enforceability. Members of the Working Group correctly pointed out that the title or form of the order for provisional measures was not decisive for purposes of enforcement of the measures in national courts.[241] Hence, this text must be coordinated with the text on enforcement.

In order to ensure that the tribunal adequately expresses its intentions on enforceability, the text might require that an order for provisional measures be issued as an interim award, and the enforceability text provide that only an order so denominated be considered enforceable. Here as elsewhere, however, function should not be sacrificed to form, and hence it is recommended that no requirement as to the form be imposed.

iii.   Paragraph (3): conditions

Chapeau. The burden for meeting the conditions for the issuance of interim measures rests with the requesting party. While the Secretariat's draft text required this party to "furnish proof", members of the Working Group correctly raised the implications for questions of evidence that might arise from the reference to "proof" and instead preferred terms such as "show" or "demonstrate". While the quality of the evidence should be left to the assessment of the arbitral tribunal, it is nonetheless appropriate to

---

241. "Working Group Report 508", *op. cit.*, fn. 226, p. 18.

leave the burden of meeting the conditions with the requesting party, rather than stipulating a more neutral formula requiring the arbitral tribunal to make the determinations that the conditions are met. The chapeau to the conditions then should read: "The arbitral tribunal may order an interim measure of protection when the requesting party has demonstrated that...."

Conditions. With the shift of the definition to follow the grant of authority provision, the conditions for the issuance of interim measures constitutes the third clause of the draft text.

The first condition is that "irreparable harm will result if the measure is not ordered". How to qualify the level of harm was a matter of discussion in the Working Group. In line with the jurisprudence of several international courts, preference was expressed for reference to "irreparable harm" rather than "a significant degree of harm", the originally proposed formulation. The former phrase reflects more accurately the basic need for interim measures than the latter phrase, and there was a decided preference for that phrase in the Working Group.

The concept of irreparable harm will provide welcome discipline to the grant of interim measures, and it is submitted here that that requirement is essential. Some consideration was given to an independent requirement of "an urgent need for the measure", but it is submitted here that urgency is implicit in the threat of irreparable harm.

The most important change made in the text during the deliberations of the Working Group was the addition of a balancing test on prospective harm – variously phrased as the balance of hardship or the balance of convenience. Specifically, it is proposed here that the requirement of irreparable harm be accompanied by an independent requirement that "that harm substantially outweighs the harm that will result to the party against whom the measure is directed if the measure is granted". It is frequently the case that an interim measure will cause hardship to the party against whom it is directed, and the arbitral tribunal must have authority to take that threat of harm into account. Of course, the tribunal's authority to order security may be used to lessen any such threat.

The second condition takes into account the merits of the dispute. The Secretariat's draft text included a requirement that the applicant show a "likelihood" of success on the merits. Most national courts do not refer to this criterion (though often there is a requirement of a serious question to be tried or litigated), and international courts and tribunals deciding disputes between states have also shied away from this formulation, considering the merits only to the extent necessary for a finding of prima facie jurisdiction.

Given the seriousness with which arbitral tribunals take their duty to treat the parties equally, a requirement that the applicant demonstrate a likelihood of success could unduly inhibit tribunals from exercising their authority out of a concern that they will be viewed as prejudging the dispute. At the same time, it is important that the tribunal be at least persuaded that there is possible merit to the claim that it is asked to order interim measures to protect. Hence, the Working Group looked for a formulation that would require the tribunal to conclude that the case was a serious one, without having to decide whether the applicant was more likely than not to succeed on the merits. "Substantial possibility" was proposed and accepted, and that formulation is used here.

128

The Secretariat draft included as an alternative provision a requirement that "the measure would be supported by a preponderance of considerations of fairness". It is submitted here that no such catch-all provision should be included. The specified conditions should capture the considerations of fairness relevant to the grant of interim measures, and they alone should guide the tribunal's discretion.

The Working Group left unresolved the question whether the specified conditions should be cumulative or alternative. It is submitted here that the notion that a requesting party may obtain interim measures on a showing of only one or two of the three specified conditions is inconsistent with their rationale and, indeed, the entire discussion of the circumstances in which interim measures should be granted. The proposed text makes clear that in order to obtain interim measures, the requesting party must demonstrate each of the conditions.

iv.   Paragraph (4): ex parte interim measures

Ex parte interim measures are those ordered without notice to the party against whom the measure is directed or before the party against whom the measure is directed has had an opportunity to respond. The authority to order ex parte interim measures risks conflict with the basic right to an opportunity to be heard. The authority of an arbitral tribunal to grant interim measures ex parte and the conditions under which it might do so prompted intensive discussion in the Working Group. The proposal here grants arbitral tribunals the authority to order ex parte interim measures.

Conditions. The only justification for interim measures sought without notice to the adverse party is a showing that, if notice were provided, the measures would be ineffective. The classic example is an attempt to restrain assets that, upon notice but before decision, could be moved from a jurisdiction where they are within reach to one where they are not.

Sometimes, notice will have been provided, and the applicant does not contest that notice is practicable, but the circumstances are such that the tribunal is asked to act before the adverse party has had an opportunity to be heard. The text recognizes the tribunal's authority to act in these circumstances as well.

Hence, the conditions for the grant of ex parte provisional measures are (a) satisfaction of the requirements applicable to interim measures generally, and (b) a showing that the measures would not be effective unless the tribunal proceeded in ex parte fashion.

Time limit. It follows from the justification for ex parte interim measures that they should be effective for only a brief period. If a party demonstrates a need to proceed in ex parte fashion, that party should act promptly once having obtained the measures to enforce the measures and prevent the harm whose threat prompted their issuance.

Any specific time limit will be arbitrary. However, the absence of a specific time limit and the use, instead, of a standard of "reasonableness" or the like may not send a sufficiently clear message as to the limited circumstances in which such measures are appropriate. The question of duration also has relevance to enforceability. It is submitted here that the text should specify a limit of twenty days.

To avoid confusion, it is also submitted that an additional sentence should state that the time limit applicable to ex parte measures does not affect the tribunal's authority to grant, confirm, extend or modify interim measures granted ex parte once the party against whom the measure was ordered has been given notice and an opportunity to be heard.

Notice. The March text included a general provision requiring "[t]he party to whom the [interim] measure ... is directed ... be given notice of the measure and an opportunity to be heard at the earliest practicable time". It is submitted here that the only special notice provision necessary in this article is that governing ex parte interim measures.

There are three possible notice scenarios. First, the applicant may be fully prepared to proceed on notice, in which case the general notice regime, requiring that all parties be given notice at the same time and by the same means as the notice provided to the tribunal, would apply. There is no need to reiterate conventional notice requirements in this article.

Second, the applicant may claim urgency, be prepared to provide notice, but contend that the tribunal must act before the party against whom the measure is directed can be heard. In that circumstance, the tribunal should require diligent efforts to provide notice and an opportunity to be heard.

Finally, the applicant may contend that notice should not be required because notice will destroy the effectiveness of the measure sought. Even here, notice should be provided as soon as the reason for excusing notice has been satisfied – that is, as soon as notice would no longer destroy the effectiveness of the measures.

As to each of the latter two situations, the proposed text requires notice at the earliest practicable time. It also includes language to clarify that the obligation set forth here does not override the tribunal's authority to proceed without notice on a proper showing.

Obligation to inform. In the Working Group, a proposal was made that the article impose on the requesting party the "obligation to inform the arbitral tribunal of all circumstances that the arbitral tribunal is likely to find relevant and material to its determination whether the requirements of that paragraph have been met". The purpose of the proposal was to help ensure that a tribunal asked to proceed ex parte had a full picture of the relevant circumstances. The proposal was consistent with the duty of full and frank disclosure imposed under certain legal systems.

As was intended, the proposal met with vigorous discussion. In particular, concern was expressed that any such obligation would conflict with fundamental expectations and, indeed, ethical obligations in many legal systems.

It is submitted here that the text is salutary but not essential so long as the enforcing court retains the authority to make an independent determination of the need to proceed ex parte, as the enforcement article proposes. In that event, the enforcing court could impose its own requirements of disclosure.

v.   Paragraph (5): security

A requirement of security is a standard means of disciplining requests for interim measures. While the tribunal is directed to weigh the balance of hardship or convenience, a condition of security provides a direct and effective means of ensuring that the party requesting the measure will bear the risk of harm done by an erroneous grant.

There was substantial debate in the Working Group as to whether security should be mandatory, particularly with respect to ex parte measures. It is submitted here that it should not. There will be circumstances where there is no real risk of harm to the restrained party, others where a condition of security would prevent the issuance of an otherwise just order, and still others where the balance of hardships points so heavily in the applicant's favor that security would be inappropriate. In all these circumstances, the tribunal should retain flexibility.

The Secretariat's text anticipated that a party other than the requesting party may be required to provide security. It is submitted here that, for the sake of clarity, this paragraph should be limited to security imposed upon the applicant as a condition to the grant of interim measures. Any other security measure would be itself an interim measure and hence adequately covered by the paragraph setting forth the permissible ends of interim measures. The proposed text would in no way impair, for example, the adverse party from proposing the provision of security as an alternative to the grant of other interim measures.

vi.   Paragraph (6): duty to inform of change in circumstances

Given the nature of interim measures, the party granted them should take on an obligation to inform the tribunal of a change in the circumstances on which they were granted. The proposal imposes such an obligation.

The drafting issue concerns the type of change giving rise to the obligation. Earlier proposals talked of a "substantial" change. It is submitted here that that phrase is not sufficiently precise. The proposal therefore imposes the requirement in the event of a "material" change going to the basis on which the measures were granted.

vii.   Paragraph (7): authority of tribunal to modify or terminate

It is generally agreed that the arbitral tribunal should retain the authority to modify or terminate any interim measures it grants. The texts before the Working Group attempted to define the circumstances in which that would be permitted. The last formulation talked of the authority to modify or terminate an interim measure "in light of additional information or a change in circumstances".

It is submitted here that the text should not attempt to limit or define the circumstances in which interim measures might be modified or terminated. Presumably, in the vast majority of cases, tribunals will modify or terminate measures they have already granted only on the basis of new information or a change of circumstances. But given the nature of provisional measures, and the potential for hurried decision making, a tribunal should also have the option just to change its mind. Hence, it is submitted here that the authority to modify or terminate should be recognized, but no attempt made to define the circumstances in which it might be exercised. In any event, any reconsideration of interim measures would have to proceed on the basis of the requirements set out in paragraph (3).

IV.   THE ENFORCEABILITY OF PROVISIONAL MEASURES

Fundamental to any discussion of provisional measures issued in international commercial arbitration is the ability of a party (or the tribunal) to have recourse to the coercive power of a state to enforce the interim order. Arbitral tribunals, as creatures of contract, possess none of the tools and mechanisms by which national courts ensure compliance with their orders.[242] Thus the question: Assuming an arbitral panel has inherent or contractual power to order interim relief, how can it be that the relief is not enforceable in a national court?

To be sure, failure to adhere to an arbitral order is a breach of the contract to arbitrate, rendering the recalcitrant party liable in damages in a judicial action.[243] But the prospect of damages at the end of the day cannot substitute for enforceable interim measures. As is apparent from the above survey of standards for obtaining judicial relief, interim measures are intended to prevent *imminent* harm or to preserve a right that is *presently* threatened; to say that a party's recourse must be to the national courts (which the party sought to avoid in the first place) in the event of that harm occurring or the loss of that right is to ignore the very purpose and rationale for interim relief, and indeed for arbitration itself.

Commentators have observed that "arbitral tribunals routinely order interim measures of protection, which parties before them, concerned not to inconvenience the ultimate trier of fact and law on the merits of the dispute, just as routinely accept".[244] But when the party against whom the order is issued fails to comply, the requesting party must turn to national courts to seek enforcement of the arbitral tribunal's award. It is that prospect that has been confronted in national courts and is currently under discussion in the UNCITRAL meetings.

---

242. As one commentator has put it, "[a]n arbitrator has no *imperium*...". Jan K. SCHAEFER, "New Solutions for Interim Measures of Protection in International Commercial Arbitration: English, German and Hong Kong Laws Compared", 2 Elec. J. Com. L. Sect. 3.3 (August 1998) at www.ejcl.org/ejcl/22/art22-2.html (last visited 5 April 2002). See also Coleen C. HIGGINS, "Interim Measures in Transnational Maritime Arbitration", 65 Tul. L. Rev. (June 1991) p. 1519 at p. 1520 ("Lacking the sovereign powers of the state, an arbitral tribunal has limited sanction power to enforce an interim ruling. Thus, the availability of court enforcement can be essential to the effectiveness of the arbitrator's rulings.").

243. D. Alan REDFERN, "Arbitration and the Courts: Interim Measures of Protection – Is the Tide About to Turn?", 30 Tex. Int'l L.J., p. 71 at p. 81 (Winter 1995) ("Of course, non-compliance could also expose the non-complying party to an action for breach of the parties' arbitration agreement...." (citing Eric A. SCHWARTZ, "The Practices and Experience of the ICC Court", in *Conservatory and Provisional Measures in International Arbitration* (ICC International Court of Arbitration 1993) p. 45 at p. 59).

244. REISMAN, et al., *op. cit.*, fn. 143, at p. 755. Of course, as the tribunal is "both [the parties'] judge and their jury", the "de facto powers" it wields over the parties by virtue of the power of ultimate decision may prompt compliance in many cases. REDFERN, *op. cit.*, fn. 243, p. 83.

1.   Enforcement of Arbitral Provisional Measures by National Courts of Selected Jurisdictions

Some international arbitral institutions, as well as some national jurisdictions, appear to take the view that if the provisional measures are granted in the form of an award, then that award could be enforced through local courts in the same way as an award on the merits of the dispute.[245] However, neither the New York Convention nor any other international instrument addresses the enforcement of interim measures by arbitral panels.[246] Thus, the *practical* outcome of an arbitration – as distinguished from the formal, final "award" – may depend not only on the substantive law as applied to the merits, but also upon the peculiarities of the lex arbitri of the seat of arbitration. This section examines the ability of parties and arbitrators to obtain judicial enforcement of arbitral provisional orders under the current lex arbitri in several jurisdictions.[247] It does not address the use of judicially ordered interim relief "in aid of" an arbitration,[248] but deals solely with the enforceability of interim orders issued by the arbitral panel.

---

245. The UNCITRAL and AAA Rules both provide for awards whereas arbitrators governed by the ICC Rules may choose between an order or an award (the former requiring reasons). The LCIA Rules do not address this question.

246. Some courts, those of the United States in particular, have relied on the enforceability of "awards" under the Convention to support enforcement of "interim awards". See below Sect. IV.5. See also Albert Jan van den BERG, "The Application of the Convention by the Courts" in A.J. van den BERG, ed., International Council for Commercial Arbitration, *Improving the Efficiency of Arbitration Agreements and Awards: 40 Years of Application of the New York Convention*, ICCA Congress Series no. 9 (1998) (hereinafter *ICCA Congress Series no. 9*) (Kluwer 1999) p. 25 at p. 28 (discussing the enforceability of interim "awards" under the New York Convention).

247. This section examines only those jurisdictions where the lex arbitri, at least in theory, does not prohibit the granting of interim relief by panels; a few jurisdictions expressly remove from the ambit of arbitral power the ability to grant such relief. See, e.g., Italian Code of Civil Procedure, Title VIII of Book IV, Art. 818 (*"Gli arbitri non possono concedere sequestri, nè altri provvedimenti cautelar.i."* (The arbitrators may not grant attachments or other interim measures of protection.).

248. Generally, national courts and arbitrators have "concurrent jurisdiction" over the granting of provisional measures, so that unless the parties have stipulated in their agreement that they shall not, they may seek provisional relief in the national courts without doing so before the tribunal. Emmanuel GAILLARD and John SAVAGE, eds., *Fouchard, Gaillard, Goldman on International Commercial Arbitration* (1999) p. 716. England has changed this dynamic by requiring the parties to seek provisional relief from the arbitral panel before seeking court assistance. See Art. 44(5) Arbitration Act 1996 (Eng.) ("In any case the court shall act [to grant interim relief] only if or to the extent that the arbitral tribunal, and any arbitral or other institution or person vested by the parties with power in that regard, has no power or is unable for the time being to act effectively.").

a.   England and Wales

The question of the enforceability of arbitral interim measures[249] in English and Welsh courts was definitively settled (at least as to arbitrations taking place in the United Kingdom[250]) by Sects. 41 and 42 of the Arbitration Act 1996.[251] Under these sections, a panel has two courses of action to obtain enforcement of an arbitral interim order: it may rely on its own powers under the Act to effect the final award as a means of coercing compliance, or it or a party may apply to a court for enforcement.

Sect. 41 permits a tribunal to issue a "peremptory order" upon application by a party should the other party fail to comply with any "order or directions" of the tribunal.[252] If the party does not comply with the "peremptory order" the tribunal may find the party in "default" and may

"(a) direct that the party in default shall not be entitled to rely upon any allegation or material which was the subject matter of the order;

(b) draw such adverse inferences from the act of non-compliance as the circumstances justify;

---

249. It is important to note that the parties to the arbitration must expressly agree that the tribunal will have the authority to issue interim orders. Read together, Sect. 39(1) and (4) of the Arbitration Act 1996 state: "Unless the parties agree to confer such power on the tribunal, the tribunal has no [power to order on a provisional basis any relief which it would have power to grant in a final award]."

250. Under pre-1996 English law, English courts could not act to enforce interim orders from arbitrations seated in foreign countries. See *Channel Tunnel Group Ltd. v. Balfour Beatty Construction Ltd.*, [1993] A.C. 334; [1993] 2 W.L.R. 262; [1993] 1 All E.R. 664; [1993] 1 Lloyd's Rep. 291 (H.L.) (observing that under Art. 12(6)(h) of the Arbitration Act 1950, there was no power to grant an interim injunction in aid of foreign arbitrations).

251. Sect. 42 Arbitration Act 1996 provides in full:

(1) Unless otherwise agreed by the parties, the court may make an order requiring a party to comply with a peremptory order made by the tribunal.

(2) An application for an order under this section may be made–

(a) by the tribunal (upon notice to the parties),

(b) by a party to the arbitral proceedings with the permission of the tribunal (and upon notice to the other parties), or

(c) where the parties have agreed that the powers of the court under this section shall be available.

(3) The court shall not act unless it is satisfied that the applicant has exhausted any available arbitral process in respect of failure to comply with the tribunal's order.

(4) No order shall be made under this section unless the court is satisfied that the person to whom the tribunal's order was directed has failed to comply with it within the time prescribed in the order or, if no time was prescribed, within a reasonable time.

(5) The leave of the court is required for any appeal from a decision of the court under this section."

252. Sect. 41(5) Arbitration Act 1996. A "'peremptory order' means an order made under Sect. 41(5) or made in exercise of any corresponding power conferred by the parties". Sect. 82(1) Arbitration Act 1996.

134

(c) proceed to an award on the basis of such materials as have been properly provided to it;

(d) make such order as it thinks fit as to the payment of costs of the arbitration incurred in consequence of the non-compliance."[253]

These powers will likely coerce most recalcitrant parties into compliance.[254] Where they do not, however, the non-compliance may sacrifice, as a practical matter, the prospect of judicial enforcement:

"If the tribunal makes an order ... in respect of the preservation of property, and this order is breached, a party may only apply for a peremptory order. It is only if the peremptory order is breached that the tribunal may order a final award, which can be enforced by the courts ... but by then the victory may be of little practical use."[255]

Another route for obtaining enforcement is via Sect. 42, which mandates that "[u]nless otherwise agreed by the parties, the court may make an order requiring a party to comply with a peremptory order made by the tribunal".[256] Application to a court for enforcement of the order may be made by the tribunal after notifying the parties, by a party with the leave of the tribunal and notice to the adverse party, or by a party sua sponte if the parties have agreed to permit direct application by themselves.[257] This mechanism, too, has limitations if the relief sought is injunctive and urgently needed; save perhaps in the last instance, the requirement that the opposing party be notified will result in a court order that is "lack[ing] the element of surprise which may be necessary

---

253. Sect. 41(7) Arbitration Act 1996. If the default relates to an order to pay security against costs, the panel may dismiss the claim. Sect. 41(6) Arbitration Act 1996.

254. As one observer noted:

"Ultimately, of course, the arbitrators' greatest source of coercive power resides in their position as arbiters of the merits of the dispute between the parties. Parties seeking to appear before the arbitrators as good citizens who have been wronged by their adversary will generally not wish to defy instructions given to them by those whom they wish to convince of the justice of their claims."

REDFERN, *op. cit.*, fn. 243, p. 81 (citing SCHWARTZ, *op. cit.*, fn. 243). However, as both Sects. 41 and 42 are optional, one wonders whether it will be long before sophisticated parties adopt express language in arbitration clauses doing just that.

255. Kelda GROVES, "Virtual Reality: Effective Injunctive Relief in Relation to International Arbitrations", 1 Int. A.L.R. (1998, no. 6) p. 188 at p. 189.

256. Sect. 42(1) Arbitration Act 1996. Note also that the parties can agree in their arbitration clause to eliminate the enforcement available under Sect. 42, but apparently must do so by express terms. See *Macob Civil Engineering Ltd. v. Morrison Construction Ltd.* [1999] 37 EG 173, para. 8 (reference in arbitration agreement that arbitrator has power to settle disputes not sufficient to eliminate Sect. 42 power).

257. Sect. 42(2) Arbitration Act 1996.

to render it effective".[258]

Other limitations on the immediate enforcement of an arbitral interim order may be the other requirements of Sect. 42. Before issuing an order to comply with the arbitral order, the court must be satisfied that the applicant has "exhausted any available arbitral process in respect of failure to comply with the tribunal's order".[259] Moreover, the court must be satisfied that the party who is subject to the order has had time to comply and has not done so.[260]

b.   France

Arts. 1442-1507, in Book IV of the French *Nouveau Code de Procédure Civile* (NCPC), control domestic and international arbitration. None of these provisions specifically addresses the power of arbitrators to grant interim measures or the enforceability of those measures in French courts. However, it is widely accepted by commentators that arbitrators are empowered to grant such relief and that courts will enforce those measures so long as they are indeed "awards" or a *"sentence arbitrale"*.[261] Enforcement of arbitral awards is accomplished by means of the exequatur procedure in the *tribunal de grande instance*.[262] According to the commentators, this procedure is available for the enforcement of partial, interim and final awards, so long as the award definitively decides an issue.[263]

---

258. GROVES, *op. cit.*, fn. 255, p. 189.

259. Sect. 42(3) Arbitration Act 1996.

260. Sect. 42(4) Arbitration Act 1996.

261. See, e.g., Yves DERAINS and Rosabel E. GOODMAN-EVERARD, "France", in ICCA *International Handbook on Commercial Arbitration*, Suppl. 26 (February 1998) p. 33. ("Like judges, also arbitrators may take interim measures of protection. They may do so in the form of interim awards, which may be enforced immediately and separately from any award on the substance.") However, nowhere does the NCPC define what constitutes an "award". In *ABC International v. Diverseylever Ltd.*, CA Paris, 1e ch., 11 April 2002, RG No 2001/10769 & 2001/15479, the court was faced with this question in the context of an action to annul a procedural order. Under French law *sentences* ("awards") are subject to judicial challenge only under the grounds listed in Arts. 1484 (domestic arbitration) and 1502 NCPC (international arbitration). Likely having in mind *Société Braspetro Oil Services (Brasoil) v. GMRA*, CA Paris 1e ch., 1 July 1999) the *ABC* court ruled that the procedural order in question could not be treated like a final *sentence* and thus could not be challenged in court, and it further specified that a *sentence* is a decision of an arbitral panel that in some way effectively and finally ends part or all of a dispute submitted to it, either expressly on the merits, or by way of a procedural decision. The court also expressly included within its definition of "award" a panel's decision on its own jurisdiction. *ABC* confirmed the court's holding in *Brasoil* that an arbitral panel's characterization of an order, as an award or otherwise, is irrelevant, as only a court can decide whether an order is in effect a *sentence* or merely a procedural order.

262. DERAINS and GOODMAN-EVERARD, *op. cit.*, fn. 261, pp. 45-47; Jean-Pierre ANCEL, "Measures Against Dilatory Tactics: The Cooperation Between Arbitrators and the Courts", in *ICCA Congress Series no. 9*, *op. cit.*, fn. 246, pp. 410-421 ("Finally, once the award has been rendered, the courts intervene to ensure its enforcement (exequatur procedure)...."); Arts. 1477-1478 NCPC.

263. DERAINS and GOODMAN-EVERARD, *op. cit.*, fn. 261, pp. 45-47; cf. *ABC International*, fn. 261.

c.   Germany

Until 1998, German law provided that an arbitration tribunal did not have the power to grant preliminary relief of any kind.[264] However, in that year the new German Arbitration Law[265] was enacted and codified in the Tenth Book, *Schiedsrichterliches Verfahren* (Arbitration Proceedings), of the *Zivilprozeßordnung* (ZPO) at Sects. 1025 to 1066. The new law is based in large part on the UNCITRAL Model Law. Sect. 1033 confers concurrent jurisdiction for interim measures on the German courts and tribunals,[266] and Sect. 1041 addresses the power of tribunals to order interim relief and the power of German courts to enforce those orders. Sect. 1041, translated, provides:

"(1) Unless otherwise agreed by the parties, the arbitral tribunal may, at the request of a party, order such interim measures of protection as the arbitral tribunal may consider necessary in respect of the subject-matter of the dispute. The arbitral tribunal may require any party to provide appropriate security in connection with such measure.

(2) The court may, at the request of a party, permit enforcement of a measure referred to in subsection 1, unless application for a corresponding interim measure has already been made to a court. It may recast such an order if necessary for the purpose of enforcing the measure.

(3) The court may, upon request, repeal or amend the decision referred to in subsection 2.

(4) If a measure ordered under subsection 1 proves to have been unjustified from the outset, the party who obtained its enforcement is obliged to compensate the other party for damage resulting from the enforcement of such measure or from his providing security in order to avoid enforcement. This claim may be put forward in the pending arbitral proceedings."[267]

---

264. Act on the Reform of the Law relating to Arbitral Proceedings of 22 December 1997 (Bundesgesetzblatt I S. 3224) (entered into force on 1 January 1998).

265. Act on the Reform of the Law relating to Arbitral Proceedings of 22 December 1997 (Bundesgesetzblatt I S. 3224) (entered into force on 1 January 1998).

266. Sect. 1033 ZPO provides:

"*Eine Schiedsvereinbarung schließt nicht aus, daß ein Gericht vor oder nach Beginn des schiedsrichterlichen Verfahrens auf Antrag einer Partei eine vorläufige oder sichernde Maßnahme in bezug auf den Streitgegenstand des schiedsrichterlichen Verfahrens anordnet.*"

(It is not incompatible with an arbitration agreement for a court to grant, before or during arbitral proceedings, an interim measure of protection relating to the subject-matter of the arbitration upon request of a party.)

The translations set forth here were prepared by the German Institution of Arbitration and the German Federal Ministry of Justice and are available at www.internationaladr.com/germany1.htm.

267. Sect. 1041 ZPO 1041. The text in German is:

"*(1) Haben die Parteien nichts anderes vereinbart, so kann das Schiedsgericht auf Antrag einer Partei*

Under Sect. 1041(2), a court may, at the request of a party, but not the tribunal, enforce an arbitral interim order. It is within the discretion of the court to enforce such orders, and the court may vary arbitral orders to comply with German law and procedure.[268] However, the standards necessary for the enforcement of the arbitral order appear to be low, requiring only a valid arbitration agreement and a finding that the order is not *unverhältnismässig*, or "wholly misbalanced".[269] Moreover, a court may not enforce an arbitral order for interim relief if a party has applied for the same relief in a judicial proceeding.

Should an arbitral order that was enforced by a court later be determined to have been unwarranted ab initio, the party who benefited from the order and its enforcement may be required to indemnify the affected party for damages resulting from the order.[270]

These new provisions of the German ZPO provide the clearest and most unfettered recourse to courts by parties seeking to enforce arbitral interim measures of any of the jurisdictions surveyed. Unlike the English system, there is no requirement in the German system that the parties seek enforcement by the tribunal and, unlike the Hong Kong regime described below, the German provisions eliminate the possibility of duplicative measures by a court. Moreover, there is no express requirement in the ZPO of notification to the affected party prior to issuance of the order, perhaps leaving the door open to the issuance and enforcement of ex parte arbitral orders.[271] Enforcement,

---

vorläufige oder sichernde Maßnahmen anordnen, die es in Bezug auf den Streitgegenstand für erforderlich hält. Das Schiedsgericht kann von jeder Partei im Zusammenhang mit einer solchen Maßnahme angemessene Sicherheit verlangen.

(2) Das Gericht kann auf Antrag einer Partei die Vollziehung einer Maßnahme nach Absatz 1 zulassen, sofern nicht schon eine entsprechende Maßnahme des einstweiligen Rechtsschutzes bei einem Gericht beantragt worden ist. Es kann die Anordnung abweichend fassen, wenn dies zur Vollziehung der Maßnahme notwendig ist.

(3) Auf Antrag kann das Gericht den Beschluß nach Absatz 2 aufheben oder ändern.

(4) Erweist sich die Anordnung einer Maßnahme nach Absatz 1 als von Anfang an ungerechtfertigt, so ist die Partei, welche ihre Vollziehung erwirkt hat, verpflichtet, dem Gegner den Schaden zu ersetzten, der ihm aus der Vollziehung der Maßnahme oder dadurch entsteht, daß er Sicherheit leistet, um die Vollziehung abzuwenden. Der Anspruch kann im anhängigen schiedsrichterlichen Verfahren geltend gemacht werden."

268. SCHAEFER, *op. cit.*, fn. 242, Sect. 4.2.2.2. The "recast" language is probably meant to allow for types of relief unknown in German law to be "recast" into the familiar *Arrest* and einstweilige Verfügung. *Ibid.*

269. KOMMISSION ZUR NEUORDNUNG DES SCHIEDSVERFAHRENSRECHTS, *Bericht mit einem Diskussionsentwurf zur Neufassung des Zehnten Buches der ZPO* (Bonn: Bundesministerium der Justiz 1994) (Report of the German Ministry of Justice on the new Arbitration Act) cited in SCHAEFER, *op. cit.*, fn. 242, Sect. 4.2.2.2.

270. Sect. 1003(4) ZPO.

271. Sect. 1042(1) ZPO which provides that *"Die Parteien sind gleich zu behandeln. Jede Partei ist rechtliches Gehör zu gewähren."* (The parties shall be treated with equality and each party shall be given a full opportunity of presenting his case.) tends to undermine this view. See SCHAEFER, *op. cit.*, fn. 242, Sect. 4.2.2.2. However, Sect. 1042(1) appears to be trumped by the language of Sect. 1063(3), which provides that *"Der Vorsitzende des Zivilsenats kann ohne vorherige Anhörung des Gegners anordnen, daß der Antragsteller bis zur Entscheidung über den Antrag die Zwangsvollstreckung aus dem Schiedsspruch betreiben oder die vorläufige oder sichernde Maßnahme des Schiedsgerichts nach § 1041 vollziehen darf."* (The presiding judge of the civil court senate may issue, without prior

in any case, requires service of the order prior to or concurrently with the start of the enforcement.

d.   Hong Kong

Issuance and enforcement of interim measures by tribunals in Hong Kong-based arbitrations are controlled by Chapter 341 of the Hong Kong Ordinances, the Arbitration Ordinance (1990, as amended 2000). The ordinance tracks the UNCITRAL Model Law, and expressly provides for the power of arbitral tribunals to issue, and courts to enforce, interim measures. Courts and arbitral tribunals have concurrent jurisdiction, with none of the legislated judicial deference found in the English system.[272] Sect. 2GB sets out the powers exercisable by the tribunal and includes the power to "make orders or give directions" for a variety of interim measures.[273]

Sect. 2GG authorizes the judicial enforcement of arbitral orders,[274] including interim measures, and provides:

---

hearing of the party opposing the application, an order to the effect that, until a decision on the request has been reached, the applicant may pursue enforcement of the award or enforce the interim measure of protection of the arbitration court pursuant to Sect. 1041.). *Ibid.*

272. See Sect. 2GC Hong Kong Ordinances Ch. 341, Arbitration Ordinance (hereinafater Arbitration Ordinance). Subsections (5) and (6) specifically provide:

"(5) The powers conferred by this section can be exercised irrespective of whether or not similar powers may be exercised under section 2GB in relation to the same dispute.

(6) The Court or a judge of the Court may decline to make an order under this section in relation to a matter referred to in subsection (1) on the ground that–

(a) the matter is currently the subject of arbitration proceedings; and

(b) the Court or the judge considers it more appropriate for the matter to be dealt with by the relevant arbitral tribunal."

273. Sect. 2GB(1) Arbitration Ordinance. The powers granted in this section include specific, enumerated powers, as well as the general power to grant injunctive relief. A panel may give orders

"(a) requiring a claimant to give security for the costs of the arbitration;

(b) requiring money in dispute to be secured;

(c) directing the discovery of documents or the delivery of interrogatories;

(d) directing evidence to be given by affidavit;

(e) in relation to relevant property–

(i) directing the inspection, photographing, preservation, custody, detention or sale of the property by the tribunal, a party to the proceedings or an expert; or

(ii) directing samples to be taken from, observations to be made of, or experiments to be conducted on the property;

(f) granting interim injunctions or directing other interim measures to be taken...."

274. The Ordinance originally specified the High Court as the enforcing court, however, following the hand-over of Hong Kong to the People's Republic of China, the Ordinance was changed to make the Court of First Instance the relevant court. See SCHAEFER, *op. cit.*, fn. 242, Sect. 4.3.2.1.

"(1) An award, order or direction made or given in or in relation to arbitration proceedings by an arbitral tribunal is enforceable in the same way as a judgment, order or direction of the Court that has the same effect, but only with the leave of the Court or a judge of the Court. If that leave is given, the Court or judge may enter judgment in terms of the award, order or direction.

(2) Notwithstanding anything in this Ordinance, this section applies to an award, order and direction made or given whether in or outside Hong Kong."

Thus, an arbitral interim order, upon the obtaining of a judicial sanction, has the same effect and force as an order that originated with a court, including the threat of contempt for failure to adhere to its terms.[275]

e. Switzerland

The *Loi fédérale sur le droit international privé*[276] (Federal Law of Private International Law) (LDIP) expressly provides for court enforcement of arbitrator-ordered provisional measures. Art. 183(1) provides tribunals the authority to grant interim relief.[277] Art. 183(2) then states: "*Si la partie concernée ne s'y soumet pas volontairement, le tribunal arbitral peut requérir le concours du juge compétent. Celui-ci applique son propre droit.*"[278]

Under the Swiss regime, only the tribunal – not the applicant for relief – may petition a court for enforcement of its order. While it may be that a tribunal would as a matter of course apply to the courts upon the request of the petitioner should the opposing party fail to comply, this procedure adds an additional layer of uncertainty as to the efficacy of such measures. However, Swiss commentators appear split as to whether Art. 183(2) precludes a party from seeking enforcement of an arbitral interim order.[279] An early commentary on the law suggested that it may not be necessary for a party or the panel to await a breach of the order by the party that is subject to the order; instead, "if the circumstances and conduct of the party concerned show from the outset that such party will not comply with the tribunal's order", then the tribunal may be able to seek preemptive assistance from the court in obtaining the party's compliance with

---

275. *Ibid.*

276. In German, *Bundesgesetzüber das Internationale Privatrecht*, and Italian, *Legge federale sul diritto internazionale privato*. The law was enacted as of 18 December 1987, Chapter 12, International Arbitration. See Tijana KOJOVIĆ "Court Enforcement of Arbitral Decisions on Provisional Relief", 18 J. Int'l Arb. (2001) p. 511 at p. 515, fn. 22.

277. Art. 183(1) LDIP states: "*Sauf convention contraire, le tribunal arbitral peut ordonner des mesures provisionnelles ou des mesures conservatoires à la demande d'une partie.*" (Unless the parties have agreed otherwise, the arbitral tribunal may, at the request of a party, order provisional or protective measures.)

278. "If the party so ordered does not comply voluntarily, the arbitral tribunal may request the assistance of the court. Such court shall apply its own law."

279. KOJOVIĆ, *op. cit.*, fn. 276, p. 515 (comparing Olivier MERKT, *Les Mesures Provisoires en Droit International Privé* (1993) p. 196 (parties may seek court enforcement), with Sebastien BESSON, *Arbitrage Internationale et Mesures Provisoires* (1998) p. 305 (Art. 183(2) precludes parties from seeking enforcement)).

the order.[280]

f.   United States of America

It is well-established in the United States that courts may issue provisional measures in aid of domestic arbitration.[281] Regrettably, however, several US courts, in an early bout of excess enthusiasm for the protection of arbitral autonomy, have erroneously held that the New York Convention bars national courts from issuing provisional measures in aid of arbitrations coming within its terms.[282]

Whatever the import of this confusion on the authority of courts to render their own interim measures in aid of arbitration, courts in the United States have generally been prepared to enforce interim measures ordered by arbitral tribunals, though the cases are

---

280. Andreas BUCHER and Pierre-Yves TSCHANZ, *International Arbitration in Switzerland* (1989) p. 89, quoted in KOJOVIĆ, *op. cit.*, fn. 276, p. 515.

281. See *Murray Oil Products Co. v. Mitsui & Co.*, 146 F.2d 381, 384 (2d Cir. 1945) (L. Hand, J.). See also *Roso-Lino Beverage Distrib., Inc. v. Coca-Cola Bottling Co. of New York*, 749 F.2d 124, 125 (2d Cir. 1984); *Ortho Pharmaceuticals Corp. v. Amgen, Inc.*, 882 F.2d 806, 812 (3d Cir. 1989); *PMS Distrib. Co., Inc. v. Huber & Shuner, A.G.*, 863 F.2d 639, 642 (9th Cir. 1988); *Teradyne v. Mostek Corp.*, 797 F.2d 43, 51 (1st Cir. 1986); *Merrill Lynch, Pierce, Fenner & Smith, Inc. v. Bradley*, 756 F.2d 1048, 1052 (4th Cir. 1985); *Sauer-Getriebe KG v. White Hydraulics, Inc.*, 715 F.2d 348, 350 (7th Cir. 1983), cert. denied, 464 U.S. 1070 (1984). But see *Merrill Lynch, Pierce, Fenner & Smith, Inc. v. Hovey*, 726 F.2d 1286, 1291 (8th Cir. 1984) (court ordered interim relief not authorized by FAA); *Merrill Lynch, Pierce, Fenner & Smith, Inc. v. Scott*, No. 83-1480 (10th Cir. 12 May 1983) (unpublished summary order to stay district court injunction during pending arbitration). The Fifth Circuit has declined to reach the issue of court ordered interim relief in aid of domestic arbitration. *RGI, Inc. v. Tucker & Associates, Inc.*, 858 F.2d 227, 230 (5th Cir. 1988) (arbitration agreement expressly authorized recourse to courts for interim relief). The better reasoned rule is the one Judge Hand outlined in Murray Oil Products, _ , but a critique of the faults of decisions to the contrary is beyond the scope of this paper.

282. Compare, e.g., *McCreary Tire & Rubber Co. v. Ceat S.p.A.*, 501 F.2d 1032, 1038 (3d Cir. 1974) (courts have no power to order interim relief in aid of arbitrations under Federal Arbitration Act and New York Convention) and *ITAD Assoc. v. Podar Bros.*, 636 F.2d 75, 77 (4th Cir. 1981) (same, citing *McCreary*) and *Cooper v. Ateliers de la Motobécane S.A.*, 442 N.E.2d 1239 (N.Y. 1982) (going beyond *McCreary* to question whether attachment would ever be appropriate in arbitration matters once a stay of judicial proceedings has been granted in favor of arbitration), with *PMS Distribut. Co. v. Huber & Suhner, A.G.*, 863 F.2d 639, 641 (9th Cir. 1988) (rejecting *McCreary* and holding courts empowered to render interim relief in aid of arbitrations) and *Teradyne, Inc. v. Mostek*, 797 F.2d 43, 47 (1st Cir. 1986) (same) and *Carolina Power & Light Co. v. Uranex*, 451 F.Supp. 1044, 1052 (N.D. Cal. 1977) (same; observing that "the availability of provisional remedies encourages rather than obstructs the use of agreements to arbitrate"). See generally John A. FRASER III, "Congress Should Address the Issue of Provisional Remedies for Intellectual Property Disputes Which are Subject to Arbitration", 13 Ohio St. J. on Disp. Resol. (1998) p. 505; Charles H. BROWER II, "What I Tell You Three Times is True: U.S. Courts and Pre-Award Interim Measure Under the New York Convention", 35 Va. J. Int'l L, p. 971, (1995) pp. 986-999; Charles N. BROWER and W. Michael TUPMAN, "Court-Ordered Provisional Measures Under the New York Convention", 80 Am. J. Int'l L. (1986) p. 24. The reasons why *McCreary* is flatly wrong as a matter of both law and policy have been well-canvassed elsewhere and are beyond the scope of this paper.

few. In *Sperry International Trade v. Government of Israel*,[283] the court found an arbitral interim order to pay proceeds of a letter of credit into escrow pending the arbitration a "final order" under the New York Convention and thus enforceable. This reasoning, while reaching the correct result, may stretch the New York Convention, which under the conventional understanding is meant to apply to awards that "put an end to a dispute".[284] In reaching the same result, the court in *Southern Seas Navigation Ltd. of Monrovia v. Petroleos Mexicanos of Mexico City*[285] provided a compelling rationale for enforcing an "Interim Ruling" by the arbitrators as a "final order" under the Federal Arbitration Act:[286]

> "Just as a district court's grant of a preliminary injunction is reviewable as a discrete and separate ruling apart from any decision on the merits, so too is an arbitration award granting similar equitable relief. No undue intrusion upon the arbitral process results from a finding that such an award is ripe for confirmation....
>
> That the arbitrators labeled their decision an 'interim' award cannot overcome the fact that if an arbitral award of equitable relief based upon a finding of irreparable harm is to have any meaning at all, the parties must be capable of enforcing or vacating it at the time it is made. Such an award is not 'interim' in the sense of being an 'intermediate' step toward a further end. Rather, it is an end in itself, for its very purpose is to clarify the parties' rights in the 'interim' period pending a final decision on the merits. The only meaningful point at which such an award may be enforced is when it is made, rather than after the arbitrators have completely concluded consideration of all the parties' claims."[287]

The court held that since the applicant had demonstrated "irreparable harm" should the tribunal not issue the order, the "award" was "ripe for confirmation".[288] Other courts have followed suit.[289]

---

283. 532 F.Supp. 901 (S.D.N.Y. 1982). The District Court in *Sperry* noted that arbitrators "have power to fashion relief that a court might not properly grant". *Ibid.* at 906. Likewise, the Second Circuit observed that tribunals are vested with traditional equity powers, so that "arbitrators [have] substantial power to fashion remedies that they believe will do justice between the parties". *Sperry Intern. Trade, Inc. v. Government of Israel*, 689 F.2d 301, 306 (2d Cir. 1982).

284. See W. Laurence CRAIG, William W. PARK and Jan PAULSSON, *International Chamber of Commerce Arbitration* (2000) Sect. 26.05 (iii).

285. 606 F.Supp. 692 (S.D.N.Y. 1985).

286. 9 U.S.C. Sect. 10(a)(4) (2002).

287. *Southern Seas Navigation*, *op. cit.*, fn. 284, p. 694.

288. *Ibid.*

289. See, e.g., *Publicis Communication v. True North Communications, Inc.*, 206 F.3d 725, 729 (7th Cir. 2000); *Yasuda Fire & Marine Ins. Co. of Europe, Ltd. v. Continental Cas. Co.*, 37 F.3d 345, 348 (7th Cir. 1994); *Pacific Reinsurance Management Corp. v. Ohio Reinsurance Corp.*, 935 F.2d 1019 (9th Cir. 1991); *Home Ins. Co. v. RHA/Pennsylvania Nursing Homes, Inc.*, 127 F. Supp.2d 482, 489 (S.D.N.Y. 2001).

2.   *Trends in the Enforcement of Arbitral Provisional Measures in National Courts*

This survey demonstrates a variety of approaches to court enforcement of arbitral provisional orders. But whether a regime places the onus for enforcement (at least initially) mostly on the panel, such as the English and Swiss systems, or whether it permits free access to the courts quickly to enforce such relief, as do Hong Kong and, to a lesser extent, Germany, or whether enforcement is somewhat ad hoc, depending on the character of the order, all of these regimes recognize that "if temporary equitable relief is to have any meaning, the relief must be enforceable at the time it is granted, not after an arbitrator's final decision on the merits".[290] What is needed, then, is a regime that will provide a degree of certainty for litigants requesting, and tribunals ordering, such relief.

3.   *A Model Law Provision for the Enforcement of Arbitral Provisional Measures*

The differing approaches to the enforcement of interim measures of protection issued by international arbitral tribunals in national courts have provided an impetus in UNCITRAL to develop a model provision to facilitate the harmonization of this area of law. The work of UNCITRAL has partially relied on the practice generated by the New York Convention as well as the UNCITRAL Model Law provisions dealing with the recognition and enforcement of arbitral awards. The issues addressed have largely revolved around how the grounds for excluding enforcement for arbitral awards apply to interim measures and what distinctive considerations need to be addressed for ex parte and inter partes interim measures.

a.   *The recent work of UNCITRAL*
The enforcement of interim measures issued by arbitral tribunals is not necessarily undertaken in a similar manner to final awards in national courts. The prevailing view has been that even if interim measures are termed an "award", the New York Convention does not cover such awards.[291] Instead, national legislation either provides expressly for recognition and enforcement or is silent on the enforceability of an arbitral tribunal's orders of interim measures.[292] Orders of interim measures are different than final awards in that the measures may have been granted ex parte or may be altered following subsequent review by the arbitral tribunal.[293] To account for these features, a national court could be empowered to modify its order as well, or to make the order for enforcement dependent on an obligation of the requesting party to inform the court promptly of any amendment to the interim measures issued by the arbitral tribunal.[294]

In preparation for the thirty-sixth session of the UNCITRAL Working Group on Arbitration, the Secretariat prepared a draft article on the enforcement of interim

---

290. *Pacific Reinsurance*, *op. cit.*, fn. 289, p. 1023.
291. "Working Paper 108", *op. cit.*, fn. 10, p. 20.
292. *Ibid.*, p. 21.
293. *Ibid.*, p. 20.
294. *Ibid.*, pp. 23-24.

measures of protection, which drew on earlier discussions.[295] An initial proposal had been based on Arts. 35 and 36 of the UNCITRAL Model Law.[296] Variant 1 of this draft provision proposed that interim measures should be enforced unless an application had already been made to a court; the arbitration agreement was not valid; the party against whom the interim measure was invoked did not have proper notice or was unable to present its case; the interim measures had been set aside or amended; the enforcing court could not have ordered the type of interim measure; or the recognition or enforcement of the interim measure would be contrary to the public policy of the relevant state. These alternatives largely drew on the grounds for recognition and enforcement of final arbitral awards, with modifications to account for the special nature of provisional measures. The other alternative, Variant 2, provided more simply that the court could order the enforcement of interim measures of protection regardless of the country in which they were issued. Variant 2 thus allowed the national court a degree of discretion rather than requiring enforcement unless certain conditions were met. The drawback of the discretionary approach was that it could result in a lack of uniformity rather than creating harmonization.[297] Overall, Variant 1 was preferred as the basis for further discussions.

When members of the Commission began discussion on this issue, it was readily agreed that consideration should be given to the enforcement of interim measures both in and outside the state where the arbitration takes place.[298] As noted, the Secretariat's proposal anticipated enforcement of an interim measure order from an arbitral tribunal regardless of the country where it was issued.

The draft article set out the grounds on which a competent court must refuse to recognize or enforce an interim measure of protection issued by an arbitral tribunal. These conditions are intended to limit the number of circumstances in which the court must refuse recognition and enforcement. The grounds for refusal are divided between, first, those that are taken into account on the motion of the respondent and, second, those taken into account on the court's own motion. The first situation is where the party against whom the measure is invoked furnishes proof to the effect that the relevant arbitration agreement is not valid;[299] that the party was not given proper notice of the appointment of an arbitrator or the institution of arbitral proceedings; or that the interim measure has been terminated, suspended, or amended by the arbitral tribunal.

A further ground for a court to refuse recognition or enforcement of an arbitral interim measure is where the party against whom the order was granted furnishes proof that essentially the same application was made to a court of the state hearing the request

---

295. "Working Paper 119", *op. cit.*, fn. 225, p. 26.

296. "Report of the Secretary-General, Settlement of Commercial Disputes: Possible uniform rules on certain issues concerning settlement of commercial disputes: written form for arbitration agreement, interim measures of protection, conciliation", UNCITRAL, 33d Sess., UN Doc. A/CN/WG.II/WP.110 (20 November – 1 December 2000) (hereinafter Working Paper 110) p. 21.

297. *Ibid.*, p. 23.

298. "Working Paper 108", *op. cit.*, fn. 10, p. 19.

299. "Working Paper 110", *op. cit.*, fn. 296, p. 41.

for enforcement or recognition. This draft provision addresses situations where a request for the same or similar measure is pending with the court; the request has been denied by the court; or the court has granted the same or a similar measure.[300]

A court may also refuse to recognize or enforce the interim measure on the basis that the measure was granted ex parte. This ground was included in response to concerns about the enforcement of ex parte interim measures, especially since the major arbitration institutions did not allow for the issuance of such measures without notice. An earlier view had been that enforcement before national courts could proceed if the ex parte interim measures were limited to a fixed period of time and that the responding party could fully present its case upon expiration of the measure and before any order maintaining or revoking the measure.[301] The Secretariat proposed several variants that would allow for such orders to be recognized or enforced. Variant 1 permits recognition and enforcement if the measure is ordered to be effective for a certain time period and the enforcement is requested before the expiry of that period. Variant 2 allows for recognition and enforcement if the arbitral tribunal has confirmed the interim measure after the other party has been able to present its case with respect to the interim measure. Variant 3 permits recognition and enforcement if the arbitral tribunal exercised its discretion in deciding that the interim measure of protection could only be effective if issued by the court without notice to the party against whom the measure is invoked.

The second situation where a court must refuse to enforce or recognize an interim measure granted by an arbitral tribunal is where the court finds that

> "[t]he measure requested is incompatible with the powers conferred upon the court by its procedural laws, unless the court decides to reformulate the measure to the extent necessary to adopt it to its own powers and procedures for the purpose of enforcing the measure."

This provision was included in response to an early proposal that only those measures that were in compliance with certain procedural conditions of the state of the court where enforcement was being sought were to be enforceable.[302] This issue is linked to the question of what degree of discretion the court should be allowed in determining how the measures would be enforced and whether the interim measures could be adapted to the procedural and enforcement system of the court.[303] To allow the court to issue an enforcement order that deviated from the interim measures issued by the arbitral tribunal raised the risk that the court would have to repeat the decision making process that had been undertaken in the arbitral tribunal.[304] This concern is not squarely addressed in the Secretariat's proposal. A provision is instead included to the effect that the court may not modify the substance of the interim measures. The court may also

---

300. "Working Paper 113", *op. cit.*, fn. 224, p. 13.
301. "Working Paper 110", *op. cit.*, fn. 296, p. 25.
302. "Working Paper 108", *op. cit.*, fn. 10, pp. 20-21.
303. *Ibid.*, p. 23.
304. "Working Paper 110", *op. cit.*, fn. 296, p. 22.

refuse to enforce where to do so would be contrary to the public policy of the state.

The party seeking recognition or enforcement is required to inform the court of any termination, suspension or amendment of the measure granted by the arbitral tribunal.

b. A proposal

The debates in UNCITRAL on the enforcement of arbitral interim measures of protection have not progressed to the same extent as those addressing the standards for the issuance of interim measures. Nonetheless, several decisions have been taken that have shaped the most recent debates. In particular, the decision was made to employ a formula that provided that interim measures were to be enforced in national courts, regardless of where the order had been made, subject to certain conditions. In making this decision, the Working Group discarded an alternative that would have provided that all awards be enforced, but at the discretion of the court. In choosing to avoid the pitfalls such discretion would create, the Commission opted for a more complex rule for the enforcement of arbitral interim measures.

It is submitted here that the better approach would be to retain a greater degree of simplicity by matching the obligation to enforce interim measures of protection to that to enforce final awards. As with the draft considered in the Working Group, the basic presumption should be that interim measures of protection ordered by arbitral tribunals will be enforced by national courts. The range of exceptions included in the current text under consideration reflects grounds for refusing recognition or enforcement of arbitral awards that are incorporated in the New York Convention and the Model Law. Rather than reiterate those grounds, enforcement of interim measures should be assimilated directly to enforcement of final awards, and hence a cross-reference to the grounds stipulated in Art. 36 of the Model Law, which was based on the New York Convention, should suffice. The draft can then address any matters on which the character of interim measures requires specific divergence – principally with respect to the question of notice and ex parte interim measures. Enactments in national jurisdictions, particularly in German law, provide guidance in drafting a straightforward text. In short, the proposal here is for radical simplicity.

In light of the survey of national jurisdictions undertaken earlier in this paper, and of the work thus far of the Working Group, it is submitted here that the text should read:

> "*Recognition and enforcement of interim measures of protection*
> 1. Interim measures of protection issued and in effect in accordance with article 17, irrespective of the country in which they were issued, and whether reflected in an interim award or otherwise, shall be recognized as binding and, upon application in writing to the competent court, be enforced subject to the provisions of articles 35 and 36, except as otherwise provided in this article. Any determination made on any ground set forth in article 36 in ruling on such an application shall be effective only for purposes of that application.
>
> 2. (a) Recognition or enforcement of interim measures of protection shall not be refused on the ground that the party against whom the measures are directed did not have notice of the proceedings on the request for the interim measures or an opportunity to be heard if

(i) the arbitral tribunal has determined that it is necessary to proceed in that manner in order to ensure that the measure is effective, and

(ii) the court independently makes the same determination.

(b) The court may condition the continued recognition or enforcement of an interim measure issued without notice or an opportunity to be heard on any conditions of notice or hearing that it may prescribe.

3. [A court may reformulate the interim measure to the extent necessary to conform the measure to its procedural law, provided that the court does not modify the substance of the interim measure.]

4. While an application for recognition or enforcement of an interim measure is pending, or an order recognizing or enforcing the interim measures is in effect, the party who is seeking or has obtained enforcement of an interim measure shall promptly inform the court of any modification, suspension, or termination of that measure."

i. Paragraph 1: enforcement of interim measures generally

When an arbitral tribunal orders interim measures, it acts on the same authority by which it renders a final award. Indeed, as canvassed here, the very purpose of interim measures is to ensure the effectiveness of the final award. It follows that, if states are prepared to lend their enforcement machinery to the enforcement of final awards, they should lend it as well to the enforcement of interim measures.

Hence, it is submitted here that the best approach to the enforcement article is to simply make interim measures subject to the same standards of enforcement as final awards. In doing so, it is further submitted, only minor adjustments will need to be made. Significantly, the enforcement clause should simply state that interim measures may be enforced upon application in writing to the competent court, subject to the provisions of Arts. 35 and 36 and the specific provisions of the enforcement article.

Consistent with the proposal made with respect to the article on authority, the proposal contemplates that interim measures shall be enforceable regardless of the form in which they are rendered. It would remain advisable, however, for a tribunal wishing to have the interim measure enforced to style it an interim award.

Proposals have been made to set forth as a ground for refusal to enforce that the measure has been modified, suspended or terminated. There should be no question that a measure that has been modified by the tribunal that issued it cannot be enforced on its original, pre-modification terms, any more than a final award that had been corrected under Art. 33 could be enforced in its uncorrected form. Equally, a measure that is no longer effective because its term has expired cannot be subject to enforcement. If modification, suspension or termination means that there is no longer a measure to enforce, they should not be treated as grounds for refusal to enforce. The proposed text inserts the phrase "and in effect" after "issued" and before "in accordance with article 17" in the first paragraph, setting out the scope of the affirmative obligation to enforce, in order to eliminate any possible confusion on the point.

The final sentence of this provision is intended to make clear that any rulings on an application for provisional measures are, indeed, provisional, and do not bind either the court or the arbitral tribunal in subsequent proceedings.

ii. Paragraph (2): enforcement of ex parte interim measures

The recognition and enforcement of ex parte interim measures poses particular issues. As discussed in the section on standards above, ex parte interim measures encroach on the fundamental right to be heard, and the right to be heard is protected in the enforcement article of the Model Law and in corresponding provisions of the New York Convention.

The Working Group canvassed a wide variety of possible safeguards that might address the concerns of those opposed to authorizing arbitral tribunals to issue ex parte interim measures. It is submitted here, as it was proposed in the Working Group, that the best and definitive safeguard would be to require the enforcing court to make an independent determination that it was necessary to proceed ex parte in order that the measure be effective.[305] Notice and an opportunity to be heard are fundamental requirements not just of arbitral procedure but of any procedure meeting minimal requirements of justice. It is therefore appropriate that a party seeking to invoke the state's judicial power to enforce the results of an arbitral process independently satisfy that judicial power of the need to depart on a temporary and provisional basis from fundamental process.

It is equally appropriate to give the enforcing court authority to condition enforcement on whatever requirements of notice and hearing it deems appropriate in the circumstances. Typically, the court will allow the proceeding to go ex parte only as long as necessary to achieve its purpose and will then arrange promptly to hear the restrained party.

The reference to the tribunal's determination on the need to proceed ex parte is intended to provide an incentive for arbitral tribunals wishing to see their interim measures enforced to lay out the basis for that finding.

It is intended that the ex parte measures be enforceable for no longer a period than the arbitral tribunal has the authority to make them effective, after which the normal regime of interim measures issued upon notice, also subject to enforcement, would come into play. For interim measures granted under Art. 17 in the enforcing state or elsewhere, that period would be twenty days.

iii. Multiple applications

There is substantial support for the inclusion in the enforcement article of a provision allowing the court to refuse enforcement if an application for the same measures has already been made to a court. It is submitted here that such a provision is inadvisable.

In a situation of genuine urgency, it will frequently be uncertain from where relief might most immediately be obtained. Parties may in such a situation file simultaneous applications in different fora. Courts would normally expect, and counsel be well advised to provide, advice as to related proceedings in other fora. But the pendency of a similar application in another forum should not automatically require a refusal to enforce. Courts are perfectly capable of assessing the need for urgency, deciding whether to go forward or await the determination of another court, and, if they wait, assessing the impact on the application before them of another court's action. Courts

---

305. "Working Group Report 508", *op. cit.*, fn. 226, p. 22.

also have means of dealing with abusive litigation.

iv.   Paragraph 3: conformity to procedural law

The Secretariat's draft text anticipates an exception to recognition and enforcement when issues of procedural law impact on the national court's means to enforce the measures granted by the arbitral tribunal. In accordance with the general assumption that interim measures of protection issued by arbitral tribunals are to be enforced in national courts, the prospect of divergence between the enforcing court's procedural law and the obligation to enforce should not provide a means of avoiding enforcement.

One solution would be to include no provision on the point. The effect would be to require enforcement on the tribunal's terms notwithstanding any such divergence. In effect, by adopting the enforcement article, the state would amend its procedural law insofar as necessary to enforce arbitral awards.

It is submitted here that the better solution is to recognize the court's authority to reformulate the measure as necessary to align the measure with its procedural laws and to achieve the goal sought in the substance of the measure issued by the arbitral tribunal. While it must be recognized that the difficulty of distinguishing between procedure and substance in the context of an interim measure may leave the enforcing court greater latitude than is intended, the judgment here is that some margin of procedural discretion will, overall, operate to facilitate enforcement rather than frustrate it.

Under either alternative, the incentive of a party requesting an interim measure to have it enforced should lead the party to request a measure whose enforcement would be compatible with the procedural law of the jurisdiction or jurisdictions in which the party expects to enforce it if need be.

v.   Paragraph 4: notice of modification, suspension or termination

The proposed text imposes an obligation on the applicant to advise the enforcing court of any change in the status of the measure sought to be enforced or already enforced.

V.   CONCLUSION

The authority to issue interim measures of protection is inherent in, and essential to, the authority of courts and tribunals. At the most basic level, courts and tribunals function to resolve disputes between parties. If they are to do so, they must have the means while the dispute is pending to control the actions of the parties that have submitted the dispute to them to the end that the ultimate decision will count. Without that prospect, the arbitral process, no less than the judicial process, would be undermined. UNCITRAL's work to define the standards by which arbitral tribunals may issue interim measures and the basis on which courts must enforce them is therefore commensurate in importance with its extremely important prior work in the field of international arbitration.

Interim Measures of Protection – a European and Continental Perspective

*Jacomijn J. van Haersolte-van Hof**

TABLE OF CONTENTS

I.   INTRODUCTION

Within UNCITRAL, over the last few years, considerable time and effort have been invested in exploring the use of interim measures in and in support of arbitration. Donald Donovan[1] has provided a general and comprehensive outline of the current status of the work of UNCITRAL and expressed his view thereon. In this contribution, an attempt will be made to comment on this topic by highlighting a number of issues. By necessity, and also to juxtapose the comments made by Donovan as an American lawyer, these comments are confined to a European perspective and in fact reflect a continental European view.

The current status is as follows. First, there is a draft Art. 17 of the UNCITRAL Model Law (UML) regarding arbitral-tribunal-ordered interim measures.[2] In the various sessions of UNCITRAL and the Working Group on Arbitration this draft provision has been fairly extensively discussed. This provision states:

"(1) Unless otherwise agreed by the parties, the arbitral tribunal may, at the request of a party, order any party to take such interim measure of protection as the arbitral tribunal may consider necessary [in respect of the subject-matter of the dispute].
(2) The party requesting the interim measure should furnish proof that:
(a) there is an urgent need for the measure applied for;
(b) a significant degree of harm will result if the interim measure is not ordered; and

---

*   Attorney, De Brauw Blackstone Westbroek.
1.   See "The Scope and Enforceability of Provisional Measures in International Commercial Arbitration: A Survey of Jurisdictions, the Work of UNCITRAL and Proposals for Moving Forward", this volume, pp. 82-149.
2.   This text was presented to the Working Group on Arbitration for its 36th session (4-8 March 2002) in A/CN.9/WG.II/WP.119

(c) there is a likelihood of the applicant for the measure succeeding on the merits of the underlying case.

(3) The arbitral tribunal may require any party to provide appropriate security in connection with such measure.

(4) An interim measure of protection is any temporary measure [, whether it is established in the form of an arbitral award or in another form,] ordered by the arbitral tribunal pending the issuance of the award by which the dispute is finally decided. For the purposes of this article reference to an interim measure includes:

Variant 1

(a) a measure to maintain the status quo pending determination of the questions at issue;

(b) a measure providing a preliminary means of securing assets out of which an award may be satisfied; or

(c) a measure to restrain conduct by a defendant to prevent current or imminent future harm.

Variant 2

(a) a measure to avoid or minimize prejudice, loss or damage; or

(b) a measure to facilitate later enforcement of an award.

(5) The arbitral tribunal may, where it is necessary to ensure that an interim measure is effective, grant a measure [for a period not exceeding [...] days] [without notice to the party against whom the measure is directed] [before the party against whom the measure is directed has had an opportunity to respond] only where:

(a) it is necessary to ensure that the measure is effective;

(b) the applicant for the measure provides appropriate security in connection with the measure;

(c) the applicant for the measure can demonstrate the urgent necessity of the measure; and

(d) [the measure would be supported by a preponderance of considerations of fairness].

[(6) The party to whom the measure under paragraph (5) is directed shall be given notice of the measure and an opportunity to be heard at the earliest practicable time.]

(7) A measure granted under paragraph (5) may be extended or modified after the party to whom it is directed has been given notice and an opportunity to respond.

[(8) An interim measure of protection may be modified or terminated [on the request of a party] if the circumstances referred to in paragraph (2) have changed after the issuance of the measure.]

[(9) The party who requested the issuance of an interim measure of protection shall, from the time of the request onwards, inform the court promptly of any substantial change of circumstances referred to in paragraph (2).]"

Furthermore, there is a draft provision in WP. 119 entitled "Enforcement of Interim

Measures of Protection" regarding the enforcement of such tribunal-ordered interim measures. This provision states:

"(1) Upon an application by an interested party, made with the approval of the arbitral tribunal, the competent court shall refuse to recognize and enforce an interim measure of protection referred to in article 17, irrespective of the country in which it was ordered, if:
(a) The party against whom the measure is invoked furnishes proof that

(i) *[Variant 1]* The arbitration agreement referred to in article 7 is not valid
[Variant 2] The arbitration agreement referred to in article 7 appears to not be valid, in which case the court may refer the issue of the [jurisdiction of the arbitral tribunal] [validity of the arbitration agreement] to be decided by the arbitral tribunal in accordance with article 16 of this Law];
(ii) The party against whom the interim measure is invoked was not given proper notice of the appointment of an arbitrator or of the arbitral proceedings [in which case the court may suspend the enforcement proceedings until the parties have been heard by the arbitral tribunal]; or
(iii) The party against whom the interim measure is invoked was unable to present its case with respect to the interim measure [in which case the court may suspend the enforcement proceedings until the parties have been heard by the arbitral tribunal]; or
(iv) The interim measure has been terminated, suspended or amended by the arbitral tribunal.
(b) The court finds that:
(i) The measure requested is incompatible with the powers conferred upon the court by its procedural laws, unless the court decides to reformulate the measure to the extent necessary to adapt it to its own powers and procedures for the purpose of enforcing the measure; or
(ii) The recognition or enforcement of the interim measure would be contrary to the public policy of this State.
(2) Upon application by an interested party, made with the approval of the arbitral tribunal, the competent court may, in its discretion, refuse to recognize and enforce an interim measure of protection referred to in article 17, irrespective of the country in which it was ordered, if the party against whom the measure is invoked furnishes proof that application for the same or similar interim measure has been made to a court in this State, regardless of whether the court has taken a decision on the application.
(3) The party who is seeking enforcement of an interim measure shall promptly inform the court of any termination, suspension or amendment of that measure.
(4) In reformulating the measure under paragraph (1)(b)(i), the court shall not modify the substance of the interim measure.
(5) Paragraph (1)(a)(iii) does not apply
[Variant 1] to an interim measure of protection that was ordered without notice to the party against whom the measure is invoked provided that the measure was

ordered to be effective for a period not exceeding [30] days and the enforcement of the measure is requested before the expiry of that period.

[Variant 2] to an interim measure of protection that was ordered without notice to the party against whom the measure is invoked provided that such interim measure is confirmed by the arbitral tribunal after the other party has been able to present its case with respect to the interim measure.

[Variant 3] if the arbitral tribunal, in its discretion, determines that, in light of the circumstances referred to in article 17(2), the interim measure of protection can be effective only if the enforcement order is issued by the court without notice to the party against whom the measure is invoked."

What is not yet available at this stage is a draft on court-ordered interim measures. Art. 9 UML contains a provision that requesting interim measures from a court, and for a court to grant these, does not constitute a violation of the arbitration agreement. Potentially, this provision could be seen as the nucleus of a provision on court-ordered interim measures, but it is far from complete, as was recognized at UNCITRAL.[3]

Finally, what is certainly not available at this stage is the necessary corollary of that, an UNCITRAL provision on the enforcement abroad of court-ordered measures issued in support of arbitration.

The purpose of this contribution is twofold. First, the existing drafts will be commented on, including some suggestions as to which elements may need to be reconsidered. In doing so, reference will be made to the practice relating to the Brussels Convention on Jurisdiction and Enforcement of Judgments in Civil and Commercial Matters (Brussels Convention),[4] and in particular the case law of the European Court of Justice (ECJ). Second, some suggestions will be made for those issues which have at this stage not yet been incorporated into actual draft provisions. Here again, apart from national experience, reference will be made to the practice under the Brussels Convention.

II.   COMMENTS ON THE EXISTING DRAFTS

This is not the time or place to attempt a detailed analysis of all aspects of Art. 17 and its corollary, the draft Enforcement Provision. Rather, it appears sensible to highlight one (obvious) issue, hopefully to contribute to a further discussion. This issue is that of ex parte measures, currently laid down in Art. 17(5). A large amount of the time available, especially in the latest discussions at UNCITRAL, seems to have been devoted to this particularly complicated aspect. Possibly, this energy could be refocused and

---

3. A/CN.9/WG.II/WP.119, para. 75.
4. 7 September 1968, Bulletin EC Supp. 2/69. In the meantime, the Brussels Convention has been converted into Regulation No. 44/2001, dated 22 December 2000, Pb EG 44 (2001) No. L 12, p. 1, which entered into force on 1 March 2002 for all EU Member States except Denmark. For practical purposes, reference will hereinafter be made to the Brussels Convention. The text of the provision most pertinent for this discussion, Art. 24 (see hereinafter), remains unchanged.

redirected.

Let us first go back one or two steps. The current draft of Art. 17 presupposes that ex parte measures are in essence a sub-category of the more general category of interim measures for which certain prerequisites apply.[5] In particular, there should be an urgent need for such a measure, there should be a significant degree of harm if the measure is not ordered and there should be the likelihood or substantial possibility of the applicant being successful on the merits of the underlying case.

Furthermore, it should be kept in mind that when UNCITRAL initiated the debate on interim measures, some sort of categorization was made at the outset. Initially three categories of measures were distinguished, namely those facilitating the conduct of the arbitral proceedings, measures to avoid loss or damage and to maintain the state of affairs, and measures to facilitate later enforcement of the award.[6]

Subsequently, a broad distinction into two categories was discussed, namely measures to avoid or minimize prejudice, loss or damage, and enforcement facilitation measures.[7] At that time, it was already recognized that the distinction between the various categories might not always be clear, and consequently it was considered that UNCITRAL's work should not reflect or encourage such distinction. However, it is suggested that a further review of this categorization would be useful, especially in the context of ex parte measures. For that purpose a determinant factor is whether a certain measure would by its very nature be frustrated without an element of surprise. If one applies this criterion it is apparent that some of the measures listed in the first category are in fact very similar to enforcement facilitation measures where there is almost always the need for a surprise measure. A freeze of assets will have little effect if it has been pre-announced. This equally applies to some of the measures listed in the first group, such as sequestration.

These measures are clearly requested in the interest of one of the parties – the party requesting the order – and the party to whom the measure is addressed will usually have a diametrically opposed interest. This is quite different for many of the other measures of the first category, such as the inspection of goods in dispute, or the sale of perishable goods. If one has a dispute about a cargo of fresh strawberries one may dispute somebody's entitlement to the cargo, but no one will dispute that the goods should be sold before there are no more strawberries left to argue about. One can then have a dispute about the price or the place where the strawberries are sold but there is no reason why such measures could not be discussed with both parties. This is even more true for the measures which require an active input of the party against whom the measure is sought, such as those where a party is ordered to continue working on a project pending the final determination of the legal dispute. To give an example: a request to decide overnight whether a soccer player can play the next day, pending

---

5. There has been some discussion whether the wording of paragraphs 2 and 5 should be amended to clarify this point further, but as far as the written record shows, there appears to be consensus that interim measures covered under paragraph 5 should at least meet the requirements of paragraph 2 (A/CN.9/508, para. 83).

6. A/CN.9/WG.II/WP.108, para. 63.

7. *Op. cit.*, fn. 3, paras. 16-18.

discussions regarding the payment of transfer monies.

In the latter type of disputes it is not immediately obvious why one should even consider the option of ex parte measures. Only where the party against whom the measure is addressed could frustrate the measure before it is issued, should one contemplate its use. So although on the one hand UNCITRAL's reluctance to include a strict categorization is understandable, some sort of classification would be useful.

The next question is, if one allows ex parte measures for a limited number of scenarios, under which conditions can these be ordered, and furthermore, is the tribunal indeed the appropriate authority to deal with these measures? To begin with the latter question, is it appropriate for an arbitral tribunal to deal with ex parte measures at all or should this authority be left to the domestic courts? The discussion at UNCITRAL has focused to a large extent, or at least the written records do, on the formal requirements and conditions. The – more principle – question outlined above has been dealt with rather summarily. There was a discussion whether allowing ex parte measures could be deemed compatible with the requirements of equal access to the tribunal and allowing a full opportunity to address one's case. This was deemed to be the case, in which context it was discussed that similar requirements apply in courts and that that has not prevented national systems from allowing the possibility of ordering ex parte measures.[8] This argument ignores, however, that court systems are not consensus-based. The attribution of court power is laid down in constitutions and comparable instruments and is a fundamental element of a state's system. Moreover, in each national system there are other, additional, safeguards, which taken together, ensure a fair and equal system of justice. So although the same fundamental principles do play a role in both court and arbitral procedures, they do not have the same significance and scope.

This leads to the second question, the prerequisite conditions for ordering ex parte measures. The current draft is based on a two-tiered system. Art. 17(2) contains the general requirements for interim measures which are supplemented in Art. 17(5). Of the general requirements, the most far-reaching is the requirement of "likelihood" or substantial possibility of success on the merits. Often, at the time when a freezing order or arrest of assets is sought, the merits of the case have not yet been sufficiently explored to come to such an evaluation. Not every national system in fact requires such a review.

As to the specific requirements, the latest draft reflects even more strongly a national-law-based attempt to accommodate these fundamental concerns for justice when this far-reaching power is given to arbitral tribunals. Earlier documents already contained an occasional – and apparently innocuous – reference to the requirement of "full and frank disclosure". The full meaning and consequences of this requirement were not spelled out until the latest session earlier this year in New York. At that time, a draft provision was discussed explicitly laying down the principle that an ex parte measure would require a party to inform the tribunal of all potentially relevant circumstances including those adverse to the requesting party's interests. This, apparently, is the Anglo-Saxon method of justifying ex parte measures. It is not argued that this is an inappropriate solution. It is, however, a concept that will be very difficult to comprehend and to apply for lawyers, certainly practitioners, coming from a different

---

8. A/CN.9/508, para. 77.

— civil law — background.

First, there might be ethical concerns, but those should not be insoluble if the requirement of disclosing adverse circumstances were explicitly incorporated in a statutory provision. But how would one apply this obligation? Under civil law systems one is not required to brief a court or tribunal on all relevant circumstances,[9] certainly not at the stage when one applies for ex parte interim measures such as a request to arrest assets. Presumably in systems where this requirement does apply there are sanctions, such as contempt of court, if one does not comply with such requirement. Those sanctions would not be available in systems where this notion is unknown and it is doubtful whether the concept would be very effective.

It may be illustrative to consider briefly an alternative method of dealing with ex parte measures. In The Netherlands, such measures, for example the request to arrest a vessel, are granted on the basis of a request in which one alleges that the requesting party has a valid claim, such as a right to payment of invoices that are due. In some cases some further requirements apply and in particular the requirement that one demonstrates a risk of concealment of the assets. In practice, a very basic and minimal explanation is sufficient. The leave for arrest is then enforceable. The safeguards boil down to the following. If leave for arrest is granted, proceedings on the merits must be instituted (before a court or tribunal) within a period prescribed by the court. Furthermore, once leave is granted and the other party is notified of the actual arrest, the respondent may institute summary proceedings requesting the lifting of the arrest. In doing so, a showing must be made that there is not a prima facie case, and the party who requested the measure will need to show the opposite. Depending on the type of measure, one can expect to be heard in court in a very short time, even in a matter of hours, for instance if a ship is about to leave, or slightly longer if there is less immediacy. If ultimately, the case on the merits is lost, there is a strict liability for what turned out to be an unlawful arrest. Additional factors playing a role in practice are first, that reasonable constraint is applied in practice, and second, and this is related thereto, that whereas it is easy for one party to make an arrest, it is equally easy for the other party to do so. There is, thus, an informal, but highly effective, system of "checks and balances". It is not proposed that this in itself is a reason to advocate the system as it is applied in The Netherlands, which is, incidentally, not one of the countries reviewed in the overview of standards for granting provisional measures prepared by Donald Donovan. Rather, the point is that each national system has a different and possibly equally effective way of dealing with ex parte measures and that one should be cautious about importing an isolated element of a foreign system by means of inclusion in the UNCITRAL Model Law. These elements are not stand-alone building bricks that can be incorporated at random.

If this is not deemed convincing, an additional consideration is proposed. So far, the discussion within UNCITRAL was focussed on the issuing of ex parte measures, and the

---

9. The recent changes in the Dutch Code of Civil Procedure do contain some elements in the direction that a party should not merely state its own views but also anticipate arguments and defenses the other party is likely to bring up. This trend is far from developed at this stage, and would also appear to go much less far than the requirement discussed by UNCITRAL.

draft provision on enforcement has not yet been discussed with the same level of attention. It certainly deserves careful attention and the position expressed in New York seems correct that it is doubtful whether interim measures ordered ex parte would still be attractive in practice if the Model Law made them unenforceable.[10]

There is a relevant precedent in this context. Art. 24 of the Brussels Convention provides that:

> "Application may be made to the courts of a Contracting State for such provisional, including protective, measures as may be available under the law of that State, even if, under this Convention, the courts of another Contracting State have jurisdiction as to the substance of the matter."

On the basis of the Convention, a decision based on this provision may in principle be enforced in the other Member States. However, case law of the ECJ confirms that ex parte measures are not covered by Art. 24, and may not be enforced in other Member States. In *Denilauler/Couchet Frères*,[11] Couchet Frères, the claimant in the main proceedings, had requested and received authorization from a French court to have Denilauler's bank assets at a German bank frozen as security. That order was enforceable and issued ex parte. Rejecting the suggestion that the Convention should apply to all judgments, whether adversarial or issued ex parte, the ECJ held that all provisions of the Convention express the intention that judicial decisions take place in such a way that the rights of defense are observed. For interim measures, special rules were contemplated. Such measures require particular care on the part of the court and detailed knowledge of the actual circumstances in which the measure is to take effect. The ECJ referred to the possibility to impose a time limit on an order or other guarantees such as bank guarantees or nominate a sequestrator. The courts of the place where the relevant assets subject to the measures sought are located were deemed best able to assess the situation. Art. 24 does not preclude the subsequent enforcement of such measures elsewhere when they are issues in adversary proceedings. The liberal and simplified enforcement procedures of the Convention do not, however, apply to ex parte measures.

To conclude, first, it is not helpful to suggest that all interim measures could potentially be ordered ex parte and that imposing additional, formal, pre-requisites is sufficient. Some measures do not lend themselves to ex parte orders at all, and if they do, it is conceivable that different requirements should apply. Second, ex parte measures are so intertwined with national systems that it is unattractive to implement one system's mechanism as a model, which may then have to be used in a very different system where it does not fit well. Third, the proof of the pudding is in the eating: even in a system as well developed as that of the Brussels Convention, enforcement of cross-border interim measures ordered ex parte was deemed incompatible with the principles of due process. That would seem to apply with even greater force in respect of tribunal-ordered measures.

---

10. *Op. cit.*, fn. 8, para. 79.
11. Judgment 21 May 1980, Case 125/79, Jur. 1980, p. 1553.

III. OMISSIONS IN THE CURRENT DRAFTS

The most striking omission at this stage is probably the lack of any draft provision dealing with court-ordered interim measures. This is particularly noticeable because UNCITRAL itself has recognized that there is a need for a provision in this respect and that it is desirable that parties have access both to the tribunal and to the court to request interim measures.[12] This is especially the case because as matters stand now, national laws are highly divergent when it comes to whether or not courts will issue measures in support of arbitration, and if so, under which circumstances and in what form and shape.[13] In some cases there is very little support of national courts, or uncertainty, and in other cases much more involvement, and some would say too much interference.

Given this divergence, it is necessary to contemplate how the boundaries between tribunal-ordered and court-ordered measures should be defined. Until now, within UNCITRAL, the focus seems to have been on the possibilities for tribunal-ordered measures, probably largely as a result of the notion that it is much more difficult to unify court-ordered measures which are, even more than tribunal-ordered measures, embedded in national systems of civil procedure.

That may be the case, but the problems of concurrent power require particular attention. A specific concern based on experience in a jurisdiction where both courts and tribunals have far-reaching powers to order interim measures, is that it is necessary to be realistic in setting out these boundaries. It is unhelpful if, possibly as a result of the good work of UNCITRAL, laws will be enacted bestowing extensive authority on tribunals to order interim measures, when ultimately these measures are unenforceable and ineffective. Such abstract powers would in practice limit the powers of courts, whereas the tribunals would not be able to fulfill the need for interim measures.

Consequently, it is crucial to deal with court-ordered interim measures, and moreover, to do so in parallel and simultaneously with the drafting of provisions on tribunal-ordered measures. UNCITRAL's question whether the Working Group might wish to consider whether a provision clarifying the issue of the courts' power should be formulated[14] should be answered with an emphatic "yes".

Two aspects in particular should be regulated: which matters are best dealt with by courts and how; and second, which courts? It follows from the above that the type of measures which require an element of surprise, security-type measures, often related to the ultimate enforcement of an award, may best be dealt with in courts. This is a fortiori true for measures involving third parties. For some measures, it is fairly obvious that the tribunal is best suited to deal with them, for example, if the requested measure requires specific expertise, which a general court may lack. Nevertheless, as a general principle it is proposed that unless there is clear reason to distinguish, the same type of provision should apply for court-ordered and for tribunal-ordered measures. For example, the current Art. 17 draft reflects that parties may exclude the possibility of tribunal-ordered interim measures. In an almost offhand sort of way, the Working

---

12. *Op. cit.*, fn. 3, para. 82; see also A/CN.9/468, para. 85.

13. A/CN.9/468, para. 86.

14. *Op. cit.*, fn. 3, para. 76.

Group discussed that a similar limitation would not be appropriate for court-ordered measures.[15] The question is why not? It is a question frequently asked by foreign practitioners faced with arbitration in countries such as The Netherlands, where far-reaching powers exist for both tribunals and courts, whether the power of the courts can be excluded or limited. Legislation clarifying the right to exclude or restrict this power would be helpful. If and to the extent a particular national system would not allow such restriction, that should be a matter to be dealt with in the implementation. Simply deleting the issue from the Model Law because of an unsupported assumption that it will not work, is unfortunate, and will only unnecessarily increase the divergence between tribunal-ordered and court-ordered measures.

Another example where the provisions regarding tribunal-ordered and court-ordered measures might be further synchronized is what to do prior to the appointment of a tribunal. The discussion in UNCITRAL shows that only court-ordered measures would appear to be feasible at this stage.[16] That is not necessarily true. This view is based on practical experience with the fairly recently amended Rules of the Netherlands Arbitration Institution (NAI). These Rules provide that prior to the appointment of a tribunal interim measures can be requested from a tribunal, which will be especially appointed to deal with such a request. In such case, the NAI will itself appoint such an arbitrator. This appointment does not mean that the normal system for appointment will not be followed for the case on the merits. It is a way, however, to obtain a speedy resolution of the issue of interim measures. Especially in countries where it is not possible to get a court date at very short notice, this route via the arbitration institutions may be attractive. UNCITRAL cannot ensure effective tribunal-ordered interim measures prior to the appointment of a tribunal, but it can point in the right direction.

Consequently, the suggestion by UNCITRAL that the Working Group might wish to consider whether provisions along the lines of those presented in respect of tribunal-related measures would be appropriate for court-ordered measures[17] should be wholeheartedly supported as well.

There is another reason why court-ordered measures should not be neglected. As the discussion at UNCITRAL has demonstrated, a key concern about tribunal-ordered measures is their enforcement. UNCITRAL stated that for court-ordered measures no regime was available and cautiously referred to the project pending before the Hague Conference on International Law. It also suggested alternative, and less tangible, methods to enhance coordination, such as sharing of information between courts.[18] Clearly, such incentives are useful, but it is important not to ignore an important instrument already available at this stage.

This instrument is the Brussels Convention and the case law developed on the basis of Art. 24 concerning interim measures in support of arbitration. This case law is by

---

15. *Op. cit.*, fn.3, para. 78.

16. See also A. REDFERN and M. HUNTER, *Law and Practice of International Commercial Arbitration* (Sweet & Maxwell, London 1999) p. 347 (stating that it is obvious that a tribunal cannot issue interim measures until it has been constituted).

17. *Op. cit.*, fn. 3, para. 78.

18. *Ibid.*, para. 84.

now famous or – some would say – notorious. In *Van Uden/Deco Line*[19] the ECJ held that even if the parties have concluded an arbitration agreement (and even if the arbitration has already commenced), Art. 24 is applicable as long as there is jurisdiction to issue interim measures on the basis of national law and certain conditions have been met. In particular, this jurisdiction is conditional on the existence of a real connecting link between the subject matter of the measures sought and the territorial jurisdiction of the State of the court addressed.[20] The corollary of the *Van Uden* decision is the ECJ's decision in *Mietz/Intership Yachting*.[21] Although this decision did not concern a case in which the parties had concluded an arbitration agreement, the ECJ confirmed its ruling in *Van Uden* also in the context of enforcement. Consequently, a decision based on Art. 24 fulfilling the *Van Uden* requirements can be enforced in other Member States.

Clearly, enforcement within Europe is only a small step, but a significant one. The plans for a Hague Convention would of course have a potentially broader territorial scope, but the Convention is not there yet, and even if it will deal with provisional measures, and it is signed and ratified, it remains to be seen how effective it will be. The Brussels Convention (or rather by now, the Regulation) is a reality.

What lessons can we learn from the case law mentioned? In *Van Uden* and *Mietz* (and in fact in *Denilauler/Couchet Frères*) the importance of the territorial link between the court addressed and the measures sought was expressed. That is clearly something to consider. Furthermore, the *Van Uden* decision demonstrates the need for unification of national rules. The ECJ accepts that such national rules create jurisdiction and then provide the mechanism for enforcement. There is hardly any check: the prohibition on exorbitant jurisdiction laid down in Art. 3 does not apply in connection to Art. 24,[22] only the substantive criteria just mentioned apply (the "real connecting link"). Moreover, there is hardly any control over the type of measure ordered: as long as it is not ex parte and some criteria have been fulfilled, even far-reaching measures such as interim payments are covered by Art. 24.

The debate within UNCITRAL has already focused on the type of measures that could be ordered, and as mentioned above, a certain amount of fine-tuning would be appropriate. When a draft is prepared on court-ordered measures, this should include provisions on jurisdiction. The need for such provisions is so acutely felt because

---

19. Judgment 17 November 1998, Case C-391/95, E.C.R. [1998] I-7091.
20. The ECJ further held that interim payment of a contractual consideration does not constitute a provisional measure within the meaning of Art. 24 unless, first, repayment to the defendant is guaranteed if the plaintiff is unsuccessful, and second, the measure sought relates only to specific assets of the defendant located or to be located in the territorial jurisdiction of the court addressed. These conditions are important for the prolific practice of interim measures relating to (advance) payments in The Netherlands, but may be of less immediate significance for the present debate. It is noteworthy, however, that the ECJ did not as a matter of principle rule out the possibility of requesting interim payment. UNCITRAL took a different position, which it may wish to reconsider, see A/CN.9/485, para 82.
21. Judgment 27 April 1999, Case C-99/96, E.C.R. [1999] I-0277.
22. *Van Uden*, para. 42.

international instruments do not otherwise fill this gap,[23] hence the reliance on national laws. Apart from the court where the assets are located, it is important to consider which other courts should be included. Many countries (certainly in continental Europe) have a general rule bestowing jurisdiction on the court of the domicile of the defendant. That may be suitable in the context of arbitration. The most obvious rule, however, is to include a reference to the court of the place of arbitration. Many national arbitration laws will do so already, but in countries where court-ordered measures are currently not available, general jurisdiction rules will not fill this gap. Finally, in doing so, it is important for the national law and therefore the model provision also to regulate the hierarchy or sequence for applying to the tribunal or to a court.[24]

IV.   CONCLUSION

To conclude, UNCITRAL has done a lot, and the drafts are an important step forward. Some aspects could be clarified and refined:

— The debate about ex parte measures seems to have taken up an excessive amount of time and effort. Setting more realistic goals and priorities would be preferable. The areas in which ex parte measures are required should be more clearly defined.
— Furthermore, it is questionable whether tribunal-ordered ex parte measures are the way to go forward. Everyone will recognize that substantial safeguards are required and these are closely connected to national systems of civil procedure. Probably they should be left to the courts.
— Moreover, even court-ordered ex parte interim measures are likely to be unenforceable in other countries, whether in support of arbitration or otherwise. The Brussels Convention is a case on point.
— This leads to the relation between tribunal-ordered and court-ordered measures and the significance of court-ordered measures. Some measures are best dealt with by courts (ex parte, enforcement-type measures); others by tribunals (specialized, technical injunctions related to the merits of the case). The basic principles should be

---

23. When the Brussels Convention was concluded, the exclusion of arbitration was reasoned by reference to the existence of "many international agreements on arbitration" already existing (Report on the Convention of 27 September on Jurisdiction and the Enforcement of Judgments in Civil and Commercial Matters, OF 1979 C 59, p. 1, commonly known as the "Jenard Report"). Jenard referred to the European Convention prepared by the Council of Europe and the New York Convention. More realistically, Advocate-General Léger in his conclusion to the *Van Uden* case concludes that the above-mentioned international agreements only relate to "very limited aspects of international disputes: those concerning arbitration as such" (Conclusion, para. 53).
24. See REDFERN and HUNTER, *op. cit.*, fn. 16, p. 349 (referring to Swiss law as an example of a law providing that one should first apply to the tribunal and only then to the court). The Dutch Code of Civil Procedure provides that if the parties have (possibly by means of the applicable arbitration rules) agreed to empower the tribunal to render an award in summary proceedings, the President of the District Court "may" declare not to have jurisdiction to render a decision in summary proceedings (Art. 1051 Code of Civil Procedure).

synchronized for both types of measures, and what should be avoided, in any event, is a sophisticated, detailed system for tribunal-ordered measures, without a counterpart for court-ordered measures. That would probably only result in decreasing the effectiveness of court-ordered measures, while court enforcement of tribunal-ordered measures remains difficult.

– Finally, one instrument that is currently available for court-ordered measures should not be ignored. The Brussels Convention is not only an important mechanism available in Europe, it can show us where to tread carefully (ex parte measures, the need for a link with the court addressed), and fundamentally, it shows us that unification of national arbitration law is of the essence.

The Enforcement of Interim Measures of Protection "Awards"

Cecil O.D. Branson, Q.C.[*]

I.   INTRODUCTION

The enforcement of international commercial arbitration awards is a favourite topic at international commercial arbitration conferences. This is understandably so as the ease of recognition and enforcement of international commercial arbitration awards has elevated this method of dispute resolution to the preferred position it finds itself in today. The present level of global trade and investment has to a significant degree been aided by the enhanced ability of those who have successfully resolved disputes with foreign parties through arbitration to recover the fruits of their victories. Uncertainty in international commercial relationships is counter-productive. Accordingly, to the extent possible, it is to be avoided or at least ameliorated. International business relationships are likely to involve aspects that are political, legal and philosophical and disputes thereunder can arise out of differences exacerbated by complexities brought about by the size of transactions, the multiplicity of parties involved, difficult technological issues and the sophistication of financing schemes. The time span of business relationships is expanding, which can exacerbate problems brought about through economic and political fluctuations and the time-limited value of the subject of the relationships.

---

[*] Member, Bar of British Columbia; member NAFTA Article 2022 Advisory Committee.
     This paper is a revision of a paper originally published by the Rocky Mountain Mineral Law Foundation in the manual of the Special Institute on International Energy and Minerals Arbitration (2002).

II.   THE NEW YORK CONVENTION, ITS HISTORY AND BENEFITS

The implementation of the United Nations Convention on Recognition and Enforcement of Foreign Arbitral Awards in 1958 (the New York Convention) has been the single most important factor which has made international commercial arbitration so successful. Art. II requires the judicial authorities of signatory States to stay court proceedings and refer to arbitration those disputes in respect of which the parties have made an agreement, unless found to be null and void, inoperative or incapable of being performed. The efficacy of this provision lies in its ability to prevent those who improperly seek to avoid their wrongdoing by delaying an ultimate decision being made against them. Probably more important are the provisions in this Convention, particularly Arts. I and V, which support the recognition and enforcement of foreign arbitral awards. Art. V mandates a competent court to recognize and enforce foreign arbitral awards subject to certain enumerated defences which are in essence limited to matters either of procedure or jurisdiction. Given that there is no comparable international treaty that deals with the recognition and enforcement of foreign court judgments, very few multilateral treaties outside of the Brussels and Lugano Conventions, and given that the largest trading nation in the world, the United States of America, has not entered into any such treaties for the recognition and enforcement of court decisions relating to commercial matters, the value of the New York Convention must be abundantly clear.

Compared with the number of reported court decisions concerning the enforcement of final awards on the substantive merits, there have been very few touching upon the enforcement of arbitral decisions relating to interim measures of protection. Nevertheless, there are now enough to allow us to attempt an analysis of the subject of this paper. To what extent, if at all, will courts treat such decisions as "awards" under the New York Convention, and, if not as such, are they enforceable under national laws concerning international commercial arbitration?

III.   JUDICIAL PRECEDENTS

In *Sperry International Trade v. Israel*,[1] the parties had entered into a contract which called upon Sperry to construct a communications system for Israel. It was a condition of the contract that Israel secure an irrevocable Letter of Credit in its favour. Differences arose between the parties and Sperry filed a demand for arbitration, claiming that Israel had fundamentally breached the contract. It sought a declaration that Israel was in breach and claimed damages. Israel denied the allegations and counterclaimed. Sperry sought from the District Court an order that Israel be enjoined from drawing down on the Letter of Credit pending an early ruling from the arbitrators concerning the draw down of funds. It obtained this, but the order was reversed by the Second Circuit on the ground that irreparable harm had not been shown. Israel then attempted to draw down the funds, but was prevented from doing so by a court order obtained by Sperry

---

1. 689 F.2d 301, 304 n.3 (2d Cir. 1982).

attaching Israel's bank account. Israel then sought an order from the court vacating the attachment order. Earlier in the morning of the day that Israel's motion was going to be heard, the arbitrators handed down an award which required both parties to escrow into a joint account the proceeds of the Letter of Credit, pending resolution of the liability and damages issues or until otherwise dealt with by the arbitrators or the courts. The following day, the court vacated the earlier court order for attachment of the bank account of Israel, but made no ruling concerning the propriety of the arbitrator's award of the previous day. Israel issued a demand to the bank to wire to it the funds in the bank account which was the subject of the attachment order; however, the bank refused to do so. The same judge who had issued the order on the previous day, on the application of Sperry, signed a show cause order against Israel as to why the award should not be confirmed. This order also directed Israel to stay the taking of any action to collect the proceeds of the Letter of Credit. Israel filed a counter-motion to vacate the arbitration award. Both applications were returnable at the same time. Israel argued that the arbitral award in question was contrary to the earlier Court of Appeals ruling which struck down the injunction forbidding Israel from drawing down on the Letter of Credit, and asserted that the arbitrators had exceeded their powers in that "a mutual, final, and definite award upon the subject matter submitted" had not yet been made.

The court stated that any judicial review of an arbitral decision had to be narrow and severely limited, and that an arbitral panel may grant equitable relief not available from a court. It then dealt with the grounds that were raised in opposition to confirmation. When it came to the argument of Israel that the arbitral tribunal ought not to have dealt with the same issue which had already been addressed by the court, it said

> "The issue before the Panel then became whether [Israel] was entitled under the terms of the contract to draw at all against the letter of credit and whether, having drawn down thereon violated the contract and intent of the parties and constituted overreaching conduct and an improper certification to the [bank] that [Israel] was entitled to draw down.... The Solomonic resolution of the Award to take the money from both parties of course does not decide the merits. The award makes sense at this stage of the arbitration."

As for the argument that the award was only interim, the court said that, although the arbitrators had not definitively resolved the question of which party, if any, is in breach of the contract, they had decided what the equities required concerning the proceeds of the Letter of Credit, which was clearly a severable issue. In the court's view, whether an award is final will depend on the terms of the contract. As a final award on a severable issue, it was clearly subject to confirmation by the court.

In contrast to *Sperry* is a Queensland case, *Resort Condominiums International Inc. v. Bolwell*.[2] In a dispute between a US franchisor of time-share entities and an Australian franchisee, the franchisor claimed that the franchisee had breached its obligations under the franchise agreement in a number of ways, including failing to pay its royalty fees, not depositing and maintaining portions of earned revenues, failing to provide an annual

---

2. [1995] 1 Q.R. 406.

audit of its operations and not allowing claimant and its auditors access to books and records of operations, as a result of which the claimant purported to cancel the licence, unilaterally. It then gave a notice to arbitrate in the United States and proceeded to the first hearing where the arbitrator made a number of decisions which were characterized as interim orders and awards which were to be operative "until such time as the arbitrator enters a final award in this matter". These included ceasing to operate as a franchisee, refraining from use of confidential or proprietary information obtained through the Licence Agreement and not altering or destroying franchise records. Also, the respondent was required to pay money into an escrow account, provide an accounting and provide certain documents. The claimant, subsequently, obtained similar orders from a US court. Enforcement of the arbitrator's order was sought in the State of Queensland, Australia. The respondent raised every conceivable defence available, thus making the decision a useful crucible within which to examine the enforceability of interim measures of protection orders issued by foreign arbitral tribunals.

The presiding judge began the operative part of his reasons by making a general statement that

> "[t]hese orders ... are clearly of an interlocutory *and* procedural nature and in no way purport to finally resolve the disputes or any of them referred ... for decision or to finally resolve the legal rights of the parties. They are provisional only and liable to be rescinded, suspended, varied or reopened by the tribunal which pronounced them...." (emphasis added)

Particular note ought to be taken here of the comment about the orders being both interlocutory *and* procedural in their nature as more will be said below about such a characterization.

The principal issue in the case was whether awards, characterized in the manner above, qualified as "arbitral awards" under the New York Convention as implemented in Queensland. The judge referred to Art. I of the Convention which says that it applies to "arbitral awards ... arising out of differences between persons". His view was that an order which gives interlocutory directions is not one which arises *directly* as a result of any differences between the parties. He saw confirmation of this in Art. V(1)(c) of the Convention which makes it a defence to enforcement where an award deals with a difference not contemplated by or not falling within the terms of the submission to arbitration, or contains decisions on matters beyond the scope of the submission to arbitration.

> "[I]t is clear that the award referred to contemplates only an award which deals with a 'difference' referred or to a 'difference' not referred and beyond the scope of the reference, and not to an order which *merely* deals with procedural or interlocutory matters."

This directs us back to the initial finding emphasized above that the orders in question were clearly of an interlocutory *and* procedural nature and in no way purported to finally resolve the disputes or any of them referred for decision.

Coming from another direction, the judge saw what he referred to as another "pointer" to his conclusion in Art. V(1)(*e*) which states that an award is unenforceable when it has not yet become binding on the parties or has been set aside or suspended by a *competent authority* of the country in which, or under the law of which that award was made. In his opinion, "competent authority" means a court and as English and Australian courts have no *inherent* power to set aside interlocutory orders, this in his view must not be the kind of decision made by an arbitral tribunal which qualifies as an award under the Convention.

The court also examined the language in Art. V(2)(*b*) which provides a public policy defence to applications for recognition and enforcement of foreign arbitral awards. This enabled him to conclude that, unlike the situation with regard to the defences mentioned in Art. V(1), where the onus was clearly on the defence, with a discretion to enforce even where none of the defences had been shown, this was not the case with the public policy defence. Thus, he found a general discretion in the court to refuse recognition and enforcement due to the broad and vexatious nature of the orders themselves, the fact that there was conflicting jurisdiction with both the United States court and the arbitral tribunal having virtually the same orders outstanding, and also the fact that there was no security required for the injunctive relief ordered, something which would be necessary under Queensland law. His findings on this issue have been the subject of negative critical comment.[3] On the other hand, the court declined to accept the argument that interim awards which don't deal with all of the issues in the submission to arbitration are not within the New York Convention. His Honour opined that as long as an interim award determined at least some of the matters at issue before the parties which were referred to the arbitration for determination, this was satisfactory. But, he went on to decide that the orders in this case were not "interim orders" under the Queensland Act as they did not "finally determine all or some of the disputes referred to the arbitrator for determination", thus again confirming the importance of his initial finding that the orders in question in no way purported to finally resolve the disputes or any of them referred for decision, or to finally resolve the legal rights of the parties.

The case *Yasuda Fire & Marine Insurance Company v. Continental Casualty Company*[4] arose out of a number of arbitrated disputes between the parties concerning responsibility for payment on reinsurance policies. The arbitral tribunal ordered that the respondent in the arbitration proceedings post an interim Letter of Credit in an amount necessary to cover a potential award. The appellate court held that this decision amounted to an award under Sect. 10(a)(4) of the United States Arbitration Act[5] which provides for "awards" to be vacated where the arbitrators exceed their powers. The appellate body followed earlier reasoning of the Ninth Circuit in *Pacific Reinsurance v. Ohio Reinsurance*,[6] which opined that "*temporary* equitable orders calculated to preserve assets or performance needed to make a potential final award more meaningful ... are final orders that can be reviewed for confirmation and enforcement by district courts under the FAA". As the sole subject of the interlocutory order in question here was the posting of

---

3. Michael PRYLES, 10 Arbitration International (1994, no. 4) p. 385.
4. 37 F.3d. 345 (7th Cir. 1994).
5. 9 U.S.C. Sect. 10(a)(4).
6. 935 F.2d 1019, 1023.

the Letter of Credit to preserve the effect of a final award, the reasoning seems to be very much in line with opinion in *Sperry International Trade v. Israel*, supra.[7]

The most recent of the decisions which this paper will use to exemplify the issues surrounding the enforcement of interim measures of protection is *Publicis Communication v. True North Communications Inc.*, a decision of the United States Court of Appeals for the Seventh Circuit.[8] This case involved the dissolution of a joint venture between two advertising companies. An issue arose over the responsibility on the part of True North to turn over to Publicis tax records that Publicis said it needed to file with the US Internal Revenue Service and the Securities and Exchange Commission. The parties agreed to arbitrate their disputes before a tribunal composed of three prominent international arbitrators. As a result of an application made to the tribunal for the release of these documents, an "order" was signed, only by the chairman of the tribunal, "for and behalf of the Arbitrators" requiring True North to turn over the documents in question. True North refused to do so. Consequently, Publicis brought on an application in Illinois for confirmation of the award. Upon the judge of first instance doing so, an appeal was taken to the Seventh Circuit Court of Appeals. It rejected the argument that the tribunal's decision was an interim order and that under the Convention only arbitral "awards" are final and subject to confirmation. In doing so, it held that whatever the tribunal chose to call its decision was not material. Indeed, it characterized the argument as one based on "extreme and untenable formalism". The "substance and impact" of the document was determinative of "whether the decision is final". The court described the issue of whether or not Publicis had to turn over the tax records as "the whole ball of wax". It was critical that "[t]he tribunal's order resolved the dispute, or was supposed to at any rate". Further, "[p]roducing the documents wasn't just some procedural matter – it was the very issue True North wanted arbitrated.... A ruling on a discrete, time sensitive issue may be final and ripe for confirmation even though other claims remain to be addressed by arbitrators." Given the admonition in this case to look beyond form to substance, are we able to wholly ignore whether the arbitral decision is an interlocutory one? Also, is it appropriate to ignore form altogether?

IV.   INTERIM SUMMARY

It might be helpful at this point to summarize the reasoning of the cases discussed. The Queensland case says that whether the issue before the arbitral tribunal is interlocutory is determinative. In *Sperry*, the decision of the arbitral tribunal was made "pending resolution of further issues to be arbitrated or until otherwise dealt with by the arbitrators or the Courts"; yet, because the order finally disposed of the issue of what to do with the proceeds of the Letter of Credit, this made it enforceable. The order was not capable of being reversed. Similarly, in *Publicis Communications* the order requiring delivery of the records was final and irreversible. Substance, in this context, was able to prevail over form, despite the manner in which the arbitral tribunal characterized its

---

7. *Op. cit.*, fn. 1.
8. 203 F.3d 725 (7th Cir. 2000).

effect. But, in the *Yasuda Fire & Marine* case the court identified the order in question as a "temporary" equitable one. Even here, one could say that the order to post the Letter of Credit was final in substance as the measure ordered was required to be undertaken; however, this could be said of any interlocutory measure. The answer may be found in the following dicta of the court: "even though the arbitration panel has yet to resolve nearly all the disputes between Yasuda [the parties], any future findings of the arbitrators will not influence the issues before us." Is this what is meant by the order being final?

From the above, we may to be able to assert a principle that, unless the arbitral tribunal's decision concerns a matter which is wholly interlocutory, if it relates to a discrete issue which is not merely procedural in its impact in that it deals with more than matters which merely facilitate the conduct of the arbitral proceedings, it may be enforced by a court. The conclusion that any decision that is not finally determinative of the substantive issues with which it deals ought not to be classified as an "award" has been advanced by authoritative writers on the subject.[9] Whether such decisions will be enforced will depend on how the court characterizes the particular measure before it. Some US courts, it is suggested, will be more likely to characterize some of the orders which were before the Queensland Court in *Resort Condominiums International v. Bolwell* as not merely procedural in their substantive effect. These will include the order to provide certain documents. The answer may well be aided through a clear categorization of the functions of interim measures of protection. While there may be varying viewpoints on how best to describe these functions, the following are suggested:

1. to facilitate the conduct of the arbitral proceedings, including:
— taking evidence
— inspection of property
— requiring discovery
— consolidation
2. to protect the integrity of the process, including:
— confidentiality
— security of information
3. to avoid loss or damage of the subject matter of the arbitration, or to preserve the status quo until final determination of the dispute, including:
— injunctions
— specific performance
— preservation of goods
— disposition of goods
— appointment of a fiduciary
4. to facilitate the enforcement of the final award, which would include:
— attachment of assets
— *Mareva* injunctions
— securing assets through the use of a third party
— providing security for the final award, and costs.

---

9. ALAN REDFERN and MARTIN HUNTER, *Law and Practice of International Commercial Arbitration*, 3d ed. (Sweet & Maxwell 1999) p. 365.

As mentioned above, this approach is in accord with the views expressed by learned authors, Redfern and Hunter.[10] About this, they say:

"In practice, the term 'award' should be reserved for decisions that finally determine the substantive issues with which they deal. (footnote omitted) This involves distinguishing between awards (which are concerned with issues) and procedural orders and directions (which are concerned with the conduct of the arbitration). Procedural orders and directions help to move the arbitration forward; they deal with such matters as the exchange of written evidence, the production of documents and the arrangements for the conduct of the hearing. They do not have the status of awards; and they may perhaps be called into question after the final award has been made (for instance as evidence of bias on the part of the arbitral tribunal)." (footnote omitted)[11]

Attractive as the approach in *Publicis* may be, it might not be wholly intellectually sound in its reasoning. In this case there was an argument made which was, unfortunately, given less consideration than it deserved by the court, which said:

"Like its formalistic argument over the difference between an award and an order, Publicis fusses that the tribunal's 30 October decision cannot be final because it was signed only by Philip. Under the United Nations arbitration rules, final awards are supposed to be signed by all three arbitrators and, if not, should explain any missing signature. UNCITRAL Arbitration Rules, Art. 32(4). This argument goes nowhere. In the first place, the tribunal chairman Philip signed the decision 'for and on behalf' of the other arbitrators. At Judge Gottschall's prompting, arbitrators Viandier and Katzenbach later signed off on the decision as well."

Contrary to the rather flippant suggestion that this legal argument was a mere "fuss", there is substance in the submission. The court may have unfairly demeaned the argument by characterizing it as "formalistic". The difference in form between an "award" and a mere "order" may well be substantive in its effect in that it demonstrates the intention of careful arbitrators. This is not a case of the parties incorrectly describing their agreement. The formal characterization by arbitrators of their decisions is the best evidence of their intention and, as such, ought to be entitled to at least the same level of deference as given to foreign judges, particularly when they are describing the legal characterization of a decision made in accordance with applicable procedural rules. If the arbitrators in the *Publicis* dispute wished to make the measure in question final all three of these experienced arbitrators would have had the foresight to sign their order as required by the combined effect of Arts. 26(2) and 32(4) of the UNCITRAL Arbitration Rules. Art. 26(4) makes it clear that "Interim measures may be established in the *form* of an interim award." Thus, *form* is dispositive, in that it determines the effect of what

---

10. *Ibid.*, pp. 361-365.
11. *Ibid.*, p. 365.

the arbitrators have done. A number of major institutional rules provide for an order for an interim measure of protection being issued in the form of an interim award. These include those of UNCITRAL,[12] AAA[13] and WIPO.[14]

Party autonomy has a special significance in arbitration law. When the parties have chosen a specific set of rules to govern their procedure, these ought to be followed unless they are so inappropriate as to offend basic concepts of fairness.

V.   LEGISLATION

Some States have enacted statutory provisions allowing for court enforcement of interim measures of protection by giving them the same legal effect as an "arbitral award" under Art. V of the New York Convention or their own more liberal laws. These jurisdictions include Australia,[15] Bermuda,[16] Ontario,[17] New Zealand[18] and Scotland.[19] When we talk

---

12. Art. 26(2) of the UNCITRAL Arbitration Rules:

"Such interim measures may be established in the form of an interim award. The arbitral tribunal shall be entitled to require security for the costs of such measures."

13. Art. 21(2) of the AAA International Arbitration Rules:

"Such interim measures may be taken in the form of an interim award, and the tribunal may require security for the costs of such measures."

14. Art. 46(c) of the WIPO Arbitration Rules:

"Measures and orders contemplated under this Article may take the form of an interim award."

15. Sect. 23 International Arbitration Act, 1974:

"Chapter VIII of the Model Law applies to orders by an arbitral tribunal under Article 17 of the Model Law requiring a party:
(a) to take an interim measure of protection; or
(b) to provide security in connection with such a measure;
as if any reference in that chapter to an arbitral award or an award were a reference to such an order."

16. Sect. 26 International Conciliation and Arbitration Act 1993, in force 29 June 1993:

"Chapter VIII of the Model Law applies to an order by an arbitral tribunal under Article 17 of the Model Law requiring a party –
(a) to take an interim measure of protection; or
(b) to provide security in connection with a measure referred to in paragraph (a), as if any reference in that Chapter to an arbitral award or an award were a reference to such an order."

17. Sect. 9 Ontario International Commercial Arbitration Act, RSO 1990, C.I-9:

"An order of the arbitral tribunal under article 17 of the Model Law for an interim measure of

about court enforcement of decisions made by arbitral tribunals concerning interim measures of protection it is important to distinguish between those decisions in respect of which the courts of the State whose laws govern the arbitration may lend assistance to the enforcement of such measures, and those which have the same force and effect as an "arbitral award" under Art. V of the New York Convention. Examples of the former are Croatia,[20] Switzerland[21] and Tunisia.[22] Only the latter will be:

— limited to the defences available under Art. V of the New York Convention;

---

protection and the provision of security in connection with it is subject to the provisions of the Model Law as if it were an award."

18. Art. 17(2) of the First Schedule to the Arbitration Act 1996, in force 1 July 1997:

"Unless otherwise agreed by the parties, articles 35 and 36 apply to orders made by an arbitral tribunal under this article as if a reference in those articles to an award were a reference to such an order."

19. Art. 17(2) of Schedule 7 to the Law Reform (Miscellaneous Provisions) (Scotland) Act 1990:

"An order under paragraph (1) of this article shall take the form of an award and articles 31, 35 and 36 shall apply accordingly."

20. Croatia, Art. 16(1)-(2) Law on Arbitration enacted October 2001:

"1. Unless otherwise agreed by the parties, the arbitral tribunal may, at the request of a party, order any party to take such interim measures of protection as the arbitral tribunal may consider necessary in respect of the subject matter of the dispute. The arbitral tribunal may require any party to provide appropriate security in connection with such measure.
2. If a party to which interim measures relate does not agree to undertake them voluntarily, the party that made the motion for such measures may request their enforcement before the competent court."

21. The Swiss Federal Private International Law Act, Art. 183:

"1. Unless the parties have agreed otherwise, the arbitral tribunal can order provisional or conservatory measures at the request of any party.
2. If the party so ordered does not comply voluntarily, the arbitral tribunal can request the assistance of the court with jurisdiction. The latter shall apply its own law."

22. Tunisia, Art. 62 Arbitration Code promulgated by Law No. 93-42 of 26 April 1993 enforced 27 October 1993:

"Unless otherwise agreed by the parties, the arbitral tribunal may, at the request of a party, order any interim measure of protection as it may consider necessary.
If the affected party, does not act in accordance with the measure, the arbitral tribunal can request the assistance of the First President of the Court of Appeal of Tunis.
In either case, the arbitral tribunal or the judge may require either party to provide a deposit on the costs necessitated by such measure."

— subject to the onus of proof being on the respondent; and
— recognized and enforced elsewhere than in the State under whose laws the arbitration was conducted.

Whether this is a good or a bad feature will be touched upon under the following heading.

VI.   SUGGESTED NEW UNCITRAL MODEL LAW PROVISIONS

The most recent, and perhaps most innovative, attempt to draft legislation regarding the enforcement of interim measures of protection is that of UNCITRAL. The UNCITRAL Working Group has before it a new article for the enforcement of interim measures of protection which reads as follows:

"(1) Upon the application to the competent court by [the arbitral tribunal or by] the interested party made with the approval of the arbitral tribunal, an interim measure of protection referred to in article 17 shall be enforced, irrespective of the country in which it was made, except that the court may at its discretion refuse enforcement if:
(a) The party against whom the measure is invoked furnishes proof that:
(i) Application for the same or similar interim measure has been made to a court in this State, whether or not the court has taken a decision on the application; or
(ii)

[Variant 1] The arbitration agreement referred to in article 7 is not valid

[Variant 2] The arbitration agreement referred to in article 7 appears not be valid, in which case the court may refer the issue of the [jurisdiction of the arbitral tribunal] [validity of the arbitration agreement] to be decided by the arbitral tribunal in accordance with article 16 of this Law]; or

(iii) The party against whom the interim measure is invoked was not given proper notice of the appointment of an arbitrator or of the arbitral proceedings or was otherwise unable to present its case with respect to the interim measure, [in which case the court may suspend the enforcement proceedings until the parties have been heard by the arbitral tribunal]; or
(iv) The interim measure has been terminated, suspended or amended by the arbitral tribunal; or
(b) The court finds that:
(i) Such a measure is incompatible with the powers conferred upon the court by its procedural laws, unless the court decides to reformulate the measure to the extent necessary to adapt it to its own powers and procedures for the purpose of enforcing the measure; or
(ii) The recognition or enforcement of the interim measure would be contrary to the public policy of this State.

(2) The party who is seeking enforcement of an interim measure shall promptly inform the court of any termination, suspension or amendment of that measure.
(3) In reformulating the measure under paragraph (1)(b)(i), the court shall not modify the substance of the interim measure.
(4) Paragraph (1)(a)(iii) does not apply to an interim measure of protection that was ordered without notice to the party against whom the measure is invoked, provided that the measure was ordered to be effective for a period not exceeding [30] days and the enforcement of the measure is requested before the expiry of that period."

The draft provision above[23] addresses some of the problems discussed earlier in this paper, and raises some new ones.

VII. POTENTIAL EFFECTS OF INTERIM MEASURES OF PROTECTION ON THIRD PARTIES

At first blush, many of us would likely accept a legislative provision which enables court enforcement of tribunal-ordered interim measures of protection as a worthwhile change in national laws. Without the coercive power available through a court, such measures granted by an arbitral tribunal lack effective authority. In addition to the lack of authoritative compulsion they do not legally affect third parties not within the jurisdiction of the arbitrators. But, a good number of attachment orders and forms of injunctive relief affect such parties. In these cases, national laws should be more justifiably concerned about third-party interests. No longer can a judiciary, with impunity, allow themselves the luxury of thinking only within the arbitration box. Furthermore, beyond third-party rights directly affected by the measures in question, there is also justification for some consideration of public interest aspects impacted.

Consider an example. A and B, two corporations, enter into an agreement with an arbitration clause in regard to which they have a dispute. In the course of the arbitration A obtains an interim measure of protection attaching a fund of money which had been deposited by B in an account with C Bank, to complete a major purchase involving D. If the transaction does not complete in a timely manner, D will suffer irreparable damage. Given the potential downsides one can appreciate the differences between enforcing a final award on the substantive merits of the dispute and enforcing an interim measure of protection preliminary to the award being made.

VIII. PARTY AUTONOMY

The draft Model Law article does not state that the parties have the right to opt out of or into this form of court intervention. A noteworthy feature of the Model Law is its respect for the autonomy of the parties as demonstrated by the inclusion of the phrase

---

23. A/CN.9/WGII/WP.113. This suggested draft was considered by the Working Group at its Session held in New York, 4-8 March 2002.

"unless otherwise agreed by the parties" or similar language in over thirty places. Australia provides that the parties must specifically opt into a similar provision in its legislation.[24] It is clear therefore, that in such cases Australian courts will enforce interim measures identified in Sect. 23, if they are granted in an international commercial arbitration. Bermuda[25] and New Zealand[26] provide that the parties may opt

---

24. *Op. cit.*, fn. 15.

25. Sect. 26 of the Bermuda International Conciliation and Arbitration Act 1993 applies Chap. VIII of the Model Law to an order by an arbitral tribunal under Art. 17 of the Model Law requiring a party to take an interim measure of protection; or to provide security in connection with such a measure, as if any reference in that chapter to an arbitral award or an award were a reference to such an order. It should be read with Sect. 36 which states

"Unless a contrary intention is expressed therein, it shall be an implied term in every arbitration agreement that the arbitral tribunal may, if the tribunal thinks fit, make an interim, interlocutory or partial award, and any reference in this Part to an award includes a reference to an interim, interlocutory or partial award."

26. Art. 17(2) of the First Schedule of the Arbitration Act 1996 reads:

"Unless otherwise agreed by the parties, Articles 35 and 36 apply to orders made by an arbitral tribunal under this Article as if a reference in those Articles to an award were a reference to such an order."

Thus, interim measures of protection ordered by arbitral tribunals are enforceable in New Zealand under Arts. 35 and 36, but not as awards under the New York Convention. This would likely prohibit application of this provision to "foreign" awards, which are not international in their character. The New Zealand legislation defines an "Award" as meaning "a decision of the arbitral tribunal on the substance of the dispute and includes any interim, interlocutory or partial award". However, these definitions are subject to the context requiring otherwise. Also, the First Schedule within which Art. 17 is to be found, is by Sect. 6 applicable if the place of arbitration is, or would be, in New Zealand; therefore, the enforcement of interim measures provision would be limited to interim measures ordered by a tribunal whose seat was in New Zealand. However, the Second Schedule, which applies to international arbitrations as defined in the Model Law contains Sect. 3 which states:

"1. For the purposes of article 19 of the First Schedule, and unless the parties agree otherwise, the parties shall be taken as having agreed that the powers conferred upon the arbitral tribunal include the power to –
....
(j) Order any party to do all such other things during the arbitral proceedings as may reasonably be needed to enable an award to be made properly and efficiently:
(k) Make an interim, interlocutory or partial award.

Then in Sect. 3(2) it is said

"[n]otwithstanding anything in article 5 of the First Schedule, the arbitral tribunal, or a party with the approval of the arbitral tribunal, may request from the court assistance in the exercise of any power conferred on the arbitral tribunal under sub-clause (1)".

out. Thus, the decision as to whether the parties wish to have those interim measures of protection which are granted by arbitral tribunals made enforceable lies with the parties. The Canadian province of Ontario, although not providing either option, applies to both international and foreign awards.[27] Given the respect paid to the autonomy of the parties concerning procedural aspects of arbitration, one might think that such an option should be available.

IX.   ARBITRAL TRIBUNAL'S ROLE IN COURT ENFORCEMENT

As it is apparent by the phrase bracketed in the *chapeau* of the new suggested article, it has not yet been finally determined whether the arbitral tribunal ought to be an applicant to the enforcement proceedings. It is hoped by this writer that this will be rejected as being contrary to the spirit of arbitration. However, the issue does raise other interesting problems relating to the role of the arbitral tribunal. For instance, due to the often urgent need for such orders they may be given orally, or in writing but without reasons. Also, being interlocutory, they are based on the specific circumstances existing at the time the orders are made. The sum of these circumstances can make it difficult for a competent enforcing court to be fully aware of the bases on which the arbitral tribunal's order was granted. Similarly, a court may not be able to recognize that a material change has occurred since the issuance of the order, if it does not know which particular circumstances were found to be most material in the eyes of the arbitral tribunal. A further significant issue concerns the extent, if at all, to which the court ought to examine the substantive merits of the case, as found by the arbitral tribunal in the first instance. It is suggested that the court should proceed on the assumption that the arbitral tribunal decided that the merits were strong enough to make such an order, with the onus of disproving this assumption upon the resisting party. The dangers of a court involving itself in the merits of the dispute have been appreciated in at least one decision.[28]

X.   GROUNDS FOR DISPUTING ENFORCEMENT

Altering the grounds on which a respondent may dispute enforcement of interim measures of protection ordered by tribunals is probably a good thing. All the defences available under Art. V of the New York Convention and in other national legislation may not be applicable to interlocutory matters. Which of these are, and whether the

---

27. Ontario, Sect. 10 International Commercial Arbitration Act, RSO C.I-9:

   "For the purposes of articles 35 and 36 of the Model Law, an arbitral award includes a commercial arbitral award made outside Canada, even if the arbitration to which it relates is not international as defined in article 1(3) of the Model Law."

28. *Relais Nordik v. Secunda Marine Services Limited* (1998) 24 Federal Trial Reporter 256, FCC, Trial Div.

new defences mentioned are appropriate, ought to be given further consideration. Where an application for the same or a similar interim measure has been made to a court, ought a court to refuse enforcement of the subsequent application? If, as in the Working Group's draft, the court's refusal of enforcement is discretionary, such a provision, it is suggested, is appropriate. Take, for instance, the circumstances in *Sperry International Trade v. Israel* mentioned above where Sperry's attempt to enjoin Israel in drawing down a Letter of Credit pending an earlier ruling from the arbitrators concerning the draw-down on funds was still before the courts, as was Israel's application to vacate the order allowing Sperry to attach Israel's bank account. These were, very arguably, similar interim measures. They should not have stood in the way of the court's enforcement of the subsequent measure which was before the court.

XI.   ENFORCING EX PARTE ORDERS

The question of interim measures of protection being granted by an arbitral tribunal on an ex parte basis is an extremely controversial one. Many arbitration statutes contain provisions forbidding such a practice. Indeed, as Holtzmann and Neuhaus make clear in their seminal text on the Model Law,[29] the fundamental precepts of Art. 18 were intended to apply both to actions taken by the arbitral tribunal and to procedural agreements reached by the parties. The arbitration legislation of many States contain similar language, which as most learned commentators have opined rules out *ex parte* applications for interim measures of protection.[30] However, a contrary opinion has been expressed.[31] The rules of many major international arbitration institutions forbid such a practice, including the AAA, ICC, LCIA, ICSID and WIPO.

XII.   JURISDICTION OF ARBITRAL TRIBUNAL

The defence raised above in Art. 36(a)(ii) of the Model Law relates to the issue of jurisdiction. Where the validity of arbitral tribunal-ordered interim measures of protection is challenged, is this a jurisdictional question which, under the Model Law should be dealt with under a procedure similar to Art. 16? If so, what approach should

---

29. HOLTZMANN and NEUHAUS, *A Guide to the UNCITRAL Model Law on International Commercial Arbitration* (Kluwer 1989).
30. Neil KAPLAN and Robert MORGAN, "National Report Hong Kong", ICCA *International Handbook on Commercial Arbitration*, Suppl. 29, December 1999, pp. 29-110; Luc DEMERYERI, "1998 Amendments to Belgian Arbitration Law", 15 Arb. Int'l (1999, no. 3) pp. 295-314; Richard A. HORNING, "Interim Relief in WIPO Arbitration"; Jan K. SCHAEFER, "New Solutions for Interim Measures of Protection in International Commercial Arbitration: English, German and Hong Kong Law Compared", Electronic Journal of Comparative Law (Aug. 1998), http://law.kub.nl/ejcl/22/art22-2.html; Tamara OYRE, *The Power of an Arbitrator to Grant Interim Relief under the Arbitration Act 1996* (South Africa).
31. Marc BLESSING in *The Conduct of Arbitral Proceedings under the Rules of Arbitration Institutions; The WIPO Arbitration Rules and Comparative Perspective*.

the court take? Should it consider the matter de novo, or would it be better that some degree of deference be given to the arbitral tribunal's decision on this subject?

XIII.   CONCLUSION

International commercial arbitration law is at a crossroads in its historical development. The ease with which assets may now be transferred from one country to another through the use of e-commerce makes the enforcement of arbitral grants of interim measures of protection more critical. It may be said that the need for the law in this area to be upgraded and harmonized is as much or greater than was the case in 1958 when the New York Convention dealt with the enforcement of foreign arbitral awards. Until such laws have been passed, can the parties protect themselves in some way? This writer suggests that, in some jurisdictions, this may be possible by drafting arbitration clauses which clearly and specifically allow for arbitral tribunals to make such orders and for their enforcement through the coercive sovereign powers available through national courts. American courts have opened the door to this in recent decisions which have recognized the right of parties to agree on an expanded review of arbitral awards.[32] Whether this will be extended to enforcement of such awards remains to be seen.

---

32. *LaPine Tech. Corp. v. Kyocera Corp.*, 130 F.3d 884 (9th Cir. 1997); *Gateway Tech., Inc. v. MCI*, 64 F.3d 993 (5th Cir. 1995). Although, to the contrary, see *Chicago Typographical Union v. Chicago Sun-Times, Inc.*, 935 F.2d 1501 (7th Cir. 1991); *Bowen v. Amoco Pipeline Co.*, 2001 WL 694508 (10th Cir. Okla.).

Party Autonomy and Interim Measures
In International Commercial Arbitration

*Christopher R. Drahozal**

I.   INTRODUCTION

Legal regimes differ on the authority of courts and arbitrators to grant interim measures in support of arbitration proceedings.[1] Some arbitration laws authorize both courts and arbitrators to award interim relief (based on the parties' agreement or otherwise);[2] some laws deny arbitrators such authority, limiting it to the courts;[3] some laws deny the courts such authority once the arbitrators have been selected;[4] while others are unclear whether and under what circumstances courts may make such orders.[5] The fundamental

---

*   Professor of Law, University of Kansas School of Law, Lawrence, KS, USA.

1. See "Note by the Secretariat, Settlement of commercial disputes: Preparation of uniform provisions on interim measures of protection", UNCITRAL, 36th Sess., UN Doc. A/CN.9/WG.II/WP.119 (30 January 2002) paras. 20-33.

2. E.g., England, Sects. 39 and 44, Arbitration Act 1996 in ICCA *International Handbook on Commercial Arbitration* (hereinafter *Handbook*), "England", Annex I (March 1997) pp. 19 and 21-22; see infra text accompanying fns. 38-40.

3. E.g., Argentina, Art. 753 National Code of Civil and Commercial Procedure in *Handbook*, *op. cit.*, fn. 2, "Argentina", Annex I (January 1985) p. 4 ("Arbitrators cannot order compulsory measures or measures leading to enforcement. They must request them from the judge who will have to lend the support of his jurisdictional powers for the most swift and effective carrying out of the arbitral proceedings."); Italy, Art. 818 Code of Civil Procedure, in *ibid.*, "Italy", Annex I (September 2000) p. 4 ("The arbitrators may not grant attachment or other interim measures of protection.").

4. E.g., United States, Sect. 8(b)(2) Revised Uniform Arbitration Act (2000) (hereinafter RUAA) www.law.upenn.edu/bll/ulc/uarba/arbitrat1213.htm (after the arbitrator is appointed, court may grant interim relief "only if the matter is urgent and the arbitrator is not able to act timely or the arbitrator cannot provide an adequate remedy").

5. E.g., United States, 9 U.S.C. Sects. 1-16, Federal Arbitration Act (silent on both court-ordered and arbitrator-ordered interim relief in non-admiralty cases). Compare, e.g., *Merrill Lynch, Pierce, Fenner & Smith, Inc. v. Salvano*, 999 F.2d 211 (7th Cir. 1993) (following majority rule that federal courts have authority to grant interim measures in support of arbitration, although holding that district court abused its discretion in continuing temporary restraining order after arbitration panel selected) with *Merrill Lynch, Pierce, Fenner & Smith, Inc. v. Hovey*, 726 F.2d 1286 (8th Cir. 1984) (holding courts may award interim relief in support of arbitration only if "qualifying contractual

question is an institutional one: Which is the appropriate party to grant interim measures – the court, the arbitration panel, or both?

This paper argues that the principle of party autonomy should determine who has the authority to award interim relief. The argument is twofold. First, empirical examination of contracting practices – what parties actually agree to in their arbitration agreements concerning interim measures – may provide important insights into how authority over interim measures should be allocated. Second, in translating those insights into statutory provisions, drafters and legislators should preserve party autonomy by permitting parties to contract around the statutory provisions, in other words, by making those provisions default rules rather than mandatory rules.

II.   ARBITRATION AGREEMENTS AND INTERIM MEASURES

Empirical data on the use of interim measures in international arbitration provides useful information in determining the appropriate allocation of authority between court and arbitrator. While experts can argue in theory about which allocation is most beneficial to the parties, better evidence comes from the parties themselves: When parties agree to arbitrate, how do they allocate authority over interim relief?

The UNCITRAL Working Group on Arbitration has recognized the usefulness of such empirical evidence in its ongoing consideration of interim measures. The Working Group identified interim measures – both court-ordered and arbitrator-ordered interim relief – as a "likely item[] for future work",[6] and indicated that its work on the subject would "have to be founded on broad empirical information".[7] As the UNCITRAL Secretary General explained:

> "The Working Group was aware that the information needed ... was not readily available and therefore requested the States and international organizations participating in the considerations of the Working Group as well as experts interested in its work to send to the Secretariat relevant information (e.g., arbitration rules, academic and practice writings, as well as examples of texts of interim measures of protection ordered omitting the names of parties and other confidential information)."[8]

I commend the Working Group for its "empirically based" approach.[9] Too often, policy judgments are made on the basis of expert opinion with too little consideration of what actually happens in the real world. Arbitration statutes, as well as commentaries

---

language" to that effect).

6. See "Report of the Working Group on Arbitration on the work of its thirty-third session", UNCITRAL, 34th Sess., UN Doc. A/CN.9/485 (20 December 2000) paras. 104-105.

7. *Ibid.*, para. 106.

8. Report of the Secretary-General, "International Commercial Arbitration: Possible Future Work", UNCITRAL, UN Doc. A/CN.9/WG.II/WP.111 (12 October 2000) para. 32.

9. *Op. cit.*, fn. 6, para. 105(b).

about arbitral practice, will benefit when their drafters take such an empirical approach.

The difficulty here, however, is in determining what parties actually do with respect to interim measures of protection.[10] Institutional arbitration rules are a good starting point.[11] Such rules are publicly available, and operate as standard contract terms that parties can incorporate by reference into their contracts. Institutions regularly review their rules and consult with user groups as to what changes should be made.[12] Thus, how those rules deal with interim measures gives some insight into what sorts of approaches are beneficial to arbitrating parties.

But an empirical examination based on institutional arbitration rules is incomplete, for at least two reasons. First, arbitration rules deal with the conduct of the arbitration proceeding and ordinarily do not address the availability of interim relief in court. As a result, they are of limited value in determining parties' preferences as to the appropriate allocation of authority between court and arbitrator.[13] Second, parties can and do change the provisions of institutional rules in their contracts.[14] Thus, any empirically based approach to the issue of interim measures would be incomplete without an examination of the provisions of parties' arbitration agreements addressing interim relief.

I am aware of only one published study of the terms of international commercial arbitration agreements: Stephen Bond's study of arbitration agreements giving rise to ICC arbitrations in 1987 and 1989.[15] That study gives no indication that any parties addressed the availability of interim measures in the ICC arbitration clauses studied.

---

10. Another way to find out what parties are doing (or at least what they say they are doing) is by conducting a survey. See, e.g., Richard W. NAIMARK and Stephanie E. KEER, "Analysis of UNCITRAL Questionnaires on Interim Relief", Mealey's Int'l Arb. Rep. (2001, no. 3) p. 23.

11. As I am focusing on the allocation of authority between courts and arbitrators over interim measures, I do not discuss arbitration awards granting interim relief.

12. See, e.g., Stephen R. BOND and Christopher R. SEPPALA, "The New (1998) Rules of Arbitration of the International Chamber of Commerce", Mealey's Int'l Arb. Rep. (1997, no. 5) p. 33 (explaining that "[t]he ICC revises its Rules of Arbitration from time to time so as to adapt them to the current needs of the international business community").

13. Arbitration statutes do address the allocation of authority between courts and arbitrators, and given competition among arbitral sites for arbitration business, might provide some evidence as to what approaches benefit the arbitrating parties. See Christopher R. DRAHOZAL, "Commercial Norms, Commercial Codes, and International Commercial Arbitration", 33 Vand. J. Transnat'l L. (2000) p. 79 at pp. 102-105.

14. Parties also may agree to change the provisions of institutional rules after a dispute arises, either before or during the hearing. That seems unlikely to be a common occurrence with interim measures, but may happen more frequently with respect to other issues.

15. Stephen R. BOND, "How to Draft an Arbitration Clause (Revisited)", ICC Int'l Ct. Arb. Bull. (Dec. 1990) p. 14 at p. 21 (reporting results of study of 237 arbitration cases filed with the ICC in 1987 and 215 cases filed in 1989; no indication that any arbitration clause addressed court or arbitrator authority to award interim relief); Stephen R. BOND, "How to Draft an Arbitration Clause", J. Int'l Arb. (June 1989) p. 65 (1987 only); see also Gary B. BORN, *International Commercial Arbitration*, 2nd ed. (2001) p. 926 ("In practice, it is unusual (although by no means unheard of) for the parties' arbitration agreement expressly to address the subject of provisional relief.").

That finding is particularly significant in that prior to 1998, the ICC rules themselves did not expressly authorize arbitrators to award interim measures.[16] If Bond's findings hold true today, they would indicate that parties do not change institutional rules concerning interim relief in their international arbitration agreements, so that such a concern is unwarranted.

By contrast, empirical evidence from domestic arbitrations in the United States suggests that parties frequently do address the availability of interim relief in their arbitration agreements. In a sample of dispute resolution clauses in franchise agreements in the United States, a sizable majority address the availability of interim relief in arbitration.[17] The provisions are of the following types.

First, only three of the thirty-four franchise agreements with arbitration clauses (8.8 percent) contain provisions authorizing arbitrators to grant interim relief. For example, the arbitration clause in the franchise agreement for Baskin-Robbins ice-cream stores provides:

"The arbitrator(s) may issue such orders for interim relief as may be deemed necessary to safeguard the rights of the parties during the arbitration, but without prejudice to the ultimate rights of the parties to the final determination of the dispute or to the rights of the FRANCHISOR to seek equitable relief from a court of competent jurisdiction at any time, even during the pendency of any arbitration proceedings initiated hereunder."[18]

Of course, all but one of the arbitration clauses (33 of 34, or 97 percent) provide for arbitration administered by the American Arbitration Association.[19] Because the AAA

---

16. See W. Laurence CRAIG, et al., *International Chamber of Commerce Arbitration*, 3rd ed. (2000) Sect. 26.05(i), p. 461 (adding that arbitration panels commonly found such authority implicit in the ICC Rules). Compare Art. 23 Rules of Arbitration of the International Chamber of Commerce (in force 1 January 1998) (expressly authorizing arbitration panel to "order any interim or conservatory measure it deems appropriate", unless the parties agree otherwise).

17. The franchise agreements studied are publicly available in some states, which require franchisors to file copies of the agreements with state regulators. For more information on the sample, see Christopher R. DRAHOZAL, "'Unfair' Arbitration Clauses", U. Ill. L. Rev. (2001) p. 695. That article contains findings on many aspects of the dispute resolution clauses studied, such as the location of the dispute resolution proceeding, the selection of arbitrators, exclusions from arbitration, and limitations on remedies and class-wide relief. The information reported in this paper on provisions dealing with interim relief, however, has not previously been published.

18. Sect. 11.1, Allied-Domecq Retailing USA Franchise Agreement (for Baskin-Robbins and Dunkin' Donuts franchises) (copy on file with author); see also Sect. 13 Fantastic Sams Conventional License Agreement (copy on file with author) ("The parties agree further that the Arbitrators may tender an interim ruling, including injunctive relief....").

19. DRAHOZAL, *op. cit.*, fn. 17, p. 728. The other clause left the choice of governing rules to the option of the franchisor. Sect. XXVI(C) GNC Franchising, Inc. Agreement (for GNC-General Nutrition Center stores) (copy on file with author) (arbitration to be administered "under the then-prevailing commercial arbitration rules of a recognized independent alternate dispute resolution service to be selected by Franchisor such as the American Arbitration Association, JAMS/Endispute or United States Mediation and Arbitration").

Commercial Arbitration Rules expressly authorize the arbitration panel to award interim relief,[20] there was little need for the parties to grant arbitrators such authority in their arbitration agreements.

Second, one (but only one) arbitration clause provides for application of the AAA's Optional Rules for Emergency Measures of Protection.[21] The Optional Rules authorize the AAA to appoint a single arbitrator to rule, on an expedited basis, on a request for emergency relief.[22] The party requesting such relief must give notice to the other party to the arbitration agreement.[23] The Optional Rules obviously are designed to address the practical problems in constituting an arbitration panel in time to rule on a request for interim relief.[24] The Rules apply, however, only when agreed to by the parties "by special agreement or in their arbitration clause",[25] and such agreements were rare in the sample.

Third, many of the arbitration clauses expressly preserve the right of the franchisor, and sometimes the franchisee as well, to go to court to seek interim relief. The Baskin-Robbins clause quoted above is one example.[26] Other examples include the following clauses:

> "MRI may seek temporary and preliminary injunctive relief from any court having jurisdiction over the controversy and the parties, in order to protect its rights set forth in Sections 8, 11, 13, and 15, while engaging or preparing to engage in arbitration of such issues."[27]

---

20. Rule R-36, American Arbitration Association Commercial Arbitration Rules (effective 1 January 2003):

    "R-36. Interim Measures
    (a) The arbitrator may take whatever interim measures he or she deems necessary, including injunctive relief and measures for the protection or conservation of property and disposition of perishable goods.
    (b) Such interim measures may take the form of an interim award, and the arbitrator may require security for the costs of such measures.
    (c) A request for interim measures addressed by a party to a judicial authority shall not be deemed incompatible with the agreement to arbitrate or a waiver of the right to arbitrate."

21. Sect. 10(c) Doctor's Associates Inc. Franchise Agreement (for Subway franchises) (copy on file with author) ("The arbitration will be held in accordance with the Commercial Arbitration Rules of the American Arbitration Association (the AAA), and under the Expedited Procedures of such rules or under the Optional Rules For Emergency Measures of Protection of the AAA, if they may apply to the Dispute.").

22. Rules O-2 & O-3 American Arbitration Association Optional Rules for Emergency Measures of Protection (effective 1 January 2003).

23. *Ibid.*, Rule O-1.

24. BORN, *op. cit.*, fn. 15, p. 934 ("provisional measures can often not practicably be obtained from the arbitrators").

25. *Op. cit.*, fn. 22, Rule O-1.

26. See supra text accompanying fn. 18.

27. Sect. 16.3 Management Recruiters Franchise Agreement (copy on file with author).

"Notwithstanding anything to the contrary contained in Paragraph F of this Section, HRI and FRANCHISEE shall each have the right in a proper case to obtain temporary restraining orders and temporary or preliminary injunctive relief from a court of competent jurisdiction, [provided,] however, that the parties shall contemporaneously submit their dispute for arbitration on the merits in accordance with Paragraph F of this Section."[28]

"The obligation herein to arbitrate shall not be binding upon either party with respect to claims relating to … requests by either party for temporary restraining orders, preliminary injunctions or other procedures in a court of competent jurisdiction to obtain interim relief when deemed necessary by such court to preserve the *status quo* or prevent irreparable injury pending resolution by arbitration of the actual dispute between the parties."[29]

Of the thirty-four arbitration clauses in the sample, sixteen (or 47.1 percent) unambiguously seek to preserve the right of the franchisor (or both the franchisor and franchisee) to seek interim measures in court, in some cases by excluding such claims altogether from arbitration. An additional ten clauses (or 29.4 percent) preserve the franchisor's (or both parties') right to interim relief, but are unclear whether the clause applies in court or only in arbitration.[30] Three more clauses (or 8.8 percent) – plus four of the ambiguous clauses – exclude actions for injunctive relief from arbitration, arguably including actions for preliminary injunctions. None of the clauses expressly deny arbitrators the authority to grant interim relief, although several likely have that effect by excluding questions of interim relief from arbitration. Only four arbitration clauses in the sample are wholly silent on interim measures.[31]

Finally, a sizable number of arbitration clauses preserve the franchisor's (or both parties') ability to seek interim measures in court by carving out disputes from arbitration for which interim measures are particularly likely to be appropriate. The most common carve-out, found in 68 percent of the arbitration clauses, is for trademark disputes, disputes for which "temporary injunctive relief to prevent further degradation of the trademark can be an important remedy".[32] The arbitration clauses either exclude such disputes from arbitration altogether or at the franchisor's option, ensuring that interim measures could be sought in court (and likely only in court) with respect to

---

28. Sect. 15(c) Harris Research, Inc. Franchise Agreement (for Chem-Dry franchises) (copy on file with author).

29. Sect. 25(f) Signs Now Corp. Franchise Agreement (copy on file with author).

30. E.g., Sect. 26 CD Warehouse, Inc. Franchise Agreement (copy on file with author) ("Nothing in this Agreement shall bar Franchisor's right to seek specific performance of the provisions of this Agreement and injunctive relief against threatened conduct that will cause it loss or damages under customary equity rules, including applicable rules for obtaining restraining orders and preliminary injunctions.").

31. The one arbitration clause not included in the categories described in this paragraph is the clause in the Doctor's Associates franchise agreement, which provides for the AAA Optional Rules for Emergency Measures of Protection to govern. See *supra* fn. 21.

32. DRAHOZAL, *op. cit.*, fn. 17, p. 740 table 10 and p. 763.

those disputes.

Thus, arbitration clauses in American franchise agreements commonly address the availability of interim relief. In many cases, the clauses provide for dual authority, by authorizing the arbitrator to grant interim measures (usually by incorporating the AAA Commercial Arbitration Rules) as well as by preserving the right of at least the franchisor to seek interim relief in court. In some cases, the clause provides for the court's authority to continue throughout the arbitration proceeding.[33] In other cases, the clause effectively deprives the arbitrator of authority to award interim measures, by excluding claims for such relief (or claims likely to require such relief) from arbitration altogether. The bottom line is that parties appear to have differing preferences for the relative authority of courts and arbitrators in granting interim relief.

The question remains, of course, as to how these results translate into the international context. The franchise agreements studied are distinguishable from international commercial contracts in a variety of respects. The most obvious distinction is between purely domestic disputes in the United States and international business disputes. Moreover, all of the franchise contracts studied were standard forms drafted by the franchisor and not individually negotiated with the franchisee; international contracts are more likely to be negotiated by the parties. Thus, one would expect to find fewer clauses in international contracts granting one party but not the other the right to go to court. Conversely, it may be that the terms of standard form contracts provide information that is more meaningful, rather than less meaningful, because the higher transaction costs of individually negotiated contracts may preclude the parties from reaching agreement on terms they otherwise might prefer.

At a minimum, these results demonstrate the need for further, updated research into the terms of international arbitration agreements. It is not enough to examine institutional arbitration rules to determine the terms to which parties agree. It also is necessary to examine their agreements to arbitrate.

III.   ARBITRATION STATUTES AND INTERIM MEASURES

The empirical evidence discussed above suggests an important role for both courts and arbitrators in ordering interim relief, and at the same time reveals a diversity in preferences as to their relative roles (at least among franchisors). How, then, should such empirical evidence be reflected in statutory policy?

At the very least, the evidence discussed above strongly suggests that statutory provisions governing interim relief in arbitration should be default rules rather than mandatory rules. Default rules are rules that the parties can contract around. The use of default rules in statutes can reduce the costs of contracting for parties by filling gaps when their contract is silent, while permitting parties that would prefer a different rule to so specify in their contract. Mandatory rules are rules that govern without regard to the terms of the parties' contract. Such rules "are justifiable if society wants to protect (1) parties within the contract, or (2) parties outside the contract. The former

---

33. See supra text accompanying fn. 27.

justification turns on parentalism; the latter on externalities".[34]

Neither justification for mandatory rules applies to any significant degree here. Parties to international arbitration agreements tend to be sophisticated parties who do not need statutory protection from the terms of their own agreements.[35] Moreover, interim relief issued by arbitrators cannot reach third parties who are not parties to the arbitration agreement. Thus, only to the extent court-ordered interim measures affect third parties (as opposed to the parties to the arbitration) might a mandatory rule be justified. Otherwise, rules governing interim relief in international arbitration should be default rules, to permit parties with differing preferences on the subject (which the above empirical evidence suggests that there are) to agree to differing provisions in their contracts.

Modern international arbitration statutes, as a general matter, properly make provisions dealing with interim measures default rules rather than mandatory rules. The UNCITRAL Model Law on International Commercial Arbitration, which has been adopted in some form in more than forty jurisdictions,[36] provides:

> "Unless otherwise agreed by the parties, the arbitral tribunal may, at the request of a party, order any party to take such interim measure of protection as the arbitral tribunal may consider necessary in respect of the subject-matter of the dispute. The arbitral tribunal may require any party to provide appropriate security in connection with such measure."[37]

The language identifying the rule as a default rule, of course, is the phrase "Unless otherwise agreed by the parties".

Likewise, the English Arbitration Act of 1996 adopts default rules both as to arbitrator-ordered interim measures and court-ordered interim measures. Sect. 39(1) provides that "[t]he parties are free to agree that the tribunal shall have power to order on a provisional basis any relief which it would have power to grant in a final award".[38]

---

34. Ian AYRES and Robert GERTNER, "Filling Gaps in Incomplete Contracts: An Economic Theory of Default Rules", 99 Yale L.J. (1989) p. 87 at p. 88; see also Ian AYRES, "Default Rules for Incomplete Contracts", in Peter NEWMAN, ed., *The New Palgrave Dictionary of Economics and the Law*, vol. 1 (1998) p. 585 at p. 586 ("While these two categories rather tautologically encompass the universe of all people, the dichotomy is still useful.").

35. Christopher R. DRAHOZAL, "Enforcing Vacated Arbitration Awards: An Economic Approach", 11 Am. Rev. Int'l Arb. (2000) p. 451 at p. 472; J. Mark RAMSEYER, "International Dispute Resolution: Law and Economics" in Koichi HAMADA, et al., eds., *Dreams and Dilemmas: Economic Friction and Dispute Resolution in the Asia-pacific* (2000) p. 464 at pp. 465-466.

36. UNCITRAL, "Status of Conventions and Model Laws" www.uncitral.org/english/status/status-e.htm (last updated 20 March 2003).

37. Art. 17 UNCITRAL Model Law on International Commercial Arbitration; see also Art. 9 *ibid.* ("It is not incompatible with an arbitration agreement for a party to request, before or during arbitral proceedings, from a court an interim measure of protection and for a court to grant such measure."). The default rule approach is continued in UNCITRAL's recent drafts of a revised Art. 17. See "Report of the Working Group on Arbitration on the work of its thirty-seventh session", UNCITRAL, 38th Sess. UN Doc. A/CN.9/523 (11 November 2002), para. 15.

38. England, Sect. 39(1) Arbitration Act 1996, *op. cit.*, fn. 2, p. 19.

In Sect. 44(1), the Act states:

> "Unless otherwise agreed by the parties, the court has for the purposes of and in relation to arbitral proceedings the same power of making orders about the matters listed below [e.g., interim measures] as it has for the purposes of and in relation to legal proceedings."[39]

That both provisions are default rules rather than mandatory rules is confirmed by Schedule 1 to the Act, which does not include either section in its list of mandatory provisions in the Act.[40]

By comparison, those national arbitration laws that restrict the power to award interim measures to the national courts effectively adopt a mandatory rule that precludes arbitrators from awarding interim relief.[41] Such statutes should be amended to permit arbitrators to award interim relief (or at least to permit the parties to authorize arbitrators to award interim relief). The content of the default rule is less important than that the rule be made a default rather than a mandatory rule.

Another problematic statute is the new Revised Uniform Arbitration Act (RUAA) in the United States.[42] The RUAA is a uniform statute promulgated by the National Conference of Commissioners on Uniform State Laws (NCCUSL) and currently in force in a handful of American states.[43] Sect. 8 of the RUAA addresses interim measures as follows:

> "(a) Before an arbitrator is appointed and is authorized and able to act, the court, upon [motion] of a party to an arbitration proceeding and for good cause shown, may enter an order for provisional remedies to protect the effectiveness of the arbitration proceeding to the same extent and under the same conditions as if the controversy were the subject of a civil action.
> (b) After an arbitrator is appointed and is authorized and able to act:
> (1) the arbitrator may issue such orders for provisional remedies, including interim awards, as the arbitrator finds necessary to protect the effectiveness of the arbitration proceeding and to promote the fair and expeditious resolution of the controversy, to the same extent and under the same conditions as if the controversy were the subject of a civil action and
> (2) a party to an arbitration proceeding may move the court for a provisional remedy only if the matter is urgent and the arbitrator is not able to act timely or the arbitrator cannot provide an adequate remedy."

The Act expressly identifies Sect. 8 as a mandatory rule (at least before a dispute arises):

---

39. *Ibid.*, Sect. 44(1), p. 21.
40. *Ibid.*, Schedule 1, p. 47.
41. See supra fn. 3.
42. Sect. 8 RUAA, *op. cit.*, fn. 4.
43. NCCUSL, "A Few Facts About the Uniform Arbitration Act" (2000) (visited 26 March 2003) www. nccusl.org/nccusl/uniformact_factsheets/uniformacts-fs-aa.asp.

"Before a controversy arises that is subject to an agreement to arbitrate, a party to the agreement may not … waive or agree to vary the effect of the requirements of" the section.[44]

The RUAA applies principally (if not exclusively) to domestic arbitration proceedings in the United States, and it might be possible to justify the treatment of interim measures as a mandatory rule on that ground. Instead, the Drafting Committee offered the following explanation for restricting the authority of courts to grant interim relief after appointment of an arbitrator:

> "In a judicial proceeding for preliminary relief, the court does not have the benefit of the arbitrator's determination of disputed issues or interpretation of the contract. Another problem for a court is that in determining the propriety of an injunction, order, writ for attachment or other security, the court must make an assessment of hardships upon the parties and the probability of success on the merits. Such determinations fly in the face of the underlying philosophy of arbitration that the parties have chosen arbitrators to decide the merits of their disputes."[45]

This explanation, while perhaps justifying a default rule restricting court-ordered interim relief, does not justify making the rule a mandatory rule instead of a default rule. The parties are better situated than the RUAA drafters or state legislatures to choose the degree of judicial involvement with the arbitration process that they prefer. The empirical evidence from franchise agreements, cited above, indicates that at least some parties prefer a greater scope of court authority to grant interim relief than is provided in the RUAA. Such parties would be better off if Sect. 8 of the RUAA were a default rule instead of a mandatory rule.[46]

---

44. Sect. 4(b)(1) RUAA, *op. cit.*, fn. 4.

45. *Ibid.* Official Cmt. 2 to Sect. 8. The Official Comments to Sect. 4 do not explain why the rule on interim relief is a mandatory rule. The Reporter to the Drafting Committee has written that "[a] key reason why the Drafting Committee included Sect. 4 was to address the adhesion situation and to put some limits on the one-sidedness of arbitration agreements". Timothy J. HEINSZ, "The Revised Uniform Arbitration Act: Modernizing, Revising, and Clarifying Arbitration Law", J. Disp. Resol. (2001) p. 1 at p. 8. But the Reporter offers no explanation as to why the restriction on court-ordered interim relief is such a rule, although he does suggest that the reason for including Sect. 8 as a mandatory rule was to limit "a party's ability … to prevent applications to a court to aid the arbitration process". *Ibid.*

46. Parties may still be able to contract around the RUAA rule, however, by excluding from the scope of the arbitration clause claims for interim relief or disputes likely to give rise to such claims. As noted above, a number of arbitration clauses in franchise agreements take precisely such an approach. See supra text accompanying fns. 30-32.

IV.   CONCLUSION

The principle of party autonomy has (at least) two important implications for the allocation of authority over interim measures between courts and arbitrators. The first implication is that it is important to consider contracting practices with respect to interim measures in determining the allocation of authority that parties prefer. Such an empirically-based approach should not be limited to reviewing institutional arbitration rules, but also should examine the provisions of parties' arbitration agreements, which may override the agreed-upon institutional rules or address issues on which the rules are silent. The empirical evidence presented here – from American franchise agreements – indicates that while many franchisors provide for shared authority over interim measures, there remain important differences among franchisors as between court-ordered and arbitrator-ordered interim relief. Thus, the second implication of the principle of party autonomy is that statutory provisions addressing interim relief should be default rules, which the parties can change by contract, rather than mandatory rules, which they cannot. Most, but not all, modern arbitration statutes have taken that approach, which benefits arbitrating parties whose preferred approach differs from that set out in the statute.

Developing Mechanisms for the Resolution of International Disputes: The UNCITRAL Model Law on International Commercial Conciliation

*Shavit Matias**

TABLE OF CONTENTS

I. INTRODUCTION: MEDIATION OF COMMERCIAL DISPUTES BETWEEN PRIVATE PARTIES

International trade, by definition, crosses borders. It includes, of course, transactions by large companies selling millions or billions of dollars of manufactured products to customers in other countries, under contracts carefully negotiated by teams of lawyers on both sides. It also includes a myriad of small transactions, such as the sale of tomatoes by a small Mexican grower to a customer across the border in the United States, underwritten agreements that may be crafted many times by the parties to the contract themselves.

Regardless of the size of the transaction, where there is trade there will inevitably be disputes. The multimillion dollar contracts between major international companies meticulously drafted by well-trained lawyers will often refer the parties to carefully constructed arbitration or conciliation processes. The agreements between less sophisticated buyers and sellers, the everyday agreements that form the delicate framework for social interaction between peoples, often do not explicitly provide for any form of dispute settlement, or, if they do, may include reference to sparsely defined

---

*   Director, Department for International Agreements and International Litigation, Ministry of Justice, Israel; Adjunct Professor, Hebrew University. The author wishes to thank Ms. Heather Kurzbauer and Ms. Judy Freedberg for their assistance in putting this paper together and many wise comments. The author would also like to thank Sir Anthony Evans, Judge Howard Holtzmann, Mr. Jernej Sekolec and Mr. Jeffrey Winton for many hours of thoughtful discussions on mechanisms for resolving international disputes. All views expressed in this paper reflect the author's personal opinions and should not be considered as views expressed in an official capacity.

mechanisms. Should a dispute arise, each side to the contract might interpret the procedure or applicability of such mechanisms differently.

In a purely domestic context, reference simply by name to an alternative dispute settlement mechanism may be less problematic in some cases, because the parties to the agreement will often (but not always) share a common cultural approach to resolution of disputes. Furthermore, the structure or parameters defining the operation of that mechanism may be defined or regulated by the domestic law.[1] By contrast, the parties to an international transaction may be separated by culture as well as an international border. They may not share a common understanding of how the different ADR processes should be conducted, how disputes should be approached, or resolved. Consequently, numerous misunderstandings can occur even with respect to the interpretation and conduct of the mechanism chosen to resolve the dispute.

The divergence of interpretation of the concepts between different cultures is very well exemplified in a study conducted by Mohamed Abu-Nimer, in which he examined the approaches of the Middle East and the West to conflict resolution processes, including mediation.

According to Abu-Nimer, the following are some of the social and cultural assumptions that shape and underlie Middle Eastern conflict resolution processes, including mediation:

> 1. Group affiliation (family, clan, religion, sect or other collective identity) is the most central and important identity that should be protected and sustained through conflict management processes.
> 2. Social norms and values rather than legal norms, are the main rules of commitment. Therefore, written agreements (or signing) are not part of the process. Instead, parties and third parties rely on established social and cultural values and norms in reaching and implementing agreements.
> 3. Codes of honor, shame and dignity are the main components which are used by the parties, mediators, and conflict resolvers to describe or establish any process.
> 4. Conflict resolution and mediation are based on hierarchical, authoritarian procedures and structures (older people, males, and powerful officials are the ones that normally should be used as mediators).[2]

By contrast, the following are some of the basic principles that have been identified

---

1. Although judging from the number of court litigations arising in many countries as a result of challenges, for example, to arbitration proceedings, a process that is, in most countries, covered by national legislation, it is clear that in domestic proceedings too there may be many difficulties and misunderstandings regarding the processes.
2. See Bashir BASHIR, "Western and Middle Eastern Approaches of Conflict Resolution" (2001) Unpublished mauscript available on file at the Mediation Department of the Ministry of Justice, Israel, summarizing ABU-NIMER's principal ideas on the subject. For more detailed reading, see also Mohamed ABU-NIMER, "Conflict Resolution in an Islamic Context: Some Conceptual Questions", 21 Peace and Change (1996) and *Nonviolence and Peace Building in Islam, Theory and Practice* (University Press of Florida 2003).

regarding approaches to conflict resolution in the Western context:

> 1. The outcome of the conflict is reflected in a written agreement, which is a central component of the conflict resolution process.
> 2. Legal formality and set procedures are an essential part of the conflict resolution.
> 3. The choice of mediators is usually task and qualification (and professionalism) oriented.[3]

According to the results of Abu-Nimer's study, therefore, there appears to be a large divergence between Middle Eastern and Western norms in terms of defining the concept of conciliation, and how it should be conducted. This divergence in norms, is, of course, relevant to many other cultures.[4] How do we bridge that gap? How do we create a mechanism for resolution of international commercial disputes with which members of different cultures can agree and feel comfortable?

A common international framework for resolving disputes may help bridge the cultural and legal gaps that may exist between the parties. And, to the extent that this framework encourages the parties to seek non-adversarial solutions through mediation and conciliation, it may enhance the opportunities for less contentious means of dispute resolution, promoting cross-border partnerships and economic growth.

Before mediation can become a viable mechanism for the resolution of international disputes, it must provide the parties with a sense of comfort with regard to the process. The parties must be able to understand, at the outset, what the mediation process entails, and they must be convinced that the mediation process will be governed by principles that will ensure a just, fair and confidential mechanism for resolving the dispute.

At present, there simply may be too much uncertainty about the mediation process for it to provide an effective alternative to more adversarial processes. In many countries, mediation is not subject to any form of regulation and there are no clearly established qualifications for mediators. In fact, in many parts of the world, a person becomes a mediator by an act of self-assertion, without any objective qualifications whatsoever. With unqualified individuals serving as mediators under ill-defined and unregulated processes, parties may have justified concerns that mediation may well result in a loss of time and money, with the possibility of prejudice towards the outcome of the case if it subsequently is brought through more adversarial processes.[5]

---

3. *Ibid.*

4. See, for example, Kevin C. CLARK, "The Philosophical Underpinning and General Workings of Chinese Mediation Systems: What Lessons Can American Mediators Learn?", 2 Pepp. Disp. Resol. L.J. (2002) p. 117; Kresimir PUHARIC, "Comparative Theme: Conciliation as a Method of Settlement of International Commercial Disputes", 4 Croat. Arbit. Yearb. p. 155; Cao PEI, "The Origins of Mediation in Traditional China", 54 Disp. Resol. J. (1999) p. 32.

5. For example, prior to the enactment of the conciliation law in Israel not so very long ago (see: Israel Courts Law (consolidated version) (1984) Conciliation, Sects. 79(c) and (d), enacted1992, amended 2000), many mediations in Israel suffered from similar or other problems. The result was that parties might have opted for this process once, but if such mediations resulted in an

A carefully drafted model law adopted by different States may help to overcome these problems.[6] By harmonizing the concepts of international commercial mediation, and establishing consistent qualifications for mediators, such a model law could well engender in private parties the familiarity and comfort with the mediation process that are needed to allow mediation to play a useful role in resolving international disputes effectively and efficiently. At the same time, a model law could also establish principles that might be used to guide the development of national laws governing mediation processes for domestic disputes.

Of course, even if such principles are established, there may still be misunderstandings and cultural differences that will increase the difficulties of resolving certain disputes. But well-formulated principles will inevitably help to create a common ground that one hopes will result in public acceptance of, and appreciation for, the opportunities that mediation can present.

II.   THE OPPORTUNITIES FOR MEDIATION OF INTERNATIONAL TRADE DISPUTES BETWEEN STATES

1.   The Evolution of Procedures for Resolving Disputes Between States

Can a model law on conciliation also enhance the use of mediation in this context in international disputes between States and between States and private parties?

For centuries, scholars, politicians and diplomats have worked to create international dispute settlement devices that would allow highly contentious disputes among States to be transformed into peaceful settlements. The basic procedures for resolving international disputes were worked out long ago, if not in classical times, then at least by the turn of the twentieth century.[7]

---

unsuccessful experience, parties usually refrained from considering the mediation process in the context of future agreements. The enactment of the law, and very significant efforts to regulate and promote mediation undertaken in the last few years by the National Center for Mediation and Dispute Resolution headed by Dr. Peretz Segal, as well as the Center for Mediation established by the Israel Bar Association, dramatically changed the situation. In the last few years the use of mediation has greatly expanded, mediation training centers and mediation services centers have sprung up all over the country, mediation and its principles are taught and promoted at universities and colleges, mediation is being taught to schoolchildren as a mechanism they can use to resolve disputes among themselves, and courts have begun regularly and systematically to refer disputes to mediation.

6. Importantly, the recently adopted US Uniform Mediation Act, enacted 16 August 2001, is being amended to bring the relevant provisions in line with the UNCITRAL Model Law.

7. See, for example, The Treaty of Peace between Sparta and Argos concluded in 418 BC, which contained a dispute resolution clause stating that:

"If there should arise a difference between any of the towns of the Peloponnesus or beyond, either as to frontiers or any other object, there shall be an arbitration. If among the allied towns they are not able to come to an agreement, the dispute will be brought before a neutral town chosen by common agreement."

More than a century ago the major nations agreed to the first Hague Convention on the Pacific Settlement of International Disputes, which established a Permanent Court of Arbitration at The Hague.[8] This convention codified, to a large extent, the same basic approaches to dispute settlement, including good offices, consultations, negotiations, inquiry, conciliation, mediation and arbitration, that still form the basis of the dispute settlement mechanisms incorporated in international agreements today. The dispute settlement mechanisms created by this Convention, and by the conventions and agreements that followed, ranged from highly simplistic dispute resolution provisions, which provided mostly for dispute resolution through diplomatic processes, to the more sophisticated third-party dispute resolution mechanisms.[9]

Hundreds of tribunals were established in the last century for the peaceful settlement of international disputes.[10] Yet, when the history of that century is finally written, it certainly will not be seen as the century in which most disputes between States or between States and private parties were peacefully resolved through pacific dispute settlement procedures. In many instances, the mechanisms available were ignored, failing to satisfy cost/benefit calculations inherent in a State's agreement to relinquish sovereignty over a disputed matter in the first place.[11] Often, when a dispute actually

---

Quoted in Jackson RALSTON, *International Arbitration From Athens to Locarno* (1929) p. 157.

8. 1899 Convention for the Pacific Settlement of International Disputes, reprinted in *Permanent Court of Arbitration Basic Documents* (The Hague 1998) pp. 1-15.

9. It is beyond the scope of this work to analyze all the different international dispute settlement mechanisms which have existed, or exist today. Several excellent references on international dispute settlement mechanisms include: Manley O. HUDSON, *International Tribunals Past and Future* (1944); C. Wilfred JENKS, *The Prospects of International Adjudication* (1964); "International Disputes, The Legal Aspects", Report of a Study Group of the David Davies Memorial Institute of International Studies (1972); A.H.A. SOONS, ed., *International Arbitration: Past and Prospects* (1988); J.G. MERRILLS, *International Dispute Settlement* (1991); Ian BROWNLIE and Surya Prakash SINHA, "The Peaceful Settlement of International Disputes in Practice", 7 Pace Int'l L. Rev. (1995) p. 257. A selective bibliography on the subject can be found in a United Nations publication, *Peaceful Settlement of Disputes between States* (1991) compiled by the Dag Hammarskjöld Library. For an excellent survey of dispute settlement mechanisms in treaties, see, e.g., *Systematic Survey of Treaties for the Pacific Settlement of Disputes 1928-1948* (United Nations Publication 1949) and *A Survey of Treaty Provisions for the Pacific Settlement of International Disputes 1949-1962* (United Nations Publication 1966).

10. See A.M. STUYT, *Survey of International Arbitrations 1794-1989*, 3rd ed. (Dordrecht 1990) Appendix II for a complete list of cases from the Permanent Court of International Justice (PCIJ)/International Court of Justice (ICJ) as well as Administrative Tribunals, Regional Tribunals and Military Tribunals, pp. 593-624.

11. The difficulties associated with the traditional dispute settlement mechanisms can be classified into two categories. First, are the problems associated with the mechanisms themselves. It would appear that many mechanisms were criticized (and consequently not widely used) for reasons associated with their structure (whether too legalistic or too diplomatic), their inability to be impartial or because of a general perception of their ineffectiveness. For an excellent analysis of these and other issues raised, see, e.g., works by HUDSON, JENKS, SOONS, MERRILLS, BROWNLIE and SINHA cited in fn. 9. Second, and not less significant, is the perception that the traditional reluctance of States to submit their disputes to a binational or multinational dispute settlement mechanism has not been overcome, despite centuries of efforts in this regard.

arose, it became apparent that the mechanism which had been established in the agreement was inappropriate as it did not appear to provide for an impartial opportunity to resolve the dispute, and generally gave at least one of the parties an overall perception of being ineffective.

When viewed in the context of this history, the current fascination legal scholars, politicians and practitioners show toward the creation of dispute settlement mechanisms that will be used more frequently, whether in a bilateral or multilateral context, is understandable. In that regard, recent experience, particularly in the context of dispute settlement mechanisms negotiated in international trade agreements, appears to represent a meaningful step forward.[12]

Throughout history dispute settlement mechanisms in international trade agreements were short and broadly defined, establishing only relatively simple procedures under which disputes were to be resolved predominately through the diplomatic process of consultations or negotiations.[13] Significantly even these diplomatic mechanisms were rarely used, and many trade disputes were, in the end, determined by the relative political and economic strength of the parties rather than through a determination of what was right or wrong through the established dispute settlement mechanism. Although a certain evolution towards more legalistic mechanisms could be discerned over the years, the mechanisms were still dominated by diplomatic procedures, and the basic reluctance of States to use the mechanisms remained.[14]

---

12. It should be noted that there have recently been established varying degrees of elaborate dispute settlement mechanisms outside of the trade field. See, e.g., the dispute settlement mechanism created under the 1982 United Nations Law of the Sea Convention. An attempt to discern an overall tendency in international relations towards more legalistic mechanisms resulting from perceived interdependence of States can be found in Marcel T. BRUS, *Third Party Dispute Settlement in an Interdependent World* (1993). An excellent summary of mechanisms for resolution of human rights claims can be found in Thomas BUERGENTHAL, David STEWART and Dinah SHELTON, *International Human Rights Law in a Nutshell* (West Publications 2002).

13. The 1870 Friendship Commerce and Navigation Treaty between the United States and El Salvador, for example, contemplated negotiations before resorting to war. The dispute resolution clause in that treaty stated that:

    "[I]f, unfortunately, any of the articles contained in this treaty should be violated or infringed in any way whatever, it is expressly stipulated that neither of the two contracting parties shall ordain or authorize any acts of reprisal, nor shall declare war against the other ... until the said party considering itself offended shall have laid before the other a statement of such injuries or damages ... demanding justice and satisfaction, and the same shall have been denied, in violation of the laws and of national right."

    General Treaty of Amity, Commerce and Consular Privileges, United States-El Salvador, 6 December 1870, Art. 13, 18th Stat. 725, T.S. No. 310.

14. For example, the United States agreed, in its Friendship Commerce and Navigation Treaties (FCNs), to the jurisdiction of the International Court of Justice (ICJ) for disputes not resolved through diplomacy, unless the parties agree to settlement by some other peaceful means. While numerous FCNs have been negotiated by the United States, disputes arising under the modern FCNs have been submitted to the ICJ only on three occasions. Both *United States Diplomatic and Consular Staff in Tehran (United States v. Iran)* 1980 I.C.J. Rep. 3, and the case of *Military and*

In the last twenty years, there has been a fundamental shift in this basic approach. Dispute settlement procedures in trade agreements have become a major focus of negotiations. The mechanisms adopted have been quite intricate, often highly legalistic, and at times have fostered the creation of sophisticated institutions capable of rendering generally acceptable rule-based determinations. Importantly, the number of trade disputes resolved through these mechanisms has steadily increased.[15]

A number of reasons can be offered for this change in emphasis.

First, the political and economic realities of recent times have contributed to the perception of a need to adopt dispute resolution mechanisms to address progressively more complex trade issues. As the world has become increasingly interdependent and countries engage in an increasing amount of trade, the ability of the stronger party to unilaterally dictate the outcome of a dispute diminishes. Such action, when attempted, can often be followed by economic retaliatory action on the part of the other party, usually affecting critical trading interests of the stronger party. Even in absence of retaliatory action, however, such behavior is no longer easily undertaken. As countries become members to an increasing number of trade agreements immediately affecting their interests, they increasingly strive to be perceived as complying with their international obligations. Use of an agreed-upon dispute settlement mechanism therefore is recognized as diminishing the likelihood of such trade wars, and the perception of unfair play.

Second, and not less important, is the fact that, in the last few decades, private economic transactions have increasingly transcended political boundaries. Businesses and corporations have become international, and investments are no longer limited to the immediate surrounding.[16] National interests, therefore, are not as clear-cut as before. While, for example, one national company may ask its government to initiate a trade measure against another country for alleged violation of international obligations, another national company that has significant investment or businesses in the violating country may oppose such measures and claim that no such violations occurred. As a result, governments are increasingly receiving mixed messages from their constituents with respect to the conduct of foreign trading partners. In such circumstances,

---

Paramilitary Activities in and against Nicaragua (Nicaragua v. United States of America) 1986 I.C.J. Rep. 14, concerned challenges to the legality of the conduct of the respondent State which involved questions of foreign policy. As a result, the respondent States disputed the ICJ's ability to pass judgment on these matters. In the third case, *Elettronica Sicula S.p.A. (ELSI) (United States v. Italy)* concerning alleged violations by Italy of its FCN through its treatment of an Italian subsidiary of Raytheon, a US company, the Court issued a judgment that Italy did not violate the treaty, 28 I.L.M. (1989) p. 111.

15. For example, while less than 300 complaints were filed under the General Agreement on Tariffs and Trade (GATT) in its fifty years of existence (See, e.g., Robert HUDEC, *Enforcing International Trade Law* (1993)) a very significant amount of complaints has been filed since 1995, when the agreements establishing the World Trade Organization (WTO) entered into force. Just in the first six months of the WTO's existence, more than fifty-three GATT complaints were filed with the dispute settlement body. And, from 1995 to date, well over 200 complaints have been filed. See WTO Internet site at www.wto.org/wto/dispute/bulletin.htm.

16. See, e.g., Jonathan T. FRIED, "Globalization and International Law – Some Thoughts for States and Citizens", 23 Queen's L.J. (1997) p. 259.

determination of the international dispute by an impartial panel can alleviate to some degree the responsibility of the government for the final determination of the matter.

Third, because of the trade liberalization policy and the astounding growth in trade since World War II, numerous trade agreements have been negotiated. As the number of trade conflicts arising from these agreements has grown, attention has focused not only on the substantive rules of the agreements, but on rules regarding conflict resolution and remedies as well. And, importantly, the nature of trade agreements has changed significantly over the last half century, considerably affecting the need for an elaborate dispute settlement mechanism. When the first multilateral trade agreements were negotiated after World War II, high tariffs and various types of import quotas constituted the primary barriers to international trade, and the primary focus of trade negotiations and agreements was the reduction of tariffs and the elimination of quotas. It was relatively easy to monitor a party's compliance with its commitments under such agreements.

As tariff rates have been reduced, and quotas eliminated through a series of negotiations, they have become less important as trade barriers. The relatively low tariff rates that remain can no longer protect domestic industries unless they are augmented by the special duties permitted to remedy the unfair practices of dumping and subsidies. As a result, the focus of international trade negotiations has shifted from simple tariff reduction to more complicated matters like disciplines on the use of anti-dumping and anti-subsidy measures and restrictions on more subtle non-trade barriers.

As trade agreements have changed to cover more complex matters, the old dispute settlement mechanisms have seemed less capable of handling the disputes that arise. It is no longer a simple matter of establishing that a party has charged duties above the ceilings established by the agreement. Now, the factual matters raised in such disputes include price adjustments and cost-of-production calculations in anti-dumping investigations, or the economic effects of the pricing of natural resources in anti-subsidy cases, or claims that government procurement procedures unfairly discriminate against foreigners, or allegations that a government has permitted anti-competitive practices that discriminate against foreign producers, or even suggestions that a government is somehow encouraging anti-import sentiment. To handle these increasingly difficult cases, it has been necessary to develop more sophisticated dispute settlement mechanisms.

Fourth, the dispute settlement mechanisms in trade agreements have become more complex over time to address specific issues and problems that have arisen under previous agreements. Each new agreement has built, to some extent, on the experience of the last. The natural tendency to work from the last agreement in negotiating the next has been reinforced to some extent by domestic political pressures which often make it difficult for governments to accept less in an agreement than they (or someone else) got in the last one. In addition, the phenomenal evolution and acceptance of judicial-like mechanisms in private international commercial arbitration, the experience gained there, and the vast body of law which emerged from these international institutions have proved a useful learning tool and background for negotiators of dispute settlement mechanisms in international trade agreements.[17]

2. Towards Mediation of International Trade Disputes Between States

The evolution of trade agreements to more complex forms of dispute settlement mechanisms has reflected a perception that more legalistic procedures were in the economic interests of the parties.[18] And, indeed, in the international commercial context whether between States or whether between States and private parties, the creation of binding sophisticated dispute settlement mechanisms is an everyday reality.

The evolution of dispute settlement provisions in trade agreements has not however been a mechanistic march towards more binding legalistic procedures. Indeed, the factors favoring more legalistic procedures have been offset by the natural inclination of independent nation States to avoid ceding sovereignty to international institutions, as well as by cultural and social inhibitions. And, as in any international negotiations, these inhibiting factors have been overcome only when doing so has been in the narrow interests of the parties.

While recognizing the necessity and value of the legalistic mechanisms, at the same time, serious concerns have been raised that these mechanisms detract from the ability of States to resolve disputes quickly and less contentiously, and that a leap has been made, from what has been traditionally a more diplomatic and negotiated process, to what now appears like an almost inevitable court-like litigation process, with very little flexibility for States to maneuver in when a dispute actually arises.[19]

---

17. In that regard the experience of the European Community (and European Union (EU)) including the establishment of legalistic dispute settlement mechanisms (including a court system) governing the application of the agreements, has also provided a meaningful impetus towards the legalistic evolution of dispute settlement mechanisms in the context of trade agreements, although unlike the situation in the EU, these agreements ordinarily do not propose a heightened degree of integration, and profess to safeguard the sovereignty of the States members to the agreements.

18. See, for example, John H. JACKSON, *The World Trading System* 1983-1988 (1989). As Jackson puts it the key to a successful dispute settlement resolution procedure is in the "bargaining chips" it creates. Jackson takes the position that it is necessary for the parties to recognize that once negotiations come to an impasse a system exists that will take over the dispute and determine the matter fairly. In absence of such system, Jackson argues, the parties are left to rely only on their respective power position. In such instances, it is no longer the party whose economic rights were violated who will have the upper hand in the dispute, but, rather, the party who is more powerful of the two. See also, "Recommendations of the American and Canadian Bar Associations Joint Working Group on the Settlement of International Disputes," 20 March 1979 (stating that only where a binding procedure can be easily triggered by either party if no settlement is reached through non-binding procedures are the parties assured that the dispute will be actually settled.)

19. There are those, for example, who, while not disagreeing that a legalistic dispute settlement mechanism may support the immediate economic interests of the parties, do disagree with the theory that a legalistic dispute settlement mechanism is desirable in international economic relations. Instead, they support the use of diplomatic means for resolution of disputes. An argument often presented by these dissenters is that insistence on legalistic mechanisms does not take into account cultural differences. While, they say, Westerners tend to focus on mechanisms and procedures, Asian, Middle Eastern and African philosophies tend towards mechanisms promoting conciliation, negotiation and mediation. In creating international dispute mechanisms

Clearly, States can always attempt to negotiate a settlement of the dispute. However, that has become more difficult once a dispute is streamlined into a legalistic process, where it seems to take on a life of its own, and where it is subject to huge publicity and private economic interests. These mechanisms, which have been so carefully negotiated and built, seem more often than not to have skipped the steps that would provide the disputants with another opportunity to resolve the dispute in a non-adversarial manner that is not as open-ended and unstructured as negotiations, but is also not as strictly legalistic and as geared towards a clear win-lose situation as a panel process, arbitration or litigation. A well-defined mediation process that can precede the more legalistic mechanism, could provide such an opportunity.

In the dispute settlement mechanisms that have been negotiated in major trade agreements to date (such as the WTO, many Bilateral Investment Treaties, or many Free Trade Agreements), mediation seems to play quite a minor role. For example, the WTO Understanding on Rules and Procedures Governing the Settlement of Disputes established an elaborate mandatory panel system that is very similar to arbitration or court proceedings, and even includes an appeals mechanism. The rules governing the mechanism stretch over twenty-four pages, yet contain only one article that addresses mediation (Art. 5). It should be noted that the article does not provide for a clear

---

therefore, these cultural differences should be taken under consideration, and there should not be an insistence on legalistic mechanisms. See, e.g., Carl GREEN, "APEC and Trans-Pacific Dispute Management", 26 Law and Policy in International Business, p. 719. The question of legalistic versus diplomatic or pragmatic dispute settlement mechanisms is commonly debated. A legalistic mechanism refers to a rule-oriented mechanism which resembles formal adjudication and which typically will have binding decisions and an enforcement mechanism. A diplomatic mechanism, on the other hand, is a flexible model for dispute resolution relying mostly on negotiations, mediation and conciliation. As a general matter, the pragmatists argue that non-binding dispute mechanisms are better suited to deal with disputes between countries. These mechanisms, the pragmatists argue, allow a country more leverage and freedom in its actions, and allow for considerations other than the immediate issue at dispute to be taken into account in fashioning the solution. See, for example, Fred L. MORRISON, "The Future of International Adjudication", 75 Minn. L. Rev. (1991) p. 827 and p. 838 (expressing the opinion that "the relative success of the GATT mechanism has been because of, not in spite of, its recognition of a political role in the process"). (It should be noted that the flexibility of the mechanism has served an important purpose in the context of international conflicts not economic in nature, and allowed for their use, in various shapes and forms, and with varying degrees of success, in territorial and other disputes. See, e.g., Saadia TOUVAL, *Mediation in the Yugoslav Wars: The Critical Years, 1990-1995* (2002).) The legalists, on the other hand, argue that only a rule-based mechanism can best resolve disputes in a fair and speedy manner, provide for predictability and stability in the field of international trade, and diminish the power differences between poor and rich nations. See, e.g., Ernst-Ulrich PETERSMANN, *Constitutional Functions and Constitutional Problems of International Economic Law* (1991) pp. xli-xlii (advancing the argument that there is a need for rule-oriented legal processes in the context of international trade disputes). See also Kenneth W. ABBOTT, "The Uruguay Round and Dispute Resolution: Building a Private-Interests System of Justice", Columbia Business Law Rev. (1992, no. 1) p. 123 (suggesting that diplomatic mechanisms may result in compromise measures and that "[c]ompromise settlements ... suggest that one may be able to profit by ignoring social norms".)

description of the process and what it entails.[20]

This vagueness, in itself, could create a disincentive to engage in what is an unclear process whose benefits are not readily apparent. Indeed, it appears that this process rarely has been formally used by disputants in the well over 200 disputes that have already arisen since the entry into force of the WTO agreements, if ever at all.[21]

How is it that States made the quantum leap from mostly diplomatic-oriented mechanisms, which had few rules or binding effect, directly to legalistic mechanisms, including binding arbitration, virtually ignoring the mechanism of mediation?

As discussed above, part of the reason for the development of the legalistic mechanisms is probably dissatisfaction with the notion that diplomatic mechanisms are suitable to resolve international trade disputes. Mediation and conciliation, processes that were never really clarified even by those who negotiated relevant agreements, were most likely classified as processes that were part of the failed diplomatic means to resolve disputes, and should therefore not be given any serious weight when building the new mechanisms.[22]

The absence of a well-defined practice of mediation for private disputes may also be partially a cause of the failure of States to adopt such practices in international disputes. There is an interdependency between tools used for resolution of disputes in the private international commercial sphere and in the public international trade sphere. Mechanisms that are viewed as successful in one usually find themselves in a relatively short time used by the other. In this regard, the Model Law on International Commercial Arbitration, which has been adopted in many States, helped create what appears today to be a well-accepted general understanding of what an arbitration is and what the process is when parties agree to an arbitration. This, in turn, allows the lawyers representing governments in trade negotiations to refer to an accepted model of arbitration when they design their dispute settlement procedures. By the same token, the absence of a model law on mediation and conciliation, and in turn an absence of a consensus on what these processes mean, has limited the ability of trade negotiators to build an effective mediation process into their agreements. A model law might well be instrumental in allowing States to use mediation more effectively in their international agreements.

---

20. Uruguay Round Understanding on Rules and Procedures Governing the Settlement of Disputes available at www.wto.org/english/docs_e/legal_e/28-dsu.doc.

21. Information available at: www.wto.org/english/tratope/dispute.htm#news. As of May 2003, no disputes resolved through mediation have been formally reported on that site. As stated in the WTO Guide to Dispute Settlement, "[c]onciliation appears to have been an underused facility of the DSU". See, Peter GALLAGHER *Guide to Dispute Settlement* (Kluwer 2002) pp. 65-66.

22. Interestingly, in the context of the current Doha negotiations for modifications to the Dispute Settlement Understanding (DSU), some countries have put forward proposals suggesting enhancement of the mediation process, including a clear structure for mediation to occur. There has not been widespread support for this as yet, and it is unclear whether these modifications will be included in this round of negotiations.

III.   CRAFTING A MODEL LAW

Two goals in particular motivated the creation of the Model Law. One goal was to create an international standard that could be adopted by States, enhance the predictability of the international mediation process, and, in turn, its use by disputing parties. As has been mentioned, a major divergence in the mediation process from one State to another may quickly render the mediation tool less effective in international disputes, in particular when small-scale contracts are involved and parties find themselves subject to varying domestic laws, practices or interpretations. One purpose of the model law was, therefore, to form a basis for harmonization among national practices.

Another goal was for the model law to serve as a reference point for States even if they do not intend to adopt the model law as such. The model law can serve as a reference both with respect to legislation concerning mediation in international disputes, or even with respect to establishing criteria and boundaries for mediation in domestic disputes. Legislators in many States do not have the resources or experience to work through all of the issues that may arise in structuring sound legislation regarding mediation. A model law can serve to raise the awareness of national legislators to issues that must be considered in this context, and to, in turn, enact legislation that is better suited to deal with the process.

When drafting a model law, there are, of course, a number of different approaches that might be followed. At one end of the spectrum, the drafters could, for example, establish a general framework that addresses only the major issues, and leaves the details to be worked out by national legislators. At the other end, the drafters could try to develop a proposal that sets forth all of the procedures in detail.

The effort to harmonize national mediation laws cannot, however, be taken too far. The model law must remain flexible in order to accommodate the different legal regimes in which it is to be employed, as this will ensure the possibility of it being accepted in as many regimes as possible. Given the purposes of a model law, an approach that bridged between these two extremes seemed most appropriate.

IV.   THE WORK OF THE UNCITRAL WORKING GROUP ON ARBITRATION AND CONCILIATION

The purpose of UNCITRAL's intergovernmental Working Group II on Arbitration and Conciliation, inaugurated in 1999, was to offer States a legislative text that would harmonize the major concerns of parties involved in the mediation/conciliation processes. Although all States expressed a concern for safeguarding the basic concept that the conciliation process not jeopardize the rights of the parties to the dispute – as might be the case if statements made during conciliation could subsequently be used as evidence in further arbitral or court proceedings, there was, however, significant disagreement on other issues – for example on whether parties should be compelled to seek conciliation before resort to more formal litigation proceedings. Overall, the Working Group was committed to preserving the flexible nature of conciliation while addressing the most important issues concerning conciliation, including the appointment of conciliators, the role of these conciliators in subsequent arbitral or court proceedings and the hotly debated issue of the enforceability of settlement agreements.

The final text of the UNCITRAL Model Law on International Commercial Conciliation deals, in a varying degree of specificity, with a wide range of issues relating to international commercial conciliation. Among other things, the Model Law:

— Provides for a definition of what is an international commercial conciliation, and who a conciliator is;
— Deals with the issue of its interpretation, and allows the parties to exclude and vary its provisions;
— Defines the stage where conciliation proceedings are deemed to commence;
— Addresses the question of appointment of conciliators, the conduct of the conciliation, and the question of communication between the conciliator and the parties;
— Addresses the question of disclosure of information provided by a party to a conciliator to other disputants in the course of a conciliation;
— Establishes the confidentiality obligation regarding all information relating to the conciliation proceeding;
— Addresses the question of admissibility of evidence obtained through a conciliation in other proceedings;
— Defines when a conciliation is to be deemed as terminated;
— Addresses the question of a conciliator acting as an arbitrator, the question of resorting to arbitral or judicial proceedings when a conciliation has been expressly agreed to by the parties, and the question of enforceability of a settlement agreement.

In brief, the Model Law provides for a definition of conciliation, basically providing that it is a mechanism for the settlement of disputes by which a neutral third person or persons (the conciliator/conciliators) is called in to assist with the dispute resolution process. The Model Law will apply as long as the definition of conciliation is met – irrespective of what the process is actually called by the parties – provided that the matters are both commercial and international in nature. However, States may choose to enact legislation affecting domestic conciliation along similar lines.

Under the Model Law, the role of the conciliator is a non-binding one. Importantly, the Model Law promotes the principle that the conciliator should be independent, impartial. Furthermore, a conciliator shall disclose any circumstance that may affect the parties.

The Model Law does not impose any obligation on the parties to conciliate; the decision of whether to impose mandatory conciliation remains a domestic one that must be determined by national laws of contract or procedure. In addition, the Model Law allows the parties the freedom to vary from its provisions, and the freedom to choose the location for the process to take place. Under the Model Law, the parties are granted full freedom to structure the conciliation proceedings, as they deem appropriate. This includes setting rules for conducting the procedure, and more. However, in absence of such agreement, the Model Law does provide for some general structure and mandates fair treatment of the parties.

Finally, the Model Law provides the parties with important safeguards and legal protections. For example, the Model Law provides that information relating to the conciliation proceeding shall, as a general matter, be kept confidential. Furthermore, the Model Law provides that certain types of evidence enumerated in the Model Law (such as admissions, personal views, proposals, etc.) revealed during the conciliation process will not be ordered disclosed by a court of law or arbitral tribunal, and should be inadmissible as evidence in subsequent proceedings should they occur. And, the Model Law prohibits the conciliator from acting as an arbitrator in any subsequent proceedings, unless parties agree otherwise. Finally, the Model Law determines when a conciliation is to be viewed as terminated, and establishes that if an agreement is reached and signed as a result of conciliation, it is to be considered both binding and enforceable.[23]

The experience of the UNCITRAL Working Group was unlike many other United Nations efforts (at least in the author's experience). The Working Group was composed of a unique group of professionals from all parts of the world – including highly qualified delegates from Egypt, Iran, Sudan, Indonesia, Singapore, China, Russia, Croatia, Finland, Switzerland, the United States, the United Kingdom, Canada and more, as well as observers from the Permanent Court of Arbitration, the Chartered Institute of Arbitrators and other institutions, all chaired by the skillful Mexican delegate, Mr. José María Abascal Zamora and the extremely knowledgeable Secretary of UNCITRAL, Jernej Sekolec. The Working Group devoted substantial time and attention to attempting to reach a model that could be accepted by as many States as possible, without regard to political considerations.

The result of the Working Group was, by its nature, a compromise. Each delegate would, no doubt, have preferred some changes in the provisions that were finally adopted. But, overall, the draft Model Law adopted by consensus of the Commission on 28 June 2002 is a well-thought-out compromise that taken with some minor variations and the addition of the explanatory notes that accompany it, can form a sound basis for many countries in building their conciliation or mediation regimes.[24]

---

23. For an excellent and thorough analysis of the law, and a much more detailed discussion on its purpose and structure, see Jernej SEKOLEC, "Introduction to the UNCITRAL Model Law on International Commercial Conciliation", ICCA *Yearbook Commercial Arbitration*, XXVII (2002) pp. 398-413.

24. The preparatory materials of the Model Law, as well as the text of the Model Law itself, are available on the UNCITRAL website (www.uncitral.org). The Model Law will be published by the UNCITRAL Secretariat together with a Guide to Enactment and Use of the Model Law that will contain, among other materials, explanatory information directed at legislators which will provide insight to users of the text.

ANNEX

UNCITRAL Model Law on International Commercial Conciliation

Adopted 28 June 2002

Article 1— Scope of application and definitions

(1) This Law applies to international[1] commercial[2] conciliation.

(2) For the purposes of this Law, "conciliator" means a sole conciliator or two or more conciliators, as the case may be.

(3) For the purposes of this Law, "conciliation" means a process, whether referred to by the expression conciliation, mediation or an expression of similar import, whereby parties request a third person or persons ("the conciliator") to assist them in their attempt to reach an amicable settlement of their dispute arising out of or relating to a contractual or other legal relationship. The conciliator does not have the authority to impose upon the parties a solution to the dispute.

(4) A conciliation is international if:

(a) The parties to an agreement to conciliate have, at the time of the conclusion of that agreement, their places of business in different States; or

(b) The State in which the parties have their places of business is different from either:

(i) The State in which a substantial part of the obligations of the commercial relationship is to be performed; or

(ii) The State with which the subject matter of the dispute is most closely connected.

(5) For the purposes of this article:

---

1. States wishing to enact this Model Law to apply to domestic as well as international conciliation may wish to consider the following changes to the text:

   - Delete the word "international" in paragraph (1) of article 1; and
   - Delete paragraphs (4), (5) and (6) of article 1.

2. The term "commercial" should be given a wide interpretation so as to cover matters arising from all relationships of a commercial nature, whether contractual or not. Relationships of a commercial nature include, but are not limited to, the following transactions: any trade transaction for the supply or exchange of goods or services; distribution agreement; commercial representation or agency; factoring; leasing; construction of works; consulting; engineering; licensing; investment; financing; banking; insurance; exploitation agreement or concession; joint venture and other forms of industrial or business cooperation; carriage of goods or passengers by air, sea, rail or road.

(a) If a party has more than one place of business, the place of business is that which has the closest relationship to the agreement to conciliate;
(b) If a party does not have a place of business, reference is to be made to the party's habitual residence.

(6) This Law also applies to a commercial conciliation when the parties agree that the conciliation is international or agree to the applicability of this Law.
(7) The parties are free to agree to exclude the applicability of this Law.
(8) Subject to the provisions of paragraph (9) of this article, this Law applies irrespective of the basis upon which the conciliation is carried out, including agreement between the parties whether reached before or after a dispute has arisen, an obligation established by law, or a direction or suggestion of a court, arbitral tribunal or competent governmental entity.
(9) This Law does not apply to:

(a) Cases where a judge or an arbitrator, in the course of judicial or arbitral proceedings, attempts to facilitate a settlement; and
(b) [...].

Article 2 – Interpretation
(1) In the interpretation of this Law, regard is to be had to its international origin and to the need to promote uniformity in its application and the observance of good faith.
(2) Questions concerning matters governed by this Law which are not expressly settled in it are to be settled in conformity with the general principles on which this Law is based.

Article 3 – Variation by agreement
Except for the provisions of article 2 and article 6, paragraph (3), the parties may agree to exclude or vary any of the provisions of this Law.

Article 4 – Commencement of conciliation proceedings[3]
(1) Conciliation proceedings in respect of a dispute that has arisen commence on the day on which the parties to that dispute agree to engage in conciliation proceedings.
(2) If a party that invited another party to conciliate does not receive an acceptance of the invitation within thirty days from the day on which the invitation was sent, or

---

3. The following text is suggested for States that might wish to adopt a provision on the suspension of the limitation period:

   Article X – Suspension of limitation period
   (1) When the conciliation proceedings commence, the running of the limitation period regarding the claim that is the subject matter of the conciliation is suspended.
   (2) Where the conciliation proceedings have terminated without a settlement agreement, the limitation period resumes running from the time the conciliation ended without a settlement agreement.

within such other period of time as specified in the invitation, the party may elect to treat this as a rejection of the invitation to conciliate.

Article 5 – Number and appointment of conciliators
(1) There shall be one conciliator, unless the parties agree that there shall be two or more conciliators.

(2) The parties shall endeavour to reach agreement on a conciliator or conciliators, unless a different procedure for their appointment has been agreed upon.

(3) Parties may seek the assistance of an institution or person in connection with the appointment of conciliators. In particular:

(a) A party may request such an institution or person to recommend suitable persons to act as conciliator; or
(b) The parties may agree that the appointment of one or more conciliators be made directly by such an institution or person.

(4) In recommending or appointing individuals to act as conciliator, the institution or person shall have regard to such considerations as are likely to secure the appointment of an independent and impartial conciliator and, where appropriate, shall take into account the advisability of appointing a conciliator of a nationality other than the nationalities of the parties.

(5) When a person is approached in connection with his or her possible appointment as conciliator, he or she shall disclose any circumstances likely to give rise to justifiable doubts as to his or her impartiality or independence. A conciliator, from the time of his or her appointment and throughout the conciliation proceedings, shall without delay disclose any such circumstances to the parties unless they have already been informed of them by him or her.

Article 6 – Conduct of conciliation
(1) The parties are free to agree, by reference to a set of rules or otherwise, on the manner in which the conciliation is to be conducted.

(2) Failing agreement on the manner in which the conciliation is to be conducted, the conciliator may conduct the conciliation proceedings in such a manner as the conciliator considers appropriate, taking into account the circumstances of the case, any wishes that the parties may express and the need for a speedy settlement of the dispute.

(3) In any case, in conducting the proceedings, the conciliator shall seek to maintain fair treatment of the parties and, in so doing, shall take into account the circumstances of the case.

(4) The conciliator may, at any stage of the conciliation proceedings, make proposals for a settlement of the dispute.

Article 7 – Communication between conciliator and parties
The conciliator may meet or communicate with the parties together or with each of them separately.

Article 8 — Disclosure of information
When the conciliator receives information concerning the dispute from a party, the conciliator may disclose the substance of that information to any other party to the conciliation. However, when a party gives any information to the conciliator, subject to a specific condition that it be kept confidential, that information shall not be disclosed to any other party to the conciliation.

Article 9 — Confidentiality
Unless otherwise agreed by the parties, all information relating to the conciliation proceedings shall be kept confidential, except where disclosure is required under the law or for the purposes of implementation or enforcement of a settlement agreement.

Article 10 — Admissibility of evidence in other proceedings
(1) A party to the conciliation proceedings, the conciliator and any third person, including those involved in the administration of the conciliation proceedings, shall not in arbitral, judicial or similar proceedings rely on, introduce as evidence or give testimony or evidence regarding any of the following:

(a) An invitation by a party to engage in conciliation proceedings or the fact that a party was willing to participate in conciliation proceedings;
(b) Views expressed or suggestions made by a party in the conciliation in respect of a possible settlement of the dispute;
(c) Statements or admissions made by a party in the course of the conciliation proceedings;
(d) Proposals made by the conciliator;
(e) The fact that a party had indicated its willingness to accept a proposal for settlement made by the conciliator;
(f) A document prepared solely for purposes of the conciliation proceedings.

(2) Paragraph (1) of this article applies irrespective of the form of the information or evidence referred to therein.
(3) The disclosure of the information referred to in paragraph (1) of this article shall not be ordered by an arbitral tribunal, court or other competent governmental authority and, if such information is offered as evidence in contravention of paragraph (1) of this article, that evidence shall be treated as inadmissible. Nevertheless, such information may be disclosed or admitted in evidence to the extent required under the law or for the purposes of implementation or enforcement of a settlement agreement.
(4) The provisions of paragraphs (1), (2) and (3) of this article apply whether or not the arbitral, judicial or similar proceedings relate to the dispute that is or was the subject matter of the conciliation proceedings.
(5) Subject to the limitations of paragraph (1) of this article, evidence that is otherwise admissible in arbitral or judicial or similar proceedings does not become inadmissible as a consequence of having been used in a conciliation.

Article 11 — Termination of conciliation proceedings
The conciliation proceedings are terminated:

207

(a) By the conclusion of a settlement agreement by the parties, on the date of the agreement;

(b) By a declaration of the conciliator, after consultation with the parties, to the effect that further efforts at conciliation are no longer justified, on the date of the declaration;

(c) By a declaration of the parties addressed to the conciliator to the effect that the conciliation proceedings are terminated, on the date of the declaration; or

(d) By a declaration of a party to the other party or parties and the conciliator, if appointed, to the effect that the conciliation proceedings are terminated, on the date of the declaration.

Article 12 – Conciliator acting as arbitrator

Unless otherwise agreed by the parties, the conciliator shall not act as an arbitrator in respect of a dispute that was or is the subject of the conciliation proceedings or in respect of another dispute that has arisen from the same contract or legal relationship or any related contract or legal relationship.

Article 13 – Resort to arbitral or judicial proceedings

Where the parties have agreed to conciliate and have expressly undertaken not to initiate during a specified period of time or until a specified event has occurred arbitral or judicial proceedings with respect to an existing or future dispute, such an undertaking shall be given effect by the arbitral tribunal or the court until the terms of the undertaking have been complied with, except to the extent necessary for a party, in its opinion, to preserve its rights. Initiation of such proceedings is not of itself to be regarded as a waiver of the agreement to conciliate or as a termination of the conciliation proceedings.

Article 14 – Enforceability of settlement agreement[4]

If the parties conclude an agreement settling a dispute, that settlement agreement is binding and enforceable ... [the enacting State may insert a description of the method of enforcing settlement agreements or refer to provisions governing such enforcement].

---

4. When implementing the procedure for enforcement of settlement agreements, an enacting State may consider the possibility of such a procedure being mandatory.

Aspects of Illegality in the Formation and Performance of Contracts

*Richard H. Kreindler**

I.   INTRODUCTION

How can, should or must an arbitral tribunal conduct itself in the face of suspected illegality of a contract in relation to which it is meant to adjudicate a dispute? How should a tribunal behave in the face of illegality which is admitted or otherwise manifest? Should the nature of the would-be illegality make a difference to the tribunal's assessment of its own jurisdiction? Of the separability of the agreement to arbitrate? Of arbitrability? When should the issue of jurisdiction hinge on whether the illicitness arguably tainted the contract ab initio, as opposed to an illegality arising or becoming apparent only in the course of later performance? Given suspected or manifest illegality, which standards of law should apply as to whether and how to proceed respecting jurisdiction, separability, arbitrability and the merits of the dispute?

It has been almost forty years since attention was sharply focussed, perhaps for the first time, on how an arbitral tribunal can, should or must conduct itself in the face of suspected or manifest illegality of a contract.[1] Since that time, various arbitral awards,[2]

---

* Partner, Shearman & Stearling, Frankfurt.

1. The issue of illegality of contract in the context of arbitration has been examined from time to time over the last several decades. However, it was particularly the award in ICC Case No. 1110 (1963) rendered by Gunnar Lagergren which cast a sharp focus on issues of competence-competence and

national court rulings[3] and commentaries[4] have come to light respecting illegality in the

---

severability of the arbitration agreement in the face of a suspected or manifestly illegal contract. Lagergren's award in ICC Case No. 1110 (1963) was reprinted for the first time in full in J.G. WETTER, "Issues of Corruption before International Arbitral Tribunals: The Authentic Text and True Meaning of Judge Gunner Lagergren's 1963 Award in ICC Case No. 1110", 10 Arb. Int'l (1994) p. 227. The award has frequently been construed to stand, inter alia, for the proposition that disputes involving allegations of corruption are non-arbitrable, and even that an arbitrator must resign his mandate in the face of a manifestly illegal contract, without rendering an award of any kind on jurisdiction or the merits:

"... the agreement between the parties contemplated the bribing of Argentine officials ... [p]arties who ally themselves in an enterprise of the present nature must realize that they have *forfeited any right to ask for assistance of the machinery of justice* (national courts or arbitral tribunals) in settling their disputes".

Ibid., p. 282 (emphasis added). At the same time, the award enunciated:

"... a general principle of law recognized by civilized nations that *contracts which seriously violate bonos mores or international public policy are invalid or at least unenforceable* and that they cannot be sanctioned by courts or arbitrators".

Ibid., p. 293 (emphasis added).

2. Subsequent awards have largely rejected Lagergren's perceived notion of non-arbitrability. They have upheld the right of the arbitrator to exercise jurisdiction to rule on the merits of a dispute involving an illegal or allegedly illegal contract. In such cases, the tribunal has often rejected the defense of voidness for, e.g., corruption on the basis that the defendant failed to substantiate the corruption claim: see, e.g., ICC Award No. 4145 (1984) *Establishment of Middle East State v. South Asian Construction Company*, ICCA Yearbook Commercial Arbitration XII (1987) (hereinafter *Yearbook*) p. 97; ICC Award No. 6286 (1991) *U.S. Partner v. German and Canadian Partners*, Yearbook XIX (1994) pp. 141-161, see p. 149 at [22]. Alternatively, in other cases the defense of voidness on the grounds of corruption or some other illegality has been sustained, whether under the applicable lex contractus or one or the other notion of international or transnational public policy: see, e.g., ICC Award No. 3916 (1981);Y. DERAINS, "Observations" following Award in ICC Case No. 4145, 112 J.D.I. (1985) pp. 987-990; Award in ICC Case No. 3916 (1982) *Iranian Party v. Greek Party*, 111 J.D.I. (1984) p. 930; see also *Omnium de Traitement et de Valorisation SA v. Hilmarton Ltd.*, Award in ICC Case No. 5622 (1988) Rev.Arb. (1993) p. 327, Yearbook XIX (1994) p. 105 (holding subject matter of dispute relating to allegedly illegal commission payment to be arbitrable, deciding on merits that commission payment claim was to be dismissed on grounds of violation of mandatory Algerian *loi de police* deemed to supersede Swiss lex contractus), award subsequently set aside by Court of Justice of Canton of Geneva, 17 November 1989, Rev.Arb. (1993) p. 315, *Yearbook* XIX (1994) p. 214, and nullification decision then upheld by Swiss Federal Tribunal.

3. See, e.g., Swiss Fed. Trib., 2 September 1993, *National Power Corp. v. Westinghouse*, ASA Bull. (1994) p. 244 at p. 247, refusing to set aside award dated 19 December 1991 which had found allegations of corruption not to have been proven. The highest Swiss court described as outdated the notion that disputes concerning allegations of corruption are not arbitrable.

4. Among the various commentators who have addressed issues of illegality of contract in a variety of forms are Ahmed S. KOSHERI and Philippe LEBOULANGER, "L'arbitrage face à la corruption et aux trafics d'influence", Rev.Arb. (1984) p. 3; Pierre MAYER, "Le contrat illicit", Rev.Arb. (1984) p. 205; Pierre LALIVE, "Ordre public transnational (ou réellement international) et arbitrage international", Rev.Arb. (1986) p. 329; Bruno OPPETIT, "Le paradoxe de la corruption

formation and performance of contracts containing an agreement to arbitrate. These awards, rulings and commentaries, emanating from varied jurisdictions and legal cultures, have displayed more elements of anecdotalism than of convergence. They have by no means given rise to a complete consensus or reconcilability of views.

Moreover, the evolution in thinking respecting the arbitrator's rights and duties in connection with illegality of contract[5] has been accompanied by a profusion of new or amended bodies of national arbitration legislation and adoption of the UNCITRAL Model Law in whole or part in certain active arbitration locales. Finally, over the last several years a number of states have acceded to multilateral conventions condemning illegal contracts, corruption, bribery of public officials, etc. These accessions have arguably contributed to, or confirmed, the development of certain national and transnational concepts of public policy in abhorrence of illegality of contracts.[6]

Against this background of significant currents and cross-currents, the present remarks intend to reconcile the different strands where possible and desirable, and in particular from the arbitrator's perspective. These remarks also intend to provide guidelines for how arbitral tribunals are to carry out their powers and duties when confronted with suspected or obvious illegality of a contract. The potential scope of the subject is indeed vast. The observations here are intentionally confined to the already broad subject areas of competence-competence of the tribunal, separability of the agreement to arbitrate, allocation of powers between the arbitrator and the national courts, and choice of the appropriate law respecting legality and illegality.[7]

à l'épreuve du droit du commerce international", 1 J.D.I. (1987) p. 5; Pierre MAYER, "La règle morale dans l'arbitrage international" in *Etudes Pierre Bellet* (1991) p. 379; Vincent HEUZÉ, "La morale, l'arbitre et le juge", Rev.Arb. (1993) p. 179; WETTER, *op. cit.*, fn. 1; Yves DERAINS, "La lutte contra la corruption – Le point de vue de l'arbitre international" in *Contribution au Congrès AIJA*, Montreux 1996; Jose ROSELL and Harvey PRAGER, "Illicit Commissions and International Arbitration: The Question of Proof", 15 Arb. Int'l (1999) p. 329.

5. In the first edition of REDFERN and HUNTER, *Law and Practice of International Commercial Arbitration* (1986) Lagergren's decision in ICC Case No. 1110 was held to be commendable, on the basis that *ex turpi causa action non oritur*; in the third edition (1999) Sect. 3-28, p. 153, the authors stated that in the intervening thirteen years the outcome and practice were likely to be different.

6. Prominent among such conventions, which have arguably contributed to a certain generalization of condemnation of corruption particularly in the public domain, are the 1997 OECD Convention on Combating Bribery of Foreign Public Officials in International Business Transactions, the 1999 Conventions of the Council of Europe, and the 2000 United Nations Convention against Transnational Organized Crime.

7. The present remarks do not seek to analyze in detail, e.g., issues of burden of proof respecting suspected or manifest illegality of the contract and/or the agreement to arbitrate. Nor do they address in particular national law prohibitions against agreements to arbitrate certain *kinds* of disputes which might result in the nullity of party agreements seeking to submit such disputes to arbitration.

II.   OVERVIEW OF THE PROBLEM OF ILLEGALITY IN ITS DIFFERENT FORMS

1.   *Definition of Illegality*

Which kinds and forms of "illegality" concern us in the present context, and which do not? There are several levels of differentiation and distinction which must be made from the arbitrator's perspective. There may be many forms and shades of illegal and illicit contracts. Not all of them necessarily enjoy generally uniform condemnation. Not all of them should necessarily be seen as consequently causing the nullity of the related agreement to arbitrate.

a.   *Overtly illegal contracts*
First, one must distinguish between certain categories of "overtly illegal contracts" and other categories which may be less overtly illegal in nature. Contracts which are overtly illegal are those whose subject matter or purpose is generally considered to offend "public morality". The offense of public morality is derived from a consensus based upon, for example, the vast majority of national legal systems, evolving notions of transnational or international public policy, emerging lex mercatoria considerations, or even local mandatory laws or *lois de police*.

Among such categories, particularly at the transnational level, are: facilitation or promotion of drug trafficking, terrorism, subversion, prostitution, child abuse, slavery and other forms of human rights violations. Generally, contracts relating to such subject matters may be considered to possess an overt illegality. That overt illegality or illicitness would render any such contract null and void ab initio according to the vast majority of national laws and any other rules of law meant to stand the scrutiny of national or international public policy.

Other categories of illicit contracts may be less overtly illegal. Where the contract or associated conduct is less obviously contemptible, the challenge to the arbitrator to determine the extent of jurisdiction, arbitrability, severability, etc. in fact becomes potentially more difficult, and not less so. Such contracts include various forms of broker, sponsor, agency, consultancy and intermediary agreements. Such agreements are invariably associated with the payment of a commission for some often ill-defined or even non-existent consideration or performance.

The reasons why the arbitrator's task here may be more difficult than in the case of an overtly illegal contract include the fact that such commission arrangements may be perfectly legal, or in any event not expressly proscribed in some countries. A further difficulty is the distinction amongst such contracts between those relating to the payment of a "commission" to a public official and those relating to the payment of a commission to a private entity. Particularly in the case of a bribe or other corrupt practice vis-à-vis a public official, the egregiousness of the conduct may be seen to rise dramatically.

b.   *Illegality and lack of assent*
Second, one must consider illicit contracts which are manifestly illegal not necessarily because of their overtly offensive nature or purpose, but rather because they simply never came into effect as purported. A graphic example is a contract which the

defendant claims, perhaps truthfully, never to have signed or otherwise assented to. An even more graphic example is a claim that the signature or other alleged manifestations of assent are in fact forgeries.

If such defense is true, the contract invariably becomes null and void ab initio. This result of nullity is indeed not unlike the first category of overtly offensive contracts involving drug trafficking, prostitution, etc.[8] A principal difference between the two categories is that the drug smuggling contract is deemed null and void even if all contracting parties assented to it. The forged contract, on the other hand, is deemed null and void because of the lack of mutual assent, and not – or not solely – by reason of its underlying subject matter.

From the perspective of the arbitrator's (possible) jurisdiction, separability and arbitrability, should there be a difference between the illicit drug smuggling contract and the illicit forged contract?[9] In fact, it may be that in the case of both contracts, unless the

---

8. See REDFERN and HUNTER, *op. cit.*, fn. 5, 3rd ed., Sect. 3-34, p. 156, holding that the validity of the arbitration agreement

    "… must depend on the reason for which the contract is found to be null and void … (giving as an example 'that's not my signature'). No amount of insistence upon the autonomy of the arbitration clause can make it valid if the respondent was not a party to it",

    citing the so-called *Pyramids* case, Award in ICC Case No. 3493 (1983), *S.P.P. (Middle East) Ltd. v. Arab Republic of Egypt*, 22 I.L.M. (1983) p. 752 at p. 767, para. 46; *Yearbook* IX (1984) p. 111; the *Cour d'appel* (CA) of Paris upheld a claim by the award debtor Egyptian Government that it was not a party to the underlying contract, with the result that the award made on the basis that it was in fact a party was set aside in France: CA Paris, 12 July 1984, *République Arabe d'Egypte v. Southern Pacific Properties Ltd.*, 112 J.D.I. (1985) p. 129, 23 I.L.M. (1984) p. 1048.

    In fact, the *Pyramids* case did not stand so much for the proposition of "that's not my signature" in the sense of a forgery or falsification. Rather, its focus was whether the term "approval, agreement and ratification" of an arbitration clause implied an intention to become a party to that clause. Extension of the arbitration agreement signed by a state-owned entity to the state is a wholly different matter than the illegality of a contract containing an arbitration clause by virtue of forgery or falsification of an assent to that contract or arbitration clause. It is the latter, the forgery or falsification scenario, which concerns us here.

9. A recent example of a prominent international dispute involving contentions of forgery, in this case forged documents submitted as evidence, was the territorial dispute between the State of Bahrain and the State of Qatar submitted to the International Court of Justice in The Hague: *International Court of Justice, Case Concerning Maritime Delimitation and Territorial Questions between Qatar and Bahrain (Qatar v. Bahrain)* Judgment of 16 March 2001, Decision No. 847, 40 I.L.M. (July 2001) p. 4. In that case, decided on the merits after a prolonged jurisdictional phase, claimant Qatar submitted, and then later retracted, various allegedly falsified historical documents respecting the 1939 award to Bahrain of the disputed Hawar Islands lying between Bahrain and Qatar.

    The official judgment has been criticized for the fact that the ICJ judgment did not make any evaluation of the series of events related to the submission and later retraction of the allegedly forged documents: see, e.g., "Faking It: Eversheds, Freshfields and the ICJ Forgeries", Legal Business, Issue 114 (May 2001) pp. 66-71. This ICJ case may be seen as relating to illegality in the formation and performance of contract as well as in the conduct of the arbitration proceedings themselves, which is a separate subject altogether.

illicitness is manifest, it must still be proven through submissions to the satisfaction of the tribunal. The allegation of illegality based on smuggling or forgery is, at least initially, only a claim, or defense, and must be proven. In all such cases where proof is still to be adduced, the tribunal must normally have jurisdiction to establish the facts of the case and take evidence. In those cases where no proof is needed because the illegality is manifest, the question of whether the tribunal has jurisdiction to make any ruling over the dispute will normally depend on whether the illicitness, additionally, leads to the voidness of the separate arbitration agreement.

c.   *Illicit contracts and public versus private parties*

Third, within the category of less overtly illegal contracts such as commission agreements, the arbitrator may need to distinguish between commission agreements providing for payment to a private party (influence peddling) and those providing for payment to a public official (bribery).[10] In the latter case, the aim of the commission payment is customarily to secure a contract award or other advantage from an agent of a state by means of what is normally considered "bribery".[11] In the former case, the commission payment may have somewhat the same nature and purpose, but not seek to corrupt an instrumentality of a government. Should this distinction matter as to whether the arbitrator has jurisdiction over a dispute relating to this type of commission agreement? Depending upon the jurisdiction, "influence peddling" vis-à-vis public officials may be illegal, but not be sanctionable in the *private* domain as long as it does not implicate a public official. Whether influence peddling even in the private domain is sanctionable will depend upon the particular form of action taken and the applicable law.

d.   *Illegality ab initio versus ex post*

Fourth, the arbitral tribunal may be called upon to make hairline distinctions between fraud in the inducement of the contract and so-called fraud in the factum. Fraud in the inducement may result in the illegality ex post of the contract. Fraud in the factum may result in its illegality ab initio.

---

10. Cf. in German law, a decision of the German Supreme Court, 8 May 1985, IV a ZR 138/83, 8 RIW 653 f. (August 1985) holding that

> "an agreement by which a foreign public official promises in criminal fashion to carry out a particular official act in exchange for payment of a bribe is void under Sect. 138 German Civil Code (*Sittenwidriges Geschäft*). The same must apply for a contract between an interested party and an intermediary when its sole or main purpose consists of establishing an agreement to pay a bribe to the responsible public official and to forward this payment to him and when the bribe is included in the commission promised to the intermediary."

11. Among the recent prominent cases of alleged bribery of public officials which became subject to arbitration included the sale of certain French naval frigates to the Republic of Taiwan by the French Thomson CSF via a Swiss "intermediary": *Frontier AG & Brunner Sociedad v. Thomson CSF*, ICC Case No. 7664 (1996).

Should the arbitrator apply a different standard respecting arbitrability and separability when the contract is deemed to have become illegal "only later", as opposed to the case where there was never any contract at all? Does it not make a difference whether the alleged fraud is manifest, as opposed to requiring the parties first to be put to their proof?

2. Circumstances of the Illegality

Wholly apart from the foregoing potential distinctions, the arbitrator may be confronted with a wide range of factual circumstances which could affect the issues of jurisdiction, arbitrability and separability.

a. Initial awareness of the illegality by all parties

First, whether the subject matter is overtly offensive or, rather, more of a "gray area" illegality, both parties were manifestly aware of the illegality ab initio. Both parties may have known of and intended the illicit nature and illicit purpose of the contract. Both parties may have known of and intended the inclusion of an agreement to arbitrate precisely to shield adjudication of any disputes from national courts which would strike down the contract as illegal.

The arbitrator must decide issues of arbitrability and separability in the context of an illegality going to the heart of both the underlying contract and the arbitration agreement. If the arbitrator does so, however, is he an "accomplice" to the illicit effort to shield adjudication from the national courts?

b. Subsequent awareness of the illegality by all parties

Second, both parties executed the contract on the assumption that it was licit in nature, and only subsequently became aware of the illegality in the course of performance. By extension, both parties included the agreement to arbitrate on the basis that it was a legitimate dispute resolution mechanism for a legitimate underlying contract.

The arbitrator must decide in the context of illegality of the main agreement. He must also decide in the context of whether the severity of the illegality should prevent him from affirming his jurisdiction on the basis of the arbitration agreement. How severe must the illegality be for the arbitrator no longer to be able to exercise jurisdiction on the basis of arbitrability and separability?

c. Illicit intention and awareness of one party

Third, one party is aware of the illegality ab initio, working, for example, through a third-party "intermediary," while the other party is unaware of the illegality. The first party did not necessarily fraudulently induce the second party to enter into the contract, but it may have induced it to enter into the contract under false pretenses. Is this not the same thing?

The arbitrator must assess the extent to which one party's good-faith reliance on the legality of the contract may influence his assessment of arbitrability and separability. Just because one of the two parties had an illicit intention, does this deprive the other party acting in good faith and in reliance on the licitness of the contract from having his day before the arbitrator?

215

d. *Reliance on the illegality as claim or defense*
Fourth, the party seeking relief in the arbitration himself committed the illegality. He seeks the benefit of an arbitral award upholding the illegality. The defendant, who is being sued for manifest non-performance, seeks to use the illegality as a means to forestall judgment against it. The arbitral tribunal may be confronted with a situation where the illegality is sanctionable under only one of several potentially applicable bodies of law.

Should the tribunal condone the illegality in order to find against a clearly defaulting defendant, or should it deny its own jurisdiction due to the illegality even though the defendant will thereby be able to abscond despite its non-performance? What if the non-performance relates to a part of the contract which may be legal and severable from the remaining, illicit portions of the contract?

e. *Contract of bribery versus contract arising out of bribery*
Fifth, the underlying contract is not alleged to represent an agreement to pay a bribe, but rather is a contract which is alleged to have arisen and been made possible as a result of an antecedent payment of an illegal bribe involving the same parties.

The tribunal must distinguish between the two contracts and decide whether its jurisdiction is in any way undermined by the circumstances which gave rise to the contract.

3. *Suspicion of Illegality versus Knowledge or Obviousness of Same*

Each of the above possible permutations may be affected by the extent to which the arbitral tribunal has a "mere" suspicion of illegality, as opposed to a firm knowledge based on the obviousness or manifest nature of the same.

Particularly in such cases, how far should arbitrators go to determine whether the contract submitted to them has been procured or performed by illegal means, or otherwise suffers from some illicitness which may render the contract and perhaps the arbitration agreement null and void, and the arbitrator defunct?

In the case of "mere" suspicion, the conviction with which the tribunal decides whether it is in a position to assert jurisdiction and render an award may be influenced by the "degree" of suspicion involved. The following issues may arise for the tribunal in the case of a suspicion falling short of concrete knowledge or admission of the illegality.

a. *Maintaining impartiality and equal treatment*
First, arguably the existence of a "mere" suspicion will place special challenges on the tribunal to maintain the requisite level of impartiality and/or independence and to ensure equal treatment. This may be the case particularly where the suspicion of illegality attaches to only one party, and not to all parties jointly. The arbitrators have a duty, for example, to maintain such impartiality and to treat the parties equally under the applicable arbitral rules, the lex arbitri and any other potentially relevant standards.[12]

---

12. See, e.g., UNCITRAL Model Law on International Commercial Arbitration, Arts. 12 and 18.

To the extent the tribunal suspects illegality on the part of one party but not of all, it must ensure that it does not allow unsubstantiated or even half-substantiated indicia of impropriety on one side to influence its even-handedness in conducting the arbitration. This is a matter of impartiality and independence. It is also an issue of equal treatment, due process and affording both sides with an opportunity to present their respective case. The extent of such "opportunity" will depend upon the applicable arbitral rules and lex arbitri.[13]

b.   Dilatory tactics and allegations of illegality

Second, where the suspicion is based primarily or solely on a "mere" allegation of illegality by the *defendant*, the tribunal may see fit to be marginally more rigorous and circumspect in its readiness to conclude that such an illegality exists. Quite apart from the not infrequent occurrence of a dilatory defendant espousing arguments primarily for the purpose of postponing or completely derailing the day of judgment, a mere allegation of illegality by the defendant should not immediately make a contract non-arbitrable which is otherwise arbitrable.

The marginally greater rigor brought to bear on the defendant may not in any way offend the arbitrator's duty of equal treatment and due process under the relevant rules and curial law. In the case of a counterclaim, it may well be that it is the claimant who then relies on a partial illegality as its defense to any liability under the counterclaim.

c.   Mutual denial of illegality

Third, it may be that *both* parties deny that the underlying contract is illegal and at least the claimant insists on its arbitrability. Should the tribunal's "mere" suspicion of a true illegality be more readily put to rest by the fact that both parties "agree" that the contract is not illegal? Or should the tribunal inquire nevertheless into the grounds for its continuing suspicion?

The fact that both parties deny an underlying illegality does not necessarily make the grounds for the tribunal's suspicion to the contrary any less compelling; indeed the fact or manner of mutual denial may actually fire the tribunal's suspicions all the more. The mutual denial may be a concerted effort to shield the illegality from the tribunal. Alternatively, it may be an attempt to seek resolution of the dispute from a private tribunal in circumstances where a national court would not be receptive.

d.   Tribunal fears of "complicity"

Fourth, when neither party asserts illegality but the tribunal's suspicion persists, should the tribunal inquire further? Similar to the third scenario above, the fact that neither party raises the issue of illegality does not necessarily make the tribunal's suspicion any less compelling.

The tribunal may fear that in the event of an underlying illegality and the rendering of an award on the merits, it would be acting as an "accomplice" to an illegal enterprise.

---

13. Art. 18 of the UNCITRAL Model Law provides for "a full opportunity of presenting his case whereas Art. 22(1) of the ICC Rules speaks, in the context of *clôture de la procédure*, of "a reasonable opportunity to present their cases".

It may fear that it is abetting an offensive undertaking, impermissibly asserting jurisdiction where none may be asserted, or contributing to a violation of local or transnational public policy or all of the above. In such case, is "mere" suspicion not enough justification for the tribunal to inquire more deeply, sua sponte, into the possible illegality?

e.   Avoiding surprise versus unduly instructing the parties
Fifth, one or both parties has asserted or denied illegality.[14] What about the parties' mutual rights of due process, equal treatment and full – or at least reasonable – opportunity to present their respective case? Here, there may be a tension between two obligations of the tribunal: to avoid surprise to the parties on the one hand and to avoid unduly instructing or aiding one party over another on the other hand.

With regard to the first obligation, if the tribunal suspects illegality and anticipates ruling on it in a way material to the ultimate award, then it must surely alert the parties to its concern. It must give them an equal – whether "full" or "reasonable"– opportunity to set forth their respective case as to such suspected illegality. With regard to the latter obligation, the tribunal's suspicion of illegality cannot translate into its unduly aiding the party which might benefit from the confirmation of such illegality. This is especially the case where that party was not aware or would not have raised the argument in its favor without the cue from the tribunal.

f.   Illegality and standard of proof
Sixth, once the tribunal has decided that its suspicion of illegality justifies further inquiry, the question arises of what standard of proof should be applied in determining illegality. It might be contended that a higher standard should be applied to the issue of illegality since the result of illicitness would be the illegality of the contract per se. Does this in fact justify imposing a higher standard of proof than any other issue under consideration?

Certain cases have indeed applied a higher standard,[15] presumably on the grounds that bribery or other corrupt behavior, like fraud, must be shown with particularity.[16] This

---

14. Cf. REDFERN and HUNTER, *op. cit.*, fn. 5, 3rd ed., Sect. 3-28, p. 153:

> "If an allegation is made in plain language in the course of the arbitration proceedings, the arbitral tribunal is under a *duty* to consider the allegation and to decide whether or not it is proved. If it is proved, then under most systems of law the agreement would be regarded as illegal and accordingly unenforceable." (emphasis added)

15. A related, but also separate issue in this regard is the allocation of the burden of proof and the extent to which the burden should shift depending upon which party is relying on an illegality argument which might result in the nullity of the contract. The normal approach to such allocation would be that the party insisting on a right has the burden, so that a defendant who refuses to perform on the basis of illegality has the burden to prove such illegality. With respect to burden of proof allocation, see also ROSELL and PRAGER, *op. cit.*, fn. 4.

16. In the *Westinghouse* arbitration, the tribunal noted that a "preponderance of the evidence" would normally apply, but that with respect to a bribery allegation "clear and convincing evidence", which was a higher standard, was required: *Westinghouse and Bruns & Roe (USA) v. National Power*

is surely a sound approach. Indeed the result of such stringency has also been that many tribunals have considered the possibility of corruption leading to the nullity of the underlying contract, but ultimately found insufficient evidence of such corruption.[17]

With respect to the standard of proof, the arbitrator should bear in mind that in most cases the reviewing court at the seat of arbitration does not, or at least should not, revisit the evidence de novo. Accordingly, there will normally be no de novo review of a finding of fraud or the lack thereof.[18] The same would generally apply in the case of enforcement proceedings, particularly of foreign awards under Art. V of the 1958 New York Convention on the Recognition and Enforcement of Foreign Arbitral Awards.

Does the absence of de novo review of the evidence place a higher burden on the arbitrator to "try to get to the bottom of" whether there was illegality? Does the lack of evidentiary review in nullification proceedings call for a greater scrutiny of illegality issues by the tribunal so that the reviewing court has as clear a picture as possible of the illegality issue although it will not be taking evidence on this matter itself?

Surely the answer must normally be no, since the arbitrator's assessment and appreciation of the evidence cannot be dictated by the constraints under which a reviewing court – which may never be called on to act – must function. The arbitrator has a right and duty to ascertain the relevant facts of the case with all appropriate means. However, this should not necessarily translate into his pursuing lines of suspicion as a surrogate for a reviewing court which is generally not meant to revisit the arbitrator's assessment of the facts in the first place.

In the *Westacre* matter,[19] for example, the English enforcing court expressed confidence in the ability of a properly constituted arbitral tribunal which had rendered a foreign award to assess the evidence regarding alleged illegality. The court made no mention of the application of a higher standard of proof. It *enforced* the foreign award, upholding the jurisdiction of the tribunal to adjudicate a matter based apparently in large part on the assumed ability of the tribunal to determine whether there was illegality:

> "It is necessary to consider both on the one hand the desirability of giving effect to the public policy against enforcement of corrupt transactions and on the other hand the public policy of sustaining international arbitration agreements ... [i]n determining whether English public policy would deny jurisdiction to arbitrators to determine the illegality issue consideration has to be given to the weight that ought to be attached to the *risk that arbitrators might reach the wrong decision in a way*

Company and the Republic of the Philippines, Award in ICC Case No. 6401 (1991) reprinted in 7 Int'l Arb. Rep. (1992) B-34; see also Award in ICC Case No. 5622 (*Hilmarton*), *op. cit.*, fn. 2, applying the standard of "beyond doubt" to a corruption allegation.

17. See, e.g., 1992 ICC Award upheld by CA Paris, 30 September 1993, *European Gas Turbines v. Westman Int'l Ltd.*, Rev.Arb. (1994) p. 359; see also *Westacre Investments Inc. v. Jugoimport–SPDR Holding Co. Ltd. & Others*, Award in ICC Case No. 7047 (1994), ASA Bull. (1995) p. 301, upheld by Swiss Fed. Trib., 30 December 1994, ASA Bull. (1995) p. 217.

18. Under the UNCITRAL Model Law, for example, the parties have no express right to appeal findings of law or fact contained in the award.

19. *Westacre Investments Inc. v. Jugoimport–SPDR Holding Co. Ltd. & Others* [1998] 4 All E.R. 570; [1998] 3 W.L.R. 770; [1998] 2 Lloyd's Rep. 111 (High Ct., Q.B.) (Com. Ct.) (1997).

which could not be challenged and thereby give effect to an underlying contract which the courts would have declined to enforce.... The opportunity for erroneous and uncorrectable findings of fact arises in all international arbitration. If much weight were to be attached to that consideration it is difficult to see that arbitrators would ever be accorded jurisdiction to determine issues of illegality." (emphasis added)

Thus, the tribunal may have a heightened duty to investigate the alleged illegality. However, the reason for sharpening this duty may reside less in the fact that a reviewing court could not revisit the issue than in the fact that allegations of illegality should in any event be pled with particularity.

At the same time, an additional justification for applying an acute standard of proof as to illegality allegations would be to ensure that contracts entered into at arm's length are not nullified on corruption or similar grounds unless the evidence truly points in that direction. Effectively, a decision to nullify a contract on the grounds of illegality is a decision to deviate from the principle of *pacta sunt servanda*.

The reasons for such deviation may be well-founded and also rest on the notion of ensuring that contracts offensive to public morals are struck down. At the same time, a deviation from *pacta sunt servanda* is likewise a deviation from a component of public policy. Therefore, these competing principles of *ordre public* must be weighed against each other carefully.

III. ILLEGALITY AND JURISDICTIONAL LIMITATIONS

1. Arbitrators versus National Courts and Illegality

Even in the context of Judge Lagergren's perceived pathbreaking – and subsequently largely criticized – analysis of the arbitration of illegality issues,[20] the focus has initially and substantially been on arbitrability in the sense of competence-competence and separability of the arbitration agreement from the allegedly or manifestly illegal main contract. This is ultimately a question of whose province is it, the arbitral tribunal's or the national court's?

a. Illegality, competence-competence and arbitrability

What is the extent to which an arbitrator has jurisdiction to decide whether he or she has jurisdiction – jurisdiction to issue an award upholding or denying jurisdiction; or to issue an award adjudicating the merits once overall jurisdiction has been upheld?

The question is central to the issue of illegality. Insofar as the allegedly or manifestly illegal contract may be null and void even ab initio, the tribunal must query whether it may still make any rulings on disputes arising out of the contract and the arbitration agreement within it. Even if the tribunal derives a jurisdictional power from the now widely accepted doctrine of competence-competence, does it retain jurisdiction where

---

20. Award in ICC Case No. 1110 (1963), *op. cit.*, fn.1.

as a result of the illegality, the contract – and perhaps the arbitration agreement – is deemed never to have come into existence?

In the past, this analysis has often been couched in terms of the allocation of power between the arbitrator on the one hand and the national courts on the other to decide challenges to the legality of the underlying contract. In recent years, with the partial exception of England and notably the United States, national legislation and uniform model legislation have largely sought to allocate such power to the arbitrator. Thus, for example, Art. 178(3) of Chapter 12 of the 1987 Swiss Private International Law Act provides succinctly:

> "The validity of an arbitration agreement cannot be contested on the ground that the main contract may not be valid."

This formulation, particularly the wording "may not", accurately reflects the predicament of the arbitrator who has only an initial suspicion of illegality and has not yet made a full determination. The formulation also fits the arbitrator who, even upon manifest proof of illegality, may not yet have determined, without further party submissions, the consequences of such illegality for the contract and possibly for the arbitration agreement itself.

In any event, a mere allegation that the contract is, or may be, invalid even to the point of being offensive to public morals should not result in the invalidity of the arbitration agreement which the contract contains. Otherwise, any and all such allegations, including those made in bad faith and those which are well intentioned but without basis, could lead to the inappropriate disenfranchisement of the arbitrator.

b.   Illegality and ipso jure invalidity of the arbitration agreement
Interestingly, the UNCITRAL Arbitration Rules (Art. 21(2)) and the UNCITRAL Model Law (Art. 16(1)) address the situation where the arbitrator has already decided, in exercise of competence-competence that the contract is and not merely "may be" invalid:

> "A decision by the arbitral tribunal that the contract is null and void shall not entail *ipso jure* the invalidity of the arbitration clause."

This provision is lacking from the Swiss Act and indeed is also missing from Art. 1040(1) of the 10th Book of the German Code of Civil Procedure, which was revised as of 1 January 1998 to implement substantially the UNCITRAL Model Law in Germany. Art. 1040(1) follows the first two sentences of the corresponding article, Art. 16(1) of the Model Law, but does not include the foregoing reference to nullity and voidness.

Does this make the Swiss and German legislation less supportive of competence-competence and the separability of the arbitration agreement in the face of the nullity of the main contract? The answer must be no. Rather, the Swiss and German approaches to the survival and independence of the arbitration agreement, even in the face of illegality, are so firm that there was no need to confuse or dilute the approach by adding the final sentence from the Model Law. The arbitration agreement does not ipso jure share the fate of the main agreement and vice versa, full stop.

In the case of German arbitration law, this is a major development as compared with the pre-1998 regime at least with respect to competence-competence (but not with respect to separability, which was already well entrenched). Prior to 1998, under former Sect. 1025 I of the German Civil Procedure Code, disputes were required to be capable of "settlement" in order to be subject to arbitration. Thus the same grounds which could nullify the main agreement could also prevent the valid conclusion of a settlement and thereby render the agreement itself invalid.[21] The ability to "settle" is no longer a prerequisite under German law for valid conclusion of an arbitration agreement apart from non-economic claims.

Therefore, those cases where previously the arbitration agreement was deemed to share the fate of nullity of the main contract must be revisited. This might even include cases of voidability on the grounds of *fraud or threat*:

> "In the case of Sect. 123 Civil Code (voidability on grounds of fraud or threat), the arbitration agreement is nevertheless voidable only where the original fraud or threat leading to the conclusion of the main agreement also *directly influenced the conclusion of the arbitration agreement....* Even if one did not have hesitation as to the applicability of Sect. 139 (Partial Voidness) in view of the independence of both agreements, the following consideration stands in opposition to the applicability of Sect. 139.... *Would the parties still have concluded the agreement to arbitrate if they had known that a dispute would arise relating to the validity of the main agreement.* Such a question arises outside of the scope of Sect. 139."[22] (emphasis added)

Having exercised his or her jurisdiction and conclusively found that the contract is illegal, the arbitrator must not necessarily then conclude that the arbitration agreement is likewise null and void. Where the tribunal concludes that the arbitration agreement shares the illegal fate of the underlying contract, it would then have to conclude that it had no basis to exercise competence-competence to make such conclusion in the first place. While this may appear potentially to tie the arbitrator in knots, the predicament is not as complicated as it may appear. Competence-competence will be obtained unless

---

21. Examples included gambling and betting demands (Sect. 762 Civil Code (*Unvollkommene Verbindlichkeit*)), illegal contracts (Sect. 134 Civil Code (*Gesetzliches Verbot*)), offensive or usurious contracts (Sect. 138 Civil Code (*Sittenwidriges Rechtsgeschäft*; *Wucher*)) etc.

22. SCHWAB/WALTER, *Schiedsgerichtsbarkeit*, 6th ed. (2000) pp. 41-42; the original German reads in relevant part as follows:

> "... *muß die Frage lauten, ob man in allen diesen Fällen, in denen der Hauptvertrag nichtig ist, auch schon unbesehen die Unwirksamkeit der Schiedsvereinbarung annehmen möchte. Dies ist gerade deshalb abzulehnen.... In den Fällen des § 123 BGB (Anfechtbarkeit wegen Täuschung oder Drohung) ist die Schiedsvereinbarung jedoch nur dann anfechtbar, wenn die für den Abschluss des Hauptvertrags ursächliche Täuschung oder Drohung auch ihren Abschluss unmittelbar beeinflußt hat.... Selbst wenn man nicht schon wegen der Selbständigkeit der beiden Verträge gegen die Anwendbarkeit von §139 (Teilnichtigkeit) Bedenken haben sollte, steht der Anwendbarkeit von §139 BGB folgende Überlegung entgegen ... ob die Parteien die Schiedsvereinbarung auch geschlossen hätten, wenn sie gewußt hätten, dass über die Wirksamkeit des Hauptvertrages Streit entsteht. Eine solche Fragestellung bewegt sich aber außerhalb von §139 BGB.*"

the nature and circumstances of the main contract's voidness inextricably also apply to the arbitration agreement so as to make it void as well.

A reason why competence-competence may still obtain is that, pursuant to prevailing trends, in the absence of an effective waiver, the tribunal's decision on its own jurisdiction will be subject to judicial control in setting aside proceedings at the seat and in enforcement proceedings at the seat or elsewhere. For this reason alone, allocation of the power to decide challenges to legality to the tribunal is not seen as a usurpation of the state courts' prerogatives. Art. V(3) of the 1961 European Convention on International Commercial Arbitration makes this point clear:

> "*Subject to any subsequent judicial control provided for under the lex fori*, the arbitrator whose jurisdiction is called into question shall be entitled to proceed with the arbitration, to rule on his own jurisdiction, and to decide upon the existence or validity of the arbitration agreement or of the contract of which the agreement forms part." (emphasis added)

c.   Illegality and prima facie analysis of the arbitration agreement
Institutional arbitration rules likewise address issues of competence-competence and arbitrability in a manner relevant to illegality. In the context of the ICC Rules of Arbitration, these issues have in part been considered in the context of a "prima facie" analysis of agreement to ICC arbitration. Upon a "finding" by the ICC Court of such a basis for agreement to ICC arbitration, any further jurisdictional questions related to illegality or otherwise have historically been referred summarily to the tribunal to-be, once it is seized with the file.

By virtue of this institutional sequence, the arbitral tribunal essentially receives its competence-competence *immediately* to hear allegations of illegality (or if not immediately, arguably subject to the signature or approval of the Terms of Reference document). Also by virtue of this sequence, the tribunal thereupon normally understands itself to have "instant" jurisdiction to render an award arising out of such illegality. This would include an award which denies the tribunal's jurisdiction on the basis of illegality. This denial of jurisdiction could be considered as the tribunal's remaining jurisdiction, since it would already have exercised "residual" jurisdiction in issuing an award denying jurisdiction in the first place.

In fact, the approach under the ICC Rules over the last few years has not been entirely conducive to clarity on the issue of how and when the arbitration may proceed in the face of allegations of corruption, bribery and the like. Under Art. 7 of the former 1988 ICC Rules, the arbitration was not to proceed where, objectively, there was "no *prima facie* agreement between the parties to arbitrate". This placed the initial burden upon the ICC Court to determine whether there were some minimal indicia of the existence of an ICC arbitration agreement between the named parties. Such determination would normally take place upon receipt of the Request for Arbitration and *before* any submissions by the named defendant. Thus the analysis was not likely to extend to issues of illegality, even in its most manifest forms.

Even where the defendant answered and called upon the ICC Court to dismiss the arbitration on the grounds of nullity, former Art. 8(3) permitted the arbitration to proceed where the ICC Court was, subjectively, "*satisfied of the prima facie existence of* such an agreement [to arbitrate]". (emphasis added) Here again, even a well-founded defense of illegality, going to the root of the arbitration agreement and fundamental public morals, would not lead to subjective "dissatisfaction" on the part of the ICC Court.

The landscape under the new 1998 ICC Arbitration Rules is slightly different. Art. 6(2) of the 1998 Rules respecting competence-competence provides that the "Court may decide ... that the arbitration shall proceed if it is *prima facie satisfied* that an arbitration agreement under the Rules of Arbitration of the ICC may exist...". It is the "satisfaction" of the ICC Court which is now prima facie, and not the existence of the agreement which is subject to the prima facie test. Moreover, the satisfaction is linked to the possible existence of an ICC arbitration agreement, and not its definitive existence.[23]

This temporizing of the ICC standard may be seen as being more in tune with the fairly far-reaching competence-competence powers of the arbitral tribunal vis-à-vis the powers of the ICC Court. It also more accurately reflects the difficulties which an arbitral institution may have at the early stage of the proceedings: on what basis can or should the tribunal responsibly seek to make any conclusory determination of illegality when it often has only perfunctory submissions of the parties to work with?

d.   Illegality and separability of the arbitration agreement
Even where competence-competence thrives, there must also be separability in order to keep the train on the rails. Bearing in mind the distinction between competence-competence on the one hand and separability on the other, Art. 6(4) of the 1998 ICC Rules makes clear that

> "[t]he Arbitral Tribunal *shall continue to have jurisdiction* to determine the respective rights of the parties and to adjudicate their claims and pleas even though the contract itself *may be non-existent or null and void*". (emphasis added)

In short, Art. 6(4) makes an important clarification. Even where the ICC Court might have been able to determine that the underlying contract is null and void by reason of

---

23. Cf. also Yves DERAINS and Eric SCHWARTZ, *A Guide to the New ICC Rules of Arbitration* (1998) p. 83:

"... it is the Court's determination that is of a *prima facie* nature and ... it is not to be inferred from the Court's decision that it has concluded that there is, in fact, an agreement".

See also Richard H. KREINDLER, "Impending Revision of the ICC Arbitration Rules – Opportunities and Hazards for Experienced and Inexperienced Users Alike", 13 J. Int'l Arb. (June 1996) p. 45 at p. 79:

"The Defendant is obliged to respond to the Request, in the manner provided for in the Rules, only to the extent it has entered into, or somehow later become bound by, an agreement with the Claimant to submit to ICC arbitration...."

See also KREINDLER, "Pitfalls and Pratfalls in the Launching of an ICC Arbitration: Practical Guidelines and Substantive Solutions", Arb. & Disp. Resol. L.J. (1993) p. 145 at p. 154 et seq.

illegality, contentions to that effect will not prevent two subsequent events: (i) the ICC Court from setting the arbitration in motion and seizing the tribunal of the file, and (ii) the arbitral tribunal from exercising power, as a result of the ICC Rules, to rule on the disputed illegality or any other disputes in view of the illegality. As long as the ICC Court was *"prima facie* satisfied" of the possible existence of an ICC arbitration agreement under Art. 6(2), above, steps (i) and (ii) under Art. 6(4) shall proceed.[24]

e.   Voidness versus non-existence of the illegal contract
The affirmation of competence-competence and separability under the ICC Rules is, on its face, actually more far-reaching than those contained in the UNCITRAL Rules and the UNCITRAL Model Law. Art. 21(2) of the UNCITRAL Arbitration Rules and Art. 16(1) of the UNCITRAL Model Law provide:

> "A decision by the arbitral tribunal that the contract is null and void shall not entail *ipso jure* the invalidity of the arbitration clause."

On their face, the UNCITRAL provisions address solely the effects of a ruling that the underlying contract is *void*, as opposed to the not necessarily identical problem of the contract's *non-existence*.

The distinction between voidness on the one hand and non-existence on the other may arise particularly in the context of allegations of "fraud in the factum", as opposed to fraud in the inducement, and has loomed large in US jurisprudence.[25] Fraud in the factum may encompass situations of forged signatures or other falsified documents going to the root of assent to the contract. In such cases, the ICC Rules may be seen as empowering the ICC Court in the first instance and the tribunal to-be in the second instance to *proceed* with the arbitration, leading to either an award on jurisdiction or an award on the merits or both.

Whether such empowerment will always be in harmony with the law at the seat of arbitration is another question and another layer of analysis. See, for example, in the United States, *Kyung In Lee v. Pacific Bullion (New York) Inc.*, 788 F.Supp. 155 (E.D.N.Y. 1992):

> "... if a party's signature were forged on a contract, it would be absurd to require arbitration".

---

24. Cf. also DERAINS and SCHWARTZ, *op. cit.,* fn. 23, p. 104:

   "Given Article 6(4), the Court will ordinarily not refrain from setting an arbitration in motion where it is alleged that the agreement containing an ICC arbitration clause is null and void or non-existent, subject, of course, to the requirements of Article 6(2)."

25. In the case of "fraud in the factum", there is "ineffective assent to the contract ... misrepresentation of the character or essential terms of a proposed contract [in such a way that] assent to the contract is impossible [and] there is no contract at all": *Cancanon v. Smith Barney, Harris, Upham & Co.*, 805 F.2d 998 (11th Cir. 1986).

Such an approach may lead to the conclusion that it is for the state courts to adjudicate disputes as to whether alleged fraud in the factum imperils the existence and validity of the arbitration agreement itself, as opposed to that of the main contract. Yet such conclusion would not appear to be in harmony with the broad powers provided for in Arts. 6(2) and 6(4) of the ICC Rules. Indeed under those provisions, even an allegation that fraud in the factum went to the forgery of the arbitration agreement alone – separately from any forgery of the main contract – might not suffice to oust the ICC tribunal of its competence-competence. By contrast, under the UNCITRAL Rules or the UNCITRAL Model Law, the tribunal is not assured of continuing to have jurisdiction even in such cases.[26]

2. Arbitral Investigation of Illegality and Ultra Petita Constraints

Even assuming the far-ranging prerogatives accorded the arbitral tribunal under, for example, Art. 6(2) and Art. 6(4) of the ICC Rules, are there no *limits* to the tribunal's ability to investigate illegality, especially when the illegality is not manifest or not even expressly alleged?

As set forth earlier, the tribunal may fear that in the event of an underlying illegality and the rendering of an award on the merits, it would be acting as an accomplice to an illegal enterprise, or contributing to a violation of local or transnational public policy. Under such circumstances and given the imperative of avoiding such "complicity", is "mere" suspicion of illegality enough justification for the tribunal to investigate, sua sponte, the possible illegality?

a. Illegality and the arbitrator's inquisitorial duties

This question will depend upon the circumstances, and thus indeed it should and must be permissible from case to case. That having been said, the challenge to the tribunal in assessing when such independent investigation is appropriate and permissible is considerable:

> "It appears however, that it is for one or other of the parties to the arbitration to make and prove the allegation. That is to say, it is not the duty of an arbitral tribunal to make and prove the allegation. That is to say, *it is not the duty of an arbitral tribunal to assume an inquisitorial role and to search officiously for evidence of corruption where none is alleged. At the same time – and this may be a difficult balance to*

---

26. DERAINS and SCHWARTZ, *op. cit.*, fn. 23, p. 105:

> "[The UNCITRAL Rules and the UNCITRAL Model Law] only deal with the effects of a decision that the contract is null and void. Moreover, even in such case, they do not, unlike Article 6(4) [of the ICC Rules], affirm that the tribunal 'shall continue to have jurisdiction,' but state rather that, in the event of such a decision, the arbitration clause shall not *ipso jure* be regarded as invalid."

strike — the arbitral tribunal should not allow itself to be used by the parties to sanction conduct which is illegal."[27] (emphasis added)

How can the tribunal weigh the risks to the proper execution of its own mission against the possible risk of ruling ultra petita on a matter which the parties did not expressly or impliedly submit to it for decision? Admittedly, the major sets of arbitration rules and model legislation do not expressly state that the arbitral tribunal may or shall decide upon its own jurisdiction even where the parties have *not* made a plea in this regard. Neither the ICC Rules[28] nor the UNCITRAL Rules or UNCITRAL Model Law so state. Indeed in the case of Art. 21 of the UNCITRAL Rules, the tribunal has the power "to rule on *objections* that it has no jurisdiction" and in the case of Art. 16(1) of the UNCITRAL Model Law, the arbitral tribunal "may rule on its own jurisdiction, including any objections with respect to the existence or validity of the arbitration agreement".

Yet what if no "objection" has been made but the tribunal still suspects an illegality potentially resulting in the nullity of the main contract and/or the agreement to arbitrate? While the powers of the tribunal in such cases do not flow expressly from such bodies of rules, the better argument must be that the tribunal may, indeed perhaps must, properly make such inquiry. The right and duty to do so may be seen as deriving from a general mandate to ensure that the tribunal's conduct and any award rendered are "enforceable at law". Such right and duty may also be linked to the overlapping mandate to ensure that the relevant public policy (whether national, transnational or otherwise) is not violated by the tribunal's acts of *omission or commission*.

b.   Self-initiated investigation of illegality and general duties
Using the ICC Rules as an example, neither Art. 6(4) nor particularly Art. 6(2) expressly prohibits the tribunal from engaging in a *self-initiated investigation* of potential illegality on the basis not of overt party pleas to this effect, but solely the tribunal's own suspicions or reasoned beliefs. There is good reason to contend that in any event Art. 35 of the ICC Rules, providing that, "[i]n all matters not expressly provided for in these Rules, the Court and the Arbitral Tribunal shall act in the spirit of these Rules and shall make every effort to make sure that the Award is enforceable at law", empowers the tribunal to make such investigation particularly where the purpose of the inquiry is to avoid arbitral conduct and/or an arbitral award which might violate the relevant public policy.

---

27. REDFERN and HUNTER, *op. cit.*, fn. 5, Sect. 3-28, p. 153. Accord, KNOEPFLER, *Corruption et arbitrage international*, Publication CEDIDAC (Lausanne 1998) p. 365.
28. In the case of the ICC Rules, DERAINS and SCHWARTZ, *op. cit.*, fn. 23, p. 100:

"Article 6(2) does not provide, however, that the Arbitral Tribunal shall otherwise decide upon its jurisdiction in the absence of a plea of one of the parties...."

Such a reading of Art. 35 finds its counterpart in certain other arbitral rules.[29] It is consistent with actual arbitral practice and of course consistent with what Art. 35 itself provides. An interpretation of Art. 35 to the effect that it has no particular stature or standing on its own but is largely a catch-all "throw-away" cannot be supported. Art. 35 is fully consistent with the mandate of the tribunal not to violate the relevant public policy or policies; what that policy or those policies require is of course another question, as addressed further below.

The absence of Art. 35 or its equivalent from the agreed arbitral rules would in no way diminish the duty of the tribunal to make every effort to ensure that any award is "enforceable at law". Arguments to the effect that Art. 35 cannot possibly require the tribunal to verify the enforceability of its actions and rulings under any and all conceivable bodies of law at multiple far-flung places of possible enforcement[30] are not on all fours with the current context.

For the question here is not the extent of due diligence which the tribunal can or should conduct under multiple bodies of public policy across the globe. The question, rather, is the extent to which the tribunal may, should or must engage in self-inquiry as to possible illegality when no party has pleaded or otherwise relied upon an illegality objection. The question also extends to the scope of due diligence when the parties have been given a reasonable opportunity to develop their competing views on a possible illegality and its consequences, but the tribunal considers the feedback insufficient to make proper determination of the illegality question.

Such a situation cannot simply be compared with the frequently encountered case where the tribunal is dissatisfied and ill-served by inept feedback from the parties on typical questions of jurisdiction or the merits unrelated to a possible illegality. In such cases, barring the limited circumstances in jurisdictions where lack of further self-inquiry could trigger a charge of manifest disregard of the law or error of law, the tribunal appropriately confines its inquiry and decision to the parties' pleas.

However, in the case of possible corruption or bribery which may offend public morals, the tribunal may fear that lack of further self-inquiry could trigger a violation of public policy. For that reason, the tribunal may see fit not to confine its inquiry to what the parties have "fed" it.

---

29. For example, Art. 32(1) of the 1998 Rules of the London Court of International Arbitration (LCIA):

"In all matters not expressly provided for in these Rules, the LCIA Court, the Arbitral Tribunal and the parties shall act in the spirit of these Rules and shall make every *reasonable* effort to ensure that an award is *legally enforceable*." (emphasis added)

30. Cf., e.g., DERAINS and SCHWARTZ, *op. cit.*, fn. 23, pp. 351-352:

"[Article 35] is not intended, however, to have any influence on the Arbitral Tribunal's resolution of substantive issues in the arbitration. Nor does it require the Arbitral Tribunal to ensure that the Award would be subject to execution in any particular country, provided that it has been rendered in accordance with the formal requirements of the place where made."

c. The duty of the arbitrator versus the arbitral institution

Indeed Art. 35 of the ICC Arbitration Rules expressly imposes a duty not only on the tribunal, but also on the ICC Court, and thereby on the entire ICC arbitral institution. On the basis of the wording of the provision ("In all matters not expressly provided for in these Rules … shall act in the spirit of these Rules …"), the argument is most often made that Art. 35 does not impose any supplemental duty on the tribunal or the ICC Court which is not already set forth in the Rules.

Art. 6(2) and Art. 6(4) give express prerogatives to the ICC Court particularly at the opening stage of the arbitration. Any tribunal-initiated inquiry into suspected illegality would, it might be reasoned, be possible only in the context of Art. 6(2) and Art. 6(4). The tribunal is bestowed with competence-competence under Art. 6(4) only after the ICC Court is "*prima facie* satisfied" under Art. 6(2). In this sense, it is reasoned, the *institution* has the power, and indeed perhaps the duty, to ascertain whether a manifest or apparent illegality exists such as to call into question the existence of the related ICC arbitration agreement.[31]

Such power would appear to emerge from the wording of Art. 6(2). Such duty would appear to emerge from Art. 35 as applied to the institution, unless by circular reasoning Art. 35 were deemed not to apply since Art. 6(2) provides that the Court "may decide" and not "shall decide". That reasoning would indeed be circular and counterproductive, since Art. 6(2) itself provides that the Court may decide, *or may not decide*, that an ICC arbitration agreement may exist. In the extreme case, where a would-be claimant files a Request for Arbitration relating to an illicit contract promoting or facilitating prostitution and containing a standard ICC arbitration clause, can the ICC Court exercise Art. 6(2) to decline to entertain the arbitration?

The answer would appear to be affirmative, and based at least in part on Art. 35.[32] When this power and duty of the institution will apply in less clear-cut cases of illegality is more problematic. In any event, the opportunity to decline to entertain the arbitration

---

31. But cf., e.g., Art. 1(3) and Art. 36 of the 1998 AAA International Arbitration Rules, which do not provide the same framework for analysis. Art. 1(3) provides:

    "These rules specify the duties and responsibilities of the administrator, the American Arbitration Association."

    Art. 36 provides:

    "The tribunal shall interpret and apply these rules insofar as they relate to its powers and duties. The administrator shall interpret and apply all other rules."

    Absent provisions and mechanisms comparable to Art. 6(2) and (4) of the ICC Rules, the AAA "administrator" would not appear to have the same rights, or duties, respecting initial illegality as may redound to the ICC Court.

32. Cf. also Art. 1(1) of Appendix I (Statutes of the International Court of Arbitration of the ICC):

    "The function of the International Court of Arbitration … is to ensure the application of the [ICC Rules], and it has all the necessary powers for that purpose."

definitely exists. In the case of a pure ad hoc arbitration, such opportunity will not arise with an institution. Instead, the national courts of appropriate jurisdiction, normally at the seat of arbitration, may be the best or only alternative for stay or dismissal of the arbitration in such overt cases of illegality.[33]

The case of a semi-administered ad hoc arbitration such as under the UNCITRAL ad hoc rules is somewhat different. There, any appointing institution stipulated in the arbitration agreement (or by default the Secretary-General of the Permanent Court of Arbitration at The Hague) will presumably be limited to functions related to appointment, as opposed to prima facie acceptance of the Request for Arbitration. To that extent, the appointing institution would appear to have no express power, or duty, to decline to entertain the arbitration in the sense of its appointment functions.

On the other hand, coming back again to the extreme case of an illicit contract relating to prostitution, the institution would arguably likewise have no obligation to participate as appointing authority if such participation constituted abetting a manifestly illegal enterprise. Support for an institutional refusal to offer its appointing services might be found directly in Art. 1(2) of the UNCITRAL Rules:

---

33. Chapter 12 of the Swiss Private International Law Act (PILA), which of course may also apply in non-institutional arbitrations with a Swiss seat and at least one non-Swiss party, presumably gives the tribunal a similar power, and even duty. Art. 186(1) provides succinctly:

"The arbitral tribunal shall decide on its own jurisdiction."

This provision may be construed to entitle the tribunal to decide on its jurisdiction, and deny it, even when not raised or attacked by any party. That decision is subject to the control of the reviewing court, the Federal Tribunal, under Art. 190(2)(b):

"Proceedings for setting aside the award may only be initiated: ....Where the arbitral tribunal has wrongly declared itself to have or not to have jurisdiction."

Cf. LALIVE, POUDRET, REYMOND, *Le Droit de l'Arbitrage Interne et International en Suisse* (1989) Art. 186, Sect. 11, reasoning that the tribunal should not necessarily always verify its own jurisdiction except, in international arbitrations, where Swiss international public policy may otherwise be violated:

"*[L]'arbitre qui constate qu'il est saisi d'une demande non arbitrable au sens de l'art. 177 doit-il se déclarer d'office incompétent? Cela paraît être le cas en arbitrage interne.... mais la loi fédérale ne contient pas de disposition semblable en matière d'arbitrage international. A notre avis et contrairement à celui de Marc Blessing (p. 53), l'art. 177 al. 1er n'est pas, comme tel, d'ordre public. S'il convient aux parties de soumettre une contestation non pécuniaire à l'arbitrage, l'arbitre ne peut pas, de ce seul fait, se déclarer d'office incompétent. En revanche il peut le faire, nous semble-t-il, s'il estime que l'ordre public international de la Suisse s'oppose à ce que la contestation don't il est saisi soit portée devant un arbitre.*" (emphasis added)

In international arbitrations in Switzerland, the standard of public policy under Art. 190(2)(*e*) (setting aside "where the award is incompatible with public policy") may be equated with Swiss notions of international public policy as opposed to local Swiss *lois de police*. In that context, the Act may be seen as authorizing self-inquiry by the tribunal into its jurisdiction vel non in the face of a suspected or manifest illegality.

"These Rules shall govern the arbitration except that where any of these Rules is in conflict with a provision of the law applicable to the arbitration from which the parties cannot derogate, that provision shall prevail."

The appointing authority is bound by the Rules. At the same time, the Rules calling for its assistance in constitution of a tribunal (whose basis is an illegal contract and also a void arbitration agreement) cannot supersede mandatory public policy. This is clear from the Rules themselves: "except that where any of these Rules is in conflict with a provision of the law applicable to the arbitration from which the parties cannot derogate". Such public policy must be deemed to encompass the nullity of manifestly offensive contracts. Neither the parties nor the appointing authority can validly derogate from such public policy.

Defining *which* national or transnational public policy should apply is, again, a potential challenge, which is addressed further below. In the case of prostitution, child labor, torture, slavery, drug trafficking and the like, there will presumably be little or no room to contend that international public policy does not offer a global proscription – even if there were somehow room to contend that some *local* public policy does not expressly proscribe such conduct.

d.   *Illegality objections, waiver and the tribunal's own inquiry*

A related question with respect to the right or duty of the tribunal to initiate its own inquiry into possible illegality concerns timing and preclusion. Some national legislation, such as Art. 186(2) of the Swiss Private International Law Act, stipulates that any objection to the jurisdiction of the tribunal "must be raised prior to any defense on the merits". Does this mean that even if the tribunal is permitted to initiate its own investigation of possible illegality and invite the parties to make submissions on the issue, the tribunal must do so before submission of the defense on the merits?

That cannot possibly be the case, as the tribunal-initiated inquiry must be deemed to be of a different nature than the party-initiated objection to jurisdiction. A primary purpose for provisions such as Art. 186(2) is to avoid last-minute and bad-faith attempts to derail the proceedings by belated pleas of lack of jurisdiction. On the other hand, the purpose of the tribunal-initiated inquiry is to verify whether the arbitrators even have the authority to act further in the proceedings. The one has little relation to the other. The position under Art. 186(2) of the Swiss Act is in any event more nuanced than its wording alone would allow one to conclude. The tribunal must generally examine *on its own motion* whether the matter in dispute is objectively arbitrable pursuant to Art. 177(1) ("Any dispute involving property can be the subject-matter of an arbitration"), and the duty to do so should be seen as being linked to verification of any violation of public policy under Art. 190(2)(*e*). There is, however, some disagreement on this issue, with certain commentators denying such right[34] and others limiting the right to cases of

---

34. LALIVE, POUDRET, REYMOND, *op. cit.*, fn. 33, Art. 186, Sect. 11 and Art. 177, Sect. 6 as evidently cited with approval by the Swiss Fed. Trib. in a decision dated 15 March 1993, consid. 5, ASA Bull. (1993) p. 398 at p. 406.

"serious doubt".[35] In the more narrow context of pleas of lack of jurisdiction under Art. 186(2) as opposed to non-arbitrability under Art. 177(1), there is likewise lack of complete agreement. On the one hand, the view has been expressed that, "for a party which remains completely passive and which, prima facie, has not concluded an arbitration agreement, the arbitral tribunal does not in principle have the power to make a ruling on jurisdiction".[36]

On the other hand, the Swiss Federal Tribunal has held that except in cases of a "sham tribunal", the existence of competence-competence "does not require that there be prima facie an agreement to arbitrate".[37]

In the context of illegality, the foregoing would indicate that in cases where the Swiss Act applies, a tribunal might not have the power to make a ruling on jurisdiction if the party that could benefit from lack of jurisdiction due to illegality did not prima facie conclude an arbitration agreement in the first place and does not raise the issue of illegality. Alternatively, where that same party did prima facie conclude an arbitration agreement and in particular where the tribunal suspects an illegality which might lead to voidness, the tribunal presumably has the power to investigate the issue on its own motion, and to render an award separately on that issue if appropriate. By extension, where the prima facie *existence* of the agreement to arbitrate is not in serious dispute, but the tribunal suspects that the agreement may not bind a particular named party for reasons of illegality, the tribunal should be entitled to investigate and to rule on its jurisdiction over that party.[38]

e.   Illegality, waiver and the party's belated plea of voidness
It may be that a *party* does after all make a plea of lack of jurisdiction based on illegality but does so belatedly. To the extent the illegality potentially embraces public policy

---

35. Robert BRINER, Art. 177, Sect. 20, in Stephen V. BERTI, ed., *International Arbitration in Switzerland* (2000) p. 324, stating:

   "[i]t should, however, be recalled that arbitral awards which violate *ordre public* are not absolutely void but only voidable, unless they violate public interests".

36. Werner WENGER, Art. 186, Sect. 37, in BERTI, *op. cit.*, fn. 35, p. 473, citing Andreas BUCHER, *Die neue internationale Schiedsgerichtsbarkeit in der Schweiz* (1989) Sect. 130.

37. WENGER, *ibid.*, citing obiter dictum in Swiss Fed. Trib. decision 120 II, 155 et seq., 163 et seq.

38. Accord, WENGER, *ibid.*:

   "The Swiss Federal Tribunal has held that *a tribunal does in any event have the power to make a jurisdictional ruling in such situations when it is not the existence but the subjective scope of an agreement to arbitrate which is in dispute....* Despite the important objections raised against this decision (Klein, De la forclusion en matière d'arbitrage international - Réflexions sur un récent arrêt, Bull. ASA 1995, 132 et seq.) it is, we submit, correct for reasons of practicability as stated by the Swiss Federal Tribunal in its judgment and in view of the close relationship between validity and subjective scope of an arbitration agreement (judgment of 19.4.1994 EAU and Others v. Westland Helicopters Ltd.; DFT 120 II 155 et seq., 163 f., and Bull ASA 1994, 404 et seq.)."(emphasis added)

concerns, the belatedness under the applicable rules or law should also be irrelevant to, or secondary to, the tribunal's continuing ability to deny jurisdiction.

The issue here is not solely procedural equality of arms or judicial economy calling for a timely raising of a jurisdictional plea. Rather, it is the root arbitrability of the dispute in the face of possible nullity of the main contract and, perhaps, the arbitration agreement. As long as the manner in which the tribunal entertains the illegality concern and allows the parties to make eleventh-hour submissions on the issue is even-handed and transparent, the tribunal should be empowered to accept the plea and make the inquiry even at a late stage.

Alternatively, the parties may *agree* that the late plea shall be entertained as an amendment to the prior procedural framework. In such cases, there is little difficulty in allowing in the further submissions. The tribunal is not per se obligated to incorporate the new plea, but if it refuses to do so it must ensure that by the refusal it treats the parties equally and with respect for their rights to an adversarial proceeding.

In the case of Art. 186 of the Swiss Act, which has been considered to be mandatory law where the Swiss Act applies,[39] query whether such a "late-breaking" illegality plea can be accepted. Where, even under the Swiss Act, the parties and tribunal have validly agreed to procedural rules (Art. 182(1) and (2)) which specify until which time a plea of non-jurisdiction is deemed to be timely, such a plea entered even later than the start of the merits phase will presumably still be timely. Where, for example, the UNCITRAL Model Law instead applies, its Art. 16(2) expressly provides that even such a plea entered after submission of the statement of defense may be allowed if the tribunal "considers the delay justified".

f. The ICC Rules and belated pleas of illegality

The ICC Rules contain no provision comparable to Art. 186(2) of the Swiss Act. Indeed none of the ICC's provisions respecting belated pleas should be seen as necessarily foreclosing a justified last-minute party plea of illegality. Such provisions are to be applied by the tribunal in the context of its overall discretion to consider the relevant circumstances. They may in any event be subject to the overall mandate of Art. 35, discussed above. In particular, ICC Rules Arts. 18(1), 19, 22(1) and 33 are noteworthy in this regard.

Art. 18(1)(c) and (d) relates to the components of the Terms of Reference. They include the claims and relief sought and, unless the tribunal considers it inappropriate, the "issues to be determined". The Terms of Reference have been regarded as a time point by which a party must make a plea of lack of jurisdiction in order for it to be timely. This view has also been taken in Swiss case law and commentary recognizing the ability to validly delay a plea of lack of jurisdiction until a point later than set forth under Art. 186(2) of the Swiss Act.[40] Query, however, whether the omission in the "list of issues to be determined" of a plea of non-jurisdiction based on illegality would foreclose

---

39. See, e.g., HEINI, KELLER, SIEHR, VISCHER and VOLKEN, *IPRG-Kommentar* (1993) Art. 186, Sect. 10.

40. See, e.g., decision of the Court of Appeal of Basle City dated 2 January 1984, ASA Bull. (1985) p. 19 at p. 22; HEINI, et. al., *op. cit.*, fn. 39, Art. 186, Sect. 11.

the right to make such a plea after signature or approval of the Terms of Reference, or the right of the tribunal to investigate such illegality at a later stage. The list of issues to be determined may not even exist if the tribunal decides not to include one, in its discretion under the 1998 ICC Rules. Moreover, even if it does exist, such list does not necessarily constitute a seamless and all-inclusive link to the petita of the party who failed to raise the illegality before the Terms of Reference entered into effect.

Therefore, under certain circumstances there should be no reason why illegality could not be raised by a party or by the tribunal at a later stage, as long as the tribunal entertains the belatedly raised issue in an even-handed and transparent manner.[41] In any event, any alleged preclusive effect under Art. 18 of the ICC Rules must be seen in the context of Art. 19 (New Claims). Art. 19 places conditions on "new claims or counterclaims" after signature or approval of the Terms of Reference. It does not purport to speak to new defenses, including objections to jurisdiction over claims or counterclaims.

Moreover, Art. 22(1) (Closing of the Proceedings) provides that "no further submission or argument may be made, or evidence produced, unless requested or authorized by the Arbitral Tribunal". Accordingly, a last-minute submission or argument alleging illegality may be requested by the tribunal based upon its own initiative or accepted upon motion of a party.

Finally, Art. 33 (Waiver) stipulates that, in particular, a party "which proceeds with the arbitration without raising its objection to ... the conduct of the proceedings, shall be deemed to have waived its right to object". In the context of the ICC Rules, the better view is that this not atypical waiver provision is not intended to foreclose justified last-minute objections to jurisdiction. Such objections should not be regarded as being encompassed by Art. 33 any more than well-founded objections to the conduct of the proceedings which may later serve as justified grounds for challenge of the award can somehow be waived by virtue of Art. 33.

g.   Waiver of illegality objections and UNCITRAL

In the context of other arbitral rules which do require that jurisdictional objections be made by a stipulated time lest they be deemed waived, such as Art. 21(2) of the UNCITRAL Rules, such a waiver provision should likewise be considered to be of only secondary importance.

Let us assume that the tribunal concludes that a last-minute illegality objection is potentially or manifestly well-founded, and that it may result in the nullity of the main

---

41. But cf. WENGER, *op. cit.*, fn. 36, Sect. 39:

"Thus, submission to the ICC Rules is to be considered as an agreement that a plea of non-jurisdiction raised in the terms of reference (Art. 18 ICC Rules) is timely, since it is not until the completion of this document that the issues to be determined by the arbitral tribunal are set down in a binding manner (ICC-Award Nr. 6140 of 31.3.1989, reported in: Bull ASA 1990, p. 257 et seq. ...)."

In light of the foregoing remarks, this restrictive interpretation cannot serve as the basis to foreclose subsequent pleas or self-initiated inquiries respecting illegality.

contract or the arbitration agreement or both. In such case, mandatory public policy concerns should entitle or compel the tribunal to entertain the late objection.

In the case of the UNCITRAL Rules, Art. 21(1)[42] by its wording suggests that the tribunal's far-reaching power to rule on jurisdictional objections is limited to "objections" to jurisdiction – that is, only if raised by a party and not as a result of the tribunal's own initiative. This conclusion is strengthened by Art. 21(4)[43] which frames jurisdictional issues in terms of "pleas concerning its jurisdiction", that are initiated by the party. At the same time, it is submitted that these provisions and the overall mechanism for confirmation or denial of jurisdiction are subject to mandatory public policy considerations. Such considerations should enable or even require the arbitrator to assess possible invalidity consequences on his own motion. Such public policy considerations must thus be seen as transcending Art. 21, and are in any event contemplated via Art. 1(2) already discussed above.

Interestingly, the UNCITRAL Model Law, Art. 16, did not follow quite the same approach as Art. 21 of the UNCITRAL Rules, and may be seen as more overtly receptive to self-initiated inquiries respecting illegality and jurisdiction. Art. 16(1) provides that the tribunal "may rule on its own jurisdiction, including any objections with respect to the existence or validity of the arbitration agreement" .

On its face, such provision does not limit the tribunal's competence-competence to "objections" to jurisdiction. Rather, this provision includes such objections as one possible component of rulings on jurisdiction. Indeed, the provision should be seen as encompassing any and all party pleas regarding jurisdiction – whether related to the existence, validity, scope or other aspects of the arbitration agreement. In any event, it would appear that the tribunal has the right and perhaps the duty to assess its own jurisdiction in the face of an illegality issue as a matter of either arbitrability or public policy concerns.[44]

---

42. Art. 21(1) UNCITRAL Rules:

  "The arbitral tribunal shall have the power to rule on *objections* that it has no jurisdiction, including any objections with respect to the existence or validity of the arbitration clause or of the separate arbitration agreement." (emphasis added)

43. Art. 21(4) UNCITRAL Rules:

  "In general, the arbitral tribunal should rule on a *plea* concerning its jurisdiction as a preliminary question...." (emphasis added)

44. Apparently, Art. 16 UNCITRAL Model Law deliberately did not follow Art. 21(1) UNCITRAL Rules in this respect. At the same time, the drafters of the Model Law considered that:

  "with the exception of certain classes of jurisdictional objections – such as those going to arbitrability or public policy – the failure to raise a plea as to jurisdiction should operate as a waiver of the point".

  Howard M. HOLTZMANN and Joseph E. NEUHAUS, *A Guide to the UNCITRAL Model Law on International Commercial Arbitration: Legislative History and Commentary* (1989) p. 479. Where

With respect, on the other hand, to the *tribunal's* belated self-inquiry justified by suspected or manifest illegality, the circumstances may call for the tribunal to initiate its inquiry at the last minute. This may be well after objections on jurisdiction have been or, under the operative deadlines, must have been submitted.

In such case, the tribunal's right or duty to do so, again based possibly in part on the notion that it seeks to avoid possible complicity in violations of public policy, should normally justify the belatedness[45] – as long as the parties are given an even-handed and reasonable opportunity to react to the tribunal's suspicions or conclusions. To surprise the parties by issuing a ruling or even obiter dictum on illegality in the award without forewarning them may or may not necessarily be an ultra petita violation, but it will almost certainly be a violation of due process and the right to a reasonable opportunity to present the case.

h.   Illegality and ultra petita

Is the arbitrator caught between a rock and a hard place by initiating his own verification of suspected illegality despite the parties' failure to plead illegality? Failure to engage in such self-inquiry might cause the arbitrator to be an "accomplice" to a contract against public morals or to issue an award which violates public policy. Initiating his own investigation, on the other hand, and in particular drawing his own conclusions as to such illegality in its award, might constitute an impermissible foray into a dispute "not contemplated by or not falling within the terms of the submission to arbitration, or contain[ing] decisions on matters beyond the scope of the submission to arbitration" in the sense of Art. 34(2)(*a*)(iii) of the Model Law or, in virtually the same wording, Art. V(1)(*c*) of the New York Convention.

Inviting the parties to make submissions on the suspected illegality might assuage concerns about each party's ability to "present his case" in the sense of Art. V(1)(*b*) of the New York Convention, but compliance with the due process commandment would not necessarily also guarantee compliance with the ultra petita commandment.

If it were correct that the arbitrator's choice resided between violating public policy and violating ultra petita, an instinctual reaction might be that in the hierarchy of mandatory norms avoiding an offense to public policy supersedes avoiding an offense to ultra petita. Whether this is in fact a correct analysis, or even an analysis which can possibly be conducted, need not be answered. The reason is that the tribunal's self-inquiry into possible illegality, whether considered a right or a duty, should normally not

---

arbitrability or public policy concerns trump the waiver provision, the same rationale may be seen as allowing or even compelling the tribunal to investigate illegality issues belatedly to the extent they go to arbitrability or public policy.

45. Cf. UN Commentary A/CN.9/264 to Art. 16 of the Model Law, which supports the foregoing observation:

"It may be mentioned that the principle of separability as adopted in Article 16(1), in contrast to some national laws which distinguish in this respect between *initial defects and later grounds of nullity, applies whatever be the nature of the defect*." (emphasis added)

be a violation of ultra petita in the first place, even where no party plea of illegality has been raised.

A second "instinctual reaction" in many such cases of illegality, which can be addressed briefly, would be that the arbitrator literally throws up his hands and decides not to proceed, but instead to resign from office.[46] It is submitted that abstention and resignation under most circumstances of illegality is neither desirable nor necessary, but rather the tribunal is entitled to proceed with the matter.

The arbitrator may not have a duty to remain in office at all costs[47] in the face of a thoroughly distasteful illicit dispute.[48] However, it is submitted that his original declaration of ability to take on the case and see it through to the end[49] should be overcome only in extreme circumstances. A distaste for the illegality of the case or a frustration with a difficulty of choice between competing mandatory norms should not normally justify resignation.

In fact, certain arbitration regulations are so strict in their provisions meant to reduce the impact of an arbitrator's dilatory conduct that an arbitrator acting conscientiously under such regulations might find it exceedingly difficult to resign even where his reason related to a fear of his "complicity" in illegality, as opposed to dilatoriness.[50] Art. 13

---

46. The arbitrator might do so if he believes that he would otherwise become involved in a breach of public policy. See, e.g., Pierre MAYER, "La règle morale dans l'arbitrage internationale", in *Etudes Offertes à Pierre Bellet* (1991) p. 379, Sect. 34. Such a resignation could be justified under, e.g., Art. 12(1) of the ICC Rules: "An arbitrator shall also be replaced ... upon the acceptance by the Court of the arbitrator's resignation...." Art. 14(1) of the UNCITRAL Model Law is somewhat more responsive in this regard: "If an arbitrator becomes *de jure* or *de facto* unable to perform his functions ... his mandate terminates if he withdraws from his office...."

47. The distinction between French domestic arbitration law and French international arbitration law is interesting in this regard. Under Art. 1462 of the French New Code of Civil Procedure applying to domestic arbitration, "[e]ach arbitrator shall carry out his or her mission until it is completed" while under Art. 1463 "[a]n arbitrator may refuse to act or be challenged only on a ground which is revealed or arises after his or her appointment". The question is what happens when, absent a more specific party agreement, in an *international* arbitration with a French seat the arbitrator resigns due to a distaste for an illegality of contract which existed and was known to him at the time of his consent to serve as arbitrator. Cf. Emmanuel GAILLARD and John SAVAGE, eds., *Fouchard Gaillard Goldman on International Commercial Arbitration,* (hereinafter *Fouchard Gaillard Goldman*) (1999) Sect. 882, p. 506, citing *TGI Paris*, réf., 15 February 1995, *Industrialexport v. K.*, Rev.Arb. (1996) p. 503, second decision, holding that, "[the judge] cannot attempt, by issuing an injunction against the defaulting arbitrator, to compel the latter to resume and pursue *a task as personal as that of judging*". (emphasis added)

48. Cf. also other arbitration legislation providing that in principle once the arbitrator has accepted office, he cannot resign without proper grounds – which begs the question of whether a thoroughgoing illegality and distastefulness for the same would constitute such grounds: e.g., Art. 1029(2) of the Dutch Code of Civil Procedure, Art. 1689 of the Belgian Judicial Code and Art. 813 of the Italian Code of Civil Procedure.

49. Cf. Art. 7(5) of the 1998 ICC Rules, providing that "[b]y accepting to serve, every arbitrator undertakes to carry out his responsibilities in accordance with these Rules".

50. For example, Art. 12(1) of the 1998 ICC Rules provides that an arbitrator's resignation must be accepted by the ICC International Court, while Art. 8 of the ICSID Arbitration Rules allows the tribunal to accept or reject the resignation of a party-appointed arbitrator.

para. 5 of the Rules of the Iran-United States Claims Tribunal is an interesting case in point, providing that arbitrators must continue to serve in all cases where they have already participated in a hearing on the substance of the dispute. In all such cases, however, presumably an arbitrator may resign without any external approval where the illegality-related grounds are properly set forth and/or affect his independence toward the parties in a manner which he did not cause.[51]

i.   Illegality, ultra petita and Terms of Reference

In any event, the difficulty of choice between ultra petita and due process does not arise here in a way which should cause the arbitrator to throw up his hands: ultra petita is a cardinal principle of international arbitration with direct relevance to standards of review and enforcement. At the same time, this commandment must be seen in the proper and realistic context. For example, the notion that the scope of the tribunal's mission can best, or even only, be monitored in an ICC or ICC-like arbitration which benefits from Terms of Reference seems to be a potential overstatement.[52]

Whether the "list of issues to be determined" is in fact a reliable and exclusive roadmap to the petita of the parties can in fact be seriously questioned. This is all the more so in the case of such "lists" which delineate the issues in intentionally generic and vague, and therefore somewhat unhelpful, terms.[53]

It may also be doubted whether vague and generic "summaries" of the parties' claims and prayers for relief in the sense of Art. 18(1)(c) of the ICC Rules, often with no specific quanta, are particularly helpful in the sense of infra or ultra petita.

There are of course many cases where Terms of Reference or comparable documents such as "constitutional orders" in non-ICC proceedings are formulated in such a way as to provide a genuinely accurate roadmap to the claims and prayers for relief. But even in such cases, it is by no means guaranteed that there will be an overlap between such document and the "differences contemplated by or ... falling within the terms of the submission to arbitration" in the sense of Art. V(1)(c) of the New York Convention.

---

51. See also *Fouchard Gaillard Goldman*, *op. cit.*, fn. 47, Sect. 1132, p. 612:

> "Arbitrators can of course resign, with or without the approval of the arbitral institution or their colleagues, if there are proper grounds to justify their resignation. For example, it may become impossible for them to pursue their functions, or a circumstance may arise, through no fault of their own, which affects their independence vis-à-vis the parties."

52. There is little doubt that a Terms of Reference agreement in the sense of Art. 18(1)(d) of the ICC Rules, including a "list of issues to be determined", may serve a number of salutary and even indispensable purposes in an arbitration. The summary of the parties' respective claims and prayers for relief as well as the "list of issues to be determined" (which, as of the 1998 ICC Rules, is at the discretion of the tribunal) have generally been regarded as a useful basis for monitoring infra and ultra petita issues leading up to and after the rendering of the award. Indeed the Working Party charged with drafting what became the 1998 ICC Rules itself noted that Terms of Reference could be helpful in ultra petita control. See generally, KREINDLER, "Impending Revision of the ICC Arbitration Rules", *op. cit.*, fn. 23, p. 99.

53. For example, "is the Claimant entitled to any or all of the relief sought as set out in Section 'x' above? If so, to which relief and in what monetary amount, if any, is the Claimant entitled?"

Arguments or differences not originally contemplated by the parties at the time of their ICC Terms of Reference – or at the time of the "constitutional order" or the like where there is no Terms of Reference per se – may well arise in the course of the later proceedings. Such arguments may even consume more attention than the originally trumpeted differences. These arguments will normally become part of the "mission" of the tribunal, and may figure as part of the final award.

The same would hold true for illegality contentions going to the nullity of the main contract and/or the agreement to arbitrate. Arguments or differences relating to illegality, even if initiated by the tribunal itself, should normally be deemed to "fall within the terms of the submission to arbitration". While an illegality analysis may not be a "difference contemplated by" the terms of the submission, it has a core relevance to arbitrability and public policy. For that reason among others, it should be seen as necessarily falling within the terms of virtually any submission to arbitration.

Moreover, there can be little doubt that a tribunal-initiated investigation of illegality is not tantamount to ultra petita. The tribunal comes to a legal conclusion as to the validity of the main contract, the claims under that contract and/or the arbitration agreement, or the unmeritoriousness of the claims due to the invalidity of the contract. Even when it does so without being expressly asked, its action should not vitiate the enforceability of an award made on this basis as long as the parties are given a reasonable opportunity to react to the tribunal's conclusion first.

The tribunal's decision following on such self-initiated investigation can "fit" into the claims and, perhaps less so, defenses already made. Alternatively, without being asked to do so the tribunal can conclude that as a result of a fundamental illegality it has no competence and render an award denying its jurisdiction on such basis as part of a duty to self-police its jurisdiction where public policy concerns apply.[54] In this regard, Wetter, writing in 1994 respecting the 1963 Lagergren award, wrote:

> "... the question whether or not a dispute is arbitrable is one which must be examined by an international arbitral tribunal of its own motion, *ex officio*, because a tribunal must satisfy itself that it does have jurisdiction legally conferred upon it by the parties...".[55]

One need not necessarily go as far as to advocate a duty ex officio even in the absence of any allegation or indication of illegality which might affect issues of arbitrability or public policy. But in the presence of such an allegation or even a suspicion on the part of the tribunal, the validity of the arbitration agreement may be at stake.

Analysis of the validity of the arbitration agreement is part and parcel of an analysis of the validity of the underlying contract. The tribunal must undertake such an analysis in the presence of a party plea of corruption or other illicit conduct which may permeate both the main contract and the arbitration agreement. Likewise, the tribunal should and perhaps must undertake this analysis on its own initiative when it suspects such a

---

54. For an interesting recent case in this regard, see Swiss Fed. Trib., 2 March 2001, *Bank Saint Petersburg v. ATA Insaat Sanayi ve Ticaret Ltd.*, ASA Bull. (2001) p. 531.

55. WETTER, *op. cit.*, fn. 1, p. 284.

thoroughgoing illegality. A similar approach was adopted in the *Westinghouse* matter[56] and may also be applied to cases of tribunal-initiated investigation of illegality.

3. *Tainting of the Arbitration Clause Notwithstanding Separability?*

The competence-competence and separability doctrines have indeed become firmly entrenched in arbitration jurisprudence and practice for the most part, including in the United States and England (to name two stragglers to the cause). Under what circumstances if ever should the tribunal "lose" even its residual competence-competence, or should it decline to act further in the proceedings, on the grounds that the *initial* assumption or attribution of competence-competence was faulty, or has been superseded by a *later* finding of fatal nullity?

a. *Illegality as fraud or duress*
Harking back to the example of "that's not my signature!", case law and commentary have increasingly held that the arbitration agreement will not "survive" where the nature of the illegality of the main contract is such as to taint the validity of the arbitration clause as well:

> "There may be instances where a defect going to the root of an agreement between parties affects both the main contract and the arbitration clause. An obvious example is *a contract obtained by threat*."[57] (emphasis added)

Thus a contract obtained under threat or duress which contains an arbitration agreement may be deemed to be void ab initio, along with the arbitration agreement itself.

Alternatively, a contract obtained as a result of corruption, or promoting or facilitating the same, may not be deemed to be void ab initio. A reason would be the notion that even corruption is a less egregious form of illicitness and/or that it does not taint effective assent to the arbitration agreement. Even a finding of voidness of the main contract in such cases will not necessarily result in the voidness of the arbitration agreement. The separability of the arbitration agreement may save it, where the same separability did not necessarily save it in the case of threat or duress:

> "With regard to the impact of bribery, it would remain to be seen whether *bribery*, if proved, affects both the main contract and the arbitration clause and renders both null and invalid."[58] (emphasis added)

In the former case, involving duress, the arbitration agreement may be deemed never to have existed. There was lack of the necessary assent. Not even competence-

---

56. *Westinghouse*, *op. cit.*, fn. 16, Preliminary Award, 19 December 1991, 7 Int'l Arb. Report 1 (1992, no. 1) B-48.

57. *Westinghouse* dictum, *op. cit.*, fn. 16 at B-13 – B-14.

58. *Ibid.*

competence arises, and there is no valid arbitration contract to "separate" from the main contract. Therefore, there is not even a residual competence-competence basis for the tribunal to render an award declaring the main contract illegal and/or declining its own jurisdiction on the basis of the voidness of the main contract and the arbitration agreement.

In the latter case, the arbitration agreement may have come into being along with the originally valid main contract. It may remain separable notwithstanding the "ensuing" illegality of the main contract. Or the main contract will be found to have been illicit from its inception, but the degree of its illicitness is not deemed to reach or relate to the continuing validity and separability of the agreement to arbitrate.

Is the basis for the foregoing distinctions – based on assent and egregiousness – crystal clear? Is there a compelling reason why the arbitration clause should "survive" in the one instance of illegality but not survive in the other, especially as one consequence of non-survival is the indirect "tolerance" of the illicitness?

What is the point of a far-reaching doctrine of separability if the arbitration agreement is not allowed to survive in order to condemn illicit contracts? For the parties to the contract agreed, at arm's length, to submit disputes under their illicit contract to binding arbitration. Is the arbitration process not still a valid one, despite the illicitness of the underlying contract formation and performance?

b.   Sustaining arbitration agreements versus giving effect to illegality
As to these questions, recent case law has not entirely unmuddied the waters. A useful focal point is England, since the entry into effect of the Arbitration Act 1996.

In the case of contracts considered to have been illegal ab initio, the longstanding common law principle in England was that the arbitration agreement – although autonomous in principle – could not exist: see, e.g., *Zinc Corporation Ltd. v. Hirsch,* [1916] 1 KB 451 and, more recently, *Dalmia Dairy Industries Ltd v. National Bank of Pakistan,* [1978] 2 Lloyd's Rep. 223.

A departure from this resistance to the separability of the arbitration agreement, also in the illegality context, emerged with the Court of Appeal decision in *Harbour Assurance Co. (UK) Ltd. v. Kansa General Insurance Co. Ltd.*, [1992] 1 Lloyd's Rep 81. The pro-separability approach of that decision has effectively been codified in Sect. 7 of the Arbitration Act 1996:

> "Unless otherwise agreed by the parties, an arbitration agreement which forms or was intended to form part of another agreement (whether or not in writing) *shall not be regarded as invalid, non-existent or ineffective because that other agreement is invalid, or did not come into existence or has become ineffective, and it shall for that purpose be treated as a distinct agreement.*" (emphasis added)

Accordingly, in proceedings to enforce an award, the English court normally cannot refuse to enforce solely on the basis that the underlying contract was illegal if that question was within the arbitral tribunal's jurisdiction and had been considered by the tribunal. This of course begs the question of under what circumstances such a question may not be within the tribunal's jurisdiction. It also raises the question of whether the tribunal indeed considered the issue, either on the basis of the pleadings of the parties or ex officio.

England having come to terms with the separability principle as enshrined in the Arbitration Act 1996, are there still limits to the principle, in the area of illegality, after 1996? It would appear that the answer is clearly yes, as case law since then illustrates.

c.   *The arbitrator as the last resort for review of evidence of illegality*

In *Westacre Investments Inc. v. Jugoimport–SPDR Holding Co. Ltd. & Others*,[59] the claimant sought to enforce, in England, an ICC international arbitral award rendered in Switzerland. The basis for the opposition to enforcement was that the award related to a consultancy agreement, expressly governed by Swiss law, which the defendant alleged was a vehicle for influence peddling. He contended that the claimant was to undertake the influence peddling in Kuwait to procure contracts for the sale of military hardware to the Government of Kuwait.

The contract was not subject to English law, nor did the alleged illicit conduct take place in England, nor for that matter did it take place in the country of the seat of arbitration (Switzerland) or the country of the applicable substantive law (also Switzerland). The ICC tribunal had addressed the allegation of illegality in the contract. It had held that neither illegality nor violation of international public policy had been established. The award also survived a challenge before the Swiss Federal Tribunal.

After new evidence was adduced respecting the true meaning and scope of the parties' "consultancy agreement", the English court had to decide whether such evidence gave rise to a defense to enforcement of the foreign award. The English court *granted* enforcement of the award, upholding the jurisdiction of the original Swiss arbitral tribunal to have decided whether illegality existed in the first place:

> "The opportunity for erroneous and uncorrectable findings of fact arises in all international arbitration. If much weight were to be attached to that consideration it is difficult to see that arbitrators would ever be accorded jurisdiction to determine issues of illegality."[60]

The enforcing court recognized that some forms of illegal contracts might not be susceptible of arbitration under English public policy. It gave a contract for illegal importation and distribution of cocaine as an example. Here, the foreign award had arguably been based on an illicit contract, but not of such an egregious nature. Whatever the amplitude of the illegality, the allegedly illicit nature of a commission scheme and its consequences had been amply argued before the prior ICC tribunal with its seat in Switzerland. The tribunal then considered and dismissed the allegation. The defendant's challenge to enforcement in England, based on illegality, thus failed and the award was enforced.

In the face of potentially new and damaging evidence indicating that the underlying contract had indeed been for purposes of corruption, the English court decided that the

---

59. *Op. cit.*, fn. 19.
60. *Ibid.*

public policy in favor of the finality of arbitral awards outweighed the public interest "in preventing the (indirect) enforcement of possibly corrupt commercial practices".[61] The public policy in favor of finality, subject to legitimate grounds for recourse, of course exists in relation to any arbitral award. Here, the mandate of finality apparently seemed all the more compelling to the enforcing court as grounds not to consider "new" evidence of illegality since illegality had already been squarely pled and considered by the ICC arbitral tribunal at the Swiss seat.

d.   The effects of a concession of illegality to the arbitrator
In the same year as *Westacre*, in *Soleimany v. Soleimany*,[62] [1998] 3 W.L.R. 811, CA, the English courts were called upon to decide whether to enforce a somewhat different award, this time a domestic English one. The basis for the opposition to enforcement was that the award related to an illegal carpet importation agreement, expressly governed by Jewish law, which the defendant alleged violated Iranian export regulations.

The contract was once again not subject to English law, nor did the alleged illicit conduct take place in England, the seat of arbitration. The English arbitral tribunal before the *Beth Din* was called upon to resolve a dispute over the division of profits from the agreement. The submission to the *Beth Din* was agreed after the dispute had arisen, and not by an arbitration agreement in the original contract.

The parties agreed to apply Jewish law and stipulated – apparently validly as a matter of the applicable substantive law – that any illegality of the underlying contract would be irrelevant to their rights and duties in the arbitration. The English tribunal addressed and acknowledged that the parties had been involved in an "illicit" enterprise involving "smugglers' fees". However, under the agreed Jewish law it awarded damages to the claimant notwithstanding the admittedly illegal contract. The tribunal thereby considered the illegality to be of no relevance since it was applying Jewish law, under which any alleged illegality would have no effect on the rights of the parties. This time, the English court *refused* enforcement of the award:

> "The court declines to enforce an illegal contract.... The parties cannot ... by procuring an arbitration conceal that they, or rather one of them, is seeking to enforce an illegal contract."[63]

Thus the defendant successfully challenged enforcement of a domestic award which had admittedly been based on an illicit contract. As in *Westacre*, the court also recognized that some forms of illegal contracts might not be susceptible of arbitration at all under English public policy:

---

61. Adam JOHNSON, "Illegal Contracts and Arbitration Clauses", 2 Int. A.L.R. (1999, no. 1) pp. 35-37.
62. [1998] 3 W.L.R. 811, 13 Int'l Arb. Rep. (1998, no. 3) (C.A. 1998) A-1.
63. [1998] 3 W.L.R. 824 A-B.

"The English Court would not recognise an agreement between … highwaymen to arbitrate their difference any more than it would recognise the original agreement to split the proceeds."[64]

Here, in contradistinction to *Westacre*, the question of illegality of the agreement had not been argued before the tribunal, and therefore not been rejected by it. On the contrary, illegality had been conceded to and acknowledged by the tribunal. Interestingly in this regard, although the enforcing court did not need to query whether illegality truly attached, in dictum it suggested, contrary to *Westacre*, that in the face of an allegation of illegality less stark than the carpet smuggling contract at issue there, the English court might see fit to inquire further, *on its own motion*, as to the illegality:

> "… *an enforcement judge, if there is prima facie evidence from one side that the award is based on an illegal contract, should inquire further to some extent.* Is there evidence on the other side to the contrary? Has the arbitrator expressly found that the underlying contract was not illegal? Or is it a fair inference that he did reach that conclusion? Is there anything to suggest that the arbitrator was incompetent to conduct such an inquiry? May there have been collusion or bad faith, so as to procure an award despite illegality?"[65] (emphasis added)

Such a dictum may be seen as running in a somewhat divergent direction from the *Westacre* court's concern that the "opportunity for erroneous and uncorrectable findings of fact arises in all international arbitration". It also runs somewhat far afield from the conclusion in that decision that the enforcing court should therefore avoid unwarranted revisiting of facts and evidence which had been before an arbitral tribunal.

On the other hand, the *Soleimany* decision is consistent with the notion that English public policy forbids the courts from being used to directly or indirectly enforce corrupt commercial practices. Ultimately, the difference in the two outcomes – *Soleimany* and *Westacre* – may be explained in large part by the failure to prove illegality in the one case and by the *admission* of the same in the other.

Thus the *Soleimany* court concluded that smuggling fell into a category of illegality where as a matter of public policy no arbitral award relating to such illegality would be enforced by an English court. One year later, the *Hilmarton* saga reached English shores. Unlike *Soleimany*, the *Hilmarton* court *granted* enforcement.[66]

e.   Illegality and enforcement of contract versus enforcement of an award
In *Hilmarton*, the basis for the opposition to enforcement was that the award related to an illegal contract for the payment of fees due under an agreement to lobby for the awarding of a public works contract in Algeria. That agreement was expressly governed by Swiss law. The defendant alleged that the agreement violated Algerian law as that of

---

64. *Ibid.*, 821 G.
65. *Ibid.*, 824 E-F.
66. *Omnium de Traitement et de Valorisation SA v. Hilmarton Ltd.* [1999] 2 All E.R. (Comm) 146 (QBD) (Comm Ct).

the place of performance. Like *Westacre* and *Soleimany*, the contract here was not subject to English law, nor did the alleged illicit conduct take place in England. Nor did the alleged illicit conduct take place in Switzerland, the seat of arbitration.

The ICC tribunal had addressed and acknowledged that the underlying agreement was illegal – under the Algerian law of performance. Notwithstanding, the tribunal had found that under the agreed Swiss law the contract was licit and not tainted by overseas illegality. This time, as in *Westacre* but not *Soleimany*, the English court granted enforcement of the award.[67]

The decision to grant enforcement in England of the prior Swiss ICC award provides a clear distinction between an action to enforce a *contract* in England and an action to enforce an *arbitral award* in England. The *Hilmarton* enforcing court found that its decision as to enforcement of the Swiss award was not an adjudication of the underlying (allegedly illicit) contract. Accordingly, the court held that in the absence of patent evidence of corruption which would give rise to mandatory public policy considerations, it was irrelevant whether the finding as to illegality would have been the same had English law applied.

The *Hilmarton* court relied on the views expressed by Waller LJ in the Court of Appeal in *Westacre*. It found that contracts for the "purchase of influence" offend English public policy. However, it also concluded that their illicit nature would not be "enough" to justify refusal of enforcement of a foreign award by an English court where such contracts were *to be performed outside England* and the foreign award had found that such contracts were *not illegal under the foreign law applicable* to the contracts in the arbitration.

Thus the *Hilmarton* court enforced a foreign (Swiss) arbitral award which had stated explicitly that the underlying contract was illegal under the law of performance (Algeria), but had concluded that under the proper law of the contract (Switzerland) the contract was licit and not tainted by overseas illegality. The enforcing court was also not in a position to second-guess the correctness of the ICC tribunal's conclusion that the illegal contract did not offend public policy at the foreign seat. Moreover, in the *Hilmarton* court's view, fraud or corruption would be sufficiently offensive to refuse enforcement of such an award in England, but a contract for the "purchase of personal influence" such as here would not.

Are *Westacre*, *Soleimany* and *Hilmarton* in fact reconcilable one with the other? It would appear that they are, largely so. An action to enforce an illegal *contract* shall be subject to English public policy, and shall normally not be successful. An action to enforce a *domestic award* which upheld an illegal contract to which *English* law applied and/or which was to be performed in England shall likewise normally not be successful. An action to enforce a domestic award which upheld an illegal contract to which a *foreign* law applied may be enforceable, unless the illegality is such as to make the underlying arbitration a

---

67. The *Hilmarton* dispute had in fact already been the subject of two ICC arbitration awards rendered in Geneva, a decision by the Swiss Federal Tribunal upholding a lower Swiss court's annulment of the first ICC award, and two decisions of the French *Cour de cassation* which refused to give effect to the prior Swiss annulment of the first ICC award and instead granted it exequatur in France.

sham and/or to make enforcement of rights arising out of the illegal contract a violation of the integrity of the English judicial process.[68]

f. Competing mandates of public policy and finality of awards

Ultimately, an action to enforce a foreign award which upheld an illegal contract to which a foreign law applied but which did not offend that foreign law's public policy shall normally be successful. An exception would be where the illegality is of such a nature as itself to offend English public policy and such offence outweighs the "competing mandate" of ensuring the finality of international arbitral awards.

What kind of illegality would suffice to cause such an offense? Again, presumably contracts promoting or facilitating corruption, drug trafficking, prostitution, torture, slavery, etc. Such matters may be seen as involving transnational or international public policy. They therefore justify striking down a foreign award not for its incompatibility with a "mere" *loi de police* of another state, but for its irreconcilability with transnational *lois de police*.

g. Sham arbitration agreements and illegality

Last but not least is *O'Callaghan v. Coral Racing Ltd.*, 1998, unreported, The Times, 26 November 1998,[69] a case demonstrating the kind of illegality which both the *Westacre* and *Soleimany* courts held would not even be susceptible to a reference to arbitration at all. In that decision, the Court of Appeal held that an arbitration clause in an indisputably illegal gaming agreement could not be regarded as a valid arbitration agreement since any "arbitration" under the circumstances, meant to be submitted to the editor of The Sporting Life, would be devoid of legal consequences. In short, the arbitration agreement itself was a sham, if also not necessarily intentionally a sham.

O'Callaghan was decided under the Arbitration Act 1950. Had it been decided under the 1996 Act, the outcome would presumably have been the same since no arbitrator could have make a valid monetary award. Focusing on separability, the Court of Appeal held that the arbitration agreement could not be severed from the overall agreement: it "must be treated as part and parcel of the void agreement, and so cannot survive independently".[70] In fact, the real explanation for the outcome was likely that the undertaking of the parties was not really to be considered as an arbitration agreement in the first place. The rejection of validity was not based so much on heinousness as on arbitrability and practicability. This is perhaps the best way to explain to Mr. O'Callaghan why the public policy condemnation of would-be agreements respecting betting on English football matches is harsher than the public policy condemnation of

---

68. See also Ewan BROWN, "Illegality and Public Policy – Enforcement of Arbitral Awards in England: *Hilmarton Limited v. Omnium de Traitement et de Valorisation S.A.*", 3 Int. A.L.R. (2000, no. 1) pp. 31-35.

69. See also HARRIS, PLANTEROSE and TECKS, *The Arbitration Act 1996: A Commentary*, 2nd ed. (2000) pp. 76-77, pp. 79-80.

70. *Ibid.*

would-be agreements respecting corruption of public officials, influence peddling and the like.[71]

Is the basis for the foregoing distinctions now clear? What about in other countries? Again, is there a compelling reason why the arbitration clause should "survive" in the one instance of illegality but not survive in the other, especially as one consequence of non-survival is the indirect "toleration" of the illicitness? As to these questions, recent case law in the United States has likewise not entirely unmuddied the waters.

h.   Challenging the arbitration agreement directly
Some US lower courts have held that the courts, and not the arbitrator, must resolve claims that an underlying contract containing an arbitration clause is illegal. Most of these cases are fairly old and they have generally done so by applying state law.[72] By contrast, more recent cases have frequently held that the arbitrator has jurisdiction to resolve such issues, as exemplified by the reasoning in the lower court decision in *Russolillo*:

> "Since the claim of illegality or violation of public policy *is not specifically directed to the arbitration clause itself*, the broad arbitration clause requires arbitration of the claim that the contract as a whole was made illegally."[73] (emphasis added)

When does the illegality of the underlying contract invalidate the arbitration clause contained in the contract, notwithstanding the competence-competence and separability doctrine, resulting in the ousting of arbitral jurisdiction? Many US courts have rejected efforts to invalidate the arbitration agreement based on the illegality of the contract. They have done so simply by taking a narrow perspective: the challenge must be to the arbitration agreement itself in order for the courts to exercise jurisdiction. If not, then the issue is for the arbitrator to decide: see, for example, the appellate court decision in

---

71. Cf. JOHNSON, *op. cit.*, fn. 61, p. 37:

> "It may appear slightly odd to Mr. O'Callagahan ... that those involved (or allegedly involved) in international corrupt trading practices and carpet smuggling should be permitted to refer their disputes to arbitration, but perfectly respectable gamblers should not. But there it is. Public policy is a funny thing."

72. See, e.g., *Durst v. Abrash*, 253 N.Y. S.2d 351 (App. Div. 1964) aff'd, 266 N.Y.S.2d 806 (1966):

> "If usurious agreements could be made enforceable by the simple device of employing arbitration clauses, the courts would be surrendering their control over public policy."

> See also, *Dickstein v. DuPont*, 320 F.Supp. 150 (D. Mass. 1970):

> "[A] claim of illegality [in a case involving allegations of antitrust violations] is a matter for this court and not the arbitrators."

73. *Russolillo v. Thomson McKinnon Securities, Inc.*, 694 F.Supp. 1042, 1045 (D. Conn. 1988); see also *Republic of the Philippines v. Westinghouse Electric Corp.*, 714 F.Supp. 1362 (D. N.J. 1989).

Lawrence v. Comprehensive Business Serv. Co., 833 F.2d 1159 (5th Cir. 1987) holding that even if the underlying contract was void from the inception, the arbitration clause is still enforceable.

Where does this all come out in view of the US Supreme Court decision in *First Options of Chicago, Inc. v. Kaplan*, which is generally considered to stand for the proposition that the existence of an arbitration agreement is the subject of an independent review by the courts except where the parties have unequivocally agreed to have the question resolved by the arbitrators?[74] The answer is not entirely clear.

First Options requires the courts to resolve questions of so-called "arbitrability" (in the somewhat peculiar American definition) unless there is "clear and unmistakable" evidence that the parties agreed to arbitrate those issues. How may this be applied to the alleged illegality of the contract and/or of the agreement to arbitrate? A binding agreement to, for example, the ICC Rules of Arbitration, the UNCITRAL Rules or many other modern sets of arbitral rules ensures application of the competence-competence and separability doctrines.

To that extent, it should be for the arbitral tribunal to resolve an illegality issue relating to the existence of the arbitration agreement. An agreement, at least of a prima facie nature, to such arbitral rules may normally be construed as the "clear and unmistakable" evidence that the parties agreed to arbitrate such issues, and not submit them to the national courts. Where the parties have not agreed to such a body of arbitral rules or where the indications of agreement to such a body of rules are not "clear and unmistakable", then presumably the courts will be entitled to decide issues of legality relating to the arbitration agreement itself.[75]

IV. WHICH LAW SHOULD THE ARBITRATOR APPLY TO ISSUES OF ILLEGALITY?

The foregoing observations and proposals regarding the arbitrator's rights and duties respecting suspected or manifest illegality cannot be seen in a substantive vacuum. Principles of competence-competence, arbitrability, separability and public policy must be applied and counterbalanced according to the relevant body or rules of law. But which one(s)?

---

74. 514 U.S. 938 (1995); 10 Int'l Arb. Rep. (1995, no. 6) A-4; *Yearbook* XXII (1997) p. 278.

75. Cf. Gary B. BORN, *International Commercial Arbitration: Commentary and Materials* (2001) p. 216:

> "… *First Options* would appear to (a) leave challenges to the legality of the underlying contract to arbitration (under *Prima Paint Corp. v. Flood & Conklin Manufacturing Co.*, 388 U.S. 395 (1967) and the separability doctrine); and (b) require judicial resolution of challenges to the legality of the arbitration agreement, unless there is clear and unmistakable evidence that the parties had agreed that such challenges were to be arbitrated".

1.   *Lex Contractus as Manifestation of Party Autonomy*

If the parties to the contract submitted to arbitration agreed, by way of a customary choice-of-law clause, to apply the "laws of Germany" to their contract, must any alleged or manifest illegality be proven under that law? Would it suffice to establish illegality under some other, "connected" body or rules of law (such as the substantive law of the seat)? Does the illegality under that other law, which is different from the one stipulated in the choice-of-law clause, mandatorily result in the illegality of the contract even under the stipulated governing law?

The substantive rights and duties of the parties (as opposed to the rights and duties of the arbitral tribunal) are governed first and foremost by the substantive law agreed, or otherwise determined, to be applicable to the contract. Invariably, the separable agreement to arbitration in that contract is likewise considered to be construed and interpreted against the background of that same agreed body of law. Accordingly, the first, and perhaps only required, step in assessing an allegation or suspicion of illegality of the main contract, and the consequences for the parties' rights and duties, will normally be that applicable substantive law.

a.   *The agreed law, the curial law and the place of performance*

Let us suppose that the tribunal concludes that the main contract promoting importation of counterfeit compact discs offends public morals under the agreed German law. Let us also suppose that such a contract does not – for the sake of argument – offend public morals under the substantive law reigning at either the non-German seat of arbitration or the non-German place of counterfeiting or importation, or both.

That fact would not prevent the tribunal from making any and all rulings flowing from its finding of illegality under the applicable German law. The rulings available to the tribunal might include an order or award denying or upholding its jurisdiction and an award granting or denying relief requested on one or both sides.

Any incompatibility of those rulings under German law with a diverging law at the seat or the place of "performance" would be irrelevant unless and to the extent that the rulings violated a mandatory norm. More specifically, in the case of the seat of arbitration that mandatory norm would need to be such as to justify nullification of the award. In the case of the place of performance, that mandatory norm should be wholly irrelevant unless enforcement of the award were sought there, and the norm justified denial of enforcement under Art. V of the New York Convention or such other basis as might apply.

b.   *The connectedness of the law of place of performance*

Would it suffice to establish illegality under some other, "connected" body or rules of law? In our prior example, there is no identity or overlap between the state of the applicable substantive law, the state in which the seat is located and the state in which the "performance" occurs. One could assume, however, a not unusual scenario in international arbitration: namely, that both the agreed substantive law and the agreed seat have nothing to do with the place of characteristic performance of the illegality – other than that the parties agreed to them.

The non-German and non-Swiss parties agreed, for example, to German substantive law and a Swiss seat in connection with an "intermediary contract" whose nexus is in neither Germany nor in Switzerland, but in Third Country X. Indeed the contract has everything to do with X, and nothing to do with Germany or Switzerland other than the "mere" party agreement. The tribunal also suspects that the parties intentionally agreed to German law and a Swiss seat so as to distance the contract as much as possible from the reach of the law of X and X's prohibition against such contracts.

This scenario is in fact a realistic modification of various elements of many of the awards and court decisions discussed already above. Where the intermediary or brokerage contract is not illegal under German law or Swiss law, what happens if it is manifestly illegal under the law of Third Country X? To the extent X is closely connected to the contract, should its public policy be followed by the tribunal deciding under German substantive law in Switzerland?

The proper result appears to be that unless the illegality under X's law rises to the level of a violation of notions of international public policy which *likewise* offend notions of international public policy in German and/or Swiss law, the illegality at X need not concern the tribunal, and cannot bind it.[76] This is not to say that the illegality of conduct in another country cannot easily render a contract immoral under the law of the seat or the law governing the contract. At the same time, the immorality resulting from the application of the foreign law should be of an egregious nature in order to supersede the agreed substantive law and contrary mandatory norms at the seat.

The fact that the law of X is, factually, closely connected to the contract – and that the laws of Germany and Switzerland respectively are not at all except for the contract terms – is, by itself, of no consequence. Even where such issues of connectivity might play a role in the national courts,[77] such consideration has no binding effect in the arbitral sphere. Conflict of law rules which might bind the national courts will not bind the arbitral tribunal, for example, at our Swiss seat. Such issues are then governed by specific legislation on international arbitration (in this case, Art. 187(1) of the Swiss Act) which supersedes any other conflicts principles.

---

76. See, e.g., Award in ICC Case No. 1399 (1967) in which the tribunal refused to avoid a contract subject to French law although it was intended to circumvent Mexican customs law ("French law is not concerned with foreign customs laws"); see also ICC Award dated 27 April 1992, upheld by CA Paris, 27 October 1994, *Lebanese Traders Distributors & Consultants LTDC v. Reynolds*, Rev.Arb. (1994) p. 709, 10 Int'l Arb. Rep. (1995, no.2) E-1 (refusal to take account of Lebanese customs regulations in distributor termination dispute); and Award in ICC Case No. 6379 (1990) *Italian principal v. Belgian distributor*, Yearbook XVII (1992) p. 212, Rev. Dr. Com. Belge (1993, no. 1) p. 146 (refusal to apply mandatory Belgian law respecting sales termination agreements in lieu of agreed Italian law); but cf. Cass. Com., 7 March 1961, *Laburthe v. Sauveroche*, Bull. Civ. III, No. 125 (1961) in which the French *Cour de cassation* held void for illegality a contract intended to provide for bribery of a public official outside France, on the grounds that French public policy did not prohibit only bribery of French officials.

77. Cf., e.g., in the European Union Art. 7(1) of the 1980 Rome Convention on the Law Applicable to Contractual Obligations, enabling courts to factor in foreign mandatory rules; Germany, Luxembourg and the United Kingdom have made the reservation pursuant to which their national courts may *not* take foreign mandatory rules into account.

Thus the illegality at X does not mandatorily result in the illegality of the contract under the stipulated governing law or under the curial law unless it fits into a egregious violation of public policy. Indeed notably in a country such as France which distinguishes between local public policy and international public policy offenses, even a violation of *local* public policy at the seat as a result of the prohibition in Country X should not mandate a finding of illegality where the parties and subject matter call for application of international, and not domestic, public policy standards.

c.   Violation of universal public policy versus local public policy
Only a fundamental violation of transcending international public policy "in the German sense" under the substantive law and "in the Swiss sense" under the curial law would call for a finding of illegality based merely on the close connection to X and X's own mandatory norms:

> "If regard is to be had to mandatory provisions ... of a law other than that of the forum or that chosen by the parties, then such provisions can only prevent the chosen law from being applied *if there is a close link between the contract and the country of that law and if they further such aims as are generally accepted by the international community.*"[78] (emphasis added)

Indeed the quite recent case of the Swiss Federal Tribunal, *Beverly Overseas SA v. Privredna Banka Zagreb*, confirms this approach: if the facts which need to be analyzed to determine the enforceability of the Swiss-based international award have no or only few links to Switzerland, then universal public policy considerations must be taken into account in addition to Swiss public policy.[79]

Whether the Swiss award would have any prospect of successful enforcement in X is, of course, an entirely different matter. To what extent the tribunal should be concerned with that problem relates, again, to the discussion of, for example, Art. 35 of the ICC Rules and the question of a duty to render an award which is "enforceable at law".

The tribunal's award respecting suspected or manifest illegality cannot make legal what would otherwise be illegal. At the same time, the arbitrator should not disregard the governing substantive law in favor of some other connected national law respecting illegality unless the application of the governing law (in disregard of the other connected law) would result in a violation of international public policy. This is no different from saying that the arbitrator need not apply the agreed or determined governing law if to do so would cause the arbitrator to violate international public policy. In such extreme cases, party autonomy is trumped by the "higher good" of international public policy.

---

78. Art. 9 of the 1991 Resolution of the Institute of International Law concerning the autonomy of the parties in international contracts between private persons or entities, reprinted in INSTITUT DE DROIT INTERNATIONAL, *"Tableau des résolutions adoptées"* (1957-91) pp. 408- 413 (1992) Rev. Crit. DIP (1992) p. 198.
79. *Beverly Overseas SA v. Privredna Banka Zagreb*, Swiss Fed. Trib., 28 March 2001, ASA Bull. (2001) p. 807 et seq.

In our scenario, the tribunal may disregard the mandatory public policy at X in favor of the agreed German law, even if German law has vastly less connection to the disputed contract than does X's law, unless such disregard would offend international public policy. And where disregard of the mandatory public policy at X would itself offend international public policy, the arbitrator has a right to apply the law of X over and above the agreed German law so as to avoid offending that transcending public policy:

> "[T]he parties are entitled to submit their legal relations to whatever law they choose, and to exclude national laws which would apply in the absence of a choice. Consequently, *the provisions of the law thus excluded can only prevail over the chosen law insofar as they are matters of public policy.*"[80] (emphasis added)

Once again, to the extent the arbitrator has a duty to render an award enforceable at law, it is submitted that it would then have a duty to apply the law of X in such case.[81] Where the provisions of foreign law are not considered to rise to the level of a transnational *loi de police,* then there should be no obligation *by the arbitrator* to apply them in lieu of the agreed substantive law:

> "... although commercial corruption is deserving of strong judicial and governmental disapproval, few would consider that it stood in the scale of opprobrium quite at the level of drug-trafficking".[82]

Likewise, where the provisions of the foreign law are considered to be valid inasmuch as the parties *agreed* to them at arm's length, they may nevertheless not be applied *by the enforcing court* if the court considers that the mandate of party autonomy must yield to the mandate of forestalling absurd results which offend public policy. In the enforcement context, that public policy may in fact be local public policy, and not necessarily transnational public policy.[83]

---

80. *Westacre, op. cit.,* fn. 19, ASA Bull. (1995) p. 301 at pp. 330-332, upheld by Swiss Fed. Trib., 30 December 1994.

81. Cf. *Fouchard Gaillard Goldman, op. cit.,* fn. 47, Sect. 1533, p. 861:

"Accordingly, arbitrators have the right – *and even the obligation* – to themselves raise the issue of whether disputed contracts or legal provisions put before them satisfy the requirements of international public policy." (emphasis added)

Citing regarding European Community antitrust law, ICC Awards No. 7315 (1992) and No. 7181 (1992).

82. *Westacre, op. cit.,* fn. 19, ASA Bull. p. 301 at p. 331.

83. *Soleimany, op. cit.,* fn. 62 [1998] 3 W.L.R. 811; 13 Int'l Arb. Rep. (1998, no. 3) (C.A. 1998) A-1 where the Court of Appeal refused to enforce an award at the London seat under Jewish law in a dispute between two Iranian refugees where the award gave effect to a contract which violated Iranian customs regulations.

2.   *Ascertaining Consensus Surrounding Transnational Public Policy*

All of the foregoing does not change the challenge confronting the arbitrator as to whether a *loi de police* or other prohibition should be regarded as local or transnational. Nor does it change the challenge of ascertaining whether in fact particular kinds of illegality which are *not* necessarily uniformly condemned still give rise to a transnational norm justifying or requiring respect by the arbitrator.

In cases where bribery or corruption are generally condemned throughout the world, what importance if any should the arbitrator attach to the fact that a particular corrupt practice is indeed widely practiced and widely accepted in a single country, and it is that country which has the closest connection to the "performance" of the contract in dispute?

In cases where the illegal act relates to disrespect of a United Nations-sanctioned embargo against one or only a few states, what importance if any should be attached to the fact that respect of the embargo constitutes a *crime* in the target country, and that target country has the closest connection to the performance?

In the case of a generally condemned corrupt practice which is nevertheless widely – perhaps even officially or statutorily – condoned in a single country, the arbitrator's task need not be complicated. The agreed substantive law should be applied except to the extent it violates generally accepted international norms. Alternatively, the tribunal may be entitled to conclude that even if the agreed substantive law is the law of that single country, it will *disregard* that governing law if applying it would contravene international public policy.

In such situations, the tribunal cannot possibly be the servant to several different masters: it must observe generally accepted international norms, even if it is thereby likely that the award will have little prospect of cross-border enforcement in that single country. Inasmuch as Art. V(2)(b) of the New York Convention should be seen as a mandatory guideline for the arbitrator,[84] he must attempt to determine whether the broad consensus internationally is embodied in the application of the agreed substantive law or not. The same would apply to alleged illegality relating to embargo measures, where arguments could be made that the measures reflect the will of only a handful of states, and not necessarily global policy:

> "[i]n no case shall an arbitrator violate principles of international public policy as to which a broad consensus has emerged in the international community".[85]

---

84. Neither fraud in the factum nor illegality is expressly mentioned as a basis for denial of enforcement under the New York Convention, although they may be deemed to be encompassed within Arts. II(3), V(1), V(2)(a) or V(2)(b) depending upon the circumstances. Notably, while the UNCITRAL Model Law grounds for setting aside an award in Art. 34 do not include corruption, the Singapore International Arbitration Act (Cap. 143), entered into force on 27 January 1995 enacting the Model Law with minor modifications, adds two additional grounds for setting aside an award, one of which is fraud or corruption (the other is breach of natural justice).

85. Art. 2 of the "Resolution on Arbitration between States, State Enterprises or State Entities, and Foreign Enterprises", adopted by the INSTITUTE OF INTERNATIONAL LAW on 12 September 1989, *Yearbook* XVI (1991) p. 236 at p. 238.

At the same time, the existence of transnational conventions, resolutions and the like condemning a particular practice does not necessarily translate into a broad consensus which might be used by the arbitrator as justification for ascertaining the existence and violation of a principle of "international public policy":

> "Despite general lip-service one hesitates to believe ... that there is an effectively practised worldwide consensus against corruption (*pots-de-vin*) as long as under the fiscal law of many industrial countries bribes paid can be deducted as business expenses and corruption is endemic in many countries and rarely seriously fought."[86]

Among the many "industrialized" countries alluded to number certain principle places of international arbitration in Western Europe.

Furthermore, query how extensive and transparent such "broad consensus" in the international community really is on some of the issues of illegality which typically affect an international commercial arbitration proceeding:

> "... even in particular areas of law one finds disappointingly few interventionist norms that are common to all or even just to the most *legal systems*: Even in the area of ordinary criminal law such common rules exist only in the narrow area of international substantive criminal law on the basis of international treaties (Genocide, drug trafficking, terrorism, slave trade, slavery, piracy)."[87]

In light of the foregoing, is an attempt to directly apply transnational *ordre public* simply too risky for an arbitrator, and therefore not his mandatory duty after all, but rather the duty of the reviewing or enforcing judge? Should the arbitrator avoid making a decision when international public policy may be such a moving target? Should the arbitrator simply resign his office where he believes that the illegality of the contract at issue is so distasteful as to prevent him from carrying out his role? The answer must be no, as set forth in the conclusion below.

V.   FACED WITH ILLEGALITY, WHAT SHOULD THE TRIBUNAL DO?

Is the arbitrator solely a manifestation and instrumentalization of party autonomy? Can his role be reduced to that of a private adjudicator of the parties' dispute, solely with power to decide the rights and duties without any broader reference to international goals of sanctioning illegality? Is the arbitrator "the servant of the parties, or of the truth"?[88]

---

86. Pierre KARRER, "Commentary to Art. 187 of Swiss Private International Law Act", Sect. 160, p. 520 in *International Arbitration in Switzerland*, *op. cit.*, fn. 35, also citing a contrario Swiss Fed. Trib., 30 December 1994, cons. 2d, 119 II 380, cons. 4b.

87. *Ibid.*, Sect. 159, p. 520.

88. ROSELL and PRAGER, *op. cit.*, fn. 4, p. 329.

The question relates not solely to the arbitrator's duty to make best efforts to render an award which is enforceable at law. The arbitrator clearly has such a duty. Nor does the question relate solely to his duty to heed mandatory international public policy, even to the point of disregarding the otherwise agreed substantive or procedural law. He clearly has this duty as well.

The issue is whether the arbitrator, having established the illegality of the contract and of the parties' performance, should confine his reaction to his role as adjudicator of the rights and duties *within the contract*, without any further consequences resulting from the parties' offense of generally accepted public morals.

1. Turning a Blind Eye to Illegality?

What could be the justification for turning a blind eye to the illegality? One school of thought would be that the tribunal is primarily a servant of the parties in their private adjudicatory process, even if the tribunal's conduct is likewise subject to concurrent review by the courts (but only if there indeed is any such review).

Accordingly, the tribunal should limit its analysis to the contractual rights and obligations of the parties, in a civil law and not penal law context. If, for example, a "commission" was not paid, then presumably the reason for the non-payment was that the bargain was not kept. This would be simply a matter of proof, and would be confined to what the contract required the parties to do – as opposed to a value judgment as to the legality of the contract.

To be sure, the arbitrator is an instrument of the parties and first and foremost an adjudicator of their internal relations. It is also true that he is charged with applying the legal standard agreed by the parties or, in the absence of agreement, as determined according to the applicable procedural and substantive rules. Indeed he is also "bound" by a valid waiver in advance of the parties' rights to challenge an award by set aside proceedings, to the extent such a waiver can validly be made and has been validly made under the applicable law including notably that of the seat.[89] Particularly in those countries, such as Switzerland, where such a waiver of possible grounds for nullification is possible based on, for example, the underlying illegality of the contract, why should the arbitrator be concerned about such illegality?

2. Determining Illegality as the Business and Duty of the Arbitrator

There are a number of reasons why the determination of the illegality, and the drawing of the consequences therefrom, remain the business and the duty of the arbitrator. Flowing from the various duties of the arbitrator discussed above is a duty to adjudicate

---

89. See, e.g., Art. 192 of the Swiss Private International Law Act:

"Provided that neither of the parties has its domicile, habitual residence or place of business in Switzerland, they can agree, in express terms either in the arbitration agreement or in a subsequent agreement, to waive the right to file an appeal; they can also exclude some of the grounds set out in Article 190 para. 2."

the dispute in its various facets. This includes the determination of the illegality, also in those situations where the tribunal may need to initiate an inquiry into the illegality itself. The fact that the parties may, in rare instances, have validly waived their right of recourse in no way softens the existence or reach of the tribunal's duties.

a.   Duties flowing from Art. V of the New York Convention

First, knowledge that the award will not be subject to review by the courts at the seat even on public policy grounds should not embolden the arbitrator to be lax in consideration of illegality. Rather, the finality of the award and the impossibility of nullification of the findings on illegality should doubly motivate the tribunal to determine the illegality and rule on it.

Of course, even an award as to which vacatur has been validly ruled out may still be subject to denial of enforcement either at the seat[90] or elsewhere. Therefore, all of the duties which may flow from Art. V of the New York Convention, and equivalent or parallel national legislation on cross-border enforcement, will enable the award debtor, or the enforcing court ex officio, to review the tribunal's award to a certain degree respecting illegality.

b.   The goal of a final and binding award

Second, where the award is normally subject to review by the courts at the seat (and elsewhere), the tribunal should still not turn a blind eye to suspected, admitted or manifest illegality of the contract and the parties. The fact that the courts at the seat and/or at a place of attempted enforcement abroad might have an opportunity to review and assess the illegality themselves does not make it any less imperative for the award already to have done so.

The award is meant, to the greatest extent possible, to be final and binding. It is meant to be based on the arbitrators' conscientious establishment of the facts and, where necessary, the law of the case on the basis of often copious and extensive taking of evidence. The reviewing or enforcing court, even if it were entitled to review certain elements of the illegality essentially de novo, cannot possibly have the same access to the evidence as did the tribunal. In most cases, the reviewing court is not allowed to conduct such an inquiry in any event. Therefore, the tribunal must not forsake the opportunities provided by the unique access which it has to the facts during the arbitration.

c.   The goal of voluntary compliance with the award

Third, the prospect of review by a court at the seat or elsewhere should not be seen as a sword of Damocles. The award is meant to be final and binding and to be carried out voluntarily by the parties, without attack at the courts of the seat and without

---

90. Art. 192(2) of the Swiss Private International Law Act provides:

"Have the parties agreed on a total waiver of their rights to file an appeal and shall the award be enforced in Switzerland, the New York Convention of June 10, 1958 on the Recognition and Enforcement of Foreign Awards applies accordingly."

compulsory enforcement there or abroad. The strength of a well-reasoned and judiciously penned award lies in large part in the hope that it will be complied with by the parties without further ado.

For this reason, the duty of the tribunal to address the illegality issue may be seen as all the more compelling. The parties may determine from the award that the tribunal has carefully considered the existence and ramifications of the illegality, and that the award stands up to scrutiny in this and all other respects which might affect its enforceability. Moreover, it is conceivable that the award will never be attacked in the first place, for whatever reason.

d. Thorough and transparent examination of the illegality issue
Fourth, precisely because of the unique position of the tribunal to assess the illegality, it should carry out its taking of the evidence respecting the illegality with a depth and transparency that any effective reviewing court can readily appreciate. The greater the doubts of the reviewing court as to the precision of the tribunal's analysis of the illegality, the greater the likelihood that the reviewing court may take it upon itself to revisit the evidence respecting the illegality.

In those jurisdictions, such as England and the United States, where the tribunal may have a statutory basis for reviewing manifest errors respecting the illegality finding, the likelihood of second-guessing by the court could rise.

e. Possible precedential value of findings respecting illegality
Fifth, it is not the primary duty of the tribunal to be concerned with the precedential value of its award, whether as a result of official reporting of its findings via subsequent court proceedings or by its entering into the bloodstream of arbitral practice and jurisprudence through unseen channels. On the other hand, in view of the importance of combating illegality and the difficulties of defining any "consensus" as to which kinds of illegality offend public policy transnationally, it is all the more important to ensure transparency and uniformity on this issue, where possible.

The award should not be rendered primarily on the basis of "how it might read" if and when published. At the same time, the fact that it is a private adjudication process does not mean that the award is rendered in a vacuum. The background of public policy concerns at the seat and elsewhere is particularly important where standards of illegality are still emerging and in need of further embellishment.

f. Illegality and social engineering
Sixth, there is no uniform code of ethics regarding illegality and corruption. Arbitrators cannot pretend to impose one of their own making. At the same time, the fact that there is no single transnational public policy even as to certain kinds of corruption and illegality does not make the goal of striving toward such uniformity any less important. Certain issues of illegality remain regional, cultural, religion-based, etc., and depend on arguably parochial needs which may make the ends justify the means in one region but not another.

These parochial standards are a product of sociopolitical conditions and cannot always be prejudged by an outsider. However, this should not prevent an arbitrator from endeavoring to establish and civilly sanction the illegality. He may do so based on the

257

standards agreed by the parties or as otherwise determined by the arbitrators, and subject to public policy as the tribunal perceives it. The arbitrator has no mandate to engage in social engineering, but it would be a mistake to assume that his office did not give him a legitimate platform from which to investigate and combat illegality, within the constraints of his mission.

g.   Toleration or perpetuation of illegal practices

Seventh, a failure or refusal to address the illegality issue head-on in arbitral proceedings could be seen as a tolerance, or indeed perpetuation, of nefarious practices. While certain practices might be tolerated and widespread in a particular country, the arbitrator should not condone or support hindrances to the elimination of those practices.

Seen less in the context of a private adjudication as in the context of transnational goals, ignoring or tolerating illegality in such situations can be seen as contributing to distortion and suppression of competitive forces as well as discouragement of future investment. The arbitrator's primary duty is not one of righting the world's wrongs. On the other hand, to the extent arbitration has become a method of choice for transnational, East-West and North-South dispute resolution, the larger implications of ignoring illegality in contracts, particularly at the state level, cannot be smoothed over.

h.   Pressure and moral suasion on state courts respecting illegality

Eighth, in those cases where the arbitrator's findings respecting illegality are attacked either at the seat or elsewhere (a possibility not available in the scheme of the International Court of Justice), the state judiciary will of course be implicated in the decision on illegality. To the extent the arbitrators have made a conscientious and unobjectionable ruling as to the existence and consequences of the illegality under the applicable standards, the reviewing or enforcing court may be obliged to decide whether to condone or reward the illegality.

This is a useful pressure and moral suasion to place on the courts, particularly in the context of their transnational obligations under Art. V(2)(b) of the New York Convention.

i.   Resignation in the face of illegality?

Ninth, resignation from office in the face of a distasteful or otherwise troublesome illegality should not be countenanced, except insofar as the reasons relate to an inability to guarantee continuing impartiality or other incapacity in carrying out the arbitrator role. Otherwise, throwing in the towel could be seen as aiding and abetting the underlying illegality and abdicating the powers and duties which the arbitrator has to civilly sanction the illegality.

Indeed resignation might be seen as a form of complicity in the original illegality where the arbitrator surrendered his opportunity to actively condemn. Depending upon the applicable rules, resignation in lieu of rendering a ruling or award at least confirming the illegality might allow the parties to seek another tribunal which could take a softer approach to the issue.

Where the tribunal concludes that it should resign on the grounds of voidness of the contract and the arbitration agreement, the tribunal might instead strive for a legitimate basis to dismiss the related claims for lack of jurisdiction by enforceable award with res judicata effect, within the confines of relevant law on competence-competence and arbitrability. For the arbitrator has just as much a duty to ensure that illegal contracts referred to him are not allowed to flourish, by rendering a corresponding award, as to ensure that legal contracts referred to him are allowed to stand, also by rendering an award.[91]

j.   Informing the arbitral institution of the illegality

Tenth, to what extent should the arbitrator who has suspected or established serious illegality inform the appointing authority or other arbitral supervisory institution to which the parties are deemed to have agreed by their arbitration clause or by operation of, for example, a bilateral investment treaty (BIT)? And in the BIT context, what about situations where, for example, tax fraud may be considered outside the jurisdiction of the arbitral tribunal inasmuch as it does not constitute a legal dispute arising directly out of an investment under Art. 25(1) of the ICSID Convention? Invariably, it may be contended that the arbitral institution shares with the arbitrators the duty of acting in the spirit of the applicable rules, including efforts to render an award enforceable at law. In the case of the ICC, this duty will arise more apparently than with certain other institutions, in view of its involvement, albeit of a largely administrative nature, in the scrutiny of the award.

Where the institution has the power, and perhaps the duty, to ascertain whether a manifest or apparent illegality exists such as to call into question the existence of the related ICC arbitration agreement, the institution may also have a right to be informed of an illegality later on, after its prima facie inspection of the basis for arbitration. There would appear to be no reason not to entitle and even obligate the arbitrator to inform the institution of such illegality, particularly in those cases where the circumstances give rise to penal sanctions which go beyond the arbitrator's review of the civil obligations between the contracting parties.

Ultimately, in extreme cases of illicitness, the institution might have no obligation to participate as appointing or administering authority if such participation constituted abetting a manifestly illegal enterprise. The appointing authority to which the parties agreed or are deemed to have agreed can no more validly derogate from mandatory public policy constraints than can the arbitrator.

In this sense, the arbitrator should inform the institution of circumstances which might cause the institution unwittingly to engage in such a derogation from mandatory

---

91. Cf. DERAINS, *op. cit*, fn. 23, p. 2 discussing the Lagergren decision:

> "*Les parties s'étant engages dans une activité réprouvée par le droit, elles ne sauraient faire appel à lui. Si cette optique procédurale est conceptuellement fort éloignée de celle qui voudrait que le caractère illicite du contrat conduise à son annulation, le résultat est pratiquement le même puisque dans les deux cas la demande d'exécution du contrat est rejetée.*"

See also Award in ICC Case No. 5622 (1988), in which the tribunal decided to proceed to the merits of the dispute and said this approach was to be preferred "since it makes it possible to declare null and void all contracts which are illicit or contrary to morality".

public policy. Providing such information to the institution should not be seen as in any way comprising the confidentiality of the relationship which may be deemed to exist between and among the parties and the tribunal.[92]

k.   Informing the penal authorities of the illegality

Eleventh, to what extent does the tribunal have a duty to inform the police or judicial authorities of a suspected or established illegality? In the case of illegality which carries no penal sanctions, there is presumably no risk that the tribunal may be deemed to have aided and abetted a criminal act.

Of course, this begs the question of which standard to use when trying to define whether the act is criminal. It also does not answer the question of whether the tribunal has a moral duty, as opposed to a duty under threat of penal sanctions, to inform the authorities.

In such cases, it would appear difficult to construct a moral duty to inform the authorities based on anything within the specific mission of the tribunal. The powers and duties of the arbitrator to condemn illegality through his role as private adjudicator would not necessarily extend to a duty to inform the penal authorities of a criminal act.

Likewise, the powers and duties of the arbitrator to take into consideration mandatory norms and public policy when rendering its award respecting the parties' civil obligations would not necessarily translate into a duty to "tell all". In an extreme case, the tribunal could obtain unique knowledge, through its appointment, of heinous acts associated with the contract containing the agreement to arbitrate.

The desire and duty to inform the authorities of the suspicion or existence of such acts, and their perpetrators, would be great, but not necessarily flow from the mission as arbitrator. In the absence of a corresponding treaty, the state courts of one country are not obliged to enforce the penal laws of another country. Why then should an arbitral tribunal do so?

At the same time, even in such cases the arbitrator will have had, and should have made use of, his or her various other tools and arsenal to firmly address any issues of illegality. The opportunities to do so within the context of competence-competence and separability are there for the taking.

---

92. The 1998 ICC Rules do not expressly provide that confidentiality attaches to the fact, pendency or outcome of the arbitration. Art. 6 of Appendix I to the Rules stipulates that the work of the ICC Court "is of a confidential nature…".

Misdeeds, Wrongful Conduct and Illegality in Arbitral Proceedings

Bernard Hanotiau[*]

I. THE ISSUE

Our topic of discussion is wrongful conduct by an arbitrator, a witness or a party to an arbitral proceeding. These misdeeds are generally intended to affect the course of the proceedings or the decision of the arbitral tribunal. Depending upon the seriousness of the misdeed, it may be illegal, subject to criminal prosecution, give rise to civil liability, or amount to fraud, corruption or violation of public policy.

Strangely enough, very little has been written on the topic. Case law is relatively scarce, except in the United States; and in most cases the misdeeds have been raised in the context of enforcement proceedings or actions to set aside the award.

---

[*] Member of the Brussels and Paris Bars, Hanotiau & van den Berg, Brussels; Professor at the Universities of Louvain and Namur, Belgium.

As we will see, it is rare to find reported arbitral awards in which a panel of arbitrators, confronted with unethical or illegal conduct in the course of an arbitration, addressed the issue in its award otherwise than in reciting the facts without criticism or comment, or, in a limited number of cases, in drawing – for example, from the absence of communication of specific documents or the production of false documents – adverse inferences on the merits.

Of course, what amounts to a misdeed does not always appear immediately in the course of the proceedings, but sometimes only after the award has been rendered. This explains why in many cases, the sanction of the conduct is sought not with the arbitral tribunal but with national courts, when an aggrieved party opposes enforcement of the award or seeks to have it set aside.

But when a misdeed comes to light in the course of the proceedings, should not one expect a positive, clear and unequivocal reaction or decision thereon by the arbitrators? This of course raises many corollary issues. How should the reaction take place? Should the matter be put to debate? What kind of action should the arbitral tribunal take? Should arbitrators ever report to professional or criminal authorities? And in institutional arbitration, what can be expected from the arbitral institution?

In the following pages, we will first summarize the various categories of misdeeds which are encountered in the course of arbitral proceedings (II), followed by the various actions and recourses offered by the law in such circumstances (international conventions, the UNCITRAL Model Law, national legislation) as well as the relevant case law (III) and finally, we will present a reflection on what may and should be expected from an arbitral tribunal or institution confronted with alleged or obvious misdeeds in the course of the proceedings.

II.   THE VARIOUS TYPES OF MISDEEDS

The misdeeds which affect arbitral proceedings may be classified in three different categories:

— arbitrators' misconduct;
— witnesses' misconduct (witnesses of fact or expert witnesses, although we will limit ourselves in this paper to the first category);
— parties' misconduct.

1.   *Arbitrators' Misconduct*

a.   Corruption
The most blatant case of arbitrators' misconduct is corruption, i.e., the acceptance payment by one party to weigh the case in its favour. Corruption, as such, is generally

very difficult to establish and we have found only one reported case where corruption was alleged by the respondent to oppose enforcement of an award.[1]

b.   Undisclosed relationship with a party

i.   Business relationship

Here we encounter a much more delicate area, i.e., situations where in the course of the arbitration, an arbitrator and a party maintain undisclosed professional, or to a lesser extent, social dealings or relationships. These are often raised after the award has been rendered, to challenge its validity or enforcement. As shown below, such claims will not be successful if the party knew of the matter during the arbitration and did not react in due time. Moreover, for claimant to have a chance to succeed, the alleged relationship must have been of a substantial nature.

ii.   Love affair

A very serious type of misconduct is the existence of a love affair between an arbitrator and a party representative or counsel for a party in the course of the arbitration.

Under the title, "Arbitrator's friendship with winning lawyer imperils huge victory. Private investigators found the pair in Chicago hotel after $ 92 million award", the Wall Street Journal published an article in 1990 which it described as "a story of sex, lawyers, videotape – and money". A Ms. Lasley, heading a team for claimant, had won a $ 92 million arbitration award on behalf of the California State Insurance Department as receiver for a bankrupt insurance concern and its reinsurance subsidiary. The chief arbitrator on the three-person panel that had made the award was Mr. McIlwain, described as "one of the most experienced and able practitioner of the art, so much so that his name is almost invariably on the short list of candidates in any major reinsurance arbitration". During the arbitration, the law firm representing respondents had already tried to disqualify Mr. McIlwain. In an expense account that Ms. Lasley had submitted in a court filing, respondents' lawyers had indeed discovered what appeared to be a forty-eight-minute telephone conversation with Mr. McIlwain. They saw this as evidence of an improper discussion of the case between the arbitrator and Ms. Lasley. The two denied, however, that the conversation ever took place and Mr. McIlwain continued as arbitrator. The final award was rendered in October 1988 but the Los Angeles federal judge whose court oversaw the arbitration refused to confirm the award and returned the case to the arbitrators. They essentially reaffirmed their findings. A second confirmation hearing before the court took place in December 1998.

A few days before the hearing, counsel for the respondents received tips from anonymous callers that Ms. Lasley and Mr. McIlwain could be found as guests in a hotel in Chicago. Investigators from New York and Chicago found that they were indeed registered in separate rooms. During three days, the investigators kept track of Ms. Lasley's whereabouts. Ms. Lasley and Mr. McIlwain were tailed to dinner and to a mall

---

1. See paragraph following fn. 66 below. The case where a party-appointed arbitrator assists the party which appointed him in drafting its submissions and receives payment for drafting may be put in the same category as corruption.

where they shopped. Late one night, the investigators used a concealed camera to videotape Ms. Lasley and Mr. McIlwain entering her suite.

Respondent filed a motion in Federal Court in Los Angeles to vacate the award on "newly discovered evidence of arbitrator's misconduct, misbehaviour and evident partiality". The couple admitted the facts but denied that any "acts of intimacy" ever took place between them. They alleged that they had decided to meet in the hotel to discuss arbitration business that had nothing to do with the case under attack. And if the couple had spent two nights in Ms. Lasley's suite, it is because she became ill and he volunteered to stay in the suite out of concern for her. They allegedly slept in separate rooms.

At the time the Wall Street Journal article was published, there was speculation that the federal judge would allow the award to stand unless it was established that the relationship between the lawyer and the arbitrator existed before the award was made; but other lawyers thought that the award would be set aside because until the award became final, Mr. McIlwain was obliged to avoid even the appearance of an improper relationship. The final decision unfortunately remains unknown.

This case is not unique. In Belgium, a few years ago, an action to set aside was introduced against an award rendered by a panel of arbitrators whose chairman was later discovered to be the lover of the counsel for claimant, the winning party. No decision was ever rendered, however. The case was settled out of court and the terms of the settlement remain unknown.

iii.   Favouritism and ex parte communications

Other types of misconduct are sometimes raised by a party either in the course of the arbitration or, more often, as grounds for objecting to the validity or the enforcement of the award:

— acts of favouritism such as a repeated failure to afford one party's attorneys equal time to make their presentations, paying attention only to the lawyers representing one side, or giving one party more favourable treatment than the other;
— ex parte communications such as holding meetings with one party in the absence of the other, or a party-appointed arbitrator having drinks every evening with the party which appointed him, or an arbitrator leaking information to the party which appointed him or reporting every day to "his" party's representative and taking instructions from him for the further conduct of the case.

iv.   Other types of misconduct

Other types of misconduct include the resignation without a valid, constraining reason, of a party-appointed arbitrator or even the chairman of the arbitral tribunal in the course of the arbitral procedure, usually just before the rendering of the award, once it becomes obvious which party is going to win the case.

2.   Witnesses' Misconduct

Cases of witnesses' misconduct cover situations in which a witness is corrupt, i.e., has been paid by a party to alter his testimony, in which a witness does not tell the truth because his employment with one of the parties is at stake, in which the witness commits perjury because he is himself interested in the outcome of the case, or in which he is partisan out of sheer nationalism, for example, in large cases involving the interests of a State or a State entity.

That witnesses lie from time to time is not a new phenomenon. This is the basic reason why testimony was given so little weight as a means of evidence in the Napoleonic Code. In international arbitration, arbitrators evaluate the weight and credibility to be given to particular testimony and are generally sufficiently experienced to make the distinction between a credible and a non-credible witness. But it may sometimes be otherwise.

The fact that a witness lied in his statement or committed perjury is not always easy to establish. It may happen however that a witness will recognize in the course of the procedure that he did not state the truth.[2] Or a subsequent investigation and comparison of the information supplied by the witness with documents available to the party challenging the testimony may lead to the objective conclusion that the witness did not tell the truth. The fact that the witness lied will not therefore always come to light in the course of the arbitral procedure but sometimes only after the award has been rendered.

One recent example is the case *S.A. Thomson CSF v. Société Brunner Sociedade Civil de Administracão Limitada & Société Frontier AG Bern*, which was submitted to the Paris Court of Appeal and was the object of two decisions on 10 September 1998 and 7 September 1999.[3] Thomson appealed the decision ordering the enforcement of an award rendered by an ICC arbitral tribunal in Geneva. It concerned the commission allegedly due to the Swiss company Frontier AG Bern by Thomson CSF at the occasion of the sale of frigates to Taiwan by Thomson. Thomson alleged before the Paris Court of Appeal that the enforcement of the award would be contrary to international public policy in that the award was based on fraudulent acts *(agissements frauduleux)* intended to influence the arbitrators (in fact, false testimony) and would accordingly declare valid a contract whose object was a traffic in influence with French public authorities. The Paris Court of Appeal ordered in its first judgment the communication of the criminal file and in the second judgment decided to suspend its decision until a judgment by the Criminal Court was rendered.

---

2. In a recent ICC case, a witness admitted during his testimony that he had lied in his statement, and that the documents the communication of which had been requested by the other party had not been shredded but indeed still existed and were in the possession of his lawyer, who was sitting next to him!

3. Rev.Arb. (2001) p. 583.

3. Parties' Misconduct

Misconduct by a party covers a wide range of situations some of which may be rather unique, like the kidnapping of an arbitrator,[4] the wiretapping of the hearing room in such a way that the conversations between the members of the adverse team are immediately reported to the lawyers on the other side, scandalous behaviour during the hearing (like shouting or screaming or trying to intimidate the panel of arbitrators with a gun). Other types of misconduct include: obstructing by all means the course of the arbitration; the exercise at various stages of undue influence on a witness to convince him to make a false statement or commit perjury; trying to bribe the arbitral tribunal or making death threats to an arbitrator who refuses to be "bought";[5] a State party having its police put pressure on an arbitrator or a panel of arbitrators by various means before or during a hearing in the country concerned ; or a party submitting to the arbitrators forged documents or trying to hide from the arbitral tribunal documents which are essential for the decision of the case. The last two categories deserve special attention. A word will then be said of the most extreme example of attempting by all means to derail the arbitration process that we are aware of – the now famous case, *Himpurna California Energy Ltd. v. Republic of Indonesia*.[6]

a. Forged documents

The leading case regarding forged documents – although not an arbitration case – is no doubt the *Qatar v. Bahrain* case of the International Court of Justice (ICJ),[7] which concerned the delimitation of boundaries between Bahrain and Qatar. The most hotly disputed of several territories at issue were the Hawar Islands, which lie between Bahrain and Qatar. In 1939, Britain, the colonial power of the time, awarded sovereignty over the Islands to Bahrain. Qatar was angered. Years of arguments followed and on 8 July 1991, Qatar introduced a claim against Bahrain at the ICJ. On 15 February 1995, the ICJ ruled that it had jurisdiction to adjudicate on the substantive issue and on 30 September 1996, Bahrain's legal team had its first chance to see eighty-two documents submitted by Qatar in support of its claim to the Hawars. They all led to the conclusion that Britain's 1939 award of the Islands to Bahrain was fraudulent. These letters were written by just about anyone of importance when the British made their 1939 decision: letters from the adviser to the Emir of Bahrain; letters from

---

4. Marie-France SCHAAD, "The Abduction of an Arbitrator – A Disturbing Account of a State's Attempt to Derail an International Arbitration", ASA Bull. (1999) p. 512; Marc GOLDSTEIN, "International Commercial Arbitration", 34 The International Lawyer (2000, no. 2).

5. In this case, the arbitrator pursued the case but took life insurance. He survived the arbitration even though the final decision was to a large extent against the State entity which had made the threats.

6. Interim Award of 26 September 1999 and Final Award of 16 October 1999, reported in ICCA *Yearbook Commercial Arbitration* XXV (2000) (hereinafter *Yearbook*) p. 109. The three arbitrators were: Prof. Pryatna Abdurrasyid (Indonesia); Mr. A.A. de Fina (Australia) and Mr. Jan Paulsson (France).

7. Judgment of 16 March 2001, *Case no. 87 Concerning Maritime Delimitation and Territorial Questions Between Qatar and Bahrain*, ICJ Reports 2001; Philippe WECKEL, "Chronique de jurisprudence internationale", Revue Générale de Droit International Public (2000) p. 443.

Ottoman officials; letters from rulers of regional powers, including Abu Dhabi and Saudi Arabia; letters from the rulers of Bahrain themselves; from Sheikhs; from judges, etc. The lawyers for Bahrain, believing that the documents were too good to be true, created a task force of renowned experts to investigate the documents. Twelve of the world's leading forgery experts were hired to examine them and concluded that not only were they forged, but that the forgery was blatant. For example, a Royal Air Force seal had been apposed on an Ottoman map. Documents purporting to have been written years apart were created from the same sheet of vintage paper that had been crudely ripped apart. On some seals, the crown of Elizabeth II was used on documents claiming to be from before her reign – 1868. Others were written by people yet to be born or by officials who would only have been ten years old at the time.

The experts' conclusions were sent to the ICJ on 25 September 1997. A year later, on 30 September 1998, Qatar informed the Court that it was withdrawing all the documents. During this period, Qatar's two lead counsels resigned from the case, while stating that their resignations were not related to the issue of forged documents. In fact, Qatar still denies today that they were forged.

By an order of 17 February 1999, "the Court, taking into account the concordant views of the Parties on the treatment of the disputed documents ... placed on record the decision of Qatar to disregard, for the purposes of the present case, the eighty-two documents whose authenticity had been challenged by Bahrain, decided that the Replies would not rely on those documents...."[8]

Bahrain finally won the case but the judgment does not contain an evaluation of the above events. The only reference to the 82 documents in the judgment is found in paragraphs 15 to 23 of the section setting out the history of the proceedings before the Court. It consists of a mere narrative. This has been criticized by a number of lawyers, and especially the lawyers for Bahrain who found Qatar's attempt to falsify history utterly repugnant, a reprehensible assault on the history and geography of Bahrain and the region.[9]

Indeed, the ICJ, which had an opportunity to establish a precedent, decided not to deal with the issue. The only comments on it are to be found in the separate opinion of Judge Fortier, the ad hoc judge for Bahrain, who considered that it was his "duty" to address the issue. Indeed, as he pointed out:

> "3. When Qatar made its application to the Court in July 1991, it based its principal contentions in support of its claim to the Hawar Islands on these 82 documents. When Qatar filed its Memorial in September 1996, its Annexes included these 82 documents. These documents played an essential role in Qatar's Memorial, serving as almost the only basis for Qatar's claim to the Hawar Islands.... Once the authenticity of these essential documents was challenged by Bahrain, Qatar did not abandon its claim to the Hawar Islands. It adduced a new argument, which was not even developed in its original Memorial as an alternative argument.

---

8. Judgment of 16 March 2001, *op. cit.,* fn. 7, para. 23.
9. Tom FREEMAN, "Dead men don't write letters", Legal Business (2001) p. 66 at p. 69.

(....)

10 [cited out of sequence] . ... Qatar's title to the Hawar Islands now rests on original title and proximity. Why was this new argument, if it has the merit that Qatar now claims for it, not developed in Qatar's original Memorial at the very least as an alternative line of approach? Qatar never answered that question....

4. I believe that the Court should not simply disregard and fail to take into consideration this unprecedented incident. In my opinion, these documents have 'polluted' and 'infected' the whole of Qatar's case....

5. Some of them resurface, directly or indirectly, at various stages of Qatar's written and oral pleadings. They remain in the record and some of them linger and are invoked occasionally in support of Qatar's alternative argument.

6. While I must accept, as I do, Qatar's disclaimer and apologies, in my opinion, I cannot consider Qatar's case without having in mind the damage that would have been done to the administration of international justice, indeed to the very position of this court, if the challenge by Bahrain of the authenticity of these documents, had not led Qatar, eventually, to inform the Court that it had 'decided to disregard all the 82 challenged documents for the purposes of the present case'."

And Judge Fortier concluded :

"11. .... I believe that the Court, in considering the Parties' conflicting versions of the facts in this case, had a duty to do more than merely narrate the Parties' respective exchange of letters following Bahrain's challenge of the authenticity of 82 documents which loomed as central to Qatar's case. I regret that it elected not to do so."

Indeed, when Qatar withdrew the documents, it stated that it would not rely on them "for the purposes of this case", quoted word for word in the decision.[10] Peter Tytell, one of the leading forgery experts on Bahrain's side, stated : "What's scary is that the Qataris are maintaining that the documents are genuine. Sure, it's all sorted out for this generation, but what about a few generations down the line? I am worried. What's going to happen 30, 40, 50 years from now, if the documents are once again 'discovered' in Qatar and taken at face value?"[11] The journalist Tom Freeman commented: "Should such a scenario arise, responsibility and accountability will be hard to come by for anyone reviewing the court's record. Bahrain's findings will be seen

---

10. See above in the text at fn. 8, the wording of the Judgment of 16 March 2001, *op. cit.*, fn. 7, para. 23.
11. Cited by Tom FREEMAN, *op. cit.*, fn. 9, p. 71.

simply as arguments denied by Qatar. No lawyer has been criticized for allowing such ropey evidence to appear. No court has condemned Qatar's action.[12]

Another leading judgment involving forged documents was rendered by the Paris Court of Appeal on 30 September 1993[13] in the case *European Gas Turbines S.A. v. Westman International Ltd*. On 11 December 1985, Alsthom Turbines à Gaz S.A. (ATG) (Alsthom), the predecessor of European Gas Turbines S.A. (EGT) and Westman International Ltd. (Westman) concluded a contract under which Westman undertook to assist Alsthom in obtaining first the "prequalification and then the contract for the supply of gas turbines for a petrochemical project at Arak, Iran". The prequalification was a first selection by the main contractor, the National Petrochemical Company of Iran (NPC), designed to limit the number of companies which could submit an offer for the project.

The contract was concluded for three years and provided for a commission fee covering "the expenses of all nature borne by Westman in order to perform its task"; the amount of the commission was to be "determined by mutual agreement before Alsthom submits its offer". Westman was subsequently prequalified but refused to pay the commission. Westman started an ICC arbitration procedure as provided for in the contract, which took place in Paris.

On 2 July 1991, the arbitral tribunal reopened the arbitral proceedings by requesting from Westman a detailed report of its expenses for the Arak project. On 9 July 1991, Westman submitted a list of expenses for a total of SF 7,104,983.00, including salaries for personnel and rent for offices in Teheran. An arbitral award in favour of Westman was rendered on 21 March 1992.

Alsthom, which had by then changed its company name to EGT, sought annulment of the award before the Paris Court of Appeal alleging that the award's enforcement would violate public policy on two grounds: first, because the award gave effect to a contract which was null and void as its real object was traffic in influence and bribery; and second, because it was based on a fraudulent report of expenses submitted by Westman in the arbitration. An expert report by an accounting firm, submitted by EGT in the annulment proceedings, showed that Westman had not paid any rent or salaries for the Arak prequalification.

The Court of Appeal dismissed EGT's first ground for annulment, finding that there was no proof that the 1985 contract was an illicit contract for traffic in influence. However, it found that the second ground for annulment was partially well-founded, and that some parts of the arbitral award were affected by the fraud committed by Westman in the arbitration. The court therefore annulled the award in so far as it was based on Westman's fraudulent accounts, applying the general principle of law *fraus omnia corrumpit*, with the exception of the arbitrators' finding that a valid sui generis

---

12. *Ibid.*
13. Paris Court of Appeal, 30 September 1993, *European Gas Turbines S.A. v. Westman International Ltd.*, Rev.Arb. (1994) p. 359 and D. BUREAU's note; Revue Critique de Droit International Privé (1994) p. 349 and V. HEUZÉ's note; *Yearbook* XX (1995) p. 198; upheld by *Cass. 1ère Civ.*, 19 December 1995, Rev.Arb. (1996) p. 49 and D. BUREAU's note.

contract (combining a brokerage contract and a contract for work) had been concluded by the parties.

b.   Documents concealed

It happens from time to time that a party refuses to submit a document to the other party or the arbitral tribunal which is central to the dispute, generally because the document contains information which goes against the party's position. The party concerned will generally argue that the relevant document cannot be found or has been shredded. Of course, it may be possible in some cases for the arbitral tribunal to order the communication of the document under a penalty (*astreinte*)[14] or to draw from the absence of communication adverse inferences which will have a direct impact on the decision of the case.

And, as we will also see below,[15] the fact that a party did not communicate a document to the other party and the tribunal which was essential for the decision of the case may also justify a subsequent annulment of the award.

c.   Obstructing the arbitration process by all available means

The facts surrounding the awards rendered by an UNCITRAL arbitral tribunal in 1999 in the *Himpurna California Energy Ltd. (HCE) v. Republic of Indonesia* (ROI) case[16] are worth mentioning to the extent they demonstrate "the extraordinary fortitude and intellectual rigor with which the members of the arbitral tribunal approached their task in this case while in a virtually constant state of siege.... International arbitrators and Counsel ... may well refer to these awards, for generations to come, for the guidance they provide in combating a deliberate campaign of sabotage against the arbitration proceedings by the state party."[17]

The dispute arose from two arbitration awards ordering PLN, a State-owned Indonesian electricity utility, to pay approximately US$ 572 million in damages to HCE and PPL, two Bermudan corporations owned by US investors which had entered into a number of contractual arrangements for the purpose of developing and operating a geothermal electricity generation facility in Indonesia. After these two awards in favour of claimants had been handed down but had not been complied with by PLN, the Indonesian government attempted to prevent a second set of arbitrations (relating to its alleged liability as PLN's guarantor) from proceeding.

To this effect, Pertamina, an instrumentality of the ROI, filed a law suit to enjoin the two new arbitration cases initiated by HCE and PPL against Indonesia. The judge at the Jakarta Central District Court entered an order enjoining the pursuit of the two cases and imposing a penalty of US$ 1 million per diem on any party that violated the order purporting to enjoin the arbitrations. The arbitral tribunal did not comply with the injunction and it held the ROI in default. The arbitrators considered that the ROI had statutory dominion over Pertamina and that the courts of Indonesia were

---

14. See, e.g., Art. 1709 bis of the Belgian Judicial Code.
15. See below at text following fn. 43.
16. See references, *op. cit.*, fn. 4 and fn. 6.
17. Marc GOLDSTEIN, *op. cit.*, fn. 4.

instrumentalities of the ROI. The tribunal held that to prevent an arbitral tribunal from fulfilling its mandate in accordance with the procedures formally agreed by the ROI in the terms of appointment was a denial of justice. Exercising their authority under Art. 16(2) of the UNCITRAL Rules, the arbitrators then decided to convene hearings at the Peace Palace at The Hague, while leaving the legal seat of the arbitration unchanged in Jakarta.

Since the arbitral tribunal was not impressed by the injunction of the Indonesian court, the ROI resorted to even more extreme means, the abduction of the Indonesian arbitrator when he arrived at the Amsterdam airport. He was escorted back to Indonesia by an Indonesian delegation. Nonetheless, the two remaining arbitrators pursued the arbitrations.

On 26 September 1999, the arbitral tribunal issued an Interim Award which held that the ROI had defaulted under the terms of appointment by failing to submit its documentary evidence in due time, without showing sufficient cause, with the result that the tribunal could make the award on the evidence before it.

On 16 October 1999, the "truncated" arbitral tribunal issued a Final Award in which it held that the ROI should not benefit from its arbitrator's absence, and ruled that the ROI was in breach of its guarantor obligations and therefore responsible for damages.

The arbitral tribunal comprehensively set forth in its Final Award the authorities in international law supporting the ability of the two remaining members of the tribunal to proceed to a final award despite the inability of the third arbitrator to participate. In particular, the tribunal relied upon the writings of Judge Stephen Schwebel, President of the International Court of Justice, to the effect that:

> "withdrawal of an arbitrator from an international arbitral tribunal which is not approved or authorized by the tribunal is wrong under customary international law and the general principles of law recognized and applied in the practice of international arbitration. It generally will constitute a violation of the treaty or contract constituting the tribunal, if not in terms, then because the intention of the parties normally cannot be deemed to have authorized such withdrawal."[18]

III. ACTIONS BEFORE NATIONAL COURTS

As we have just seen, in a number of cases, a strong and committed arbitral tribunal will be in a position to overcome in the course of the proceedings the obstacles or difficulties created by a party's (or an arbitrator's or witness') misconduct or misdeed. We will come back to this in Sect IV. We will first examine what remedies are available before national courts, usually after the award has been rendered.

---

18. *Yearbook* XXV (2000) p. 195.

1. During the Arbitral Proceedings

The assistance of national courts may be needed to solve problems created by a party's, witness' or arbitrator's misconduct in the course of the arbitral procedure, especially in the context of an ad hoc arbitration. The recourse will be governed by the applicable national law of procedure. National laws on arbitration generally do not contain specific provisions concerning misdeeds, wrongful conduct and illegality in arbitral proceedings. Most of the time, they only touch upon the matter indirectly, in the grounds for annulment or refusal of enforcement. The only provisions contained in national statutes in relation to misdeeds and misconduct concern the challenge of an arbitrator for lack of impartiality or independence or the means for an arbitral tribunal to deal with allegedly false documents produced by a party.[19]

2. Actions to Set Aside the Award

a. The UNCITRAL Model Law

According to Art. 34 of the UNCITRAL Model Law, an award may be set aside when it is in conflict with the public policy of the state where the arbitration took place. According to a leading commentary on the Model Law, the procedural defects that might lead to setting aside an award should be limited to serious or gross violations or to non-compliance only with mandatory provisions. Moreover, a causal link should exist between the procedural defect and the award, such as that the error probably affected the result.[20]

Redfern and Hunter also point out[21] that when the Model Law was being drafted, some doubt was expressed as to whether the public policy ground would cover injustices that might result from corruption of an arbitrator or a witness, admitted mistakes or discovery of new evidence. Some of these concerns have been addressed, for example, in Australia. There, the Model Law has been amended to define further the term "public policy" as it is used in Art. 34 of the Model Law so as to include situations where the award was induced or affected by fraud, corruption or breach of natural justice that occurred in connection with the making of the award.

b. The United States Federal Arbitration Act

In the United States, the bases upon which an award may be vacated under the Federal

---

19. See, e.g., Art. 1696(5) of the Belgian Judicial Code which provides that:

> "The Arbitral Tribunal may not order the verification of signatures nor rule on an objection relating to the production of documents or upon the alleged falseness of documents. In this case, it will leave it to the parties to bring the matter to the court of first instance within a determined period."

20. H. HOLTZMANN and J. NEUHAUS, *A Guide to the UNCITRAL Model Law on International Commercial Arbitration: Legislative History and Commentary* (Kluwer 1989) pp. 921-922.

21. *Law and Practice of International Commercial Arbitration*, 2nd ed. (Kluwer) p. 444. See also HOLTZMANN and NEUHAUS, *op. cit.*, fn. 20, p. 913.

Arbitration Act (FAA) are set forth in Sect. 10, whose relevant parts read as follows :

> "(1) Where the award was procured by corruption, fraud, or undue means;
> (2) where there was evident partiality or corruption in the arbitrators, or either of them
> (....)"

i.   Award procured by fraud, corruption, undue means

The case law[22] essentially merges these three grounds for vacating an arbitration award – fraud, corruption, and undue means – into a single appellation: fraud. For fraud to justify vacatur: (1) the petitioner must establish the existence of the fraud by clear and convincing evidence, (2) the fraud must not have been discoverable upon the exercise of due diligence prior to or during the arbitration, and (3) the petitioner must demonstrate that the fraud materially related to an issue in the arbitration.[23]

The most commonly asserted "fraud" is perjury. The most common reason courts reject claims of "fraud" is that the party seeking to vacate the award could have discovered the fraud prior to the conclusion of the arbitration.[24]

In a recent case,[25] the court found that the petitioner failed to prove any of the three prerequisites for finding fraud. The alleged fraud concerned an eyewitness who claimed she had been pressured by the defendant's counsel to commit perjury. She signed an affidavit stating that she had received a "mixed message" from counsel, who "tried to tell [her] what the truth was".[26] The court held that the witness' testimony was ambiguous, not "clear and convincing" evidence of fraud, that the testimony could have been discovered earlier had the petitioner sought to compel the witness' appearance at the hearing, and that the alleged effort to suborn perjury did not affect the outcome of the arbitration, because the witness never ended up testifying.

Actions to set aside based on non-disclosure of evidence or interference of a party

---

22. G. RATH, D. BOCH and T. BURKE, "Judicial Review of Arbitration Awards", SF 86 ALI-ABA 705 (2001).

23. *Bonar v. Dean Witter Reynolds, Inc.*, 835 F.2d 1378, 1383 (11th Cir. 1988) (vacating arbitration award where prevailing party's expert witness had falsified his credentials); *Karpinnen v. Karl Kiefer Machine Co.*, 187 F.2d. 32 (2d Cir. 1951) (refusal to set aside where the matter on which the witness testified was remote from, and had no material bearing on, the issues before the arbitrators); *Mobile Oil Indonesia v. Asamera Oil Ltd.*, 487 F.Supp. 63 (S.D.N.Y. 1980) (claimant did not meet burden of showing that the award was procured by the false testimony); see also, *Coppola v. Charles Schwab & Co.*, 969 F.2d 1042 (2d Cir. 1991); *Terk Technologies Corp. v. Dockery*, 86 F.Supp.2d. 706 (E.D. Mich. 2000).

24. See, e.g., *O.R. Securities, Inc. v. Professional Planning Associates, Inc.*, 857 F.2d 742 (11th Cir. 1998) (failure to cross-examine witness with respect to suspicious testimony barred later claim of fraud); *Lafarge Conseils et Etudes, S.A. v. Kaiser Cement & Gypsum Corp.*, 791 F.2d 1334 (9th Cir. 1986) (failure to issue subpoena to person suspected of tampering with exhibits vitiated claim of fraud); *Valentino v. Smith*, Fed. Sec. L. Rep. (CCH) Sect. 97, 256 (W.D. Okla. 30 September 1992) (no fraud where inconsistencies in customer's testimony could have been raised before the arbitrators).

25. *Merrill Lynch, Pierce, Fenner & Smith, Inc. v. Lambros*, 1998 WL 154629 (M.D. Fla. 9 March 1998).

26. *Ibid.*, at 6.

with the arbitration are usually dismissed because the three conditions listed above place such a high burden of proof on claimant that they are rarely met.[27]

ii.   Evident partiality or corruption of arbitrators

"Evident partiality" is not defined in the FAA, and courts have struggled to flesh out the concept. Most take an individualized approach, analyzing the unique factual setting of each case, instead of trying to apply a uniform definition.[28]

In general, mere "appearance of bias" is not enough. Evident partiality exists only where "a reasonable person would have to conclude that an arbitrator was partial to one party".[29] The alleged partiality must be "direct, definite, and capable of demonstration rather than remote, uncertain, and speculative".[30] The party asserting partiality must establish specific facts that indicate improper motives on the part of the arbitrators.[31] If, however, an arbitrator failed to disclose a substantial relationship between himself and a party, the less demanding "appearance of bias" standard then applies.[32]

In assessing claims of bias, courts consider factors including "the arbitrator's financial interest in the outcome, the nature of the relationship between the arbitrator and the allegedly favoured party, and whether the relationship existed during the arbitration".[33]

---

27. On non-disclosure of evidence, see, e.g., *Pontiac Trail Medical Clinic, P.C. v. Paine Webber Inc.*,1993 US app. LEXIS 20280 (6th Cir. 1993); *Shearson Hayden Stone, Inc., v. Liang*, 653 F.2d 310 (7th Cir. 1981); *Iron City Industrial Cleaning Corp. v. Laundry & Dry Cleaners International Union*, 316 F.Supp. 1373 (W.D. Pa. 1970); *Biotronik Mess.-und Therapiegeraete GmbH & Co. v. Medford Medical Instrument Co.*, 415 F.Supp. 133 (D.C. N.J. 1976); *O.R. Sec. v. Professional Planning Associate Assocs.*, 857 F.2d 742 (11th Cir. 1988); *Dean Foods Co. v. USW*, 911 F.Supp., 1116 (N.D. Ind. 1995); *Baltia Air Lines v. Transaction Management*, 98 F.3d 640 (App. D.C. Dist. Col. 1994). On disruption or interference with arbitration, see *Newark Stereotypers' Union v. Newark Morning Ledger Co.*, 397 F.2d 594 (3d Cir. 1968) (alleged threats by the president of a newspaper company involved in an arbitration with a union to cease doing business with the current employer of an expert witness for the union if the witness continued to testify for the union. The court stated that the merits of the controversy submitted to arbitration were not dependent upon the attitude of the newspaper company's president towards the witness' employer and that the award in favour of the newspaper company was amply supported by the record); *Mantle v. Upper Deck Co.*, 956 F.Supp. 719 (N.D. Tex. 1997); *Vita Food Products v. Sklar*, 1995 U.S. Dist. LEXIS 8160 (N.D. Ill. 1995).

28. See *Int'l Bhd. of Elec. Workers, Local Union No. 323 v. Coral Elec. Corp.*, 104 F.R.D. 88, 89 (S.D. Fla. 1985) ("'Evident partiality', like obscenity, is an elusive concept: one knows it when one sees it.... No jurist has yet coined an exacting legal standard for 'evident partiality', although many have tried.").

29. *Local 814, Int'l Bhd. of Teamsters v. J&B Systems Installers & Moving, Inc.*, 878 F.2d 38, 40 (2d Cir. 1989).

30. *Lifecare Intern. Inc. v. CD Medical, Inc.*, 68 F.3d 429, 433 (11th Cir. 1995); *York Hannover Holding AG v. American Arbitration Assn and others*, 11 May 1993 (D.C. S.D.N.Y) Yearbook XX (1995) p. 856; *Health Services Managt Corp. v. Hughes*, 975 F.2d 1253 (7th Cir. 1992); *International Produce v. A/S Rosshavet*, 638 F.2d 548 (2d Cir. 1981).

31. *Dawahare v. Spencer*, 210 F.3d 666 (6th Cir. 2000).

32. *Park v. First Union Brokerage Services, Inc.*, 926 F.Supp. 1085, 1088 (M.D. Fla. 1996).

33. *Sun Ref. & Mktg. Col. v. Statheros Shipping Corp. of Monrovia*, 761 F.Supp. 293, 299 (S.D.N.Y.) aff'd, 948 F.2d 1277 (2d Cir. 1991).

Complaints of favouritism or unfair evidentiary rulings do not establish partiality.[34]

As a practical matter, courts seem more willing to credit allegations of evident partiality when they are based on arbitrators' failure to disclose conflicts of interest or past dealings with the parties.[35] But in any case, for a business relationship to justify the vacating of an award, it must be a significant and ongoing relationship.[36]

Challenges based on allegations of overt acts of favouritism rarely succeed.[37] Ex parte contacts between an arbitrator and a party may justify the setting aside of an award if the merits of the case were discussed and evaluated.[38]

---

34. *Sisti v. Merrill, Lynch, Pierce, Fenner & Smith*, 1991 U.S. Dist. LEXIS 15817 (E.D. Va. 22 April 1991) (evident partiality may not be shown through alleged "procedural or evidentiary errors, by legitimate efforts to move the case along, or by failure to follow the rules of evidence".).

35. See, e.g., *Wages v. Smith Barney Harris Upham & Co.*, 937 P.2d 715 (Ariz. 1997) (vacating award for evident partiality where the tribunal's chairperson failed to reveal that he had twice sued the respondent firm on behalf of investors, and one of the cases involved claims virtually identical to those being asserted by claimants); *Rollings v. Paine Webber Inc.*, Cal.App. 2 Dist. (No. B058271 23 February 1993) (unpublished) (vacating award where arbitrator failed to disclose that, at the time of the arbitration hearing, he was a defendant in a separate arbitration matter where the party suing him was represented by the same counsel representing the customer in the arbitration).

36. *Commonwealth Coatings Corp. v. Continental Casualty Co.* (1968) 393 US 145, 21 L.Ed.2d 301, 89 S.Ct 337.

37. See, e.g., *Areca, Inc. v. Oppenheimer & Co.*, 960 F.Supp. 52 (S.D.N.Y. 1997) (rejecting allegations of pro-industry bias that were based on arbitrators' refusal to hear certain testimony and limitation of certain evidence); *Pompano Windy City Partners, Ltd. v. Bear Stearns & Co.*, 794 F.Supp. 1265 (S.D.N.Y. 1992) (evident partiality was not established by pattern of alleged improper rulings and the appointment of an arbitrator who was a former Director of Arbitration [of the National Association of Securities Dealers]); *Carpenter v. Brooks*, 534 S.E. 2d 641 (N.C. Ct. App. 2000) (the panel's occasional impatience with repetitive testimony and its legitimate efforts to move the proceedings along, the panel's questioning of witnesses, even though perceived by plaintiff as hostile, and the panel's exclusion of evidence relating to the broker's handling of other customers' accounts as irrelevant, did not evince bias, impartiality or misconduct sufficient to vacate an award under the FAA); *Holodnak v. Avco Corp.*, 381 F.Supp. 191 (D.C. Conn. 1974) (award vacated, the transcript of the hearing disclosed open hostility toward the employee); *Billward Painting Co. v. Partner's Dist. Council no. 3*, 1990 U.S. Dist. LEXIS 11898 (W.D. Mo.1990) (award vacated because of evidence that arbitrators prejudged the dispute).

38. *Metropolitan Property & Casualty Ins. Co. v. J.C. Penny Casualty Ins. Co.*, 780 F.Supp. 885 (D.C. Conn. 1991) (award vacated, the court stated that even a party-appointed arbitrator has a responsibility not only to the parties but also to the process itself and must observe high standards of conduct so that the integrity and fairness of the process will be preserved); *David Spector & Security Industrial Ltd. v. Dov Torenberg & others*, 852 F.Supp. 201 (S.D.N.Y. 1994) and *Yearbook* XX (1995) p. 962 (refusal to set aside. The court stated that, "[i]n order to vacate an award based on an ex parte conversation, a party must show that this conversation deprived him of a fair hearing and influenced the outcome of the arbitration.... Generally, the subject matter of the conversation must have gone to the heart of the dispute's merits, and an award will therefore not be vacated if the conversation concerned a merely peripheral matter"); *Konkar Maritime Enterprises, S.A. v. Compagnie Belge d'Affrètement*, 668 F.Supp. 267 (S.D.N.Y. 1987) (award not vacated, because the losing party could not show prejudice resulting from the ex parte communications).

c.   The United Kingdom Arbitration Act 1996

According to Sect. 68 of the Arbitration Act 1996, a party may apply to the court challenging an award on the ground of serious irregularity affecting the tribunal, the proceedings or the award. However, a party may lose the right to object if it continues to take part in the proceedings without making its objections in due time.[39] According to Sect. 68(2) :

> "[s]erious irregularity means an irregularity of one or more of the following kinds which the court considers has caused or will cause substantial injustice to the applicant....
> (g) The award being obtained by fraud or the award or the way in which it was procured being contrary to public policy;
> (....)
> (i) Any irregularity in the conduct of the proceedings or in the award which is admitted by the tribunal or by any arbitral or other institution or person vested by the parties with powers in relation to the proceedings or the award."

Para. 3 of Sect. 68 further provides that:

> "[i]f there is shown to be serious irregularity affecting the tribunal, the proceedings or the award, the court may—
> (a) remit the award to the tribunal, in whole or in part, for reconsideration,
> (b) set the award aside[40] in whole or in part, or
> (c) declare the award to be of no effect, in whole or in part".

According to leading commentators,[41] fraud implies some act of deceit perpetrated against the tribunal (e.g., providing the tribunal with falsified certificates of ownership of property claimed) or against the other party (i.e., if the tribunal was a party to the fraud). On the other hand, the reference in the section to public policy is intended to cover circumstances which, though not amounting to fraud, would be similarly offensive, such as bribery of the tribunal.[42]

d.   The French Code of Civil Procedure

According to Art. 1504 of the French Code of Civil Procedure, an arbitral award made in France in an international arbitration may be the subject of an action to set aside in the cases set forth in Art. 1502. Art. 1502(5) of the Code provides that recognition or enforcement of an award will be refused where it would be contrary to international public policy. In other words, an award made in France can be set aside if it is contrary

---

39. Sect. 73.

40. See, in relation to the setting aside of a judgment, the leading case, *Odyssey Re (London) Ltd and Anor v. OIC Run-off Ltd* (formerly *Orion Insurance Co Plc*), Court of Appeal, 13 March 2000, 2001 Lloyd's Law Reports 1 (test for setting aside when there is perjured evidence).

41. *Russell on Arbitration*, 21st ed. (Sweet & Maxwell, London 1997) p. 421, note 57.

42. *Ibid.,* note 58.

to international public policy.

The requirements of international public policy concern both the merits of the dispute and the arbitral procedure. A case is cited in *Fouchard Goldman Gaillard* in which a party had deceived the arbitrators by submitting false documents, even though the fraud was not discovered until after the award was made, as being among the situations which violate international public policy.[43] Another situation is the case where the award has been obtained by fraud following the retention by a party of documents which were fundamental for the solution of the dispute.[44] According to the Paris Court of Appeal, in order to justify the annulment of the award, the alleged fraud "*suppose notamment que des pièces intéressant la solution du litige aient été frauduleusement dissimulées aux arbitres et que leur décision ait été ainsi surprise*". The fraudulent retention will be taken into consideration only if it appears that the decision of the arbitral tribunal would have been different had the documents been communicated.[45] The Paris Court of Appeal also decided in another case[46] that the court's control extends to all elements of law or fact enabling the court to justify the possible application of the rule of international public policy.[47]

It is equally argued that the dignity and impartiality of the judicial process is also a matter of public policy.[48]

In order to be admissible before the French courts, a ground for setting the award aside must have been raised whenever possible before the arbitral tribunal itself. A violation of international public policy is however, by its nature, the only ground which cannot be ratified by the parties. Nevertheless, where the claim against the award could have provided the basis for a challenge of the arbitrators but no challenge was made, French courts consider the action available under Art. 1502(5) to be no longer

---

43. Emmanuel GAILLARD and John SAVAGE, eds., *Fouchard, Gaillard Goldman on International Commercial Arbitration* (Kluwer 1999) (hereinafter *Fouchard Gaillard Goldman*) p. 958, citing the *Westman* case (*op. cit.*, fn. 13). See also, Paris Court of Appeal, 20 April 2000, *Société Ivoir-Café v. Banque Africaine de Développement*, Rev.Arb. (2001) p. 583 and note Jean-Baptiste RACINE. Three partial awards and one final award were rendered in this case concerning the non-performance of a loan agreement by Banque Africaine de Développement which was finally condemned to pay damages to Ivoir-Café. However, Ivoir-Café was not satisfied by the awards and decided to start an action to set aside. The main complaint was that the award gave effect to a procedural fraud and therefore violated international public policy. Ivoir-Café alleged that the drafter of an audit report had submitted to the arbitral tribunal a fraudulent document (a forged invoice). A criminal complaint was also filed by Ivoir-Café against the drafter of the report. The complaint alleged perjury and the drafting and use of a forged document. The Court of Appeal decided to suspend the procedure on the basis of the principle, "*Le criminel tient le civil en état*."

44. Paris Court of Appeal, 17 June 1997, *Société Eiffage v. Société Butec*, Rev.Arb. (1997) p. 583 and note D. BUREAU.

45. See also Paris Court of Appeal, 29 January 1997, Rev.Arb. (1997) p. 429 and note Y. DERAINS.

46. 27 February 1997, *Banque Franco Tunisienne – BFT v. ABCI*, Rev.Arb. (1997) p. 587.

47. "*Lorsqu'il est saisi pour ce motif, sur le fondement de l'article 1502-5 ° du Nouveau Code de Procédure Civile, le juge de l'annulation doit exercer son contrôle sur tous les éléments de droit ou de fait permettant de justifier l'application ou non de la règle d'ordre public international.*"

48. *Fouchard Gaillard Goldman*, *op. cit.*, fn. 43, p. 958.

admissible.[49] On the other hand, a party will naturally not be penalized for having failed to raise an objection before the arbitral tribunal if it only became aware of the grounds for that objection after the award had been made.[50]

Another recourse, called *recours en révision*, is also possible against an award rendered in domestic and international cases in France, which have been obtained by fraudulent means. In domestic cases, such recourse may be brought before the Court of Appeal in case the award has been obtained by fraud, retention of documents or through the production of documents, affidavits or testimonies which later appear to be false or to have been forged.[51] Although in international cases, the *recours en révision* is excluded by Art. 1507 of the French Code of Civil Procedure, the French Supreme Court has decided in the *Fougerolles* case[52] that it could be exceptionally admitted in case of fraud (for example, the retention of important documents) when the arbitral tribunal remains constituted after the award has been rendered or may be constituted anew.

e.   The Belgian Judicial Code (Code Judiciaire)
According to Art. 1704(2)(a) and (3)(a), (b) and (c) of the Judicial Code, an arbitral award may be set aside :

— if it is contrary to public policy;
— if it was obtained by fraud;
— if it is based on evidence that has been declared false by a judicial decision having res judicata or on evidence recognized as false;
— if, after it was made, a document or other piece of evidence was discovered which would have had a decisive influence on the award and which was withheld by the other party.

In all four cases, the application is valid even if the applicant had knowledge of the relevant facts during the arbitration proceedings and did not invoke them at that time.[53]

The fraud referred to in Art. 1704(3) of the judicial code may be the fact of a party, a party's representative or the arbitrators themselves.[54]

It also seems that the false evidence referred to in Art. 1704(3) does not include evidence resulting from the hearing of a party, witness or an expert.[55]

---

49. *Ibid.*, p. 928, citing Paris Court of Appeal, 2 June 1989, *Gemanco v. S.A.E.P.A.*, Rev.Arb. (1991) p. 87, 2nd decision.

50. *Ibid.*, p. 928.

51. Arts.1491 and 595 French Code of Civil Procedure.

52. *Soc. Fougerolle c. Soc. Procofrance*, 25 May 1992, Rev.Arb. (1993) p. 91; JDI (1992) p. 974 and note LOQUIN; Rev.crit.dip. (1992) p. 699 and note OPPETIT. See also de BOISSÉSON, "L'arbitrage et la fraude", Rev.Arb. (1993) p. 3.

53. Art. 1704(4).

54. Parliamentary documents, Chamber of Representatives, session 1970-1971, no. 988/1, p. 26, no. 121; P. de BOURNONVILLE, *Droit judiciaire: L'arbitrage* (Larcier 2000) p. 213, no. 6 and references cited.

55. P. de BOURNONVILLE, *loc.cit.*, fn. 54.

f.   The Swiss Law on Private International Law

According to Art. 190 of the Swiss Law on Private International Law, an award can be set aside if it has violated the principle of equal treatment of the parties (d) or if the decision violates public policy (e). It is considered that fundamental procedural errors might be qualified a violation of procedural public policy.[56]

An award is also subject to "*révision*" by the Federal Court when a criminal court has determined that the award was influenced by a crime or delict to the detriment of the party which has introduced the recourse. If a criminal procedure is not possible, the evidence may be administered by other means.[57]

3.   Refusal of Enforcement of the Award

Like the New York Convention,[58] national provisions on enforcement of arbitral awards generally provide for refusal of enforcement in case the award violates international public policy.[59]

It was on the ground of a violation of international public policy that enforcement of an award was refused in France where one of the arbitrators, who was also sitting in a parallel arbitration, communicated erroneous information to the arbitral tribunal that was likely to influence the tribunal's decision. The *Cour de cassation* held that this "had created an imbalance between the parties in violation of the parties' rights to a fair hearing, so that the award made (outside France) in such conditions contravened French public policy" within the meaning of Arts. 1502(5) of the new Code of Civil Procedure and V(2)(*b*) of the New York Convention.[60]

In the United States, courts have rarely refused enforcement of an award despite a claim that to do so would violate the public policy of the United States because the arbitrator considered improper testimony or evidence. For example, in *National Oil Corp. v. Libyan Sun Oil Co.*,[61] the court confirmed an international arbitration award of US$ 20 million in favour of a Libyan government corporation arising out of the failure of an American oil corporation to perform an oil exploration contract after the US government barred Americans from traveling to Libya. This came despite the claim that enforcement of the award would violate the public policy of the US in that the testimony of a witness for the Libyan corporation was false and misleading, depriving the American corporation of its due process rights and that therefore, the court should not enforce the

---

56. S. BERTI, ed., *International Arbitration in Switzerland*, (Kluwer 2000) p. 584; Swiss Federal Court, 11 March 1992, Rev.Arb. (1993) p. 115, note P.Y. TSCHANZ.

57. Art. 137(a) of the Federal Statute on Judicial Organization which applies by analogy. See, e.g., the decision of the Federal Court, 11 March 1992, ASA Bulletin (1992) p. 356.

58. Art. V(2)(*b*) New York Convention.

59. For example, Art. 1502(5) of the French Code of Civil Procedure, Art. 1723(2) of the Belgian Judicial Code, Sect. 103(3) of the United Kingdom Arbitration Act 1996, Art. 31(1)(*b*)(2) of the UNCITRAL Model Law.

60. *Cass. 1e Civ.*, 24 March 1998, *Excelsior Film TV v. UGC-PH*, Dalloz, IR 105 (1998); JCP, Ed. G., Pt. IV, No. 2128 (1998); 126 JDI (1999) p.155 and A.E. KAHN's note. *Fouchard Gaillard Goldman*, *op. cit.*, fn. 43, p. 958.

61. 733 F.Supp. 800 (D. Del. 1990).

award under Art. V(2)(*b*) of the New York Convention. The court rejected the argument that the witness' testimony was false and misleading and added that if some of the statements were incorrect, this fact was not material. In any event, the court stated that for fraud to justify vacating an arbitration award, it must not have been discoverable upon the exercise of due diligence prior to the arbitration; in the instant case, the oil company had six months' prior notice that the witness was going to testify and what he was going to testify about, but did not even bother to cross-examine the witness at the arbitration.[62]

Pleas that enforcement of an award should be refused because the arbitrator was biased or prejudiced are also rarely successful in the United States.[63] According to the consolidated commentary on Art. V(2)(*b*) of the New York Convention,[64] courts will refuse the enforcement of an award for lack of impartiality of an arbitrator only when the arbitrator has effectively not acted in an impartial manner. For example, in relation to an AAA arbitration that had taken place in New York, the District Court rejected allegations of bias of the presiding arbitrator because, inter alia, he was said to have paid attention only to the lawyer member of the panel and not to the businessman member of the panel.[65] In this decision, the District Court noted : "In the Second Circuit, a party must show more than 'partiality'. The challenging party must show that a 'reasonable person' would have to conclude that an arbitrator was partial to one party to the arbitration."[66]

Corruption may also be a ground for refusal of enforcement of an award on the basis of Art. V(2)(*b*) of the New York Convention if it is raised in due time. In a case recently

---

62. See also, *Waterside Ocean Nav. Co., Inc. v. International Nav. Ltd.*, 737 F.2d 150 (2d Cir. 1984) and in England, *Westacre Investments Inc. v. Jugoimport-SPDR Holding Co. Ltd. and others*, [2000] Q.B. 28: the defendants had applied to set aside the leave to enforce the award. In the course of the hearing, they sought leave to re-amend their points of defense to allege that a number of witnesses called by the plaintiffs at the arbitration had given perjured evidence and that since the award had been obtained by fraud and/or manifestly dishonest evidence it would be contrary to public policy to enforce it. The defendants' application for leave to re-amend was refused. The Court held:

"that normally the issue could not be reopened unless the evidence to establish the fraud was not available to the party alleging fraud at the time of the hearing before the arbitrators; that where the allegation was of perjury the evidence must be so strong that it could reasonably be expected to be decisive at a hearing, and must if unanswered be decisive; that in the instant case the defendants had shown no good reason why they should not have raised with the Swiss Federal Tribunal within the 90 day period allowed the allegation that the award had been obtained by perjured evidence; and that, accordingly, the defendants should not be granted leave to amend".

63. *In Matter of Andros Compania Maritima, S.A. of Kissavos*, 579 F.2d 691 (2d Cir. 1978); *Transmarine Seaways Corp. of Monrovia v. Marc Rich & Co. A.G.*, 480 F.Supp., 352 (S.D.N.Y. 1979); *Brandeis Intsel Ltd. v. Calabrian Chemicals Corp.*, 656 F.Supp. 160 (S.D.N.Y. 1987).

64. *Yearbook* XXI (1996) p. 506.

65. *York Hanover Holding AG v. American Arbitration Association, op. cit.*, fn. 30.

66. See also Hong Kong Court of Appeal, 22 May 1997, *Yearbook* XXIII (1998) p. 660 and Court of Final Appeal of the Hong Kong Special Administrative Region, 9 February 1999, *Yearbook* XXIVa (1999) p. 652 (enforcement granted, no proof of actual bias).

decided by the United States Court of Appeals for the Second Circuit on 23 March 1998,[67] enforcement was granted despite a claim of corruption. In 1991 and 1992, IDTS had entered into contracts for the purchase of non-ferrous metals from Techno. The contracts contained arbitration clauses providing for arbitration at the International Court of Commercial Arbitration of the Chamber of Commerce and Industry of the Russian Federation in Moscow. Disputes arose under the contracts and in the ensuing arbitration, two awards were made in Techno's favour for approximately US$ 200 million. Techno subsequently sought enforcement of the awards. IDTS opposed the enforcement arguing that the Arbitration Court was corrupt, as it had "tested" their integrity and found them willing to take bribes. The District Court granted the motion for an order to confirm the awards. IDTS appealed but the Court of Appeals affirmed the order of the court below, finding that IDTS had knowledge of concrete facts[68] possibly indicating the corruption of the Arbitration Court but despite this knowledge had remained silent. It had thus waived whatever objections it had to the tribunal.

4. Other Criminal or Civil Procedures

a. Against an arbitrator

The author of a recent in-depth comparative analysis on the liability of international arbitrators[69] concludes her article as follows:

> "Arbitrators currently have immunity from complaints regarding their arbitral actions. The scope of this immunity largely depends upon the law of the relevant jurisdiction and the applicable institutional rules. The United States is the only country that has nearly absolute immunity for arbitral acts. In contrast, most other countries have forms of qualified immunity while others appear to have liability limited only by the terms of the *receptum arbitri* and the applicable law."[70]

---

67. *AAOT Foreign Economic Association (VO) Technostroyexport (Techno) v. International Development & Trade Services, Inc.*, 139 F.3d 980 and *Yearbook* XXIV (1999) p. 813.

68. "Following the initiation of the arbitration proceedings, IDTS sent an interpreter – Tamara Sicular – to Moscow to file papers, clarify the status of the cases and gain an understanding of the procedures that would be followed. On 14 July 1993, Sicular met with Sergey Orlov, the Secretary of the Arbitration Court, and his superior at the Chamber of Commerce. According to IDTS, Sicular, on her own initiative and to test the integrity of the Court, asked Orlov whether the Court could be bought. Orlov responded affirmatively and offered to 'fix' the cases for IDTS in exchange for a substantial payment. His superior later that day told Sicular he would personally assist IDTS 'sort out' the arbitration. On the next day, Orlov presented Sicular with his plan which called for a payment of US$ 1 million for which he would rig the tribunal. There followed a series of communications with Orlov over the next two months in which Sicular ostensibly sought to gather further evidence and establish that the Arbitration Court and its officials were corrupt. They ended inconclusively in September 1993, without any payment being made."

69. Susan D. FRANCK, "The Liability of International Arbitrators: A Comparative Analysis and Proposal for Qualified Immunity", 20 N.Y.L.Sch. J. Int'l & Comp. L., p.1.

70. *Ibid.*, p. 19.

In the United States, an arbitrator is absolutely immune from civil liability for all acts related to his decision-making function. The scope of immunity even extends to situations where the arbitrator was careless, grossly negligent, or intentionally acted in a fraudulent manner. Instead of imposing liability for bad faith behaviours such as fraud and conspiracy, the American cases hold that the arbitrators' inappropriate behaviour merely prevented them from collecting their arbitral fees.[71] On the other hand, statutes that establish criminal sanctions for a limited form of arbitral misconduct, namely bribery, are common. For example, in California, arbitrators who asked for, received or agreed to receive bribes to influence their decisions are guilty of a crime and can be jailed for up to four years.[72]

England's new Arbitration Act 1996 provides arbitrators with a statutory basis for immunity in tort, contract or otherwise. There are only two specific situations justifying liability: if an arbitral act or omission is done "in bad faith" or if a court determines withdrawal is unreasonable.

In many countries, whether the issue is addressed by statute or not, it is considered that arbitrators may in principle be liable in tort or in contract subject to limited immunity. They may be prosecuted if they commit a criminal offence. They may be liable in tort or in contract but most of the time, only in cases of intentional misconduct or gross negligence.[73, 74]

The potential liability of arbitrators is further restricted by the rules of the various institutions. The London Court of International Arbitration (LCIA) provides that no arbitrator "shall be liable to any party howsoever for any act or omission in connection with any arbitration conducted" under the auspices of the LCIA.[75] However, the LCIA does provide an exception when the arbitrator can be liable for "conscious or deliberate wrongdoing".[76] The World Intellectual Property Organization (WIPO) also has a similar standard for immunity where "[e]xcept in respect of deliberate wrongdoing, the arbitrator or arbitrators ... shall not be liable to a party for any act or omission in connection with the arbitration".[77] Similarly, although they do not have the force of law unless the parties incorporate them in their agreement, the International Bar Association's Ethics for International Arbitrators provide for immunity except in cases of "willful or reckless disregard of their legal obligations".[78]

The International Chamber of Commerce (ICC), on the other hand, provides that arbitrators will not "be liable to any person for any act or omission in connection with

---

71. *Ibid.*, p. 9 and cases cited.

72. *Ibid.*

73. See the analysis of the law of the various countries by Susan D. FRANCK in the article quoted above, fn. 69 and the various reports contained in Julian LEW, ed., *The Immunity of Arbitrators* (Lloyd's of London Press Ltd. 1990).

74. This is the case in France; see the references cited by *Fouchard Gaillard Goldman, op. cit.*, fn. 43, p. 598.

75. Art. 31(1) LCIA Rules.

76. *Ibid.*

77. WIPO Arbitration Rules, Art. 77.

78. International Bar Association, *Ethics for International Arbitrators*, "Introductory Note", 26 I.L.M. (1987) p. 583, *Yearbook* XII (1987) p. 199.

the arbitration".[79] The Nederlands Arbitrage Instituut (NAI) also provides that no arbitrator "can be held liable for any act or omission with regard to an arbitration governed by the [NAI] Rules".[80] Beyond the fact that in some jurisdictions, liability for gross negligence or intentional wrongs cannot be excluded in advance by contract, the question whether such a broad exclusion of liability is appropriate from a moral point of view has been seriously questioned.[81]

b. Against a witness or a party representative

Sworn testimony is relatively uncommon in international commercial arbitration. Further, criminal sanctions against perjury are in most cases only available when the witness has testified under oath.[82] By way of example, we will successively review the laws of England, Switzerland and Austria on this issue.

In England, the law relating to false testimony is governed by the Perjury Act 1911. Under the Act, a person who is lawfully sworn as a witness in a judicial proceeding and who makes a statement, material in that proceeding which he knows to be false or does not believe to be true, is guilty of perjury and liable to imprisonment and/or a fine. It is accepted that "judicial proceeding" includes proceedings before any tribunal, including an arbitral tribunal. However, when false statements are made not under oath, prosecutions are possible only in so far as the declarant is required to make the statement under any public general Act of Parliament.[83] It seems therefore that as long as the public court system does not step in, the orders of arbitrators to appear and to testify are mere invitations by private people lacking any coercive authority. As a consequence, a witness not complying with an arbitral order cannot be punished. The same must be true for a witness who does not tell the truth. This of course does not mean that the perpetrator may not be criminally liable under a different offence.[84]

In Switzerland, on the other hand, the criminal code expressly extends the offences of sworn and unsworn false testimony to arbitral proceedings.[85] However, Swiss law makes another distinction: false testimony committed by a party is punished less severely than the same offence committed by a witness. Moreover, in order to commit a crime, a party must have been reminded to tell the truth and to be aware of the criminal consequences of false testimony. Under these circumstances, a party who knowingly and willfully gives false sworn or unsworn testimony faces a penalty of imprisonment for a term of up to three years; in the case of perjury, i.e., false sworn testimony, there is a

---

79. Art. 34 ICC Arbitration Rules.
80. Art. 66 NAI Rules.
81. See, for example, Pierre LALIVE, "Sur l'irresponsabilité arbitrale" in *Etudes de Procédure et d'Arbitrage en l'honneur de Jean-François Poudret* (Lausanne 1999) p. 419.
82. This is the case in Belgium and also in France with the difference that in France, arbitrators are not allowed to administer an oath. Art.1461(2) NCPC. See, in general, Marianne ROTH, "False Testimony at International Arbitration Hearings Conducted in England and Switzerland", Journal of International Arbitration (1994) p. 5.
83. Sect. V; subsects. b and c.
84. ROTH, *op. cit.*, fn. 82, p. 22.
85. Art. 309 St. G.B.

required minimum period of imprisonment of at least three months.[86] With regard to witnesses, the term of imprisonment is increased to five years; the required minimum period for perjury amounts to six months.[87]

Moreover, contrary to the English Perjury Act 1911, even when a false statement is completely immaterial to the final decision, a lying witness is guilty of false testimony and may be imprisoned, but only up to six months.[88]

However, all the above provisions punish false oral testimony, but do not include false written statements, although the latter might fall under Art. 251 of the Criminal Code.

In Austria, Sect. 288 of the Austrian Criminal Code of 1974 criminalizes false testimony only if it is given before a court. However, if the arbitral tribunal invokes court assistance for taking testimony and the evidence is taken by a judge on behalf of the arbitrators, it seems that Sect. 288 St G.B. applies, which makes false testimony given before a court a criminal offence.

It should also be pointed out that under Austrian criminal law, unsworn false testimony given by a party is not punishable. Sect. 288 only sanctions unsworn false testimony by witnesses and perjury, i.e., sworn false testimony, regardless of whether it is committed by a witness or a party.

When a witness is judged guilty of a criminal offence, he is normally also declared liable for the civil consequences of his conduct. Moreover, in the civil law system, witnesses may be subject to suit for damages resulting from their false statement provided that the general requirements for tort liability are fulfilled. It is enough for the plaintiff to show that the defendant unlawfully caused an injury by his or her fault and that the injury caused a damage.[89]

In the United States, on the other hand, communications taking place during the course of a judicial proceeding are absolutely privileged by the so-called witness immunity rule which bars any civil liability arising out of a witness' conduct at court proceedings. The same rule applies in arbitration.[90]

IV.   THE ROLE OF THE ARBITRAL TRIBUNAL AND THE ARBITRATION INSTITUTION

In my experience, and as was also clearly evidenced by the *Bahrain/Qatar* case, the tendency of international judges and arbitrators when faced with an issue of misdeed in arbitral proceedings is often to avoid any sort of direct confrontation. They certainly entertain a moral judgment on the inadmissibility or illegality of the relevant conduct but they often avoid expressing it. Why is this so?

If one takes the ICJ case, it is probable that the Court considered that since the eighty-two documents had been withdrawn, it did not have to decide the issue and it

---

86. Art. 306 St. G.B.
87. Art. 307 St. G.B.
88. *Ibid.*
89. ROTH, *op. cit.*, fn. 82, p. 38.
90. *Ibid.*, p. 42.

could not express an opinion on Qatar's conduct without going through the evidence to reach a decision on Qatar's alleged forgery. Qatar had moreover expressed apologies. The fact that the ICJ's jurisdiction is based on consent, that the ultimate goal of the UN Charter is keeping the peace and also that a moral condemnation might have endangered the enforcement of the judgment, are probably reasons why the Court limited itself to a recital of the events.

Faced with the issue of forged documents or other types of misdeeds, international arbitrators invariably take the wrongful or illegal conduct into consideration by awarding in favour of the other party or drawing adverse inferences. But they often do not go beyond these measures. It is probable that most arbitrators consider that their duty is to decide the case and that from the moment the claim of the party which is at the origin of the misdeed is dismissed, it is not appropriate or useful to blame further. It might jeopardize the enforcement of the award or even incite the party which has "lost face" to start an action to set aside.[91]

But this raises a fundamental issue concerning the role of the arbitrator. Should the arbitrator limit himself to deciding the dispute and avoid anything which might trouble the peaceful atmosphere of the arbitral setting, or does he have moral or legal duties which impose an obligation on him to go beyond this?

From a legal point of view, an arbitrator does not have to include in the award elements which are not a necessary justification of its decision. But on the other hand, he is appointed *intuitu personae*, in consideration of his legal as well as moral qualities and character. In this respect, if the arbitrator should indeed avoid doing anything which could jeopardize or make more difficult the enforcement of the award, this should not cause him a priori to abstain from expressing a judgment on blatant irregularities in the arbitral proceedings. Arbitrators must behave according to high moral and ethical standards and must make sure that the same standards apply during the arbitral process.

Moreover, arbitrators are guardians of international public policy which includes the dignity and impartiality of the arbitral process.[92] As Professor Lando wrote,[93]

"The arbitrator will have to consider not only the interests of the parties but also those of international commercial arbitration considered as an institution. Today arbitration still enjoys the prestige which has induced the liberality shown to it by

---

91. On the other hand, if the misdeed, a false testimony, is not recited and criticized and the party concerned nevertheless decides to attack the validity of the award, an occasion has been lost by the arbitrators to show the court the bad faith of that party.

92. See above fn. 48. In the *Metropolitan Property* case, cited at fn. 38, a US District Court vacated an award on the basis of ex parte communications between an arbitrator and the party who appointed him stating that even a party appointed arbitrator has a responsibility to the process itself and must observe high standards of conduct so that the integrity and fairness of the process will be preserved. See also Thomas CLAY, *L'arbitre* (Dalloz 2001) no. 799, p. 616: *"L'arbitre a l'obligation de vérifier que l'instance arbitrale se déroule dans le respect strict des garanties fondamentales de bonne justice. Il est à ce titre garant du respect des droits de la défense, du principe du contradictoire et de l'égalité des litigants."*

93. O. LANDO, "Conflicts of Law Rules for Arbitrators" in *Festschrift für K. Zweigert* (1981) p. 157 at p. 172.

most Western countries. If it becomes known that arbitration is being used as a device for evading the public policy of states which have a governmental interest in regulating certain business transactions, its reputation may suffer."

In the same vein, Derains also wrote that:

> "*L'arbitre a des devoirs vis-à-vis des parties pour le compte desquelles il remplit sa mission, mais il en a aussi vis-à-vis de la communauté du commerce international, la Societas Mercatorum, laquelle a besoin à la fois de l'arbitrage et de relations harmonieuses avec les Etats. Or, s'il suffisait de recourir à l'arbitrage pour se soustraire à des lois de police ayant un titre légitime à s'appliquer, c'est bientôt la survie de l'arbitrage lui-même qui serait mise en cause par les Etats qui l'ont favorisé jusqu'ici. L'arbitrage international est un instrument au service des parties et à cet égard, il est indispensable qu'il préserve son autonomie vis-à-vis des Etats. Mais cette autonomie n'est acceptable par la communauté internationale que si l'arbitrage est capable d'être autre chose que le comptable d'intérêts particuliers et s'il sait sauvegarder un certain nombre de valeurs supérieures à ces intérêts.*"[94]

As a consequence of their legal and moral obligations, arbitrators should in the first place raise ex officio all violations of international public policy. Moreover, those violations and more generally, all substantial violations – whether unethical, wrongful or illegal – of the fundamental principles of arbitral procedure, should be clearly, directly, immediately and efficiently dealt with by the arbitral tribunal. Of course, the attitude of the arbitrators will depend upon the circumstances of the case, the type of wrongful conduct and the moment at which the issue arises. What one expects is a strong and proactive arbitral tribunal, committed to the integrity and fairness of the arbitral process and to the values of justice and good morals. Depending upon the type of situation, the arbitrators should use all available legal means to oppose the attempt at obstructing or derailing the arbitral process by a party, as in the *HCE v. ROI* case;[95] after having given each side the opportunity to comment on a misdeed or an illegality in the procedure, they will intimate – whenever possible – to the wrongdoer to immediately discontinue its wrongful course of conduct. They will order, when appropriate, the immediate communication of concealed documents under subpoena when available, draw adverse inferences, or even, in extreme situations, grant the request of the other party to dismiss the case. In their award, they will not only recite and stigmatize the facts but to the extent the latter are clearly established, they will also, whenever appropriate, express a judgment on the attitude of the party which is at the origin of the misdeed.

If the misdeed is in fact the arbitrator's, the co-arbitrator or the chairman, depending upon the circumstances, should raise the issue with him and if the facts are established, put him on notice to put an immediate end to the misconduct, and report to the

---

94. Y. DERAINS, "Les tendances de la jurisprudence arbitrale internationale", JDI (1993) p. 829 at p. 846 and note under ICC award no. 6142 of 1990, JDI (1990) p. 1039 ; "Pouvoirs et obligations de l'arbitre" in *Competition and Arbitration Law* (ICC Institute) p. 251 at pp. 257-258.

95. See above fn. 37 et seq.

institution to allow it to take the measures which on the basis of its rules, appear appropriate.[96]

But in all cases, the arbitral tribunal should avoid any unnecessary measure, action or expression which might jeopardize or make the enforcement of the award more difficult.

On the other hand, I think it is normally the parties and not the arbitrators who should report a case of unethical conduct on the part of a lawyer or an expert to the bar or other professional authorities. If a particular misdeed could be categorized as a criminal offence, parties should report to the district attorney. The arbitrators should if necessary draw the attention of the parties to their responsibilities in this respect. The issue needs to be further discussed and analyzed, however, given the great variety of national statutes and rules and the fact that in many jurisdictions, the rule of professional secrecy applies to members of the bar but not to arbitrators as such. The matter becomes further complicated when the offence has not been committed at the seat of the arbitration.

Finally, what may be expected from arbitral institutions in the various cases of misconduct described above? It appears that institutions consider that their role in this area is relatively limited and that it is for the arbitral tribunal to take the decisions which appear appropriate depending upon the circumstances. The only type of situation in which institutions have a specific role to play is in relation to a misconduct by an arbitrator, as the latter is bound by strict rules of ethics. If he does not comply with these rules, he may be removed, either following a challenge by one of the parties, or ex officio by the institution itself.[97] Other types of misconduct should definitely be reported to the institution but apart from unofficial contacts between the secretariat and the counsel for the party concerned, there is little that institutions are able or willing to do. The appropriate action or decision on these issues is the responsibility of the arbitral tribunal.

---

96. See also IBA Ethics no. 5(4):

"If an arbitrator becomes aware that a fellow arbitrator has been in improper communication with a party, he may inform the remaining arbitrators and they should together determine what action should be taken. Normally, the appropriate initial course of action is for the offending arbitrator to be requested to refrain from making any further improper communications with the party. Where the offending arbitrator fails or refuses to refrain from improper communications, the remaining arbitrators may inform the innocent party in order that he may consider what action he should take. An arbitrator may act unilaterally to inform a party of the conduct of another arbitrator in order to allow the said party to consider a challenge of the offending arbitrator only in extreme circumstances, and after communicating its intention to its fellow arbitrators in writing."

97. Art. 12 ICC Rules; Art. 10 LCIA Rules.

Corruption and Other Illegality in the Formation and Performance Of Contracts and in the Conduct of Arbitration Relating Thereto

*Karen Mills**

I.   INTRODUCTION

Asia has no monopoly on corruption. Ubiquitous and pernicious, corruption respects neither international boundaries nor national laws. It is so widespread not only in Asia but also in Europe,[1] Africa and South America, probably providing a significant portion of civil servants' family income, that it is simply accepted as a way of life and rarely even mentioned. This "everyday" corruption is seen as just another cost of living, although it is often on this level that cosmetic attempts to clean up are directed. Corruption on the general private business level, where kickbacks are given to procurement personnel and "grease" to regulatory officials – the "cancer of commerce" – is also generally widespread and becomes an element in the transaction's costing that has to be borne by the businessman and/or ultimate consumer.

---

* Karim Sani Law Firm, Jakarta, Indonesia; J.D., F. CI Arb., F. SI Arb., F. HKI Arb., Chartered Arbitrator.
1. See, e.g., THEIL and DICKEY, "Europe's Dirty Secret", Newsweek (international edition) 24 April 2002.

But it is corruption at a higher level – in public infrastructure projects – that is of more serious concern. The cost of this type of corruption, augmented by multiple profit-margins along the way, has to be borne by the taxpayer. Moreover, we must also differentiate between infrastructure projects of a commercial nature, such as construction of a road or airport or development of an oilfield or mine, and those for the provision of basic needs of and services to the populace, such as clean water, electricity and telecommunications. In these latter cases, the cost and other damage of the corruption must be borne doubly by the populace – as recipients of the public services and as taxpayers.

Unfortunately it is unlikely that the governments of the countries in which corruption is rife will be able, or even have much political will, to eradicate it. Possibly not ever. So many of those in power are too involved, or their families are. And it is generally accepted that, at least in Indonesia, most of the middle class has grown out of this corruption – starting their businesses or funding their children's higher education from the fruits of this "black economy" or its trickle-down. No wonder there are few sincere efforts to reform.

Arbitrations in any jurisdiction often run across corruption in its more common, lower, levels. But it is on the higher level, with public infrastructure projects, that it is most imperative that the greatest degree of diligence in scrutiny for corruption must be applied by a tribunal because, although, as mentioned above, it is the populace that will be most affected, the populace has no advocate in the arbitral reference. We, as arbitrators, take on this additional responsibility, sitting as we do *in locus curiae*. One might even question whether public policy should not reserve to the courts of the land disputes affecting the livelihood of its populace, seeing that the populace never agreed to have foreign arbitrators determine their interests: what they will have to pay for electricity, water or telecommunications, and whether the same will be available to them even if they are able so to pay.

In order to fight corruption, we must be able to recognize it. And to do that requires an understanding of how it is manifest in the applicable venue which, in turn, requires more than a little knowledge of the politics and culture of that venue. It would be nothing short of negligence were we to believe we can evaluate Asian conduct by western paradigm.

This paper will discuss some of the ways corruption works, particularly in infrastructure projects, and how we, as arbitrators, might deal with it. Corruption of arbitrators is also discussed. Indonesia is used as an example because that is the jurisdiction in which this writer is based; because the country is notorious for the depth and breadth of its corrupt systems; and also because there have been some high profile Indonesian infrastructure arbitrations recently as a result of the Asian economic crisis, and we may be seeing more in due course.

II.   HOW CORRUPTION IS MANIFEST

Where foreign, or even local, contractors wish to invest in infrastructure projects, they normally seek a concession of some sort from the local and / or central government, such as an exclusive right over a certain geographical area, either for exploration and exploitation or for market. This concession is akin to a monopoly of sorts, or a license to control the area and receive "rents". The officials vested with the authority to grant such concessions also see that authority as their right to rents, or to obtain personal profit from the exercise appropriate to the quantum of the concession being awarded. This, of necessity, increases the cost to the host government or its people, since the investor will seek to recoup from project revenue, or even from project costs, the improper payments it has made.

When such a contract breaks down, which it is likely to do where its terms are stacked against the host country, the result of the collusion of unscrupulous foreign businessmen with officials acting contrary to the mandate of their position can be devastating losses to their nation and its people. Failure on the part of a tribunal to recognize this can have, and has in fact had, disastrous results.

1. Corruption in the Awarding of the Project

Indonesian law requires any contract of greater than a virtually nominal value[2] that in any way affects the state treasury to be bid at open[3] or limited[4] tender, and any contact that is not so tendered is invalid.[5] Tender is essential to ensure that both pricing and quality are competitive. In infrastructure projects tender is all the more necessary so that the populace affected will not be overcharged for, or deprived of, its basic needs.[6]

Probably only three or at most four of the twenty-seven independent power projects awarded in Indonesia since the early 1990s were tendered. The rest were "arranged" through collusion and corrupt means. Interestingly none of those few projects that were tendered have been the subject of arbitrations thus far. Technically all of the contracts upon which the recent arbitrations have been held were thus illegal and invalid.

With or without tender, there is often something of an underground "auction" where the prospective investors not only have to compete for the official terms, but also for the underground payment to be made to the licensing or awarding officials themselves. This kind of corruption may be initiated by the officials, but is more often initiated by the foreign investors who, over the years, have learned that the easiest way to obtain a project is handsomely to reward those with the power to grant it. Often heads of state

---

2. Indonesian Rupiah 50,000,000, roughly equivalent to US$ 5,000.00 at current exchange rate.

3. Openly publicized and open to any number of bidders.

4. Requiring tender by at least five selected bidders.

5. See, inter alia, Art. 33 of the Indonesian Constitution of 1945; the Indonesian Mining Law (Law No. 37 of 1967); the Oil and Gas Law (Law No. 44 of 1960) and Presidential Decree No. 16 of 1994.

6. See, inter alia, Asian Wall Street Journal, 9 February 1994; WALDMAN and SOLOMON, "US Deals in Indonesia Draw Flak", Asian Wall Street Journal, 24 December 1998; Dan MURPHY, "Trouble on the Grid", Far Eastern Economic Review, 21 October 1999; and "The Fate of 26 IPP Projects", Petrominer magazine, 21 August 1998, in which it is noted: "In accomplishing the contracts, practices of collusion, corruption and nepotism were rampant, resulting in the high price of private electricity."

(such as Soeharto during his reign) or other powerful politicians simply order the granting authorities to award the contracts to companies owned or controlled by their family members or cronies.

2. Foreign Government Intervention

Where substantial infrastructure projects are involved we may even find the government of the investor playing a role in the "corruption" by exerting political or economic pressure upon the host country government to award the contract to its nationals rather than to others. Some European countries, as well as Japan and South Korea, have long been noted for lobbying host governments to move business to their nationals, whether or not the host country even needs these projects. Recently the United States has joined in this kind of lobbying.

> "Corruption can lead not only to individual agreements that are not the best deals that could have been negotiated, from the public point of view, but also to more capacity than needed, since each contract can carry some side payments. The former head of PLN has, for example, stated publicly that he was 'told' to sign power agreements, even though it was clear that the total amount of power being contracted exceed likely demand and distribution capacity."[7]

In April of 1995 the then CEO of Indonesia's state-owned electricity provider, Perusahaan Listrik Negara (PLN) was summoned to Hanover, Germany, to attend a ceremony with Soeharto, Helmut Kohl and then Technology Minister (and later President), Habibie, at which a number of projects involving Germany and Indonesia were signed. At the ceremony he was ordered to sign the contract for the Paiton II electricity generation plant, a substantial project to which he had never agreed.[8]

Pressure by the US government is normally aggressive and political in nature, tending to disregard the improprieties of the US companies it is seeking to assist, despite the Foreign Corrupt Practices Act (FCPA).[9] In 1994 US government officials made several visits to Indonesia to try to push deals through for consortia led by US companies. In

---

7. Louis T. WELLS, "Private Foreign Investment in Infrastructure: Managing Non-commercial Risk", paper prepared for World Bank conference in Rome, Italy, September 1999, Sect. 2.4.

8. See, inter alia, "The Fate of 26 IPP Projects", *op cit.*, fn. 6, in which former President Director of PLN, Djiteng Marsudi, is paraphrased as stating:

   "This (Paiton II) project owned by Germany's Siemens, Britain's Power Gen and Bumipertiwi Tatapradipta, is controlled by Soeharto's son Bambang Trihatmodjo. The signing of the contract was conducted in 1995 during a state visit of the then Indonesia's President Soeharto to Germany. Refusing to sign means suicide. This was how on the average the contracts with the IPP's usually came about."

9. US companies will try to persuade us that their conduct does not violate the FCPA because their payments are made to, and/or partnerships forged with, not the sitting government officials themselves but only their cronies and family members.

January of that year there were three delegations of US officials, one led by then Treasury Secretary Lloyd Bentsen, to try to push the Paiton I project.[10] In December of that same year, the late US Secretary of Commerce, Ron Brown, came to visit Indonesia just at the time that the terms of several private geothermal power contracts were being negotiated with US companies. Although many of the commercial terms were still in dispute and PLN could not accept the financial ramifications of the combination of 100 percent "take-or-pay" provisions with ease to expand scope of production being pushed by the foreign consortia, nor certain other terms, the US government and OPIC, backed by the national oil company, Pertamina, which had a hand in the awarding (without tender) of these contracts in the first place, put political pressure on the Soeharto government to speed up the negotiations so that the contracts could be signed during Brown's visit. Much to the dismay of PLN, its then President Director was "ordered" to sign five such contracts[11] at a ceremony to mark Brown's visit, and to accept the terms being pushed by Pertamina and the foreign investors, regardless of their imbalance and the fact that doing so would result in production of more power than Indonesia would need in the proposed time frame, and for which inflated payment would have to be made in US dollars in violation of applicable law.[12]

3. Influential Partners

Most infrastructure projects in Indonesia have been granted to consortia involving one or more foreign companies and one or more local companies. Although most fields do not impose any legal requirement for a local partner, it is often made clear to the foreign party or parties that they will only be awarded the contract if they take a designated local entity as partner. These entities normally belong to a crony or family member of one of the top governing officials: if not of the President, then of the Vice President or a powerful Minister.

> "The independent power programme attracted a swarm of Suharto cronies in the early 1990's. Virtually all 27 private power contracts have relatives of former President Suharto or cabinet ministers as partners and virtually none of them were awarded on the basis of competitive bidding. 'The way to get your project approved was to have very strong political back-up, or a member of Suharto family on your team' says Djiteng Marsudi, a former PLN president who oversaw the contracts. 'I couldn't stop it.'"[13]

It was recently noted in the international press how surprising it was that there was no participation of the Soehartos in any of the fixed-line telecommunications joint

---

10. See Asian Wall Street Journal, 9 February 1994, and WALDMAN and SOLOMON, *op. cit.*, fn. 6.
11. For the Dieng, Kamojang, Karaha Bodas, Patuha and Wayang Windu projects.
12. Presidential Decree No. 37 of 1992.
13. Dan MURPHY, *op. cit.*, fn. 6.

operations (known as KSOs) awarded to foreign contractors.[14] Probably the "family" knew at the time that only cellular services, in which they are heavily involved, would prove profitable and thus were not interested in the KSO programme. But the fact remains that it has long been universally understood that without the "right" partner no contractor – foreign or local – would be likely to win a major project, tendered or not. Needless to say, the "right" partner is not an inexpensive proposition.

4. Free Carry

And make no mistake: the local partners rarely, if ever, make any capital contribution to the project. They will normally be given a share of between 10 percent and 30 percent of the project in return for their "liaison" services only. Usually these local partners will also be paid princely sums up front, and/or given the opportunity to convert part or all of their share to cash at an early juncture, such as by selling a portion back to the foreign parties at inflated value. This "free-carry" and other outlays must be grossed-up into the pricing. Other opportunities to profit at initial stages may also be granted. In one major coal-powered electricity project the local partner's affiliate was appointed as the sole supplier of coal. And in many, if not all, private power projects, including those subject to recent arbitrations, the local partners' affiliates or principals were granted various ambiguous consulting contracts at high rates. All of this is costed to the project and will eventually be borne by the populace.

5. Overpricing and Fictitious Payments

Another form that corruption may take is overpricing in supply and service contracts. Generally one member of a contractor consortium will act as, or designate an affiliate to be, main contractor for the procurement and construction. In this way that partner stands between the project company and its suppliers and service providers, often re-invoicing the project at highly inflated costs for plant, equipment, supplies and services. Japanese, French and German contractors are notorious for such practices, and we are seeing a similar trend with US-based companies as well.

The foreign partner, or its parent, may act as intermediary in "arranging" the financing for the project, and charge inordinately large commissions and/or finder's fees for such "services". In one of the cases which went to arbitration more than US$ 40,000,000 of such fees were claimed as "costs", while such funds had simply been moved from one pocket to the other of the claimant's group. In the end this double windfall to the foreign claimants will fall upon the Indonesian taxpayers to bear.

Project funds may also be siphoned off into private pockets through the creation of

---

14. See Asian Wall Street Journal, 15 April, 2002: "Telkom Will Take Control of Private Phone Company":

"Foreign Bidders: Eager to get a piece of Indonesia's then-booming economy, dozens of foreign companies had bid to be Telkom's KSO partners. In a surprise outcome, none of the foreign winners were partnered with relatives of then-President Suharto, a rare case in which his family didn't get a role in infrastructure development."

fictitious payments and obligations. Fake invoices and receipts are easy to generate, and commonly used to justify skimming of cash in every kind of business, at least in developing countries. Where questioned, the burden of proof to establish the authenticity of these should be shifted to the party claiming reimbursement for any such alleged payments. In one of the recent arbitrations the claimants claimed over US$ 8,000,000 for unexplained consulting fees paid to related parties. In the same reference, claimants were also awarded over US$ 7,000,000 as reimbursement for alleged purchases of project-related land, despite the fact that the underlying contracts make it very clear that all land would be provided by, and be and remain the property of, Pertamina. No land title documentation was provided and very substantial payments were justified by the presentation of unofficial receipts allegedly issued by local community officials and some only by book entries with no receipts at all. Those payments were characterized by independent financial advisors from a "Big-5" accounting house as more than suspicious and as one of the more common means applied in Indonesian projects to hide corrupt payments and/or skim off cash.

III.   WHAT SHOULD A TRIBUNAL DO WHEN THERE IS ANY INDICATION OF CORRUPTION?

1.   Jurisdiction

Where the corruption is clear and is of a nature that calls into question the validity of the underlying contract, the question which faces the tribunal is whether or not it has jurisdiction to adjudicate a dispute falling under such contract. If, under the governing law, the corruption or illegality is of a nature that gives rise only to the right to invalidate the contract, clearly under the doctrine of separability the arbitration may continue and the tribunal is then faced with the question of how to treat the corruption as a legal or factual matter. On the other hand, where under the governing law the nature of the corruption voids the contract in its entirety ab initio, then the question becomes whether the arbitration clause ever existed and consequently whether the tribunal has jurisdiction to adjudicate at all. The writer is advised that Mr. Kreindler has discussed this issue very thoroughly in his paper for this session and thus we need not cover the same ground here.[15] We must not neglect to consider, however, the omnipresent potential conflict between the interest of every arbitrator to earn his arbitration fee and the interests of justice which might rightly call for relinquishment of jurisdiction in some such cases.

Let us then consider the situation where the corruption or illegality does not obliterate the arbitral jurisdiction, but indeed calls into question substantive matters affecting the rendering of the award.

---

15. See this volume, pp. 209-260.

2.   In-Depth Examination

It is clear that, like most crimes and intentional misconduct, and perhaps more so, acts of corruption and collusion are specifically designed not to be able to be identified or detected. That is why the kinds of payments referred to above are made in such circuitous manner. It is an unfortunate fact of life that probably the majority of infrastructure projects in developing countries contain elements of such corruption. Possibly all do. How can we, as arbitrators sitting on tribunals established to adjudicate disputes that have arisen under such projects, ensure that we do not allow ourselves to overlook such corruption and, by so doing, perpetuate the damage that has been inflicted thereby?

Requiring a party which was not party to the questionable transaction and which has no access to data or documentation maintained by the other party to present evidence or prove the corruption of such activities is not only unrealistic but may be tantamount to aiding and abetting such corruption. This is particularly true in civil law jurisdictions where there are no discovery procedures to allow access to documentation in the possession of the other party. It is in this kind of situation that we, as arbitrators, must take particular care not to allow ourselves to be "railroaded" or tricked by the same kind of unscrupulous conduct that brought about the corrupt practices in the first place.

Clearly if we are to uphold justice, and not only the letter of questionable contracts, the most rigorous examination must be made in any case which smacks of corruption or illegality. Such an examination cannot be restricted only to documents and evidence presented by the parties themselves. Certainly the corrupt party will make every effort to obscure or disguise the corrupt conduct. And often the party victim of such corruption, which in infrastructure projects may be the government-related party, will have been denied access to the evidence necessary to establish it and/or, worse, prohibited from presenting what evidence they may have by the very officials who benefited. Where there is any indication of corruption at all, it would be nothing short of negligent were we simply to look the other way and reward possible wrongdoers for their misdeeds. Often a study of the history of the institutions involved, and of the local and international press which tends diligently to police such situations in its role as purveyor of transparency, can enlighten us to the reality of the situation when the evidence produced by the parties is lacking. At the very least, before embarking on an assignment to arbitrate a major infrastructure dispute, we will need to know who holds what power in the subject society and how the exercise of such power is funded.

3.   Shifting of Burden of Proof

Because of the near impossibility to "prove" corruption, where there is a reasonable indication of corruption, an appropriate way to make a determination may be to shift the burden of proof to the allegedly corrupt party to establish that the legal and good faith requirements were in fact duly met.

For example, where the allegation is failure to tender, had tender in fact been held it would be a simple matter for the tendering party to produce its tender documents and official notice of award to disprove the allegation. But how can the party not involved "prove" the negative: that no tender was in fact held? Where the allegation is overpricing, the party handling the payment need only show that the purchase price paid by it and the price charged to the project do not differ by a material amount. Where true, such proof is easy to obtain. But how can the party who did not handle the transaction prove how much "discrepancy" was pocketed by the contractor?

4. Sanctions

In many jurisdictions, and certainly in Indonesia, no jurisdiction to impose criminal sanctions is granted to an arbitral tribunal. Their jurisdiction may only cover commercial matters and only those which the parties themselves would have legal authority to settle.[16] Thus only commercial sanctions may be imposed or financial relief denied, as appropriate. Mention of the misconduct may be made in the award and, if verging on serious criminal behavior, the court in which the award is sought to be enforced may take it upon itself to take action against the offender. This writer has not heard of any such case, but it would not be inappropriate in certain situations.

At the very least, whatever action a tribunal deems appropriate to take, it should guard very closely against rewarding an arbitrating party for corrupt or illegal practices. Questionable payments which a claimant fails to substantiate and funds that have been siphoned off by a claimant should not, under any circumstances, be awarded to them again.

IV. MISCONDUCT/CORRUPTION OF ARBITRATORS

1. Financial Corruption

Of the types of misdeeds that may occur in the conduct of an arbitrator, the most intolerable is financial corruption. We must always keep in mind the omnipresent interest of every arbitrator to earn his fee and the ramifications that may have: tendency to assume or confirm jurisdiction so that the fee may be earned; prolonging and complicating, or allowing a party to complicate, a reference so as to bill more days or hours (where the fee is based on time); leaning towards a party or its counsel that is more likely to have the opportunity to re-appoint the arbitrator in a future reference;[17] as well as the rare (let us hope) but nonetheless occasional case in which an arbitrator's income will be directly proportional to the award. This latter is, by definition, the most difficult to identify and certainly to prove, but it is also the most devastating to balancing the rights of parties and to the interests of justice.

Financial corruption can be all the more likely in references in which each party directly pays the fees of its party-appointed arbitrator and only the fee of the chair is shared. This can lead to a perception on the part of a party-appointed arbitrator that he

---

16. Art. 5, Law No. 30 of 1999 (the Arbitration Law).
17. For example, the scandal relating to HMO arbitration with Kaiser Permanente and other HMO medical providers in California in recent years (see various reporting by Transparency International: http://www.transparency.org/press_moni.html).

should be acting as advocate for the party that appointed (and pays) him.

The writer has reviewed a number of contracts, particularly those prepared by UK firms, that call for arbitration before two party-appointed arbitrators and only if those two do not agree will they mutually appoint a third who will act as "referee", while the two party-appointed arbitrators become advocates for their own point of view. This arrangement may have had some success in the "old days", before US litigators got into the act and arbitration was widely understood to be a cooperative effort between gentlemen counsel mutually seeking to reach the "truth", rather than the "no-holds-barred" all out war it has become today. In today's world this system is nothing short of dangerous. It should not be encouraged in any situation for it will certainly breed intellectual corruption if not outright financial corruption.

2. Intellectual Corruption

Intellectual corruption is certainly far more common. Preconceived notions, prejudices and opinions of an arbitrator will always threaten to color his impartiality and ability to see the matter in a clear and balanced manner. We seem to be seeing this more and more where western arbitrators sit to adjudicate disputes between western and "Third World" parties. Intellectual corruption in these cases may range from simple cultural misunderstanding through cultural bias to actual racism. There is, unfortunately, still a widespread prejudice on the part of many westerners who perceive that Third World cultures are inferior to, and its citizens less intelligent than, their own countrymen or their own race. A western arbitrator may pay greater credence to a western witness than to an Asian one, even where the local witness may be a recognized expert in his or her field. The western witness not only speaks the same, or a similar language, as the western arbitrator, but also approaches his analysis from the western point of view, even though this may be completely irrelevant to the project or contract at hand. Our challenge is to guard against falling into this ethnocentric trap.

The courts of any country are often suspected of being nationalistically biased. But court judgments will be subject to review by a higher court, whereas an arbitral award invariably will not. Therefore, although arbitrators have more freedom to allow their personal prejudices to govern, we must be very much on our guard against such a tendency precisely because there is no effective review of the awards which we render.

It is thus our duty, if we accept an appointment to adjudicate a dispute involving a culture of which we are not conversant, to make every effort to familiarize ourselves with the cultural idiosyncrasies of the parties. And when governments or government-related bodies are involved, a study of the history and political environment is also essential.

For example, a visitor to Indonesia, such as a foreign arbitrator, will see it as a single homogeneous culture. But everyone living or working in Indonesia is aware of the vast cultural diversity to the extent that one needs to know from which of Indonesia's hundreds of ethnic groups[18] a person comes in order even to understand what he or she

---

18. According to the US Central Intelligence Agency, there are over 300 distinct cultures. See VREELAND et. al., *Area Handbook for Indonesia*, 3rd ed. (Washington, DC, 1975).

says. Javanese (from central and east Java) are the most self-contained and courteous people in the world and will rarely give an open and full response to any question, for fear of offending someone. On the other hand, the Bataks (from north Sumatra) are extremely outspoken and forceful. Other cultures fall somewhere in between or have their own idiosyncrasies. How can a foreign arbitrator unfamiliar with the culture hope to assess witness testimony without in-depth study of the local culture?

V.   WHAT SHOULD AN ARBITRATOR DO WHEN FACED WITH CORRUPTION ON THE TRIBUNAL?

This is, of course, the most difficult question to address. If one arbitrator in a panel of three suspects one of the others of corruption, prejudice or even bad faith, the first course of action would be to discuss the matter directly with the offending arbitrator. If after such discussion, the concerned arbitrator is not satisfied, he must look to the law and the rules governing the reference. If the reference is administered by an institution, the matter should be brought to the attention of it supervisory board. If, however, it is an ad hoc arbitration and no guidance is provided in the governing law or rules, what can be done? As long as the second arbitrator sees eye to eye with the investigating arbitrator, no harm may be inflicted on the parties if the award reflects the views of their non-corrupt majority. However, if the offending arbitrator is able to influence the third arbitrator to his point view, and a miscarriage of justice will result from the award, the investigating arbitrator is left with a difficult dilemma. Of course he may write a dissenting opinion; or possibly make a report to the law society with jurisdiction over the offending arbitrator. Unfortunately many arbitrators are not lawyers and there may be no professional organization to which they are answerable.

There is no easy answer to this question, and as a result it is probable that such conduct normally passes unremedied and unsanctioned. But this must, of necessity, result in a miscarriage of justice and leads to perpetuation of the corrupt conduct. One solution might be for the arbitrator who believes there has been corruption by one or more of the others, and that corruption has resulted in an unjust award, not only to write a dissenting opinion, stating his perception therein, but also to step down from the tribunal, making his reasons clear. This may or may not rectify the damage in the instant case, but it would at least bring the offender to the public view and perhaps prevent further such damage.

There has been considerable discussion in recent arbitration conferences about the need for a mechanism for review of arbitral awards that are not otherwise subject thereto. As the New York Convention[19] imposed certain standards for enforcement of foreign arbitral awards, and the UNCITRAL Rules have provided an international standard of procedural rules for ad hoc arbitrations, perhaps the time has come to go the next step, by providing an UNCITRAL-based award review board to ensure such misconduct as corruption, breach of natural justice and willful disregard for governing

---

19. 1958 United Nations Convention on the Recognition and Enforcement of Foreign Arbitral Awards.

law shall not pass unrectified.

VI.   CONCLUSION

Arbitrators hold a unique position in international commerce. The jurisdiction with which we are often invested spans international cultures and a multitude of diverse laws and legal systems. No judge in any court has such responsibility. Part of that responsibility is to ensure that corrupt practices cannot take hold of the arbitral process. Where arbitrating in a culture with which we are not familiar, it is not an easy task to identify the corruption and deal with it in an effective way. We must exercise the most rigorous degree of sensitivity and scrutiny so as not to fail.

This responsibility seems to feed a growing trend among some western arbitrators to consider that international arbitration stands above the law of any individual jurisdiction, and that such arbitrators are more powerful than the governments and courts of the jurisdictions in which they operate, and thereby qualified to make awards unencumbered by local laws, policies, politics and customs. But arbitrators are only human. But we must not forget that we, too, are fallible and not allow the position of power granted to us as arbitrators to create in us such arrogance as to eclipse the fact that we are still subject to the laws of the lands in which we operate. When we enter into a culture which we do not understand, operating under laws with which we are not familiar, with an attitude towards respect for and compliance with such laws that is also alien to us, and particularly those with a history of corrupt practices, we can no longer rely entirely upon our own judgment and instincts which have been forged in our own and similar societies.

Cultural understanding and sensitivity, or the lack thereof, is perhaps the single major cause of international disputes in the first place. Let us not fall into the same trap as does the western businessman who closes a deal in unknown territory without first doing his homework. Without judicial review of our awards we are under a far higher obligation to be as diligent and vigilant as we are able to ensure that we do not become an unwitting party to corruption and injustice.

The Challenge of Awards on the Basis of Criminal Acts

*Christoph Liebscher**

I.   INTRODUCTION

This paper will briefly compare the possibility to challenge an award on the basis of criminal acts under the arbitration laws of Austria, England, France, Germany and Switzerland.

In three different situations arbitration may be faced with crime:

— when the arbitration agreement itself is obtained by a criminal act, e.g., fraud,[1]
— when the underlying transaction is illegal, or
— when criminal acts have occurred in connection with or influenced the course of the arbitration proceedings.

This paper will deal with the third aspect.

Due to the fact that the situation in challenge and enforcement proceedings is comparable and given the fact that court decisions are not abundant, some court decisions in enforcement proceedings are included as well.

II.   GROUNDS FOR CHALLENGE

1.   *General Aspects*

a.   Austria
Statutory law allows the challenge of an award because of certain criminal acts.

---

*   Attorney-at-law, Wolf Theiss, Vienna-Prague-Belgrade-Bratislava-Zagreb-Ljubljana; MBA (INSEAD), FCIArb.
1.   Cf. for France: Cass. 11 June 1991, *Orri v. Société des Lubrifiants Elf Aquitaine*, Rev Arb (1992) p. 73 with note by D. COHEN; M. de BOISSÉSON, "L'arbitrage et la fraude (à propos de l'arrêt *Fougerolle*, rendu par la Cour de Cassation le 25 May 1992)", Rev Arb (1993) p. 3 at p. 5 et seq.

Generally, according to Sect. 595(1) no. 7 Code of Civil Procedure (CCP) an award may be challenged for certain reasons which would also allow the reopening of a court case pursuant to Sect. 530 nos. 1-7 CCP. From these seven cases only numbers 1-3 refer to criminal acts:

i.   Forgery of an official document or certificate (Sect. 530 (1) no. 1 CCP)
Applying Sect. 530(1) no. 1 CCP to arbitration allows the award to be set aside if it is based on a document which is forged or falsified. Sects. 223 (falsification of official documents), 224 (falsification of protected documents) or 228 (false certification or legalization of documents) Penal Code are the main offences in this context. Examples of this type of criminal act are the forging of receipts,[2] registration plates[3] or passports.[4]

ii.   False testimony (Sect. 530(1) no. 2 CCP)
This second ground for setting aside applies where false testimony is given pursuant to Sect. 288 Penal Code. It covers the false testimony of witnesses and experts as well as perjury committed by a witness, expert or party. This provision refers only to court proceedings. The question therefore arises whether false evidence given before an arbitral tribunal allows the challenge of an award pursuant to Sect. 595(2) no. 7 in conjunction with Sect. 530(1) no. 2 CCP.

The Supreme Court has ruled that false testimony before an arbitral tribunal does not constitute a criminal act under Austrian law and that it does not lead to criminal prosecution in Austria.[5] Therefore, such false testimony cannot form the basis for the setting aside of an award. Sect. 530(1) no. 2 CCP will only apply in the – rather rare – cases where the arbitral tribunal bases its award on the false testimony given in municipal court proceedings.

Written witness statements which are not correct do not per se allow a challenge.[6]

Sect. 530(1) no. 3 CCP contains a catalogue of diverse criminal acts committed by the representative of the party or of the opposing party, or by the opposing party itself such as wilful misrepresentation, embezzlement, fraud, forgery of public seals, indirect false recording or certification, suppression of documents and displacement of border marks. As regards false testimony or allegations of a party, this in itself does not constitute the element of "deceit" as required for fraud by Sect. 146 Penal Code.[7] However, if additional means of deception are employed, such as falsified or forged documents, this amounts to the criminal act of fraud viz. procedural fraud.[8]

In all of the above cases the award may only be challenged on the basis of a final and binding criminal conviction (Sect. 539 CCP) and if there is a causal link between the

---

2. OGH 5 December 1978 (1978) 51 SZ no. 172.
3. OGH 1 June 1965 [1966] EvBl no. 43.
4. OGH 3 November 1982 [1983] ZVR no. 88.
5. OGH 1 December 1954 Neuteufel no. 277.
6. OGH 13 May 1931 [1931] GH 214.
7. OGH 2 March 1971 [1971] EvBl no. 256; 12 April 1969 [1970] EvBl no. 186.
8. OGH 10 December 1975 [1976] EvBl no. 162; 1 December 1970 [1971] EvBl no. 241; 19 May 1967 [1968] EvBl no. 248; 3 March 1966 (1966) 37 SSt no. 7.

criminal act and the award (Sect. 530(1) CCP).[9]

b. England

One of the irregularities under Sect. 68(2)(g) Arbitration Act 1996 (AA 1996) is that an award may be challenged if it was obtained by fraud, or if the award was otherwise obtained contrary to public policy. It is generally recognized that English public policy can be violated by a failure to comply with requirements of natural justice or on the ground of illegality.[10]

"Fraud" has been defined as "some act of deceit perpetrated on the arbitral tribunal (e.g., providing the arbitral tribunal with falsified certificates of ownership of property claimed), or on the other party (i.e., if the arbitral tribunal was a party to the fraud)".[11]

It is also considered to be a ground for challenge if evidence is suppressed due to a fraudulent act by one of the parties.[12]

Sect. 68(2)(g) AA 1996 was at issue in *Cuflet Chartering*.[13] The claimant alleged that the respondent had misled it by conduct, which would violate public policy. The owner sued the charterers for unpaid hire. The charterers did not serve a reply and entered into settlement negotiations. The arbitrator extended the time for filing the reply but made clear that it would render an award were the new time limit not met. Moore-Bick J. summarized as follows:

> "It will be apparent from this brief summary of ... submissions that Cuflet's case turns not simply on the allegation that the [respondents] acted in a devious and underhand manner, but that they did so in a way which misled Cuflet into thinking that they had taken steps to prevent [the arbitrator] from proceeding to an award and that if Cuflet had been aware of the true position it could and would have taken steps itself to protect its interests."[14]

Further, Moore-Bick J. indicated the necessary requirements to be able to invoke fraud under Sect. 68(2)(g) AA 1996 as follows:

> "Public policy is capable of covering a wide variety of matters and it is neither necessary nor desirable in this case to attempt to define the circumstances in which sub-section (2)(g) is capable of being invoked. However, where, as in the present case, one party to arbitration proceedings bases his complaint on the manner in which the other conducted himself in relation to the proceedings, I doubt whether anything short of unconscionable conduct would justify the Court in setting aside the award. [The arbitrator] was therefore right in my judgement

---

9. OGH 28 February 1990 [1992] RZ no. 63; KODEK in W. RECHBERGER, *Kommentar zur ZPO*, 2nd ed. (Vienna 2000) Sect. 530, marg. no. 3.

10. R. MERKIN, *Arbitration Law*, (London/Hong Kong 2001) marg. nos 17.58.1 et seq.

11. D. SUTTON and J. GILL, *Russell on Arbitration* (London 2003) marg. no. 8-046 in fn. 14.

12. MERKIN, *op. cit.*, fn. 10, marg. no. 18.6.

13. *Cuflet Chartering v. Carousel Shipping (The "Marie H")* [2001] 1 Lloyd's Rep 707 (QBD (Comm. Ct)).

14. *Ibid.*

to concede that it would not be enough to show that the owners had inadvertently misled Cuflet, however carelessly they might have expressed themselves. However, once it is recognised that the allegation is one of serious impropriety, it must also be recognised that cogent evidence will be required to satisfy the Court that the owners did behave in such a manner."[15]

If one takes the view that the requirement of "serious irregularity" implies some behaviour on the part of the arbitral tribunal,[16] then the scope for a challenge will be very limited. A challenge may then only be successful if the arbitral tribunal did not properly react to criminal acts tainting the arbitration which it could have discovered. Under this condition also criminal acts other than fraud may permit a challenge.

c.   France
Prior to the 1981 reform an award could be challenged in the courts when criminal acts were discovered after the award was made.[17]

The reform removed this possibility, which was severely criticized.[18] According to Sect. 1507 NCCP the revision procedure provided by Sect. 1491 NCCP does not apply to international arbitration.

In *Fougerolle*,[19] nevertheless, the Supreme Court somewhat lessened the impact of the situation by stating that as a consequence of the general principles of law relating to fraud – despite the fact that Sect. 1507 NCCP excludes a revision of an award – such revision of an award by the arbitral tribunal is, by way of exception, to be permitted in the case of fraud as long as the arbitral tribunal remains constituted after making the award or if it can be reconstituted.

Fougerolle, a subcontractor, raised a claim against the main contractor. After an award was rendered, which denied the claim, Fougerolle discovered that the main contractor had actually raised a claim against the customer on the same grounds, in particular because of bad soil conditions. However, the Supreme Court rejected the challenge of the award. The Supreme Court held that the main contractor could believe in good faith that the documents concerning its claims against the customer were not of relevance in the arbitration.

The question remains as to what happens if the arbitral tribunal no longer exists and cannot be reconstituted.[20] It has been proposed that in such a case either a challenge

---

15. *Ibid.*
16. MERKIN, *op. cit.*, fn. 10, marg. no. 13.35.
17. E. GAILLARD and J. SAVAGE, eds., *Fouchard, Gaillard Goldman on International Commercial Arbitration* (The Hague/London/Boston 1999) marg. no. 1599.
18. Cf., e.g., P. MAYER "L'insertion de la sentence dans l'ordre juridique francais" in Y. DERAINS, *Droit et pratique de l'arbitrage international en France* (Paris 1984) p. 89; E. LOQUIN, "Perspectives pour une réforme des voies de Recours", Rev Arb (1992) p. 321; P. BELLET and E. MEZGER, "L'arbitrage international dans le nouveau code de procédure civile", Rev Crit DIP (1981) p. 611 at p. 654.
19. Cass. 25 May 1992, *Fougerolle v. Procofrance*, 119 JDI (1992) p. 974.
20. Cf. de BOISSÉSON, *op. cit.*, fn. 1, p. 11.

under Sect. 1502 NCCP would be possible[21] or that a new arbitral tribunal should be constituted to decide on the request for revision.[22]

In any case, *Fougerolle* provides for a remedy which is to be addressed to the arbitral tribunal.[23]

In *Westman* the Supreme Court confirmed that an award obtained on the basis of expense accounts although no expenses were incurred violates (international) public policy.[24] Following the principle *fraus omnia corrumpit* the award was set aside as it was based on documents serving to prove expenses which had never been incurred.

Recently, the Paris Court of Appeal confirmed that the international public policy set forth in Sect. 1502(5) NCCP is violated if "fraudulent manoeuvres" by a party influenced the arbitrators' decision.[25]

However, according to Sect. 595 NCCP a revision could be based on three different types of criminal acts: fraud by a party (Sect. 595(1) no. 1 NCCP), false documents (Sect. 595(1) no. 3 NCCP) and false attestations or testimony (Sect. 595(1) no. 4 NCCP). In addition, Sect. 595(1) no. 2 NCCP provides for revision if a relevant document is discovered which was withheld by another party.

On the face of the text it could be argued that only the first case of fraud seems to be covered by this jurisprudence. This would consequently mean that no challenge could be made in the other cases. However, the Supreme Court held that the use of forged documents to support an allegation constitutes fraud under Sect. 595(1) no. 1 NCCP if the party was aware of the forgery.[26] Therefore, all four cases imply fraudulent activity.[27]

Criminal acts committed by a third party without the involvement of a party to the arbitration will not allow a challenge.

A challenge can only be successful if the fraudulent act was decisive for the outcome of the arbitration.[28]

---

21. J. SCAPEL, "L'arbitrage et la fraude (à propos de l'arrêt *Fougerolle*, rendu par la Cour de Cassation le 25 May 1992)", Dalloz Affaires (1999) p. 1431 at p. 1434; D. BUREAU note, Rev Arb (1996) p. 50 at p. 53 et seq.

22. I. FADLALLAH "Nouveau recul de la révision au fond: motivation et fraude dans la contrôle des sentences arbitrales internationales", Gaz Pal (2000, no. 336) p. 5 at p. 10.

23. Cf. for a critcial review of this approach Y. DERAINS, "La révision des sentences dans l'arbitrage international" in R. BRINER, L.Y. FORTIER, K.P. BERGER and J. BREDOW, *Law of International Business and Dispute Settlement in the 21st Century – Liber Amicorum Karl-Heinz Böckstiegel*, p. 165.

24. Cass. 19 December 1995, *Westman International v. European Gas Turbines*, Rev Arb (1996) p. 49 with note by J.-B. BUREAU.

25. CA Paris 1 March 2001, *Republic of Congo and another v. Commisimpex*, Rev Arb (2001) p. 583 with note by J.B. RACINE; 10 September 1998, *Thomson v. Brunner Sociedade Civil de Administracao Limitada and another*, Rev Arb (2001) p. 583 with note by J.-B. RACINE.

26. Cass. 22 October 1981, *Chipusso-Ello v. Russo*, Gaz Pal (1982 no. 1) p. 107.

27. S. GUINCHARD, *Droit et Pratique de la Procédure civile* (Paris 2000) marg. no. 6226 with further references; SCAPEL, *op. cit.*, fn. 21, p. 1436.

28. Cass. 17 March 1983, *Lagrange v. Aubignat*, Gaz Pal (1983 no. 2) p. 227.

d.   Germany

The former provision of Sect. 1041(6) former CCP referred to Sect. 580 CCP, which allows the reopening of a court case in certain instances.

The parliamentary documents[29] as well as a recent decision of the Supreme Court[30] stress that the grounds referred to in Sect. 1041(6) former CCP are now deemed to be included in the new Sect. 1059(2)(2)(b) CCP (violation of public policy).[31] Thus, nothing has changed in respect of the continued applicability of Sect. 580(1)-(6) CCP to arbitration. The Supreme Court considers these provisions as part of procedural public policy.[32]

According to Sect. 581 CCP a successful challenge of an award on the basis of criminal acts can only be made on the basis of a legally binding conviction on the grounds provided in Sect. 580(1)-(5) CCP.[33] The only possible exception from this requirement is where the criminal proceedings were not started for reasons other than the lack of evidence.[34] The Supreme Court has confirmed the applicability of these rules to arbitration.[35] Additionally, pursuant to Sect. 582 CCP it is necessary for the applicant to have not been able to assert the ground for revision at an earlier stage of the proceedings, although it acted diligently.

The individual criminal acts are the following:

Sect. 580(1) CCP concerns the case of sworn parties giving false testimony either in an intentional or in a grossly negligent manner.[36] The courts have held that in order to fulfil these requirements it is sufficient for the testimony to be false even only as regards an auxiliary point.[37]

Statutory law also allows a reopening of the case if the false testimony of a party was not given under oath; in this scenario Sect. 580(4) CCP applies rather than Sect. 580(1).[38] However, as the arbitral tribunal cannot administer an oath[39] this can only apply where testimony under oath is given before a municipal court, e.g., assisting the arbitral tribunal pursuant to Sect. 1050 CCP.

Sect. 580(2) CCP deals with the issue of a document which was falsely drawn up or forged. The document must have played a decisive role in the arbitration proceedings.

29. Parliamentary documents in K.P. BERGER, *Das neue Recht der Schiedsgerichtsbarkeit – The New German Arbitration Law* (Cologne 1998) p. 288.

30. BGH 2 November 2000 [2001] no. 2 RPS 12.

31. J.-P. LACHMANN, *Handbuch für die Schiedsgerichtspraxis,* 2nd ed.(Cologne 2002) marg. no. 1229; K.-H. SCHWAB and G. WALTER, *Schiedsgerichtsbarkeit*, 6th ed. (Munich 2000) chap. 24 marg. no. 51.

32. BGH 2 November 2000 [2001] NJW 373.

33. SCHWAB and WALTER, *op. cit.* fn. 31, chap. 24 marg. no. 51.

34. BGH 2 November 2000 (2001) 145 BGHZ 376.

35. Cf. fn. 32.

36. HARTMANN in A. BAUMBACH, W. LAUTERBACH, J. ALBERS and P. HARTMANN, *Zivilprozeßordnung*, 60th ed. (Munich 2002) Sect. 580, marg. no. 3.

37. RG 28 June 1932 (1932) 137 RGZ 90.

38. GREGER in R. ZÖLLER, *Zivilprozeßordnung*, 21st ed. (Cologne 2002) Sect. 580, marg. no. 8.

39. SCHWAB and WALTER, *op. cit.*, fn. 31, Chap. 17, marg. no. 1.

It is irrelevant who the forger was or who had knowledge of the act.[40] Sect. 580(2) CCP includes the falsification or forgery of electronic documents.[41]

Sect. 580(3) CCP concerns the false testimony of a witness or expert. Under Sect. 580(3) CCP it is not decisive whether the witness was under oath.[42] The provisions of the Penal Code which are applicable to this case are: Sects. 153 (false unsworn testimony), 154 (perjury), 155 (solemn affirmation), 156 (negligent false statutory declaration) and 163 (negligent false oath; negligent false statutory declaration). It is sufficient that the false testimony concerns only a possibly irrelevant point.[43] The reason for this lies in the fact that the credibility of the testimony is of tantamount importance. Thus, intended falsification in the smallest part of the testimony is likely to lead to the disqualification of it in its entirety.[44] Despite the clear wording of Sect. 580(3) CCP only false testimony of witnesses or experts can lead to the reopening of the case. False testimony by other persons participating in the proceedings (such as the parties themselves) does not allow the application of Sect. 580(3) CCP if they were not sworn, and could possibly only result in claims for damage against the person submitting the false declaration.[45]

Sect. 580(4) CCP relates to criminal acts committed by a representative of the party, by a party,[46] or by its representative in the proceedings which were decisive for the outcome of the arbitration proceedings. The following sections are amongst the provisions of the Penal Code which could find application in this context: Sects. 156 (negligent false statutory declaration), 160 (inducement to falsely testify), 239 (deprivation of liberty), 240 (duress), 263 (fraud),[47] 266 (breach of trust) and 356 (prevarication).[48]

Sect. 580(5) CCP sanctions a violation of the judge's official duties vis-à-vis the parties. Sects. 331 (acceptance of an advantage), 332 (bribery and corruption) and 336 (failure to perform official services) Penal Code are amongst the provisions held to be applicable.[49]

e.   Switzerland
The Swiss Private International Law Act (PILA) fails to provide specific provision for setting aside an award because it is based on a criminal act.

The Supreme Court explicitly recognized this shortcoming of the statutory law and

---

40. Cf. *ibid.*, Chap. 24, marg. no. 52.

41. GREGER, *op. cit.*, fn. 38, Sect. 580, marg. no. 9.

42. RG 18 December 1933 (1934) 143 RGZ 46.

43. RG 28 June 1932 (1932) 137 RGZ 90; HARTMANN, *op. cit.*, fn. 36, Sect. 580, marg. no. 5.

44. HARTMANN, *op. cit.*, fn. 36, Sect. 580, marg. nos 3 and 5.

45. OVG Koblenz 28 August 1974 [1974] RdL 333; GREGER, *op. cit.*, fn. 38, Sect. 580, marg. no. 3.

46. HARTMANN, *op cit.*, fn. 36, Sect. 580, marg. no. 6.

47. *Op. cit.*, fn. 30.

48. SCHWAB and WALTER, *op. cit.*, fn. 31, Chap. 24, marg. no. 52.

49. *Ibid.*

thus held that it is up to its own discretion to fill this gap.[50] In doing so, the Supreme Court ruled that the provisions of the Federal Judicial Organization Act (OG) concerning the revision of judgments are to be applied by analogy in international arbitration.[51] Therefore, the Supreme Court and not the arbitral tribunal is competent to decide on a request for revision.[52]

The Supreme Court's view of applying the OG to fill the gap is not shared by the majority of scholars.[53] Rather, scholars point out that awards which were brought about by criminal acts can be set aside pursuant to Sect. 190(2)(a) PILA (public policy).[54] Other scholars, however, see the lack of a specific ground for setting aside an award due to criminal acts as a clear disadvantage and support the Supreme Court's view that the courts should develop this ground for challenging an award.[55]

According to the Supreme Court, Sects. 137 and 140 to 143 OG must be applied to fill the *lacuna* as described above. Therefore, pursuant to Sect. 137(a) OG the application for the revision of an award is permissible where in the course of criminal proceedings it is revealed that criminal acts which tainted the award have taken place to the disadvantage of the applicant.[56] The provision further sets forth that the fact of whether the criminal act led to a conviction is of no relevance.

Sect. 137 OG allows the application for a revision even in cases where it was impossible to initiate criminal proceedings as long as the criminal acts are evidenced by other means.

Relevant criminal acts are for example fraud (Sect. 146 Penal Code), false testimony of a party (Sect. 306 Penal Code) or false testimony of a witness or expert (Sect. 307 Penal Code), forgery of official documents (Sects. 251-255 Penal Code), active or passive corruption (Sect. 322 Penal Code) or the offering or accepting of a bribe (Sect. 322 Penal Code).

2.   Fraud by Omission

One of the practical issues in this context is the question whether the omission of a party to submit facts or evidence can allow the challenge of an award.

---

50. BG 11 March 1992 BGE 118 II 199.

51. *Ibid.*

52. BG 1 November 1996, Bull ASA (1997) p. 116.

53. See, e.g., T. RÜEDE and R. HADENFELDT, *Schweizerisches Schiedsgerichtsrecht*, 2nd ed. (Zurich 1993) p. 365; A. BUCHER, *Die neue internationale Schiedsgerichtsbarkeit in der Schweiz* (Basel 1989) marg. nos 408 et seq.; further references in P. LALIVE, P. POUDRET and G. REYMOND, *Le droit de l'arbitrage interne et international en Suisse* (Lausanne 1989) Art. 191, para. 5.

54. RÜEDE and HADENFELDT, *op. cit.*, fn. 53, p. 366 with further references.

55. LALIVE, POUDRET and REYMOND, *op. cit.*, fn. 53, Art. 191, para. 5.

56. A. RIGOZZI and M. SCHÖLL, *Die Revision von Schiedssprüchen nach dem 12. Kapitel des IPRG* (Basel 2002) p. 33.

a.   Austria

Numerous scholars hold that Sect. 178 CCP obliges the parties in court proceedings to submit all relevant facts and not to withhold material facts even if they may be disadvantageous for the party's position.[57] The only exception applies to the concealment of facts which are sufficient to amount to a dishonour or criminal liability for the party itself. These facts may be concealed without this being regarded as constituting a breach of this duty.[58]

However, it seems that fraud cannot be committed by pure omission; an active element, such as submitting forged documents, seems to be required.[59]

b.   England

In court proceedings, according to Rule 31 of the Civil Procedure Rules (CPR), the parties are under a duty of disclosure of evidence, which continues during the entirety of the proceedings. Under the standard disclosure procedure the parties are required to disclose documents they rely on, those which can adversely affect their or the other parties' case, or those which it is required to disclose by a relevant practice direction (Rule 31(6) CPR). However, the duty of a party to disclose is limited to documents "which are or have been in his control" (Rule 31(8) CPR).

A comparable rule is missing in the Arbitration Act 1996. It seems that such a duty only exists where the parties have provided for disclosure or where such disclosure has been ordered by the arbitral tribunal under Sect. 40(2)(a) AA 1996.

A case involving Sect. 68(2)(g) AA 1996 which dealt with the issue of fraud is *Profilati v. Painewebber*.[60]

In this case Moore-Bick J. was concerned with the withholding of a document in arbitration proceedings which would have altered the arbitral tribunal's decision, and with the question of whether such a deliberate withholding could amount to a fraudulent act. The arbitral tribunal had issued an order to disclose documents "relating to the transaction". The respondent's counsel thought the documents at issue were not covered by the order as they related to a different transaction.

Moore-Bick J. held :

> "Where an important document which ought to have been disclosed is deliberately withheld and as a result the party withholding it has obtained an award in his favour the Court may well consider that he has procured that award in a manner contrary to public policy. After all, such conduct is not far removed from fraud."

After a closer examination of the Arbitration Act 1996 and the previous law, the court, nevertheless, came to the conclusion that a mere withholding of documents as

---

57. See, e.g., H. FASCHING, *Lehrbuch des österreichischen Zivilprozeßrechts*, 2nd ed. (Vienna 1990) marg. no. 653 with further references.

58. R. HOLZHAMMER, *Österreichisches Zivilprozeßrecht*, 2nd ed. (Vienna/New York 1976) p. 153.

59. *Op. cit.*, fns. 7 and 8; BERTEL, "Der Prozeßbetrug", AnwBl (1976) p. 203 at p. 203.

60. *Profilati Italia v. Painewebber and another* [2001] 1 Lloyd's Rep 715 (QBD (Comm. Ct)).

was done in this case could not amount to fraudulent behaviour and had to be classified as a mere "innocent failure":

> "An application to challenge the award may only be made on the grounds of serious irregularity which is itself carefully defined in subsection (2). The Court has no general jurisdiction to interfere with the working of the arbitral process and some of the grounds on which the Court would formerly have acted [under the pre-1996 Act regime] find no place in Section 68. One such ground, which is particularly relevant to the present case, is the discovery of new evidence: the Court no longer has the power to remit an award simply on the grounds that new evidence has come to light. I agree with Lord Goldsmith that to allow a challenge to the award to be made on the grounds of an innocent failure to give proper disclosure would be contrary both to the spirit and to the wording of the Act."

This seems to allow the conclusion that the deliberate withholding of material evidence could allow a challenge.[61]

c.   France

"Fraud" is not to be equated with a "simple lie" or silence which misleads the arbitral tribunal.[62] In divorce proceedings before municipal courts the Supreme Court held that the fact that a party did not disclose adultery as well as the existence of an illegitimate child does not allow a revision of the judgment. A revision would be permitted only if the party defended itself against an allegation made in this respect by specifically fraudulent manoeuvres.[63]

However, in *Eiffage* the Paris Court of Appeal held that the fraudulent dissimulation of relevant documents is procedural fraud, which allows the challenge of the award.[64] This could be seen to imply that a dissimulation with the intent to deceive the arbitral tribunal would indeed justify a challenge. However, given the established jurisprudence in respect of state court proceedings a different rule for the challenge of awards does not seem to be justified.

d.   Germany

Sect. 138 CCP provides that in court proceedings the parties have to make complete and truthful submissions. It seems to remain undecided whether this also applies in arbitration.[65] In any case, the Supreme Court denied an obligation of the parties to raise issues which are not in their favour.[66]

---

61. MERKIN, *op. cit.*, fn. 10, marg. no. 18.20.
62. S. GUINCHARD, *op. cit.*, fn. 27, marg. nos 6221 et seq. with further references.
63. Cass. 24 January 1996, *A. v. G.*, Juris-Data no. 000283.
64. CA Paris 17 June 1997, *Eiffage v. Butec*, Rev Arb (1997) p. 583 with note by BUREAU; see also 10 September 1998, *Thomson v. Brunner Sociedade Civil de Administracao Limitada and another*, *op. cit.*, fn. 25.
65. BGH 30 January 1957 (1957) 23 BGHZ 198.
66. BGH 11 June 1990 (1991) 104 ZZP 203.

However, in a recent case the Supreme Court found that fraud committed by the representative of a party, which led to the rendering of an award on agreed terms, would allow a challenge because procedural public policy was violated. This person had dissimulated the fact that annual accounts which were of relevance in the arbitration had been made in violation of generally accepted accounting principles (GAAP).[67]

e.   Switzerland

In state court proceedings the parties are not obliged to submit facts, which are detrimental to their own position.[68] This does not seem to be different in international arbitration.

III.   TIME LIMIT FOR FILING THE CHALLENGE

1.   Austria

The time limit for applications under Sect. 595(1)(7) which refers to Sect. 530 CCP is governed by the provisions concerning the application to reopen the case.

These provisions set a time limit of four weeks from receipt and thereby binding legal effect of the criminal sentence.[69] The courts read the provision for reopening a case because of a criminal action differently. The time limit starts to run from the day a diligent claimant is able to obtain information about the relevant decision.[70]

However, ten years after the award, a challenge for reopening the case can no longer be made (Sect. 534(3) CCP).

2.   England

Any challenge of an award shall be brought within twenty-eight days from the date of the award or, if there has been any arbitral process of appeal or review, from the date when the applicant or appellant was notified of the result of this process (Sect. 70(3) AA 1996).

However, the time limit may be extended by the court in accordance with Sect. 79 AA 1996. Paragraph 3 provides that:

> "[t]he court shall not exercise its power to extend a time limit unless it is satisfied—
> (a) that any available recourse to the tribunal, or to any arbitral or other institution or person vested by the parties with power in that regard, has first been exhausted, and

---

67. BGH 2 November 2000, *op. cit.*, fn. 30.
68. With respect to Zurich see R. FRANK, *Kommentar zur zürcherischen Zivilprozessordnung* (Zurich 1997) Sect. 50, marg. no. 16.
69. RECHBERGER and MELIS in RECHBERGER, *op. cit.*, fn. 9, Sect. 597, marg. no. 3.
70. OGH 3 July 1928 (1928) 10 SZ no. 198; 26 June 1928 (1928) 10 SZ no. 191.

(b) that a substantial injustice would otherwise be done".

It is generally admitted that the applicant for extension of time must demonstrate:

"(a) an adequate reason for delay ...
(b) a good arguable case for remitting or setting aside the award ...
(c) that the balance of prejudice as between the parties lies in favor of the grant of an extension of time ...".[71]

In one case, the court did not extend the time limit due to the fact that the application to challenge the award mainly relied on new evidence, which could have been presented to the arbitral tribunal.[72]

In *AOOT Kalmneft v. Glencore International*[73] Colman J. put forward the facts he would consider when confronted with an application for the extension of a time limit:

"(i) the length of the delay;
(ii) whether, in permitting the time limit to expire and the subsequent delay to occur, the party was acting reasonably in all the circumstances;
(iii) whether the respondent to the application or the arbitrator caused or contributed to the delay;
(iv) whether the respondent to the application would by reason of the delay suffer irremediable prejudice in addition to the mere loss of time if the application were permitted to proceed;
(v) whether the arbitration has continued during the period of delay and, if so, what impact on the progress of the arbitration or the costs incurred in respect of the determination of the application by the court might now have;
(vi) the strength of the application;
(vii) whether in the broadest sense it would be unfair to the applicant for him to be denied the opportunity of having the application determined".[74]

3.   France

Pursuant to Sect. 1505 NCCP the challenge of an award "shall be brought before the court of appeal of the place where the award was made" at the latest one month after the enforcement order was issued. The general rules of the NCCP on time limits for

---

71. MERKIN, *op. cit.*, fn. 10, marg. no. 18.34 with further references; FYFE and DAHLBERG, Int ALR (2002) p. 9.
72. *Ranko Group v. Antarctic Maritime ("The Robin")* 1998 ADRLN 35 (QBD) cited in SHACKELTON, Int ALR (1999) p. 53 in fn. 30; in this respect, see also Civil Procedure Rules, rule 22, Practice Direction 49 G.
73. *AOOT Kalmneft v. Glencore International* [2001] 2 All ER (Comm) 577 (QBD).
74. *Ibid.*, para. 59.

recourse do not apply.[75] For applicants whose residence or corporate seat is abroad this time limit is extended by two months bringing the time limit to three months in total (Sect. 644(2) NCCP).

In case of fraud a revision must be filed within two months after the party obtained knowledge of the reason to request a revision (Sect. 596 NCCP). However, it is held that no new remedy against awards was introduced by the case law[76] so that it seems that the general period of time of one month after enforcement applies also to challenges based on fraud.

4.   Germany

Sect. 1059(3) CCP states:

> "Unless the parties have agreed otherwise, an application to the court for setting aside may not be made after three months have elapsed. The period of time shall commence on the day on which the party making the application had received the award. If a request had been made under section 1058 [for the correction or interpretation of the award], the time limit shall be extended by not more than one month from receipt of the decision on the request. No application for setting aside the award may be made once the award has been declared enforceable by a German court."

For the sake of legal certainty the time limit of three months is a strict one and no exceptions may be made, not even if grounds for challenge are discovered at a later date.[77] There is no special rule for the challenge of awards due to criminal acts. The parliamentary documents explicitly state that the general time limit also applies to the continued application of Sect. 1041(1) no. 6 former CCP (see above Sect. II.1.d) which are considered part of public policy under Sect. 1059(2) no. 2 (b) CCP.[78] Should the time limit already have expired when the crime or the new facts or evidence are discovered, the remedy offered for this problem is a claim for damages.[79]

5.   Switzerland

A challenge of an award must be made within thirty days from the issuing of the award (Sect. 89(1) OG).[80] Pursuant to Sect. 140(1)(b) OG an application for revision on the

---

75. See, e.g., Cass. 18 October 2001, *Mège v. Michaud and another*, Rev Arb (2002) p. 157 with note by PINSOLLE.

76. GAILLARD and SAVAGE, eds., *op. cit.*, fn. 17, marg. no. 1599.

77. SCHWAB and WALTER, *op. cit.*, fn. 31, Chap. 25, marg. no. 12; ALBERS in *op. cit.* fn. 36, Sect. 1059, marg. no. 12.

78. Parliamentary documents in BERGER, *op. cit.*, fn. 29, p. 289.

79. *Ibid.*

80. BERTI and SCHNYDER in *Berti, Honsell, Vogt and Schnyder*, Art. 191, marg. no. 9.

grounds of criminal acts may be brought within ninety days from the date of the criminal conviction.

IV.   SUMMARY

This brief comparison shows the following:

Five jurisdictions which, on a global scale, have very similar social systems and whose arbitration laws have seen a great degree of harmonization over the past decades come to rather different solutions when dealing with the challenge of awards because of criminal acts.

The fraud committed by a party allows a challenge in all five jurisdictions. Two different cases can be distinguished. The fraud can either by committed by an act, e.g., the submission of a document forged by the party, or by an omission, e.g., withholding critical evidence.

With respect to the second case, the issue is whether silence can amount to fraud. This seems to be denied in all five jurisdictions.

The extent to which other criminal acts, in particular criminal acts committed by other persons than the parties, permit a challenge varies greatly. It seems that these do not allow a challenge in England and France, whereas the opposite is true for Austria, Germany and Switzerland.

The time limit for filing a challenge plays an important role. The situation in France and Germany may not allow challenges to be made in time. England has a flexible rule and it may be assumed that an extension of the time limit to challenge an award may be granted in case of fraud. Only Austria and Switzerland assure on a statutory basis that challenges on the basis of criminal acts can be made within a certain time limit after the crime has been discovered.

Harmonization may be beneficial in two areas in particular: the extent of the duty of a party to disclose relevant evidence and facts and the time limit for filing a challenge.

The Detection of Forgery and Fraud

*Peter V. Tytell**

The origins of many of the basic features of our lives are lost in the mists of time. Like the invention of the wheel or the domestication of plants and animals, the exact date of the discovery of writing is unknown. However, human nature being what it is, it is fairly safe to assume that whenever the first documents were written, it was only a few days later that the first forgeries were produced. Questioned document examiners evolved immediately thereafter.

The ancients were well aware of the problems caused by forged documents. Cicero reproached Anthony with having made huge profits through forgery.[1] The historian Procopius mentioned a certain Priscus of Emesa whose forgeries were so good that only the forger himself could reveal them, and Suetonius noted that the young Titus was so accomplished at the imitation of handwriting that he could have been the prince of forgers. It is hardly surprising that Roman law provided for adjudication of the authenticity of written instruments, allowing the judge to call in experts to give testimony on the genuineness of writings by comparing the disputed material with admitted writings.[2] Such procedures persisted over the centuries in ecclesiastical courts, in the French, German, as well as other codes following the Roman tradition, and eventually even entering the common law courts of England and the United States.[3] Today's venues have similar procedures for similar reasons.[4]

The ancient craft of the forger has continued into the twenty-first century with the computer, scanner, printer, copier and the fax machine functioning as merely new tools for the contemporary forger, replacing or supplementing traditional handwork. The ends are the same: to change the perception of the past, be it the distant history of a nation or the recent story of a transaction; it can involve a treaty between empires or a contract between individuals. The basic methodology has been consistent through the ages: simulation, alteration, obliteration, insertion, combination and transposition have been used to create a misleading document.[5]

---

* Forensic document examiner. Correspondence concerning this paper should be addressed to Peter V. Tytell, 116 Fulton Street, New York, NY 10038-2712, USA. E-mail: typeter@aol.com

1. Marcus Tullius CICERO, *Second Philippic*, e.g., at IV, XXXVIII, etc.
2. *Enactments of Justinian*, Novel 49.2; Novel 73.7.
3. See, J. Newton BAKER, *Law of Disputed and Forged Documents* (Michie, Charlottesville, VA, 1955) Sects. 3-13; Maggie GUIRAL, *La valeur de la preuve dans l'expertise des écritures* (Bosc Frères and Riou, Lyon 1927) pp. 9-22.
4. See, e.g., Fed. R. Evid. 901(b)(3).
5. "Forgers have been as consistent over the ages in their choice of media as they have been diverse in their personalities and interests. A relatively restricted group of colors makes the forger's palette, now as two millennia ago. After all, the forger has to carry out a limited range of tasks, one that has not altered greatly over time. He must give his text the appearance – the linguistic appearance as a text and the physical appearance as a document – of something from a period dramatically earlier than and different from his own. He must, in other words, imagine two things:

The document examiner also has access to a wondrous variety of modern tools that extend basic human perception, but still endeavors to answer one or more of the timeless adverbial questions, often summarized as the six *w*'s: *w*ho, *w*hat, *w*here, *w*hen, *w*hy, and ho*w*. The basic methodology for answering these questions is a recursive three-step process of examination, comparison, and evaluation that document examiners have studied for a century.[6] Today this approach is characterized by the wider forensic community as the A.C.E. Method: Analysis, Comparison, and Evaluation.[7] However, unlike most forensic disciplines that rarely find application in civil litigation, document examination is equally applicable to civil and criminal cases.

The important role played by document examiners in civil litigation or arbitration[8] may be something of a surprise to attorneys who associate document examination with forged check cases in police court. Dr. Hans Gross, founder of modern criminalistics, noted long ago that "... lawyers find a certain difficulty in understanding the nature of fraud because it is by no means easy to fix the exact line of demarcation between civil

---

what a text would have looked like *when it was written* and what it should look *like now that he has found it.*" (emphasis in the original)

Anthony GRAFTON, *Forgers and Critics: Creativity and Duplicity in Western Scholarship* (Princeton University Press 1990) pp. 49-50.

6. "... the investigation of documents presents problems which in the main are to be solved by the study, comparison and interpretation of that which in some form is actually present before the court".

Albert S. OSBORN, *Questioned Documents* (Lawyers' Co-operative Publishing Co., Rochester, NY 1910) p. 89.

7. "1. *Analysis.* The 'unknown' item must be classified according to its properties or characteristics. These properties may be directly observable, measurable, or implied, but they are the parts which make up the whole.
2. *Comparison.* ... a comparison is made of the properties of the item found through analysis with the known or recorded properties of others whose identity is unquestioned.
3. *Evaluation.* It is not sufficient that the comparison disclose similarities or dissimilarities in any of the characteristic properties of knowns and unknowns. Each property will have a certain value for identification purposes, determined chiefly by its relative frequency of occurrence. The weight or significance of each must be considered."

Royston A. HUBER, "Expert Witnesses: In defense of expert witnesses in general and of document examiners in particular", 2 Criminal Law Quarterly (1959) p. 276 at p. 289.

8. See, e.g., International Court of Justice, *Case Concerning Maritime Delimitation and Territorial Questions between Qatar and Bahrain*, Judgment of 16 March 2001, Decision No. 847, 40 ILM (July 2001) p. 4 (hereinafter *Qatar v. Bahrain*). In the Judgment a narrative of the document issue is found in paras. 15 to 23 of the section setting out the history of the proceedings before the Court as well as in the various Orders of the Court and other documents mentioned therein. The issue is more fully discussed in the Separate Opinion of Judge Fortier. (The author had some involvement with this matter and will therefore refer to it with what may appear unseemly frequency.)

wrongs and criminal wrongs".[9] Part of this confusion may stem from the extra burden that should be borne by the attorney in a civil case; it includes the work that would be done in a criminal case by the police investigator or inquiring magistrate, and can even go beyond that. These tasks are implicit in the three words, *questioned document examination*. Someone must raise a *question*, someone must gain access to the *document* for *examination*, and usually someone must also obtain appropriate comparison *documents* to facilitate the *examination*. In criminal cases that "someone" is from the police, the prosecution, or the court; in civil matters the burden is on counsel.

In the first instance, someone must question a document. After all, the examiner does not generally seek out documents to examine; they are submitted to the examiner because some real or potential question has been raised. In criminal cases it is usually the victim who will complain to the police, and in civil cases it is often a party who will initially question a document, rightly or wrongly, often with the exclamation "That's not my signature! I would never sign that!" However, parties are usually unable to carefully review the numerous bulging boxes of documents that are increasingly the standard fare in litigation.[10] It is the duty of counsel and counsel's junior associates to wade through the masses of copies and copies of those copies to find the documents that should be contested. There are various circumstances when litigators, litigants and even judges or arbitrators will immediately question a document. Unfortunately, however, there are too many cases where documents are allowed to pass by unchallenged.

The attorney first reviewing the documents must constantly doubt and must constantly question the documents presented, all the documents, not just those brought forth by an adversary, but also those coming from nominally friendly parties, and those from counsel's own client. It certainly falls to the attorney's perception of the meaning of due diligence as to the degree of care with which documents from his/her own side will be vetted, as well as the level of trust that will be placed in the documents received from an adversary. However, it behooves the prudent lawyer to consider the circumstances of the appearance of a document in the context of the case. Is it a surprise to those who are familiar with the background of the matter? Does it come late in the day, after numerous unanswered requests for discovery, and then appear to resolve issues raised during the proceedings in favor of the party producing it?[11] Is it just too

---

9. J. Collyer ADAM, *(Hans Gross) Criminal Investigation a Practical Textbook for Magistrates, Police Officers and Lawyers Adapted from the System Der Kriminalistik of Dr. Hans Gross* (Sweet & Maxwell, London 1924) p. 520. "… *weil die Grenze zwischen zivilem und strafbarem Unrecht nirgends scharf zu ziehen ist*". Hans GROSS, *Handbuch für Untersuchungsrichter als System der Kriminalistik,* II (Schweitzer 4 Aufl. Munich 1904) p. 306.

10. Consider the recently announced International Court of Justice (ICJ) Practice Directions: "The Court has noticed an excessive tendency towards the proliferation and protraction of annexes to written pleadings. It strongly urges parties to append to their pleadings only strictly selected documents." International Court of Justice, Practice Direction III, Annex to Press Communiqué No. 2001/32, 31 October 2001.

11. "Plaintiffs' excuse for the sudden materialization of this purported lease, hard on the heels of defendants' cross motion for summary judgment on the ground of Statute of Frauds, was that in the rush to commence this litigation, they had 'completely forgot[ten]' about the document."

convenient?[12]

The attorney should also scrutinize the document itself and consider the many aspects of the document that might not be correct. Dr. Gross wrote of the "'great blunder' (*grosse bêtise*)(*grosse Dummheit*) which is almost inevitable in the greatest crimes and which the most expert forger rarely fails to commit".[13] All of this and more is part of the work of the questioned document examiner, which is not limited to the examination of handwriting – which itself includes cursive- or script-style writing, handprinting, signatures, numerals, and other written marks or signs – but encompasses all the features of a document, from ink to inscription, from paper to printer, from signature to staple.[14]

Glatter, et al. v. Borton, et al., 649 N.Y.S.2d 677 (App. Div. 1996).

12. The cynical New Yorker knows the caveat that when something seems too good to be true, it probably isn't true.

13. ADAM, *op. cit.*, fn. 9, p. 521; GROSS, *op. cit.*, fn. 9, vol. II, p. 307. A case from William WILLS, *Principles of Circumstantial Evidence* (London 1862) is also recounted.

"A certain Alexander Humphreys attempted in the High Court of Judiciary, Edinburgh, in the year 1839, to procure large sums of money, relying upon ancient documents. These documents were marvelously counterfeited, but it was discovered that one of them, dated December 7, 1639, had been signed by the Chancellor Archbishop Spottiswood, who had died on Nov. 26, 1639. The forger, who had consulted the list of Chancellors, only knew that Lord Loudon, this successor of Spottiswood, had not entered on his functions until 1641 and thought that Spottiswood had been Chancellor up to that time; he was ignorant that between the two there had been an exceptional interregnum of two years."

ADAM, *op. cit.*, fn. 9, pp. 521-522; GROSS, *op. cit.*, fn. 9, vol. II, p. 308. This same form of "great blunder" in *Qatar v. Bahrain* is nicely summarized in the title of Tom FREEMAN's article on the case "Dead men don't write letters", Legal Business (May 2001) p. 66. These and other "great blunders" were detectable by those familiar with the details of the relevant history even from an examination of copies. Finding other "great blunders" required examination of the originals.

Adam, a public prosecutor in Madras, recounted another similar blunder from the subcontinent: "In a recent case in Southern India a pro-note, put in as having been made, stamped, and dated in 1900, bore a stamp with the King's head, which stamp did not, of course, exist in that year." ADAM, *op. cit.*, fn. 9, p. 524. Use of the Royal Arms from the wrong reign was also found on a number of the documents submitted in *Qatar v. Bahrain*.

14. The scope of the examiner's activities includes

"examinations, comparisons, and analyses of documents in order to: establish genuineness or non-genuineness, or to expose forgery, or to reveal alterations, additions, or deletions, identify or eliminate persons as the source of handwriting, identify or eliminate the source of typewriting or other impression, marks, or relative evidence, and write reports or give testimony, when needed, to aid the users of the examiner's services in understanding the examiner's findings. (....)

Examiners in this field are sometimes known by the term 'handwriting experts'. Forensic document examination includes expertise in handwriting identification. Handwriting includes cursive or script style writing, handprinting, signatures, numerals, and other written marks or signs. Forensic document examination does not involve the employment of calligraphic or engrossing skills, nor does it involve a study of handwriting in an attempt to create a personality profile or otherwise analyze or judge the writer's personality or character. (....)

When an attorney does contact a document examiner because questions have been raised about a document or in exercising caution or due diligence, the examiner can be expected to request immediately that the original document be submitted for examination. In situations involving comparisons (e.g., signature authentication) there will also be a request for known documents of the appropriate nature and number. Both of these requests are vital to the proper conduct of a complete examination. Among the principal limitations that lead to less-than-definite opinions from document examiners are the submission of poor-quality copies, or of inadequate knowns, or both.

Considering the prevalence in today's society of photocopies, microfilm records and now digital imaging of records in both public and private archives, this insistence on original documents may sound old-fashioned. However, it is this very acceptance of copies that provides an opportunity to the falsifier of documents. Important features of the ink, paper and other physical aspects of the document can only be discovered through examination of the original.[15] Furthermore, it should be self-evident that the original will provide the maximum amount of information regarding the details of handwriting. Some fine detail is lost in even the best photocopies, and even the gross outline of the writing can be difficult to make out in high contrast microfilm or digital images. Unfortunately, it is common for document examiners to receive a fax of a copy of a copy of a fax with barely legible printed text and a few random marks where the signature once appeared. This is not the sort of the material that generally leads to a definite opinion. Convincing an attorney to put in the extra effort to find the originals, be it from the adversary or the client, can be the most arduous part of the case for the document examiner. The level of resistance to this seemingly logical, straightforward request and the reason(s) offered for the resistance, can often be very revealing.

When a request for the original is met with a reply that there is no original, and that all that remains is a photocopy, some explanation for this situation is required. A traditional explanation is that after the document was signed, the original was taken by the party who now denies all knowledge of the transaction and only a copy was retained by the other party. Whatever the explanation, the document examiner in search of an

---

Typical problems in this field are: the identification of handwriting, typewriting; the identification or elimination of the source of and the output of other mechanical or electronic imaging devices such as printers, copying machines, facsimile equipment, and the like; the identification or elimination of ink, paper, and writing instruments; the establishment of the date, source, history, sequence of preparation, alterations or additions to documents, and relationships of documents. Other problems are the decipherment and sometimes the restoration, or both, of obscured, deleted, or damaged parts of documents. The work often includes a study of the information carried by a document for discovery of evidence of spuriousness, identification of persons, or to show significant relationships."

"E444 The Scope of Work of the Forensic Document Examiner" in *Annual Book of ASTM Standards*, vol. 14.02 (American Society for Testing and Materials, West Conshohocken, PA 2002).

15. In *Qatar v. Bahrain* the significant findings of the many examinations that could only be performed on the original challenged documents seem to have justified the considerable efforts of Bahrain's counsel in gaining access to most of the originals. (Of the eighty-two documents challenged by Bahrain, only seventy-six originals were submitted to the Registrar of the Court. The whereabouts of the others or the reasons for their unavailability is still not known to the author.)

original will ask to examine the "original copy" (i.e., the actual piece of paper that was found in the file, the one supposed to come out of the copy machine after the signing).[16] Locating the "original copy" is often complicated by the law office norm of copying and recopying every sheet of paper in the file to attach to each motion or response. While many attorneys will carefully segregate the actual items received from a client or an adversary and work from a set of copies, document examiners are accustomed to watching lawyers and their staffs shuffle frenetically through stacks of paper and compare copies to locate the least indistinct image.

Even when the original is unavailable, it is still possible to conduct certain examinations with copies. Examination of the copy and comparison to appropriate known copies can provide information to support or contradict the story of the document's preparation. Through use, mechanical devices like photocopiers develop individuality that can serve to identify the work product of a particular device. The gradual development of these characteristics, plus various maintenance cycles and other transient factors, can be used to date a particular copy from the machine or to fix its preparation within a period of time.

Many examinations of documents, like many other forensic examinations, are based on a comparison of the questioned material with appropriate knowns, regardless of whether originals or copies are involved. Questioned signatures, hand-printing or handwriting must be compared with a group of similar known signatures, hand-printing or handwriting that is both qualitatively and quantitatively adequate. The strength of any opinion from such an examination rests upon the adequacy of the known comparison material. While the document examiner may suggest sources for known documents, the burden of finding a sufficient quantity of appropriate knowns also falls on the attorney.

Known samples for handwriting examinations and some other kinds of examinations can be considered to fall into two major categories: those prepared specifically for the purpose of examination, referred to as request or dictated exemplars; and those initially prepared for other purposes, referred to as collected or normal-course-of-business knowns. Both classes are useful, each having its own advantages and drawbacks. In general, the knowns should include comparable material in the same type of writing (i.e., signatures to compare with signatures, block printing to compare with block printing) and should be from documents of a similar nature. It is not really possible to compare a symbolic signature of a few loops and lines allegedly written by Thomas Atkins on an important contract with the block capital printing of an envelope address, especially when the envelope address does not contain the letters of Mr. Atkins' name. It is also advisable (and sometimes vital) for the knowns to be contemporaneous with the questioned material. An individual's signature or writing may change over time or with the circumstances. This is particularly important with regard to individuals whose

---

16. The document examiner is today confronted with the output of a variety of devices (e.g., computer, computer printer, photocopier, fax) often used in such combinations that the words *original* and *copy* become relative rather than absolute terms.

writing may be affected by accident, physical deterioration, illness, etc.[17]

The search for knowns may also reveal a "great blunder" by the fabricator of a non-genuine document. It is not unusual for simulated signatures to be copied from a model signature taken from the wrong time period, for instance in cases where signatures written in the last days of a person's life are used to create documents dated years earlier, often part of an extensive program of posthumous retroactive estate planning. It is not uncommon that the search for appropriate knowns will turn up the "model" or "prototype" signature used to manufacture a document by means of tracing or by transposition using a photocopier, computer scanner or other means. Often the model is to be found within the litigation papers, even in the attorney's own files (e.g., on affidavits, motions, responses) or in the underlying correspondence or other interactions between the parties.[18]

Regardless of the class of known writing, there is another factor that must be considered. Knowns must be proven authentic for the purpose of use in a proceeding. It is an unfortunate expert who is informed at the last minute that some or even all of the knowns relied upon have not been admitted into evidence. Protestations are passed off with a breezy, "We know he wrote it, you gave a report, just say so on the stand, you don't need those charts." The examiner foolhardy enough to take the stand will be handicapped by the lack of charts or the suspicious blanks on the charts where exemplars not properly before the court or tribunal have been blocked out. On cross-examination,

---

17. These are requirements that almost rise to the level of common sense and are hardly unique to document examiners. For instance, in the examination of Chinese art:

"In subjecting a work of art to comparison, we must first have authentic examples. These touchstone works must be well established and similar in subject matter and approximate dating. In other words, a figure painting of artist's middle period cannot serve as a comparison for a flower painting of his late period."

Wan-go WENG, "A Tall Pine and Daoist Immortal: An Examination of a Painting Attributed to Chen Hongshou" in Judith G. SMITH and Wen C. FONG, eds., *Issues of Authenticity in Chinese Painting* (Metropolitan Museum of Art New York 1999) pp. 171-172.

18. In *Qatar v. Bahrain*, twenty-six documents (dating from 1930 to 1944) bore at least one impression of a signature stamp reading "C. Dalrymple Belgrave". While this version of Belgrave's signature did not agree with any of the signatures used for the Belgrave signature stamps found on known documents dating from 1926 to 1948, it did match his signature on an original document dated 22 December 1938 (a date later than about half the twenty-six suspect documents). Mokhtar AMIN, Mohammed Ezz-el-Din SOBHI and Peter TYTELL, "Expert Forensic Document Examination Report III", pp. 3-8, in Jawad S. AL-ARAYED, (Agent for the State of Bahrain), 31 December 1997, Letter to the President of the Court, submitted by the Agent for the State of Bahrain. This document, addressed to H.B.M's Political Agent, Bahrain, is Bahrain's reply (counterclaim) in response to Qatar's claim to the Hawar Islands. (*Ibid.*, Appendix 4, Vol. II, Tab 8.) It is one of the basic documents that should be reviewed by anyone studying the background of the dispute underlying the ICJ case and is specifically mentioned several times in the ICJ Judgment (in paras. 57, 124, 132, and 142). There may be a certain element of irony in the choice of this signature as the model for the stamp used to create so many non-genuine documents or perhaps a misconstruing of the last sentence of this document which reads: "If the Shaikh of Qatar has any proof of his claim to ownership he should produce it."

it is the expert who will have to reconcile the inconsistencies between the meager testimony and a report based upon more known writing. Alternatively, the use of improperly authenticated knowns can be grounds for a successful appeal.[19] The onus for any such a debacle must be shared by the expert who did not verify the admissibility of the standards and by the attorney who did not lay a proper foundation for the expert's testimony.

Depending on the rules applied, the standard of proof for knowns can vary from beyond a reasonable doubt to a mere preponderance of the evidence; however, in practice, known documents generally must be proven to the satisfaction of the court or arbitrator to be genuine by evidence sufficient to support such a finding whatever that may be.[20] Modes of proof can include acknowledgment by the adverse party and other traditional methods.[21] However, "[t]here is no precise method by which a specimen must be proved to be genuine and the methods of proof may be either direct or circumstantial",[22] especially where a "chain of circumstances in the evidence is so complete that there can be no doubt that [the defendant] wrote" the standards,[23] or

---

19. Where the known writings were admitted because they were government records, but no authentication of the defendants' signatures was offered.

"Not having proved to be genuine, the signatures on the public documents were inadmissible as standards of comparison. In these circumstances the foundation for the expert's opinion cannot stand, and his opinion falls with it. The opinion evidence was erroneously admitted, it was prejudicial, and the case must, accordingly, be reversed for a new trial."

US v. Wagner, 475 F.2d 121 (10th Cir. 1973).
20. Proper standard of proof is that there be sufficient evidence so that jury finding of genuineness would not be subject to reversal as against weight of evidence. *US v. American Radiator & Standard Sanitary Corp.*, (3d Cir.) 433 F.2d 174, cert. denied, 401 US 948.
21. See *People v. Molineux*, 168 NY 264 at 328 (1901):

"Thus the genuineness of a writing may be established: [1] by the concession of the person sought to be charged with the disputed writing made at or for the purpose of the trial, or by his testimony; [2] or by witnesses who saw the standards written, or to whom, or in whose hearing, the person sought to be charged acknowledged the writing thereof; [3] or by witnesses whose familiarity with the handwriting of the person who is claimed to have written the standard enables them to testify to a belief as to its genuineness; [4] or by evidence showing that the reputed writer of the standard has acquiesced in or recognized the same, or that it has been adopted and acted upon by him in his business transactions or other concerns."

22. Probation file introduced through testimony of probation officer. "There is no precise method by which a specimen must be proved to be genuine and the proof may be either direct or circumstantial," citing *Dean v. US*, 246 F. 568 (5th Cir. 1917). "The courts have not restricted the manner in which specimens may be proved genuine and each case must be viewed on its own facts." *US v. White*, 444 F.2d 1274 at 1280 (1971) cert. denied, 440 US 949.
23. Letters to family: "two letters addressed to appellant's wife and internally identifiable as having been written by appellant. The chain of circumstances in the evidence is so complete that there can be no doubt that Wolfish wrote the two letters beginning: 'Dear Marcia & Children'." *US v. Wolfish*, 525 F.2d 457 (2d Cir. 1975).

where "[o]nly baseless speculation could assign these documents to any hand other than that of appellant".[24] However, whatever the applicable rules may be, the rules must be considered, the appropriate procedures must be followed and the required standard of proof must be met.

With all due respect to the reasons counsel believes the knowns to be valid, the document examiner should still review the knowns to verify that they all stem from a single source. Material submitted as knowns for one individual can include extraneous material from another person. This type of contamination can mislead the document examiner to a wrong conclusion if it is missed. Sometimes files with genuine knowns are "salted" with the work of the same fabricator who produced the questioned document.[25] Regardless of how comprehensive the attorney thinks the collection of knowns submitted for examination to be, it is probable that the document examiner will ask for more.

There is one obvious, simple and straightforward method of obtaining handwriting exemplars that should be avoided: asking the client to provide them on the spot. The courts have long frowned upon *post litem motam* writings[26] "on the ground that they [are] objectionable as self-serving exemplars prepared especially for trial"[27] observing that,

> "[u]nquestionably, a defendant has a strong motive to alter his writing so as to render it dissimilar to an incriminating document alleged by the prosecution to be in his hand. Accordingly, any handwriting sample prepared for the specific purpose of showing dissimilarity of handwriting is inherently suspect and should not be admitted into evidence."[28]

While this rule bars a party from making what could be considered a self-serving declaration and closes the door to the possibility of fraud, such writings may be offered by an adverse party.[29] Document examiners are warned against *post litem motam* exemplars from their earliest training. Since violation of this warning has all too often

---

24. See *US v. Liguori*, 373 F.2d 304 (2d Cir. 1967).

> "Appellant also claims that the standards used by the handwriting expert to show that Liguori has written a note which accompanied the narcotics sent to Miss Moree were improperly admitted in evidence because it was not established that Liguori had written the standards. However, the standards consisted of appellant's lease application, key application, automobile registration and chauffeur's application. The expert testified that they were all, including the note, written by the same person. Only baseless speculation could assign these documents to any hand other than that of appellant."

25. This happened in the affair of the Hitler diaries fabricated by Kujau.

26. "Writings created *post litem motam* are inadmissible in favor of a party creating them." *People v. Molineux*, *op. cit.*, fn. 21, p. 326.

27. *US v. Lam Muk Chiu*, 522 F.2d 330 at 331 (2d Cir. 1975).

28. *Ibid.*, at 332. *Citing Hickory v. United States*, 151 US 303 (1874).

29. *People v. Molineux*, *loc. cit.* fn. 21.

caused problems,[30] document examiners seem to take this caution much more seriously than lawyers.

Once the attorney has done what can be done to gain access to the original documents and obtain the appropriate known material, the examination can proceed. The exact examination(s) will vary with case circumstances and the resulting opinion(s) may be definitive or qualified. The nature of the findings may be inconclusive or they can confirm counsel's fondest wishes or worst fears. Whatever the results, it is the examiner's responsibility to present the results neutrally.[31] It is often the duty of the document examiner to render what is sometimes termed an "adverse report" to the counsel or party who submitted documents for examination. These adverse opinions are accepted with varying degrees of grace or resignation, or lack thereof. Once the bad news has settled in, counsel must deal with the facts for what they are.

In closing, a few of the attorney's options in these matters should be considered. An appropriate response can be to submit the documents to another examiner. It may well be prudent to seek a second opinion, but this can descend into opinion shopping in hopes of finding a more pleasing result based on the ancient legal presumption that for every expert there is an equal and opposite expert. Thankfully, upright experts do prove this to be a rebuttable presumption.[32]

Counsel may be able to accept the facts in the document examiner's report and find logical or at least useable arguments to explain them away. These explanations may be correct, but may include statements that can come back to haunt at a later point in the proceedings. If the facts are too difficult to dismiss, the attorney may be able to withdraw the documents or set them aside and continue the case with other evidence.[33] However, such "mid-course corrections" after the proceedings are well underway can be embarrassing[34] and could raise serious questions as to the worth of the fallback

---

30. Jan BECK, "Sources of Error in Forensic Handwriting Evaluation", 40 Journal of Forensic Sciences (January 1995, no. 1) pp. 78-82.

31. Appendix 12 to the British Commercial Court Guide states that the document examiner has a duty as an expert to help the Court on the matters within his/her expertise and that this duty overrides any obligation to the person from whom instructions or payment may be received.

32. In *Qatar v. Bahrain* the two American document examiners who reviewed the report of the experts for Bahrain not only confirmed virtually all of the significant findings leading to the determination that the suspect documents were not genuine, but they located even more flaws in the documents. They concluded that virtually all the suspect documents "contain faults or flaws which cannot be refuted or rebutted". David A. CROWN and Brian B. CAREY, "Forensic Document Examination Report" II, 14 in Abdullah bin Abdulatif AL-MUSLEMANI (Agent of the State of Qatar), 30 September 1998, Interim Report submitted by the State of Qatar. Vol. II, Annex III.

33. As when "Qatar stated ... that it had 'decided [to] disregard all the 82 challenged documents for the purposes of the present case so as to enable the Court to address the merits of the case without further procedural complications'." (ICJ Judgment in *Qatar v. Bahrain*, para. 20, quoting AL-MUSLEMANI, *op. cit.*, fn. 32, vol. I.)

34. As when "[b]y letter of 15 December 1998, the Agent of Qatar expressed '[his Government's] regret at the situation that [had] arisen and the inconvenience that this [had] caused to the Court and Bahrain'". ICJ Judgment, *Qatar v. Bahrain*, para. 20.

position and underlying merit of the claim,[35] and might be disallowed by the court.[36] In extreme cases it may be necessary for counsel to advise the party to give up the case entirely. Depending on professional or ethical considerations, the attorney may choose to withdraw from the case. To continue to proffer or challenge a document in the face of convincing adverse opinion(s) runs the risk of incurring serious sanctions for the attorney, the client, or both.[37]

In sum, the prudent attorney should cast a wary eye on all documents, regardless of their source, and question those that seem in the least suspicious. It could even be considered due diligence to have a crucial document examined before it is offered in evidence or disclosed to any party. The various kinds information that can be provided by the document examiner can be of great help to the litigator, even when the opinion is an adverse one.

---

35. See, e.g., the Separate Opinion of Judge Fortier in *Qatar v. Bahrain*.
36. *Opals on Ice Lingerie v. Bodylines, Inc.*, No. 99 CV 3761 (ILG) 2002 WL 718850 (E.D.N.Y. 5 March 2002).
37. See, e.g., Fed.R.Civ.P. 11; 26(g)(3); 37(a) and (c); N.Y.C.P.L.R. 3126. The concept is hardly a new one; compare *Enactments of Justinian*, Novel 18.8 (a party denying a document is genuine that his opponent proves to be genuine is liable to double damages).

The Psychological Aspects

of

Dispute Resolution

Psychological Aspects of Dispute Resolution: Issues for International Arbitration

*Shari Seidman Diamond**

To set the stage for talking about the psychology of dispute resolution as it actually occurs, consider first the *ideal* tribunal and setting for resolution of a legal dispute. The ideal litigants fully and honestly present all relevant and no irrelevant information to the tribunal. The ideal tribunal, learned in the applicable law, is strictly objective, without either incentives or inclinations to find the position of one side more persuasive than that of the other side. The applicable law is clear once the relevant facts have been decided. Civilized exchange is the rule and emotional outbursts do not occur. Proceedings are well-organized and efficient. The decision is correct and the litigants on both sides go away accepting that justice has been done. It is an attractive picture, but I do not know how many real proceedings in which you have participated match this ideal, or indeed if *anyone* has ever been lucky enough to have had such an experience. In my too-many years of watching how legal disputes are resolved in the United States, I would be hard-pressed to identify a single proceeding that would fully measure up to this standard. After all, in the real world we deal with human beings – litigants, witnesses, arbitrators and judges – who, even if they come to court or arbitration proceedings with good intentions, also come with human motivations, biases and weaknesses. Dispute resolution, whatever the tribunal, is always a perilous undertaking. Evidence in the abstract tends to look different from evidence in the concrete. Decision-makers filter evidence and arguments through different lenses. Those features may explain why a wise senior partner in the firm where I practiced law would counsel supremely confident clients considering litigation that no matter how strong they thought their case was on the merits, they could be certain of winning it no more than 75 percent of the time.

---

* Howard J. Trienens Professor of Law and Professor of Psychology, Northwestern University Law School; Research Fellow, American Bar Foundation. I am very grateful to my colleagues Bryant Garth, Janice Nadler and Mary Rose and the organizers of the ICCA Conference, Neil Kaplan and Arthur Marriott, for their comments and suggestions.

My focus here is on two features of the psychology of dispute resolution that have particular implications for arbitration. The first is the psychology of dispute resolution procedures from the viewpoint of the litigants. That is, what is it that makes the procedure appear fair to the disputants? The second, not totally unrelated to the first, is how the psychology of the decision-maker can affect the actual outcome of the case. I'll close with a challenge for the international arbitration community, based on what we do not yet know about decision-making in the innovative and evolving world of international arbitration.

I.   THE DISPUTE RESOLUTION PROCESS

The parties on the opposite sides of any dispute – whether it is a drainage dispute between neighbors or a multi-million Euro loss allegedly caused by a breach of contract – engage in dispute resolution for vindication, that is, to win. At the simplest level, no matter what a judge or panel of arbitrators decides, one of the parties must go away with less than they wanted. But, as I will suggest to you here, that simple picture of dispute resolution is misleading – and the *process* by which a trial or arbitration is conducted can have a powerful effect on the psychology and reactions of the prevailing party. Perhaps more importantly, it will also affect the reactions of the *losing* party and the willingness of that party to accept the decision of the tribunal without requiring further enforcement efforts – which of course can be a concern in international arbitration.

In stressing the psychological dimensions of dispute resolution, I do not mean to ignore the powerful economic concerns of the parties. Indeed, I should disclose that in one of my two identities as a research psychologist and as an attorney, I was trained at what has been referred to in the United States as the center for law and economics, the University of Chicago. I have a healthy respect for the power of economics in explaining human behavior. What I mean to stress here, however, is that the economic story is an incomplete one when it comes to understanding dispute resolution and, in particular, to understanding how parties react to their experiences in arbitration and litigation.

1.   How Does Procedure Matter?

One view that a decision-making tribunal might take is that its exclusive responsibility in dispute resolution is to arrive at a correct decision. A more sophisticated way to describe this obligation is to characterize it as the responsibility to arrive at a decision that is consistent with the evidence and appropriately guided by the relevant law. Both descriptions, I suggest to you, are too limited from both a psychological and a practical view. If the goals of dispute resolution include legitimacy for the tribunal, the willingness of the parties to accept the decision of the tribunal without coercion or need for further enforcement efforts, and the likelihood that the parties will be willing to submit to arbitration in the future, then it is clear that other critical features of the tribunal's activities are crucial as well.

In making the case for the importance of these other features, I will draw heavily on the work of many scholars who, particularly in the past twenty-five years, have studied the process of dispute resolution and its consequences – John Thibaut, Laurens Walker and more recently Tom Tyler, E. Allan Lind and Yuen J. Huo, among others. Before much of this work on procedural justice began, the dominant thrust of research on dispute resolution focused on distributive justice.[1] Distributive justice occurs when parties competing for scarce resources receive fair allocations as the outcome. Under what circumstances would various outcomes be viewed as fair? Researchers had discovered, for example, that people in work settings were strongly affected by equity[2] concerns in judging the fairness of pay and promotion decisions – that is, they perceived differential outcomes as fair when those different outcomes could be attributed to differences in contributions – for example, if one party put in more time, or contributed greater expertise. The research has only limited value for our concerns here, however, because it also found that people tend to exaggerate the value of their own contributions, much as the parties to a contract dispute tend to overvalue their own efforts to fulfill contract terms and to undervalue the efforts of the opposing party. Thus, in practical terms, it is hard to provide opposing parties with the level of compensation they believe reflects the value of their own contribution – creating the seemingly intractable problem of making people satisfied with outcomes in what game theorists call a zero-sum game: what one party wins, the other must lose.

Against this backdrop, Thibaut and Walker[3] began a new set of investigations, focusing on the *procedures* used to reach allocation decisions. Their early studies showed that the level of satisfaction people felt with the decision of a third party was strongly influenced by their perceptions of the fairness of the procedures used by the third party to reach that decision. That is, even when actual outcomes were held constant and even when those outcomes were negative, the perceived fairness of the procedures strongly influenced the party's satisfaction with the verdict and willingness to accept the legitimacy of the decision.[4] Perhaps most important for its application to international arbitration, these and more recent studies of procedural justice show that people are more willing to accept decisions[5] and to adhere to agreements over time[6] when they perceive those decisions as having been produced by fair procedures. Moreover, the authority and perceived legitimacy of the institutions that produce the decisions are

---

1. See, e.g., J. Stacy ADAMS, "Inequity in Social Exchange", 2 Advances in Experimental Social Psychology (1965) p. 267.
2. Equity was defined as the apportionment of outcomes in proportion to each individual's contributions to those outcomes.
3. John THIBAUT and Laurens WALKER, *Procedural Justice: A Psychological Analysis* (1975).
4. For a description, see Tom R. TYLER, "Social Justice: Outcome and Procedure", 35 International Journal of Psychology (2000) p. 117.
5. For recent examples, see E. Allan LIND, Carol T. KULIK, Maureen AMBROSE and Maria V. de VERA PARK, "Individual and Corporate Dispute Resolution: Using Procedural Fairness as a Decision Heuristic", 38 Administrative Science Quarterly (1993) p. 224; Roselle L. WISSLER, "Mediation and Adjudication in Small Claims Court", 29 Law & Society Review (1995) p. 323.
6. See, e.g., D.G. PRUITT, R.S. PEIRCE, J.M. ZUBEK, G.L. WELTON and T.H. NOCHAJSKI, "Goal Achievement, Procedural Justice, and the Success of Mediation", 1 The International Journal of Conflict Management (1990) p. 33; D. PRUITT, R.S. PEIRCE, N.B. McGILLICUDDY, G.L. WELTON and L.M. CASTRIANNO, "Long-term Success in Mediation", 17 Law and Human Behavior (1993) p. 17 .

enhanced when the procedures used to produce the decisions are viewed as fair – again, even when those decisions involved unfavorable outcomes. The value of enhanced authority and legitimacy for international arbitration is clear: contracting parties will be more willing to include an arbitration clause in their agreements if they recognize the fairness and legitimacy of the institution that will resolve any disputes that arise.

What then are the procedural characteristics that cause disputants to perceive the process of reaching a decision on their dispute as fair? Distilling twenty-five years of research, psychologists have identified several features that consistently emerge as powerful components of perceptions about the fairness of procedures for dispute resolution.[7] They include: (1) *neutrality*, that is, did the decision-maker treat the disputants in an evenhanded, nondiscriminatory way? (2) *trust*, that is, did the decision-maker fully consider the views and needs of the disputants? and (3) *treatment with respect and dignity*, that is, was the decision-maker appropriately polite and respectful in dealing with the disputants and the dispute? All three of these features can be influenced, if not controlled, through a combination of the choice of the decision-maker and how the decision-maker behaves in the course of conducting the proceeding and arriving at a decision. The choice of an arbitrator, not surprisingly, can be significant and contested terrain, because it will affect the expectations of the parties to the arbitration proceedings and can thereby affect their reactions. The choice of senior judges, professional notables and leading continental academics as the principal arbitrators[8] in the early days of international arbitration reflects the value of the social capital that they brought to arbitration through their prestige and reputation. As international arbitration has become more common, procedure should play a larger role in affecting how disputants evaluate their arbitration experience.

It is instructive to look at both the overlap and the difference between the set of questions that disputants are likely to consider about procedural justice and the list of criteria for the choice of an arbitrator identified by Mauro Rubino-Sammartano.[9] He lists eight criteria (p. 320). Three of them relate to the nuts and bolts of conducting an arbitration proceeding: skills in the appropriate language, time availability and availability to travel, if required. One, the experience of the arbitrator, relates to the important issue of expertise, although the experience of the arbitrator can be a double-edged sword when perceptions of fairness are at issue: a positive feature if the expertise arises in a neutral way, for example, from judicial experience, but a potential liability if, for example, the potential arbitrator's experience and expertise arose from long employment in one sector of an industry or in the country of one party to a dispute. The remaining characteristics, that is, the nationality of the arbitrator, the possession of a

---

7. See E. Allan LIND, "Procedural Justice, Disputing, and Reactions to Legal Authorities" in A. SARAT, M. CONSTABLE, D. ENGEL, V. HANS and S. LAWRENCE, eds., *Everyday Practices and Trouble Cases* (1996) p. 177; Tom R. TYLER and E. Allan LIND, "A Relational Model of Authority in Groups", 25 Advances in Experimental Social Psychology (1992) p. 115; see also Tom R. TYLER, *op. cit.* fn. 4.

8. Yves DEZALAY and Bryant GARTH, *Dealing in Virtue: International Commercial Arbitration and the Construction of a Transnational Legal Order* (1996).

9. *International Arbitration: Law and Practice* (2001).

balanced mind, independence and impartiality more directly implicate the three features that promote a sense of procedural justice.

2. Perceived Trust

Trust has a surprisingly powerful effect on all interactions, including negotiations and other forms of dispute resolution. In today's age of E-mails and electronic information exchange, researchers have been investigating the effects of trust on the negotiation of conflicts and formation of contracts between strangers. In a series of intriguing experiments,[10] they have shown that a brief non-substantive get-acquainted telephone conversation with a stranger before a negotiation conducted by E-mail can affect both the likelihood of an impasse in the negotiations and the joint profitability of the agreements that the parties reach if they do reach an agreement. Half of the pairs of participants in the study were given some biographical information about one another and were instructed to have a five-minute social conversation on the telephone in which they could discuss anything but business or the negotiation. The other half had no pre-negotiation conversation with their partner. All of the pairs then conducted a negotiation by E-mail over the course of the next week. The rapport stimulated by the telephone conversation led to greater trust and lower rates of impasse in the negotiations for those who had spoken before the E-mail negotiation began. The results of this study and others like it not only emphasize the importance of trust, but also should give pause to some of the enthusiasm recently expressed about the ability of new technology to eliminate in-person proceedings in the name of efficiency.

Just as trust leads negotiators to be more willing to work at reaching a jointly acceptable resolution, if parties perceive an arbitrator or other third party decision-maker as motivated to consider fully the concerns and needs of the parties, that perception instills confidence that the parties are being treated fairly. In arbitrations or court hearings, trust that the third-party decision-maker will consider fully the disputant's views and needs thus can have a substantial effect on perceptions of procedural justice. When parties turn to a tribunal to reach a decision on their dispute, it means that they have failed to settle their differences themselves and that they are choosing or being forced to bring in a stranger to resolve the dispute. This loss of control is threatening, and one way in which the threat can be addressed is to ensure that the party retains some crucial input in the process. Thus, the opportunity for what has been called "voice" plays an important role in the perceived fairness of the hearing. "Voice" may be expressed orally or in a written form, but constraints placed on what the party has an opportunity to present can influence the party's sense of fairness. For example, a party may want to show the tribunal a document that has not been authenticated, or provide testimony that amounts to inadmissible hearsay or opinion evidence. When rules of evidence prevent this material from being presented, those

---

10. Michael MORRIS, Janice NADLER, Terri KURTZBERG and Leigh THOMPSON, "Schmooze or Lose: Social Friction and Lubrication in E-Mail Negotiations", 6 Group Dynamics (2002) p. 89; Janice NADLER, "Electronically-Mediated Dispute Resolution and E-commerce", 17 Negotiation Journal (2001) p. 333.

exclusions are often a source of frustration to parties who want to share what they see as relevant information. One of the attractions of some alternative dispute resolution procedures, such as mediation, is that those procedures generally do not limit the parties from expressing themselves fully and on their own terms, even if some of what they say is not directly on point or does not carry the standard indicators of reliability.

There is some ambiguity about why voice is so important. One possibility is that the opportunity to tell one's side of the story fully is in itself a crucial element in dispute resolution – that expression is an end in itself. Alternatively, the importance of voice may arise only from its perceived instrumental character, that is, that the party feels that if he is given the opportunity to speak on the issue, the decision-maker will use what has been said in arriving at a decision. The best evidence suggests that both expressive and instrumental motivations give voice its importance. Researchers find that people value the opportunity to speak in the course of a proceeding even when they believe that what they are saying is having little or no impact on the decisions being made. For example, in a study by Lind, Kanfer and Earley,[11] participants who were given an opportunity to express their views either before or after a decision was imposed on them both rated the decision process as fairer than participants who were never given an opportunity to voice their positions. Those who voiced their positions before the decision was reached, however, rated the procedure as fairer than those who had the opportunity to speak only after the decision was reached. Participation effects on the judged fairness of procedures are enhanced when people believe that what they are saying is affecting the outcome of the dispute.[12] Moreover, people tend to overestimate the amount of control they do have,[13] so to the extent that opportunity for voice bolsters a sense of control, it is likely to enhance impressions of fairness even when the views expressed do not actually influence the decisions that are made.

From an arbitrator's perspective, building feelings of trust by maximizing the opportunity for the parties to have voice has some disadvantages in terms of efficiency – it may require substantial patience and may even argue for permitting some material to be presented that the arbitrators anticipate that they will not rely on in reaching their decision. Nonetheless, a more permissive approach than one that, for example, might be permitted under the strict rules of evidence in an American jury trial, may have the advantage of bolstering the parties' sense of fairness with the proceedings. Of course, an arbitrator can go too far in permitting the parties to generate evidence that the tribunal will not consider. In their ground-breaking study of international commercial arbitration, Dezalay and Garth[14] report on the fascinating interview research in which

---

11. "Voice, Control, and Procedural Justice: Instrumental and Noninstrumental Concerns in Fairness Judgments", 59 Journal of Personality and Social Psychology (1990) p. 952.

12. See, e.g., D.L. SHAPIRO and J. BRETT, "Comparing Three Processes Underlying Judgments of Procedural Justice: A Field Study of Mediation and Arbitration", 65 Journal of Personality and Social Psychology (1993) p. 1167.

13. See, e.g., P.C. EARLEY and E.A. LIND, "Procedural Justice and Participation in Task Selection: The Role of Control in Mediating Justice Judgments", 52 Journal of Personality and Social Psychology (1987) p. 1148; A. PEPITONE, "Motivational Effects in Social Perception", 3 Human Relations (1950) p. 57.

14. Yves DEZALAY and Bryant G. GARTH, *op. cit.*, fn. 8.

no doubt many of you participated. In one interview, the respondent reported the following story (with identities appropriately protected) about an arbitration in which he had participated: the chairman of the panel permitted the parties to hold witness hearings, although the norm was not to do so.[15] The parties arranged to have most of the hearings transcribed by a court reporter and had the transcripts delivered to the arbitration panel. The last volume was unavailable in time to submit it. When the attorney explained that he could not argue a particular point because of the absence of the transcript, the chairman expressed surprise and revealed that the transcripts were for the parties rather than for the panel and that the panel would not ever read them. The disappointed attorneys for both sides had anticipated that the panel would appreciate their efforts. The attorney who Dezalay and Garth interviewed characterized the miscommunication about the value of what the parties had done as a disaster, presumably because of the unnecessary expense that had resulted and the assumptions that the parties had made about what the panel would consider in reaching its decision. Although the tribunal had permitted an extra opportunity for voice, confronted with the evidence that the additional material they provided was destined to fall on deaf ears, the opportunity was identified as an empty – and costly – one. The key is maximum, but not an unduly expensive or deceptive, opportunity for the parties to present their case.

3. Perceived Neutrality

A second and powerful element in procedural justice is the perception of *neutrality* on the part of the decision-maker – that is, the belief that one is being accorded evenhanded treatment, that the playing field for dispute resolution is level. Respect for the fact-finding ability and legal expertise of the decision-maker is not sufficient. Honesty, unbiased treatment and consistency are also requirements if an authority is to be perceived as neutral. Most legal systems recognize the importance of apparent neutrality in their proceedings. Judges in the United States, for example, are required to recuse themselves from cases in which they have a conflict of interest, for example, in the form of stock ownership in one of the parties. Disqualification is mandatory for conduct that calls a judge's impartiality into question.[16] Nonetheless, a variety of features undermine the appearance, if not the fact, of neutrality. Perhaps the most common example that exists in the United States is where state court judges are elected to their judicial positions either at the trial or appellate level. In thirty-eight of the fifty states, judges must raise funds to support their election campaigns from the very attorneys who appear in their courts. Other sources that undermine the appearance of neutrality may arise when a judge breaks the normal pattern of silence[17] and makes statements about a case

---

15. *Ibid.*, p. 108.
16. See 28 U.S.C. Sect. 455(a); *In re School Asbestos Litig.*, 977 F.2d 764, 783 (3d Cir. 1992).
17. A judge "shall disqualify himself in any proceeding in which his impartiality might reasonably be questioned". 28 U.S.C. Sect. 455(a). The standard for disqualification under Sect. 455(a) is an objective one. The question is whether a reasonable and informed observer would question the judge's impartiality. See *In re Barry*, 946 F.2d 913, 914 (D.C. Cir. 1991); see also *In re Aguinda*, 241 F.3d 194, 201 (2d Cir. 2001); Richard E. FLAMM, *Judicial Disqualification*, Sect. 24.2.1

before hearing all of the evidence or during a pending appeal, as Judge Jackson did last year in the Microsoft antitrust litigation. In that instance, the Court of Appeals found that most of Judge Jackson's findings had been correct, but remanded the case to another judge for re-hearing on the remaining issues because of the inappropriate statements Judge Jackson had made in interviews with reporters in the course of the trial, and publicly while the case was on appeal.

Another factor involving the appearance of partiality may arise if the judge formerly practiced law with one of the law firms or lawyers appearing in the judge's courtroom. The legal system operates on the presumption that the judge can put aside any natural affinity for her former colleagues as long as she no longer has a financial relationship with the firm. Standard practice requires a disclosure of the prior affiliation, but not a disqualification of the judge from hearing the case.

The make-up of the typical three-arbitrator panel implicitly acknowledges the dangers of partiality by permitting each of the parties to nominate one of the arbitrators. While each arbitrator is formally expected to play a judicial role that answers to the neutral goal of legal accuracy, the structure of the tribunal recognizes that legal accuracy may be open to multiple interpretations. The party-nominated members of the panel increase the likelihood that the arguments and vote of at least one member of the tribunal will be informed by what each party believes is the correct way to view the dispute. Thus, the mixed structure of the arbitration panel both provides some measure of neutrality through balance and incorporates opportunity for voice within the tribunal. Two difficult problems remain, however. The party-selected members of the panel must balance dual demands on their loyalty: to the party that selected them and to the law as represented by the panel as a whole and the evidence presented in the case. Second, a third member of the panel must be selected who has no marked association with or evident inclination to favor one of the parties. The party-selected members can control the choice of the chair only if they can agree. It is unclear how well this system provides the balance it is intended to create. What is missing is research on the frequency and choice of chairpersons in arbitration panels, and a study of how their selection affects process and outcomes, and how it affects the ultimate satisfaction of the parties with the proceedings.

If the system of arbitration is increasingly to attract cases, it is crucial that it be perceived as both efficient and impartial. Moreover, a presumption of impartiality must be maintained within the community of international arbitrators whose colleagues may appear before them as counsel on one day, and may sit beside them on the same panel of arbitrators on another occasion. Yet the arbitration context presents an unusually complicated set of interlocking loyalties and incentives. As a result, there is ample room for loyalties to influence judgments, whether consciously or unconsciously, and for parties or their representatives who are not part of this network of colleagues to be concerned about the neutrality of the tribunal. The controversial[18] approach taken by the ICC, the "declaration of independence" requiring the disclosure of any significant relationship between the proposed arbitrators and counsel for the parties to the

---

(1996).

18. DEZALAY and GARTH, *op. cit.*, fn. 8, p. 48.

arbitration, implicitly acknowledges the potential costs that partiality or the appearance of partiality can have for the health of the process. Indeed, the evidence from studies of procedural justice suggests that the attention to how parties will perceive the neutrality of the arbitration panel is warranted.

It is, as Dezalay and Garth have pointed out,[19] no accident that much international commercial arbitration takes place in locations that are not local to either party. Despite the extra costs and inconvenience that a distant location can impose, a detached location suggests an image and perhaps a reality of independence for the tribunal that would be more difficult to project on the home turf of one or the other of the parties.

4. Treatment with Dignity and Respect

The third key component of procedural justice judgments from the point of view of a disputant is *treatment with dignity and respect*. Such treatment conveys to disputants not only that they are valued participants in the proceeding but also that the proceeding itself is being treated as important. Politeness and respect are ways to impress on participants the seriousness with which the occasion is being treated. In one study, Lind and his colleagues[20] interviewed litigants whose cases had been subjected to arbitration, trial or settlement conferences. They found that litigants perceived arbitration as very fair because it was viewed as dignified, while they viewed settlement conferences as unfair because they were seen as undignified. While formality can promote a feeling of dignity, formality is not the key. Both arbitrations and trials were viewed as dignified, although arbitrations tend to be less formal than trials. The sources of perceived dignity are politeness and respect.

5. Process and Outcomes

My discussion thus far has focused on the nature of proceedings that can instill confidence in the parties. The comfort and positive reactions of litigants are of course important in and of themselves. To the extent that litigants are satisfied with their treatment, they will have good words to say about both arbitration and the arbitrators! But building perceptions of procedural justice has an additional important pay-off: it increases the likelihood that the parties will accept and comply with the findings of the tribunal. In a study of litigants whose cases were subjected to mandatory non-binding arbitration in eight US courts, Lind, Kulik, Ambrose and de Vera Park[21] measured the rate at which litigants (both corporate and individual) exercised their right to a trial at the conclusion of the arbitration. Not surprisingly, litigants with more positive *outcomes* were more likely to accept the arbitration decision and less likely to opt for a trial. But

---

19. *Ibid.*, p. 69.
20. E. Allan LIND, Robert J. MacCOUN, Patricia A. EBENSER, William L.F. FELSTINER, Deborah R. HENSLER, Judith RESNIK and Tom R. TYLER, "In the Eye of the Beholder: Tort Litigants' Evaluations of Their Experiences in the Civil Justice System", 24 Law & Society Review (1990) p. 953.
21. *Op. cit.*, fn. 5, p. 224.

importantly, there was a separate and independent predictor of whether the arbitration award was rejected – namely, a litigant's perception of the procedural fairness of the arbitration proceeding.

Up to this point, I have not referred to the actual quality of decision-making. Does that mean that I am suggesting a focus on mere window dressing by stressing factors that influence perceptions of procedural justice – a kind of soporific for the disputants that lacks substance? Avoid the appearance of bias, but not actual bias? Not at all. Party concerns about fairness are serious. One reason that we cannot assume fairness is because many forces operate to undermine evenhanded treatment of litigants, even given the best of intentions by the decision-makers responsible for producing fair and just outcomes. I turn now to this prickly subject: the psychology of the decision-maker.

II.   THE PSYCHOLOGY OF THE DECISION-MAKER

What affects the ultimate decision in a legal dispute? In general, the strongest predictors of decisions are the weight of the evidence and the applicable law, but they are not the only influences. The judgments of even highly-educated professionals are influenced by psychological factors that affect how they view evidence and how they reach decisions. As a result, in a close case, these factors can influence outcomes, albeit quite unconsciously and without any intentional distortion. Three common psychological sources of influence include: (1) *affinity effects*, which arise from the tendency to share the perspective of those who come from a similar background and have had a similar set of prior experiences; (2) *self-serving or egocentric bias*, the tendency for decision-makers to resolve ambiguity and interpret facts in the direction that is most favorable to themselves; and (3) *expectancy effects*, the tendency to arrive at interpretations that are consistent with expectations.

Affinity effects occur when decision-makers are influenced by their cultural backgrounds, their prior experiences, and their personal associations in formulating their understanding of and judging the behavior they must consider in reaching their decisions. A classic study of decision-making in commercial arbitration demonstrated this influence.[22] Haggard and Mentschikoff had twenty different panels of arbitrators listen to a tape of the same contract dispute. The panel members were American Arbitration Association arbitrators, and half of them were brokers, while the remaining half were manufacturers. The case involved a contract dispute in which the plaintiff, a distributor who had agreed to purchase goods from the defendant, claimed that the defendant, a broker with the sole right to import the goods, had not been entitled to cancel the contract between the two parties. Each of the arbitrators indicated whether he would have decided the case in favor of the plaintiff or the defendant. A comparison between the manufacturer arbitrators and the broker arbitrators indicated that the

---

22. Ernest A. HAGGARD and Soia MENTSCHIKOFF (1977a) "Responsible Decision Making in Dispute Settlement" in J.L. TAPP and F.J. LEVINE, eds., *Law, Justice, and the Individual in Society: Psychological and Legal Issues*, p. 277; Soia MENTSCHIKOFF and Ernest A. HAGGARD (1977b), "Decision Making and Decision Consensus in Commercial Arbitration" in *ibid.*, p. 295.

brokers were far more likely to favor a decision for the broker defendant than were the manufacturers. The difference in the pattern of responses was not attributable to nefarious motives, or even to any form of personal loyalty to a particular party, but rather emerged from the natural alignment of interests based on shared experience. It is important to recognize that what we are often inclined to characterize as bias may reflect this shared perspective that emerges naturally from shared experiences. Thus, whether or not we call it bias, a shared cultural background can foster an unconscious shared perspective that would be perceived as bias by an observer from a different cultural background. Whatever the label, however, the result is an advantaging of one party over another or a tendency to see a witness with a particular background as more or less credible than a witness who has a different background.

A second psychological influence on decision-makers is the *self-serving or egocentric bias*, the tendency for people to reach judgments that are biased in a self-serving direction.[23] Although the most prominent example of the dangers of this bias occurred recently in the troubles of the accounting and auditing firm of Arthur Anderson in the American ENRON scandal, the bias is ubiquitous – people "tend to conflate what is personally beneficial with what is fair or moral".[24] Studies of highly educated professionals, such as physicians and accountants, reveal that despite codes of ethics, in the face of good intentions, and without conscious awareness, judgments tend to move in the direction of self-interest. Thus, physicians tend to order more tests and longer treatments when they receive additional income as a result.[25] Similarly, when accountants were asked to evaluate the dollar amount of inventory loss that an insured suffered in a fire, the amount of loss they set was dramatically higher when they were told that their client was the insured than when they were told it was the insurance company.[26]

Finally, *expectations* alone, without affinity or self-interest, influence how evidence is viewed. Whatever their source, beliefs about the world and preconceived notions about the likely credibility of particular types of witnesses affect how decision-makers evaluate evidence. Decision-makers in all settings ordinarily scrutinize more carefully and are more likely to reject information that is inconsistent with their beliefs and

---

23. See David M. MESSICK and Keith SENTIS, "Fairness, Preference, and Fairness Biases" in D.M. MESSICK and K.S. COOK, eds., *Equity Theory: Psychological and Sociological Perspectives* (1983) p. 69.

24. George LOEWENSTEIN, "Behavioral Decision Theory and Business Ethics: Skewed Trade-Offs between Self and Others" in David M. MESSICK and Ann E. TENBREUSEL, eds., *Codes of Conduct* (1996) p. 214 at p. 221; Max H. BAZERMAN and George LOEWENSTEIN, "Taking the Bias Out of Bean Counting", 79 Harvard Business Review (2001) p. 28.

25. George J. ANNAS and Frances H. MILLER, "The Empire of Death: How Culture and Economics Affect Informed Consent in the U.S., the U.K., and Japan", 20 American Journal of Law & Medicine (1994) p. 357.

26. Lawrence A. PONEMON, "The Objectivity of Accountants' Litigation Support Judgments", 70 Acct. Rev. (1995) p. 467.

expectations.[27] It is generally easier for people to remember information that is consistent with their other beliefs than information that is inconsistent with it,[28] and ambiguous information tends to be interpreted as consistent with already held beliefs.[29] Professionals are not immune from this tendency. Indeed, the expectations that arise from their experience are part of their expertise. Nonetheless, expectations can also distort what the professional sees, introducing a confirmatory bias. Thus, when scientists were asked to evaluate a piece of research, their judgments about the quality of the research were influenced by whether the outcome supported the scientist's prior beliefs.[30]

Of course, physicians, auditors and scientists are typically not attorneys, and the arbitrators in the study I described earlier were not attorneys or judges or legal scholars. One might therefore be tempted to conclude that legal training can eliminate or at least reduce some of these distortions in judgment. Although we have some evidence to suggest that similar distortions arise even when decision-makers are legally trained, the most systematic source of evidence comes from the extensive literature on judicial decision-making by American judges. This work is particularly interesting in revealing the influence of the background of the decision-maker on decision-making because much of the research has been done on federal appellate court judges who are appointed for life. Their lifetime tenure means that these judges are not subject to concerns about re-appointment that may lurk in the back of the consciousness of judges selected for a term of years or arbitrators who are appointed on a case-by-case basis. Because they generally sit in panels of three and, unlike some tribunals,[31] are free to reach non-unanimous verdicts, it is possible to study the nature and extent to which differences among judges deciding the same case reach different decisions. Political scientists and recently, some legal scholars, have examined the pattern of decision-making by these federal judges for evidence that background characteristics of the judges can explain some portion of the variation in their decisions. In a recent example of this genre of research, Brodney, Schiavoni and Merritt[32] (1999) looked at appellate cases reviewing unfair labor practice

27. C.G. LORD, L. ROSS and M.R. LEPPER, "Biased Assimilation and Attitude Polarization: The Effects of Prior Theories on Subsequently Considered Evidence", 37 Journal of Personality and Social Psychology (1979) p. 2098.

28. A. LOCKSELY, C. STANGOR, C. HEPBURN, E. GROSOVSKY and M. HOCHSTRASSER "The Ambiguity of Recognition Memory Tests of Schema Theories", 16 Cognitive Psychology (1984) p. 421.

29. R.P. VALLONE, L. ROSS and M.R. LEPPER, "The Hostile Media Phenomenon: Biased Perception and Perceptions of Media Bias Coverage of the Beirut Massacre", 49 Journal of Personality & Social Psychology (1985) p. 577.

30. Jonathan J. KOEHLER, "The Influence of Prior Beliefs on Scientific Judgments of Evidence Quality", 56 Organizational Behavior and Human Decision Processes (1993) p. 28.

31. In the Dutch legal system, for example, public dissent is not permitted. That is, majority decisions are announced publicly as if they were unanimous. Peter VAN KOPPEN and Jan TEN KATE, "Individual Differences in Judicial Behavior: Personal Characteristics and Private Law Decision-making", 18 Law & Society Review (1984) p. 225 at p. 227, fn. 1.

32. James J. BRUDNEY, Sara SCHIAVONI and Deborah J. MERRITT, "Judicial Hostility Toward Labor Unions? Applying the Social Background Model to a Celebrated Concern", 60 Ohio State Law Journal (1999) p. 1675.

claims issued by the federal courts of appeals over a seven-year period. According to a strictly legal model of how cases are decided, attributes of a judge's background should provide no information that will help to predict judicial decisions. In contrast, a social background perspective, while acknowledging the influence of case-specific facts and legal precedent, posits that biographical factors, such as personal traits, educational background and pre-judicial activities also help to explain judicial decisions.[33] Brodney and his co-authors found, as have others, empirical support for the social background perspective. For example, whether the judge attended an elite college and whether the judge had experience as a practicing attorney representing management in labor matters were significant predictors of the positions that the judge took toward labor union claims about unfair labor practices.[34] A purely doctrinal explanation of appellate court decisions cannot account for these results.

The influence of social background as well as the research showing that judges are subject to cognitive biases in the evaluation of evidence[35] explain only a part of judicial decision-making. There is little doubt that the primary influence on judicial decisions is the evidence and applicable law. Nonetheless, the research reveals that when the evidence or law is somewhat ambiguous, there is ample room for non-evidentiary and extra-legal considerations to influence outcomes. The variety of perspectives that naturally arises across individuals with differing backgrounds is one rationale for the American jury. To reach a verdict, multiple citizens must pool their diverse experiences and perceptions.

The best judges try hard to provide both sides to a dispute with an equal opportunity to persuade the court of the virtue of their positions, but it would be naive to assume that they always succeed. The same struggle occurs in the attempt to ensure that arbitrators have the attributes identified by Mauro Rubino-Sammartano that include "possession of a balanced mind", "independence" and "impartiality".[36] The choice in international arbitration to avoid selecting a chairman from the same country as one of the parties is a further reflection of the effort to produce, and convey the appearance of producing, a fair and balanced tribunal.

It would be unrealistic, however, to ignore the possibility that structural features of arbitrator selection can influence the perspective of a party-appointed arbitrator, and it is here that I want to take up Neil Kaplan's invitation to be somewhat obstreperous. Let me suggest that there is a parallel to international arbitration panels that you may not, at first glance, recognize: to the party-appointed expert in litigation that is a standard feature of the adversary system in the United States. The party-appointed

---

33. See, e.g., Jilda M. ALIOTTA, "Combining Judges' Attributes and Case Characteristics: An Alternative Approach to Explaining Supreme Court Decisionmaking", 71 Judicature (1988) p. 277; see generally Lawrence BAUM, *The Puzzle of Judicial Behavior* (1997).

34. The surprising result was that judges who had prior experience representing management clients were more likely to support labor union claims than were judges who lacked that prior experience.

35. Cognitive biases affect both judicial and lay judgments, although judges appear to be less affected by some biases than are laypersons. See, e.g., Chris GUTHRIE, Jeffrey J. RACHLINSKI and Andrew J. WISTRICH, "Inside the Judicial Mind", 86 Cornell L. Rev. (2001) p. 777.

36. *Op. cit.*, fn. 9, p. 320.

arbitrator is expected to understand the perspective of the party that appointed him, and to make certain that the chairperson and the other party-appointed arbitrator are fully informed as well. At the same time, the party-appointed arbitrator cannot display partiality. To do so not only would be inconsistent with the duty of the arbitrator to exercise independent judgment, but also would have consequences for the arbitrator's reputation and would undermine his ability to influence his fellow panel members. Of course, in light of the affinities discussed earlier and the ability of a party to "'shop' for arbitrators with specific backgrounds and experience" in order to identify an arbitrator likely to be receptive to the party's perspective,[37] the party-appointed arbitrator is likely to be more sympathetic to the position of the appointing party, even if the ultimate weight of the evidence favors the opposing party and the panel reaches a unanimous decision on the appropriate verdict.

How similar is this picture to the position of the party-appointed expert? The expert testifies under oath at trial, with an obligation to provide truthful answers to the questions he is asked. Moreover, this expert has a professional reputation to protect, and not only that reputation but the nature of his testimony will follow him in future cases. In fact, what the party-appointed expert says, unlike the questions or deliberation behavior of the party-appointed arbitrator, will become part of a public record. Parties, of course, can search for experts who have taken, or are likely to take, positions that favor the view that the party wants to advance. For example, recently a spate of cases has been making their way through American courts in which the plaintiffs allege that they have been stroke victims as a result of taking the drug Parlodel to suppress lactation after giving birth. Medical experts testifying for the plaintiffs in these cases are on record for having taken the position that Parlodel can cause strokes; experts for the defendants, not surprisingly, have reached the opposite conclusion. Each is more likely to find evidence persuasive that the plaintiff in the specific case did or did not experience a stroke due to her Parlodel exposure to the extent that it is consistent with the earlier views they have expressed.[38]

American party-appointed experts are currently the subject of much critical comment in the United States,[39] as they have been in England,[40] and some efforts have been made to reduce their role and their influence by substituting or at least supplementing them with court-appointed experts. Parties and the attorneys who represent them are generally opposed to court-appointed experts. I suspect that the reason is very close to those that have encouraged the system of party-appointed arbitrators and the values of procedural justice. Some degree of party control encourages a sense of fairness that a tribunal, even one that decides against you, has received and considered all of the

---

37. See James H. CARTER, "Improving Life with the Party-Appointed Arbitrator: Clearer Conduct Guidelines for 'Nonneutrals'", 11 The American Review of International Arbitration (2001) p. 295 at p. 296.

38. See, e.g., *Siharath v. Sandoz*, 131 F.Supp. 2d 1347 (N.D. Ga. 2001); *Brasher v. Sandoz*, 160 F.Supp. 2d 1291 (N.D. Ala. 2001)

39. Joe S. CECIL and Thomas E. WILLGING, *Court-Appointed Experts: Defining the Role of Experts Appointed Under Federal Rule of Evidence* (Federal Judicial Center 1993) p.706.

40. Lord WOOLF, *Access to Justice* (1996).

information you think should be part of its deliberations. The value of party control may be particularly crucial for the legitimacy of international arbitration in which parties may come to the table from not only different legal systems, but also with cultural differences that affect their perspectives (e.g., on what behaviors are appropriate).[41]

One intriguing feature of the three-member international arbitration panel that may act as an important constraint on partiality does not exist for a party-appointed expert. While the prospect of repeat business is a potential incentive in both situations, the reputation of an arbitrator as fair and unbiased should increase the likelihood that he or she will receive appointments as the third member of the arbitration panel. If that incentive does affect behavior, there may be important differences in the behavior of arbitrators who frequently occupy the chairman's seat and those who do not. Unfortunately, there is no study that has tested either that hypothesis or indeed many hypotheses about patterns in arbitration. Thus, although we can draw from the general literature on dispute resolution to point to the influence of perceptions of procedural justice on parties' reactions to arbitration, there is no clear analog we can draw on to examine the effects of the structure of international arbitration on the behavior of arbitrators.

III.   CONCLUDING REMARKS

This examination of the psychology of dispute resolution and its application to international arbitration reveals how procedures can have a crucial effect on the reactions of litigants and on their willingness to accept decisions even when those decisions do not favor them. It also shows why it is unrealistic to expect even highly trained and well-motivated arbitrators to be unaffected by their own prior experiences and backgrounds in the way they evaluate evidence. As a result, procedures loom large in ensuring that the methods of dispute resolution maximize both the appearance and the reality of procedural and substantive justice.

The discussion to this point leaves many questions unanswered about the operation of international arbitration that can be addressed only by examining the actual behavior of international arbitration panels as they decide cases. For example, does the chairperson behave differently when selected by the parties or by the party-selected arbitrators than when the ICC or another arbitral institution appoints the chair? Does adversarial behavior by one of the party-appointed arbitrators invariably stimulate adversarial behavior in the other party-appointed arbitrator? With what effect? When the arbitrators are all from the same country (or from a particular country), are they more likely to agree on procedures? On outcomes? If one of the advocates is an English barrister who is a member of the same chambers as one of the arbitrators, does that connection affect the judgment of the panel? If so, in what way? Answers to these and other questions can contribute to the health of international arbitration by correcting misimpressions that are based on anecdotes or unusual cases, and can signal where

---

41. See., e.g., Joseph SANDERS and V. Lee HAMILTON, "Legal Cultures and Punishment Repertoires in Japan, Russia, and the United States", 26 Law & Society Review (1992) p. 117.

reforms may be appropriate. Although the exciting, but relatively young, world of international arbitration has spawned a large body of scholarship and commentary, most of the writing on the subject has been limited by the requirements of confidentiality that are a distinctive feature of international arbitration. There has been no study of international arbitration in which researchers have systematically observed and analyzed the actual behavior and decision-making process. Lest you think that such a research agenda for international arbitration merely represents another unrealistic professorial pipe dream, I want to close with an example to show that such apparently sensitive research can be carried out.

The jury in the United States is a constitutionally protected cultural icon, although it is frequently the subject of criticism. Its deliberations are confidential, and researchers interested in studying the jury have, for the past fifty years, set up mock cases and juries to study and interviewed jurors in real cases after their jury service was completed[42] because they were not permitted to observe actual jury deliberations. Recently, with the permission of the Arizona Supreme Court, we were able, with the consent of the litigants and their attorneys, to videotape jury deliberations in fifty trials. The research was done with the understanding that only the researchers would have access to the tapes, and that any published results would not disclose the identity of the parties or their attorneys. Although the work is still in progress, my expectation – and that of those who have supported the research – is that this close study of a series of trials can provide insights and suggestions that could not be assembled through less direct means of study. Indeed, the project already has had that result[43] – but that is a subject for another occasion. I mention it here only to provide an example of research carried out on what would appear on the surface to be an impossible institution to study directly, and to invite you to consider new ways, consistent with the demands of confidentiality, to examine the psychology of dispute resolution in the exciting forum you have created.

---

42. Post-trial interviews with jurors are not permitted in some countries (e.g., England).

43. Shari Seidman DIAMOND, Neil VIDMAR, Mary ROSE, Leslie ELLIS and Beth MURPHY, "Juror Discussions During Civil Trials: Studying an Arizona Innovation", 45 Az. L. Rev. (2003) p. 1; Shari Seidman DIAMOND and Neil VIDMAR, "Jury Room Ruminations on Forbidden Topics", 87 Va. L. Rev. (2001) p. 1857.

The Psychological Aspects of Dispute Resolution

*Anne Marie Whitesell**

Shari Diamond's paper[1] discusses the important role that psychology plays in successful dispute resolution. She has highlighted the fact that the level of satisfaction of the parties and their ultimate acceptance of the decision are strongly influenced by their perceptions of the fairness of the procedure.

Shari Diamond has identified three factors leading to a perception of fairness: perceived neutrality, perceived trust and treatment with respect and dignity. She has discussed how these three factors are influenced by the choice of the decision-maker and the conduct of the procedure.

Theresa Giovannini's[2] paper presents several examples of behavior by arbitrators which could weaken the parties' perception of the fairness of the procedure.

What I propose to do now is to discuss the psychological aspects seen from the perspective of an arbitral institution and, more specifically, that of the ICC International Court of Arbitration (the Court). I will try to highlight the vital role that the institution plays in dealing with these psychological aspects, in particular when compared to ad hoc arbitration.

I will do this first by addressing the two key elements discussed by Shari Diamond – the choice of the decision-maker and the conduct of the procedure – with a view to demonstrating the role that the institution plays in increasing the parties' perception of the fairness of the procedure.

I.   CHOICE OF THE DECISION-MAKER

No one present here today needs to be told that the choice of the decision-maker is in all likelihood the most important factor in increasing the parties' perception of the fairness of a procedure. In international arbitration this is probably even truer than in a domestic setting. The active participation of the parties in that choice is a key element. In ICC cases last year, approximately 69 percent of the arbitrators were proposed by the

---

*   Secretary-General, International Court of Arbitration of the International Chamber of Commerce, Paris, France. This article represents the personal views of the author and should not be interpreted as binding upon the ICC or the ICC International Court of Arbitration.
1. See this volume, pp. 327-342.
2. See this volume, pp. 348-352.

parties or the co-arbitrators. The Court appointed only 31 percent of the arbitrators.[3] As to the choice of the number of arbitrators – i.e., whether to have a sole arbitrator or a three-member arbitral tribunal – interestingly, the decision to have a three-member tribunal in 90.4 percent of the cases was the result of the arbitration clause or a subsequent agreement of the parties; in only 9.6 percent of the cases was the decision to submit the matter to a three-member tribunal the result of a Court decision.[4]

Once the decision as to the number of arbitrators has been made, the statistics are interesting too. In cases submitted to a sole arbitrator last year, 83 percent of those arbitrators were appointed by the Court. When there was a three-member panel, in 57 percent of the cases, the chairman was chosen by the parties or the co-arbitrators. Therefore, the Court appointed the chairman in only 43 percent of the cases. Ninety-six percent of the co-arbitrators were proposed by the parties.

It thus appears that the parties are playing a highly active role in the choice of the decision-maker, which, as Shari Diamond says, allows them to feel that they have some control and heightens their psychological acceptance of the procedure.

We now turn to the choice of the persons acting as arbitrators in ICC cases. Shari Diamond has drawn attention to the fact that the choice of the decision-maker will often "affect the expectations of the parties to the arbitration proceedings ... thereby affect[ing] their reactions". She highlights the important influence of the background of the person, nationality-wise, culturally and professionally. She further stresses the critical effect of a perception of neutrality.

The ICC Rules provide that "[i]n confirming or appointing arbitrators, the Court shall consider the prospective arbitrator's nationality, residence and other relationships with the countries of which the parties or the other arbitrators are nationals and the prospective arbitrator's availability and ability to conduct the arbitration in accordance with these Rules".[5] As concerns neutrality, when the Court appoints a sole arbitrator or chairman, such person "shall be of a nationality other than those of the parties",[6] unless the parties have not objected to the Court choosing someone from a country of which any of the parties is a national.

Neutrality is also privileged by the Court's use of its national committee system in making appointments. When the Court is to appoint an arbitrator, based upon the elements of each case (i.e., nationalities involved, possible languages, applicable law, place of arbitration, specific requirements of the clause, the need for specific expertise), the Court requests a proposal from one of approximately eighty different national committees. This decentralized system ensures that arbitrators are not being selected

---

3. In 2001, 57.1 percent of the arbitrators were proposed directly by the parties, 11.5 percent were proposed by the co-arbitrators, and 31.4 percent were appointed by the Court.

4. Art. 8(2) of the ICC Rules of Arbitration (ICC Rules) provides:

"Where the parties have not agreed upon the number of arbitrators, the Court shall appoint a sole arbitrator, save where it appears to the Court that the dispute is such as to warrant the appointment of three arbitrators."

5. Art. 9(1) ICC Rules.

6. Art. 9(5) ICC Rules.

by the Court from any pre-established list and allows for the appointment of arbitrators with appropriate qualifications from all over the world. In selecting the national committee to be invited to make a proposal, the Court also takes into account political, regional and cultural considerations. Efforts are made to find the appropriate balance among the members of the tribunal. In constituting a tribunal, the Court seeks to consider all elements that will promote greater acceptance of the award.

Another central element for Shari Diamond's factors of perceived neutrality and trust is independence. Every arbitrator acting in an ICC proceeding must be and remain independent of the parties involved in the arbitration.[7] Shari Diamond has referred to what she surprisingly calls the "controversial approach of the ICC statement of independence". The statement of independence requires the disclosure of "any facts or circumstances which might be of such a nature as to call into question the arbitrator's independence in the eyes of the parties".[8] Here, the psychological aspect is fully evident in the terminology itself. The ICC standard for disclosure is based on facts viewed "in the eyes of the parties".[9] The requirement of a statement of independence and the fact that every ICC arbitrator must be either appointed or confirmed by the Court heightens the parties' perception that the decision-maker will be neutral and can be trusted.[10]

The need for perceived neutrality can also be seen particularly in multi-party cases. Under the ICC Rules, when either multiple claimants or multiple respondents do not jointly nominate an arbitrator, the Court "may appoint each member of the Arbitral Tribunal and shall designate one of them to act as chairman".[11] By appointing all three members, the Court avoids the risk of a party thereafter claiming that it did not receive equal treatment in the constitution of the tribunal.

Subsequent to the appointment stage, the parties may reach a point where their perception of the neutrality or their trust in the decision-maker is called into question, leading to issues of challenge, resignation or replacement. The role of the arbitral institution is primordial in such cases, allowing an evaluation of the well-foundedness of such change in perception.[12]

---

7. Art. 7(1) ICC Rules.
8. Art. 7(2) ICC Rules.
9. It should be clarified that this is the standard for disclosure and not for confirmation or appointment of arbitrators by the Court.
10. When there are reasonable grounds for an objection, the Court decides not to confirm an arbitrator. This occurred seventeen times in 2001. It should be noted that 948 arbitrators were either appointed or confirmed by the Court in 2001. Included in this number are the arbitrators who were confirmed by the Secretary-General of the Court pursuant to Art. 9(2).
11. Art. 10(2) ICC Rules.
12. In 2001, thirty-three challenges were brought before the Court, of which only two were accepted. During 2001, the Court accepted seventeen resignations and replaced two arbitrators pursuant to Art. 12(2).

II.   CONDUCT OF THE PROCEDURE

Shari Diamond has discussed how perceived neutrality, perceived trust and treatment with dignity are influenced by the conduct of the procedure.[13] Once again, I would like to highlight the important role that institutional arbitration, and in particular ICC arbitration, plays in enhancing these elements during the conduct of the procedure.

In institutional arbitration, the parties may be reassured by the fact that the procedure is overseen by a neutral body other than the decision-maker. In ICC arbitration, both the Secretariat of the Court and the Court itself carefully monitor all stages of the proceedings. The different functions performed by the Secretariat and the Court may affect the parties' perceptions of the conduct of the case.

On the Secretariat level, the parties know that there is a professional staff available to discuss any problems encountered during the procedure. In the event of a potential problem, the Secretariat is able to contact the arbitral tribunal without revealing the identity of the party that has voiced concern. Additionally, the staff members are in a position to discuss with the chairman or co-arbitrators various difficulties that may arise within the tribunal. As the members of the Secretariat are able to communicate in approximately twenty languages, this allows both the parties and the arbitrators to feel more at ease within the system.

The fact that the Secretariat is copied on all correspondence between the parties and the arbitrators helps to reassure the parties that their case is being handled fairly and neutrally. The parties and the arbitrators also know that the Secretariat is following up on time-limits and keeping the Court informed about deadlines under the ICC Rules. This creates a certain psychological pressure which can have a positive effect on the efficiency of the proceeding.

The Court itself exercises various functions which serve to reinforce the parties' perceptions of neutrality and trust. Among the most critical of these functions is the Court's scrutiny of awards.[14] As the parties are aware that their award has been reviewed by a neutral body, this has a major effect on their psychological acceptance of the award. The Court is able to draw on the various legal and cultural backgrounds of its over 100 different members in carrying out the scrutiny process. The international composition of the Court allows culturally diverse parties to feel that their points of view have been taken into account. This aids the parties to have greater trust in an award that has gone through the system.

The parties and the arbitrators know that an award has been examined with a view to ensuring its maximum enforceability. The scrutiny process permits suggested modifications to be carried out by the arbitrators, possibly making the decision more acceptable to the parties. For example, on certain occasions, the Court has requested

---

13. The parties' desire to exercise control, which we have seen in their choice of the decision-maker, is also apparent for certain procedural elements. For example, in 2001, the parties agreed upon the applicable law in their contract in 78.4 percent of the cases. Similarly, the place of arbitration was agreed between the parties, either in the arbitration clause or in a subsequent agreement, in 83.7 percent of the cases.

14. See Art. 27 ICC Rules.

drafting changes of text concerning the behavior of parties which the parties might have found to be offensive. Also, as a result of the scrutiny process, there have been majority awards that have become unanimous awards once the arbitrators considered the comments received from the Court. For both the parties and the arbitrators, this allowed for an award that was perceived as more authoritative.

Another important role played by the Court in enhancing the parties' sense of trust and fairness relates to the financial administration of the procedure. In all ICC cases, the Court fixes the arbitrators' fees and expenses. Any separate fee arrangement between the parties and the arbitrators is prohibited.[15] This fundamental principle of the ICC Rules takes away the possibility of psychological pressure being exercised by the arbitral tribunal on the parties.

I have tried to illustrate how institutional arbitration can aid in the perception of neutrality and trust by the parties, allowing for successful dispute resolution. But now I would like to approach the topic from a different perspective. Both Shari Diamond and Theresa Giovannini have talked about the important role that psychology plays in helping parties to feel that the process is fair and just. The focus has been on how the parties perceive the process. I would submit that this is a one-sided point of view.

I would like to speak now about how psychology is used by the parties as a strategic weapon. Not all parties act disingenuously and thus psychology is not always used to ensure a fairer procedure.

Some examples of the psychological tactics that are employed by parties are:

— strategic filings of requests to be claimant rather than respondent — in several cases, both sides stated that they were the claimant;
— objections to confirmation of arbitrators and groundless challenges;
— choices of arbitrators who are not well-suited to a procedure, based on language skills for example;
— intentional drafting of clauses that cannot be respected — for example, ICC arbitration to be administered by another institution;
— refusal to pay advances on costs;
— refusal to quantify claims;
— intentional complication of the procedure and use of delaying tactics in order to force a settlement;
— seeking of security for costs where not founded;
— refusal of consolidation of procedures.

In such examples, the balance of experience between the parties and the arbitral tribunal is essential to prevent the use of psychological elements to derail the procedure.

This brings us back to the first topic of the Congress: control of the procedure. The motion concerned who should control the procedure – the parties or the arbitrators? I would maintain that the institution also has a vital role to play, by ensuring that the psychological aspects receive appropriate treatment.

---

15. See Art. 2(4) of Appendix III of the ICC Rules.

The Psychological Aspects of Dispute Resolution: Commentary

*Teresa Giovannini**

TABLE OF CONTENTS   Page

I.   INTRODUCTION

Professor Diamond has presented the scenario of ideal arbitration proceedings, where both the tribunal and counsel behave in a perfectly balanced way. The tribunal shows no interest or inclination in finding the position of one side more persuasive than that of the other. Civilized exchange is the rule and emotional outbursts do not occur. As pointed out by Professor Diamond, in such ideal proceedings: "Proceedings are well organized and efficient. The decision is correct and the litigants on both sides go away accepting that justice has been done."[1]

Unfortunately, we do not live in such an ideal world.

The purpose of my comments on Professor Diamond's report is to give you some practical examples of arbitral tribunals' psychological misbehaviors, which – while clearly not constituting grounds for challenge, be it of the tribunal itself or of one of its members, or of the award itself – can seriously undermine the "value of enhanced authority and legitimacy for international arbitration".[2]

II.   THE TRIBUNAL'S ATTITUDE

Our distinguished speaker mentioned the importance of parties' perception of the fairness of procedures in the process of accepting the final verdict. With respect thereto, Professor Diamond focused in particular on (i) perceived trust and (ii) perceived neutrality.

As to the issue of perceived trust, Professor Diamond underlined the importance for parties to "have their day in court". But this requirement sometimes leads the arbitrators to lose the distance and perceived neutrality they are supposed to keep during the entire proceedings, as shown by the following examples.

I was involved as lead counsel in a case where a claim for tort (misrepresentation) was

---

*   Partner, Lalive & Partners, Geneva.
1. See this volume, pp. 327-342 at p. 327.
2. *Ibid.*, at p. 330.

put forth by my side. During the coffee break of one of the preliminary hearings, the chairman (a very experienced arbitrator) "confidentially" told me that I should better base my claim on a contractual basis, and explained the reasons for that approach to me.

I did what he suggested, and amended my claim with the correlative investment of time and money for the client and myself. There is no question that the chairman was acting in good faith and wanted to do me a favor, so to say.

Contrary to my expectations, I could have done without this advice. As it turned out, the case was a hopeless one and we lost it, both on extra-contractual and contractual grounds.

I gave a lot of thought to this event afterwards, trying to understand the reasons for this "advice" that was not requested from the chairman or from any of the party-appointed arbitrators. My conclusion was the following: the arbitrator – on the basis of the confidence and the mission he or she had been entrusted with – sometimes feels that he or she should show concern about the case on a personal basis. This is in my view a clear psychological trap – the need for recognition by counsel, whatever the outcome of the dispute may be. This trap must be avoided, as it causes frustration for parties and their counsel.

A similar situation arises when the "perceived neutrality" on the part of the decision-maker – the tribunal or of one of its members – is at stake. In this respect, Professor Diamond has mentioned the problem of the balance that the party-appointed arbitrators have to strike between the loyalty due to the party that selected them and the loyalty due to the law as represented by the panel as a whole and the evidence presented in the case.

The issue of the party-appointed arbitrator's loyalty towards the party that selected him or her actually gives rise to what I consider to be a clear deviation from the parties' understanding and expectations from a tribunal in which they place their trust. The most common example is when one of the party-appointed arbitrators "argues" the case in support of the position brought forward by the party that appointed him or her. In practice, and all of us have witnessed such situations, the party-appointed arbitrator puts questions to the witnesses which, far from giving the impression that the tribunal as a whole is trying to ascertain facts, clearly indicates that he or she feels duty bound to support one position rather than another.

This behavior, far from creating trust, triggers suspicion, both on the part of other arbitrators and on the side of the other party. The other arbitrators will obviously be very careful in considering this arbitrator's positions in the deliberations on the final decision, with the consequent weakening of this arbitrator's influence on the final outcome. This arbitrator's view is clearly tainted, therefore subject to careful verification by the other arbitrators. As counsel, I greatly fear this kind of intervention from an arbitrator appointed by the side I represent, and I seriously question the advantages of having the arbitrator appointed by the opposite side behaving that way. In two recent arbitration cases where I was counsel, and which were chaired by very experienced arbitrators, this attitude of clear and open support towards the party that appointed the arbitrator concerned was adopted by the opposite side's arbitrator. I remain convinced that the opposite side's position was not helped by this attitude, regardless of the outcome of the dispute. I also feel that when the party that appointed the arbitrator loses the case, the trust that the party had towards the arbitrator becomes much more undermined than it would have been without this kind of intervention.

Another example all of us surely have come across is the case where one of the party-appointed arbitrators continuously whispers in the chairperson's ear during the hearings. Professor Lalive told me of a case where such behavior was adopted by the arbitrator appointed by the opposite side, while the arbitrator nominated by his client, a government, continued behaving in a very discrete and impassive way. Pierre Lalive's client reacted very strongly to that attitude, considering – rightly or wrongly – that the chairperson was clearly inclined to consider the opposite side's arguments more favorably.

I am firmly convinced that trust in an arbitrator is not synonymous with the expectation of a partisan attitude. In our capacity as arbitrators, we are entrusted – and the word is chosen on purpose – with this role because of our supposed or actual skills and capacities to lead a fair trial. But, judges we are, and judges we must remain. There is no room for arguing a case, this is not what we are hired for. There is no room for partiality, there is no room for expression of personal considerations or feelings. We must remain open to any possible decision until the very end of the proceedings, when all the facts are gathered, and not give the parties any indications in connection thereto before the final award is rendered. Attitudes of physical proximity – as the one I mentioned of the arbitrator whispering to the chairperson – must be carefully avoided and the chairperson must unequivocally discipline arbitrators in breach thereof.

III.   THE OUTCOME OF THE DISPUTE AND HOW IT IS PRESENTED TO THE PARTIES

Beyond these examples of personal attitudes of arbitrators, the way the tribunal examines the facts of the case and reflects this thorough examination in the award are clearly crucial for "the party's satisfaction with the verdict and willingness to accept the legitimacy of the decision ... and the fairness and legitimacy of the institution".[3] Unfortunately, as shown by the following example, this is not always the case.

I was counsel in a case where a fishing company had ordered six fishing boats worth US$ 3 million each. The first four were actually delivered by the shipyard with so many defects that the fishing company decided to rescind the contract. As it happens, the remaining two boats were never delivered, and did not even receive the "release" upon completion of their construction by the relevant port authorities. At the time of the proceedings, the shipyard was bankrupt.

In the award, the tribunal held that the fishing company had to pay for what it had received, namely the six boats. End of discussion. The same result could have been reached by saying that the rescission was not justified, that the fishing company was responsible for not having required the shipyard to deliver the two remaining boats, for example. The tribunal's statement that the company had to pay for what it received simply showed that the tribunal had not paid attention to the fact that the two boats not only were never delivered, but in addition, had never been in a state to be delivered and – due to the construction company's bankruptcy – could never be delivered in the future.

---

3. *Ibid.*, at p. 329.

Such superficial and clearly erroneous arbitral awards destroy any trust parties can have in a particular panel, but more importantly, also destroy the parties' trust in arbitration as a valid and serious alternative dispute resolution mechanism. I remember the client's reaction when reading the award: he simply said that the award was of such a mediocre level that even a district court in his country (it was a North African country) would have been frightened to render a decision of the kind. In addition, such a decision could have been appealed, while the award was clearly not appealable. For sure, this fishing company will never resort to arbitration again.

Conversely, however, I have had the opportunity to feel how much trust the following behavior can give the parties and their counsel. In a recent case relating to the dissolution of a joint venture, the tribunal, after the closing of the proceedings, issued an Order by which it gave its tentative "inclination" regarding the outcome of the dispute and – simultaneously – put some additional questions to the parties. Albeit deprived of any reasoning, the tribunal answered each substantive issue raised by both parties in that Order, reserving any modifications of its final judgment depending upon the parties' answers to the questions put.

This Order actually gave the parties the possibility to see – before the final award was issued – that any and all issues raised were duly taken into consideration by the tribunal and also to realize that the tribunal had actually understood the core of the dispute. Indeed, the losing party tried – through the answers required by the tribunal – to redress the situation through what it considered its strongest arguments. In that case, it was in vain. But clearly, the losing party had been given a "voice" in a very efficient process.

Professor Diamond also mentioned the "decision-making process".[4] Besides the arbitrators' cultural backgrounds, prior experiences and personal associations referred to by our speaker, the decision-making process also gives rise to behavior patterns which can ruin the other arbitrators' trust. For example, there are arbitrators who, when they see that the point of view they are defending, is not being adhered to by the other members of the tribunal, systematically threaten not to sign the award or to issue a dissenting opinion. This situation is clearly unfair and surely incompatible with the balance an ideal tribunal must keep, namely – as underlined by Professor Diamond – a tribunal without either interest or inclination to find the position of one side more persuasive than that of the other.[5] This must be reflected not only in the hearings but also in the deliberations themselves.

IV.   CONCLUSION

The little time allocated to me does not allow me to give further examples of the difficulty of achieving the "ideal tribunal" or the "ideal proceedings". But the organizers of this session dedicated to The Psychological Aspects of Dispute Resolution were right in holding that the knowledge of the law, be it procedural or substantial, and compliance

---

4. *Ibid.*, at p. 342
5. *Ibid.*

with it by the parties and the tribunal, is not sufficient to create trust in arbitration as a valid alternative dispute resolution mechanism. Trust and perceived neutrality require adequate psychological behaviors. These are not among the least of all of our interests and challenges, particularly as arbitrators.

Arbitration under

Investment Treaties

Public Interest and Investment Treaty Arbitration

Nigel Blackaby[*]

I.   INTRODUCTION

Treaty arbitration often raises fundamental issues of public interest which are usually absent from international commercial arbitration. It is said that arbitrators are not guardians of the public interest and should simply resolve the dispute inter partes without looking at the wider political and economic impact of the issues in debate. Such an approach may be appropriate in a private dispute but is that still the case when measures of democratically elected governments are reviewed for their compliance with norms of international law?

The conflict between the essentially private nature of arbitration and the often public nature of the issues at stake in investment treaty arbitrations have caused this nascent institution to come under increasing criticism from the media, public interest groups and even the states themselves. As the United States Government argued in the context of one such case:[1]

---

[*]   Partner, Freshfields Bruckhaus Deringer International Arbitration Group, Paris.
      This paper was delivered at the Swiss Arbitration Association Conference on Investment Treaties and Arbitration, held in Zurich on 25 January 2002.

1. *Methanex Corporation v. United States of America.*

"[investor-state disputes are] to be distinguished from a typical commercial arbitration on the basis that a State [is] the Respondent, the issues [have] to be decided in accordance with a treaty and the principles of public international law and a decision on the dispute could have a significant effect extending beyond the two Disputing Parties".

A recent New York Times article[2] commenced as follows:

"Their meetings are secret. Their members are generally unknown. The decisions they reach need not be fully disclosed. Yet the way a group of international tribunals handles disputes between investors and foreign governments can lead to national laws being revoked and environmental regulations changed. And it is all in the name of protecting foreign investors under NAFTA."

The interests of states are at stake in these cases. Arbitrators' awards, even if unable to declare state measures invalid, may have a direct and significant impact on the state's future conduct and the national budget. Taxpayers in states which are the subject of an adverse award may legitimately demand to know why their money is being paid out to disgruntled foreign investors. But the criticisms should not simply be dismissed as the ranting of anti-globalizationists. There is some legitimacy behind the hyperbole and the legitimate complaints need to be identified so that they can be addressed.

There is a risk of this new child in the world of international arbitration dying in infancy, delicate and overprotected by its parents from exposure to the outside world. The arbitration community should not take the role of the overprotective parents, suffocating its natural development and depriving it of survival skills in the outside world by reciting the mantra of confidentiality. Concrete steps can be taken to everyone's advantage to ensure that investment treaty arbitration matures into a powerful tool for the effective protection of foreign investment and thereby a motor for international commerce, whilst at the same time balancing the legitimate concerns that have been expressed. To do that we need to understand and seek to reconcile competing public interests.

II.   PUBLIC INTEREST IN INVESTOR PROTECTION

I start from the proposition that there is an overriding public interest in effective foreign investment protection. It is no coincidence that the number of bilateral treaties for the promotion and protection of investment has mushroomed from about 500 treaties in 1992 to some 2,000 treaties today. States recognize that effective investor protection promotes foreign investment – they proudly display their record in this regard on their foreign investment propaganda, promising a secure environment for such investments underpinned by effective international law standards. As the tribunal in *Amco v. Indonesia*

---

2. 11 March 2002. See also the Washington Post, "Fast Track Attack on America's Values" (5 December 2001).

noted:[3] "To protect investment is to protect the general interest of development and of developing countries."

Those standards are ineffective without a practical enforcement mechanism. Many early treaties stipulated a wide range of protection for foreign investment but were only backed up by inter-state remedies, little better than customary international law rights of diplomatic protection. These provided little comfort to the foreign investor. They depended on the willingness of the state to trigger formal inter-state arbitration by espousing the claim of the investor. The dispute was inevitably politicized as the state weighed up the concerns of antagonizing the state against the importance of the investment in question. The small or medium investor would rarely carry the weight to cause the scales to tip in its favour.

It is simply unrealistic to assume that such remedies would ever effectively police an investment protection regime. Indeed, one of the motivating factors for the Convention on the Settlement of Investment Disputes between States and Nationals of Other States (the ICSID Convention) was to remove investment disputes from the realm of diplomatic protection through direct access to an international remedy. As Professor Schreuer notes in his Commentary:[4] "The dispute settlement process is depoliticized and subjected to objective legal criteria. Moreover there is no requirement to exhaust local remedies before resorting to ICSID arbitration unless this has been made an explicit condition of consent by the host State."

In the recent Senate Ways and Means Committee Hearings on the Free Trade Area of the Americas, the question of an appropriate dispute resolution mechanism was discussed. Dan Price, one of the Chapter 11 NAFTA negotiators noted in these hearings that: "Limiting investment dispute settlement to a state-to-state procedure will politicize disputes, leaving investors, particularly small and medium sized enterprises, with little recourse save what their government cares to give them after weighing the diplomatic pros and cons of bringing any particular claim."

As a consequence, the foreign investor's interest is only guaranteed by a direct right of access to a neutral and effective dispute resolution procedure to enforce the specific rights afforded to their investment by the relevant treaty. This has the salutary effect of depoliticizing the dispute, reducing investment risk and thereby increasing cross-border investment. Nearly all modern treaties follow this model by providing investors with a right to trigger international arbitration unilaterally without the sanction of their home state once a "cooling-off" period for negotiations has been completed.

This public interest in investor protection needs to be balanced against the increasing concerns voiced as to the nature of the process which is then engaged. Unless these concerns are addressed, states themselves may step back in the next generation of such treaties or in a possible future multilateral investment protection treaty and limit direct access to adjudication of disputes by foreign investors.

Indeed, this "backlash" may already be starting. In the debate surrounding the dispute resolution provisions of the future Free Trade Area of the Americas, it has been suggested that direct access to dispute resolution be abrogated. In an attempt to curb

---

3. *Amco v. Indonesia* (Decision on Jurisdiction), 1 ICSID Reports 400.
4. Ch. SCHREUER, *The ICSID Convention: A Commentary*, p. 398.

some of the wilder investor claims, the NAFTA Free Trade Commission has issued "Notes of Interpretation" of Art. 1105 by clarifying that its scope is not intended to go beyond that of customary international law.[5] Since the scope of this article is the subject of pending claims, the policy makers have been accused of "changing the rules in midgame".[6]

A more drastic "backlash" through removal of the direct right of action for the investor might be stopped in its tracks by seeking to address the concerns expressed by the critics. We first need to understand the competing public interests at stake in this debate which might be resumed as the public interest in transparency, the public interest in an independent and impartial tribunal and the public interest in the uniform development of the law.

III.   PUBLIC INTEREST IN TRANSPARENCY

The first and principal criticism of investor/state arbitration is its opacity. This stems from the nature of arbitration itself. The notion of three private individuals deciding a commercial dispute behind closed doors which will only affect the rights of the parties behind the doors does not offend fundamental principles of justice. Parties should be able to elect to dispose of their rights, including the disposal of their right to a judicial resolution of disputes by the inclusion of an arbitration clause.

The possibility of those same three private individuals deciding whether measures taken by a legitimate government are compatible with an international treaty is more problematic, especially where the decision on the merits is without appeal. This is a fortiori the case when those three individuals condemn that government to pay eight-figure dollar sums from its coffers, paid for by its taxpayers, who have not been permitted access to the process. When that process permits the provincial judge of one state to have the ultimate word on the legality of measures passed by another state in the context of annulment proceedings,[7] eyebrows may be raised. As Barton Legum, an attorney with the Office of the Legal Adviser of the US State Department recently observed:[8] "Conducting arbitrations implicating the public interest in conditions of secrecy is unacceptable."

Many of the decisions issued by tribunals, especially in the NAFTA context, raise extremely sensitive issues: in *SD Myers*, a tribunal punished Canada for blocking the export to the United States of hazardous waste products;[9] in a settlement of the *Ethyl*

---

5. Reproduced in 13 World Trade & Arbitration Materials (2001, no. 6) pp. 139-140.

6. Attributed to Henri ALVAREZ, "Is NAFTA the Law of the Land?", The American Lawyer (March 2002).

7. In the case of *Metalclad v. United Mexican States*, ICSID Case No. ARB 97/1, the seat of the arbitration under an ICSID Additional Facility case had been fixed as Vancouver. The Mexican Government was unhappy with the award and petitioned to have it set aside by the British Columbia Supreme Court. The Court took jurisdiction and partially set the award aside.

8. *Op. cit.,* fn. 6.

9. *S.D. Myers, Inc. v. Government of Canada*, Partial Award of 13 November 2000, 40 ILM (2001, no. 6) p. 1408.

case, the Canadian government lifted restrictions on manufacturing an ethanol-based petrol additive that it considered hazardous; in *Metalclad*, the Mexican government was ordered to pay US\$ 16 million compensation because it refused to permit the construction of a toxic waste processing plant;[10] in *Methanex*, a Canadian corporation is challenging California's decision to phase out the use of a gasoline additive containing methanol.[11]

The public interests raised by these issues are not limited to NAFTA. A claim is pending against the Republic of Bolivia concerning the expropriation of a water concession following civil disturbances as a result of privatization and price increases necessary to improve the quality of the water system.[12] In two cases brought against Argentina, the legality of the generalized government measures effectively revoking the legal framework applicable to tariff structures as a result of the economic crisis will be reviewed.[13]

The current opacity occurs at various levels: first, the knowledge of the dispute's existence; secondly, the access to the process itself and finally the access to the resulting decision.

1. Public Awareness of the Dispute

There is a concern that public awareness of an investor-state dispute, which may address issues of general public concern, and which will risk depleting that country's resources through a damages award, may be under the control of the parties. Whilst the existence of ICSID cases is posted on its website with details of the tribunal[14] and NAFTA cases benefit from publication as a result of access-to-information legislation,[15] investor-state cases involving other jurisdictions decided ad hoc under the UNCITRAL rules, or pursuant to the rules of the ICC or Stockholm Chamber of Commerce may go wholly unnoticed unless the parties agree otherwise. In such a case how can public interest be protected?

2. Public Access to the Process

Even if the existence of the dispute is public, the hearings remain private, thereby preventing an informed debate on either the quality of the process itself or substantive

---

10. *Metalclad Corporation v. United Mexican States*, Award of 25 August 2000.

11. *Methanex Corporation v. United States of America*, claim pending.

12. *Aguas del Tunari S.A. v. Republic of Bolivia* (ARB/02/3) (the author declares his interest as counsel to the claimant). The issues arising from the case are discussed in "Leasing the Rain", The New Yorker (8 April 2002).

13. *CMS Gas and Transmission Company v. Republic of Argentina* (ARB/01/8) (the author declares his interest as counsel to the claimant) and *LG&E Energy Corp. (and others) v. Republic of Argentina* (ARB/02/1). The cases were discussed in a Bloomberg News article "CMS Energy, Powergen Unit, Lenders Challenge Argentine Policies" of 25 April 2002.

14. See www.worldbank.org/icsid.

15. See, for example, the website www.naftaclaims.com which contains all publicly available material on the NAFTA claims, including briefs and interim decisions.

issues which might touch on matters of public interest, such as environmental protection. The clamour for public access to the hearings on such issues of public importance is therefore understandable. At the same time, it is important that the process is not re-politicized or turned into a media circus.

One means of addressing the concern is to permit the access and/or intervention of interested third parties in the procedure as amici curiae. The arbitrators in the *Methanex* case concluded that their tribunal had the power to accept submissions from amici curiae as a matter of jurisdiction in an arbitration governed by the UNCITRAL Rules but, considering the matter to be premature, declined to articulate detailed criteria.[16] The tribunal concluded that the public interest could play an important role in the decision and that admission of amicus briefs could counter some of the suspicion which had built up in connection with the secrecy of the proceedings.

Transparency is not merely aimed at ensuring that third parties get their say on issues of public importance. It also encourages good government. Citizens of Mexico, India or Russia ought not simply to be told: "your money has just been used to satisfy an international arbitration award", the details of which cannot be divulged. Democratically elected governments are accountable to their electorate and should come under scrutiny in the political process if they are engaged in conduct contrary to their international obligations. Transparency through access to the record and to hearings ought therefore to discourage governments from acting in an arbitrary way towards foreign investors.

Public access is unlikely to open the floodgates. The arbitrations are often of a technical nature and only of specific interest to a small number of public interest groups. Public access to the European Court in Luxembourg has not caused lines to form before the commencement of each hearing and that institution has not been turned into a media circus.

## 3.	Public Access to the Awards

A related issue of transparency is the publicity and availability of awards. In a new and developing area of law such as this where there are few decided cases, nearly every decision draws new lines. Yet access to such decisions can remain a lottery. ICSID does an excellent job in encouraging parties to consent to publication and then offers the widest circulation through its Foreign Investment Law Journal. However, is it right that these cases, all of which (for better or worse) take on an exaggerated precedential value due to the dearth of authority, are only accessible at the parties' discretion? This affects not only the general public's right to access and consider the substantive decision but also the lawyer's right to present the best case for his or her client by accessing and addressing all relevant precedent.

This is a real problem. Access to many of the decisions is through a network of law firms active in this area: whilst it benefits the members of that "magic circle" it is not right that those firms should have a wider array of jurisprudence with which to fight their case. Access should be equal to all – whether the sole practitioners in middle

---

16. *Methanex Corporation v. United States of America*, Decision on Petitions from Third Persons to Act as Amici Curiae dated 15 January 2001.

America (who have been active in these cases) or the international law firm in Paris or Washington.

IV.   PUBLIC INTEREST IN AN INDEPENDENT AND IMPARTIAL TRIBUNAL

Most commentators suggest that the role of an arbitrator is private and contractual: the arbitrator is charged with the "mission" of resolving a particular dispute between specific parties. But international arbitrators have traditionally had an advantage over their judicial colleagues: their decisions are usually not published. They can focus on the case at hand and ignore wider implications on the development of jurisprudence since, absent enforcement measures or an application for setting aside, the decision will be known only to a few. The sporadic nature of such publication has deterred a general culture of looking for arbitral precedents other than with respect to purely procedural issues. As a result, the judicial tension between the need for justice in the specific case and the danger of creating an unfortunate precedent, particularly acute in common law systems of stare decisis, does not arise for the arbitrator. There is not the same underlying fear that (as any English or American law student will recall) "hard cases make bad law".

In the light of the increased publicity of investor-state awards, the treaty arbitrator has a new responsibility for establishing a corpus of law. This responsibility may cause problems where the arbitrator is instructed as counsel in a similar case. Unlike commercial arbitration where applicable law varies, the arbitrators in these cases are consistently applying a limited number of concepts under public international law. It is important therefore that the arbitrator's mind not be subconsciously influenced against a certain interpretation of a treaty if the published award would cause him or her problems in a pending case in which they were acting as counsel.

The other concern voiced is that of "secret courts" of which "the members are generally unknown". Arbitration clearly provides parties with the right to select a decision-maker of their choice, but there is no minimum requirement to be an ICSID or investment treaty arbitrator. Whilst there is a corpus of eminent lawyers who act as arbitrators in this area, there is no means of preventing the appointment of decision-makers whose abilities or knowledge of the area of law are questionable. In the absence of any right of appeal on matters of substance, the complete liberty with which the parties may act can give rise to concerns.

V.   PUBLIC INTEREST IN THE UNIFORM DEVELOPMENT OF THE LAW

Recent criticism has also been focused as a result of two allegedly inconsistent awards brought under two investment treaties and two different tribunals but on the basis of identical facts (the *Lauder* cases).[17] Such inconsistency in decisions on state liability is a

---

17. *Lauder v. Czech Republic*, Final Award of 3 September 2001 and *CME Czech Republic BV v. Czech Republic*, Final Award of 13 September 2001. See also "Czech Mate", The American Lawyer (March 2002).

matter of concern. Yet it is difficult to see how it can be avoided given that individual shareholders up a chain of ownership might establish a separate and independent right to bring such a claim and start a separate arbitration under different treaties depending on their nationality.

The classic investor-state arbitration scenario arises out of a specific state measure taken in respect of a specific foreign investment, often involving claims of expropriation or discrimination. A new and far more radical scenario arises where the state has passed general measures which affect whole classes of foreign investor in alleged breaches of standard treaty protections. This is the current case with the Argentine crisis. Argentina's Emergency Law and related regulations removed the right for public utilities to charge in dollars, converted tariffs from dollars to pesos at a rate of 1:1 and abolished the indexation of tariffs to US dollar indices. These measures affect all regulated public utilities in the gas, electricity and water sectors in a virtually identical manner. Most of these public utilities were privatized in the 1990s and bought by foreign investors who have now lost all value in their Argentine assets as they are unable to fund dollar denominated debt. Many of the foreign investors have sought to benefit from Argentina's extensive network of bilateral investment treaties (BITs) and two claims are already pending before ICSID on virtually identical facts. In a few months time the number of claims could have tripled as the compulsory negotiation periods expire.

In such circumstances, each tribunal will have to reach an independent decision on the compatibility of the measures with the treaty rights in question with a corresponding risk of inconsistent decisions. The prestige of the arbitration institution risks severe erosion if such inconsistencies occur. This is the first time that the institution of investor-state arbitration has faced such concerns – in earlier financial crises, the state in question had either concluded few BITs or investors did not seek to enforce their rights.

VI.   POSSIBLE SOLUTIONS

Returning to the overriding public interest in effective investor-state dispute resolution, how can this be achieved whilst at the same time responding to the issues raised? There are two approaches. The first is the "bottom up" approach that takes into account the current position with all its faults and vested interests. The "top down" approach takes a more utopian view and asks the question how the concerns could be best addressed without taking account of any of the existing constraints. Neither approach will be able to result in an overnight revolution.

1.   "Bottom-up" Reform

Many of the problems are inherent in the current model treaty structures and 2000 treaties are unlikely to be renegotiated quickly. The better hope would be for a true multilateral investment treaty which would gradually replace all bilateral treaties between signatory states and incorporate the modifications to the dispute settlement process. A first review could be undertaken in the context of the negotiation of the Free

Trade Area of the Americas Agreement which, if successful, could provide a model for a wider multilateral investment treaty. Another approach could be at the level of the capital exporting states' model treaties. Many such states negotiate with capital importing states on the basis of a model which is then modified in the course of the negotiation.[18]

Another means of engineering change (also not easy) could be through modifications to the ICSID Rules or the execution of a supplement to the ICC or UNCITRAL Rules to apply in the event of arbitrations commenced pursuant to investment treaties.

So what changes could be proposed?

a.   Existence of claims

A new generation treaty (or rule changes) could provide for express publicity of all new claims, along the lines of the information provided by ICSID on its website. Consideration could also be given to ensure that, subject to business confidentiality concerns, the main submissions be made publicly available. As Dan Price noted in his evidence to the Senate as to how the NAFTA system might be improved in the future FTAA Treaty:

> "The FTAA parties should consider increasing the transparency of the process by ensuring that the briefs and arbitration proceedings are open to public view, subject to reasonable protections for confidential business information."

b.   Access to hearings

The next generation of treaties or rule changes should consider allowing access to the arbitration hearings from affected third parties, upon prior application as amici curiae. Whilst the *Methanex* decision is to be welcomed, it would be appropriate to institutionalize the rules for admission of third-party public-interest groups, either as participants or observers. There are as yet no clear rules with respect to this delicate question. Arbitrators might wish to look to the experience of the WTO Appellate Body which has permitted such intervention.

c.   Access to awards

There should be a systematic publication of all awards in investor-state cases to ensure the development of a proper corpus of law with equal access to investors and states. This will also reduce the risk of inconsistent decisions.

d.   Arbitrators

In order to avoid criticism of the arbitrators, consideration should be given to the establishment of minimum criteria for the admission of arbitrators to act in these types of disputes. There should also be consideration of a reform to the manner in which the

---

18. See, e.g., the Model Treaties annexed to DOLZER and STEVENS, *Bilateral Investment Treaties* (1995).

ICSID List is established. It includes many names with little or no experience in this field and omits some of the major practitioners. A more radical approach (dependent on the creation of a more appropriate list) could be the nomination of all members of the tribunal by a neutral institution such as ICSID.

e.   Appeal process

Arbitration is usually a process without appeal. This sits well with the exigencies of commerce but needs to be reconsidered in the field of investor-state arbitration where the policies of a state are under question and the precedential value of a particular case can become exaggerated due to the dearth of other authority. An appeal on specific points of law would avoid the risk of an aberrant decision and be more likely to result in coherent jurisprudence. It would also (in non-ICSID cases) avoid the implication of national courts in the review process as happened in the case of *Metalclad*. The process could be engineered along the lines of the ICSID ad hoc annulment panels but with a wider remit.

2.   "Top-down" Reform

A more radical solution which could be considered in the context of the FTAA or any multilateral investment agreement would be the creation of a permanent judicial body, whose members would be drawn from eminent practitioners with an equal balance of members from capital-importing and capital-exporting states.

The hearings of such an institution would be public, and its decisions published and developed into a consistent body of jurisprudence. One need only look at the use of Iran-US Claims Tribunal jurisprudence in investor-state cases to see what a valuable source of law that institution has been. There would be no lengthy tribunal appointment process and a panel of judges would be selected randomly upon filing of a claim (possibly respecting a balance of at least one judge from a capital-exporting country and a capital-importing country on each panel). There would be a procedure for the admission of amicus curiae briefs from third parties.

In this way, the overriding public interest in investor-triggered dispute resolution would be preserved but it would be insulated from much of the criticism levelled at the current process by the public and the states alike. The process would be fully transparent, there would be an institutionalised right of access to third party groups, there would be a developing and accessible case law and no risk of arbitrator/counsel conflict of interest. There would be no appeal from its decisions and no equivalent of a setting aside procedure other than claims of judicial bias. Its process would include a procedure where cases with identical or similar issues would be stayed to avoid the risk of inconsistent decisions.

Such an institution, I believe, would have the necessary authority to silence the current critics while protecting the investor.

Detractors might decry a transfer of sovereignty to a supranational court. But its authority would stem from the state's consent in the applicable treaty – it would have no compulsory jurisdiction. Others might claim that there is already a plethora of judicial institutions and there is no need for another. But this institution would be at the very heart of investor protection and have an ever-increasing role given the growth in world trade.

Of course, the implementation of such an institution would be an enormous exercise – it is highly unlikely that states will sit down and renegotiate their 2000 BITs. However, in the context of a possible multilateral investment treaty or even initially in the context of the FTAA, it is an idea which should not be ignored.

One thing is clear: unless the criticisms of the current system are addressed (either more modestly or in the grand plan), this new child of the arbitration world may be stunted in its growth. International trade and investment would suffer as a result and a great opportunity would have been lost.

The Role of the Arbitrators in Investment Treaty Arbitration

*Karl-Heinz Böckstiegel**

I.   INTRODUCTORY NOTE

It is not by accident that arbitration under investment treaties has been a focus of interest in recent years in meetings and publications on international arbitration. Not only has the number of cases in this field increased dramatically in the last few years, but this kind of arbitration also distinguishes itself from other international commercial arbitration by quite a number of special features and difficulties which could easily be the subject of a full-day meeting, as was organized earlier this year by the Swiss Arbitration Association in Zurich.

Twice, during the ICCA Congress in London I had to review the version of my paper as it had been included in the Conference Folder distributed to the participants.

First, after Sally Fitzgerald, in the Opening Debate of Monday morning, made a specific reference to what she – and Jan Paulsson in a recent publication[1] – called the "Böckstiegel Method" of conducting arbitrations, I had to examine whether my remarks on the role of the arbitrator in this paper are in contradiction to what is described as that method. They are not. And, indeed, they are in conformity with the result of the general vote after that debate to the effect that the majority abstained indicating thereby

---

* Professor Emeritus of International Business Law, University of Cologne; President, German Institution of Arbitration (DIS); Member of ICCA.
1. Jan PAULSSON, "The Timely Arbitrator – Reflections on the Böckstiegel Method" in Robert BRINER, Yves FORTIER, Klaus Peter BERGER and Jens BREDOW, eds., *Law of International Business and Dispute Settlement in the 21st Century – Liber Amicorum Karl-Heinz Böckstiegel* (Cologne 2001) p. 607 et seq.

that neither the parties alone nor the arbitrators alone can be said to control the arbitration.

Second, on the next day of the Congress in her comments on psychological aspects of dispute settlement, Teresa Giovannini,[2] as an example of how a positive interaction between the arbitrators and the parties might be promoted, mentioned a Procedural Order in a recent arbitration by which the arbitrators had informed the parties of their present inclinations and asked for certain specific information and comments in this regard before the tribunal came to its final decision. Since I had chaired the tribunal that issued that Order, again, a reexamination of my paper was due but, to my relief, showed no conflict to this paper.

This was important, as I have been asked to deal with the role of the arbitrator in investment treaty arbitration. My remarks are subject to the following qualifications: For understandable reasons, the contributions of each panelist have been limited in volume which means that I can only highlight certain major aspects and raise certain specific questions regarding the subject while detailed consideration must be left to further discussion. And secondly, my considerations are to be seen under the influence of my own subjective experience in the field which primarily comes from investment treaty arbitration cases under the ICSID and NAFTA Rules, and also from more general investment arbitrations under the ICC, LCIA and UNCITRAL Rules.

II.   LEGAL FRAMEWORK

The topic already qualifies the legal framework for the kind of arbitration we are dealing with. The dominant features are the almost 2,000 bilateral investment treaties (BITs) though which multilateral treaties such as NAFTA, the treaties of the European Union and of MERCOSUR and, at a later stage, perhaps also of the World Trade Organization (WTO) come into play.

But in addition thereto, the law to be applied by arbitrators in this kind of arbitration may also include customary international law and general principles of law for such questions as the compensation standards for expropriation, and the national law of the host country either as the law applicable to an investment contract or as the object of examination regarding the question whether, in the given case, a taking "tantamount to expropriation" of the investment has been effected by way of law or court measures rather than by way of executive acts of the host state.

And then, of course, an additional legal framework has to be taken into account regarding the arbitral procedure. This may again include to some extent treaties in public international law, such as the BITs, NAFTA or the ICSID Convention, but will also include lower-ranking law, particularly the arbitration rules of the institution chosen, such as those of ICSID, ICC, LCIA or UNCITRAL.

---

2. See Teresa GIOVANNINI, "The Psychological Aspects of Dispute Resolution", this volume, pp. 348-352.

III.   SELECTION OF ARBITRATORS

The often-repeated truism that arbitration can only be as good as the arbitrators are, is also valid for investment treaty arbitration. Therefore, the process of selecting arbitrators for investment treaty arbitration not only is of relevance for the quality of the arbitral procedure, but also for what the parties can expect as the outcome of the case in substance. It is thus not surprising that parties and their counsel will exercise extremely thorough due diligence in selecting arbitrators for these cases which quite often deal with very large amounts in dispute.

The usual set-up that we know from international commercial arbitration to the effect that the parties nominate one arbitrator and either the parties or these nominated arbitrators can try to agree on a third arbitrator to preside over the procedure is subject to some qualification in investment treaty arbitration. These qualifications are either found in certain BITs or in the other legal framework mentioned above. If we look at the most frequently used system of investment treaty arbitration, namely the ICSID system, we find that Art. 37 of the ICSID Convention provides for the just-mentioned traditional procedure of appointment, but that Rule 3 of the ICSID Arbitration Rules then provides further limitations regarding the procedure and the persons to be nominated. Similarly, insofar as a party does not nominate an arbitrator or no agreement can be reached regarding the chairman of the tribunal, the usual solution that the arbitral institution then takes over in appointing such missing arbitrators is again qualified by Arts. 38 to 40 of the ICSID Convention and by Rule 4 of the ICSID Arbitration Rules. In this context, to avoid a considerable reduction in the number and kind of candidates for appointments from the ICSID Panel of Arbitrators, it is highly recommended to the parties and the arbitrators appointed by them to make every effort to agree on a president of the tribunal who is acceptable to all concerned. It is a bad start for an arbitral procedure if, right from the beginning, a party or the parties feel uncomfortable with the chairman or president of the arbitral tribunal, irrespective of whether such hesitation is justified or not.

In addition to these formal criteria of appointment, experience from many cases shows that it is extremely helpful for the quality of the subsequent arbitral procedure and the substance of an award resulting therefrom if all arbitrators appointed are not only acquainted with the law and practice of international investment and regular commercial arbitration, but also with the relevant fields of public international law and the principles of its interpretation and application, such as the Vienna Convention on the Law of Treaties. In making use of their discretion, the parties and the party-appointed arbitrators have to be aware of the interrelation between Art. 39 of the ICSID Convention which attempts to discourage the appointment of so-called national arbitrators and Rule 1(3) of the ICSID Arbitration Rules which tries to close a loophole left by that Article in a way that is not easy to grasp. The corresponding provision of the ICSID Additional Facility Arbitration Rules is easier to understand, because it includes text paraphrasing the basic rule of Art. 39 of the ICSID Convention.

IV.   BETWEEN PARTY AUTONOMY AND PROACTIVE ARBITRATORS

From international commercial arbitration, we know party autonomy as the dominating factor regarding the arbitral procedure. It is mostly exercised simply by choosing the arbitration rules of an arbitral institution, but it may also be and not seldom is exercised by the parties agreeing on specific aspects of the procedure either already in their arbitration clauses or arbitration agreements or, after the start of the arbitration case, between the parties' counsel.

Also in investment treaty arbitration, the consensual character of proceedings is not only considered as the cornerstone of the arbitral procedure, but should also be accepted in practice by the institution and the arbitrators to the greatest extent possible in shaping the arbitral procedure. As there is no arbitration without the consent of the parties, any consent of the parties regarding certain procedural aspects must also be taken into account.

However, there are limitations, particularly those imposed by mandatory provisions in the investment treaties or the procedural legal frameworks the parties have chosen. If we look again at the most relevant example in practice, namely the ICSID system, we find quite a number of provisions from which neither the parties can derogate by consent nor from which the arbitrators can derogate by using their discretion on how to conduct the procedure. First, there are several provisions designed to assure the effectiveness of the arbitral process and in particular of the arbitral tribunal as a decision-making body, particularly ICSID Convention Arts. 41(2) on the competence-competence of the arbitral tribunal, 42(2) prohibiting a finding of *non liquet*, 45(2) in case a party fails to appear, and 48(3) obliging the tribunal to deal with every question submitted to it and to state the reasons upon which the finding is based. Other ICSID Convention Articles seek to assure the integrity and impartiality of the process, particularly Art. 36 regulating the request for arbitration. Similarly, certain provisions of the ICSID Convention seek to promote the integrity and impartiality of the arbitrators and their role in the process. Thus, Art. 39 discourages the appointment of so-called national arbitrators, Art. 40(2) provides a high threshold for the personal qualification of arbitrators, Arts. 57 and 58 provide for the possible disqualification of an arbitrator, Art. 21(a) provides that the arbitrator's immunity may only be waived by ICSID itself, and Art. 48(3) obliges the arbitrators to state the reasons for their findings in the award. Further limits may be found in the ICSID Institution Rules and Administrative and Financial Regulations.

The interrelation between such mandatory rules on the one hand and valid implementation of party autonomy on the other hand provides the legal framework within which the arbitrators may use the discretion they are generally granted in all institutional rules as well as the UNCITRAL Arbitration Rules for ad hoc arbitrations regarding the conduct of the procedure.

This still grants considerable room for the arbitrators between a more passive role and a far-reaching proactive role. Where a tribunal places itself within this discretionary area will, to a large extent, depend on the experience and the national and legal background of the arbitrators concerned and particularly of the chairman of the tribunal.

Here, I cannot resist repeating the example that Eloise Obadia[3] gives of the extremely proactive arbitrator: In one of his fables, "The Cat, the Weasel and the Small Rabbit", Jean de la Fontaine reports on a dispute between a weasel and a rabbit regarding ownership of a piece of land. The weasel and the rabbit agreed to have their dispute settled by a cat known as "the expert arbitrator in all issues". Without even giving them an opportunity to present their case, the cat ate both of them. This is obviously a very speedy and efficient method of solving a dispute though some may hesitate to transfer it to our world of human arbitrations.

Generally speaking, over the years, arbitrators have tended to become more proactive in shaping the procedure, not only in normal commercial arbitration, but also in investment treaty arbitration. This is exemplified not only by deciding on procedural aspects which, up to that point in the procedure, have neither been ruled upon by consent of the parties nor by provisions in the respective arbitration rules, but also by discussing with the parties whether their consent on certain procedural aspects really provides the best method of efficiently dealing with the case at stake. If the parties have selected experienced arbitrators, it will quite often occur that these arbitrators detect certain weaknesses or problems in the intended procedure and are in a position to propose solutions to deal with them. Also from the point of view of the parties and their counsel, it will often be preferable to have frequent consultations between the parties and the arbitrators concerning procedural aspects as well as substantive issues of the case rather than filing written submissions and presenting oral presentations to a basically silent tribunal whose procedural as well as substantive decisions are absolutely unpredictable for the parties who thus do not know whether they speak to what the tribunal considers relevant.

V.   INTERNAL COOPERATION BETWEEN PRESIDING AND CO-ARBITRATORS

The internal relationship and cooperation between the members of an arbitral tribunal are not subjects which are widely addressed or ruled upon in the legal framework indicated earlier in this presentation. What we normally do find is a provision to the effect that the tribunal shall decide questions by a majority of the votes of all its members, such as Art. 48 of the ICSID Convention. In this context, two basically different solutions appear for the case that no majority is found because each of the three members of the tribunal maintains a different solution. If no additional ruling is provided by the applicable procedural framework, the tribunal will have to continue deliberating the matter until at least two of its members can agree to form a majority on a certain solution. This is the situation under the ICSID Convention as well as the UNCITRAL Rules. On the other hand, Art. 25 of the ICC Rules and Art. 26.3 of the LCIA Rules provide that, failing a majority decision on any issue, the chairman of the arbitral tribunal shall decide that issue. Issuing procedural orders will mostly be delegated to the chairman of the tribunal either by the applicable arbitration rules or by an agreement at

---

3. Eloïse M. OBADIA, "How Proactive Arbitrators Really Are in Conducting Arbitral Proceedings: An ICSID Perspective", 16 News from ICSID (1999, no. 2) p. 8 et seq.

the start of the procedure. Normally, such procedural decisions will require consultations between the members of the tribunal, but for practical purposes and to avoid delay, routine decisions, such as the extension of time limits, are often delegated to be decided by the chairman alone.

Beyond this legal framework, the practical and human relationship among the members of the tribunal will have a major impact on the conduct of the procedure and the outcome of the case. In investment treaty arbitration as well as in other commercial arbitrations it does, of course, occur that a party-appointed arbitrator, though not challenged or challengeable for lack of impartiality, may in practice consider and use his role as having to represent the interest of the parties that appointed him within the tribunal. In fact, parties and their counsel when selecting an arbitrator may stress such an expectation both from the investor's side as well as perhaps even more from the side of the host state involved in the case. While one may well consider it a responsibility of the party-appointed arbitrator to make sure that the written and oral submissions of the party that appointed him are taken well into account in the deliberations of the tribunal, experience shows that a party-appointed arbitrator playing the role of the advocate of the party within the tribunal is self-defeating. If the chairman of a tribunal gets that latter impression from the behaviour of a party-appointed arbitrator, this arbitrator's influence on the deliberation and decision process of the tribunal will decrease considerably. Thus, even from the party's point of view it is not in that party's interest to select and pressure an arbitrator to that effect.

This is, of course, even more so if the other members of the tribunal and particularly the chairman find out that a party-appointed arbitrator, in breach of his obligation of confidentiality, continues to communicate with the party that has appointed him during the arbitral process.

The above situation should be distinguished from the often-occurring situation that fully objective and impartial arbitrators nevertheless disagree considerably on certain issues in the case. This is absolutely natural and happens frequently. Here, it is the obligation of the chairman of the tribunal to provide for a full discussion of such disagreements, but also to find an appropriate time to end such discussion by a decision even if it is "only" a majority decision. In such cases, it is preferable to include the dissenting arguments in the reasoning of the award itself as well as the reason why the majority felt otherwise. In order to enable this, the dissenting arbitrator has at least a *nobile officium* to present his dissenting arguments at such a stage of the procedure that they can be considered when drafting the award. This may not exclude the option of a separate dissenting opinion of the arbitrator.

VI.   ADMINISTRATIVE SUPPORT TO ARBITRATORS

Investment treaty arbitration cases will often bring about such a volume and number of submissions and documents as well as statements by witnesses and experts that dealing with the mere logistics becomes a considerable problem for the arbitral tribunal. This is so irrespective of whether the applicable arbitration system provides for a far-reaching administrative support by the institution, as does the ICSID system, or leaves the issuing of procedural orders etc. to the tribunal and its chairman, as do the ICC, LCIA and

UNCITRAL Rules. In such large cases, it may well be appropriate and, in spite of the additional costs involved, also in the interest of the parties to enable the arbitrators to concentrate on their traditional function, if a secretary or assistant to the arbitral tribunal is appointed to deal with the logistics of the case. However, if there is such an appointment, the arbitrators will have to ensure that they remain solely responsible for procedural and substantive decisions.

VII.   DUTIES OF ARBITRATORS

The fundamental duty of the arbitrators is to come to a reasoned decision on the claims put before them after giving the parties an equal and full opportunity to present their case. The above-mentioned legal framework for investment treaty arbitration, particularly the applicable treaties of public international law and even more so the applicable arbitration rules, provide a great number of provisions implementing and qualifying this fundamental duty. As we have seen, some of these provisions are mandatory and thus create absolute duties, others are simply guidelines which the arbitrators may chose not to apply, with or without the consent of the parties, for an efficient procedure in the case before them. There is no need and no room in this short presentation to deal with all of these provisions.

Rather, it seems appropriate to briefly mention duties which are found less explicitly in the legal framework. The first such duty is the availability of the arbitrator. Particularly in the field of investment treaty arbitration where the parties and their counsel tend to choose particularly experienced arbitrators, such arbitrators may have many other commitments and perhaps other pending cases which then turn out to prevent the arbitrator from being sufficiently available for the new case. Obviously, neither the parties nor their counsel nor the institution can expect, when appointing an experienced international arbitrator, that this arbitrator has an unlimited availability for the new case. But practice shows that it is highly recommendable during the appointment process to examine whether the prospective arbitrator is available for the major foreseeable work involved with the new case: i.e., an early procedural meeting, work on submissions as they come in and communications with the other arbitrators, sufficient periods for perhaps a hearing on jurisdiction found necessary and an evidentiary hearing on the merits at a later stage.

Though one may not consider it a formal duty of the arbitrator, it is again highly recommendable for the arbitrators and particularly the chairman of the tribunal to ensure, at an early stage of the arbitral procedure, an exchange of communications among the parties, their counsel and the tribunal on the major aspects of the further conduct of the procedure. Usually, the best way of doing this will be a personal meeting between the arbitrators and the parties as is provided for by ICSID Arbitration Rule 13 within sixty days after the constitution of the tribunal. It is highly important in order to avoid misunderstandings on the parties' part and to assure that they can fully present their case in an efficient procedure that the parties' counsel knows the "rules of the game" in some detail before major submissions are drafted and one meets for the evidentiary hearing. The drafting of such submissions and the preparation of statements by witnesses and experts will depend very much on how they are used later, at which stage no further submission of documents is permitted, and what their relevance is during and after the evidentiary hearing.

VIII.   PARTICULARITIES DUE TO STATES AS PARTIES

The mere fact that a state or state institution is involved as one of the parties in investment treaty arbitration leads to certain particularities of the arbitral procedure not appearing in normal commercial arbitration between private enterprises. Again, the limitations for this paper do not allow going into many details in this regard, and this author must resist the temptation of elaborating such details which he has treated extensively in other publications.[4] But at least a few major aspects regarding the role of arbitrators in this context may be briefly mentioned.

First of all, of course, the arbitrator will have to examine and take into account any specific rules provided by the above-mentioned legal framework. More of such rules are naturally found in the ICSID system which has been shaped for the involvement of states as parties. Reference can here be made not only to Art. 64 of the ICSID Convention regarding disputes between Contracting States, but regarding the usual case between a foreign investor and a host state, to Arts. 25 to 27 regarding jurisdiction, and Arts. 53 to 55 regarding recognition and enforcement of awards.

Next, in spite of the confidentiality of the procedure itself, the arbitrators have to be aware that often they are involved in a semi-public dispute settlement procedure, because the representatives of the host state will have to report back to administrative and political authorities at home in application of mandatory national law provisions. This may also lead to public interest groups and private interest groups trying to get involved. And, at least under the procedure of Chapter 11 of NAFTA, the respective governments of the three states may file submissions to the tribunal even if not directly involved as a party in the case.

For similar reasons, the arbitrators will have to be aware much more than in private commercial arbitrations that their decisions may be considered as precedent for future cases as they become known to interested outside observers either by official publication or by other means of information. I still recall that, when I was chairing the first NAFTA investment arbitration and a dispute arose already regarding the place of arbitration,[5] the tribunal felt obliged to ask for a full briefing from the parties in this regard and to issue a formal separate and reasoned decision on the place of arbitration which, indeed, was then made publicly available and used in later arbitrations.

---

4. K.-H. BÖCKSTIEGEL, *Arbitration and State Enterprises — A Survey on the National and International State of the Law and Pratice* (Deventer/Netherlands and Paris/France 1984) 113 pp; K.-H. BÖCKSTIEGEL, ed., *Acts of State and Arbitration*, vol. 12 of Series of the German Institution of Arbitration (DIS) (Cologne 1997) 301 pp; K.-H. BÖCKSTIEGEL, "The Legal Rules Applicable in International Commercial Arbitration Involving States or State-Controlled Enterprises" in: *ICC International Arbitration — 60 Years On — A Look at the Future* (Paris 1984) p. 117 et seq.

5. NAFTA/UNCITRAL Decision of 28 November 1997 by Tribunal consisting of K.-H. Böckstiegel (Chair), Charles Brower and Marc Lalonde (Co-Arbitrators), published in ICCA *Yearbook Commercial Arbitration* XXIVa (1999) p. 211 et seq.

The involvement of states in investment treaty arbitration also brings up a difficulty not unknown in private commercial arbitration, but qualified in certain ways in investment treaty arbitration, namely that a party is poorly represented in the procedure. This will normally not be the case on the side of the investor which mostly tends to be a potent private enterprise, but does occur for the side of the host state of the investment which may be a small and poor developing country. All those involved in international arbitration are well aware of the strong influence it can have on the conduct of the procedure and the outcome of the case if the representatives and also counsel of the parties are not acquainted with international dispute settlement and neither logistically nor legally in a position to conduct a full and efficient presentation of the case of that party. Sometimes, this is not simply a matter of the financial funds not being available to hire an internationally experienced law firm, but is caused by the fact that the administrative civil servants of the state either have the duty or the personal pride to insist on representing the case themselves. In such cases, the arbitrators will have to follow the difficult route of taking this weakness on the side of one party into account without a breach of their obligation of equal treatment of the parties.

IX.   TAKING EVIDENCE

As in commercial arbitrations, in investment treaty arbitration the taking of evidence is also often on the one hand a highly disputed and on the other hand a highly important aspect of the procedure. In most regards, the questions arising are not specific to investment treaty arbitration and thus need not to be reiterated here. The above-mentioned legal framework will normally include some rather general provisions on the taking of evidence by documents and statements of witnesses and experts. Most details are left to the discretion of the arbitrators in conducting the procedure.

Unlike the practice of years ago, it has become a common feature of modern international arbitration that, at a relatively early stage of the procedure, the parties are obliged to submit all documents as well as statements of witnesses and experts on which they want to rely in order to give the other party an equitable opportunity to respond and supply rebuttal evidence and also in order to come to an evidentiary hearing which can concentrate on disputed factual issues after all the basic evidence is "on the table".

In practice, disputes tend to arise mostly on requests of a party for disclosure of certain documents by the other party, even if US-style discovery has not become common in international arbitration. Here, also in investment treaty arbitration, the new IBA Rules on the taking of evidence in international commercial arbitration may be chosen and are in fact often chosen as a guideline and a compromise between the traditional procedures in the common law and the civil law legal systems.

X.   PROMOTION OF AMICABLE SETTLEMENTS BY THE ARBITRATORS?

Another aspect of international arbitration which is widely discussed in recent years and on which one finds very different law, traditions and opinions between the various legal systems of the world is the question whether and to which extent the arbitrators are permitted or even encouraged to play a role in promoting amicable settlements between the parties. In certain legal systems, such as those of China, Japan and Germany, at least in domestic arbitrations parties will expect the arbitrators to play such a role and, in fact, the majority of arbitration cases will end by amicable settlement with or without an award by consent. But in many other jurisdictions, such a role for the arbitrator is either not permitted or at least not the practice. As the parties may often have an interest in concluding the dispute by an amicable settlement rather than by an award because this gives them a better basis for future business relations, starting primarily with a respective discussion at the ICCA Conference in Seoul,[6] many commentators have suggested to give arbitrators a more active role in this regard.

However, there is little reason to discuss this further in the context of investment treaty arbitration, because in most cases this is not a practical option. The foreign investor, if he alleges expropriation, will often not be inclined to a settlement, because in any case he does not intend to invest again in that particular host country. On the other hand, the representatives of the host state, either due to administrative or political pressure, may not have the authority or may not dare to take the responsibility for an amicable settlement which would normally entail having to admit that the state is at fault to some extent.

XI.   FINAL NOTE

I hope the above considerations, short as they had to be, have nevertheless shown that, on the one hand, investment treaty arbitration brings up many of the features and difficulties one is used to in international commercial arbitration between private enterprises. But on the other hand, as could be shown, there are a considerable number of specific legal provisions, interests and practical aspects due to the particular situation in which a foreign investor and a host state are involved as parties to the dispute. The arbitrator in such cases will have to take into account both the general experience of commercial arbitration and the particularities of this kind of arbitration to shape the procedure in such a way that both the investor and the host state are provided sufficient opportunities to present their case from their rather different backgrounds and interests in order to enable the arbitrators to come to convincing or at least adequate decisions.

---

6. Proceedings of the ICCA International Arbitration Conference, Seoul, Korea, 10-12 October 1996, *International Dispute Resolution: Towards an International Arbitration Culture,* ICCA Congress Series No. 8 (1998) p. 55 et seq.

Some Objections to Jurisdiction in Investor-State Arbitration

*Pierre Lalive**

TABLE OF CONTENTS

I.   INTRODUCTION

As a subject for this presentation, I have chosen "some objections to jurisdiction in investor-State arbitration" and this choice would seem to call, if not for an apology, at least for an explanation.

It is hardly necessary to emphasize the importance and increasing number of investment treaties today, whether multilateral like the 1965 Convention on the Settlement of Investment Disputes between States and Nationals of Other States (Washington Convention) or the Energy Charter Treaty, regional like NAFTA, Mercosur or the Agreement of Cartagena, or bilateral, like the some hundred treaties signed by Switzerland since 1961.

In an important paper on arbitration under BITs (2001), Antonio Parra, the distinguished Deputy Secretary General of the International Centre for Settlement of Investment Disputes (ICSID) was able to mention some 2,000 Bilateral Investment Treaties (BITs) signed by more than 170 countries. Similarly, Professor Siqueiros, writing last year on "the Mexican experience",[1] stated that "[d]isputes between investors and sovereign Governments are becoming increasingly frequent", having regard to "the gradual economic interdependence among developed and emergent economies, the growth of regional and sub-regional trade agreements and the proliferation of bilateral investment treaties ..." which explained that "investor-State arbitration has had special

---

*   Attorney, Lalive & Partners; Professor Emeritus, Geneva University; Honorary President of the Swiss Arbitration Association and of the ICC Institute of World Business Law; Member of ICCA.
1. José Luis SIQUEIROS, "An Overview of Arbitration Mechanisms between States and Investors – The Mexican Experience", Journal of World Investment (2001, no. 2) p. 249.

significance throughout the world, particularly in Latin America".

Now, to future historians and many observers, it may well seem to constitute an extraordinary progress of the rule of law and of international relations in general, that so many modern States have been willing to enter into binding commitments (of course in the exercise of their sovereignty, and not as an "abandonment" of their sovereignty as was sometimes contended!). It is remarkable that so many States are or seem ready to accept, under certain conditions, to submit disputes with a foreign private investor to outside adjudication.

The progress is indisputable, as is proved by the case load of ICSID or by recent developments in NAFTA, to mention but those examples. But I would suggest that the overall picture is perhaps less "rosy" than appears at first sight, and that a more realistic approach should also take into account the many and indeed traditional manifestations of State reluctance to accept binding adjudication by third parties. After all, this phenomenon has long been observed in public international law, e.g., with regard to the acceptance by States of the "optional clause"[2] of the International Court of Justice (ICJ), and in the number of objections to its jurisdiction.

Let me state at the outset that the deep and traditional reluctance of governments to undertake binding arbitration commitments (in the broad sense of the term "arbitration") is perfectly understandable and indeed sometimes quite justified on the part of responsible State authorities. Be that as it may, in spite of the remarkable progress accomplished by some pioneers like the late Aron Broches, it is unlikely that the tendency of States or governments to object to arbitral jurisdiction will diminish.

This remark is not pessimistic but merely realistic. A fact which leads me to hesitate to answer in the affirmative the stimulating question posed in the program for this Congress: "Will governments view with favor the increasing role and authority of arbitrators and institutions in the regulation of trade and investment disputes?"

Before I come to my first section (Procedure), I should perhaps mention a caveat. It is of course quite out of the question to attempt here anything like a complete survey of preliminary objections to jurisdiction, in the context of investor-State arbitration. What is possible, within the limited scope of this presentation, is only to give a few selected examples of such objections borrowed from recent international practice.

It is hoped that such examples (which sometimes may be named and sometimes should remain nameless) will suffice to give some idea of the difficulties in this domain, difficulties which some practitioners always keep in mind and others appear too often to ignore or underestimate at their cost! And by "practitioners", I do not mean only investors and their counsel, but also diplomats and government advisers called upon to draft BITs or to apply them.

II.   PROCEDURE

The importance, frequency and practical effects of objections to jurisdiction in investor-State arbitration are obvious. A proper understanding of the problem does require in my

---

2. Art. 36(2) Statute of the ICJ.

submission, first of all, some consideration of its procedural aspects. And no practitioner in arbitration, whether counsel or arbitrator, can hope to have a solid grasp of "investor-State arbitration" without a fairly thorough knowledge of international procedure and practice.

I have no intention to deal here with, or even to mention, the many procedural issues that may arise in investor-State arbitration. Some of them are quite specific, such as a choice or conflict between an international treaty forum and a domestic one, private or administrative; or issues such as confidentiality, representation of the public interest, or admissibility of an *amicus curiae* brief.[3]

I should like to limit my observations in this section to one question, i.e., the conduct of the proceedings in case of a challenge to the arbitrator's jurisdiction. I shall take as a convenient starting point Art. 41 of the Washington Convention where it states that:

"1. The Tribunal shall be the judge of his own competence.

2. Any objection by a party to the dispute that that dispute is not within the jurisdiction of the Centre, or for other reasons is not within the competence of the Tribunal, shall be considered by the Tribunal which shall determine whether to deal with it as a preliminary question or to join it to merits of the dispute."

The so-called principle of "competence-competence" does not call here for any comment: it is quasi-universally accepted.[4] What is perhaps interesting to note is that the Rule was accepted without any discussion during the elaboration of the Washington Convention.[5]

The principle may be seen as a counterpart of Art. 25 (1) (in fine) of the Washington Convention according to which "when the parties have given their consent, no party may withdraw its consent unilaterally", for instance, by defending some restrictive interpretation of its own consent.

It may also be noted that the power of the arbitral tribunal to be the judge of its own jurisdiction, a power recognized by general international law, has never been seriously disputed in ICSID proceedings. Also, the tribunal's power has an exclusive character, vis-à-vis other national or international organs, including State courts.[6]

An important practical question is raised by Art. 41(2) of the Washington Convention: "Should the Arbitral Tribunal deal with the objection as a preliminary question or should it join the objection to the merits of the dispute?" The choice between the two methods is of capital importance for the parties.

Art. 41 of the Washington Convention is based on a long and consistent practice of both the Permanent Court of International Justice (PCIJ) and the ICJ. It is interesting

---

3. Accepted for the first time in NAFTA in *Methanex v. USA*.

4. See, e.g., Art. 36(6) Statute of the ICJ; Art. 21 UNCITRAL Arbitration Rules (1976), Art. 16 UNCITRAL Model Law (1985).

5. 1 ICSID Reports 31.

6. As clearly decided, e.g., in the first ICSID case: *Holiday Inns v. Morocco*, ICSID Case No. ARB/72/1; or in the case *LETCO v. Liberia*.

to note that the practice of joining preliminary objections to the merits of the case was initiated by the PCIJ for the first time in 1933 in the *Administration of the Prince von Pless* case[7] and then in the case of the *Railway Panevezys – Saldutiskis*.[8]

In the *Prince von Pless Administration* case the PCIJ stated:

> "The question ... appears to be inextricably bound up with the facts induced by the Applicant and can only be decided on the basis of a full knowledge of these facts, such as can only be obtained from the proceedings on the merits.
>
> At the present stage of the proceedings a decision cannot be taken either as to the preliminary character of the objections or on the question whether they are well founded; any such decision would raise questions of fact and law in regard to which the Parties are in several respects in disagreement and which are too closely linked to the merits for the Court to adjudicate upon them at the present stage; ... if it were now to pass upon these objections, the Court would run the risk of adjudicating on questions which appertain to the merits of the case or of prejudging the solutions.
>
> Whereas the Court may order the joinder of preliminary objections to the merits whenever the interest of the good administration of Justice requires it."[9]

In 1936 the court considered that "the questions raised by the first of these objections ... are too intimately related and too closely interconnected for the court to be able to adjudicate upon the former without prejudging the latter"[10] – so the court joined the objections to the merits, considering that, in that way, it would be: "in a better position to adjudicate with a full knowledge of the facts" upon the objections.[11]

A leading case must be quoted, the famous *Barcelona Traction* case (24 July 1964), which contains a full review of the problem. At that time, Art. 62 of the Rules of Court of the ICJ expressly provided for the possibility of a joinder.

Confronted with four preliminary objections, the ICJ noted that:

> "... this is not a case where the allegation [of the Respondent] ... stands out as a clear-cut issue of a preliminary character that can be determined on its own. It is inextricably interwoven with the issues of denial of justice which constitute the major part of the merits...."[12]

Another citation from the same judgment may be particularly worth keeping in mind by arbitrators when they hesitate or feel somewhat at a loss as to the better course to be adopted under Art. 41 of the Washington Convention: Should they decide the objection "as a preliminary question" or "join it to the merits"?

---

7. 1933 P.C.I.J., Ser. A/B, No. 3, p. 149.
8. 1938 P.C.I.J., Ser. A/B, No. 75, p. 56.
9. 1933 P.C.I.J., Ser. A/B, No. 52, p. 14.
10. 1936 P.C.I.J., Ser. A/B, No. 9, p. 66.
11. *Ibid.*, Pajzs, Cskaky, Esterhazy preliminary objections.
12. 1964 I.C.J. Rep. 46.

The Court felt that it "could not pronounce [upon the third objection] at this stage in full confidence that it was in possession of all the elements that might have a bearing on its decision".[13] Furthermore, the court found it necessary to add the following rather remarkable statement:

> "The Court is not called upon to specify which particular points, relative to the questions of fact and law involved by the third Objection, it considers an examination of the merits might help to clarify, or for what reasons it might do so. The Court will therefore content itself by saying that it decides to join this Objection to the merit because – to quote the Permanent Court in the *Pajzs, Csáky, Esterházy* case (P.C.I.J., Series A/B, No. 66 at p. 9) 'the … proceedings on the merits … will place the Court in a better position to adjudicate with a full knowledge of the facts' and because 'the question raised by … these objections and those arising … on the merits are too intimately related and too closely interconnected for the Court to be able to adjudicate upon the former without prejudging the latter'."[14]

Lastly, two recent decisions of the ICJ adopted the same position: The *Lockerbie* case and the *Nigeria-Cameroon* case.

One may also mention in passing that the express mention of a joinder disappeared from the Rules of Court in 1972 (a change confirmed in 1978); it was replaced by the possibility for the Court to declare that the objection "does not possess, in the circumstances of the case, an exclusively preliminary character".[15]

The interpretation of this new formula is a matter for doctrinal debate and it is doubtful whether this change was one of substance or not, and intended to wipe out "virtually consistent case law itself corresponding to a widely felt need and existing independently of the Rules of 1936-1946".[16]

As Judge Charles De Visscher rightly observed, the joining of objections to the merits "is, to a large extent, a question to be decided on a case by case basis".[17] What must be stressed is that the interest of the defending State, which objects to the jurisdiction, is not only or not always to prevent the dispute from being adjudicated: the State may have a legitimate interest in also preventing the discussion of the case before the tribunal.

As Sir Hersch Lauterpacht stated:

> "The reasons of caution which counsel the occasional joinder of preliminary objections to the merits may, in turn, be mitigated by other considerations. A defendant Government which pleads to the jurisdiction of the Court ought not,

---

13. *Ibid.*
14. *Ibid.*
15. I.C.J. Rules of Court (1972) as amended 1978 and 5 December 2000.
16. See Shabtai ROSENNE, *Law and Practice of International Court 1920-1926*, 3rd ed. (Martinus Nijhoff 1997) p. 924.
17. Charles De VISSCHER, *Aspects récents du droit procedural de la Cour International de Justice* (Paris 1966) p. 106

without good reasons, and without its consent, to be expected to submit to the effort, expense and uncertainty of engaging in proceedings on the merits."[18]

However, the number of cases in which an objection to jurisdiction has been joined to the merits, either by the ICJ or by an international arbitral tribunal is too significant to allow the opinion, (mistakenly expressed by some writers and one or two judges) that the decision to join is exceptional. The text of Art. 41 of the Washington Convention should suffice to prove the contrary.

The practice of ICSID arbitral tribunals confirms that view. In a number of cases the objection was joined to the merits.[19] One reason is clearly expressed in the *SOABI v. Senegal* decision:

> "Neither the letter nor the spirit of the various documents put forward by the Parties, as support for their respective positions on the jurisdiction of the Tribunal ... could properly be appreciated, save after a full consideration of the actual subject matter of the Application.... In the result, the Objection to Jurisdiction must be joined to the arguments on the merits, and will be addressed at the same time as the latter."[20]

It is now time to conclude this "procedural introduction" and to turn to an examination of the objections themselves.

Whenever challenges to jurisdiction are raised – and they seem to be becoming more and more frequent in "investor-State arbitration" – the arbitrator is likely to consider issuing an interim award, or he may be requested to do so.

The same is true, mutatis mutandis, with regard to objections to admissibility (but there is no need here to deal with this notion, or to attempt to define or distinguish the two concepts). However, issuing such an interim award, and deciding at the outset whether or not there is jurisdiction, is far from being always possible, or simply convenient.

Questions of jurisdiction (or admissibility) and merits are often closely intertwined – and the parties themselves, in their arguments on jurisdiction, often illustrate, unconsciously or not, this close connection. It is therefore a common feature of recent arbitral practice, whether investor-State or other international types, that arbitrators frequently prefer to join the objection to the merits – a fact which, needless to say, cannot be interpreted as indicating any *favor jurisdictionis* on the part of the arbitral tribunal!

---

18. Sir Hersch LAUTERPACHT, *The Development of International Law* (London 1958) p. 113.
19. See, e.g., *Amco v. Indonesia* (1983) 1 ICSID Reports 390; *Klöckner v. Cameroon* (1983) 2 ICSID Reports 1318; *Atlantic Triton v. Guinea* (1986) 3 ICSID Reports 39 et seq.
20. *SOABI v. Senegal* (1984) 2 ICSID Reports 180-189.

III.   NATIONALITY

A strong objection to jurisdiction that a State may raise (as did Zaire in the case of *American Manufacturing and Trading* in 1997) is that the dispute is a purely domestic one, because the investor happens to be a national of the host State. Another possible objection is that the claimant is a national of a State that is not a party to the Washington Convention, or has not ratified a particular BIT. Let me just mention one example of each situation.

In a case which shall remain anonymous, the claimant, after leaving his country of origin in Europe, settled in Latin America and acquired the nationality of State X. Many years later, following a revolution, during which his assets were confiscated, he returned to his country of origin, of which he was still a citizen. The question was whether he was or was not a *dual national*.

It requires no particular effort of interpretation to discover that the Washington Convention is exclusively established, as its very title indicates, for the purpose of settling investment disputes "between States and Nationals *of Other States*".

It is enough to quote here a leading commentary of the Washington Convention by Schreuer:

> "For natural persons, possession of the host State's nationality is an absolute bar to becoming a Party to ICSID proceedings: the dual national would be disqualified from invoking the ICSID clause in the BIT.... The individual investor's only chance to gain access to the Centre may be to relinquish the host State's nationality before consent to ICSID's jurisdiction is perfected...."

The author adds that:

> "... the investor would have to ensure that the renunciation of the nationality is valid under the host State's law....."[21]

In the concrete case I have in mind, the parties were in complete disagreement on both the facts and the law relating to the possibility for a citizen of the State in question to relinquish his nationality and/or of being deprived of it, either formally by decree or indirectly, in particular circumstances.

In passing, I may draw your attention to the difficulty which international arbitrators may experience when called upon to interpret and apply not only public international law, but also domestic constitutional and public law of a particular State regarding its nationality.

It is worth adding that, during the drafting of the Washington Convention, "the problem of compulsory granting of nationality was discussed and the opinion was expressed that this would not be a permissible way for a State to evade its obligation to submit a dispute to the Center ... but it was decided that this question could be left to

---

21. Ch. SCHREUER, *The ICSID Convention: A Commentary* (2001) pp. 265, 272.

the decision of the Arbitral Tribunal".[22]

In the *Banro American Resource and SAKIMA v. Democratic Republic of Congo* case[23] the difficulty was of a different nature.

This case is particularly interesting since it illustrates in the clearest manner the specific characteristics of what may be called the ICSID system. The objection of Congo derived from the fact that Banro Resource Corp. had Canadian nationality and Canada had not ratified the Washington Convention. Nor is Canada a party today (for reasons unknown to me).

As stated in the unpublished *Banro-Congo* Award, ICSID arbitration is not open to investors (whether natural or juridical persons) who are not nationals of a State party to the Washington Convention, or are nationals of host States that are not parties to this Convention. As is well known, "one of the central features of the system is that, by becoming a party to the Convention, the State of which the investor is a national automatically waives its right to provide the latter with diplomatic protection".[24]

A curious characteristic, perhaps unique, of this case is that Canada exercised its diplomatic protection vis-à-vis Congo, while the American subsidiary of the Canadian group Banro relied upon the ICSID arbitration clause – a device which the arbitral tribunal considered unacceptable.

A fundamental feature of the system (quite apart from the necessity of the State involved to be a party to the Washington Convention) is of course the fact that the ratification of the Convention is not enough: to be bound to accept ICSID arbitration requires that both parties, the host State and the investor, must have provided written consent to the jurisdiction.[25]

Leaving aside this well-known feature, I should like to draw attention to two other aspects in the *Banro* case, which can only be mentioned in a somewhat sketchy manner:

Canada, as already stated, is not a party to the Washington Convention. Under the Mining Convention, the term "Banro" meant Banro Resource, a Canadian company. That company had consented to arbitrate future disputes with Congo, under the Mining Convention, and Congo had (contrary to Canada) ratified the Washington Convention.

The request for arbitration had been filed, not by the Canadian corporation, but by its American subsidiary, in order to bypass the serious obstacle posed by the fact that Canada was not a party to ICSID.

The award clearly states that "if Banro American and its Congolese subsidiary are to be considered the Claimants, the condition that the Claimant must possess the nationality of a 'Contracting State' would be met; however, the condition pertaining to the consent of the parties would no longer be met".[26]

Since the Company Banro Resource, being Canadian, could not, although a party to the Mining Convention with the Congolese State, benefit from ICSID arbitration, it had used its American subsidiary, as already noted, to file the request. But at least two

---

22. *Ibid.*, fn. 47, p. 272.
23. ICSID ARB/98/7 (1 September 2000).
24. The full text of the award has not been published.
25. Preamble Washington Convention
26. *Banro American Resource and SAKIMA v. Congo*, Award, paras. 72-73.

obstacles had to be overcome: (1) Congo had indeed consented to submit to ICSID arbitration, but only, at least expressly, disputes *involving the Canadian company*, but not disputes involving the (formal) claimant, the subsidiary Banro American (and its Congolese subsidiary) and (2)The Mining Convention did *not* provide for consent by Banro American, at least explicitly, but it was argued that it had consented indirectly, in one of two possible ways, either as a majority shareholder of the Congolese subsidiary or in its capacity as an "affiliate company", since the Canadian corporation had transferred its shares in the Congolese subsidiary, a transfer which included (so the argument went) the right to have recourse to ICSID arbitration.

This line of argument was rejected by the tribunal on the grounds that "Banro Resource, a Canadian company, never had, at any time, *jus standi* before ICSID. Having never existed for the benefit of Banro Resource, the right to access to ICSID cannot be viewed as having been 'extended' or 'transferred' to its affiliate, Banro American."[27]

An important lesson must be drawn from this decision, which can be summed up as follows: a contractual clause purporting to give access to ICSID arbitration cannot, when "it is inapplicable vis-à-vis the beneficiary that it expressly mentions" (for reasons of nationality), "take effect and apply vis-à-vis another entity to which it would have been 'extended' or 'transferred'".

And the tribunal, referring to the Mining Convention in that case as a "poorly constructed instrument, full of all kinds of contradictions and uncertainties", found it "difficult to understand how the Parties to the Mining Convention were able to insert in the contract a clause so manifestly deprived of its object and purpose and so manifestly inapplicable"![28]

Another possible approach to this fundamental problem of *jus standi* would have been for the arbitral tribunal to lift or pierce the corporate veil of the Banro Group and, going "beyond procedural appearances" and looking at the financial reality, to conclude that the real or actual claimant was not the signatory of the request for arbitration, Banro American, but its parent company. The result of this approach would then be that one of the conditions of ICSID jurisdiction would be met, i.e., the condition of consent of the parties, but the other condition of the jurisdiction of the tribunal would not be met, the nationality of the claimant!

IV. ABSENCE OF INVESTMENT

It may be tempting for a defendant State to argue, as a basis for an objection to jurisdiction, that either there was no investment whatever, or no investment under the definition of the BIT or under the particular contract, or to argue that, if there was an investment, it was not a "foreign" investment.

In the ICSID case *American Manufacturing and Trading (AMT) v. République du Zaïre*[29] the State of Zaire objected that the Claimant AMT (of American nationality) had never

---

27. *Ibid.*, para. 74.
28. *Ibid.*, para. 75.
29. 21 February 1997, Journal du droit international (Clunet) (1998) p. 243.

invested directly in its own name in Zaire and that it was merely a partner of a local company, Sinza; from which it followed that the dispute existed only between the State and one of its own nationals, therefore falling outside the scope of the Washington Convention.

After joining the question of jurisdiction to the merits, the tribunal decided that none of the objections was justified, and it held, in particular, that there had been consent by both parties.

In a somewhat similar case of 1996, *Tradex v. Albania*,[30] the respondent State objected to the jurisdiction of the ICSID tribunal, in particular on the grounds that, under the applicable law of Albania, Tradex was not a foreign investor. This objection was rejected by the tribunal.

About the *Tradex* case, I should perhaps add in passing that, according to a second objection, the dispute did not relate to an "expropriation" within the meaning of the applicable law, and therefore was not one concerning a "legal dispute arising directly out of an investment" under Art. 25 of the Washington Convention.

V.   THE QUESTION OF ASSIGNMENT

It may well be that, in a particular case, the existence of one of the conditions for jurisdiction (and/or for admissibility) whether nationality, consent in writing, quality of "investor", etc. ...) happens to be doubtful or even absent. It may be, more precisely, that an investor or alleged investor fears that the possible institution of proceedings would give rise to valid objections. Then, in order to circumvent that difficulty, the investor may consider acting, in one way or another, through another party, who would be better qualified as a formal claimant.

In the context of questions of nationality, and of dual nationality, I have mentioned a case in which an individual, who may be called "the original Investor", decided to assign or transfer to a legal person of foreign nationality (a foundation) the majority of his shares. We have also seen that, in the case *Banro Resource v. RDC*, in a context of a group of companies, assignments had taken place between a Canadian parent company, one of its American subsidiaries and Congolese subsidiaries (or sub-sub).

In the first example, the respondent State, the host State, had objected, not unexpectedly, to ICSID jurisdiction as regards the assignee, the foreign foundation. On various, connected, grounds. It argued that the foundation had been created before the relevant BIT had been concluded and ratified (a treaty said to be non-retroactive). It was said also that the foundation was not an investor. And in any case the host State – if it had consented in writing to ICSID arbitration as regards the individual, the assignor – had never expressed such a consent with regard to the assignee.

This involves a series of highly delicate questions of private international law, concerning the formal and the substantial validity of an international assignment of contractual rights and what law governs the validity (and the opposability) of such a contractual assignment of the investor's rights, as well as questions of public

---

30. 14 ICSID Review (1999) p. 161.

international law.

They can only be mentioned here in passing, on the level of public international law and within the context of the Washington Convention, an important question is whether, in case of assignment of the investor's rights, jurisdiction ratione personae can or cannot be presumed in favour on the claimant.

The case of transfer or assignment of the investor's rights is probably the most important but not the only situation where the identification of the claimant has created difficulties for ICSID arbitral tribunals. It may be said, in general terms, that these tribunals have shown a certain absence of formalism, a certain flexibility, in that respect. This was the case in two situations in particular, as the tribunal summed up in the *Banro* award:

> "When the request was made by a member company of a group of companies while the instrument expressed the consent of another company of this group; and when, following the transfer of shares, the request came from the transferee company while the consent had been given by the company making the transfer."[31]

Two well-known illustrations are the first ICSID case, *Holiday Inns v. Morocco* (when the request was filed by the parent companies, while consent had been given by their subsidiaries), and the case *AMCO v. Indonesia*, in a similar situation. In the latter case, it was noted that the goal of an arbitration clause – which is to ensure the protection of the investor – cannot be reached if the competence of the tribunal is limited to disputes referred to it by the subsidiaries mentioned in the arbitration clause – a subsidiary which is in a final analysis merely an instrumentality through which the parent company was to realize the investment.

With regard to the question of transfer, or assignment, of rights, it was stated that: "The right to avail oneself of arbitration is tied to the investment and can therefore be transferred at the same time as the shares, provided that the host State approved the transfer of the shares"[32] – to which some decisions have added: provided it did not oppose the assignment.

It should be noted that consent expressed by a subsidiary has rather easily been considered to have been given by the parent company (the actual investor), while the converse is less true. Furthermore "the extension of consent to subsidiaries that are not designated or not yet created, even following a transfer of shares, is readily accepted".[33]

To conclude on the question of assignments between companies that are members of the same group, a fundamental distinction should be kept in mind between questions of private law and questions of international law. The first category relates to or governs the relationship among companies of the same group and it answers the question whether rights assigned by contractual instrument to one company of the group apply to another company of that group. But the question of whether, under the Washington

---

31. *Op. cit.*, fn. 26, para. 10.

32. *AMCO v. Indonesia*, Resubmitted Case, Award 5 June 1990, 1 ICSID Reports (1993) 569.

33. *Op. cit.*, fn. 26, para. 87.

Convention, the conditions are fulfilled that are required for a State to be considered as a contracting State is governed by international law.

Lastly, a particularly interesting observation made by the arbitral tribunal in the *Banro* case deserves to be cited: After referring to the "flexible approach" of many ICSID tribunals regarding the *jus standi* of subsidiaries and parent companies, the tribunal noted:

> "What the Claimants are asking to the Tribunal in the present case, is not to uncover the reality behind the matter or to find a true investor behind the formalities and procedural appearances, but rather; on the contrary, to base its inquiry on the formal and procedural appearance and to turn a blind eye to the reality behind the relationships deriving from the investment."[34]

VI. SOME OTHER OBJECTIONS TO JURISDICTION

1. *Absence of Prior "Amiable" Consultations or Negotiations?*

A few remarks need be made, at this stage, on another fairly frequent objection to jurisdiction (or, as some would prefer, objections to *admissibility* of a request for arbitration), an objection based on the alleged absence of prior consultations or prior amiable negotiations. According to Antonio Parra, "the provisions of *most BITs* on the settlement of investment disputes urge that such disputes be resolved amicably" (emphasis added)[35] and he gives as typical examples that of the 1994 India-United Kingdom BIT and that of the 1992 Romania-United States BIT.

A great majority of BITs and some national investment laws foresee, as a common condition for the institution of proceedings, that a negotiated settlement should have been attempted. In two cases I have mentioned (*AMT v. Zaire* and *Tradex v. Albania*) the consent clauses, respectively, were subject to the following condition: "if the dispute cannot be resolved through consultation and negotiation ..." and "if the dispute cannot be settled amicably".

As everybody knows, this kind of formula is to be found not only in treaties but in most contractual arbitration clauses and, unless it contains some precisions regarding the consultation period and a notification, it offers ideal *dilatory* opportunities for the defendant.

It would seem that a not insignificant number of BITs have been drafted no doubt by great diplomats but by people largely ignorant of international arbitration and unaware of the perils of nice and vague formulas.

In some BITs however, one finds an article providing for a written notification of a request to begin consultation, together with the clause that arbitration may be requested if no amicable solution is found within six months from that notification.

In the *Tradex v. Albania* case, already mentioned, the arbitral tribunal examined five

---

34. *Op. cit.*, fn. 26.
35. 12 ICSID Review (1997, no. 2) p. 322

letters sent by the investor to the government and concluded that these letters were "a sufficient good faith effort to reach an amicable settlement within the meaning of" the applicable law.[36]

Similarly, in *AMT v. Zaire* (ICSID arbitration), the State raised without success the objection based on prior consultation providing that any dispute should, *if* possible, be settled by way of consultation.[37] The tribunal observed as a fact that the investor had indisputably made several attempts at serious negotiations, but that they had been fruitless. When an arbitration clause in a contract or in a BIT provides that the parties should attempt to reach a friendly settlement *whenever* possible, it is of course a matter of interpretation of the common intention of the parties in each particular case; no general answer or rule can be suggested.

To conclude, reference may be made to an excellent study by Professor Tibor Varady, of Budapest, on what he calls the "courtesy trap".[38] The courtesy trap demonstrates, on the basis of many cases, that such "declarations" of good intentions are not innocuous and that "placed within the Arbitration Agreement, even if it is just meant to be a gesture – become a possible stepping stone of various procedural gambits".[39]

The result may be that resort to arbitration is considered to be premature, or on the contrary, belated. Varady also shows, however, that the very success of amiable negotiations "might also cause discomfort. Particularly if it is not a full success."[40]

2.   Non-Exhaustion of Local Remedies

There is a clear analogy between the condition of prior amiable negotiations and that of prior exhaustion of local remedies, and both can be relied upon, in practice, by a State wishing to object to the jurisdiction of the arbitrator or to the admissibility of the request.

While many BITs specify that the host State shall give its consent to arbitration, some of them preserve expressly the right of the host State to require that internal remedies be exhausted and this,[41] curiously enough "with no time-limit for rendering a final judicial decision, so considerable delay in fulfilling the commitment to arbitrate is of course possible".[42]

A possible answer to that objection comes immediately to mind, as suggested by international law cases and doctrinal writings on the subject. It may well be that no real remedy is available under the local law, or that, in practical terms, there are no "local remedies to exhaust". An attempt to obtain redress before the courts of the host State would be "obviously futile" under the circumstances.

---

36. 14 ICSID Review (1999, no. 7) p. 159 at p.182.

37. Art. VIII of the Bilateral Treaty between Zaire and the United States of America of 1984.

38. Tibor VARADY, "The Courtesy Trap", J. Int'l.Arb (1997, no. 4) pp. 5-12.

39. *Ibid.*, p. 6.

40. *Ibid.*, p. 10.

41. See, e.g., 1990 Switzerland-Jamaica BIT.

42. J.-Ch. LIEBESKIND, "State-Investor Dispute Settlement Clauses in Swiss Bilateral Investment Treaties", 20 ASA Bulletin (2002, no. 1) p. 27.

3. Choice of Local or Choice of International Forum?

Several BITs contain a provision stipulating that disputes which have not been settled amicably may, at the choice of the *investor*, be submitted either to the domestic courts of the host State or to international arbitration (sometimes ICSID, sometimes UNCITRAL or ICC).

In some treaties, such provision is supplemented by another, according to which the investor's choice of one of the other forum, once made, shall be final. A few years ago, an international dispute was submitted to ICSID arbitration, in rather unusual circumstances, which enabled the respondent State to raise the following preliminary objections to jurisdiction.

Prior to filing his request with the ICSID Secretariat in Washington, the investor had resorted twice to the courts of the host State, for two specific reasons. First, in order to obtain the restitution of some documents proving his ownership of assets which had been confiscated by that State – a petition which was successful – and second, in order to obtain the restitution, or at least the indemnification, of a particular immovable asset located in the host State.

The host State objected to ICSID jurisdiction on the second basis. It contended that by submitting a petition or a claim to the local courts the investor had necessarily opted in favour of domestic jurisdiction and waived its right to benefit from ICSID arbitration. In other words, the choice of forum offered by a provision of the BIT to the investor had been exercised once and for all. It was said to be both global and final.

Lack of space does not allow a discussion of that particular problem undoubtedly of great interest both from a theoretical and a practical point of view. Two general observations may perhaps be made, however. First, the investor's option should, of course, be exercised in good faith and according to the general principles of public international law, just as there should likewise be no abuse of the right to object to jurisdiction. Second, there can be no universally valid answer to the problem. It is a question of interpretation of the consent of the parties, and in particular of the consent of the host State, to decide whether, in a given BIT, the intention was to offer, or not, a global and final choice to the investor. The most that can be said, in general terms, is that the admission of partial choices is likely to create serious practical difficulties, and even conflicts between international jurisdiction and domestic, national jurisdiction.

Quite independently of the particular question of the choice of forum in BIT provisions, conflicts between national and international adjudicating bodies are a source of very great difficulties, which have sometimes occupied ICSID tribunals. An example is ICSID's very first case, *Holiday Inns / Occidental Petroleum v. Morocco*, where the arbitral tribunal affirmed, in the clearest possible manner, the superiority of international tribunals and the duty of the Moroccan courts, either to suspend their decision or to adapt it to the pronouncements of the ICSID tribunal.

In the *Waste Management Inc. v. Mexico* case,[43] an arbitral tribunal (presided over by B. Cremades) declined jurisdiction, because the investor, having maintained, or instituted new proceedings before Mexican courts, had thereby ipso facto annulled its written

---

43. 15 ICSID Review (2000, no. 1) p. 211.

consent to NAFTA arbitration. It was held by the majority that these two kinds of proceedings (judicial and arbitral), although based on different legal arguments, related to the same alleged breaches of the Mexican State.

In a strong dissenting opinion, Mr. Keith Highet considered that the two kinds of proceedings were substantially distinct, the one relating to contractual obligations under Mexican law, the other to the breach of obligations based on NAFTA. In favour of the majority decision, it can be argued that investors should not be permitted to attempt to obtain double compensation in what is substantially the same dispute. Cumulation of proceedings should be discouraged.

Under the heading of "the problem of overlapping jurisdictions and remedies" B. Cremades has, in a recent article, rightly observed that :

> "The multiplicity of sources of law and dispute resolution mechanisms creates a real risk of overlapping and duplicated claims.... Many investment treaties require either irrevocable election by an investor between international arbitration and domestic litigation, or an express waiver of other dispute settlement procedures, as a pre-condition to access to investor-State arbitration."[44]

An example of election is Art. 8 of the France-Argentina BIT, which offers a choice of fora to the investor but makes it clear that "once an Investor has submitted the dispute either to the jurisdictions of the Contracting Parties involved or to international arbitration, the choice of one or the other of these procedures shall be final". (What remains to be solved is the precise interpretation of the words "the dispute", and the question whether such dispute could be "divided" by the investor.)

An example of a waiver is provided by Art. 1121 of NAFTA, with respect to conditions precedent to submission of a claim to arbitration.

Cremades observes that: "Notwithstanding these mechanisms, however, the overlapping sources of law have created substantial complexities in investor-State arbitrations, and are likely to continue to do so."[45] It is impossible to disagree with this opinion: there is no doubt that the frequent "overlap of an investment treaty and a contract as competing sources of law is a significant current issue for investor-State arbitrations", as shown by recent decisions.

In the case *Compania de Aguas del Aconquija S.A. and Vivendi Universal v. Argentine Republic*,[46] the tribunal held that the BIT claims involved allegations that would also amount to breaches of the concession agreement, which was a matter within the exclusive jurisdiction of domestic courts. Hence a decision that the claimants could only pursue a claim under the BIT after having exhausted the remedies in a domestic court of the defendant and suffer a denial of justice there! (Award subject to an annulment proceedings.)

---

44. "The Brave New World of Global Arbitration", 3 Journal of World Investment (2002, no. 2) pp. 189-190.
45. *Ibid.*, p. 190.
46. ICSID Award, 21 November 2000, 40 ILM 457 (2001).

VII.   CONCLUSION

At the end of this survey, both rapid and long, of "some" objections to jurisdiction in investor-State arbitration, the conclusion can be brief: In this era of globalization and worldwide integration of markets, we are witnessing an extraordinary growth of arbitration in the field of foreign direct investment. However the proliferation of BITs should not lead hastily to over-optimistic judgments.

When a private investor is evaluating what kind of legal protection is offered by a particular State, it is probably not enough for him to take into account (together with the draft contract that is being negotiated) the fact that the State is a party to the Washington Convention and/or has ratified a BIT with his own national State. What should also be taken into consideration is what may be called the "arbitral record" of that host State, and its past conduct in judicial or arbitral proceedings. And I should borrow the last word from a recent article by a London Barrister, Mr. Chatterjee, who rightly observes that "[d]espite the judicial guidelines developed by ICSID tribunals on the competence of those tribunals over their relatively long history, challenges to the jurisdiction of those tribunals under Article 25, Washington Convention have become a common phenomenon".

The New Face of Investment Arbitration:
Capital Exporters as Host States under NAFTA Chapter 11

*Guillermo Aguilar Alvarez** and*
*William W. Park*** ****

TABLE OF CONTENTS

---

* Partner, SAI Law and Economics; Principal Legal Counsel for Mexico during the negotiation and implementation of NAFTA; Member of ICCA.

** Professor of Law, Boston University; Vice-President, London Court of International Arbitration.

*** The authors wish to dedicate this paper to the memory of Michel Gaudet, Chairman of the ICC International Court of Arbitration from 1977 to 1988.

I.   THE CONTOURS OF INVESTMENT ARBITRATION

1.   Double Standards

The French writer Jules Romains describes a character in one of his novels as a man who likes honesty but only in others.[1] Some observers perceive a similar double standard toward investment arbitration in certain emerging American attitudes toward investment arbitration. Many business and political leaders still support arbitration as the preferred method to resolve disputes between host countries and foreign investors. However, recent trade legislation has significantly impaired the vigor of future treaty-based arbitration of investment disputes,[2] and vocal opposition to investment arbitration has been expressed by important segments of the media and several non-governmental organizations.

Traditionally, American multinationals imposed arbitration as the mechanism for settling investment disputes with foreign countries, particularly in Latin America. Arbitration was justified as a way to level the playing field and to reduce the prospect of the host state "hometown justice", thereby safeguarding assets from expropriation without compensation. Foreign investment was seen as a net good for both investor and host state, helping to reduce poverty through international economic cooperation. And arbitration was perceived as one way to promote respect for the rule of law underpinning investment stability.

The argument ran as follows. No supranational courts possess mandatory jurisdiction to decide the appropriate indemnity for nationalized assets.[3] Assertions of diplomatic protection being absent, litigation in the expropriating country remains the default mechanism for adjudicating investment disputes.[4] Consequently, the real or imagined bias of host country judges can create an anxiety that inhibits wealth-creating

---

1. A foreign emissary who helped himself to a share of the bribes his government paid French newspapers was shocked that intermediaries had skimmed from these payments. ROMAINS writes, *"M. Coubersky, lequel se charge de prélever sur ces millions une gorgée abondante, semble trouver mauvais que les intermédiaires aient une soif parente de la sienne. C'est un homme qui aime l'honnêteté d'autrui."* Jules ROMAINS, *Les Hommes de bonne volonté* (1958) Part 9 (Montée des Périls) Sect. XXX (Réponse de Marc Strigelius) vol. II (Robert Laffont Edition 1988) p. 335.
2. See discussion infra of Trade Act of 2002. See also Edward ALLEN, "Washington Alters Line on US Investor Protection", Financial Times, 2 October 2002, p. 13, describing how the United States in its bilateral trade negotiations with Chile and Singapore has attempted to limit the legal recourse available to investors who believe their property has been expropriated without compensation by foreign host states.
3. The experience of the International Court of Justice (ICJ) is limited both by tradition and by jurisdictional constraints. For one commercial case that did reach the ICJ, see *Elettronica Sicula SPA (ELSI) (United States v. Italy)*, 1989 ICJ 15 (finding no illegal taking of property when Italy requisitioned a plant and equipment owned by US nationals in order to prevent planned liquidation).
4. In most cases one would expect investors to prefer arbitration to the more cumbersome process of having their country assert diplomatic protection. Exceptions might arise when the legal basis of the claim was weak and the investor state had a degree of clout with the host country.

transactions and discourages cross-border economic cooperation,[5] and will inevitably either thwart cross-border economic cooperation or add to its cost.[6]

Arbitration responds to this apprehension by providing a forum that is more neutral than host country courts, both politically and procedurally. Investor confidence can be bolstered by the relative impartiality of international tribunals, which inspire greater certainty that the contract will be interpreted in line with the parties' shared *ex ante* expectations.

After January 1994, when NAFTA came into force,[7] the rifle sights were turned in the opposite direction, however, and the United States and Canada became respondents in cases brought by investors based in other NAFTA countries.[8] Not surprisingly, when claims for unfair treatment were filed *against* the US government, arbitration looked different than when American companies were the investors.[9]

As Americans and Canadians began to understand the host state perspective, praise for arbitration's neutrality began to have competition in the form of complaints about infringement of national sovereignty and democracy. The level playing field no longer appeared as an unalloyed benefit. NAFTA was said to undermine legitimate governmental regulations, challenge legislative prerogatives and open decision making to ill-informed foreign tribunals.

The NAFTA process was attacked for the confidentiality of its proceedings ("lack of transparency"), uncertainty and absence of accountability to domestic constituents. A dispute resolution process that had been fair for the rest of the world came to be seen as a tool to put business before public interest. These concerns bring to mind the

---

5. The perception of litigation bias may be as significant as its reality. A study of US federal civil actions between 1986 and 1994 found that foreigners actually fared better than domestic parties. See Kevin CLERMONT and Theodore EISENBERG, "Xenophilia in American Courts", 109 Harv. L. Rev. (1996) p. 1122 at pp. 1133-1134. One explanation for this finding lies in a fear of judicial and jury partiality that leads foreign litigants to settle rather than continue to final judgment unless their cases are particularly strong.

6. To illustrate, imagine an attractive investment abroad in Country X where there is doubt that local courts will be fair to a foreign party, and another efficient opportunity in the investor's home country. Depending on the size of the disparity between the expected returns, many risk-averse merchants will choose the lower return coupled with the fairer legal system. See generally William W. PARK, "Neutrality, Predictability and Economic Cooperation", 12 J. Int'l Arb. (1995, no. 4) p. 99.

7. North American Free Trade Agreement, 32 ILM (1993) p. 289; 1993 WL 574441. NAFTA was enacted in the United States on 8 December 1993, 107 Stat. 2057.

8. NAFTA Chapter 11 protects "investors of another Party" (Art. 1101), defined in Art. 1139 to include "a national or an enterprise of such Party". See also general definitions of Art. 201, including as an "enterprise of a Party" an enterprise "constituted or organized under the law of a Party".

9. See Charles BROWER and Lee STEVEN, "Who Then Should Judge?: Developing the International Rule of Law under NAFTA, Chapter 11", 2 Chi. J. Int'l. L. (2001) p. 93; see also Charles H. BROWER II, "Investor-State Disputes Under NAFTA: A Tale of Fear and Equilibrium", 29 Pepperdine L. Rev. (2001) p. 43.

principles espoused by the 19th-century Argentine economist Carlos Calvo in his attempt to protect the economic sovereignty of Latin America.[10]

In the present climate of public opinion, many Americans and Canadians fail to understand why arbitration should be available for foreign investors. Taking for granted the fairness of their own judicial systems, Americans in particular are often surprised that not everyone feels comfortable with civil juries and the prospect of large punitive damages.[11]

Regardless of whether such self-perceptions are valid, the fact remains that when NAFTA was being negotiated, it was the United States that insisted on arbitration as a protection for foreign investment. The business community's long-standing hesitation toward foreign litigation made it vital to bolster confidence that investors would receive a "fair shake" in the event of controversy with the host government.

NAFTA also stipulated substantive standards of investor protection that would require interpretation. Reciprocal lack of trust among the three countries made it unlikely that host state courts would be acceptable to construe and apply these standards. Understandably, this investor protection scheme was based upon equality of treatment among the three countries. For Mexico to accept arbitration of investment disputes within its borders, Canada and the United States had to respect a similar dispute resolution process. It would have been unwise and unworkable for Chapter 11 to be applied by American and Canadian courts when claims were brought against the United States and Canada, but to have arbitrators appointed for claims against Mexico.

2. Historical Context

To some extent NAFTA brings investment arbitration full circle, to a time 200 years ago when the United States was principally a debtor nation. In 1794 the so-called "Jay Treaty" (named for its American negotiator John Jay, later Chief Justice of the US Supreme Court) gave British creditors the right to arbitrate claims of alleged despoliation by American citizens and residents.[12]

More recently, however, it was African and Latin American nations that were required by multinational corporations to submit investment disputes to arbitration, either through arbitration clauses contained in custom-tailored concession agreements

---

10. See discussion infra.

11. For evidence of foreign fear of litigation bias in American courts, see discussion infra of the *Loewen* case. See also CLERMONT and EISENBERG, *op. cit.*, fn. 5.

12. Treaty of Amity, Commerce and Navigation, London, 19 November 1794, US-UK, 8 Stat. 116. The treaty addressed difficulties arising from the 1783 Treaty of Paris ending the American Revolution. Under Art. 6, damages for British creditors were to be determined by five Commissioners. Two were appointed by the British and two by the United States, with the fifth chosen unanimously by the others, in default of which selection would be by lot from between two candidates, one proposed by each side. For an intriguing comparison of modern investment arbitration and the Jay Treaty, see Barton LEGUM, "Federalism, NAFTA Chapter Eleven and the Jay Treaty of 1794", 18 News from ICSID (Spring 2001): Remarks presented at panel discussion on "Investment Disputes and NAFTA Chapter 11" at 95th Annual Meeting of the American Society of International Law, Washington, DC, 4-7 April 2001.

or through bilateral and multilateral investment treaties.[13] Such arbitration has often implicated natural resources and elements of industrial infrastructure no less critical to the economic sovereignty and well-being of those countries than the NAFTA cases that have caused controversy in the United States and Canada.

In many instances investment arbitration was not a happy experience for the host state, often serving as little more than an extension of gunboat diplomacy in state-to-state proceedings where private investors participated only vicariously through their governments. Latin American states were often forced to submit disputes to European sovereigns such as Britain's Queen Victoria, Russia's Tsar Alexander II, Germany's Kaiser Wilhelm II and King Léopold I of Belgium, whose predispositions and sympathies did not always inspire confidence among developing countries.[14]

Not surprisingly, host states reacted to what they perceived as foreign control of their economies. Invoking principles articulated by the Argentine economist Carlos Calvo, Latin American countries came to require similar treatment for foreign and domestic investors, which effectively eliminated both diplomatic protection and arbitration as options.[15] In 1974 the Calvo doctrine was pushed further in the so-called "New International Economic Order" adopted by the United Nations General Assembly in an attempt (unsuccessful as history has shown)[16] to require host state courts rather than international arbitrators to determine the measure of compensation for expropriated property.[17]

Ultimately an increasing number of capital-importing countries came to realize that their self-interest was served by agreeing to arbitrate investment disputes. The greater

---

13. Treaty-based arbitration might take place under the auspices of the World Bank's International Centre for Settlement of Investment Disputes (discussed infra) or one of the many Bilateral Investment Treaties. See generally Rudolf DOLZER and Margrete STEVENS, *Bilateral Investment Treaties* (1995); Eloïse OBADIA, "ICSID, Investment Treaties and Arbitration: Current and Emerging Issues", 18 News from ICSID (Autumn 2001) p. 14; Matthew COBB, "Development of Arbitration in Foreign Investment", 16 Int'l Arb. Rep. (April 2001) p. 48; Kazutake OKUMA, "Investment Disputes Settlement", 34 Seinan Law Review (2002) p. 75.

14. See survey in Lionel M. SUMMERS, "Arbitration and Latin America", 3 Cal. W. L. J. (2001, no. 1) pp. 6-7.

15. Calvo first announced his doctrine in 1868, in *Le Droit international théorique et pratique*. The principle that foreign nations should not intervene in South America to protect private property and debts included several elements: investor submission to local jurisdiction and local law, waiver of home state protection and surrender of rights under customary public international law. See generally, Kurt LIPSTEIN, "The Place of the Calvo Clause in International Law", *British Year Book of International Law* (1945) p. 130 (concluding at p. 145 that "before international tribunals the Calvo Clause is ineffective").

16. Thomas WAELDE, "Requiem for New International Order" in G. HAFNER et al., eds., *Liber Amicorum for I. Seidl-Hohenveldern* (1998) p. 771.

17. Art. 2(2)(c) Charter of Rights and Duties of States provides that compensation should be "appropriate" as determined under "the domestic law of the nationalizing State and by its tribunals". See William W. PARK, "Legal Issues in the Third World's Economic Development", 61 B. U. L. Rev. (1981) p. 1321. This principle was rejected in *Texaco Overseas Petroleum Co. (TOPCO)/California Asiatic Oil Co. (CALASIATIC) v. Libya*, 17 ILM (1978) p. 1. See also *Libyan American Oil Co. (LIAMCO) v. Libya*, 482 F.Supp. 1175 (D.D.C. 1980), vac'd without op., 684 F.2d (D.C. Cir. 1981) p. 1032.

the risk, the higher the cost of investment. Thus untrustworthy enforcement mechanisms tend to chill cross-border economic cooperation to the detriment of those countries that depend most on foreign capital for development. To the extent that arbitration promotes respect for implicit bargains between investor and host country, it commends itself to developing countries as a matter of sound international economic policy.

II.   NAFTA CHAPTER 11

1.   Safeguarding Cross-Border Investment[18]

NAFTA Chapter 11 gives business managers from a member country the opportunity to arbitrate investment grievances with the government of another NAFTA country, regardless of whether an agreement to arbitrate actually exists in a negotiated investment concession.[19] This private right to direct action eliminates recourse to traditional state-to-state negotiations, in which a foreign investor asked for his country's intervention (diplomatic protection) against the host state.

The first part of Chapter 11 (Sect. A) imposes the substantive norms for cross-border investment, forbidding discrimination against investors from another member country,[20] and requiring "fair and equitable" treatment as well as compensation for nationalized

---

18. See generally Henri C. ALVAREZ, "Arbitration Under the North American Free Trade Agreement", 16 Arb. Int'l (2000) p. 393; Axelle LEMAIRE, "Le Nouveau visage de l'arbitrage entre état et investisseur étranger: le chapitre 11 de l'ALENA", Rev. arb. (2001) p. 43; Todd WEILER, "Substantive Law Developments in NAFTA Arbitration", 16 Int'l Arb. Rep. (December 2001) p. 69; Leon TRAKMAN, "Arbitrating Investment Disputes Under NAFTA", 18 J. Int'l Arb. (2001, no. 4) p. 385; William S. DODGE, "National Courts and International Arbitration: Exhaustion of Remedies and Res Judicata Under Chapter Eleven of NAFTA", 23 Hastings Int'l & Comp. L. Rev. (2000) p. 357; Patrick DUMBERRY, "The NAFTA Investment Dispute Settlement Mechanism: A Review of the Latest Case Law", 2 J. World Investment (2001) p. 151; Todd WEILER, "NAFTA Investment Arbitration and the Growth of International Economic Law", 36 Canadian Bus. L. J. (2002) p. 405; Chris TOLLESFON, "Games Without Frontiers: Investor Claims and Citizen Submissions Under the NAFTA Regime", 12 Yale J. Int'l L. (2002) p. 141.

19. See generally Todd WEILER, "The Ethyl Arbitration: First of Its Kind and a Harbinger of Things to Come", 11 Am. Rev. Int'l Arb. (2000) p. 187.

20. Each member country must treat NAFTA investors and their investments no less favorably than its own investors (Art. 1102, concerning National Treatment) and investors of other countries (Art. 1103, concerning Most-Favored-Nation Treatment). In *S.D. Myers, Inc. v. Government of Canada*, a Partial Award of 13 November 2000 articulated the national treatment standard to require consideration as to whether the NAFTA investor is in the same "economic and business sector" as the national investor. A measure breaches the national treatment standard if (i) it creates a disproportionate benefit for nationals over non-nationals, (ii) the measure, on its face, appears to favor nationals over non-nationals and (iii) there must be a practical impact required, not merely motive or intent. Political subdivisions must treat foreign investors no less favorably than the best treatment accorded to investors of the country to which the subdivision belongs. For example, Massachusetts must treat investors from Quebec no less favorably than it treats investors from New York or Pennsylvania.

property.[21] An entity incorporated and with substantial business activities[22] in a NAFTA country qualifies as an investor without regard to any "origin of capital" limitations.[23] Thus a Mexican corporation owned by French shareholders qualifies as an investor under NAFTA Chapter 11.

The compensation criteria adopted by NAFTA Chapter 11 were intended to be compatible with standards traditionally advocated by the United States.[24] Expropriation must be justified by a public purpose and applied on a non-discriminatory basis.[25] Compensation must be "equivalent to the fair market value" of the investment at the date of expropriation, must be "paid without delay and be fully realizable", and must bear interest at a commercially reasonable rate until the date of actual payment. If paid other than in a hard currency,[26] compensation must be in an amount which, at market rates of exchange, would convert into a sum no less than the hard currency equivalent of market value on the payment date. Compensation will not be affected because market awareness of the pending expropriation drove down the property's price.[27]

The second portion of Chapter 11 (Sect. B) goes on to provide arbitration as a

---

21. Art. 1102 prohibits discrimination by requiring "national treatment", while Art. 1105 requires respect for international law, including "fair and equitable treatment" as a minimum standard. Proper compensation for nationalized property is mandated by Art. 1110.

22. See Art. 1113(2).

23. See definitions in Arts. 201 and 1139. Moreover, standing to bring a claim may be based on citizenship regardless of residence. See Interim Award in *Feldman (a.k.a. Karpa) v. United Mexican States*, 40 ILM (2001) p. 615, which determined, inter alia, that permanent residence in Mexico did not deprive a US citizen of the right to arbitrate claims concerning tobacco export tax rebates.

24. While the terms "prompt, adequate and effective" do not appear in the text of Chapter 11, some observers consider the combination of Art. 1110 factors ("paid without delay", "fair market value" and "fully realizable") to amount to the same result. See *Restatement (Third) Foreign Relations Law*, Sect. 712, comments "c" and "d", and "Reporter's note 2" (1987) stating that for compensation to be "just" it must be "paid at the time of taking", "in an amount equivalent to the value of the property taken" and "in a form economically usable by the foreign national". The expression "prompt, adequate and effective" originates in a communication to Mexico from US Secretary of State Cordell Hull on 22 August 1938. See *Banco Nacional de Cuba v. Chase Manhattan Bank*, 658 F.2d (2d Cir. 1981) p. 875 at p. 888. Compare the standard under *Restatement* Sect. 712 with the United Nations' Charter of Rights and Duties of States Art. 2(2)(c), providing that compensation should be "appropriate" as determined under "the domestic law of the nationalizing State and by its tribunals". See William W. PARK, *op. cit.*, fn. 17, p. 1321.

25. Art. 1110(1) NAFTA adopts a four-part structure, requiring that the expropriation (1) have a public purpose, (2) be applied on a non-discriminatory basis, (3) "in accordance with due process of law and Art. 1105(1)" ["fair and equitable treatment"] and (4) result in "payment of compensation in accordance with paragraphs 2 through 6 [of Art. 1110]", which adopt the fair market value standard.

26. Art. 1110 NAFTA speaks of a "G-7 currency", which includes the currencies of Canada, France, Germany, Italy, Japan, the United Kingdom and the United States. 32 ILM (1993) p. 641. For France, Germany and Italy, members of the European Union's common currency union, the currency would now be the euro. By contrast, the United Kingdom at present maintains its own currency.

27. Art. 1110(2) NAFTA provides that fair market value "shall not reflect any change in value occurring because the intended expropriation had become known earlier".

remedy for a host state's breach of its duties. An aggrieved investor[28] may choose either (i) arbitration supervised by the International Centre for Settlement of Investment Disputes (ICSID) (part of the World Bank group)[29] or (ii) a proceeding conducted under arbitration rules adopted by the United Nations Commission on International Trade Law (UNCITRAL).[30] Disputes raising common questions of fact or law may be consolidated into a single arbitration.[31]

Should the investor want ICSID arbitration there is a slight limitation. Neither Mexico nor Canada is yet party to the Washington Convention establishing ICSID. Consequently ICSID-style arbitration must proceed under the so-called ICSID Additional Facility designed for cases in which the Washington Convention does not apply. As discussed below, this will have significant consequences when one side wishes to mount a challenge to the arbitration.

2. The Role of the Arbitral Situs

a. Current alternatives

When a dissatisfied loser in NAFTA arbitration seeks to have an award set aside, the choice of arbitral forum may have a significant impact on the role played by courts at the arbitral situs.[32] To understand the impact of local law, a brief contrast might be helpful. Under "pure" ICSID arbitration, the Washington Convention forecloses challenge to awards on normal statutory grounds[33] in favor of ICSID's special system of quality

---

28. Claims may be made either directly or on behalf of an enterprise owned by the investor under Art. 1116 NAFTA.

29. Established under the 1965 Washington Convention, ICSID normally has jurisdiction over investment disputes between a state that is a party to the Convention and an investor from another Convention State. The Convention on the Settlement of Investment Disputes Between States and Nationals of Other States, 18 March 1965, entered into force 14 October 1966. See generally DOLZER and STEVENS, op. cit., fn.13, pp. 130-146.

30. Art. 1120 NAFTA. Unless otherwise agreed, the place of arbitration must be in the territory of a country that is a party to both NAFTA and the New York Arbitration Convention. See Art. 1130 NAFTA, referring to a "Party [a NAFTA member] that is a party to the New York Convention".

31. Art. 1126 NAFTA.

32. See generally, David WILLIAMS, "Challenging Investment Treaaty Arbitration Awards: Issues Concerning the Forum Arising from the *Metalclad* Case", this volume at pp. 444-467.

33. For ICSID arbitration in the United States, this rule has never been tested in a court action raising the conflict between the Federal Arbitration Act (allowing motions to vacate awards) and the Washington Convention (which excludes such vacatur). The US Constitution in Art. VI(2) lists both treaties and federal statutes as the "supreme Law of the Land", without establishing a hierarchy. On some matters statutes clearly override treaties. See, e.g., Pub. L. No. 96-499 Sect. 1125, providing that no treaty shall require "exemption from (or reduction of) any tax imposed" on gains from disposition of US realty. When Congress is silent courts look to canons of statutory interpretation such as "last in time prevails" or "specific restricts general". See Detlev VAGTS, "The United States and Its Treaties: Observance and Breach", 95 Am. J. Int'l L. (2001) p. 313.

control under its own internal challenge procedure.[34]

However, since Canada and Mexico are not parties to the Washington Convention, investors currently have only two options for arbitral procedure: (i) the UNCITRAL Rules, which are entirely ad hoc, and (ii) the ICSID Additional Facility, supervised by ICSID but *outside* its treaty framework.

Whether under the UNCITRAL or Additional Facility Rules, arbitration will go forward within the framework of either the New York Convention[35] or the Panama Convention,[36] both of which require deference to valid arbitration agreements and awards but say nothing about proper or improper annulment standards.[37] In contrast to ICSID, the New York and Panama Conventions leave each country free to establish its own grounds for vacating awards made within its territory.

The consequence of arbitration under the rules of UNCITRAL or the Additional Facility is that NAFTA awards are now subject to the judicial review mechanisms that exist at the place of arbitration.[38] Art. 1136(3)(b) NAFTA explicitly contemplates such review. Award enforcement for arbitration under "Additional Facility" or UNCITRAL rules may not be sought until a court either dismisses or allows an application to revise, set aside, or annul the award and there is no further appeal, or three months have elapsed without such application being made.

---

34. See Art. 52, 1965 Washington Convention, *ICSID Basic Documents* (1985) p. 25. See generally W. Michael REISMAN, *Systems of Control in International Adjudication and Arbitration* (Duke 1992) pp. 46-50.

35. Convention on the Recognition and Enforcement of Foreign Arbitral Awards, 330 U.N.T.S. 38, 21 U.S.T. 2517, T.I.A.S. No. 6997 (1958).

36. Inter-American Convention on International Commercial Arbitration of 1975, set forth in 9 U.S.C. Chapter III.

37. At present the United States and Mexico, but not Canada, are parties to the Panama Convention. In the United States, when both Conventions are applicable, the Panama Convention prevails. See 9 U.S.C. Sect. 305. While similar in their basic structure, the New York and Panama Conventions differ in significant respects. For example, the Panama Convention does not require judges to refer parties to arbitration, or set forth conditions that must be satisfied by the party seeking award enforcement. Moreover, only the Panama Convention contains reference to arbitration rules (those of the Inter-American Commercial Arbitration Commission) that apply in default of party choice. See generally, Albert Jan van den BERG, "The New York Convention 1958 and Panama Convention 1975: Redundancy or Compatibility?", 4 Arb. Int'l (1989) p. 229; John BOWMAN, "The Panama Convention and Its Implementation under the Federal Arbitration Act", 11 Am. Rev. Int'l Arb. (2000) p. 116.

38. In the United States award "finality" has been interpreted to mean final as allowed under relevant arbitration laws. See, e.g., *M&C Corp. v. Erwin Behr GmbH & Co., KG*, 87 F.3d 844, 847 (6th Cir. 1996); *Iran Aircraft Industries v. Avco Corp.*, 980 F.2d 141, 145 (2d Cir. 1992). Compare the situation in Ontario. In *Noble China Inc. v. Lei*, 42 Ont. Rep. (3d) 69, 87 (1998), the UNCITRAL Model Law exclusion of judicial review was deemed to foreclose a motion to set aside an award, although the court noted that evidence of bias might have led to a different result. The authors are not aware of any analogous interpretations of award "finality" in Mexico, which adopted the UNCITRAL Model Law in June 1993.

b.   Metalclad

The much-discussed *Metalclad* case[39] illustrates the role currently given to the arbitral situs, by which judicial scrutiny of awards varies in function of the monitoring standards deemed appropriate by the relevant court. An "Additional Facility" award had granted damages to an American company for expropriation of a hazardous waste disposal facility. Regulatory action by a Mexican municipality had prevented a subsidiary of a US company from operating. Arbitrators had found that Mexican regulatory action denied "fair and equitable treatment" and constituted expropriation without adequate compensation. Mexico then petitioned to have the award set aside by the British Columbia Supreme Court, which had jurisdiction by virtue of the arbitration's official situs fixed in Vancouver.[40]

As a preliminary matter the court had to decide between application of two different provincial arbitration statutes. The International Commercial Arbitration Act (based on the UNCITRAL Model Law) provides a relatively narrow scope of review, while the Commercial Arbitration Act (which catches arbitration excluded from the International Act) allows a more generous role for court intervention, including appeal on points of law.

Surprisingly, the choice turned on the meaning of "commercial" rather than "international". The International Act requires that the arbitration be commercial as well as international. Mexico argued against application of the International Act on the grounds that the arbitration related to a regulatory rather than commercial relationship.

The court disagreed, finding that the arbitration was commercial in the sense that it "arose out of a relationship of investing".[41] Characterizing the arbitration by reference to the underlying transaction (a cross-border investment) placed the dispute within the terms of the International Act, which meant that court scrutiny focused on whether the award exceeded the arbitrators' powers or violated public policy.

As to the substance of the challenge, the Canadian court found that some but not all of the arbitrators' findings exceeded their jurisdiction. In particular, the court held that the tribunal went beyond its authority in finding that Mexico breached a NAFTA requirement of "transparency" in the sense that investment requirements should be knowable and free from doubt. In finding a transparency requirement, the arbitral tribunal "did not simply interpret the wording of Art. 1105 [but] misstated the

---

39. See *Metalclad v. United Mexican States*, ICSID Case No. ARB(AF)/97/1, Award of 30 August 2000, reprinted in 16 Int'l Arb. Rep. (January 2001) p. 62, finding expropriation without adequate compensation where a US-owned company was prevented by Mexican municipality from operating hazardous waste facility in Mexico. See Clyde PEARCE and Jack COE, "Arbitration under NAFTA Chapter 11 – Some Pragmatic Reflections Upon the First Case Filed Against Mexico", 23 Hastings Int'l & Comp. L. Rev. (2001) p. 311; Todd WEILER, "Metalclad v. Mexico: A Play in Three Parts", 2 J. World Investment (2001) p. 685. For the British Columbia decision on vacatur, see *United Mexican States v. Metalclad*, Vancouver Court Registry Case No. L 002904, Mr. Justice Tysoe, decided 2 May 2001, reprinted in 16 Int'l Arb. Rep. (May 2001) p. A-1.

40. For convenience, hearings had been held in Washington, DC.

41. See British Columbia Slip Opinion at para. 44.

applicable law ... and then made its decision on [that] basis".[42] Nevertheless, the court upheld the bulk of the award, given that one prong of the arbitrators' reasoning fell within their jurisdiction.[43] Consequently, only a portion of the award (dealing with interest) was set aside and remitted for recalculation.[44]

The practical lesson to be learned from *Metalclad* is that courts at the place of arbitration will have the last word in an arbitration. Consequently, care should be taken in selecting a venue where judges exercise a control function over the arbitration's basic procedural integrity (looking at matters such as bias, excess of authority and due process) but do not second guess the arbitrator on the substantive merits of the dispute.[45]

From the American perspective, the decision in *Metalclad* seemed quite normal. An investor from the United States was found to have been treated unfairly by a political subdivision of Mexico. Thus the proper way to resolve the dispute was the relatively neutral mechanism of arbitration rather than Mexican courts. As discussed below, however, when the shoe is on the other foot perceptions of fairness may be quite different, and the industrialized countries may not be enthusiastic about playing by the same rules.

3. Investor Protection in Practice

Considerable grist for the arbitration mill has been supplied by two particular aspects of Chapter 11: the matters of (i) "minimum standard of treatment" and (ii) compensation standards for expropriation. Several recent cases illustrate the way NAFTA has been applied in practice in these areas.

a. Minimum standards of treatment
Art. 1105 (1) NAFTA requires each country to "accord to investments of investors of another Party treatment in accordance with international law, including fair and equitable treatment and full protection and security". Although the meaning of "international law" has been the object of controversy,[46] at least two conclusions seem warranted. First, the "fair and equitable standard" is not complied with by simply

---

42. *Ibid.*, para. 70. This aspect of the case presents an example of how the line between excess of jurisdiction and simple error of law is often quite thin. The concept of transparency had been defined earlier in the decision at para. 28.

43. The court agreed that the arbitrators were correct in resting their decision on an "ecological decree" as tantamount to expropriation. Thus excess of authority was deemed to exist in only two out of the three breaches of NAFTA found by the arbitrators.

44. This decision has caused some scholars to argue in favor of a supra-national appellate mechanism to replace review of awards by national courts. See Jack J. COE, Jr., "Domestic Court Control of Investment Awards – Necessary Evil or Achilles Heel within NAFTA and the Proposed FTAA", 19 J. Int'l Arb. (2002) p. 185; William S. DODGE, "*Metalclad Corp v. Mexico*", 95 Am. J. Int'l L. 910 (2001) p. 918.

45. See William W. PARK, "Duty and Discretion in International Arbitration", 93 Am. J. Int'l L. (1999) p. 805.

46. See discussion of Free Trade Commission *Notes of Interpretation*, infra.

extending national or most-favored-nation treatment to NAFTA investors. Second, reference to "full protection and security" adopts the settled principle that a nation is liable for failure to exercise due diligence to prevent injuries to an investor caused by third parties.[47]

In *Metalclad*[48] Mexico was held to be in breach of Art. 1105(1) as a result of a lack of "orderly process" and "timely disposition" in relation to a NAFTA investor acting under the expectation that it would be treated fairly and justly in accordance with NAFTA. In *S.D. Myers*[49] treatment of NAFTA investors was held to fall below this minimum standard of treatment even in a situation where government conduct was not discriminatory. A breach of Art. 1105(1) thus occurs when the NAFTA investor is treated in such an unjust or arbitrary manner as to rise to a level unacceptable from the international perspective.

It is worth noting that several aspects of what might loosely be considered fair treatment are the subject of separate NAFTA provisions. For example, under Art. 1106 a NAFTA country may not "impose or enforce 'performance requirements' in connection with investments in its territory", which include achievement of export levels, domestic procurement requirements, minimum local content, trade balancing, product mandating or the transfer of technology.[50] NAFTA also grants investors an explicit right to choose senior managers (Art. 1107) and the right to convert local currency into foreign currency at the prevailing market rate of exchange, in order to repatriate earnings, proceeds of a sale, loan repayments or other investment-related transactions (Art. 1109).

b.   Expropriation

A NAFTA member country may directly or indirectly expropriate private property provided that it does so: (i) for a public purpose; (ii) on a non-discriminatory basis; (iii) in accordance with due process of law; and (iv) on payment of prompt, adequate and effective compensation. Art. 1110 extends protection against uncompensated expropriation to measures "tantamount to nationalization or expropriation", thus

---

47. Ian BROWNLIE, *System of the Law of Nations: State Responsibility* (1983) p. 161; ICSID Case ARB/87/3.

48. *Metalclad Corporation v. Government of the United Mexican States*, Award of 25 August 2000, discussed supra.

49. *S.D. Myers, Inc. v. Government of Canada*, Partial Award of 13 November 2000, reprinted in 40 ILM (2001) p. 1408. US investor hoped to capture a large portion of the Canadian market for destruction of PCBs by sending materials to Ohio facilities, a competitive advantage over Canadian facilities further away. Canadian environmental authorities responded to Canadian lobbying with an emergency ban preventing export of PCB waste.

50. In two early cases testing this requirement, arbitral tribunals hearing claims against Canada have failed to find improper imposition of performance requirements. See *Pope & Talbot, Inc. v. Government of Canada*, Interim Award on Merits of 26 June 2000; final award 31 May 2002 (US investor claimed damages in connection with Canadian softwood export prohibitions; the tribunal dismissed all but the claim that Canada had engaged in denial of fair treatment); *S.D. Myers, Inc. v. Government of Canada*, Partial Award of 13 November 2000 (tribunal found that the export ban in question was not a requirement on "the conduct or operation of the investment").

encompassing takings that have often been referred to as "creeping" expropriation. In all cases compensation for expropriation must be paid without delay, be equal to the fair market value of the investment prior to the expropriation, include interest, and be fully realizable and freely transferable.

While "tantamount to expropriation" is not defined in NAFTA, this well-established concept has been applied to cover not only openly avowed state takings of property, but also "other actions that have the effect of 'taking' the property, in whole or in large part, outright or in stages [including] when [a state] subjects alien property to taxation, regulation, or other action that is confiscatory, or that prevents, unreasonably interferes with, or unduly delays, effective enjoyment of an alien's property.[51] "An indirect expropriation may occur if the investor's expected entitlement to the benefits are impaired by host state interference, even if property is not legally taken by the State",[52] or when the host state itself acquires nothing of value but "at least has been the instrument of its redistribution".[53]

Several Chapter 11 arbitrations, including *Azinian*,[54] *Metalclad*,[55] *Pope & Talbot*[56] and

---

51. See *Restatement (Third) Foreign Relations Law*, *op. cit.*, fn. 24, Sect. 712. ICSID cases that have addressed indirect expropriation include *Amco Asia Corp. v. Republic of Indonesia*, ARB/81/1; *Liberian Eastern Timber Corp. v. Government of Liberia*, ARB/83/2 and *Southern Pacific Properties Ltd. v. Arab Republic of Egypt*, ARB/84/3. See generally references to works by DOLZER, HIGGINS and WESTON cited infra, fn. 89.

52. Istvan POSGANY, "Bilateral Investment Treaties: Some Recent Examples", Foreign Investment Law Journal (1987) p. 964.

53. Allahyar MOURI, *The International Law of Expropriation as Reflected in the Work of the Iran-U.S. Claims Tribunal* (1994) p. 66; *Poehlmann v. Spinnerei AG*, 3 U.S. Ct. Rest. App. 701-702, 704-710 (1952).

54. *Robert Azinian v. United Mexican States*, Award on Merits of 1 November 1999. US investors contracted with a local municipality to provide waste treatment services. The tribunal concluded that the claimant had not shown the Mexican actions to be illegal under international law.

55. *Metalclad Corporation v. Government of the United Mexican States*, Award on Merits of 25 August 2000. The tribunal ruled that "Expropriation under NAFTA includes not only open, deliberate and acknowledged takings of property, such as outright seizure or formal or obligatory transfer of title in favor of the host State, but also covert or incidental interference with the use of property which has the effect of depriving the owner, in whole or in significant part, of the use or reasonably-to-be-expected economic benefit of the property even if not necessarily to the obvious benefit of the host State." At p. 33, para. 103, the tribunal also applied an "effects" test and held that the motivation or intent of the adoption of an environmental decree was not relevant to a determination under NAFTA Art. 1110.

56. *Pope & Talbot, Inc. v. Government of Canada*, Interim Award on Merits of 26 June 2000; Final Award 31 May 2002. In the Interim Award of June 2000 the tribunal dismissed all but the claim that Canada had denied fair treatment under Art. 1105, but indicated that "creeping expropriation could be conducted by regulation, and a blanket exception for regulatory measures would create a gaping loophole in the international protection against expropriation". *Ibid.*, p. 35, para. 99. On whether there was an expropriation, the arbitral tribunal indicated that the test is "whether the interference is sufficiently restricted to support a conclusion that the property has been *taken* from the owner". See generally, Patrick DUMBERRY, "The Quest to Define 'Fair and Equitable Treatment' for Investors under International Law", 3 J. World Investment (2002) p. 657.

S.D. Myers,[57] have addressed the question of what constitutes expropriation. Thus far none would seem to have departed from traditional notions of customary international law.

III. ARBITRATION AND THE NEW HOST STATES

1. Three Illustrations

Three Canadian claims against the United States illustrate how a traditional investor country has seen the tables turned by mandatory arbitration with foreign investors.[58] Each case involves complaints about an American state rather than the federal government. In *Methanex* California banned gasoline additives manufactured from a feedstock produced by a Canadian company; in *Loewen*, a Mississippi jury awarded $ 500 million against a Manitoba funeral director; and in *Mondev* the Supreme Judicial Court of Massachusetts upheld the city of Boston in refusing to sell land to a Montreal real estate developer.

The reaction common to all three cases is that arbitration becomes problematic when American interests may be adjudicated outside American courts. The protest is pregnant with irony when we remember how often the United States has imposed arbitration on other countries,[59] and how US negotiators advocated arbitration to promote the security of American investments over Mexico's longstanding opposition thereto.[60]

a. Methanex[61]

When California became concerned about risks to drinking water as a result of leakage from underground fuel storage tanks, its Governor banned gasoline containing a

---

57. *S.D. Myers, Inc. v. Government of Canada*, Partial Award of 13 November 2000. The tribunal decided that the term "tantamount" in NAFTA Art. 1110 means "equivalent" and is intended to capture acts of creeping expropriation but does not broaden the scope of expropriation under customary international law.

58. The fourth claim against the United States, filed on 19 July 2000 by ADF Group of Quebec, involved a "Buy American" requirement of the Federal Highway Administration that interfered with participation in a Virginia highway project by a Canadian manufacturer of complex steel components.

59. See W. Laurence CRAIG, William W. PARK and Jan PAULSSON, *International Chamber of Commerce Arbitration*, 3rd ed. (2000) Chapter 36.

60. The NAFTA Statement of Administrative Action makes this point: "The NAFTA provides a historic investor-state dispute settlement mechanism, so that individual U.S. companies no longer face an unbalanced environment in an investment dispute with the Mexican government but can seek arbitration outside Mexico by an independent body." See North American Free Trade Agreement, texts of Agreement, Implementing Bill, Statement of Administrative Action and Required Supporting Statements, House Document 103-159, vol. 1, p. 685.

61. *Methanex Corp. v. USA*, Amended Claim filed 12 February 2001 by Jones, Day, Reavis & Pogue, Washington, DC. Available through www.naftaclaims.com.

methanol-based gasoline additive called "MTBE".[62] A Canadian corporation producing feedstock for this additive responded by filing an arbitration claim arguing discrimination, denial of minimum standard of treatment and improper expropriation of its investment.[63]

The filing of the claim led to protests by environmentalists and the US Environmental Protection Agency (EPA). Charges were made that NAFTA Chapter 11, by allowing corporations to recover for unfair treatment, favored corporate profits over legitimate exercise of sovereignty by local governments. This arbitral process was attacked as undemocratic, cloaked in secrecy, lacking adequate rights of appeal and protection for equally injured domestic producers. NAFTA was further criticized as denying the American public a right to protect its water and air.[64]

b. Loewen

In *Loewen v. USA*,[65] a Mississippi jury verdict led to claims of failure to grant "fair and equitable treatment" and expropriation without adequate compensation. The jury had awarded half a billion dollars in favor of a Mississippi funeral director who claimed that a Canadian buyer had breached a contract for the purchase of his funeral parlors. When the Canadian attempted to appeal, he found that state law required the posting of a bond as security for payment of the judgment equal to 125 percent of the amount awarded. In this case the sum would have been $ 625 million, high enough to force a substantial settlement.

The Canadian defendant then filed a NAFTA Chapter 11 claim against the United

---

62. It is significant that the claimant Methanex does not produce MTBE (Methyl tertiary butyl ether), but rather the feedstock (methanol) for the banned additive. This fact seems to have played a part in the recent Partial Award in this case. The arbitral tribunal appears to have posited that the connection between methanol and the ban was too remote in the context of NAFTA Art. 1101, since the government measure did not apply to the investor's product itself. The ban was effective 31 December 2001. See Exec. Order No. D-5-99 promulgated by Governor Gray Davis.

63. Violations were alleged with respect to Arts. 1102, 1105 and 1110 NAFTA. Methanex Corp. Notice of Intent to Submit a Claim to Arbitration Under Art. 1119, Sect. B, Chapter 11 of NAFTA, filed 2 July 1999. The arbitration proceeding was brought under the UNCITRAL Rules and has already resulted in an interim ruling. See *Methanex Corp v. United States*, 15 January 2001, 16 Int'l Arb. Rep. (2001, no. 1) p. D-1, "Decision on Authority to Accept Amicus Submissions", finding that it "could be appropriate" for an environmental group to make submissions. Art. 15(1) UNCITRAL Rules permits conduct of the proceedings "in such manner as [the tribunal] considers appropriate".

64. For a survey of the criticisms of NAFTA provoked by *Methanex*, see generally Lucien J. DHOOGE, "The Revenge of the Trail Smelter: Environmental Regulation as Expropriation Pursuant to the North American Free Trade Agreement", 38 Am. Bus. L. J. (2001) p. 475 at pp. 478-479, notes 18-25.

65. *Loewen Group, Inc. v. U.S.A.* (ICSID Case No. ARB (AF)/98/3) Interim Award on Jurisdiction, 5 January 2001. The US$ 500 million verdict included US$ 400 million in punitive damages. The basis of the claim was Arts. 1105 and 1110 NAFTA. The rich tapestry of this dispute is set forth in Jonathan HARR, "The Burial", The New Yorker (1 November 1999) p. 70, describing the backgrounds of the Mississippi plaintiff, Jeremiah O'Keefe, his Florida lawyer, Willy Gary, the allegedly xenophobic comments to the jury, and the circumstances surrounding the US$ 175 million settlement.

States in an ICSID Additional Facility arbitration. The merits of the case are still being arbitrated, but an interim award did decide that a court judgment can be considered a governmental "measure" that might give rise to liability for discrimination, failure to grant "fair and equitable treatment" and expropriation without adequate compensation.

c.   Mondev

In the final example, a Quebec corporation commenced arbitration arising from a decision by the Massachusetts Supreme Judicial Court dismissing an action against the City of Boston for breach of a contract to sell property in connection with municipal redevelopment, and against the Boston Redevelopment Authority for tortuous interference with contractual relations.[66] The developers had entered into an agreement with Boston to acquire a parcel of downtown real estate. When the city balked at going through with the transfer, the failure was ultimately excused on the basis that the Canadian investment vehicle did not "follow the steps" required under the agreement, since its offer to buy the parcel had not manifested a "precise time and place for passing papers".[67] The claim against the Boston Redevelopment Authority was dismissed on the basis that this public body was immune from tort liability under the Massachusetts Tort Claims Act.[68]

Aggrieved by the court decision, the Montreal investor brought a $50 million claim under the ICSID Additional Facility alleging discrimination, expropriation without compensation and denial of "fair and equitable treatment". The decision of the Massachusetts Supreme Judicial Court endorsing the denial of the developer's right to purchase the land was described as "unprincipled" and "arbitrary".[69]

One can understand that such a proceeding might surprise many Americans. What could be more likely to fall within the power of the Supreme Judicial Court of Massachusetts than an action relating to land in Boston? Imagine, however, the reverse situation, in which rights of similarly situated Boston investors are rebuffed by a foreign court. It is not hard to imagine New England voices crying foul play.[70]

---

66. *Mondev International Ltd. v. United States of America* (ICSID Case No. ARB (AF)/99/2) in an Award notified to the Parties on 11 October 2002, the arbitral tribunal dismissed Mondev's claims, finding that the American court decisions "did not involve any violation of Art. 1105(1) of NAFTA or otherwise". The party-nominated arbitrators were James Crawford (for claimant) and Stephen Schwebel (for respondent United States), and the Presiding Arbitrator is Ninian Stephen. See also *Lafayette Place Associates v. Boston Redevelopment Authority*, 427 Mass. 509, 694 N.E.2d (1998) p. 820. Operating in Boston through the limited partnership, Mondev had agreed to participate in a project originating in an attempt to rehabilitate the so-called "combat zone", a dilapidated area near Boston's downtown shopping district. Although the Supreme Judicial Court found the contract with Boston to be enforceable, the developers were deemed to have forfeited their rights due to lack of evidence that they were ready, able and willing to close the sale.

67. *Ibid.*, p. 520.

68. *Ibid.*, pp. 531-533. See MGL, c. 258, Sects. 1, 10(c).

69. *Mondev International Ltd. v. USA*, Notice of Arbitration, ICSID Case No. ARB(AF)/99/2 (1 September 1999) p. 74.

70. The story in the Boston newspapers might read something like this: "Xenophobic judge in Ruritania refused to enforce a promise to sell property to an American company. Investor asks why it should take the trouble of entering into contracts when local judiciary excuses breach of

2.   Reactions and Complaints

As the first Chapter 11 cases were filed against the United States and Canada,[71] voices began to be heard saying that investment arbitration infringes national prerogatives. Investor protection has been presented by activists as a subterfuge to challenge laws simply because they have a negative impact on the foreign capitalist.[72] In one *New York Times* article NAFTA arbitration was thus described,

> "Their meetings are secret. Their members are generally unknown. The decisions they reach need not be fully disclosed. Yet the way a small group of international tribunals handles disputes between investors and foreign governments has led to national laws being revoked, justice systems questioned and environmental regulations challenged."[73]

a.   "Fast track attack on America's values"

Among the most negative reactions to investment arbitration, a December 2001 advertisement in the *Washington Post* attacked investment arbitration under the headline "Fast Track Attack on America's Values", which appeared against the background of the preamble to the US Constitution ("We the people ...") with captions that read: "Secret Courts for Corporations" and "Taxpayer Dollars for Foreign Polluters".[74]

---

agreement on a technicality, citing nothing more than absence of a 'precise time and place for passing papers'. The seller was granted total immunity from liability."

71. Twenty-seven notices of intent (not all of which have been followed by claims) have been brought under Chapter 11 to date: nine against Canada (Ethyl, S.D. Myers, Sun Belt, Pope & Talbot, UPS, Ketcham Investments, Crompton, Trammel Crow and Signa); ten against Mexico (Metalclad, Karpa (a.k.a. Feldman), Adams, Azinian, Waste Management Services I and II, Calmark Commercial Development, Halchette, GAMI Investments Inc. and Fireman's Fund); eight against the United States (Loewen, Methanex, Mondev, ADF Group, Canfor, Tembec, Kenex and Doman and Kenex). Cases raising environment issues include *Metalclad, Methanex, Ethyl, S.D. Myers* and *Crompton*.

72. See generally, BROWER and STEVEN, *op. cit.*, fn. 9, p. 198; Daniel M. PRICE, "Some Observations on Chapter Eleven of NAFTA", 23 Hastings Int'l. & Comp. L. Rev. (2000) p. 421; Frederick M. ABBOTT, "The Political Economy of NAFTA Chapter Eleven: Equality Before the Law and the Boundaries of North American Integration", 23 Hastings Int'l & Comp. L. Rev. (2000) p. 303 at p. 306.

73. See, e.g., Anthony DE PALMA, "NAFTA's Powerful Little Secret", New York Times, Sunday Late Edition, (11 March 2001) Sect. 3, p. 1. For an attempt at a more broad-based rebuttal of claims that international trade undermines governmental regulatory structures, see Ronald A. CASS and John HARING, "Domestic Regulation and International Trade: Where's the Race? Lessons from Telecommunications and Export Controls", in Daniel KENNEDY and James SOUTHWICK, eds., *The Political Economy of International Trade: Essays in Honor of Robert E. Hudec* (2002).

74. Sponsored by Ralph Nader's "Public Citizen's Global Trade Watch", the publication referred to possible extension of a NAFTA provision permitting "foreign corporations to sue the federal government in secret tribunals, demanding our tax dollars as payment for complying with U.S. health, safety and pollution laws". The advertisement continued that foreign manufacturers of

The full-page advertisement urged rejection of the trade bill (ultimately passed by one vote in the House of Representatives) giving the President "fast track" authority to negotiate agreements in the Free Trade Area of the Americas (FTAA). These agreements could extend to thirty-four Western Hemisphere countries based on the NAFTA model.

In one well-publicized television show hosted by Bill Moyers, NAFTA was labeled a "sophisticated extortion racket", and "an end-run around the Constitution" in which "secret NAFTA tribunals can force taxpayers to pay billions of dollars in lawsuits".[75]

Environmentalists have been particularly vocal in saying that NAFTA makes it possible to undermine legitimate governmental regulations.[76] Chapter 11 arbitration is portrayed as a forum insulated from rightful domestic political and legal safeguards.[77] The World Wildlife Fund and the Institute for Sustainable Development published a report entitled "Private Rights, Public Problems", which labels NAFTA Chapter 11 arbitration as "one-sided" and "lacking transparency", and concludes that arbitration is "shockingly unsuited to the task of balancing private rights against public goods".[78]

---

toxic chemicals could use "private courts" (i.e., arbitration) "to sue U.S. taxpayers ... if zoning rules kept them from building a chemical plant near a school". Referring to arbitration's confidentiality, the advertisement said that "even the identity of judges can be kept secret indefinitely", ending with the rhetorical question, "Whose side is Congress on – foreign corporations or the American people?" See Washington Post (5 December 2001) p. A-5, placed by the Global Trade Watch division of Public Citizen (www.citizen.org).

75. The transcript of the PBS special series "Trading Democracy" (aired 1 February 2002) can be obtained on www.pbs.org/now/transcript.

76. No administrative veto prohibits arbitration of disputes implicating environmental measures. NAFTA simply provides that nothing in Chapter 11 shall be construed as preventing adoption of measures "to ensure that investment activity ... is undertaken in a manner sensitive to environmental concerns". See Art. 1114 NAFTA.

77. See, e.g., comments at "Public Citizen" web page (www.citizen.org). See also Howard MANN and Konrad von MOLTKE, "NAFTA's Chapter 11 and the Environment: Addressing the Impacts of the Investor-State Process on the Environment", International Institute for Sustainable Development Working Paper (1999) (http://iisd1.iisd.ca/pdf/nafta.pdf). Complaints include the "virtually unfettered right of foreign investors to initiate direct actions against their host governments" and the "aggressive use of this process to challenge public policy and public welfare measures". The authors complain about "uncertainty and unpredictability for environmental regulations", lack of procedural or public interest safeguards, "non-transparent, secretive and non-appealable" arbitration, all of which mean that host governments must "pay foreign investors in order to be able to effectively regulate the environment". See also Todd WEILER, "A First Look at the Interim Merits Award in *S.D. Myers v. Canada*: It Is Possible to Balance Legitimate Environmental Concerns with Investment Protection", 24 Hastings Int'l & Comp. L. Rev. (2001) p. 173; Joseph DE PENCIER, "Investment, Environment and Dispute Settlement: Arbitration Under NAFTA Chapter Eleven", 23 Hastings Int'l & Comp. L. Rev. (2000) p. 409.

78. Howard MANN, "Private Rights, Public Goods", International Institute for Sustainable Development and World Wildlife Fund (2001) p. 46. The report by Dr. Mann, a lawyer based in Ottawa, led to follow-up commentary in Canada and the United States that furthered the negative characterization of NAFTA. See Mark THOMSEN, "Companies Using NAFTA to Undermine Legitimate Regulations", 12 June 2001, reported at www.socialfunds.com/news; Chantal BLOUIN, "NAFTA Goes Too Far on Investor Protection", North-South Institute (31 August 2001) reported at www.nsi-ins.ca/ensi/news.

Members of Congress also complain that NAFTA tribunals override health and labor laws, and express alarm that the US federal government might be held liable for the idiosyncratic acts of local authorities and state courts.[79] During debate on an appropriations bill, a Congressman lamented that the Justice Department might have to sue local governments to enforce NAFTA decisions, and in a burst of fervor proclaimed, "This is nuts! … We must stand together to protect the sovereignty of American laws."[80]

A recent indication of American discontent with the NAFTA model for investment dispute resolution came in response to legislative efforts to extend trade benefits to Latin American countries. The Chairman of the Senate Finance Committee wrote to the Bush Administration endorsing attempts to deny foreign investors any substantive rights not given to American investors, to establish an appellate review of NAFTA awards,[81] and to support government screening of arbitration requests to reduce the prospect that they are ever considered by arbitrators.[82]

While not all legislators accepted the wisdom of such measures,[83] some went even further. Senator Kerry of Massachusetts proposed amendments to the Andean Trade

---

79. See debate on HR 2670, an appropriations bill for the Commerce, Justice and State Departments, at 145 Cong. Rec., HR, 106th Congress, 1st Session, 5 August 1999, at H-7368. Federal statute prohibits challenge of state laws inconsistent with NAFTA, "except in an action brought by the United States [i.e., the federal government] for the purposes of declaring such law or application invalid". 19 U.S.C. Sect. 3312(b)(2), codifying Sect. 102(b) of NAFTA Implementation Act. Similar protections apply to state laws in conflict with Uruguay Round trade agreements. 19 U.S.C. Sect. 3512(b)(2). An amendment to the bill offered by Rep. Kucinich (Ohio) would have prohibited the Department of Justice from using appropriated funds to challenge state laws that run afoul of NAFTA, for example, the Mississippi bond requirement in *Loewen*. The amendment failed 196 to 226.

80. 145 Cong. Rec., HR, 106th Congress, 1st Session, 5 August 1999, at H-7368. Congressman TIERNEY (Massachusetts) expressed concern that the pace of globalization might result in "sacrificing state and local laws at the altar of ill-defined international investor rights". Congressman SHOWS (Mississippi) opposed allowing "American taxpayer dollars [to] pay American lawyers to help a foreign corporation fight American state laws in court", *ibid.* Congressman BONIOR (Michigan) added, "The question … is very clear: Should the rights of an investor come before the rights to enact a chemical ban to prevent cancer?", *ibid.* Observers will note, of course, that NAFTA prohibits discrimination, not the right to ban carcinogens. The essence of the concern would seem to be that arbitrators hearing anti-discrimination claims might strike down otherwise valid health regulations.

81. Letter of 26 March 2002 from Max Baucus to Trade Representative Robert Zoellick, discussed in Rossella BREVETTI, "Baucus Welcomes Options Administration Is Considering on Investor-State Disputes", 19 BNA Int'l Trade 13 (28 March 2002) p. 529.

82. A similar screening mechanism already exists with respect to expropriation claims that implicate tax measures. See Art. 2103(6) NAFTA, discussed infra.

83. On 28 March 2002 the Senate Finance Committee's ranking Republican Charles Grassley urged Trade Representative Zoellick to reject such screening. See Rossella BREVETTI, "Grassley Urges Zoellick to Reject Government Screening for Investor Suits", Regulation Law & Economics, No. 62, 1 (April 2002) p. A 6. Industry groups, including the National Association of Manufacturers, have also expressed concern for the preservation of investor protections for American-owned businesses abroad. See BREVETTI, *op. cit.*, fn. 81. See also discussion of HR 3005 in Chris RUGABER and Rossella BREVETTI, "In Partisan Markup, House Ways and Means Approves TPA Legislation", International Trade Reporter Current Reports (11 October 2001).

Preferences Act which would have given the investor state[84] the right to prohibit arbitration on the basis that the claim "lacks legal merit" and established a "single appellate body" to review decisions in investment arbitration.[85]

As finally enacted, the 2002 trade legislation includes provisions for "mechanisms to eliminate frivolous claims", an appellate body to "provide coherence" to interpretations of trade agreement investment provisions and a mandate to make arbitration proceedings public and allow amicus curiae submissions from business, labor non-governmental organizations.[86]

b.   "Cone of silence"
Some groups in Canada have likewise complained bitterly about NAFTA, alleging that it serves "to limit the legitimate rights of governments to regulate".[87] An editorial in The Globe and Mail criticized the confidentiality inherent in arbitration as a "cone of silence", claiming that "lawsuits against the Canadian government under NAFTA's Chapter 11 end up being composed almost entirely of rumour and leaks rather than official documents".[88]

---

84. While some might imagine that this veto right would be given to the host state, in fact the Kerry proposals accorded this to the "competent authority in the investor's country". See SA 3430, proposed Sect. 2102(b)(3)(H)(i) & (ii). This approach follows the lines of traditional practice in matters of state responsibility, with a capital-exporting country espousing its national's claim in order to assert protection of the investor's foreign assets.

85. The Kerry proposals would also have modified the substantive contours of what NAFTA arbitrators could award, requiring, inter alia, that trade agreements with investment provisions (i) ensure that foreign investors receive no greater legal rights than American citizens; (ii) exclude compensation for regulatory measures that cause "mere diminution" in the value of property; and (iii) ensure that standards for minimum treatment grant foreigners no greater legal rights than possessed by American citizens under the Constitution's due process clause. See Kerry amendment to Andean Trade Preference Expansion Act, H. R. 3009 (107th Con. 2nd Sess.), Senate Amendment 3430 to Sect. 2102(b) of the Andean Trade Preferences Act, Cong. Rec. 16 May 2002 S 4504. The amendment was tabled 21 May 2002.

86. See Sect. 2102(b)(3) of Trade Act of 2002 (P.L. 107-210), 16 Stat. 933, codified 19 U.S.C. 3802.

87. See Nihal SHERIF, "Canadian Memo Identifies Options for Changing NAFTA Investment Rules", Inside US Trade (12 February 1999) p. 20 (commenting upon a memo of the Canadian Department of Foreign Affairs and International Trade). See also discussion of *Pope & Talbot v. Canada*, Award of 26 June 2000, 16 Int'l Arb. Rep. (July 2001) p. 20, which finds that Canadian export controls on softwood lumber discriminated against an Oregon investor; Final Award 31 May 2002. See also WEILER, *op. cit.*, fn. 77, p. 173; Joseph DE PENCIER, "Investment, Environment and Dispute Settlement: Arbitration Under NAFTA Chapter Eleven", 23 Hastings Int'l & Comp. L. Rev. (2000) p. 409.

88. "NAFTA Cone of Silence", The Globe and Mail (26 August 1998) p. A 14. Responses to this editorial include letters to the editor by Sergio Marchi (Canadian Trade Minister), who asserted that investor rights must not "inhibit the sovereign responsibility of governments to legislate and regulate in the public interest", (The Globe and Mail (31 August 1998) p. A 12) and Maude BARLOW, who asserted that NAFTA was the "first international treaty in history to grant foreign investors the right to bypass their own governments in a trade dispute and sue the government of another country for cash compensation" and that NAFTA arbitrators were all "trade bureaucrats" (The Globe and Mail (5 September 1998) p. D 7).

3. Understandable Concerns

Many host state concerns about NAFTA arbitration are understandable. Considerable ambiguity exists with respect to what constitutes "fair and equitable" treatment. The law on expropriation is also relatively malleable, with little consensus on the standards that determine when administrative regulations give rise to a governmental taking that requires compensation. Must a claimant show an abuse of power by the host government? Must the nationalization include an element of bad faith? May a foreign investor recover in circumstances where the claim of a domestic owner would fail?

The crux of the problem is that not all discrimination is outright and abrupt. Arbitrary taking of property may occur in a gradual fashion through abusive manipulation of the legal system. Various names have been applied to such de facto nationalization: "creeping expropriation", "indirect expropriation", and "constructive expropriation", as well as measures "tantamount to" or "equivalent to" expropriation.[89] Indirect nationalization through improper administrative measures has long served as a back door to deprive the investor of its assets.[90] In some cases a taking might occur through non-action, as when a state refuses to interfere with popular seizure of foreign property or fails to fulfill a contractual obligation to grant fiscal benefits.

Expropriation under the guise of otherwise valid regulations is often easier to recognize than to define, as illustrated by the practice of the Overseas Private Investment Corporation (OPIC).[91] A federally chartered agency of the United States government, OPIC insures American investors against expropriation and currency inconvertibility in connection with their foreign investments.[92] Notwithstanding OPIC's broad definition of expropriation,[93] the experience of investors seeking reimbursement

---

89. See generally Burns H. WESTON, "Constructive Takings under International Law: A Modest Foray into the Problem of 'Creeping Expropriation'", 16 Va. J. Int'l L. 103 (1975); Rosalyn HIGGINS, "The Taking of Property by the State: Recent Developments in International Law", 176 Recueil des cours (The Hague 1982) p. 259; Rudolf DOLZER, "Indirect Expropriation of Alien Property", 1 ICSID Review–Foreign Investment Law J. (1986) p. 41. See also discussion of Overseas Private Investment Corporation (OPIC) infra. See generally, Markham BALL, "Assessing Damages in Claims by Investors Against States", 16 ICSID Review–Foreign Investment Law J. (Autumn 2001) p. 408.

90. See, e.g., Barcelona Traction, Light and Power Co., Ltd. (Belgium v. Spain) (2d Phase), 1970 ICJ 3; 9 ILM (1970) p. 227. By refusal to authorize transfer of foreign currency to pay Sterling bond interest, Spain allegedly engineered the bankruptcy of a Canadian owned company as a way to deprive the parent of its property. See also V.V. VEEDER, "The Lena Goldfields Arbitration: The Historical Roots of Three Ideas", 47 Int'l & Comp. L. Q. (1998) p. 747 (discussion of Goldfields v. USSR, Judgment of 3 September 1930).

91. See generally Vance KOVEN, "Expropriation and the 'Jurisprudence' of OPIC", 22 Harvard Int'l L. J. (1981) p. 269; Wolfgang PETER, Arbitration and Renegotiation of International Investment Agreements, 2nd ed. (1995) pp. 348-357.

92. The Contract of Insurance provides for controversies between OPIC and the investor to be settled by arbitration.

93. OPIC's current Program Handbook (available at www.opic.gov) defines expropriation coverage as protection against "nationalization, confiscation or expropriation of an enterprise, including 'creeping' expropriation – unlawful government actions that deprive the investor of fundamental

has not always been consistent.[94] In many instances jurists will find difficulty establishing intellectually rigorous standards, and thus will be consigned to a "we-know-it-when-we-see-it" attitude toward de facto takings.

Not all scholars see the case law of expropriation as a threat to environmental regulations. One thoughtful study of regulatory takings has identified a number of standards applied in nationalization cases, such as proportionality, necessity and non-discrimination.[95] Not every governmental measure that diminishes the worth of an investment will require compensation, and some balance must be struck between the right to regulate and the preservation of property values. At the least, the investor has the right to be concerned with uncertainty and surprise and breaches of prior commitments.[96]

To some extent the United States may have become a victim of its own success. In the past, Americans sometimes persuaded arbitrators to adopt broad standards providing "protection and security" that might override otherwise legitimate domestic laws.[97] Regulations which in a domestic context constituted normal protection of the public interest appeared in a cross-border transaction as violations of international law. Thus

---

rights in a project" but excluding losses due to "lawful regulation or taxation" and "actions provoked or instigated by the investor". *Ibid.* at p. 11. See also www.opic.gov/finance/products/expropriation.htm; Jonathan HADDON, PLI Presentation, 784 PLI/Comm (February 1999) p. 271.

94. In one case OPIC acknowledges that rights could be denied through a "chain of conduct", but found that the investor's control over its assets continued even after it lost managerial and shareholder control of the investment vehicle. See *Cabot Int'l Capital Corp., Contract 8383*, Memorandum of Determination (27 December 1980). See also *Revere Copper & Brass, Inc. v. OPIC*, American Arbitration Association Award, 17 ILM (1978) p. 1321, motion to vacate denied, D.C. Cir. (26 February 1980), cert. denied, 100 S.Ct. 2964 (1980). At that time the OPIC Contract of Insurance defined "expropriatory action" to include actions that prevent (a) payment of amounts due in respect of securities, (b) effective exercise of fundamental rights, (c) disposition of securities, (d) exercise of effective control or (e) repatriation of earnings.

95. See Thomas WAELDE and Abba KOLO, "Environmental Regulation, Investment Protection and 'Regulatory Taking' in International Law", 50 Int'l & Comp. L. Q. (2001) p. 811.

96. WAELDE and KOLO conclude, "[I]t is unlikely that courts or arbitrators will find a compensable expropriation in cases where governments issue environmental regulation for legitimate purposes in accordance with the state of scientific knowledge and accepted international guidelines." *Ibid.*, p. 846. The authors remain optimistic that regulatory taking would be found "only when the environment becomes a pretext for domestic protectionism and when elements of discrimination or breach of governmental commitments or [when regulation has been used] to extract benefits unrelated to the legitimate purpose of the regulation ...". *Ibid.*

97. See, e.g., *American Mfg. & Trading (AMT) v. Zaire*, 36 ILM (1997) p. 1531, arising under the US-Zaire 1984 Bilateral Investment Treaty and involving destruction to property of an American subsidiary by the Zaire army. Referring to the host state's "obligation of vigilance" to "ensure the full enjoyment of protection and security of [the US company's] investment", the arbitral tribunal stated that Zaire "should not be permitted to invoke its own legislation to detract from any such obligation". *Ibid.*, p. 1548. The case is cited in *Methanex* Amended Claim (12 February 2001) p. 65.

Americans were, in Shakespeare's words, "hoist with their own petard",[98] having contributed to the creation of pro-investor substantive standards applied by international tribunals, and to a blurring of distinctions between state-private proceedings ("mixed arbitration") and commercial arbitration exclusively among private parties.

4.   The Free Trade Commission Notes of Interpretation

Initially the NAFTA countries had expected that the ebb and flow of arbitral wisdom would create a body of case law providing sound investment protection. However, NAFTA also included a safety valve that permitted member countries to interpret Chapter 11 through the Free Trade Commission.[99]

During the summer of 2001, however, the NAFTA Free Trade Commission issued *Notes of Interpretation* related to several matters currently sub judice in Chapter 11 cases. Under the *Notes of Interpretation*, the requirements of Art. 1105 NAFTA were restated to indicate that a breach of another NAFTA provision or a separate international agreement will not in itself establish that "fair and equitable treatment" has been denied.[100] Moreover, the *Notes of Interpretation* limit the meaning of international law to "customary" minimum standards,[101] thus preventing recourse to other sources of international law that might either impose or relax restrictions on host State treatment of foreign investors.[102]

To some, these *Notes of Interpretation* constitute de facto modification of NAFTA that departs from the original meaning of Chapter 11, and thus require approval pursuant to Art. 2202 in accordance with "applicable legal procedures of each Party". One award

---

98. See *Hamlet*, Act III, Scene 4 ("for 'tis sport to have the engineer hoist with his own petard") in which the Prince of Denmark makes plans to catch the conspirators in his father's murder.

99. Art. 1131(2) states, "An interpretation by the [Free Trade] Commission of a provision of this Agreement shall be binding on a Tribunal established under [Chapter 11 Sect. B]."

100. See NAFTA Free Trade Commission, Notes of Interpretation of Certain Chapter 11 Provisions, 31 July 2001, Part B, reprinted in 13 World Trade & Arbitration Materials (December 2001) p. 139. In addition, the "Notes of Interpretation" address the criticism that Chapter 11 arbitration is not "transparent". Under the heading "Access to Documents" the Notes provide that "Nothing in the NAFTA imposes a general duty of confidentiality on the disputing parties to a Chapter Eleven arbitration." In this context, it is worth noting that for decades before NAFTA, expropriation claims against developing countries had been arbitrated in confidential proceedings under ICSID, UNCITRAL and ICC Rules without complaint from the industrialized investor nations.

101. The Free Trade Commission stated, inter alia, that Art. 1105 "prescribes the customary international law minimum standard of treatment of aliens as the minimum standard of treatment to be afforded to investments of investors of another Party" and that neither "fair and equitable treatment" nor "full protection and security" require "treatment in addition to or beyond that which is required by the customary international law minimum standard of treatment of aliens".

102. For example, a Multilateral Agreement on Investment (reached in the future within the OECD or the WTO) might refine concepts such as "regulatory taking" in a way different from customary international law. Or a WTO standards agreement might also become an issue. However, while such a standards agreement might constitute international law, it is unlikely that it would relate to investor protection in the context of NAFTA.

has suggested that *Notes of Interpretation* which fail to respect the text of NAFTA would not be binding on arbitrators deciding Chapter 11 disputes.[103]

To date no satisfactory way has been found to resolve the potential conflict between the requirements for amendment under Art. 2202 and the provisions of Art. 1131 that permit Free Trade Commission interpretations. If the requirement of proper approval for amendments is to make any sense, some limits must exist on the power of the Commission to change the meaning of the established text.

The conflict does not yield to easy analysis.[104] On the one hand, arbitrator disregard of Commission interpretations could result in different results by different tribunals, thus reducing the consistency and efficiency of investment arbitration. On the other hand, the Commission's de facto amendment of NAFTA would imperil the stability and predictability of the investor protection regime so laboriously negotiated in 1994.

IV.   OLD PROBLEMS, NEW PERSPECTIVES

1.   International Commercial Decision Making

The fuss over NAFTA Chapter 11 is essentially about who controls economic dispute resolution. Most of the current questions about investment arbitration did not originate with NAFTA. Rather, the perceived novelty of the rhetoric derives from a change in the angle from which arbitration is observed. Misgivings are new only in that Canada and the United States now articulate variations on themes long advanced by Latin American and African countries forced to arbitrate disputes over natural resources, the environment and other vital elements of national life. Changing hats from a capital exporter's fedora to a host state's sombrero, the United States has come to a new appreciation of the predicaments experienced by capital importers.[105]

The debate is not only about *what* standards apply, but about *who* decides matters with a direct effect on the economic interests of both the investor and the host state. The substantive norms governing expropriation and treatment of aliens remain basically unchanged, in that international law has long held states liable for injury to aliens. The unique aspect of NAFTA lies in its creation of a private right of action by which foreign investors bypass the political hurdles to obtaining the diplomatic protection of their

---

103. See Final Award in *Pope & Talbot*, 31 May 2001 (ordering Canada to pay $ 461,556 plus interest in damages). At fn. 37 (para. 47) the Award states, "[W]ere the Tribunal required to make a determination whether the [NAFTA Free Trade] Commission's action is an interpretation or an amendment, it would choose the latter." The tribunal continued, however, that such a determination was "not required" and thus its analysis "proceeded on the basis that the Commission's action was an 'interpretation'". Tribunal composed of Lord Dervaird, Presiding Arbitrator, Hon. Benjamin J. Greenberg and Mr. Murray J. Belman.

104. Presumably attempts to address potential conflicts would require recourse to Art. 31, Vienna Convention on the Law of Treaties, 23 May 1969, U.N. Doc. A/Conf. 39/27, entered into force 27 January 1980, 63 AJIL (1969) p. 875, 8 ILM (1969) p. 679.

105. See M. SORNARAJAH, *The Settlement of Foreign Investment Disputes* (2000); Wolfgang PETER, *Arbitration and Renegotiation of International Investment Agreements*, 2nd ed. (1995).

home country.

To some observers, NAFTA arbitral tribunals appear as courts of appeal on vital regulatory matters that discriminate against foreign investment or constitute illegal taking of an alien-owned property. In fact, however, Chapter 11 tribunals have no such power, but may review only government measures that violate the NAFTA treaty obligations.[106]

Consequently, disquiet arises over the prospect that arbitrators may decide differently than would national judges. In some instances this means that foreign claimants will receive better treatment than domestic courts give similarly situated local claimants. Such differences should not be surprising. Business managers have traditionally favored arbitration in overseas transactions precisely because an arbitrator may see things more dispassionately than a host state judge. Moreover, investors from industrialized countries have long insisted on fair dealing for themselves, regardless of how poorly a host state might treat its own people.

Anti-NAFTA concerns rest in part on what has traditionally been considered a strong point of international arbitration: the general predisposition of those chosen to arbitrate international disputes. Experienced commercial arbitrators generally will see their mandate as giving effect to the parties' shared ex ante expectations, finding the facts and applying the law in the most dispassionate and correct fashion possible. Quite understandably, arbitrators do not normally see themselves as guardians of the public interest.[107] In the context of NAFTA Chapter 11, these arbitral virtues may at some point be affected by the more public dimensions of the controverted investments.

Ironically, NAFTA Chapter 11 gives ingenious lawyers the opportunity to present on

---

106. In a Chapter 11 arbitration brought by American investors against Mexico, the arbitral tribunal noted,

> "The possibility of holding a State internationally liable for judicial decisions does not, however, entitle a claimant to seek international review of the national court decisions as though the international jurisdiction seized has plenary jurisdiction. This is not true generally, and it is not true for NAFTA. What must be shown is that the court decision itself constitutes a violation of the treaty.... Claimants must show either a denial of justice, or a pretense of form to achieve an internationally unlawful end."

> *Azinian v. United Mexican States* (ICSID Case No. ARB(AF)/97/2) Award on Merits of 1 November 1999, para. 99, p. 29.

107. This does not mean, however, that an arbitrator can ignore mandatory public norms (*lois de police*) imposed by the place of contract performance. See Pierre MAYER, "Mandatory Rules of Law in International Arbitration", 2 Arb. Int'l (1986) p. 274; Pierre MAYER, "Les Lois de Police Etrangères", J. Dr. Int'l (1981) p. 277; Pierre MAYER, "Reflections on the International Arbitrator's Duty to Apply the Law", 17 Arb. Int'l (2001) p. 235 (noting that "the relationship linking an arbitrator to the law is much more complex than the relationship that ties judges to it"). See generally Abul F.M. MANIRUZZAMAN, "International Arbitrator and Mandatory Public Law Rules in the Context of State Contracts: An Overview", 7 J. Int'l Arb. (September 1999) p. 53; Abul F.M. MANIRUZZAMAN, "Internationalization of Foreign Investment Agreements", 1 J. World Investment (December 2000) p. 293; Abul F.M. MANIRUZZAMAN, "The Lex Mercatoria and International Contracts: A Challenge for International Commercial Arbitration?", 14 Am. U. Int'l L. Rev. (1999) p. 659.

an international level the type of "due process" and "equal protection" arguments which in some ways are analogous to the principles invoked in the south of the United States during the civil rights era. Forty years ago, however, federal courts were invoking such principles to set aside rules that worked against African Americans. Now it is the Canadians who charge discrimination by state courts, and in an ironic role reversal the federal government has become the champion of states' rights.

Concerns expressed by opponents of NAFTA also overlap many misgivings raised in the so-called "globalization" debate, which has attracted so much attention by protests at international trade meetings from Seattle to Genoa. Not all observers today accept Riccardo's theory of comparative advantage or share the assumption that cross-border trade and investment bring the world a net benefit. In particular such criticism is likely to be made by groups that in former times might have endorsed either socialism or the "New International Economic Order".[108] "Such opposition was partly responsible for collapse of the OECD-sponsored Multilateral Agreement on Investment."[109]

Members of the US Congress commend trading partners who accept international arbitration as a potential tool to address foreign trade violations.[110] Yet when the United States is on the receiving end of a request for arbitration, protests are heard about "American laws being overridden" by NAFTA tribunals.[111] American legislators warn against "sacrificing state and local laws at the altar of ill-defined international investor rights"[112] and suggest that under NAFTA "the rights of an investor come before the rights to enact a chemical ban to prevent cancer".[113]

2. Playing by the Same Rules

Calling into question the very notion of neutral binding arbitration is fundamentally unsound. Ultimately, any disregard of basic ground rules for fair international investment dispute resolution will cause significant harm to American interests when foreign governments follow suit, impairing neutral mechanisms to protect American investment abroad.

---

108. See discussion of Charter of Economic Rights and Duties and States in PARK, *op. cit.*, fn. 17.
109. See Edward GRAHAM, "National Treatment of Foreign Investment: Exceptions and Conditions", 31 Cornell Int'l L. J. 599 (1998). In France, opposition to globalization under the slogan "*L'AMI c'est l'ennemi*" ("MAI is the enemy") built on the double entendre of AMI (the French acronym for MAI as well as the word for friend).
110. See 134 Cong. Rec. 26930-32. Senator Jesse HELMS (arch-opponent of restrictions on American power) urged the United States to withhold economic aid from Costa Rica until it agreed to arbitrate an expropriation dispute with an American citizen named J. Royal Parker. See also, 146 Cong. Rec. H3031, concerning Turkey's agreement to arbitrate investment disputes with foreigners.
111. See 145 Cong. Rec. at H-7368. Statement by Rep. SHOWS (Mississippi) concerning amendment of HR 2670.
112. *Ibid.*, Statement by Rep. TIERNEY (Massachusetts).
113. *Ibid.*, Statement of Rep. BONIOR (Michigan). In the same debate Rep. ROS-LEHTINEN (Florida) asked rhetorically, "Are my colleagues to allow families' health and that of our children, our friends and neighbors to be threatened because of foreign bureaucrats?" *ibid.* at H-7370.

Arguments that the federal government is not responsible for acts of state authorities toward foreigners (as in the context of *Methanex, Loewen* and *Mondev*) are not convincing. The United States has long presumed that foreign governments must repair damage caused by political subdivisions.[114] Indeed, in *Metalclad* the fuss was about actions by a municipality rather than the Mexican federal government. And notions of federal responsibility for local misdeeds has a long history within the United States.[115]

Cynics might say that one should not be surprised at double standards. Selective application of procedural standards, however, can have profoundly disconcerting consequences for wealth creation and economic cooperation. American legal principles tend to be exported. Thus the United States should take special pains to project the qualities of fair play and evenhandedness that promote undistorted participation in the global marketplace. In today's heterogeneous world, cross-border investment will be chilled without a willingness of all countries to accept arbitration. Sauce for the goose ought to be sauce for the gander as well.[116] Promotion of procedural inequality can only backfire to injure the long-term commercial interests of investor states.

As a practical matter, the nature of anti-NAFTA rhetoric often captures popular sentiment more easily than the sound arguments against distortion of cross-border capital flows. The lobby that invokes "pure air and water" and "sovereignty" has a message with a more urgent ring than the theme of international economic cooperation, notwithstanding the unfortunate aggregate consequences that flow from measures that discourage transnational wealth creation.

V. LIMITING THE SCOPE OF INVESTMENT ARBITRATION

1. *Overview*

NAFTA's drafters recognized that they were combining a trade agreement with an investment treaty, and that arbitration of investment disputes might have a disruptive effect on other NAFTA commitments including trade in goods and procurement. Moreover, there was recognition that investment arbitration posed special problems with respect to vital national prerogatives in tax and financial services.

The compromises made to reconcile NAFTA's competing goals implicated a multiplicity of concerns. Those worth special note include the following:

---

114. See Ian BROWNLIE, *Principles of Public International Law*, 5th ed., p. 451, fn. 107, giving examples of arbitrations in which federal states have been held responsible for acts of their constituent units, including the *Youmans Claim* (1926, RIAA IV) p. 110, the *Mallen Claim* (1927, RIAA IV) p. 173 and the *Pellat Claim* (1929, RIAA V) p. 534.

115. In support of the so-called alienage jurisdiction of federal courts (covering disputes between aliens and American citizens), Alexander Hamilton argued that the "peace of the whole ought not to be left at the disposal of a part". Hamilton asserted, "The Union will undoubtedly be answerable to foreign powers for the conduct of its members." See Alexander HAMILTON, James MADISON and John JAY in C. ROSSITER, ed., *The Federalist Papers No. 18* (1961) p. 476, quoted in Gary BORN, *International Civil Litigation in United States Courts*, 3rd ed. (1996) p. 11.

116. Or as the French would say, *On ne peux pas faire deux poids et deux mesures*.

(i)   inconsistencies between Chapter 11 and other NAFTA chapters are resolved in favor of the latter;[117]

(ii)   investment was limited by a definition *numerus clausus*, indicating what 'investment means' rather than what 'investment includes';[118]

(iii)   excluded from the definition of investment were loans to state enterprises, and money claims arising solely from contracts for the sale of goods or services or the extension of commercial credit such as trade financing;[119]

(iv)   interpretations of NAFTA's Free Trade Commission shall be binding on Chapter 11 arbitral tribunals;[120]

(v)   the creation of intellectual property rights will generally not give rise to rights to claim compensation for expropriation;[121]

(vi)   non-discriminatory measures of general application will not be considered tantamount to expropriation of a loan or debt security merely because they impose an increased cost that causes debtor default.[122]

Of particular interest are the limitations on investment arbitration that implicate tax and finance, two areas of particular sensitivity to economic sovereignty. As discussed below, member states have the right in certain circumstances to block or to modify Chapter 11 arbitration in both of these domains.

2.   *Expropriation Through Fiscal Measures*

a.   *Distinguishing normal and abnormal taxation*
Few areas illustrate the complex interaction of arbitration and sovereignty concerns more sharply than taxation. The power to raise revenue by forced levies is an attribute of sovereignty that is less negotiable than others.[123] Yet uncompensated nationalization often takes the form of excessive fiscal measures, designed either to force the foreign owner to abandon the investment by taxing away its economic value, or to subject an investor's competitors to a more favorable tax regime. While escaping precise definition, such subtler forms of expropriation can deprive an investor of wealth arbitrarily as effectively as explicit nationalization.

Evaluating such "creeping expropriation" does not lend itself to facile analysis. Distinctions must be made between normal and excessive taxation, a task that implicates

---

117. Art. 1112 NAFTA.

118. Art. 1138 NAFTA.

119. Art. 1139 NAFTA.

120. Art. 1132 NAFTA.

121. Art. 1110 NAFTA does not apply to the creation or limitation of intellectual property rights to the extent consistent with Chapter XVII, which addresses intellectual property explicitly.

122. Art. 1110(8) NAFTA.

123. One remembers that it was a tax revolt that forced King John of England to sign the Magna Charta in 1215. And few scholars challenge Lord Mansfield's "Revenue Rule" preventing enforcement of foreign tax judgments. See *Holman v. Johnson*, 98 Engl. Rep. 1120 (K.B. 1775). For later articulations of this principle, See *HM Queen v. Gilbertson*, 597 F.2d 1161 (9th Cir. 1979); *United States v. Boots*, 80 F.3d 580 (1st Cir. 1996).

culturally influenced notions of the "right" level of tax.[124] From one perspective taxation constitutes a form of asset seizure (echoed in the American catch phrase "the power to tax is the power to destroy")[125] in which fiscal authorities take money from its current owner (the taxpayer) and give it to someone else (the state).

The competing characterizations of tax may be distinctions without a difference, however. Fiscal measures inevitably involve an element of expropriation. The only question is whether they are "normal" taxes or are the type of punitive measure intended to confiscate foreign investment.

b.   The NAFTA "tax veto"

The problematic nature of using arbitration to settle claims that taxation constitutes "creeping expropriation" was foreseen when NAFTA was drafted. The Chapter 11 dispute resolution process would be misused and corrupted if "ordinary" fiscal measures gave rise to expropriation claims. Consequently, the fiscal administrations of host and investor countries have been given the task of making a preliminary cut between normal and abnormal taxes.

If an alleged expropriation is accomplished through "taxation measures", the competent fiscal authorities of the relevant states may veto the investor's right to arbitrate.[126] At the time of advising the host state of its intention to commence arbitration, the investor must also submit the tax measure to the appropriate fiscal authorities. The investor may proceed to arbitration only if the competent authorities "do not agree to consider the issue or, having agreed to consider it, fail to agree that the measure is not an expropriation".[127]

This awkwardly drafted "negative deadlock" provision gives the competent authorities six months to decide the question, failing which the investor may proceed to

---

124. Justice Holmes distinguished between a penalty intended as a "discouragement" to behavior and a tax that "may be part of an encouragement [to actions] when seen in its organic connection with the whole". *Compañía General de Tabaco de Filipinas v. Collector of Internal Revenue*, 275 U.S. 87 (1927) at 100.

125. The original US Supreme Court citation was: "An unlimited power to tax involves, necessarily, a power to destroy; because there is a limit beyond which no institution and no property can bear taxation." *McCulloch v. Maryland*, 17 U.S. (4 Wheat.) 316, 327 (1819), striking down a state tax on a federally chartered bank.

126. Art. 2103(6) NAFTA states that Art. 1110 provisions concerning expropriation "shall apply to taxation measures except that no investor may invoke that Article as the basis for a claim [for investment dispute resolution], where it has been determined pursuant to this paragraph that the measure is not an expropriation". Thus far, at least one case (the Karpa claim against Mexico) implicated tax measures. The competent authorities agreed that one of the three measures was not an expropriation, and thus the arbitration did not go forward on that question. As to two other measures, however, there was no agreement, and thus for those issues the arbitration proceeded.

127. It is uncertain whether an investor's disregard of reference to the competent authorities (either in bad faith or due to an innocent misunderstanding) would provide an opportunity for sua sponte intervention by tax authorities. Whether or not permitted, state intervention would not seem mandated. Rather, without an opinion from the relevant fiscal authorities, an expropriation claim would lie beyond the arbitrators' jurisdiction.

arbitration.[128] In attempting to distinguish normal from excessive taxation, fiscal authorities inevitably can be expected to rely on culturally influenced notions of tax.[129]

NAFTA does not suggest that tax matters cannot be arbitrated. Rather, the treaty says that fiscal authorities in host *and* investor states together may block the arbitral proceedings by agreeing "that the [tax] measure is not an expropriation".[130] Thus if the United States is accused of expropriating a Canadian investor's property, investment arbitration would be barred only if both the US Department of the Treasury and the Canadian Department of Finance concluded that no expropriation had taken place.[131] Presumably the Canadian authorities would hesitate to acquiesce in the plundering of its citizens merely because such theft was dressed in fiscal garb. Thus the capital exporter's government is given a protective role, in that refusal to join the veto authorizes arbitration.

The tax veto by its terms applies only to claims of improper expropriation under NAFTA Art. 1110. By contrast, claims for breaches of other host state duties, such as "fair and equitable treatment", might possibly escape the jurisdiction of the respective national fiscal authorities.

c.   Double taxation and investment arbitration

The perception of arbitration as an abdication of sovereignty will likely affect attempts to eliminate another barrier to cross-border investment arbitration: asymmetrical transfer pricing adjustments by national tax authorities. Frequently the tax treatment of a subsidiary in one country (in the form of deductions, for example) does not accord with that of the parent in the other country (where items of income might be included). The lack of fiscal symmetry creates an economic double taxation that distorts cross-

---

128. The English language version contains a slight ambiguity, providing for arbitration to go forward "[i]f the competent authorities do not agree to consider the issue or, having agreed to consider it, fail to agree that the measure is not an expropriation within a period of six months of such referral [by the investor]". To interpret the six-month limit as applying only to competent authorities who agreed to hear the matter (as contrasted to ignoring or refusing to consider the investor's request), would make little sense in this context.

129. For example, Americans can be expected to look to the US tax system, based on the same approach used to characterize "income tax" for purposes of the foreign tax credit. See, e.g., Treas. Reg. Sect. 901-2(a); *Bank of America Nat'l Trust & Savings Ass'n v. United States*, 459 F.2d 513, 515 (Ct. Cl. 1972) ("It is now settled that the question of whether a foreign tax is an 'income tax' … must be decided under criteria established by our revenue laws and court decisions, and that the foreign tax must be the substantial equivalent of an income tax as the term is understood in the United States.")

130. The text of Art. 2103(6) NAFTA does not make clear whether a "tax veto" requires unanimity of all three competent authorities, or only from the tax administrations of the investor and host state. In practice only the latter two administrations would be directly concerned, although the third country might argue for inclusion on the theory that such decisions have policy implications affecting all NAFTA members.

131. See NAFTA Annex 2103(6). The competent authority for the United States would be the Assistant Secretary of the Treasury (Tax Policy), for Canada it would be the Assistant Deputy Minister for Tax Policy, and for Mexico it would be the Deputy Minister of Revenue of the *Secretaría de Hacienda y Crédito Público* (Ministry of Finance and Public Credit).

border capital flows.

When two countries disagree on how to interpret an income tax treaty, the task of resolving the difference falls either to national court actions or to joint efforts by the tax administrations to work out differences on a voluntary basis. Neither alternative is satisfactory. Judicial proceedings lack political neutrality and yield inconsistent results. And the process for "mutual agreement" among competent fiscal authorities is fraught with delays and uncertainty.

In response, scholars[132] and non-governmental organizations have suggested arbitration as a means to address income tax treaty disputes. To date, however, income tax treaty arbitration remains more aspiration than reality.[133] While some treaties include language raising the prospect of arbitration, these provisions operate only if the two countries agree after a controversy arises. Such provisions have never been implemented, due to the contracting states' inability to reach accord when a dispute actually occurs. Only the new Austro-German treaty imposes a duty to arbitrate treaty differences without further negotiation.

To remedy this, the International Chamber of Commerce and the Organization for Economic Cooperation and Development have issued policy papers suggesting arbitration of such tax overlaps.[134] The International Fiscal Association (IFA) has commissioned a study on the topic,[135] and the Tax Council Policy Institute and the American Society of International Law have both organized discussions of the topic.

Objections to these sensible suggestions include the alleged infringement of sovereignty constituted by arbitration, with much of the argument echoing a less sophisticated version of the complaints voiced about NAFTA Chapter 11. However, as

---

132. See, e.g., Gustaf LINDENCRONA and Nils MATTSON, *Arbitration in Taxation* (1981); David R. TILLINGHAST, "Choice of Issues to be Submitted to Arbitration Under Income Tax Conventions", in H. ALPERT and K. van RAAD, eds., *Essays on International Taxation* (1993) p. 349; Jean-Marie HENCKAERTS, "EC Arbitration Convention for Transfer Pricing Disputes", 10 J. Int'l Arb. (September 1993) p. 111; Paul R. McDANIEL, "NAFTA and Formulary Apportionment", in ALPERT and van RAAD *op. cit.*, p. 293; William W. PARK, "Finality and Fairness in Tax Arbitration", 11 J. Int'l Arb. (June 1994) p. 19; Proceedings of IFA Seminar in Florence, "Resolution of Tax Treaty Conflicts by Arbitration", 18 IFA Seminar Series (October 1993). IFA revisited the topic in seminar presentations at its Congress in Eilat, Israel, October 1999.

133. One practitioner has remarked a bit whimsically that ever since 1981, tax arbitration is "an idea whose time is about to come". See David R. TILLINGHAST, "Choice of Issues to be Submitted to Arbitration Under Income Tax Conventions" in H. ALPERT and K. van RAAD, eds., *op. cit.*, fn. 132, p. 349.

134. See, e.g., ORGANIZATION FOR ECONOMIC COOPERATION AND DEVELOPMENT, COMMITTEE ON FISCAL AFFAIRS, "The Role of Arbitration Procedures in Resolving Tax Disputes", DAFFE/CFA (95) (11 January 1995) p. 12; INTERNATIONAL CHAMBER OF COMMERCE COMMISSION ON TAXATION, "Arbitration in International Tax Matters", Doc. No. 180/438 (3 May 2000) www.iccwbo.org/home/statements_rules/statements/2000/arbitration_tax.asp; INTERNATIONAL CHAMBER OF COMMERCE COMMISSION ON TAXATION, Arbitration in International Tax Matters, Draft Bilateral Convention Article, Doc. No. 180/455 Rev. (10 September 2001).

135. See also International Fiscal Association, "Resolution of Tax Treaty Conflicts by Arbitration", 18th IFA Congress Seminar Series (Kluwer 1993).

Rudyard Kipling might write, this is another story for another day.

3.   Financial Services

NAFTA provisions on financial services generally trump inconsistent stipulations in Chapter 11.[136] Under Chapter 14, the host state can invoke prudential concerns related to protection of depositors, financial markets and the maintenance of safe and sound financial institutions.[137] On request of a member state, arbitrators must refer the matter to the NAFTA Financial Services Committee (Committee) for a decision on whether the prudential concerns are valid defenses to an investor's claim, which decision is binding on the tribunal.[138]

If the Committee makes no decision within sixty days, the host state or the investor's country may request establishment of an arbitral panel convened under under the NAFTA's institutional (state-to-state) dispute resolution provisions.[139] The panel's report, like the Committee's decision, binds the arbitrators. If no request for such dispute resolution has been made within ten days of the expiration of the sixty days for panel action, the arbitral tribunal may proceed to adjudicate the claim.

VI.   CONCLUSION

Thirty years ago the line between host and investor states was fairly clear. Nations such as Libya and Mexico were the host states; the United States and Canada were the investors. Today, however, NAFTA Chapter 11 has led to a role reversal, with the United States and Canada learning the "down side" of arbitration.

When one country finds itself in an unwanted arbitration, the temptation is to label the proceeding as an infringement on sovereignty. As a practical matter, of course, sovereignty may end up being a slippery and unhelpful abstraction of malleable substance, serving simply as a justification for the exercise of unfettered government

---

136. Art. 1101(3) NAFTA provides that Chapter 11 "does not apply to measures adopted or maintained by a [NAFTA country] to the extent that they are covered by Chapter Fourteen (Financial Services)". Under Art. 1401, the "minimum standard of treatment" provisions (Art. 1105) do not apply to investment in financial services.

137. Pursuant to Art. 1410, none of the investment protections prevent a NAFTA Party from adopting reasonable measures for prudential reasons such as "protection of investors, depositors ... financial market participants ... the maintenance of the safety [and] soundness ... of financial institutions, and ensuring the integrity and stability of a [country's] financial system", nor from taking non-discriminatory measure of general application in pursuit of monetary and credit or exchange rate policies.

138. See Art. 1415(2) NAFTA. The term "Committee" is defined in Annex 2001.2(A). The term "Tribunal" carries over the Chapter 11 taxonomy for the body of arbitrators deciding a particular dispute.

139. See Arts. 1415(3) and 2008 et seq. NAFTA. Such an arbitral panel is to be constituted in accordance with Art. 1414 (see Art. 1415(3)), chosen from a special financial services roster to render a decision.

power.[140] One scholar has referred to "the unique character of governments" as one of those "predictably unpredictable variables" that make the fundamental problems of law "short term experiments" at best.[141]

National welfare has generally been enhanced by bilateral and multilateral treaties facilitating economic cooperation, even if their provisions on occasion supplement or override domestic law. As evidenced by almost half a century of treaty-based international arbitration under the New York Arbitration Convention, an occasional "wrong" decision is a small price for promoting general welfare through cross-border investment that results in a net aggregate gain to the countries involved. With NAFTA investment arbitration as with any dispute resolution system, clarification and adjustment may be in order. However, overly general critiques of investment arbitration risk doing more harm than good, in the end backfiring to injure both the long- and short-term national interests.

If investment arbitration is to fulfill its promise, however, some mechanism must be found to promote greater sensitivity to vital host state interest. Otherwise investor-government arbitration may fall prey to public pressure arising from a backlash against investor victories in some of the more visible NAFTA arbitrations.[142] In the larger picture, the ebb and flow of arbitration's wisdom may have to accommodate political reality.

As in other areas where law and policy interact, the devil is in the detail. It is less than self-evident (at least to the authors) what exactly should be done to reduce the prospect of harsh legislative responses to NAFTA arbitration. In all events caution must remain a significant part of the process for bringing order to the resolution of investment disputes.

Notes of Interpretation to promote reconciliation of the arbitral process and public interest may end up as the least troublesome path. However, for the Free Trade Commission to engage in de facto amendment of NAFTA would imperil the stability of investor protection, and in some instances might provoke arbitrator disregard of

---

140. Taken from the Latin *super*, meaning "above", sovereignty reflects a power said to be "above others: *au dessus des autres, die höchste Staatsgewalt* or *por encima de los demás*". Historians sometimes talk of "Westphalian" sovereignty, derived from the 1648 Treaty of Westphalia ending the Thirty Years' War in a way that granted substantial autonomy to local princes. Other uses of sovereignty include reference to autonomy of political subdivision on certain matters and recognition of one state by another. See generally, W. Michael REISMAN, "Sovereignty and Human Rights in Contemporary International Law" in G. FOX and B. ROTH, eds., *Democratic Governance and International Law* (2000) p. 239 (exploring sovereignty of populations in contrast to that of rulers); Stephen D. KRASNER, "Globalization and Sovereignty" in D. SMITH, D. SOLINGER and S. TOPIK, eds., *States and Sovereignty in the Global Economy* (1999).

141. W. Michael REISMAN, "International Arbitration and Sovereignty", 18 Arb. Int'l (2002) p. 231, adapted from 12th Annual Workshop of Institute for Transnational Arbitration, 21 June 2001, Dallas, Texas.

142. See Michael GOLDHABER, "Czech Mate", American Lawyer (March 2002) p. 82. While generally positive about investment arbitration (indicating how an American investor was able to vindicate an expropriation claim against the Czech Republic), the article quotes David Rivkin of the New York firm Debevoise & Plimpton as warning of a hostile reaction should the Canadian investor win in the *Loewen* arbitration, discussed supra.

Commission interpretations.[143] In all events, solutions that rely on government screening of an arbitration's substantive legal merits risk doing significant damage to the fabric of cross-border economic cooperation and wealth creation.[144]

---

143. See fn. 37 of Final Award in *Pope & Talbot* (at para. 47) discussed at fn. 103. The process for amendment of NAFTA requires approval in accordance with "applicable legal procedures of each Party". See Art. 2202 NAFTA.
144. See discussion supra of H.R. 3005 and H.R. 3009.

Bilateral Investment Treaties of Japan and Resolution of Disputes With Respect to Foreign Direct Investment

Shuji Yanase[*]

I.   INTRODUCTION

Japan has entered into very few Bilateral Investment Treaties (BITs) in comparison to other countries with a comparable accumulated balance of foreign direct investments. Why has Japan entered into so few BITs? Is this attributable to some policy of the Japanese Government? Will government policy change and, as a result, will the number of BITs entered into by Japan rapidly increase in the near future? How can the level of

---

[*]   Partner of Nagashima Ohno & Tsunematsu in Tokyo, Japan.

foreign direct investment by Japanese companies be so significant without provision for the protection of such investment through BITs? Is there any reason that Japanese companies have not relied on the protection of BITs? How do Japanese companies tend to approach foreign direct investment? I attempt to answer these questions by examining Japanese BITs and the impact they have had on foreign direct investments as well as describing the business mentality of Japanese companies investing abroad.

II.   BILATERAL INVESTMENT TREATIES ENTERED INTO BY JAPAN

1.   Eleven BITs

Japan is party to eleven BITs as follows:

	Other Party	Year of Execution	Effective Since
1.	Egypt	1977	1978
2.	Sri Lanka	1982	1982
3.	China	1988	1989
4.	Turkey	1992	1993
5.	Hong Kong	1997	1997
6.	Pakistan	1998	May 2002
7.	Bangladesh	1998	1999
8.	Russia	1998	2000
9.	Mongolia	2001	March 2002
10.	Korea	December 2001	___ [1]
11.	Singapore	January 2002	___ [2]

(1) The BIT with Korea has not yet come into effect.
(2) The treaty with Singapore is known as The Japan-Singapore Economic Partnership Agreement. The treaty was approved by the Japanese Parliament on 8 May 2002 but was not effective at the time of writing (May 2002).

BITs with Saudi Arabia, Vietnam and Indonesia are currently under negotiation.

According to the United Nations Conference on Trade and Development (UNCTAD) website, 1,914 BITs were concluded worldwide by the end of 2000. The number of BITs entered into by Japan is extremely small as compared with the numbers of BITs concluded by other countries.[1]

---

1. According to the UNCTAD database on BITs, the top thirty-one countries in terms of number of BITs concluded as of 1 January 2000 had an aggregate of 1,919 BITs. Of the top twenty-five countries, Germany ranked number one with 124 BITs and the twenty-fourth and twenty-fifth

2.   Foreign Direct Investment by Japanese Investors and Protection Prior to BITs

Under the Foreign Exchange and Foreign Trade Law of Japan as amended (FEL) (Law No. 228 of 1949), foreign direct investment generally means equity investment in 10% or more of the total share capital of a foreign legal entity and the extension of long-term loans to a foreign legal entity in which such equity investment is made; equity investment in and extension of long-term loans to a foreign legal entity with which a long-term relationship exists by way of technology licensing, secondment of directors and officers or long-term supply of materials or products; and disbursement of funds to establish a branch office, manufacturing plant or other place of business in a foreign country.[2] The term "foreign direct investment", as used in this report, is not necessarily intended to have precisely the same meaning as that in the FEL, but rather, is intended to refer broadly to the disbursement of funds from Japan to foreign countries for the purposes set out above.

Japan may be regarded as one of the top five countries in the world in terms of accumulated balance of foreign direct investment.[3] At the end of 2000, the United States ranked first with a total balance of foreign direct investments totaling US$1,244,654 million,[4] while Japan's total balance was US$ 278,445 million.[5]

Foreign direct investment by Japanese investors began in the 1970s and increased rapidly during the 1980s. In the five-year period from 1980 through 1984, foreign direct investments by Japanese investors represented 12.1% of total foreign investments worldwide. During this period, Japan ranked third in the world after the United States and the United Kingdom.[6] Until 1980, the majority of Japan's foreign direct investment was in developing Asian countries, but since the 1980's direct investment in North America and Europe has been increasing.[7] The overview as set out in these paragraphs should remain accurate notwithstanding that the precise meaning of "direct foreign investment" or "foreign investment" as used in the statistics discussed in these paragraphs has not been scrutinized.

The Japanese Government relied on an overseas investment insurance system as well as commercial and navigation treaties to provide protection for foreign direct investment by Japanese investors prior to relying on the conclusion of BITs for foreign investment protection. The overseas investment insurance system was introduced in 1956. Under this system, risks including nationalization, war and repatriation are underwritten by the

---

ranked countries entered into thirty-nine BITs each. The United Kingdom and the United States of America entered into ninety-two and forty-three BITs, respectively.

2. Art. 23(2) FEL and Art. 12(4) of the Cabinet Order under the FEL.
3. Extrapolated from statistical data taken from the IMF's *Balance of Payment Statistics Yearbook* 1998. Unfortunately, no uniform statistics as to the accumulated balance of direct foreign investments from various countries are available.
4. "Japan External Trade Organization Investment Report" (2002) (hereinafter JETRO Investment Report) (2002), information provided by the US Department of Commerce.
5. *Ibid.*, information provided by the Ministry of Finance of Japan and Bank of Japan.
6. OECD Foreign Revenues and Expenditures Statistics.
7. Statistics published by the Ministry of Finance of Japan ("Economic Cooperation Report" 1986).

Japanese Government.[8]

Until recently, investment protection clauses in commercial and navigation treaties have served as another framework used to protect foreign direct investments. Currently, Japan has entered into commercial and navigation treaties with twenty-seven countries, of which the following nine treaties include provision for most-favoured-nation treatment and fair compensation in the event of the nationalization of property:

Other Party	Year of Execution	Effective Since
1. India	1958	1958
2. Malaysia/Singapore	1960	1960
3. Cuba	1960	1961
4. Pakistan	1960	1961
5. Peru	1961	1961
6. Indonesia	1961	1963
7. El Salvador	1963	1964
8. Argentina	1961	1967
9. Mexico	1979	1980

Most of these treaties were concluded before foreign direct investments by Japanese investors started to show a material increase.

3.   *Recent Examples of BITs Entered into by Japan*

Since 1977, Japan has concluded BITs to provide specific protections to foreign direct investments by Japanese investors. Nine of the eleven BITs Japan concluded (including the Treaty with Mongolia in 2001) are "conventional" BITs as compared to the Japan-Korea BIT (December 2001) and the Japan-Singapore BIT (January 2002).

Each of the nine BITs includes a provision that each contracting state shall accord to investments of investors of the other contracting state treatment no less favourable than that accorded to its own nationals or companies or those of any third country. These provisions are applicable in full to the post-establishment stage of investment (namely after foreign investments are made) but do not require such most-favoured-nation treatment with respect to the pre-establishment stage. Thus, with respect to the establishment of a venture, acquisition of a venture or acquisition of securities, real estate or other property for investment purposes, the host contracting state does not

---

8. The 1956 Amendment to the Export Insurance Law of Japan (Law No. 73, 1956) introduced overseas investment insurance to cover loss of equity interest against the risks of nationalization and war for the first time. The law was further amended in 1970 to expand the insurance coverage to the loss of loans and other indebtedness extended to a joint venture partner and real estate, mining rights and intellectual property rights in connection with overseas projects.

commit itself to afford such most-favoured-nation treatment to nationals or companies of the other contracting state. In these cases, most-favoured-nation treatment applies only after the investment is made in the host contracting state. The BITs also include provisions concerning dispute resolution.

Two new clauses have been added in the Japan-Korea BIT and the Japan-Singapore BIT: a most-favoured-nation clause covering the pre-establishment stage and a comprehensive prohibition against those measures which impose restrictions on the foreign investor by requiring, for instance, local content, equilibrium of imports and exports, transfer of technology, equity investments or research and development commitments.[9,10]

4. Policy of the Japanese Government

The Japan-Korea and Japan-Singapore BITs, executed in December 2001 and January 2002 respectively, are considered to be the "new generation" of Japanese BITs because of the application of the most-favoured-nation clause during the pre-establishment stage and the incorporation of a comprehensive prohibition clause. In February 2002, I had a meeting with officials from the Ministry of Foreign Affairs of Japan to discuss the Japanese Government policy with regard to BITs and the protection of foreign direct investment by Japanese investors. According to these officials, the Japanese Government recognizes that since there are no comprehensive multi-national investment rules, BITs constitute an important source of investment rules. Accordingly, the Government of Japan will endeavour to enter into BITs with other countries, including the APEC[11] member states in which a number of Japanese companies have investments. However, as further elaborated by the Japanese Government, it is not, and will not be, the policy of the Japanese Government to simply increase the number of BITs and compromise its policy to secure the new generation BITs by settling for BITs which incorporate only terms which other countries are prepared to accept. In order to make its BITs more meaningful, Japan will continue to seek to secure the new generation type of BITs (such as those with Korea and Singapore) rather than opting for a numerical increase in the number of BITs. The Japanese Government will also continue to take an interest in efforts being made in relation to multilateral agreements on investment.

---

9. Before the Japan-Korea and Japan-Singapore BITs, certain BITs included aspects of such comprehensive prohibition clauses. In the Japan-Russia and Japan-Mongolia BITs there are certain provisions prohibiting performance demands. The Japan-Russia BIT prohibits local contents demands, export restrictions and import-export equilibrium demands (Art. 16). The BIT with Mongolia prohibits local contents demands and restrictions on import and export (Art. 15). A local contents demand typically requires that the finished product should include locally produced components and parts at a specified percentage in terms of value.

10. A transparency clause is also a new clause included in recent BITs. The Japan-Russia and Japan-Mongolia BITs require that each treaty party make public all laws, regulations, administrative procedures and judicial decisions that pertain to or affect investments.

11. The Asia-Pacific Economic Cooperation was founded in 1989 and has twenty-one members from around the Pacific Rim.

5.   Dispute Resolution Clauses in BITs

The Convention on the Settlement of Investment Disputes Between States and Nationals of Other States (Washington Convention) took effect in Japan on 16 September 1967. In many cases, BITs provide for the written consent to the jurisdiction of the International Centre for Settlement of Investment Disputes (ICSID) established under the Washington Convention.[12] With the exception of the Japan-Hong Kong BIT, which provides for resolution in accordance with the Arbitration Rules of the United Nations Commission on International Trade Law (UNCITRAL) all the Japanese BITs include a dispute resolution clause providing for referral, subject to certain conditions (including the exhaustion of local procedures), of any dispute between a contracting state and an investor from the other contracting state with respect to such investor's investments within the territory of the first contracting state, to conciliation or arbitration in accordance with the provisions of the Washington Convention. Art. 10 of the Japan-Mongolia BIT reproduced in Annex 1 is an example of a typical dispute resolution clause in Japanese BITs. A BIT concluded between Japan and China in 1988 provides that disputes shall be submitted to a conciliation board or an arbitration tribunal to be established *with reference* to the Washington Convention (emphasis added). China was not a party to the Washington Convention in 1988.

Alternatively, under the Japan-Russia and Japan-Mongolia BITs, a legal dispute that arises out of investments made by an investor may, at the investor's request, be submitted to arbitration under the UNCITRAL Arbitration Rules. According to the officials I met at the Ministry of Foreign Affairs of Japan in February 2002, the Japanese Government holds the opinion that a conciliation or an arbitration in accordance with the Washington Convention, or an arbitration in accordance with the UNCITRAL Arbitration Rules, would be appropriate for resolution of disputes between a state party to a treaty and an investor from the other state party.

6.   Resolution of Disputes Between a Japanese Company and a Country with Which Japan Has a BIT

At the February 2002 meeting mentioned above, I asked the government officials whether they had heard of any dispute where a Japanese company sought protection pursuant to a BIT to which Japan is a party. According to the officials, the Ministry of Foreign Affairs of Japan is sometimes consulted with respect to whether there is any remedy available under a BIT. According to their knowledge, there has never been a case where Japan has initiated discussion with another contracting state to a BIT or where a Japanese company has initiated proceedings under a BIT. There has been no report of any dispute where a Japanese company has initiated any such procedure. Japan has never

---

12. The Japan-Turkey BIT imposes a duty to consent to submit a dispute to conciliation or arbitration in accordance with the Washington Convention.

been a party to any dispute on investments under BITs entered into by Japan.[13] It appears that the Japanese Government has not devoted much attention to the conciliation or arbitration procedures that may take place under the BITs or to whether such procedures provide adequate protection to a Japanese company. In Japan, it appears to be assumed that the rules in the BITs in and of themselves establish an adequate framework to govern the behaviour of and the relationship among all relevant parties.

7.   *Have BITs Increased Foreign Direct Investment by Japanese Investors?*

In order to examine whether the conclusion of BITs has had any material impact on encouraging foreign direct investment, the Ministry of Foreign Affairs of Japan has compiled data showing the level of annual foreign direct investment in certain countries with which Japan has concluded BITs. The following table shows the annual amount of foreign direct investment in each country for the years 1989 through 1999:

---

13. According to the officials of the Ministry of Foreign Affairs of Japan, Japan has not been a party to any dispute under a BIT initiated by a contracting state or a company of such contracting state against Japan under a BIT.

Foreign Direct Investment in Countries/Areas with which Japan Has BITs[1]
(In Billions of Yen)

	Egypt[3]	Sri Lanka[4]	China	Turkey	Hong Kong	Bangladesh	Russia[5]
1989	0.6	0.1	**58.7**[2]	5.3	250.2	0.7	2.5
1990	0	0.7	51.1	8.5	261	6	3.6
1991	0	0.5	78.7	4.1	126	1.2	7.4
1992	0	2.4	138.1	7	96.6	7.9	5.7
1993	0.7	2	195.4	**15.1**[2]	144.7	1.7	2.6
1994	0.8	1	268.3	7.9	117.9	0.2	2
1995	0.1	5.6	431.9	9.9	110.6	0.1	2.9
1996	0.1	3	282.8	12	167.5	1.2	2
1997	1.9	33.2	243.8	2.1	**85.3**[2]	0.8	1.2
1998	0	4.6	136.3	0.7	77	0.4	1.6
1999	1.1	2.1	83.8	1.3	108.3	**0**[2]	0.7

(1) Source: Statistics published by the Ministry of Finance of Japan, "Amounts of Foreign Direct Investment in Countries/Political Regions".
(2) The amounts in **bold** show the amount for the year in which the BIT with such country took effect.
(3) The Japan-Egypt BIT took effect in 1978.
(4) The Japan-Sri Lanka BIT took effect in 1982.
(5) The Japan-Russia BIT took effect in 2000. The amounts in 1991 and the years preceding 1991 show foreign direct investment in the USSR.

The data do not indicate that the conclusion of BITs has had any material impact on the amount of foreign direct investment in the relevant foreign country.

Obviously, the expected return on investment will be a critical factor in determining whether foreign direct investment should be made in a specific country. In many cases, the expected return on investment may not be limited to dividends, interest and capital gains, but may also include synergies which may enable the investing company to effectively compete with its competitors in the domestic or world-wide market. Importantly, the total amount of foreign direct investment by Japanese investors should have been affected by the capital resources of Japanese companies and the industrial structure of Japan. The table above indicates that the impact of BITs has been minor when compared to these factors.

III.   DISPUTES WITH RESPECT TO FOREIGN DIRECT INVESTMENT

The dispute resolution provisions of BITs apply only to disputes between an investor and the host contracting state or between the two contracting states. However, many disputes with respect to foreign direct investment are between private parties to investment contracts, including joint venture companies created by such private parties. By looking at how Japanese companies tend to approach their foreign direct investments, and at the risks involved in such investments, we will be able to understand the degree of importance of BITs to Japanese companies.

1.   Mandate to Avoid Disputes – Disputes Are Failure

If a businessman fails to prevent a difference in opinion from growing into a dispute or, at minimum, fails to find a solution once a dispute has arisen, thereby necessitating the intervention of a third party (whether such third party is a court or a conciliator or arbitration body) for settlement of such dispute, this is regarded as a gross failure by the businessman in the performance of his duties. In recent years this view seems to have gained some support in the United States and in Europe due to the enormous costs, both in terms of money and time, involved in the dispute resolution process. It goes without saying that this view is widely accepted in Japanese society, not only because of the monetary cost involved in dispute resolution, but also because of the strong Japanese social stigma attached to the failure to avoid disputes.

2.   Traditional Philosophy

"Rain wouldn't beat me" by Kenji Miyazawa (1896-1933) is one of the best-known poems in Japan.[14] The poem has appeared in school textbooks in Japan for many years. When I ask myself why Japan has only eleven BITs despite having a large accumulated balance of foreign direct investment, the following phrase from that poem comes to mind, "in the north, if there's a fight or a lawsuit tell them to stop it because it doesn't get them anywhere". This poem was not published while the poet was alive, but was found in his notebook as a mental sketch of the ideal person the poet wished to become. This ideal person is clearly drawn from his image of *bosatsu* in Buddhism. The universe, consisting of man and nature, continuously evolves. Truth and justice exist and change as the universe evolves. With this profound philosophy in mind, laws and regulations and provisions in contracts must inevitably be adjusted to accommodate such changes in order to maintain their justification.

Two relevant points arise from this way of thinking. First, written words and provisions, whether they are provisions of laws or regulations, or provisions of contracts, or whether they constitute express promises between two persons, do not necessarily constitute the ultimate rules according to which a person should behave. In

---

14. A reprint of the English translation of the poem reprinted in Annex 2 can also be found at: www.k-space.net/tops, the site that introduces the Japanese poet Kenji Miyazawa to the English-speaking community (The Mental Sketches of Kenji Miyazawa).

other words, it is not sufficient for a person to abide by mere words. In order for a person to be regarded as a good person, he must always look at the reality of the situation and make his own judgment to determine what is just under the given circumstances. Second, enforcement by force is not appropriate. Every person is expected to understand matters and to behave voluntarily and properly in a manner as expected by society and it is not acceptable, and in many cases is even disgraceful, for a person to have to be told what he should do. No difference in opinion should continue to develop into a dispute.

This way of thinking is completely different from the traditional Western philosophy that individuals should have different opinions, that all opinions are to be respected and that decisions are to be made by the will of the majority. The Japanese way of thinking may be condemned as being anti-democratic, because in actual human society it allows an unwarranted power to prevail over people of different opinions. The Japanese way of thinking tends to encourage people to postpone any decision, or not to vote on controversial matters.

Leaving these and other interesting issues without further discussion, I would postulate that this type of mentality encourages Japanese companies to make every effort to resolve differences in opinion or interests before they grow into disputes.[15]

3. Efforts to Avoid Disputes

Frequent traffic and contacts among nations by a large number of people have resulted in the culture of other parts of the world affecting, or in certain instances even replacing, the conventional Japanese way of thinking. Today many Japanese companies are vigorously fighting before the courts in foreign countries, although it would be fair to say that they are the defendants in most cases. Nevertheless, the Japanese mentality has led Japanese businessmen to make every effort to understand the people in the foreign countries where their companies have made investments and to find solutions for differences of opinion or interests, without resorting to third-party dispute resolution mechanisms. These efforts can be seen in the preparations for investment in foreign countries made by a Japanese company.

---

15. There is, of course, a practical business reason for making such effort. In order for a Japanese company to do business profitably in foreign countries, it must make every effort to foresee risks and avoid disputes that would not arise in the conduct of its domestic business in Japan. This is particularly true if the revenues and profits from the overseas business will not be large enough to absorb risks and dispute resolution expenses that would not arise in connection with its domestic business in Japan.

IV.   CONSIDERATIONS IN DEVELOPING INVESTMENT CONTRACTS

1.   *Non-Pecuniary Factors*

Let us assume that a Japanese company intends to enter into a joint venture agreement with the government of a foreign country or a company based in a foreign country to establish and operate a joint venture company in that country. The Japanese client comes to us as legal counsel to seek our assistance when starting negotiations with its potential partner in that foreign country. Our first job would be to help the client draft a letter of intent to be executed at the initial stage. We carefully listen to the client to understand the background of the current negotiations and the client presents his reasons for pursuing the proposed project and states the purpose of the proposed project in the context of its international strategy. In addition, the client and legal counsel try to envision the future of the proposed project.

All these matters are examined so as to enable us to assist the client to formulate the optimum structure for the proposed project and the most suitable allocation of roles and functions to be undertaken by each joint venture partner to ensure the ultimate success of the proposed project. Proper reflection and determination of such matters in the project documentation is important to create the best possible structure for the project in order to minimize potential conflicts in the future.

In my experience in representing Japanese companies making direct investments abroad, I have come to recognize certain features of Japanese companies at this initial stage of a potential investment project in a foreign country as important for the avoidance of future disputes. As such, my discussion with the client will invariably involve a discussion of the following:

– A strong will to succeed
Does management have a strong will to succeed? Of course the client's reply will be "yes". The real question is whether the client is truly prepared to endure hard times when difficulty arises. This question may be posed in different ways. How important is the proposed project to management? Is there a real need for success? Do the employees hold the same views as management with respect to these questions? If management and employees share the view that the project's success is vital to the future of the company, they will endure any future hardships that may arise from insufficient understanding of potential problems inherent in the proposed project.

– Willingness to understand and live with the different culture
Do management and the client's employees understand the culture of the foreign country? They usually understand, to some extent, the differences between the foreign culture and Japanese culture, but it seems inevitable that they will be shocked by such differences as the project proceeds. The shock can however be overcome by a strong determination to succeed and by the willingness of management and the employees to understand and live with the "different" culture.

— Determination to live with the management and employees of the joint venture partner

Are management and employees deeply committed to live with the management and employees of their joint venture partner? Tough negotiations with the other side sometimes make us feel it is impossible to understand the demands, responses and behaviour of the other party. Once I asked a Japanese businessman, after extremely tough negotiations with the other party lasting until five o'clock in the morning, "Are you prepared to get along with these people for many years to come if the project agreements are signed?" It was my first question to him before we resumed negotiations that same morning. Without hesitation, he replied to me, "Yes." I was deeply impressed with his patience and strong determination to succeed, and we resumed the negotiations to make the deal. Several years later, the joint venture company created as a result of these negotiations was listed on the major stock exchanges of the relevant country.

— Common interests of the parties

What are the common interests of the parties? What is their point of departure? Will both the parties benefit from the project, and if so, how, and to what extent? At what stage of the project will the interests of the parties diverge? Is the client willing to allow its partner to pursue its own interests? These questions should be frankly and openly discussed by the parties. If the parties do not have a mutual understanding on these matters, they may be surprised to see the difference in interests that develops in the future, and it may not be easy for the parties to reach a mutual understanding on such matters at that time.

— What is the client's definition of success for the project?

Is the project feasible for the client? What is the client's definition of success for the project? How quickly can such success be achieved?

One can see from the series of questions above that we are focusing on elements of foreign direct investment other than the power of capital. The money invested by a Japanese company must be utilized by those who will undertake and implement the project. Without the enthusiasm, energy, effort and hard work of such individuals, the invested capital cannot produce a profit. If the project does not contribute to or benefit the society in which it operates, the project is not entitled to any return.

2. Risk Factors Leading to Disputes

It is not and should not be the purpose of negotiations to produce an investment contract favourable to only one side (i.e., to one's own client). Negotiation can and should be a process for the parties to stimulate each other to find and identify future potential issues and problems, to carefully consider such future issues and problems and to create solutions satisfactory to each of them. Good (and may I add, successful) negotiations enhance the mutual trust of the parties. In order to prepare for foreign direct investment, we must consider the risk factors associated with the proposed investment. Let us look at the risk factors which may develop into or lead to disputes in the future and which, therefore, should be carefully examined before any direct foreign investment is made. These risk factors may be categorized as follows:

— Purpose of the project
The parties may start the project with a common interest, but their interests are probably not identical. In what respects are they different? How can each party accommodate the other party's interests?

— Future potential disputes
What sort of disputes can be expected in the future?

— Political situation
Can the project survive future shifts in political power within the relevant foreign country?

— Economy
Is the economy of the relevant foreign country mature enough to make the proposed project feasible?

— Society
Are there cultural or social norms that could make it impossible or difficult to secure management and/or labour in the same way as is done in other countries?

— Nationalization
What if the project is nationalized? What remedy or compensation should be incorporated into the investment contract to address this concern, assuming that such risk is not negligible?

— Deadlock
Under what circumstances is a deadlock likely to arise and in what manner is it likely to occur? Which party has more to lose in a deadlock situation? Is there any way to prevent the deadlock? What are the possible methods of dealing with a deadlock situation?

— Disinvestment
Are there situations where the client would prefer to effect a disinvestment from the project? How can this be achieved?

— Different mandatory rules of law
There are certain countries which have mandatory provisions of law which differ from those of other countries. This is due to different public policies reflected in the corporate law framework. Do such different mandatory provisions of law exist, and if so, what is their potential impact on the proposed project?

— Role and function of law
Are reliable lawyers available in the relevant foreign country? Are lawyers respected? Will a contract be respected and abided by? How valuable will the project agreements be if we wish to insist upon the compliance of the other party? Does the relevant law

provide sufficient sanctions for non-compliance to encourage the other party to comply?

– Courts and arbitration
Is the court system in the relevant foreign country reliable? If the government or a governmental body is a party to the investment contract, one would probably not want to elect to submit to the courts of that country and would instead propose international arbitration. Will an arbitration scheme function as expected?

– Return on investment
How quickly can a proper investment return be realized? If realization of an adequate minimum investment return can be expected in a short period of time, all of the risk factors enumerated above may develop into a difficult situation only after such minimum investment return has already been secured. In such a case, our analysis of such project risks would be substantially different.

3.   *Disputes Are Sometimes Inevitable*

My practice in assisting Japanese companies with their foreign direct investment projects started in the early 1970s. In most cases, I was asked to help these companies develop and prepare project agreements. However, inevitably, there have been occasions where I have been asked to assist clients in their disputes with their joint venture partners. Mentioned below are three major disputes in relation to which I assisted Japanese companies in the 1990s in connection with their foreign direct investment.

The first case was the result of a deadlock in the management of a joint venture company in Hong Kong. The client obtained an injunction from the Hong Kong court to enjoin the management nominated by the other party from exercising its managerial power. A settlement of the dispute was negotiated to buy out the other party's equity interest in the joint venture company. In this case, the non-Japanese party had expected a profit from the business in a manner and at a level which was in fact unacceptable to the Japanese company. The client first came to us only after the dispute had already arisen.

The second case involved a dispute over the appointment of the CEO of a joint venture company in India. An application was brought by the client before an Indian court for an injunction to stop corporate procedures for the appointment of a person nominated by the joint venture partner as CEO. The client requested international arbitration in accordance with the terms of the joint venture agreement. The case was amicably settled during the arbitration process, and the joint venture company has operated successfully since then with cooperation between the parties on the same good level as before the dispute.

The third case involved an attempt by a joint venture partner to acquire control of the joint venture company by way of a capital increase. An injunction was obtained in Hong Kong by the client. The dispute was resolved by way of a negotiated settlement whereby the parties agreed to split the investment between themselves to enable each to independently pursue his respective business.

Disputes are sometimes inevitable; however, once a dispute arises even Japanese companies, which are normally very slow in taking the initiative to bring legal action, will take swift and decisive action against the other party. Conflicts of interest are inevitable as circumstances change and disputes develop despite provisions in joint venture agreements which one party considers to be clear.

4.   How to Avoid or Resolve Disputes

Disputes arise when a party seeks to change an existing relationship and create a new relationship different from the existing relationship. If the new relationship is within the scope of the provisions of the parties' existing investment agreement, or at least within the expectations or understandings of the parties, it may be possible to develop such a new relationship through amicable discussions between the parties and, perhaps, by amendment of the existing investment agreement. If, on the other hand, the new relationship is not only beyond the scope of the existing investment agreement, but also beyond or contrary to the expectations or understanding of the parties, any attempt to create a new relationship or order could very likely develop into a dispute.

The parties can attempt to deal with such potential points of dispute by either trying to provide for such changing circumstances in the initial investment agreement, or trying to find ways to accommodate the other party's proposal for a new relationship or order. The former can only be achieved (if at all) by careful analysis of the proposed transaction and the risks involved in it, and the latter can only be accomplished by endeavouring to understand the other party's new situation and needs rather than simply insisting upon the rights set out in the provisions of the existing investment agreement.

Even after the dispute resolution process commences, there will be good reason to attempt to achieve a reasonable and amicable settlement, in light of the fact that a situation has developed where either one party is no longer satisfied with the existing investment agreement or the existing investment agreement, although susceptible to various possible interpretations, no longer properly addresses the new situation. Provisions of investment contracts; provisions of BITs and other treaties; provisions of injunctive court orders; the expected outcome of litigation, arbitration, conciliation and/or meditation; and progress in identifying relevant issues in these proceedings all serve to provide a basis for settlement between the parties. A careful analysis of risk, and an effort to prepare an investment contract that will accommodate future changes that may occur as the project proceeds, as well as a serious willingness to understand the partner's interests and to address conflicts of interest to create a new relationship appropriately reflecting the parties respective interests, will together make it possible to avoid or amicably settle disputes.

5.   Disputes Under BITs

Having reviewed risks and disputes with respect to foreign direct investment, it can be seen that those which involve BITs constitute only a portion of such potential disputes, although if such BIT-governed types of disputes were to arise, they would likely be quite fundamental and serious. Given the likely seriousness of such a BIT-governed dispute and the fact that a sovereign state will, by definition, be party to such dispute, a number of serious and complex issues will likely arise in connection with arbitrations under BITs. However, Japan and Japanese companies have not played a significant role as parties to arbitrations under BITs, at least thus far.

V.   CONCLUSION

The BITs concluded by Japan do not appear to have played an important role in foreign direct investment by Japanese investors. Instead, it appears that foreign direct investment has been influenced more by economic conditions in Japan and in those countries in which foreign direct investments have been made. Neither the Japanese Government nor Japanese companies have placed much emphasis on BITs as a vehicle for the protection of foreign investments. Disputes in relation to foreign direct investment by Japanese companies have been avoided or resolved by such companies' own efforts, rather than through the reliance on dispute resolution clauses in BITs with Japan. Such efforts are the natural outcome of the business mentality of Japanese companies which reflects the conventional and very traditional tendency in Japanese culture which respects the amicable settlement of conflicts. These efforts remain important and will become increasingly so, not only for Japanese companies but also for companies of other nationalities, in view of the increasing volume of foreign direct investment in the growing global economy and the significant expense involved in the resolution of disputes through the involvement of a third party whether in the form of a court, conciliation body or arbitral tribunal. Frequent traffic and contact among nations have prompted interactive exchanges of cultures from different parts of the world. As a consequence, the Japanese Government and Japanese companies will ultimately become closer in their attitude and behaviour to the governments and companies of other countries in relation to dispute resolutions and to BITs, while foreign companies will also likely learn something from Japanese methods of risk management and dispute resolution. The increasing accumulated balance of foreign direct investment, particularly through active cross-border merger and acquisitions transactions in recent years will also increase the need for proper resolution of cross-border disputes. International arbitration institutions should be prepared to offer appropriate facilities for such disputes. Japanese companies will, gradually but inevitably, play a significant part in the development of international arbitration.

ANNEX 1

Article 10 of the Japan-Mongolia BIT

1. Any dispute between an investor of either Contracting Party and the other Contracting Party with respect to investment within the territory of such other Contracting Party shall, as far as possible, be settled amicably through consultation between the parties to the dispute. This shall not be construed so as to prevent an investor of the former Contracting Party from seeking administrative or judicial settlement within the territory of such other Contracting Party.

2. If any legal dispute that may arise out of investment made by an investor of either Contracting Party cannot be settled through such consultation, the dispute shall at the request of the investor concerned be submitted to either:

(1) conciliation or arbitration in accordance with the provision of the Convention on the Settlement of Investment Disputes between States and Nationals of Other States done at Washington, March 18, 1965 so long as the Convention is in force between the Contracting Parties, or conciliation or arbitration under the Additional Facility Rules of the International Centre for Settlement of Investment Disputes so long as the Convention is not in force between the Contracting Parties; or

(2) arbitration under the Arbitration Rules of the United Nations Commission on International Trade Law, adopted by the United Nations Commission on International Trade Law on April 28, 1976.

3. A Contracting Party which is a party to a legal dispute referred to in paragraph 2 of this Article shall give its consent to the submission of the dispute to international conciliation or arbitration referred to in paragraph 2 in accordance with the provisions of the present Article

4. The decision of the arbitrators shall be final and binding upon both parties to the dispute. This decision shall be executed by the applicable laws and regulations concerning the execution of decision in force in the country in whose territories such execution is sought.

5. So long as an investor of either Contracting Party is seeking administrative or judicial settlement within the territory of the other Contracting Party concerning a dispute that may arise out of investment made by such investor, or in the event that a final judicial settlement on such dispute has been made, such dispute shall not be submitted to arbitration referred to in the provisions of the present Article.

6. In case a legal dispute arises out of investment made by a company of either Contracting Party and such company is controlled by investors of the other Contracting Party on the date on which such company makes a request to the former Contracting Party to submit the dispute to conciliation or arbitration, such company of the former Contracting Party shall be treated for the purposes of the provisions of the present Article as a company of such other Contracting Party.

ANNEX 2

rain wouldn't beat me

Kenji Miyazawa

rain wouldn't beat me
wind wouldn't beat me
snow nor heat could defeat me
have a healthy body
possess no greed
never get angry
always with a tranquil smile
have four cups of brown rice a day
and some beans and vegetables
do not count myself
in anything
have profound knowledge and understanding
and keep it in mind
live in a small thatched hut
behind some pine trees in a field
in the east, if there a sick child
go and look after him
in the west, if there's a tired mother
go and carry that bunch of rice plants for her
in the south, if there's a dying man
go and tell him he need not be frightened
in the north, if there's a fight or a lawsuit
tell them to stop it because it doesn't get them anywhere
shed tears when a drought strikes
walk helplessly when stricken with a cold summer
be called blockhead by everyone
never be praised
yet burden to no one
such a person
i wish to be

Challenging Investment Treaty Arbitration Awards – Issues Concerning the Forum Arising from the *Metalclad* Case

David A.R. Williams QC *

TABLE OF CONTENTS   Page

I.   INTRODUCTION

This paper addresses certain issues which have arisen in the light of the *Metalclad* case.[1] The first is whether it is appropriate that the forum for challenge should depend on the dispute resolution mechanism imposed by the particular treaty or selected by the investor claimant. Next, the *Metalclad* case produced a situation where the court of a Canadian province was requested to determine whether Mexico was liable for a breach of a treaty. Is this consistent with traditional concepts of sovereignty? Some have suggested that it is inappropriate for a state court of one country to be deciding whether the government of another has breached its international obligations. Such questions are traditionally for the International Court of Justice or international tribunals or commissions. The third issue accepts that where ICSID Rules are applied, the problem is avoided due to the internal review mechanism of the ICSID but asks what is the real scope of such a challenge under ICSID rules? The annulment procedure of ICSID would be a preferable forum, but its nature and extent is not yet settled.

The issues thus stated seem to have a familiar ring. They remind us of the haphazard way in which national courts come to address enforcement issues under the New York Convention and the fact that occasionally they are required to grapple with questions of

---

* Barrister and Arbitrator of 9 Princes Street Chambers, Auckland, New Zealand and Essex Court Chambers, London; former Justice of the High Court of New Zealand.
1. Decision of the Tribunal: ICSID case no. ARB (AF)/97/1, rendered on 30 August 2000. Decision of the Supreme Court of British Columbia in judicial review application: [2001] BCSC 664, 2 May 2001, Tysoe, J.

state policy under the public policy exception. The difficulties in some such cases have led to suggestions for the formation of an International Court of Arbitral Awards which would hopefully engage with such sensitive enforcement issues in a more consistent and neutral way. But this is to anticipate the ultimate questions and possible solutions. It is first necessary to explain by brief reference to the history of investment treaty arbitration and the *Metalclad* case how these issues have arisen.

II.   BRIEF SUMMARY OF THE DEVELOPMENT OF INVESTMENT TREATY ARBITRATION

There is enormous literature on the topic and what is offered here is the briefest of summaries. The development of treaty-based foreign-investment dispute resolution mechanisms arose out of the need to supplement customary international law rules at a time when newly independent states required foreign capital in order to develop their economies. They were often unable to attract foreign investment and wealth-creating international transactions in the absence of reliable protections for investors. The first bilateral investment treaty (BIT) was signed in 1959. Early BITs involved reciprocal undertakings between states whereby each state guaranteed a minimum standard of treatment to investors of the other state. These treaties did not confer any rights on investors which they could enforce directly against a host state. Instead, disputes had to be resolved between the state parties to the treaties under the established rules of international law which have been helpfully summarized as follows:[2]

> "For most purposes, individuals and private business organisations have no standing under international law. A complaint that a state has breached its international obligations can be made only by another state. Historically, this was as true in the area of foreign investments as in any other. If a private investor experienced an injury as a result of an action by a state in breach of its international obligations, the investor's only means of redress was to seek to have its national government take action on its behalf."

Such dispute resolution procedures depended upon states being prepared to sponsor claims and pursue them through time-consuming intergovernmental arbitration or other dispute resolution methods. From the 1960s, however, there emerged a trend towards foreign investors having the right to bring actions directly against host states. Initially, host states recognized the legal personality of foreign investors by contract but the most significant development was the 1965 Convention on the Settlement of Investment Disputes Between States and Nationals of Other States (the ICSID Convention). This Convention created the International Centre for Settlement of Investment Disputes (ICSID) and permitted foreign investors to refer a dispute with a state party directly to the Centre, if consent was obtained in writing. The significance of the Convention and the subsequent utilization of its dispute resolution procedure in BITs and multilateral

---

2. CREMADES, "Promoting and Protecting International Investments", Int ALR (2000) p. 53 at p. 56.

investment treaties (MITs) has been helpfully summarized by Professor Sir Elihu Lauterpacht QC in his Foreword to Professor Schreuer's magisterial Commentary on the ICSID Convention:[3]

"At the time the Convention was concluded, some of its most important features represented significant new developments, though in the light of subsequent advances in international law they now appear almost commonplace. For the first time a system was instituted under which non-State entities — corporations or individuals — could sue States directly, in which State immunity was much restricted; under which international law could be applied directly to the relationship between the investor and the host State; in which the operation of the local remedies rule was excluded; and in which the tribunal's award would be directly enforceable within the territories of the States parties.

The system was at first limited to cases where both the national State of the investor and the State party to the case were Parties to the Convention. This meant that if one party to the dispute did not meet this requirement, the matter could not be submitted to ICSID, even if both parties so wished. This problem was solved in 1978 by the creation by the Bank of the "Additional Facility" which permits recourse — albeit imperfect — to the main elements of the ICSID system even if only one party meets the requirement, provided that both have given their consent.

Consent to jurisdiction under the system was originally foreseen as deriving principally from express references to it in the arbitration clauses of investment contracts. However, the sources of consent have been significantly widened by the development of recourse to ICSID on the basis of provisions in inter-State bilateral investment protection and investment guarantee agreements as well as by multilateral arrangements such as the North American Free Trade Agreement. Professor Brigitte Stern has recently produced a striking analysis of the 29 cases pending at the beginning of 2000; five were founded on an arbitration clause; two on an arbitration agreement; one on a national law; and the remaining 21 on multilateral or bilateral treaties. On the basis of the more detailed analysis of which these figures form a part, Professor Stern has concluded that 'we are walking with giant steps towards a general system of compulsory arbitration against States for all matters relating to international investments, at the initiative of the private actors of international economic relations'."

The sources of consent in BITs or MITs came to be seen as the making of an offer to resolve disputes by ICSID arbitration which an investor could accept by referring a dispute to the Centre, a system which has been characterized as arbitration without

---

3. LAUTERPACHT, "Foreword" in SCHREUER, *The ICSID Convention: A Commentary* (2001) pp. xi-xii.

privity.[4] Blanket consents to arbitration became common in the 1970s and the number of BITs containing such provisions increased dramatically in the 1980s and 1990s. It is estimated that over 2,000 BITs have been formed. Countries continue to conclude numerous BITs containing the usual investor-to-state dispute settlement provisions. According to the United Nations Conference on Trade and Development, 158 BITs were concluded in 1999 alone (the latest year for which data is available).

MITs, which transcend the reciprocal basis of BITs, constitute a further significant step in the evolution of a global foreign investment dispute resolution system. MITs such as the 1992 North American Free Trade Agreement (NAFTA) between the USA, Canada and Mexico, and the 1994 Energy Charter Treaty (ECT) between the European Communities and forty-nine mostly European states, are trade and investment treaties which involve numerous states and have considerable potential for expansion. Under MITs, an investor based in one state obtains a right of direct action against however many states are parties to the treaty. The future expansion of existing MITs and the creation of new ones will cement in place the new international law norm whereby private investors are recognized as having standing under treaties to bring international arbitral proceedings against states.

III.   DISPUTE RESOLUTION UNDER INVESTMENT TREATIES

The following summary is included only as a necessary prelude to discussion of the specific topic of the forum for challenging an investment treaty arbitration award. It is natural in this connection to refer to the NAFTA since it has provided the most interesting case law in the area and of course *Metalclad* is a NAFTA case.

The NAFTA, which entered into force on 1 January 1994, is the most interesting and significant MIT. First, the expansiveness of the grounds upon which foreign investors may directly bring arbitral proceedings against host states was unprecedented and has established a model for future MITs. It goes beyond the usual BIT standard of investor treatment – no less favourable than is accorded to investors from other states or to the state's own investors – to a minimum standard under which each party is obliged to accord to investors of another party treatment "in accordance with international law, including fair and equitable treatment and full protection and security".[5] Its scope is very extensive because Chapter 11 applies with limited restrictions to all measures adopted or maintained by the state party relating to investors of another party and contains a very

---

4. PAULSSON, "Arbitration Without Privity", 10 ICSID Rev—Foreign Investment LJ (1995) p. 232. However, some authors have disagreed with this description. Sornarajah describes the idea as a "mere slogan without substance", stating that jurisdiction is exercised with alleged consent between the parties. The consent is constructed on the basis of an offer to arbitrate by the host state contained in a tready document that is unilaterally accepted by the foreign investor. See M. SORNARAJAH, *The Settlement of Foreign Investment Disputes* (Kluwer Law International, The Hague, 2000) pp. 208-209.

5. Art. 1105(1) NAFTA. The NAFTA case law on this article is discussed in WEILER, "Substantive Law Developments in NAFTA Arbitration", 16 Mealey's International Arbitration Report (2001) p. 69.

broad definition of measure including "any law, regulation, procedure, requirement or practice".[6] This means that it includes not only the actions of central government legislatures and executives, but also the actions of state enterprises, domestic courts and municipal and state governments.[7] Furthermore, the treaty covers virtually all types of investment. By comparison, the ECT which entered into force in 1998, confers many of the same rights on investors, but relates solely to the energy sector.

The NAFTA Treaty was intended to encourage the settlement of disputes through negotiation and accordingly contains a number of preliminary steps that must be followed before an investor may submit a dispute to arbitration. For example, the disputing parties are required first to attempt to settle a claim through consultation and negotiation[8] and may not initiate arbitral proceedings until six months have elapsed since the events giving rise to the claim.[9] At least ninety days before the claim is submitted, the investor must deliver to the disputing party written notice of its intention to submit a claim to arbitration.[10] Alleged non-compliance with these and other procedural requirements is often raised as a preliminary jurisdictional defence.[11]

---

6. Art. 1120 NAFTA.
7. Two issues arise as to the breadth of Art. 1105. The first issue is what is included in international law. On the one hand is the argument that it includes only customary international law, whilst on the other is the argument that a broader definition is appropriate, particularly in the light of the definitions of international law contained in the Statute of the International Court of Justice, which many regard as the definitive definition. Art. 38(1) of the Statute provides:

   "1. The Court, whose function is to decide in accordance with international law such disputes as are submitted to it, shall apply:
   a. international conventions, whether general or particular, establishing rules expressly recognized by the contesting states;
   b. international custom, as evidence of a general practice accepted as law;
   c. the general principles of law recognized by civilized nations;
   d. subject to the provisions of Article 59, judicial decisions and the teachings of the most highly qualified publicists of the various nations, as subsidiary means for the determination of rules of law."

   This means that Art. 1105 may extend beyond the customary norms by which states consider themselves and other states to be bound. It may extend to treaty commitments (for example, the WTO obligations), international judicial decisions, and the opinions of eminent international law jurists.
   The other issue is whether "fair and equitable treatment and full protection and security" form part of the minimum international law standard or are additional to it. There are currently conflicting arbitral decisions rendered under the NAFTA treaty as to which see WEILER, supra note 5, pp. 79-83. The issue was also considered by the reviewing court in *Metalclad*, discussed below.
8. Art. 1118 NAFTA.
9. Art. 1120 NAFTA.
10. Art. 1119 NAFTA.
11. See, e.g., *Tradex Hellas S.A. (Greece) v. Albania*, 24 December 1996, reprinted in ICCA *Yearbook Commercial Arbitration* XXV (2000) (hereinafter *Yearbook*) p. 221 at p. 223 (challenging the jurisdiction of the tribunal on the grounds that the claimant did not make a good-faith effort to resolve the dispute amicably before resorting to arbitration as required by the arbitration

The minimum standard of treatment in Art. 1105 creates an international standard against which the conduct of the state parties may be judged. This article is the one that can lead to the result, deeply concerning to some commentators, that a domestic court at the seat of an arbitration may have to assess whether the host state has met its obligations under international law if the court is called upon to review an international arbitration conducted under the ICSID Additional Facility Rules or the UNCITRAL Rules.

IV.   THE LACK OF UNIFORMITY RESULTING FROM THE INVESTOR'S RIGHT TO SELECT THE FORUM

NAFTA permits an aggrieved investor to select arbitration under:

> "(a) the ICSID Convention, provided that both the disputing Party and the Party of the investor are parties to the Convention;
> (b) the Additional Facility Rules of ICSID, provided that either the disputing Party or the Party of the investor, but not both, is a party to the ICSID Convention; or
> (c) the UNCITRAL Arbitration Rules".[12]

Under Art. 26 of the ECT, apart from the ICSID Convention or its Additional Facility, the investor is given the choice of the courts and administrative tribunals of the host state, previously agreed procedures, UNCITRAL arbitration, and arbitration in the framework of the Arbitration Institute of the Stockholm Chamber of Commerce.

In pure ICSID arbitration, the ICSID Convention creates a supranational system which excludes appeal, thus foreclosing challenges to awards on traditional New York Convention grounds.[13] The autonomous character of ICSID arbitration is clearly stated in Art. 26 which provides that consent of the parties to arbitration under the Convention shall unless otherwise stated be deemed consent to such arbitration to the exclusion of any other remedies. By submitting to ICSID arbitration the parties therefore have the assurance that they may take full advantage of procedural rules specifically adapted to their needs and, equally important, that the administration of these rules will be exempt from the scrutiny or control of domestic courts and states that are parties to the Convention. ICSID itself supplies the only remedies available to a losing party, namely as to the interpretation of the meaning or scope of the award;

---

be met before a tribunal could consider the claim).

12. Art. 1120 NAFTA.

13. This supranational nature of the ICSID system was discussed in a New Zealand case where a stay of proceedings was granted against the New Zealand Government which had commenced proceedings in breach of a contract which provided for reference of investment disputes to ICSID. The judge noted that ICSID arbitration constituted a self-contained machinery functioning in total independence from domestic legal systems: *Mobil Oil NZ Ltd v. Attorney-General* [1989] 2 NZLR 649; 4 ICSID Reports 117.

revision on the grounds of discovery of a previously unknown factor of decisive importance; and annulment of the award by an *ad hoc* Review Committee. In short, ICSID itself is expected to supply its own internal quality control systems.

ICSID normally has jurisdiction over investment disputes between a state that is a party to the Convention and an investor from another Convention state.[14] With reference to NAFTA, since Mexico and Canada are not yet parties to the ICSID Convention, ICSID must supervise arbitration involving these countries under its Additional Facility regime, designed for cases in which the Convention does not apply and the investor chooses ICSID arbitration instead of arbitration under the UNCITRAL Rules. Under the ICSID Additional Facility regime, the litigants use ICSID rules and supervisory personnel outside the ICSID Convention framework. As with awards made under the UNCITRAL Rules, an award's finality thus depends on the judicial review mechanisms at the place of arbitration, and in some countries awards are subjected to mandatory judicial control.[15] Thus an important feature in NAFTA (and ECT) arbitration is that an investor's choice of arbitral rules can produce a different result as to the scope and standard of review of the arbitral award and the procedure for review. As to NAFTA, this is because Chapter 11 of the NAFTA Treaty does not specifically address the question of review or recourse against arbitral awards made pursuant to the Treaty.

In summary, if an investment treaty claimant selects ICSID arbitration under the Washington Convention (which as noted earlier is not yet available to NAFTA investors because neither Canada nor Mexico has ratified the Convention) the review process is internalized within ICSID itself and parties may not challenge enforcement of the award in domestic courts by way of appeal or other remedy.[16] However, neither the ICSID Additional Facility Rules nor the UNCITRAL Rules provide a procedure for review or recourse against awards. The matter is left to the courts at the seat of arbitration and the scope and procedure of review will be determined by the applicable international commercial arbitration legislation at the seat of arbitration. This is implicitly confirmed by Art. V(1)(*e*) of the 1958 New York Convention, which provides that one of the grounds for refusing recognition or enforcement of an arbitral award is that it has been set aside by a competent authority of the state in which the award was made. It is also confirmed by Art. 1136 of the NAFTA, which provides in relevant part:

> "Article 1136: Finality and Enforcement of an Award
> 3. A disputing party may not seek enforcement of a final award until:
> …
> (b) in the case of a final award under the ICSID Additional Facility Rules or the UNCITRAL Arbitration Rules

---

14. Convention on the Settlement of Investment Disputes Between States and Nationals of Other States, 4 ILM (1965) p. 532.
15. See Art. 1136 NAFTA, 32 ILM (1993) p. 646.
16. Art. 53 ICSID Convention. Each Contracting State must recognize an award rendered pursuant to the Convention as binding and enforce the pecuniary obligations imposed by that award within its territories as if it were a final judgment of a court in that State.

(i) three months have elapsed from the date the award was rendered and no disputing party has commenced a proceeding to revise, set aside or annul the award, or

(ii) a court has dismissed or allowed an application to revise, set aside or annul the award and there is no further appeal."

Art. 1130 of the NAFTA provides that unless the disputing parties agree otherwise, an arbitral tribunal must hold an arbitration in the territory of a party that is a party to the New York Convention. Currently, this means that the scope of review will be determined by the international commercial arbitration legislation in either Canada, Mexico or the United States, depending upon the seat selected by the arbitral tribunal. Generally speaking the legislation in each of the three jurisdictions incorporates the grounds for refusing recognition and enforcement of awards contained in Art. V of the New York Convention, which are replicated in Art. 34 of the UNCITRAL Model Law.[17] However, courts in the three jurisdictions may interpret and apply the grounds differently, and in particular may differ as to what constitutes a sufficient public policy imperative to justify the setting aside of an award or the refusal to grant it recognition and enforcement.

The ultimate question is whether the lack of a uniform forum in investment treaty

---

17. Art. V of the New York Convention provides:

"1. Recognition and enforcement of the award may be refused, at the request of the party against whom it is invoked, only if that party furnishes to the competent authority where the recognition and enforcement is sought, proof that:

(a) The parties to the agreement referred to in article II were, under the law applicable to them, under some incapacity, or the said agreement is not valid under the law to which the parties have subjected it or, failing any indication thereon, under the law of the country where the award was made; or

(b) The party against whom the award is invoked was not given proper notice of the appointment of the arbitrator or of the arbitration proceedings or was otherwise unable to present his case; or

(c) The award deals with a difference not contemplated by or not falling within the terms of the submission to arbitration, or it contains decisions on matters beyond the scope of the submission to arbitration, provided that, if the decisions on matters beyond the scope of the submission to arbitration, provided that, if the decisions on matters submitted to arbitration can be separated from those not so submitted, that part of the award which contains decisions on matters submitted to arbitration may be recognized and enforced; or

(d) The composition of the arbitral authority or the arbitral procedure was not in accordance with the agreement of the parties, or failing such agreement, was not in accordance with the law of the country where the arbitration took place; or

(e) The award has not yet become binding, on the parties, or has been set aside or suspended by a competent authority of the country in which, or under the law of which, that award was made.

2. Recognition and enforcement of an arbitral award may also be refused if the competent authority in the country where recognition and enforcement is sought finds that:

(a) The subject matter of the difference is not capable of settlement by arbitration under the law of that country; or

(b) The recognition or enforcement of the award would be contrary to the public policy of that country."

and enforcement.

The ultimate question is whether the lack of a uniform forum in investment treaty claims is avoidable or, if not, whether it really matters. At a basic level some alternatives have to be offered under investment treaties which provide investors with the right to arbitrate directly against state parties because of the undeniable fact that not all states are party to the ICSID Convention. Moreover, if one key object of such treaties is to encourage investor confidence then the provision of alternative fora may help to serve that purpose by presenting widely different alternatives to claimants. If the choice of the claimant investor may possibly lead to different outcomes then surely that is primarily a matter for the investor to consider. The lack of uniformity appears to be no different in character from that which often exists under forum selection options available in both domestic and international litigation.

V.   DOMESTIC COURT REVIEW OF INVESTMENT TREATY AWARDS: THE *METALCLAD* CASE

The *Metalclad*[18] case, the first in which an application was made to a domestic court to set aside an arbitral award rendered under the provisions of the NAFTA, highlights the issues involved when a domestic court is called upon to review an arbitral award rendered by a NAFTA tribunal. Metalclad, a US company, instituted international arbitral proceedings against the United Mexican States in a dispute arising from the construction by Metalclad of a landfill and waste treatment facility in a Mexican state. Metalclad had purchased a Mexican company called Coterin from Mexican nationals and federal authorities in Mexico had assured Metalclad that its subsidiary Coterin would have no difficulty obtaining the necessary consents to complete and operate the facility. Metalclad subsequently concluded an agreement with Mexican federal environmental agencies as to the operation of the facility and proceeded with construction. However, the Mexican company did not have a permit from the local municipality, which obtained an injunction in respect of the agreement with the federal authorities. Subsequent negotiations to obtain a permit from the municipality were unsuccessful. After arbitral proceedings had been issued, the State Government declared the area in which the facility had been built to be a permanent ecological reserve, which almost certainly meant that Metalclad would never be able to operate the facility for its intended purpose. Metalclad elected arbitration under the Additional Facility Rules of ICSID. Pursuant to the NAFTA, the tribunal, in consultation with the parties, determined that the place of arbitration would be Vancouver, British Columbia, Canada although the hearings took place in Washington, DC.[19]

The tribunal found that the actions of Mexico and the municipal authority breached Mexico's obligation to afford Metalclad's investment a standard of treatment which was in accordance with international law, including fair and equitable treatment pursuant to

---

18. *United Mexican States v. Metalclad Corp.* [2001] BCSC 664, Tysoe, J.

19. ICSID (Additional Facility) Case no. ARB(AF)/97/1. The tribunal (Professor Sir Elihu Lauterpacht QC CBE, Mr. Benjamin R. Civiletti, and Mr. Jose Luis Siqueiros) rendered an award on 30 August 2000.

relied upon Art. 102(1) of the NAFTA which lists objectives and principles of the treaty, including transparency and the substantial increase in investment opportunities. The tribunal considered that, pursuant to Art. 31 of the Vienna Convention on the Law of Treaties and Art. 1131 of the NAFTA, which require that treaty provisions be interpreted in the light of the treaty's overall objectives, the principle of transparency was relevant to the interpretation and application of Art. 1105.

Second, the tribunal found that the same actions were tantamount to expropriation prohibited by Art. 1110. In the tribunal's view the denial of a right to operate the facility after the earlier assurances was a measure tantamount to expropriation of the investment. The tribunal also stated, although it did not consider this to be necessary for the decision, that the issuance of the ecological decree was also a measure tantamount to expropriation because it permanently barred operation of the facility. The tribunal awarded Metalclad damages of nearly US$ 17 million.

Mexico applied to the Supreme Court of British Columbia to have the award set aside. There was naturally great interest in how the court would approach the case and Canada and the province of Quebec joined as intervenors. As to the appropriate standard of review, the court was required to decide which of two different British Columbia Arbitration Acts, the International Commercial Arbitration Act or the domestic Commercial Arbitration Act, applied to a review of a NAFTA award. The choice depended not upon whether the arbitration was international or domestic, but upon whether the arbitration was commercial pursuant to the definitions in Sect. 1(b) of the International Commercial Arbitration Act, which provided in relevant part:

"An arbitration is commercial if it arises out of a relationship of a commercial nature including, but not limited to, the following…
(d) an exploitation agreement or concession;…
(p) investing."

The choice was fundamental to Mexico's application because whilst the Commercial Arbitration Act allowed for appeals on a question of law, the International Commercial Arbitration Act did not, and it restricted applications for the review or setting aside of an award to the grounds contained in Art. 34 of the UNCITRAL Model Law which replicate those for refusal of enforcement in Art. V of the New York Convention.

Mexico, and the Canadian Government as intervenor, argued that the dispute between the parties did not have a sufficiently significant commercial nature for the International Commercial Arbitration Act to apply. There was an important distinction between arbitration pursuant to a private agreement between international commercial parties and arbitration pursuant to an international treaty, the existence of the treaty giving the dispute a public law character. Furthermore the relationship between the parties was a regulatory relationship, not a commercial one. The Court rejected this view, and noted the wide definition of "commercial" in the International Commercial Arbitration Act. This classification was supported by the legislative history of the UNCITRAL Model Law. The Court also held that the regulatory aspect of the dispute was incidental as Chapter 11 of the NAFTA was intended to deal with the treatment of investors. This brought the dispute within the International Commercial Arbitration Act and accordingly its limited grounds for review applied to the dispute.[20] Unable to appeal on a question of law, Mexico relied primarily upon Sect. 34(2)(a)(iv) of the International Commercial Arbitration Act, which permitted the court to set aside an award of the tribunal if the decision was beyond the scope of the submission to arbitration.[21] This ground of challenge contemplates a situation in which an award has been made by a tribunal that did have jurisdiction to deal with the dispute but which exceeded its powers by dealing with matters that had not been submitted to it. Redfern and Hunter[22] suggest that it is becoming increasingly common for this issue to be raised as a first line of defence by losing parties.

The court emphasized the narrowness of the review permitted by the Act and cited the decision of the British Columbia Court of Appeal in *Quintette Coal Ltd v. Nippon Steel Corp* as follows:[23]

> "It is important to parties to future such arbitrations and to the integrity of the process itself that the court express its views on the degree of deference to be accorded the decision of the arbitrators. The reasons advanced in the cases discussed above for restraint in the exercise of judicial review are highly persuasive. The 'concerns of international comity, respect for the capacities of foreign and transnational tribunals, and sensitivity to the need of the international commercial system for predictability in the resolution of disputes' spoken of by Blackmun J. [in *Mitsubishi Motors Corp. v. Soler Chrysler-Plymouth Inc.*, 473 U.S. 614 (1985)] are as compelling in this jurisdiction as they are in the United States or elsewhere. It is meet therefore, as a matter of policy, to adopt a standard which seeks to preserve the autonomy of the forum selected by the parties and to minimize judicial intervention when reviewing international commercial arbitral awards in British Columbia."

It will be recalled that the tribunal found that Mexico had breached its international law obligations under Art. 1105 of the NAFTA by not providing a transparent regulatory environment for investment. Mexico submitted first that the tribunal's reliance on the transparency issue for its finding of a breach of Art. 1105 was in excess of jurisdiction and went beyond the scope of the submission to arbitration and secondly

---

20. *Op. cit.*, fn. 19, paras. 39-49.
21. Sect. 34(2)(a)(iv) provides:

"An arbitral award may be set aside by the Supreme Court only if
(a) the party making the application furnishes proof that...
(iv) the arbitral award deals with a dispute not contemplated by or not falling within the terms of the submission to arbitration, or if contains decisions on matters beyond the scope of the submission to arbitration..."

The International Commercial Arbitration Act of course provides the same ground for refusal of enforcement of an award. The ground derives from Art. V(1) of the New York Convention.
22. REDFERN and HUNTER, *Law and Practice of International Arbitration*, 3d ed. (1999) p. 464.
23. [1991] 1 WWR 219, 229.

of jurisdiction and went beyond the scope of the submission to arbitration and secondly that the tribunal similarly erred in going beyond the transparency provisions contained in the NAFTA and creating new transparency obligations. It argued that the international law standard contained in Art. 1105 did not require a transparent regulatory environment. Mexico further asserted that the tribunal's finding that measures taken by Mexican authorities were tantamount to expropriation pursuant to Art. 1110 of the NAFTA was also unsound because the finding was based in large part on the alleged breach of Art. 1105 by failing to provide a transparent business environment.

The court held that the submission to arbitration was confined to Metalclad's claim that Mexico had breached Arts. 1105 and 1110. In respect of Art. 1105, the court decided that in order to determine whether the tribunal had made a decision which was outside the scope of the submission to arbitration, it was necessary to determine whether the tribunal had applied the correct legal standard for determining whether Mexico was under an obligation pursuant to Art. 1105 to provide a transparent regulatory environment.

The Court determined that the tribunal had failed to apply the correct law. The legal standard in Art. 1105 was the minimum standard of treatment required by customary international law. His Honour further held that the reference in Art. 1105 to "fair and equitable treatment and full protection and security" was not additional to the customary international law standard but was merely an example of it.[24] The court observed that the tribunal gave no evidence for a finding that customary international law required a transparent regulatory system and if the tribunal's belief that such a standard could be applied was based upon matters of fairness and equity in the circumstances, the tribunal's decision was not merely a misinterpretation of the wording of Art. 1105 but a misstatement of the applicable law.[25] Tysoe, J. further observed that Art. 102(1) lists transparency as a rule or principle by which the NAFTA objectives are to be carried out. It is not an objective for the purposes of Art. 31(1) of the Vienna Convention. The rules and principles are elaborated in specific chapters, and transparency is implemented through Chapter 18, not Chapter 11. The principles in Art. 102(1) were not intended to be used in the interpretation of all provisions of the NAFTA. The state parties provided in the NAFTA that investors could bring proceedings only in respect of the undertakings in Chapter 11 and certain undertakings in Chapter 15, and breaches of any other provisions were to be dealt with between the states.[26]

The court went on to hold that the tribunal's finding that Mexico's conduct prior to the issuance of the ecological decree was tantamount to expropriation, was based in large part on the finding of a breach of Art. 1105. However, Metalclad was still entitled to compensation because the court had no jurisdiction to set aside the tribunal's finding that the ecological decree was tantamount to expropriation. This finding was not in any way based on a breach of Art. 1105 and no other sound basis had been advanced by Mexico for setting aside the tribunal's conclusion in respect of the ecological decree.

---

24. *Op. cit.*, fn. 19, paras. 62-65. The court held that "including" could not ordinarily be read as "plus".

25. *Ibid.*, para. 70.

26. *Ibid.*, Art. 1116 NAFTA.

tribunal's definition of expropriation was "extremely broad", including incidental interference with the use of property, the court did not have jurisdiction to set aside the award.[27] Accordingly the award of damages remained largely intact, the only change being an adjustment to the interest component as Mexico had breached Chapter 11's protections at a later stage than determined by the tribunal. Mexico commenced an appeal against this decision in May 2001, but abandoned it in October of that year, perhaps concerned that it would risk losing foreign investment if it refused to honour the award and settle the dispute.

VI.   ANALYSIS OF THE *METALCLAD* DECISION

Metalclad may be presented as an example of why it is inappropriate for a national court to enter upon matters of international law when reviewing an international arbitral decision. However, in many respects an analysis of the *Metalclad* decision suggests that there is no reason to be overly concerned. First, the court rejected the view of the state parties to the NAFTA that awards rendered pursuant to Chapter 11 could be subject to wider review in domestic courts than ordinary international commercial arbitral awards. The court also dismissed the notion that the treaty gave the dispute a non-commercial public law character which would justify wider review than is justified in standard international commercial disputes.

Secondly, the court readily accepted that it did not have jurisdiction to set aside the tribunal's finding that the ecological decree was tantamount to expropriation. The court held that it did not have jurisdiction to set aside an interpretation, even if the interpretation was "patently unreasonable".[28] The interpretation of Art. 1110 was a matter for the expert tribunal, which the court did not have jurisdiction to second guess.

Thirdly, the court avoided the tendency, which some *ad hoc* annulment committees constituted under the Washington Convention appear to have adopted, of automatically annulling an award if found to contain any errors. Instead, the court considered the award in its entirety and held that even though Mexico succeeded on the Art. 1105 point, the tribunal's finding on the ecological decree could not be set aside.

Fourthly, the court, although not deciding the issue, inclined to the view that a patently unreasonable finding disregarding relevant evidence was not a ground for setting aside an award.

Fifthly, the court took a strict approach to proof of public policy exception when rejecting claims that allegedly improper acts by Metalclad rendered the award in conflict with the public policy in British Columbia. Finally, the court rightly refused to apply the proposition, said to derive from the ICSID *ad hoc* annulment committee decisions in *Klöckner*, *Amco* and *MINE*, discussed below, that an arbitral award should be set aside if it does not address all arguments made by the parties which would have changed the outcome of the award if the arguments had been accepted.

Overall there is an argument for concluding that the British Columbian court,

---

27. *Ibid.*, para. 99.

28. *Ibid.*, paras. 99-100.

exercising jurisdiction under the grounds contained in the New York Convention and UNCITRAL Model Law, performed rather better than the first *ad hoc* annulment committees in ICSID international arbitration (see below).

However, in respect of Art. 1105 it is debatable whether the court kept within the bounds of the narrow standard of review which it correctly held applied to the dispute, and whether its interpretation of Art. 1105 was correct. It has been suggested that the case really turned on the interpretation of Art. 1105, not application of the correct law and so the Court should not have second-guessed the tribunal's views on Art. 1105.[29] In *Quintette*, the parties submitted the interpretation of a contractual provision to the tribunal, and in subsequent proceedings the Court held that it was not permitted to substitute its interpretation of the provision in place of the interpretation of the tribunal. It has been argued that Art. 1105, as an undertaking by the state party, is analogous to a contractual provision and it was therefore for the tribunal, not the Court, to determine the standard of treatment required by the provision. An eminent three-member international tribunal was asked in *Metalclad* to rule on the extent of the obligations undertaken, and the domestic court should not have asserted jurisdiction to set aside the award.

The right to review awards on the ground of excess of authority is a feature of numerous arbitration laws including the US Federal Arbitration Act (Sect. 10), the French New Code of Civil Procedure (Art. 1502), the Swiss Federal Private International Law Act (Art. 190) and the UNCITRAL Model Law (Art. 34). It is a ground that would seem on its face to preclude review for errors of law. However, as Professor William Park[30] has noted, the text of such a law must be read in the context of its application and this ground "may allow wiggle room for an over zealous judge to examine a dispute's legal merits under the guise of correcting arbitrator excess of authority". Some may consider that is what occurred in *Metalclad*. If the review of the award had been undertaken by a US court the standard of review would very likely have been much more deferential as is shown for example by the decision of the US court of Appeals for the District of Columbia in the *LIAMCO*[31] case which followed and applied the well-known passage from *Parsons & Whittemore*:[32]

---

29. See, e.g.,the criticisms of the decision in WEILER, "*Metalclad v. Mexico*: A Play in Three Parts" in WAELDE, ed., Internet Journal of the Centre for Energy, Petroleum and Mineral Law and Policy. Available at: www.dundee.ac.uk/cepmlp/journal/html/article9-20.html.

30. PARK, "Why Courts Review Arbitral Awards" in *Law of International Business and Dispute Settlement in the 21st Century*, Liber Amicorum in honour of Karl-Heinz Bockstiegel (2001) pp. 597-598.

31. *Libyan American Oil Company (LIAMCO) v. Libyan Arab Republic*, Yearbook VII (1982) p. 382.

32. *Parsons & Whittemore Overseas Co Inc v. Société Generale De L'industrie du Papier* 508 F. 2d 969, 976-977 (1974). Numerous other cases exhibiting the same narrow approach to excess of authority claims are conveniently collected together in Born, *International Commercial Arbitration*, 2d ed. (2001) pp. 852-855. However, as to the precise issue of deciding issues not within the scope of the submission there are some cases (listed in fn. 13, pp. 856-857) which adopt an approach similar to that taken in *Metalclad*. However, BORN notes that "doubt about the scope of the parties' submissions are resolved in some national legal systems (including the United States) in favour of coverage".

"This defense to enforcement of a foreign award, like the others already discussed, should be construed narrowly. Once again a narrow construction would comport with the enforcement-facilitating thrust of the Convention.... Overseas must therefore overcome a powerful presumption that the arbitral body acted within its powers.... [t]he Convention ... does not sanction second-guessing the arbitrator's construction of the parties' agreement. The appellant's attempt to invoke this defence, however, calls upon the court to ignore this limitation on its decision-making powers and usurp the arbitrator's role. The district court took a proper view of its own jurisdiction in refusing to grant relief on this ground."

In *LIAMCO* it was asserted that the tribunal had exceeded its jurisdiction by awarding damages for consequential loss when the relevant contract excluded such recovery. The court refused to engage in an in-depth review of the law of contract to ascertain whether the assertion was soundly based, holding that it would not be proper for the court to usurp the role of the tribunal and second guess the arbitrators' construction of the contract.

Whatever one's view of the court's decision, the *Metalclad* case illustrates the fine balance between the exercise of judicial control to ensure that tribunals remain within the scope of the submission to arbitration, and inappropriate interference with a tribunal's award on matters of mixed fact and law. The distinction can be a very fine one. As long ago as 1978 the English Court of Appeal remarked that "the distinction between an error which entails absence of jurisdiction and an error made within jurisdiction is [so] fine ... that it is rapidly being eroded".[33] In *Metalclad* the court in effect took the view that it could set aside a decision which was inconsistent with its view of the applicable law. In respect of Art. 1105, the court concluded that the tribunal had not simply interpreted the wording of Art. 1105. Rather, it had misstated the applicable law to include transparency obligations and then made its decision on the basis of the concept of transparency. It had thus applied a legal standard of its own creation, and accordingly the court was entitled to set aside that part of the decision. However, if the court does not disagree with the tribunal as to the legal standard, the matter is properly one of application of the standard, which the court should leave to the tribunal.

In summary, the difference is between misreading the scope of the arbitration agreement and in doing so setting an incorrect legal standard, in which case the court has jurisdiction to intervene, and making a "mistake" in applying a correct standard implicit or explicit in the arbitration agreement in which case the court should not have jurisdiction to intervene.

The remaining issue is the use of interpretative notes by the NAFTA Free Trade Commission as a means of revising erroneous or unacceptable judicial decisions relating to NAFTA awards. It is possible to argue that this technique is an adequate safeguard for cases where a national court misreads the true scope of state responsibility under the NAFTA. The question as to whether the court in *Metalclad* correctly interpreted Art. 1105 as restricting the applicable law – "international law, including fair and equitable

---

33. *Pearlman v. Governors of Harrow School* [1978] 3 WLR 736, 743 (CA).

1105 as restricting the applicable law – "international law, including fair and equitable treatment and full protection and security" – to customary international law has been the subject of an interpretative note issued by the NAFTA Free Trade Commission. Art. 2001 of the NAFTA provides for the establishment of the Commission, consisting of a representative from each state party (typically the international trade ministers), which has the power to issue binding interpretations of NAFTA provisions.[34] After the decision in *Metalclad*, the Commission, reflecting state party concern about the litigation, issued an interpretative note on 31 July 2001, which included the following:

> "*B. Minimum Standard of Treatment in Accordance with International Law*
> 1. Article 1105(1) prescribes the customary law minimum standard of treatment of aliens as the minimum standard to be afforded to investments of investors of another Party.
> 2. The concepts of 'fair and equitable treatment' and 'full protection and security' do not require treatment in addition to or beyond that which is required by the customary international law minimum standard of treatment of aliens.
> 3. A determination that there has been a breach of another provision of the NAFTA, or of a separate international agreement, does not establish that there has been a breach of Article 1105(1)."

This interpretation, which was an endorsement of Tysoe, J.'s approach, is vulnerable to the criticism that it is not an interpretation at all, but a rewriting of Art. 1105. It has been criticized by Professor Sir Robert Jennings QC.[35] He argues that the note twisted the intention of Art. 1105. First, Art. 1105 does not prescribe that the "international law" standard is limited to the customary international law treatment of aliens, and interpolation of the word "customary" is highly questionable. It is difficult to justify limiting "international law" to customary international law in the light of the much wider definition contained in Art. 38(1) of the Statute of the International Court of Justice, which is widely regarded as the authoritative definition.[36] However, it may be that the state parties "scarcely intended" to incorporate all present and future international law obligations by the simple words in Art. 1105.[37]

Second, Sir Robert Jennings has argued that subsuming "fair and equitable treatment" within customary international law is flawed because it gives the additional words no meaning. Additionally, the interpretation is inconsistent with the interpretation given to many BITs requiring "fair and equitable treatment". However, the ordinary meaning of "including" makes it difficult to argue that the state parties intended "fair and equitable treatment" to be additional to the minimum international law standard. Furthermore,

---

34. *Ibid.*, Art. 1131(2) NAFTA.
35. "Second Opinion of Professor Sir Robert Jennings, QC", produced in the *Methanex* arbitration on 6 September 2001.
36. Van DUZER, "NAFTA Chapter 11 to Date: The Progress of a Work in Progress", paper presented at a Conference on Chapter 11 held at Carleton University (Ottawa January 2002). Available at: www.carleton.ca/ctpl/ch11papers/vanduzer.htm.
37. *Ibid.*

as the state parties have argued, the wording of Art. 1105 is different from that of the Model Bilateral Investment Treaty 1987, leading to the "natural inference" that the parties intended to depart from the Model BIT approach.[38]

Professor Weiler has also criticized the interpretative note, arguing that the note is really an amendment to the plain meaning of Art. 1105.[39] Eight out of the nine international arbitrators in the *Metalclad, Pope & Talbot*[40] and *S D Myers*[41] NAFTA arbitrations held that limiting Art. 1105 to customary international law is not supported by the wording of the provision. Professor Weiler further argues that tribunals or courts may be forced to reject the Free Trade Commission's interpretation. Art. 1131(1) provides that a tribunal shall decide a dispute in accordance with the NAFTA and international law. Tribunals cannot ignore their obligation to apply the customary international law of treaty interpretation unless the state parties amend the NAFTA to exclude it. Additionally, Art. 102(2) requires that the state parties shall interpret and apply the provisions of the NAFTA in the light of its objectives and in accordance with international law.

The principle of good faith expressed in the *pacta sunt servanda* rule, now incorporated in Art. 26 of the Vienna Convention, prohibits the Commission from using its interpretative authority to impose changes to the NAFTA which cannot be supported by the customary rules of treaty interpretation.[42] In any event, Professor Weiler argues that the presumption against retrospectivity in treaty interpretation may mean that it will be some time before the interpretative note can have any effect.[43]

A final point to keep in mind is that any problems which may be considered to exist under the Chapter 11 procedure have to be considered in the broader picture of the NAFTA. The three state parties jointly published a report on the NAFTA in 2001. Between 1994 and 2000, trade between the NAFTA countries increased by 128 percent, from US\$ 297 billion to US\$ 676 billion.[44] The Canadian Minister for International Trade, the Hon. Pierre Pettigrew, observed in a recent speech that in spite of all the laws and regulations passed by NAFTA governments since 1994, there have been very few investor-state disputes in which the Chapter 11 arbitration provisions have been necessary.[45] At the end of February 2002, the Chapter 11 provisions had been invoked in only twenty-three cases. Of these, tribunals have rendered decisions in only five cases; fourteen cases are ongoing, although some are effectively inactive; three claims were not pursued; and one was settled. *Metalclad* is the only decision to have been

---

38. See Tysoe, J.'s judgment in *Metalclad, op. cit.*, fn. 19, para. 65.
39. WEILER, "NAFTA Art. 1105 and the Free Trade Commission: Just Sour Grapes, or Something More Serious?", 29 International Business Lawyer (2001) p. 491 at p. 496.
40. *Pope & Talbot Inc v. Canada*, Award rendered on 10 April 2001.
41. *S D Myers Inc v. Canada*, Partial Award rendered on 13 November 2000.
42. WEILER, *op. cit.*, fn. 39, p. 496.
43. *Ibid.*, p. 495. However, it is suggested in van DUZER, *op. cit.*, fn. 36, that despite the residual uncertainty, the NAFTA Free Trade Commission's ruling will severely curtail attempts to take an expansive approach to Art. 1105.
44. "NAFTA at Seven: Building on a North American Partnership".
45. Speech delivered to the House of Commons during a motion on investor-state dispute settlement, 1 May 2001.

case.[46] The fundamental worth of the Chapter 11 system is that it encourages investors to invest in other NAFTA states in the knowledge that an international dispute resolution procedure is available.

VII.   THE NATURE AND SCOPE OF REVIEW UNDER ICSID

The third issue calls for a brief analysis of the ICSID annulment mechanism.[47] Sect. 5 of the Convention provides for interpretation, revision and annulment of awards. Art. 50 permits either party to an award to request an interpretation as to the meaning or scope of an award; and Art. 51 permits either party to request revision of an award if new evidence is discovered which is "of such a nature as decisively to affect the award". These provisions are straightforward. However, the annulment provisions have proved in practice to be controversial. Art. 52(1) provides:

> "Either party may request annulment of the award by an application in writing addressed to the Secretary-General on one or more of the following grounds:
> (a) that the Tribunal was not properly constituted;
> (b) that the Tribunal has manifestly exceeded its powers;
> (c) that there was corruption on the part of a member of the Tribunal;
> (d) that there has been a serious departure from a fundamental rule of procedure; or
> (e) that the award has failed to state the reasons on which it is based."

The application must be made within 120 days after the date on which the award was rendered (Art. 52(2)) or, in the case of applications made on the ground of corruption, within 120 days of the discovery of the corruption and within three years after the date on which the award was rendered. Art. 52(3) requires the chairman, upon receipt of the request, to appoint from the Panel of Arbitrators a three-member *ad hoc* committee, which will have authority to annul the award or any part of it on any of the grounds listed in Art. 52(1). If the award is annulled, the dispute must be submitted upon the request of either party to a new tribunal.

It is most unlikely that there will be breaches of Art. 52(1)(a) or (c). The constitution of tribunals is organized by experienced professionals at the ICSID Centre and tribunals are made up of distinguished international arbitrators. In any event the existence of such grounds is undoubtedly proper. However, the remaining three grounds are contentious. Early drafts of the Convention did not provide for annulment and the words "manifest", "serious" and "fundamental" indicate that the *ad hoc* committee's powers were intended to be very limited.[48]

---

46. Canada applied for review in the Trial Division of the Federal Court on 8 February 2001 (Court file no. T 25-01). A hearing date has not been set at this stage.
47. For a comprehensive analysis see SCHREUER, *op. cit.*, fn. 3, pp. 881-1075.
48. REDFERN, "ICSID – Losing its Appeal?", 3 Arbitration International (1987) p. 98 at p. 99 and pp. 102-103.

The parties negotiating the ICSID Convention wished to promote the finality of awards. Whilst some form of review procedure was necessary in the interests of justice, the Convention makes it clear that the annulment procedure is not an appeal. There is no standing committee to hear annulment applications, and the committee constituted to hear a particular application may decide only whether the award should be annulled. It has no power to revise an award on the merits. The procedural rules applying to tribunal proceedings also apply to annulment proceedings.

As to the ICSID case law on annulment, nine requests for annulment have been registered.[49] These cases involved *Klöckner v. Cameroon* (twice),[50] *Amco v. Indonesia* (twice),[51] *MINE v. Guinea*,[52] *SPP v. Egypt*,[53] *Compañía de Aguas del Aconquija SA and Vivendi v. Argentina*,[54] *Wena Hotels v. Egypt*[55] and *Philippe Gruslin v. Malaysia*.[56] *Ad hoc* annulment committees have reached decisions in response to six of these requests.[57]

An issue which has arisen is the degree of discretion which an *ad hoc* committee may exercise. The *Klöckner* committee considered that where a ground for annulment has been made out, the committee must annul the award in whole or in part, the parties to the dispute having an absolute right to strict compliance with the Convention's provisions regardless of the materiality of non-compliance. However, the committee in the *MINE* case considered that there was limited discretion where annulment would unjustifiably undermine the binding force and finality of awards. This would seem a better balance, given that parties will lose confidence in ICSID arbitration if a dispute must be referred to a new tribunal even where the irregularity did not materially affect the original award.

VIII.   ANALYSIS OF ANNULMENT CASES

It is proposed to concentrate on the early annulment cases, beginning with *Klöckner v. Cameroon* where the parties had concluded a series of contracts for the supply and management of a fertilizer factory. After a period of unprofitable operation the factory was shut down by the Cameroonian Government. Klöckner filed a request for ICSID arbitration claiming the balance of the price of the factory. The Government counter-

---

49. For a general survey of early ICSID annulment cases, see SCHREUER, *op. cit.*, fn. 3, pp. 807-903; and REDFERN, *ibid.*, p. 103, et seq.
50. *Klöckner Industrie-Anlagen GmbH v. United Republic of Cameroon & Société Camerounaise des Engrais*, Case no. ARB/81/2.
51. *Amco Asia Corporation v. Republic of Indonesia*, Case no. ARB/81/1.
52. *Maritime International Nominees Establishment v. Republic of Guinea*, Case no. ARB/84/4.
53. *Southern Pacific Properties (Middle East) Ltd v. Arab Republic of Egypt*, Case no. ARB/84/3.
54. *Compañía de Aguas del Aconquija SA & Vivendi Universal v. Argentine Republic*, Case no. ARB/97/3.
55. *Wena Hotels Ltd v. Arab Republic of Egypt*, Case no. ARB/98/4.
56. *Philippe Gruslin v. Malaysia*, Case no. ARB/99/3.
57. In *SPP v. Egypt*, the case was settled before a decision by the *ad hoc* Committee was reached. Proceedings in *Compañía de Aguas del Aconquija SA v. Argentina* and *Philippe Gruslin v. Malaysia* are pending, although in the latter case the Secretary-General has moved that the *ad hoc* Committee discontinue the proceeding due to lack of payment.

claimed damages for losses it had incurred in the project. The tribunal rejected both the claim and the counterclaim.[58] Klöckner requested annulment invoking three of the grounds listed in Art. 52(1): manifest excess of powers; serious departure from a fundamental rule of procedure; and failure to state the reasons for the award. The decision of the *ad hoc* Committee (*Klöckner I*) annulled the award.[59] It found that the tribunal, by postulating rather than demonstrating the existence of relevant principles, had failed to apply the proper law, thereby manifestly exceeding its powers. The *ad hoc* Committee also found that the tribunal had failed in its duty to state reasons by failing to deal with several crucial questions that had been submitted to it.

The dispute was resubmitted to a second tribunal which rendered an award that has remained unpublished. Both parties requested annulment of the second award. The decision of the second *ad hoc* Committee (*Klöckner II*) rejected the requests for annulment.[60]

Amco v. Indonesia[61] arose from agreements to develop and manage a hotel and office block in Indonesia. The project proceeded and the hotel was in operation when in 1980 a dispute arose between the investor and its local partner PT Wisma. As a consequence, PT Wisma took over control of the hotel with the assistance of members of the Indonesian armed forces. Shortly thereafter, the Indonesian authorities revoked the claimant's investment licence citing as grounds that the investor had not itself discharged its management obligations but had handed management over to another company and that the investor had not invested the full US$ 3 million in equity capital. Amco submitted a request for ICSID arbitration. After finding that it had jurisdiction[62] the tribunal made an award in favour of the claimant. Indonesia requested annulment relying on three of the grounds listed in Art. 52(1): excess of powers; serious departure from a fundamental rule of procedure; and failure to state reasons for the award.

The decision of the *ad hoc* Committee (*Amco I*) annulled the award, with the exception of the tribunal's finding as to the illegality of the hotel's armed takeover.[63] The *ad hoc* Committee found that the tribunal had correctly identified the proper law but had failed to apply it when calculating the shortfall of the amount that had been invested. It followed that the tribunal's finding as to the illegality of the withdrawal of the investment licence, its findings on the amount of damages and its rejection of certain Indonesian counter-claims had to be annulled as well. The case was resubmitted to a new tribunal which rendered a preliminary Decision on Jurisdiction[64] determining

---

58. *Klöckner v. Cameroon*, Award, 21 October 1983, 2 ICSID Reports 9.

59. *Klöckner v. Cameroon*, Decision on Annulment, 3 May 1985, 2 ICSID Reports 95.

60. Decision reached on 17 May 1990.

61. For a more extensive summary on this highly complex case see 1 ICSID Reports 377.

62. *Amco v. Indonesia*, Decision on Jurisdiction, 25 September 1983, 1 ICSID Reports 389.

63. *Amco v. Indonesia*, Decision on Annulment, 16 May 1986, 1 ICSID Reports 509. See also LEIGH, "Arbitration – Annulment of Arbitral Award for Failure to Apply Law Applicable Under ICSID Convention and Failure to State Sufficiently Pertinent Reasons", 81 American Journal of International Law (1987) p. 222.

64. *Amco v. Indonesia,* Resubmitted Case: Decision on Jurisdiction, 10 May 1988, 1 ICSID Reports 543. See also CURTIS, "Amco v Indonesia", 83 American Journal of International Law (1988) p. 106.

mainly which parts of the award had been annulled and which were res judicata. In a new award on the merits,[65] the new tribunal awarded damages to Amco for the general disturbance entailed by the loss of the right to manage. Both parties requested annulment of the second award. The decision of the second *ad hoc* Committee (*Amco II*) rejected the requests for annulment.[66]

MINE v. Guinea[67] arose from contracts for the creation of facilities to ship bauxite. The tribunal held that Guinea had breached its contractual obligation and awarded damages to MINE.[68] The parties had agreed on Guinean law and the tribunal applied the corresponding provisions of the French Civil Code on breach of contract. The tribunal awarded lost profits but rejected the profit projections submitted by MINE as too speculative. Guinea requested annulment of the award. It claimed excess of powers, a serious departure from a fundamental rule of procedure and failure to state reasons for the award. The *ad hoc* Committee[69] did not annul the portion of the award which had found Guinea to be in breach of contract. It did annul the damages section of the award. In the *ad hoc* Committee's view, the tribunal had correctly applied the proper law, but it had failed to deal with questions raised by Guinea, the answers to which might have affected the damages awarded. In addition, the tribunal had contradicted itself in adopting its damages theory.

MINE resubmitted the damages question for decision by a new tribunal. The parties subsequently reached a settlement and by agreement the proceedings were discontinued.[70]

As is well known, the decisions annulling awards in *Klöckner I* and *Amco I* have attracted severe criticism.[71] Professor Schreuer summarizes this criticism as follows and gives an interesting overall assessment (footnotes omitted):[72]

> "It has been argued that the two *ad hoc* Committees exceeded their authority by re-examining the merits of the cases, thereby transgressing the line between annulment and appeal. The extensive interpretation the two *ad hoc* Committees applied to their review function was said to have affected one of arbitration's primary goals, the finality of awards. In *Amco v. Indonesia*, the new tribunal also intimated that the *ad hoc* Committee had made findings that were *obiter* to the annulment function, and had expressed views beyond its jurisdiction *ratione materiae*. It has also been argued that in *SPP v. Egypt* the uncertainty surrounding the outcome of annulment proceedings was used for leverage to obtain a favourable settlement, or at least as delaying tactics to postpone compliance.

---

65. *Amco v. Indonesia*, Resubmitted Case: Award, 5 June 1990, 1 ICSID Reports 569. See also GAILLARD, "Observations", 118 Journal du Droit International (1991) pp. 181-188.

66. Decision, 17 December 1992.

67. For a more extensive summary of this case see 4 ICSID Reports 55.

68. *MINE v. Guinea*, Award, 6 January 1988, 4 ICSID Reports 61.

69. *MINE v. Guinea*, Decision on Annulment, 22 December 1989, 4 ICSID Reports 79.

70. Order taking note of the discontinuance issued by the Secretary-General on 20 November 1990.

71. See SCHREUER, *op. cit.*, fn. 3, pp. 901-902, fns. 56-62.

72. *Ibid.*, pp. 901-903.

Some authors even spoke of a breakdown of ICSID's control system, which posed a grave risk to the institution's future effectiveness. A number of suggestions were made to reform the system.

A small group of commentators have defended the approach adopted in these early annulment cases. They have described any transgressions by the two *ad hoc* Committees as minor or have actually welcomed the activist role taken by them.

Subsequent *ad hoc* committees have adopted a much more cautious approach. The decision in *MINE* addresses most of the concerns that had been voiced with regard to the earlier two Decisions. The refusal to annul the Awards in *Klöckner II* and *Amco II* speaks for itself. It may, therefore, be said that after a difficult start the system of annulment has now found its proper balance."

Since Professor Schreuer made those comments there has been one further annulment decision. On 5 February 2002, the *ad hoc* Committee in *Wena Hotels v. Egypt* dismissed the request for annulment, upholding the tribunal's award in its entirety.[73] However, the decision is not yet available.

As to the methodology of *ad hoc* committees and their interpretation of Art. 52 there seems to be little uniformity. While it is apparently accepted that any problems of interpretation have to be resolved in accordance with the principles and rules of treaty interpretation generally recognized in international law,[74] there has been no explicit adoption of either a restrictive or expansive approach to the grounds for annulment. The *MINE ad hoc* Committee said:[75]

"The fact that annulment is a limited ... remedy might suggest either that the terms of Article 52(1) ... should be strictly construed or, on the contrary, that they should be given a liberal interpretation since they represent the only remedy against unjust awards. The Committee has no difficulty in rejecting either suggestion. In its view, Article 52(1) should be interpreted in accordance with its object and purpose, which excludes ... review ... on the merits and ... an unwarranted refusal to give full effect to it within the limited but important area for which it was intended."

However, the *Klöckner I ad hoc* Committee[76] has noted that the language of Art. 52 which includes the words "manifestly exceeded its powers" and "a serious departure from a fundamental rule of procedure" demands a cautious approach. There has been no consistent view as to a presumption in favour of the validity of awards.[77] Overall one has the impression that predicting the outcome of annulment proceedings is difficult in view of the absence of any authoritative statement of the relevant principles and the changing personnel of annulment committees.

---

73. Noted at www.worldbank.org/icsid/cases/conclude.htm.
74. *Amco v. Indonesia*, Decision on Annulment, 16 May 1986, 1 ICSID Reports 514.
75. *MINE v. Guinea*, Decision on Annulment, 22 December 1989, 4 ICSID Reports 85, para. 4.05.
76. *Klöckner v. Cameroon*, Decision on Annulment, 3 May 1985, 2 ICSID Reports 97.
77. SCHREUER, *op. cit.*, fn. 3, p. 986.

IX.   DISCUSSION OF POSSIBLE SOLUTIONS – CONCLUDING OBSERVATIONS

To the extent that a national court may be regarded as an inappropriate forum for determining matters of state responsibility or international public policy a number of possible alternatives may be suggested. First, as mentioned at the outset, there have in the past been suggestions for an International Court of Arbitral Awards. At the LCIA Centennial Conference in 1995 a proposal of this kind was advanced by Judge Holtzmann[78] and supported by Judge Schwebel.[79] Judge Holtzmann's proposed court would have exclusive jurisdiction over questions of whether recognition and enforcement of an international arbitration award may be refused for any of the reasons set forth in Art. V of the New York Convention. Each New York Convention state would undertake an international treaty obligation to execute judgments of the new international court with respect to persons and property within its territory. The new court would also have the power to impose damages on states which did not fulfil that obligation. The new court would not only take over the functions now performed by municipal courts under the New York Convention but would also be substituted for municipal courts at the place of arbitration with respect to applications for setting aside or enforcing awards. This he considered would be valuable because it would facilitate international contract negotiations by removing a difficulty which parties often faced in reaching agreement on the choice of a place of arbitration of any future disputes. Judge Holtzmann considered that the new court should apply international public policy rather than attempt to discover and effectuate the public policy of any particular state. Bearing in mind the ambitious and far-reaching nature of his proposal it is of great interest to note that Judge Holtzmann himself considered that while the proposed new international court would be highly useful, the need for it must be kept in proper perspective. He accepted first that in most cases no issues arise as to enforceability of awards because parties comply with them voluntarily and, secondly, that recognition and enforcement of awards is rarely refused by domestic courts.

Judge Stephen M. Schwebel supported Judge Holtzmann's proposal and urged the introduction of a new international convention drafted by UNCITRAL. Interestingly Judge Schwebel proposed that "the new Court would not be entitled to consider the merits of disputes which had been referred to arbitration, or the merits of resultant arbitral awards except insofar as examination of the validity of an arbitral award might require, as typically it would not". The court's primary concern would be for the integrity of the arbitral process. The Holtzmann/Schwebel proposal does not appear to have been actively pursued since.

Secondly, for purposes of certainty, and to address sovereignty concerns about domestic courts of one state determining the treaty obligations of another state, there may be merit in proposals to establish a permanent NAFTA appeals tribunal, composed

---

78. HOLTZMANN, "Task for the 21st Century: Creating a New International Court for Resolving Disputes on the Enforceability of Arbitral Awards" in HUNTER, MARRIOTT and VEEDER, eds., *The Internationalisation of International Arbitration* (1995) pp. 109-114.

79. SCHWEBEL, "The Creation and Operation of an International Court of Arbitral Awards" in *ibid.*, pp. 115-123.

of a panel of experienced international arbitrators.[80] However, a development along these lines is likely to be some years away.

Thirdly, to the extent that ICSID is often likely to be the selected dispute resolution method, there have been suggestions that ICSID should have a permanent review institution.[81] It is perhaps unfortunate that the Convention did not create such a body.[82] The parties to the Convention were mindful not to create a strong appeals procedure, and wished applications for annulment to be rare. The absence of a permanent body makes the system less predictable. This has been compounded by the express rejection by the *AMCO ad hoc* Committee of a precedent-based approach. This proposal would help overcome the difficulties in securing complete consistency of personnel in successive *ad hoc* annulment committees, a matter discussed by Professor Schreuer in his recent treatise.[83] However, as Professor Schreuer points out,[84] the creation of a permanent ICSID tribunal would require an amendment to the Convention, not a promising possibility.

It would be imprudent to form any definitive conclusions as to the need for all or any such possible changes on the basis of the one single-judge decision in *Metalclad*. The conflicting principles of finality and fairness/correctness will often produce different outcomes in different cases and, as Professor Park has said, equilibrium in judicial review is not easily attainable and "legislators and courts must engage in a process of legal fine tuning that seeks a reasonable counterpoise between arbitral autonomy and judicial control mechanisms".[85] Moreover, to the extent that some degree of uncertainty is developing in the wake of the move away from traditional concepts of international state responsibility toward a general system of compulsory arbitration against states in respect of investment disputes, there is no need for unnecessary alarm. We are in a period of innovation and change as the old norms disappear and new principles and practices take time to settle.[86]

---

80. See HART and DYMOND, "NAFTA Chapter 11: Precedents, Principles, and Prospects", in *op. cit.*, fn. 36, at www.carleton.ca/ctpl/ch11papers/hartdymond.htm.

81. See, e.g. REDFERN, *op. cit.*, fn. p. 48 at p. 102.

82. PINSOLLE, "The Annulment of ICSID Arbitral Awards", 1 J. World Investment (no. 1) p. 243.

83. SCHREUER, *op. cit.*, fn. 3, p. 1014.

84. *Ibid.*, p. 1016.

85. *Op. cit.*, fn. 30.

86. One recalls the eloquent ending to Grant GILMORE's work on *The Death of Contract* (1974) pp. 102-103:

> "I have one final thought. We have become used to the idea that, in literature and the arts, there are alternating rhythms of classicism and romanticism. During classical periods ... everything is neat, tidy and logical; theorists and critics reign supreme; formal rules of structure and composition are stated to the general acclaim.... But the classical aesthetic, once it has been formulated, regularly breaks down in a protracted romantic agony. The romantics spurn the exquisitely stated rules of the preceding period.... At the height of a romantic period, everything is confused, sprawling, formless and chaotic – as well as, frequently, extremely interesting. Then, the romantic energy having spent itself, there is a new classical reformulation – and so the rhythms continue. Perhaps we should admit the possibility of such alternating rhythms in the process of the law."

Postscript

Postscript

*V. V. Veeder**

I. INTRODUCTION

As the last speaker, it is my solemn duty in this "Postscript" to summarize each and every idea, argument, question and answer to which you have been exposed over the last three days. All in thirty minutes. And like me, you must be wondering: how is he going to do it? Until a moment ago, I was hoping to be introduced by Arthur Marriott with the same succinct introduction which he inflicted on the LCIA's Acting President last Sunday night; but to my despair, Arthur is not here; and I still have twenty-nine minutes to go. And now I think: if they really wanted a summary or a synthesis, they were wrong to choose me. And anyway, now that I am up here, I can probably say whatever I want. I can change the topic of this "Postscript" standing here; and at an ICCA Conference, possession of the lectern is 10/10ths of the law.

And so that is what we are going to do. In the next twenty-eight minutes, I shall not refer to anything or to anybody you have heard since Sunday at this ICCA Congress. It is possible that, like Yogi Berra, you will experience a sensation of *déjà entendu* all over again; but as arbitration specialists, we can only talk about one subject. And if at the end you really do not like this postscript, please remember that the alternative was much, much worse; and anyway, that it is Arthur Marriott's fault for not introducing me.

---

* Turkey-Handler and Turkey, Essex Court Chambers, London.

II.   TURKEY ARBITRATION

Long ago, in Ireland, as recalled by Mr. Justice Megarry and recorded in Lord Bingham's Freshfields Arbitration Lecture,[1] disputes were resolved by placing a hungry turkey at the end of a long table facing a single line of corn leading to the far end of the table. There the stream of corn split into two separate streams: one leading sharply left towards the respondent party and the other sharply right to the claimant party. As the turkey ate its way down the table, its eventual destination after the critical T-junction, left or right, determined the result of the arbitration.

As a method of dispute resolution, Turkey Arbitration was quick, cheap and final: it was final because, regrettably, the parties ate the turkey. Until very recently, this is all we knew about Turkey Arbitrations. But a few weeks ago, an important arbitration archive was discovered. It seems that Turkey Arbitration was widespread in the earliest of times. Indeed, we need to go back far beyond the 14th century, Lord Mustill's usual starting-point for any proper understanding of the roots of modern commercial arbitration.

From these archives, it appears Turkey Arbitration was widely used by the Druids. They called themselves the International Cluck-Cluck Arbitration or I-C-C-A. In Ancient Britain, as you will know, it was probably the Druids who built the Great Stone Circle at Stonehenge.[2] But, with this archive, we can predict that the Druids will soon become known as the true founders of Turkey Arbitration and as far as we can know, the forebears of modern international commercial arbitration. (As far as we know, because like most good things in those times, it may well be that Turkey Arbitration came from China – or even Turkey).

These archives include a near verbatim account of a Famous Turkey Arbitration, taking place at a Special Congress of senior Druids. This account was recorded by three scribes named as Sister Freedberg, Sister Borelli and Sister Kurzbauer, working with another Druid as general editor, Brother van den Berg. And this is what they described:

III.   THE DEBATE

The Turkey Arbitration began, as always, with the Turkey standing at the head of the table, assisted by the parties' respective Turkey-Handlers, and of course, the Turkey's Secretary. However, at that moment, a furious debate broke out between four senior Druids. It concerned a question which might seem odd to us now, maybe a question designed more for entertainment than intellectual analysis; but it was plainly a very important question to these Druids. The question was: "Do the parties, not the Turkey,

---

1. Lord BINGHAM, "The Problem of Delay in Arbitration", Arb Int (1989) p. 333. (The eventual demise of Turkey Arbitration is surmised in the present author's "Evidence: the Practitioner in International Commercial Arbitration", *Forum du droit international* (1999) p. 228 at p. 231, having much to do with the problems of the "truncated turkey"). I am most grateful to Daniel Wehrli for bringing to my attention Benjamin Zephaniah's poem.
2. Actually, it wasn't; but with Druids, myth is stronger than fact.

control the Turkey?"

Under the watchful eye of the Chief Druid, Brother Alvarez, Brother Smit and Sister Kaufmann-Kohler argued it was the parties who controlled the Turkey. Brother Smit, as a skilful ruse to confuse his opponents, also argued exactly the contrary; but by the end of his address, his meaning was clear – more or less. Sister Kaufmann-Kohler contended that the Turkey could never be bound by any procedural agreement between the parties: Turkeys could not read; and indeed most Turkeys were intellectually challenged. Brother Mustill and Sister Fitzgerald argued nonetheless that it was the Turkey that controlled the Turkey. In previous years, however, Brother Mustill had apparently argued the exact opposite. He was a very wise Druid; and apparently, it did not always appear to him now as it appeared to have appeared to him then.

The debate raged furiously all morning amongst the other Druids. Brother Beresford-Hartwell said the Turkey was a mere employee of the parties, a servant if not in fact a domestic animal. But Brother Mustill said that was impossible: the Turkey was an independent professional person, with a juridical status in Druid law far above the mere rules of Druid contract. Brother Staughton, speaking in a language few Druids could understand, argued that it was the dispute of the parties and not the Turkey; and the parties could compromise their dispute by a settlement at any time, bringing the arbitration and the Turkey to an immediate end. At this point, in his usual unprovocative way, Brother Lalive said the question under debate was totally misleading raising a totally false problem.

And Brother Mustill now said the question was totally misconceived. It depended on what you meant by the word "control", and the word "parties", and the word "turkey", and also the word "the"; and also on the significance of the "?". Indeed, it all depended. Another Druid here interrupted to say that it also depended on the meaning of the word "is" (a word which appears to be entirely missing from the text of the question, as recorded); and anyway he had never touched that Turkey – but this quotation from Brother Clinton is very obscure. It was probably some private Druid joke. At the reference to misconception, however, Brother Brower brought up the question of sex. Some Druid always did.

It is again not easy for us thousands of years later to understand the subtle relevance of this particular argument. It is clear from the archives, however, that many Druids had already noticed that this very elderly Turkey had a strange smile. One Druid said it was clear that this old Turkey had never had sex, ever. Brother Smit said that he thought the Turkey had it almost every day – almost on Monday, almost on Tuesday, almost on Wednesday etc. – but always only almost. But another Druid said: "No: I know this old Turkey: he only has it once every ten years." "But why does he look so happy?", asked a Druid; "Because after ten long years", came the reply "tonight is the night".

The debate then descended into an orgy of insults; and the Druids divided into two opposing camps. Some Druids criticized Turkeys generally, they called it "Turkey-bashing". Other Druids blamed the specialist Turkey-Handlers, the elite corps of well-paid Druids who conducted Turkey Arbitrations for disputant parties. These Druids even thought that the whole process of Turkey Arbitration had been taken over by the Turkey-Handlers. They described a desperate power-struggle between the Turkeys and the Turkey-Handlers. This part of the debate is of course quite impossible for us now to understand. We all know very well that any complex arbitration today requires both skilled arbitrators and skilled advocates; and one cannot work without the other. No one today would think of blaming all lawyers or all arbitrators. Of course, we would all criticize *bad* lawyers and *bad* arbitrators; but none of us here would fall into the same facile criticism exchanged by these ancient Druids.

The result of the debate was apparently inconclusive. It was plainly a great and exciting debate; but perhaps the Druids eventually thought the question of limited practical importance – or conversely, as Brother Holtzmann suggested, so important that this Druid ICCA Congress could not possibly pronounce on it, one way or the other, without compromising the whole future of Turkey Arbitration, if not the whole Druid world. Or maybe it was time for the Druid's lunch.

IV.   INTERIM MEASURES

The Druids understood very well that Turkey Arbitration was a careful, contemplative process. The Turkey took time as it deliberated over and gobbled up each grain on its way to its decisive destination. It took even longer in a special new form called "slow-track" arbitration, which eventually became the normal method of Turkey Arbitration. But what happened to the dispute in the meantime, as the Turkey deliberated with itself? An urgent temporary decision might be required to preserve the status quo. So the Druids invented something called "interim measures of protection".

Here Brother Donovan[3] produced a preliminary draft carved in stone, most of which seemed good common sense to most Druids, except for one part of the obelisk called the "ex parte" part, an obscure Druid term which we cannot now understand. Whatever this was, it was roundly condemned by Sister van Hof,[4] a Dutch Druid. Another Druid from Gaul, Brother Gaillard explained that the answer lay not in heavy stone carvings but in private contract; and he described the *référé* procedure newly practised by the Gaulish Druids.

This was how it worked in Paris. Pending the Turkey's determination of the dispute, a starving mouse would be released on a thin, parallel stream of corn, to make a provisional decision which would constitute "interim measures". Being smaller and faster than a Turkey, with a leaner appetite, this decision could be available quickly and cheaply. Although a mouse was not the intellectual equivalent of a Turkey, this procedure was becoming popular in Gaul; and Brother Briner, it seems, kept a permanent stable of starving mice ready for instant appointment to this most useful procedure. Through all this, the Third Druid, Brother Sekelec, kept the debate calm. What skills he had to deploy over these coarse and unruly Druids: he must have been some kind of Druid Diplomat.

---

3. See this volume, pp. 82-149.
4. See this volume, pp. 150-162.

V. WRITTEN FORM

But still the Turkey could not start his contemplative perambulation down the table. At this point, Brother Landau[5] raised the question of the form of the Turkey Arbitration Agreement.

He argued that it should never take the written form; and he spoke eloquently with a mass of research to support his arguments. Indeed, he achieved the near impossible: he spoke in footnotes. As the sun rose and fell, he proved his case to the entire satisfaction of almost all the Druids. No one could justify the waste of obelisks, stone masons, money and time required to satisfy a rule that Turkey Arbitration Agreements should be made in writing; and no Druid could think of a good reason why there should ever be a written form, notwithstanding the parties' oral consent, as a ritualistic pre-condition of Turkey Arbitration.

But since the Druids had no such written rule and could not believe that anyone would be foolish enough ever to introduce such a rule in the future, this debate raised no practical problem for the Druids; and the exchange was less lively than before. Possibly the Druids were by now intellectually exhausted. Or maybe it was time for their tea.

VI. CONCILIATION

The next debate concerned the Model Law on Turkey Conciliation. There was a great contribution from Sister Matias,[6] but Brother Sekolec stopped the most interesting part of the debate: how conciliation settlements could be enforced throughout the Druid world. Or perhaps they could not be enforced; and as the Druid diplomat, he was rightly protecting the Druids' feelings against premature disappointment. The archives reveal nothing more; and it is possible that this part of the debate was being reserved for another future congress or working group elsewhere.

VII. OTHER DRUID TOPICS

The Congress continued over the next several days, much facilitated by the absence of alcohol at midday. Whether this was a local tradition or the frugality of the occasion, the scribes do not reveal. The archives next describe a debate about illegality. Brother Kreindler[7] described in detail what naughty parties did; and how Turkeys could be corrupted by evil and particularly evil doings by Turkey-Handlers. Sister Mills[8] expressed the despairing conclusion that corruption was rife throughout the world of Druids. It was true that the Druid world was venal and corrupt; but most Druids felt

---

5. See this volume, pp. 19-81.
6. See this volume, pp. 190-208.
7. See this volume, pp. 209-260.
8. See this volume, pp. 288-299.

that was not true of Turkey Arbitration. Corruption could make good headlines and fine stories; but it was the rare exception amongst Turkeys, if and when it occurred at all. Indeed, if Turkey Arbitrators had grown rich from corruption in Turkey Arbitration, how come they were still Turkeys practising Turkey Arbitration with that process's inevitable finality?

Brother Hanotiau[9] then described how love was also impermissible in Turkey Arbitration, particularly between a Turkey and the parties or their respective Turkey-Handlers. Love was thoroughly incompatible with the Turkey's duty of independence and impartiality. The Druids were puzzled at his survey: If love and evil were both forbidden, what was left?

Sister Majeed here interposed to say that, culturally, it was very important for the Turkey to attend with cultural sympathy to both sides of each grain of corn, particularly the eastern, rather than the western side. And Brother Hussain expressed concern that some Turkeys attended more to the north side of the grain and less to the south. All this sounds reasonable to us now; but apparently to many Druids then, there was much concern at these statements.

There was then reference to a famous story of the allegedly kidnapped Turkey. Apparently, it was said, one party had abducted a Turkey midway through an arbitration, wrung its neck, plucked its feathers, stuffed and roasted it in order deliberately to thwart the arbitral process. The Druids felt there was probably another side to this story. There usually was. Maybe this party did not actually stuff the Turkey; or maybe the whole thing was only a question of timing. But if this other side of the story is never told, then only the first side can be publicly known; and the Druids felt that no one could complain at being misunderstood. Nevertheless, it was not felt that Turkey-kidnapping had become a practical problem for Turkey Arbitration, not yet.

Questions of general naughtiness were then pursued by Brothers Lew and Paulsson. Surprisingly one Druid, Brother Tytell,[10] even showed the others how to forge documents. Seen from our modern perspective, was this really wise? It could have lead to the most important disputes being subjected to forgeries. And then there was more bashing, again, of the specialist Turkey-Handlers; and still more discussion of cultural differences between both Turkeys and Turkey-Handlers. It seems that we are wrong in thinking that Druids formed a homogeneous society: in fact their flowing white robes hid vast differences between North Druids, South Druids, East Druids and West Druids – and Turkey-Handlers. Brother Craig was nevertheless very optimistic: he expressed great confidence in the new facilities for training young Turkey-Handlers, especially in Vienna; and he also described breeding developments to produce a Model Super-Turkey which would eliminate many national differences in Turkeys.

Sister Diamond[11] spoke next on the psychology of the Turkey: it had to be neutral, it had to earn the trust of the parties and it had to treat them with respect and dignity. Less was said about the parties' treatment of the Turkey: the age of deference to Turkeys was clearly over; and the Druids all knew of cases where the losing party had

---

9. See this volume, pp. 261-287.

10. See this volume, pp. 314-324.

11. See this volume, pp. 327-342.

not hesitated to denigrate the adjudicating Turkey. This is of course all foreign to us now: no party would now criticize arbitrators for anything. Brother Abraham, Sister Whitesell[12] and Sister Giovannini[13] then added their generous contributions; and all were well received by the Druids.

The last debate was conducted by Brothers Blackaby,[14] Böckstiegel,[15] Lalive,[16] Park, Aguilar Alvarez,[17] Yanase[18] and Williams.[19] Space does not permit us to describe this debate here; but it is surprising that these Druids in ancient times had such sophisticated concepts for international investment. Or is it possible that these archives were doctored by a malevolent Druid who attended Brother Tytell's lecture? Whatever the explanation, we must be cautious in reading this account of so-called "Turkey Arbitration under Investment Treaties".

Here the records suddenly come to an end. Maybe Brother van den Berg's editorial functions were diverted to completing the second edition of his famous comparative work on the enforcement of Turkey Arbitration Awards; but then maybe not. There was obviously supposed to be a summary of this ICCA Congress in the form of a postscript; but the designated Druid probably failed or refused to do it. Or perhaps he was introduced by Brother Marriott.

VIII.   *PLUS ÇA CHANGE, PLUS C'EST LA MÊME CHOSE*

Let us now leave Turkey Arbitration and move forward several thousand years, to an issue which, unlike Turkey Arbitration, increasingly bedevils transnational commercial arbitration. In 1925, Alfred Hayes wrote a poem which became a famous American song:

> "I dreamed I saw Joe Hill Last night
> Alive as You and Me
> Says I: 'But Joe, you're ten years dead'
> 'I never died' says he ...
>
> 'In Salt Lake City, Joe by God' says I
> Him standing by my bed
> 'They framed you on a murder charge'
> says Joe: 'But I ain't dead' ...."

---

12. See this volume, pp. 343-347.
13. See this volume, pp. 348-352.
14. See this volume, pp. 355-365.
15. See this volume, pp. 366-375.
16. See this volume, pp. 376-391.
17. See this volume, pp. 392-425.
18. See this volume, pp. 426-443.
19. See this volume, pp. 444-467.

But Joe Hill was dead: he was executed at sunrise on 19 November 1915 in the Utah State Penitentiary; and Joe Hill was not his real name. He was baptised Joel Emmanuel Haggland in Gavle, in Sweden; and he was a Swedish national. After his trial in Salt Lake City, widely perceived as a denial of justice around the world, the Swedish Government appealed for clemency towards their citizen, as did President Woodrow Wilson. But the Governor of Utah disregarded all appeals; and Joe Hill was executed. *Plus ça change* ....
As we heard from Donald Donovan at this ICCA Congress, history repeated itself recently with the two cases brought before the International Court of Justice by Paraguay and Germany; and the United States' subsequent refusal to stay the execution of their foreign nationals in violation of the ICJ's orders on interim measures. These cases represent an unprecedented assertion of national sovereignty by a state otherwise firmly committed to justice and the rule of international law, in word and deed.

How all this relates to international commercial arbitration was well put by Fali Nariman at the UN birthday celebrations for the New York Convention a few years ago, when he cited the Paraguay case. As he explained, public policy, or state policy, or overriding national interest, even or particularly if democratically expressed, can arise in any country at any time, North, South, East and West. Let not the first world, with false indignation, point the finger too readily at countries other than its own, including now Pakistan or Bangladesh or Indonesia as we have heard this week. Equally, let us be aware that the whirlwind of powerful state interests can deprive the developing and the developed world of the best advantages of international commercial arbitration in banking, investment and trade, so vital to their long-term common interests. There is no easy or quick solution; but in the conflict between short-term state interests and these long-term advantages, let us not like the Druids disembowel the Turkey and destroy international commercial arbitration where that process is most needed.

ICCA is the world's arbitration forum where, thankfully, everyone can speak out, right or wrong – from North and South, East and West, both Turkeys and Turkey-Handlers. If right, we all learn; and if wrong, it is possible that an answer can eventually be found. In the field of international commercial arbitration, there is only one reality; and that is the perception of reality, even if it is sometimes a misperception. It is not easy today being an international arbitrator or practitioner; it may become increasingly difficult; but at ICCA Congresses such as this, possible solutions and apparent problems can be debated across all the world's frontiers, cultures and misperceptions. And that open debate ensures that international arbitration today is far better than the Druids' Turkey Arbitration.

An Irrelevant Annex
(Or the Anthem of the Turkey Arbitrator)

Talking Turkeys

Benjamin Zepaniah

Be nice to yu turkeys dis christmas
Cos turkeys jus wanna hav fun
Turkeys are cool, turkeys are wicked
An every turkey has a Mum.
Be nice to yu turkeys dis christmas,
Don't eat it, keep it alive,
It could be yu mate an not on yu plate
Say, Yo! Turkey I'm on your side.

I got lots of friends who are turkeys
An all of dem fear christmas time,
Dey wanna enjoy it, dey say humans destroy it
An humans are out of dere mind,
Yeah, I got lots of friends who are turkeys
Dey all hav a right to a life,
Not to be caged up an genetically made up
By any farmer an his wife.

Turkeys jus wanna play reggae
Turkeys jus wanna hip-hop
Can yu imagine a nice young turkey saying,
"I cannot wait for de chop"?
Turkeys like getting presents, dey wanna watch christmas TV,
Turkeys hav brains an turkeys feel pain
In many ways like yu and me.

I once knew a turkey called Turkey
He said "Benji explain to me please.
Who put de turkey in christmas
An what happen to christmas trees?"
I said, "I am not too sure turkey
But it's nothing to do wid Christ Mass
Humans get greedy an waste more dan need be
An business men mek loadsa cash."

Be nice to yu turkey dis christmas
Invite dem indoors fe sum greens

479

Let dem eat cake an let them partake
In a plate of organic grown beans,
Be nice to yu turkey dis christmas
An spare dem de cut of de knife,
Join Turkeys United and dey'll be delighted
An yu will mek new friends FOR LIFE.

ICCA LONDON CONGRESS LIST OF PARTICIPANTS

Argentina

Tawil, Guido Santiago
M & M Bomchil
Suipacha 268, 12th Floor
1008 Buenos Aires

Australia

Bannon, Frank
Clayton Utz
PO Box H3
Australia Square
Sydney, NSW 2000

Bonnell, Max
Mallesons Stephen Jaques
Level 53 Governor Phillip Tower
1 Farrer Place
Sydney, NSW 2000

Derrington, Sarah
University of Queensland
T C Beirne School of Law
Brisbane, Queensland 4072

George, Patrick
Minter Ellison
88 Phillip Street
Sydney, NSW 2000

Griffith, Gavan
205 William Street
Melbourne, Victoria 3000

Hoyle, Jonathan R.
Clayton Utz
PO Box H3
Australia Square
Sydney, NSW 2000

Pryles, Michael
Minter Ellison
525 Collins Street
Melbourne, Victoria 3000

Austria

Binder, Peter
Wolf Theiss & Partners
Schubertring 6
1010 Vienna

Castello, James
Freshfields Bruckhaus Deringer
Seilergasse 16
1010 Vienna

Frosch, Gunther
Petsch Frosch & Klein
Eschenbachgasse 11
1010 Vienna

Heger, Susanne
Law Office Dr Susanne Heger
Mariahilfer Strasse 105/2/11
1060 Vienna

Liebscher, Christoph
Wolf Theiss & Partners
Schubertring 6
1010 Vienna

Melis, Werner
Honorary Vice President of ICCA
Baier Lambert
Rotenturmstrasse 12
1010 Vienna

Pitkowitz, Nikolaus
Graf Maxl & Pitkowitz
Stadiongasse 2
1010 Vienna

Reiner, Andreas
ARP Andreas Reiner & Partner
Freyung 6/12
1010 Vienna

Sekolec, Jernej
Secretary, UNCITRAL
Vienna International Centre
PO Box 500
1400 Vienna

Wolff, Arthur
Baier Lambert
Johannesgasse 22
1010 Vienna

Bahrain

Zainal, Yousif
GCC Commercial Arbitration Centre
PO Box 16100
Al Adliya
Manama

Belgium

Barnum, John
McGuirewoods LLP
Avenue Louise 250, Bte 64
1050 Brussels

Van den Berg, Albert Jan
Member of ICCA
Hanotiau & Van den Berg
Avenue Louise 480
1050 Brussels

Hanotiau, Bernard
Hanotiau & van den Berg
Avenue Louise 480
1050 Brussels

Van Houtte, Hans
Louvain Law School
Tiensestraat 41
3000 Leuven

Van Houtte, Vera
Stibbe
47-51 Rue Henri Wafelaerts
1060 Brussels

Linsmeau, Jacqueline
Association Gregoire
Rue Camille Lemonnier 63
1050 Brussels

Verbist, Herman
Bogaert & Vandemeulebroeke
(Landwell)
Woluwedal 20
1932 Sint-Stevens-Woluwe

Wazen, Sarah
Hanotiau & van den Berg
Avenue Louise 480
1050 Brussels

Bermuda

Elkinson, Jeffrey
Clarendon House
Church Street
Hamilton HMCX

Woloniecki, Jan
Attride-Stirling & Woloniecki
Crawford House
50 Cedar Avenue
PO Box HM2879
Hamilton HMLX

Brazil

Muriel, Marcelo Antonio
Pinheiro Neto Advogados
Rua Boa Vista 254 9°
Centro
01014-907 Sao Paulo-SP

Nehring Netto, Carlos
Member of ICCA
Nehring e Associados Advocacia
Av. Paulista 1294-12. ander
01310-915 Sao Paulo-SP

Bulgaria

Chernev, Silvy
Court of Arbitration at the
Bulgarian Chamber of Commerce
and Industry
42 Parchevich Street
1000 Sofia

Ivanova, Rouja
Court of Arbitration at the
Bulgarian Chamber of Commerce
and Industry
42 Parchevich Street
1000 Sofia

Cameroon

Ndoky Dikoume, Josue Dumont
Ndoky Law Firm
1473 Rue Galeieni
PO Box 12994
Douala

Canada

Alvarez, Henri
Fasken Martineau DuMoulin LLP
2100-1075 West Georgia Street
Vancouver BC V6E 3G2

Barin, Babak
Stikeman Elliott
1155 René-Lévesque Blvd West
Montreal QC H3B 3V2

Branson, Cecil
886 Walker's Hook Road
Salt Spring Island BC V8K 1B6

Chiasson, Edward
Borden Ladner Gervais LLP
1200-200 Burrard Street
Vancouver BC V7X 1T2

Davidson, Paul
Canadian Arbitration Conciliation &
Amicable Composition Centre
c/o Dept. of Law
Carleton University
Ottawa ON K15 2B8

Doig, Brenda
Torys LLP
79 Wellington Street W, Suite 3000
Box 270 TD Centre
Toronto ON M5K 1N2

Flaherty, Pat
Torys LLP
79 Wellington Street W, Suite 3000
Box 270 TD Centre
Toronto ON M5K 1N2

Fortier, Yves L.
Ogilvy Renault
1981 McGill College Ave., Suite 1100
Montreal QC H3A 3C1

Gauthier, Paule
Desjardins Ducharme Stein Monast
1150 Claire Fontaine, Suite 300
Quebec City QC G1T 5G4

Irving, Colin K.
Irving Mitchell & Associates
4119 Sherbrooke Street West
Montreal QC H3Z 1A7

Lalonde, Marc
Member of ICCA
Stikeman Elliott
1155 René-Lévesque Blvd West, 40th Floor
Montreal QC H3B 3V2

Leon, Barry
Torys LLP
79 Wellington Street W, Suite 3000
Box 270 TD Centre
Toronto ON M5K 1N2

Ouimet, Eric
Brouillette Charpentier Fortin GP
1100 René-Lévesque Blvd West, 25th Floor
Montreal QC H3B SC9

Prujiner, Alain
Laval University
354 de la Corniche
Nicholas QC G7A 2Y4 St.

Rowley, J. William
McMillan Binch
PO Box 38
200 Bay Street
South Tower Royal Bank Plaza
Toronto ON M5J 2JZ

Tobin, Anthony G.V.
Law Chambers of Anthony G.V. Tobin
816-938 Howe Street
Vancouver BC V6Z 1N9

China

Aglionby, Andrew
Baker & McKenzie
14th Floor, Hutchison House
10 Harcourt Road
Central, Hong Kong

An, Rui
CIETAC
6/F Golden Land Building
32 Liang Ma Qiao Road
Chaoyang District
100016 Beijing

Barrington, Louise
Aculex Transnational Inc
16/F Double Building.
22 Stanley Ct
Central
Hong Kong

Beaumont, Ben
1702 Winway Building
50 Wellington Street
Hong Kong

Caldwell, Peter S.
Caldwell Ltd
1133 Central Building
1 Pedder Street
Central
Hong Kong

Cheng, Teresa Yeuk Wah
Hong Kong International
Arbitration Centre
38/F Two Exchange Square
8 Connaught Place
Central
Hong Kong

Cheung, Yuk-ming
Banz Asia Ltd
Unit C 4/F Yun Tat Centre
70 Wuhu Street
Hunghom
Hong Kong

Coleman, Russell
Temple Chambers
One Pacific Place, 16th Floor
88 Queensway
Hong Kong

Downey, Martin John
Denton Wilde Sapte
43/F Cheung Kong Centre
2 Queen's Road
Central
Hong Kong

Gearing, Matthew
Allen & Overy
Three Exchange Square, 9th Floor
Central
Hong Kong

Jeffries, Andrew
Allen & Overy
Three Exchange Square, 9th Floor
Central
Hong Kong

Kang, Ming
CIETAC
6/F Golden Land Building
32 Liang Ma Qiao Road
Chaoyang District
100016 Beijing

Kwok, Ernest
Koo & Partners
21-22/F Bank of China Tower
1 Garden Road
Hong Kong

Li, Hu
CIETAC
6/F Golden Land Building
32 Liang Ma Qiao Road
Chaoyang District
100016 Beijing

Liang, Hua
CIETAC
6/F Golden Land Building
32 Liang Ma Qiao Road
Chaoyang District
100016 Beijing

Liu, Wenjie
CIETAC
6/F Golden Land Building
32 Liang Ma Qiao Road
Chaoyang District
100016 Beijing

Lu, Ren
CIETAC
Shanghai Commission
7/F Jinling Mansion No. 28
Jinling Road W
200021 Shanghai

Sandborg, David
City University of Hong Kong
School of Law
83 Tat Chee Avenue
Hong Kong

Tang, Houzhi
Advisory Member of ICCA
CIETAC
6/F Golden Land Building
32 Liang Ma Qiao Road
Chaoyang District
100016 Beijing

Tao, Jingzhou
Coudert Brothers LLP
Jing Guang Centre, 27th Floor
Chaoyang District
100020 Beijing

To, Christopher
Hong Kong International
Arbitration Centre
38/F Two Exchange Square
8 Connaught Place
Central, Hong Kong

Wall, Colin J.
Commercial Mediation & Arbitration Service
1206 Workingview Commercial Building
Yi Wa Street
Causeway Bay
Hong Kong

Wang, Jie
CIETAC
6/F Golden Land Building
32 Liang Ma Qiao Road
Chaoyang District
100016 Beijing

Wang, Sheng Chang
Member of ICCA
CIETAC
6/F Golden Land Building
32 Liang Ma Qiao Road
Chaoyang District
100016 Beijing

Wang, Zuxing
CIETAC
Shenzhen Commission
19/F Block B, Zhong Yin Building

5015 Caitian Road
Futian District
518026 Shenzhen

Xia, Fang
CIETAC
Shanghai Commission
7/F Jinling Mansion No. 28
Jinling Road W
200021 Shanghai

Xie, Weimin
CIETAC, Shenzhen Commission
19/F Block B, Zhong Yin Building
5015 Caitian Road
Futian District
518026 Shenzhen

Yang, Chunlei
CIETAC
6/F Golden Land Building
32 Liang Ma Qiao Road
Chaoyang District
100016 Beijing

Colombia

Bernal, Rafael
Cra 62 No. 125C 09
Bogata

Croatia

Uzelac, Alan
Permanent Arbitration Court
Croatian Chamber of Commerce
Rooseveltov Trg 2
10000 Zagreb

Czech Republic

Klein, Bohuslav
Arbitration Court Prague
Dlouha 13
11000 Prague 1

Pohunek, Milos
Arbitration Court Prague
Dlouha 13
11000 Prague 1

485

Denmark

Dalgaard-Knudsen, Frants
Plesner Svane Grønborg
Esplanaden 34
1263 Copenhagen K

Gernaa, Henriette
Gorrissen Federspiel Kierkegaard
HC Andersens Boulevard 12
1533 Copenhagen V

Philip, Allan
Philip & Partners
Vognmagergade 7
PO Box 2227
1018 Copenhagen K

Egypt

Aboul-Enein, Mohamed
Cairo Regional Centre for
International Commercial Arbitration
1, Al-Saleh Ayoub Street
Zamalek
Cairo

El-Kosheri, Ahmed
Member of ICCA
Kosheri Rashed & Riad
16, Maamal El-Sokkar Street
Garden City
11451 Cairo

Sharaf Eldin, Ahmed
Arbitration Centre
Ainshams University
70 Nagt Farid Street
Mohandessin
Cairo

Finland

Moller, Gustaf
Board of Arbitration of the
Central Chamber of Commerce of Finland
Ritarikatu 7 A 7
00170 Helsinki

France

Banifatemi, Yas
Shearman & Sterling
114, Av. des Champs Elysées
75008 Paris

Baum, Axel H.
Hughes Hubbard & Reed
47, Av. Georges Mandel
75116 Paris

Blackaby, Nigel
Freshfields Bruckhaus Deringer
69, Bd Haussmann
75008 Paris

Blumrosen , Alexander
Bernard-Hertz-Bejot
8, rue Murille
75008 Paris

de Boisséson, Matthieu
Darrios Villey Maillot Brochier
63, Av. Victor Hugo
75116 Paris

Bond, Stephen R.
White & Case
11, Bd de la Madeleine
75001 Paris

Buchman, Louis
Caubet Chouchana Meyer
49, Av. des Champs Elysées
75008 Paris

Buehler, Michael
Jones Day Reavis & Pogue
120, rue du Faubourg St. Honoré
75008 Paris

Colaiuta, Virginie
Coudert Freres
52, Av. des Champs Elysées
75008 Paris

Craig, William L.
Coudert Freres
52, Av. des Champs Elysées
75008 Paris

David, Nicolas
Total Fina Elf
Tour Coupole
92078 Paris La Defense Cedex

Decker, Micheline
13, rue Fortuny
75017 Paris

Degos, Louis
SCP B. Moreau
3, rue la Boetie
75008 Paris

Delvolvé, Jean-Louis
Delvolvé Rouche
5, rue Margueritte
75017 Paris

Derains, Yves
Member of ICCA
SCP Derains & Associés
167 bis, Av. Victor Hugo
75116 Paris

Ford, Alexandra
Arbitration Chamber of Paris
61, Bourse de Commerce
2, rue de Viarmes
75040 Cedex 1 Paris

Gaillard, Emmanuel
Shearman & Sterling
114, Av. des Champs Elysées
75008 Paris

Gelinas, Paul A.
69, Av. Victor Hugo
75783 Paris Cedex 16

Hascher, Dominique
Court of Appeal
34, Quai des Orfevres
75001 Paris

Henry, Marc
Lovells
37, Av. Pierre 1er de Serbie
75008 Paris

Hertzfeld, Jeffrey M.
Salans Hertzfeld & Heilbronn
9, rue Boissy d'Anglas
75008 Paris

Honlet, Jean-Christophe
Salans Hertzfeld & Heilbronn
9, rue Boissy d'Anglas
75008 Paris

Houalla-Simon, Nadine-Marie
SCP Bore-Xavier
36, Av. Georges Mandel
75116 Paris

Jarvin, Sigvard
Jones Day Reavis & Pogue
120, rue du Faubourg Saint-Honoré
75008 Paris

Kuckenburg, Joachim
De Busschere Kuckenburg
128, Bd Saint-Germain
75006 Paris

Leurent, Bruno
Salans Hertzfeld & Heilbronn
9, rue Boissy d'Anglas
75008 Paris

Malinvaud, Carole
Cabinet Gide Loyrette Nouel
26, Cours Albert 1er
75008 Paris

Moreau, Bertrand
SCP B. Moreau
3, rue la Boetie
75008 Paris

Mourre, Alexis
Castaldi Mourre Sprague
3, rue du Boccador
75008 Paris

Nouel, Philippe
Cabinet Gide Loyrette Nouel
26, Cours Albert 1er
75008 Paris

Paulsson, Jan
Member of ICCA
Freshfields Bruckhaus Deringer
69, Bd Haussmann
75008 Paris

Pinsolle, Philippe
Shearman & Sterling
114, Av. des Champs Elysées
75008 Paris

Plantey, Alain
Advisory Member of ICCA
6, Av. Sully Prudhomme
75007 Paris

Pointon, Gerald
Delvolvé Rouche
5, rue Margueritte
75017 Paris

Rosell, José
Rosell & Associés
147, Av. de Malakoff
75116 Paris

Rouche, Jean
Delvolvé Rouche
5, rue Margueritte
75017 Paris

Schwartz, Eric
Freshfields Bruckhaus Deringer
69, Bd Haussmann
75008 Paris

Timsit, Jean
Conflict Resolution Centre
91, rue de Mironesnil
75008 Paris

Vuillard, Emmanuel
Alstom Transport SA
25, Av. Kleber
75795 Paris Cedex 16

Webster, Thomas
Gravel Otto
32, Av. de l'Opera
75002 Paris

Whitesell, Anne Marie
International Chamber of Commerce
International Court of Arbitration
38, Cours Albert 1er
75008 Paris

Willems, Jane
Lazareff & Associés
20, Av. de Wagram
75008 Paris

Germany

Böckstiegel, Karl-Heinz
Member of ICCA
Parkstraße 38
51427 Bergisch-Gladbach

Von Bodungen, Thilo
Lovells Boesebeck Droste
Marstallstraße 8
80539 Munich

Bredow, Jens
German Institution of Arbitration
Adenauerallee 148
53113 Bonn

Darwazeh, Nadia
Shearman & Sterling
Gervinusstraße 17
60322 Frankfurt

Glossner, Ottoarndt
Member of ICCA
Ludwig-Sauerstraße 33
61476 Kronberg

Huechting, Heinrich
Gohmann Wrede Haas Kappus & Hartmann
Wachtstraße 17-24
28195 Bremen

Hunter, Robert
Lovells
Damstadter Landstraße 125
60598 Frankfurt

Kreindler, Richard
Shearman & Sterling
Gervinusstraße 17
60322 Frankfurt

Mark, Juergen
Baker & McKenzie
Neuer Zollhof 3
40221 Dusseldorf

Nicklisch, Fritz
University of Heidelberg
Am Baechelchen 35
60388 Frankfurt

Pickrahn, Guenter
Baker & McKenzie
Bethmannstraße 50-54
60311 Frankfurt

Raeschke-Kessler, Hilmar
am Dickhauterplatz 18
76275 Karlsruhe-Ettlingen

Sachs, Klaus
CMS Hasche Sigle
Briennerstraße II/V
80333 Munich

Schafer, Erik
Cohausz & Florack
Kanzlerstraße 8a
40472 Dusseldorf

Semler, Franz-Jorg
CMS Hasche Sigle
9 Schoettlestraße
70597 Stuttgart

Trappe, Johannes
Wessing Rechtsanwalte
Neuer Wall 44
20354 Hamburg

Wilske, Stephan
Gleiss Lutz
Maybachstraße 6
70469 Stuttgart

Greece

Dimolitsa, Antonias
A. Dimolitsa & Associates
12 Milioni Street
10673 Athens

Economou, George
Chrysses Demetriades & Co
126 Kolokotroni Street
18535 Piraeus

Koch, Christopher
Georgana & Koch
8 Merlin Street
10671 Athens

Hungary

Horváth, Evá
Arbitration Court
Hungarian Chamber of Commerce
Kossuth Lajos tér 6-8
1055 Budapest

Szász, Iván
Vice President of ICCA
Squire, Sanders & Dempsey LLP
Andrassy ut 64
1062 Budapest

India

Dave, Dushyant A.
Atlantis Building
43, Prithviraj Road
110 011 New Delhi

Dhankhar, Jagdeep
House No. 128
Sector 40
Gurgaon

Dholakia, S.K.
D-97 Panchasneel Enclave
110 017 New Delhi

Nankani, Vikram
218-220 Himalaya House
Palton Road
400 001 Bombay

Nariman, Fali S.
Honorary President of ICCA
F-21/22 Hauz Khas Enclave
110 016 New Delhi

Popat, D.M.
Mulla & Mulla & Craigie Blunt & Caroe
Mulla House
51, Mahatma Gandhi Raod
400 001 Port Mumbai

Sharma, M.
Steel Authority of India
Ispat Bhawan
Lodi Road
110 003 New Delhi

Indonesia

Mills, Karen
Karim Sani Law Firm
Level 11
Wisma Danamon Aetna Life
Jl Jend Sudirman Kav 45-46
12930 Jakarta

Stone, Nick
JL Poncol No. 3
Cipete
12420 Jakarta

Sukirno, Timur
Hadiputranto Hadinoto & Partners
Jakarta Stock Exchange Building
Tower II
21st Floor
JL Jenderal Sudirman Kav 52-53
12190 Jakarta

Iran

Seifi, Seyed Jamal
Dr Jamal Seifi & Associates
125 Karimkhan-Zand Ave.,
1st Floor
15856 Tehran

Ireland

Anglade, Leila
Law Faculty UCD
Belfield
Dublin 4

Bunni, Nael
Member of ICCA
Bunni & Associates Ltd
42 Thormanby Road
Howth
County Dublin

Israel

Matias, Shavit
Department for International Agreements and
International Litigation
State of Israel
2nd Hashlosha Street
61092 Tel Aviv

Italy

Anglani, Angelo
Ughi e Nunziante
Via XX Settembre No. 1
00187 Rome

Azzali, Stefano
Chamber of National and International
Arbitration
Palazzo Mezzanotte
Piazza Affari 6
20123 Milan

Bernini, Giorgio
Honorary President of ICCA
Studio Bernini Associato a Baker & McKenzie
Via Mascarella 94-96
40126 Bologna

De Berti, Giovanni
De Berti Jacchia
Foro Buonaparte 20
20121 Milan

Borelli, Silvia
ICCA Editorial Staff
Via Carlo Mayr 161
44100 Ferrara

Caldelli, Valeria
ASA-Azienda Servizi Ambientali spa
Via del Gazometro No. 9
57100 Livorno

Crivellaro, Antonio
Bonelli Erede Pappalardo
Via Barozzi 1
20122 Milan

Dotto, Massimo Francesco
CMS Adonnino Ascoli & Cavasola Scamoni
Via A. Depretis 86
00184 Rome

Ferrante, Mauro
Advisory Member of ICCA
Associazione Italiana per l'Arbitrato
Via Venti Settembre 5
00187 Rome

Grieco, Antonio
Grieco & Associati
Via Piemonte 39
00187 Rome

Najar, Jean-Claude
GE Oil & Gas
Via F Matteucci 2
50127 Florence

Opilio, Laura
CMS Adonnino Ascoli & Cavasola
Scamoni
Via A. Depretis 86
00184 Rome

Riccomagno, Mario
Studio Legale Riccomagno
Via Assarotti 7
16122 Genoa

Rubino-Sammartano, Mauro
President, European Court of Arbitration
Viale Cassiodoro 3
20145 Milan

Japan

Oghigian, Haig
Jones Day Reavis & Pogue
Syiroyam MT Building 6F
4-1-17 Toranomon
Minato-Ku
105-0001 Tokyo

Taniguchi, Yasuhei
Member of ICCA
Matsuo & Kosugi
7-14-16 Ginza
Chuo-Ku
104-0061 Tokyo

Tateishi, Takao
Tokyo Maritime Arbitration
Commission (TOMAC)
3F Wajun Building
Koishikaw 2-22-2
Bunkyo-Ku
112-0002 Tokyo

Yanase, Shuji
Nagashima Ohno & Tsunematsu
Kioicho Building
3-12 Kioicho
Chiyoda-Ku
102-0094 Tokyo

Jordan

Aljazy, Omar
90 Queen Nour Street
PO Box 921409
11192 Amman

Korea

Kim, Grant
Kim & Chang
Seyang Building
Naeja-Dong 223
Chongro-ku
110-720 Seoul

Kim, Jong-Hee
Korean Commercial Arbitration Board
Trade Tower, 43rd Floor
Korean World Trade Center
159 Samsung-Dong Kangnam-ku
135-729 Seoul

Lee, Jae-Woo
Korean Commercial Arbitration Board
Trade Tower, 43rd Floor
Korean World Trade Center
159 Samsung-Dong Kangnam-ku
135-729 Seoul

Latvia

Udris, Ziedonis
Skudra & Udris
Marijas Street 13/3
Berga Bazars
1050 Riga

Lebanon

Comair-Obeid, Nayla
Obeid Law Firm
Sami el Solh Ave.
Makarem B19
1162234 Beirut

Liechtenstein

Burger, Johannes
Marxer & Partner
Heiligkreuz 6
9490 Vaduz

Fischer, Martin Ulrich
Marxer & Partner
Heiligkreuz 6
9490 Vaduz

Lithuania

Skibarka, Laimonas
Lideika Petrauskas Valiunas & Partners
Labdariu 5
2001 Vilnius

Madagascar

Jakoba, Raphael
Madagascar Arbitration & Mediation Centre
c/o Usaid Madagascar Villa
Vonisoa III Ave. Dr Ravohangy Anosy
Antananarivo

Malaysia

Abraham, Cecil
Member of ICCA

Shearn Delamore & Co.
Wisma Hamzah, 7th Floor
Kwong Hing
No. 1 Leboh Ampang
50100 Kuala Lumpur

Farid, Fuzet
Messrs Azmi & Associates
Menara Keck Seng, 14th Floor
203 Jalan Bukit Bintang
55100 Kuala Lumpur

Pradhan, Vinayak
SKRINE
Unit No. 50-8-1, 8th Floor
Wisma UOA Damansara
Damansara Heights
50490 Kuala Lumpur

Shankar, Mahadev
Zaid Ibrahim & Co
Menara Milenium, Level 19
Jalan Damanlela
Bukit Damansara
50490 Kuala Lumpur

Mexico

Aguilar-Alvarez, Guillermo
Member of ICCA
SAI Consultores SC
Prol. Paseo de la Reforma 600-103
Santa Fe Peña Blanca
01210 Mexico DF

Santibanez, Carmen Lucia
Camily y Valero SC
Temistocies 236 Dep 201
Col Polanco
Mexico DF

Zamora, Rodrigo
Bufete Zamora Pierce
Porfirio Diaz 102-4
Col Nochebuena
03720 Mexico City DF

The Netherlands

Ameli, Koorosh H.
Iran-US Claims Tribunal

Parkweg 13
2585 JH The Hague

Bitten, Jan Willem
Netherlands Arbitration Institute
Weena 666
3012 CN Rotterdam

Daly, Brooks W.
Permanent Court of Arbitration
International Bureau
Peace Palace
Carnegieplein 2
2517 The Hague

De Ly, Filip
Erasmus University Rotterdam
Johan Buziaulaan 33
3584 ZT Utrecht

Freedberg, Judith
Managing Editor ICCA
Permanent Court of Arbitration
International Bureau
Peace Palace
Carnegieplein 2
2517 KJ The Hague

Van Haersolte-van Hof, Jacomijn
De Brauw Blackstone Westbroek
PO Box 90851
2509 LW The Hague

Van den Hout, Tjaco T.
Permanent Court of Arbitration
International Bureau
Peace Palace
Carnegieplein 2
2517 KJ The Hague

Kurzbauer, Heather
Assistant Managing Editor ICCA
Permanent Court of Arbitration
International Bureau
Peace Palace
Carnegieplein 2
2517 KJ The Hague

Roorda, Peter
Stibbe
Strawinskylaan 2001
1077 ZZ Amsterdam

Sanders, Pieter
Honorary President of ICCA
Burg. Knappertlaan 134
3177 BD Schiedam

Shifman, Bette E.
Permanent Court of Arbitration
International Bureau
Peace Palace
Carnegieplein 2
2517 KJ The Hague

Wackie Eysten, Piet
De Brauw Blackstone Westbroek Linklaters
PO Box 90851
2509 LW The Hague

De Witt Wijnen, Otto L.O.
Weena 750
3014 DA Rotterdam

New Zealand

Kennedy-Grant, Tómas
Shortland Street
PO Box 4074
Auckland

McVeagh, Russell
Mobil on the Park
157 Lambton Quay
Wellington

Williams, David
PO Box 405
Shortland Street
Auckland

Nigeria

Balogun, Joseph O.K.
St Matthew-Daniel Balogun & Associates
Kajola House, 5th Floor
62/64 Campbell Street
Lagos

Busari, Olatunde
Akinwunmi & Busari
21 Boyle Street, 6th Floor
Onikan
Lagos

493

Fagbohunlu, John Babatunde
Aluko & Oyebode
35 Moloney Street
Lagos

Gadzama, Joe Kyari
Kyari Chambers
4A Suez Crescent
PO Box 8822, Zone 4
Abuja

Oddiri, Eunice
Regional Centre for International
Commercial Arbitration
1 Alfred Rewane Road
Ikoyi
Lagos

Ojo San, Bayo
Bayo Ojo & Co
Stallion House, 13th Floor, Suite 4
2 Ajose Adeogun Street
Victoria Island
Lagos

Okara, Lyna
Khalil & Associates
Parklane Boulevard, Suite 12
Civic Centre PH
Rivers State
PO Box 8119
Port Harcourt

Oyekunle, Tinuade
Honorary Vice President of ICCA
Tinuade Oyekunle & Co
17 Olujobi Street
Gbagada Phase I
Anthony
Lagos

Richard, Godwin N.
33 Moloney Street
Lagos

Ufot, Dorothy
Dorothy Ufot & Co
Okoi Arikfo House, 4th Floor
5 Idowu Taylor Street
Victoria Island
Lagos

The Philippines

Feliciano, Florentino
224 University Ave.
Ayala Alabang Villa Muntinlupa
Metro Manila

Poland

Wardynski, Tomasz
Wardynski & Partners
Al Ujazdowskie 12
00478 Warsaw

Romania

Babiuc, Victor
President of the Court of International
Commercial Arbitration
Chamber of Commerce & Industry of
Romania
2 Octavian Goga Blvd., Sector 3
Bucharest

Bacanu, Ion
Court of International Commercial
Arbitration
Chamber of Commerce & Industry of
Romania
2 Octavian Goga Blvd., Sector 3
Bucharest

Florescu, Grigore
Court of International Commercial
Arbitration
Chamber of Commerce & Industry of
Romania
2 Octavian Goga Blvd., Sector 3
Bucharest

Russian Federation

Avanesova, Galina
International Industrial Bank
23/8 Bolshaya Dmitrovka Street
103009 Moscow

Bardina, Marina
International Commercial Arbitration Court
at the Russian Federation Chamber of

Commerce and Industry
6 Ilyinka Street
103684 Moscow

Cheltsova, Natalia
Ilim Pulp Enterprises
17 Marata Street
191025 St. Petersburg

Ekimov, Maxim
TomskPodvodTruboprovodstroy

Ekimova, Irina
TomskPodvodTruboprovodstroy

Ekimova, Larisa
TomskPodvodTruboprovodstroy

Eliseev, Boris
JSC Aeroflot-Russian Airlines
Building 9
37 Leningradskiy Avenue
125167 Moscow

Gladkov, Dimitri
Debevoise & Plimpton
13/2 Bolshoi Palashevsky Per
103104 Moscow

Grishchenko, Anatoly
Rosenergoatom

Kabarukhina, Angelina
JSC Tagmet
1 Zavodskaya Street
347924 Taganrog

Kalatcheva, Alexander
JSC Primorskoe Morskoe
Parokhodstvo
Administrativny Gorodok
Nakhodka-4
692900 Moscow

Khvalei, Vladimir
Baker & McKenzie
B Strochenovski Pereulok 22/25
113054 Moscow

Kisseleva, Svetlana
JSC Volga Balakhninskiy
Bumkombinat
1 Gorkogo Street

Balakhna
606407 Nizegorodskiy Region

Komarov, Alexander
Member of ICCA
International Commercial Arbitration Court
at the Russian Federation Chamber of
Commerce and Industry
6 Ilyinka Street
103684 Moscow

Korotkov, Sergey
GM Russia
11 Gogolevskiy Boulevard
119019 Moscow

Kostin, Alexey
Arbitration Commission under MICEX
13/1 Bolshoy Kislovskij
103009 Moscow

Koutylkina, Ekaterina
Zapadno-Sibirskiy Metallurgical
Complex

Krivoroutchko, Evgueni
JSC Omskenergo
10 Partizanskaya Street
Omsk
644037 Moscow

Kutsubin, Sergey
Dolomanov & Partners
Pokrovskiy Boulevard 4/17, Building 1
101000 Moscow

Lebedev, Sergei
Honorary Vice President of ICCA
International Commercial Arbitration Court
at the Russian Federation Chamber of
Commerce and Industry
6 Ilyinka Street
103684 Moscow

Leonova, Zinaida
Bank Rossiyskiy Kredit
26/9 Smolensky Boulevard
121002 Moscow

Maruzhenkov, Sergey
Mezhdunarodnaya Kaliynaya Company

Matveev, Sergey
Corus Trading (UK) Ltd
5 Gogolevskiy Avenue
Building 2
Moscow

Mintchenko, Alexandre
JSC Tagmet
1 Zavodskaya Street
347924 Taganrog

Mnatsakanian, Karina
Sofos Quatro
Office 311-312
Building 1
21 Malaya Nikitskaya Street
121069 Moscow

Okuneva, Natalia
JSC Electrosila
139 Moskovskiy Avenue
196105 St. Petersburg

Orekhov, Anatoly
SIBIR-Airline
Ob-4
633104 Moscow

Rylskaia, Natalia
JSC Stroytransgas
65 Novocheremushinskaya Street
117418 Moscow

Ryzhikh, Alexander
UKOS-Moscow
26 Ulanskiy Pereulok
103045 Moscow

Saranchuk, Konstantin
Flotjurservice
37-2 Prospect Vernadskogo
117415 Moscow

Savchenko, Victor
Sviazinvest

Shmakov, Alexandre
Vegas-Lex
5 Gazetny Pereulok
101999 Moscow

Simantchev, Anatoli
JSC Belon

56B Khmelnitskogo Street
630110 Novosibirsk

Vinogradova, Elena
Institute of State and Law of the RAN
10 Znamenka Street
119841 Moscow

Vylegjanina, E.
Res-Lex
16 Rozhdestvensky Boulevard
Moscow

Zimenkova, Olga
International Commercial Arbitration Court
at the Russian Federation Chamber of
Commerce and Industry
6 Ilyinka Street
103684 Moscow

Zykin, Ivan
International Commercial Arbitration Court
at the Russian Federation Chamber of
Commerce and Industry
6 Ilyinka Street
103684 Moscow

Scotland

Dervaird, Lord
4 Moray Place
EH3 6DS Edinburgh

Dundas, Hew R.
Dundas Energy Services
One St. Colme Street
EH3 6AA Edinburgh

Singapore

Gregson, Neale
Watson Farley & Williams
16 Collyer Quay
#12-02 Hitachi Tower
049318 Singapore

Howell, David J.
Baker & McKenzie
1 Temasek Avenue
#27-01Millenia Tower
039192 Singapore

Hwang, Michael
Vice President of ICCA
Allen & Gledhill
36 Robinson Road
#18-01 City House
068877 Singapore

Khoo, Warren L. H .
Singapore International Arbitration Centre
City Hall Building
St. Andrews Road
178957 Singapore

Lau, Christopher
Ang & Partners
150 Beach Road
#32-00 The Gateway West
189720 Singapore

Lee, Fook Choon
Integral Marine Consultants Ltd
29 Binjai Park
589831 Singapore

Rajah, Chelva
The Arbitration Chambers
65 Chulia Street
#31-06 OCBC Centre
049513 Singapore

Savage, John
Shearman & Sterling Stamford
6 Battery Road #19-02
049909 Singapore

Smith, Gordon
Baker & McKenzie
1 Temasek Avenue
#27-01 Millenia Tower
039192 Singapore

Slovenia

Balazic, Vladimir
Supreme Court
Tavcarjeva 9
1000 Ljubljana

Puharic, Kreso
Permanent Court of Arbitration
Chamber of Commerce & Industry

Dimiceva 13
1000 Ljubljana

Spain

Cairns, David
B. Cremades y Asociados
Goya 18 2°
28001 Madrid

Cremades, Bernardo M. Sanz-Pastor
Member of ICCA
B. Cremades y Asociados
Goya 18 2°
28001 Madrid

de Nadal, Elisabeth
Cuatrecasas
Paseo de Gracia 111
08008 Barcelona

Fernandez-Armesto, Juan
Universidad Pontificia Comillas
Icade
General Pardinas 102
28006 Madrid

Fernandez-Ballesteros, Miguel Angel
Gomez-Acebo & Pombo
Castellana 164
28046 Madrid

Fortun, Alberto
Cuatrecasas
Velazquez 63
28001 Madrid

Mantilla-Serrano, Fernando
Garrigues
Jose Abascal 45
2803 Madrid

Quintana, Inigo
Cuatrecasas
Alameda Mazarredo 5
48001 Bilbao

Sweden

Bagner, Hans
Vinge KB

497

Smalandsgatan 20
PO Box 1703
11187 Stockholm

Bendrik, Mats
Cederquist KB
Box 1670
11196 Stockholm

Brocker, Stefan
Mannheimer Swartling
PO Box 2235
40314 Gothenburg

Franke, Ulf
Secretary General of ICCA
Arbitration Institute of the Stockholm
Chamber of Commerce
PO Box 16050
10321 Stockholm

Gernandt, Johan
Gernandt & Danielsson
Nybrogatan 11
PO Box 5747
11487 Stockholm

Hober, Kaj
Mannheimer Swartling
Box 1711
11187 Stockholm

Johansson, Tom
Cederquist KB
Box 1670
11196 Stockholm

Kadelburger, John
Bird & Bird
Box 5348, Stureplan 2
10247 Stockholm

Lundblad, Claes
Mannheimer Swartling
Box 2235
40314 Gothenburg

Magnusson, Annette
Arbitration Institute of the
Stockholm Chamber of Commerce
PO Box 16050
10321 Stockholm

Nilsson, Bo G.H.
RydinCarlsten Advokåtbyra AB
PO Box 1766
11187 Stockholm

Ragnwaldh, Jacob
Mannheimer Swartling
Box 1711
11187 Stockholm

Romlov, Robert
Advokåtfirman Vinge
PO Box 11025
40421 Gothenburg

Soderlund, Christer
Advokåtfirman Vinge
Box 1703
11187 Stockholm

Wiwen-Nilsson, Tore
Mannheimer Swartling
PO Box 4291
20314 Malmö

Switzerland

Aggarwal, Raghu
Thesenacherstrasse 14
8126 Zumikon
Zurich

Bergh, Bettina A.
Tavernier Tschanz
11 bis, rue Toepffer
1206 Geneva

Blessing, Marc
Baer & Karrer
Seefeldstrasse 19
8024 Zurich

Briner, Robert
Member of ICCA
Lenz & Staehelin
25 Grand Rue
1211 Geneva

Brown-Berset, Dominique
Froriep Renggli
4, rue Charles-Bonnet
1211 Geneva

Dasser, Felix
Homburger
Weinbergstrasse 56/58, PO Box 338
8035 Zurich

Desax, Marcus
Pestalozzi Lachenal Patry
Löwenstrasse 1
8001 Zurich

Dessemontet, François
University of Lausanne
Chateau des Augustins
1015 Lausanne

Favre-Bulle, Xavier
Lenz & Staehelin
25 Grand Rue
1211 Geneva

Giovannini, Teresa
Lalive & Partners
6, rue de l'Athénée
1205 Geneva

Habegger, Philipp
Walder Wyss & Partners
Münstergasse 2
PO Box 2990
8022 Zurich

Hirsch, Laurent
Hirsch Kobel Heritier
8, rue Eynard
1205 Geneva

Ibig, Eugene
Lenz & Staehelin
25 Grand Rue
1201 Geneva

Imhoos, Christophe
J P & C Imhoos & Partners
1, place du Port
1204 Geneva

Kaelin-Nauer, Claudia
Froriep Renggli
Bellerivestrasse 201
8034 Zurich

Karrer, Pierre A.
Pestalozzi Lachenal Patry

Löwenstrasse 1
8001 Zurich

Kaufmann-Kohler, Gabrielle
Member of ICCA
Schellenberg Wittmer
PO Box 3054
1211 Geneva

Knoepfler, François
Knoepfler Gabus Gehrig & Partners
Serre 4
2000 Neuchatel

Koenig, Gino B.
Gloor & Sieger
Utoquai 37
PO Box 581
8024 Zurich

Lalive, Pierre
Member of ICCA
Lalive & Partners
6, rue de l'Athénée
1205 Geneva

Levy, Laurent
Schellenberg Wittmer
PO Box 3054
1211 Geneva

Peter, Wolfgang
Python Schifferli Peter & Partners
9, rue Massot
1206 Geneva

Preti, Philippe
Baker & McKenzie
4, chemin des Vergers
1208 Geneva

Reymond, Claude
Reymond Bonnard Maire Freymond
Tschumy Thevenaz
5, rue du Grand-Chene
PO Box 3633
1002 Lausanne

Roncaglia, Renato
Law Office of R. Roncaglia
7, place du Molard
1204 Geneva

Roney, David P.
Schellenberg Wittmer
PO Box 3054
1211 Geneva

Schneider, Michael E.
Lalive & Partners
6, rue de l'Athénée
1211 Geneva

Von Segesser, Georg
Schellenberg Wittmer
Löwenstrasse 19
PO Box 6333
8023 Zurich

Tschanz, Pierre-Yves
Tavernier Tschanz
11 bis, rue Toepffer
1206 Geneva

Vulliemin, Jean-Marie
Etude Froriep Renggli
4, rue Charles-Bonnet
1211 Geneva

Wehrli, Daniel
Gloor & Sieger
Utoquai 37
PO Box 581
8024 Zurich

Wenger, Werner
Wenger Plattner
Aeschenvorstadt 55
4010 Basel

Wiebecke, Martin
Anwaltsbüro Wiebecke
Kohlrainstrasse 10
8700 Küsnacht/Zurich

Wiegand, Wolfgang
University of Berne
Choisystrasse 7
3008 Berne

Wühler, Norbert
International Organisation for Migration
17, route des Morillons
1211 Geneva

Syria

Sarkis, Sami
5 Tajhiz Street
PO Box 4223
Damascus

Taiwan

Li, Nigel N.T.
Lee & Li/The Chinese Arbitration
Association
7th Floor, 201 Tun Hua North Road
105 Taipei

Turkey

Kartal, Ali
Aybay & Aybay
Siraselviler Cad 87-8
80060 Istanbul

Uganda

Ahamed, Sayed
Ahamed & Ahamed
PO Box 5522
Kampala

Ukraine

Logvynenko, Volodymyr
Ukraerorukh
76a Vozdukhoflotskiy Ave.
03151 Kiev

Pobirchenko, Igor
International Commercial
Arbitration Court at the Ukrainian
Chamber of Commerce and Industry
33 Bolshaya Zhytouirskaja Street
01601 Kiev

Shchygol, Volodymyr
JSC Ukrtransnafta
80 Artema Street
04050 Kiev

Smykovskyy, Vasyl
JSC Ukrtransnafta
80 Artema Street
04050 Kiev

United Arab Emirates

Abu-Nura, Barakat
Zakum Development Company
PO Box 46808
Abu Dhabi

Galadari, Ziad Abdulla
Galadari & Associates
PO Box 7992
Dubai

Al-Mehairi, Mohamed
Dubai Chamber of Commerce
PO Box 1457
Dubai

United Kingdom

Asouzu, Amazu A.
King's College London School of Law
The Strand
London WC2R 2LS

Bassi, Rajinder
Shearman & Sterling
Broadgate West
9 Appold Street
London EC2A 2AP

Beechey, John
Clifford Chance LLP
200 Aldersgate Street
London EC1A 4JJ

Benedettelli, Massimo
Freshfields Bruckhaus Deringer
65 Fleet Street
London EC4Y 1HS

Benton, Derek
Martindale-Hubbell
Holden House
57 Rathbone Place
London W1T 1LD

Beresford Hartwell, Geoffrey
BHA
Cromwell House
78 Manor Road
Wallington Surrey SM6 8RZ

Berkeley, Andrew W.A.
ICC United Kingdom
49 Arden Road
London N3 3AD

Bhesania, Zarina
Debevoise & Plimpton
Tower 42
Old Broad Street
London EC2N 1HQ

Blanch, Juliet
Norton Rose
Kempson House
Camomile Street
PO Box 570
London EC3A 7AN

Bowsher, Michael
Monckton Chambers
4 Raymond Buildings
Gray's Inn
London WC1R 5BP

Brower, Charles N.
20 Essex Street Chambers
20 Essex Street
London WC2R 3AL

Brynmor Thomas, David
Herbert Smith
Exchange House
Primrose Street
London EC2A 2HS

Bunch, Anthony
Masons
30 Aylesbury Street
London EC1R OER

Burr, Andrew
Atkin Chambers
1 Atkin Building
Gray's Inn
London WC1R 5AT

Canning, David
High-Point Rendel
61 Southwark Street
London SE1 1SA

Capper, Phillip
Lovells
65 Holborn Viaduct
London EC1A 2DY

Clark, Victoria
Hammond Suddards Edge
7 Devonshire Square
Cutlers Gardens
London EC2M 4YH

Colbridge, Christopher
Shearman & Sterling
Broadgate West
9 Appold Street
London EC2A 2AP

Colvin, Andrew
1 Dr Johnson's Buildings
Temple
London EC4Y 7AX

Connerty, Anthony
Lamb Chambers
Temple
London EC4Y 7AS

Constantatos, Sapfo
Allen & Overy
One New Change
London EC4M 9QQ

Conybeare Williams, Helen
Jones Day Reavis & Pogue
Bucklersbury House
3 Queen Victoria Street
London EC4N 8NA

Critchlow, Julian
Fenwick Elliott
353 Strand
London WC2R OHT

Croall, Philip
Freshfields Bruckhaus Deringer
65 Fleet Street
London EC4Y 1HS

Crowter, Harold
Harold Crowter Associates
Kings Chambers
Queens Road
Coventry CV1 3EH

Davis, Michael
Herbert Smith
Exchange House
Primrose Street
London EC2A 2HS

Dobry, George
6 New Square
Lincoln's Inn
London WC2A 3QS

Dunning, Graham
Essex Court Chambers
24 Lincoln's Inn Fields
London WC2A 3ED

Dutson, Stuart
Linklaters & Alliance
1 Silk Street
London EC2Y 8HQ

Eastwood, Gillian
Freshfields Bruckhaus Deringer
65 Fleet Street
London EC4Y 1HS

Evans, Anthony
Essex Court Chambers
24 Lincoln's Inn Fields
London WC2A 3EG

Flannery, Louis
S. J. Berwin
222 Gray's Inn Road
London WC1X 8XF

Fletcher, Nicholas
Clifford Chance LLP
200 Aldersgate Street
London EC1A 4JJ

Foyle, Andrew
Lovells
65 Holborn Viaduct
London EC1A 2DY

Franck, Susan
Allen & Overy
One New Change
London EC4M 9QQ

Frangesrides, Maria
Coudert Brothers
60 Cannon Street
London EC4N 6JP

Friel, Steven
Debevoise & Plimpton
Tower 42
Old Broad Street
London EC2N 1HQ

Frommel, Stefan
Institute of Advanced Legal Studies
Flat 19, 169 Queen's Gate
London SW7 5HE

Gardner, Christopher
Lamb Chambers
Temple
London EC4Y 7AS
United Kingdom

Gascoigne, Ian
Eversheds
Senator House
85 Queen Victoria Street
London EC4V 4JL

Gill, Judith
Allen & Overy
One New Change
London EC4M 9QQ

Goldberg, David
Kennedys
Longbow House
14-20 Chiswell Street
London EC1Y 4TW

Greig, Peter J.
Contract Management Associates
The Old Vicarage
Nether Stowey
Bridgewater
Somerset TA5 1LJ

Hacking, David
Littleton Chambers

3 King's Bench Walk North
Temple
London EC4Y 7HR

Hall, Nina
Vinson & Elkins
Citypoint 33rd Floor
1 Ropemaker Street
London EC2Y 9UE

Harverd, Arthur
Carter Backer Winter
Hill House
Highgate Hill
London N19 5UU

Haydn-Williams, Jonathan
Taylor Joynson Garrett
Carmelite House
50 Victoria Embankment
London EC4Y ODX

Heaps, John
Eversheds
Senator House
85 Queen Victoria Street
London EC4V 4JL

Heneghan, Patrick
Skadden Arps Slate Meagher & Flom LLP
One Canada Square
Canary Wharf
London E14 5DJ

Hickman, Damian
International Dispute Resolution Centre
8 Breams Buildings
London EC4A 1HP

Hill, Julian
Old Angle
Dartmouth Row
Greenwich
London SE10 8AN

Hossain, Ajmalul
29 Bedford Row
London WC1R 4HE

Hunter, Ian
Essex Court Chambers
24 Lincoln's Inn Fields
London WC2A 3ED

Hunter, J. Martin
Member of ICCA
Essex Court Chambers
24 Lincoln's Inn Fields
London WC2A 3ED

Jacobs, Richard
Essex Court Chambers
24 Lincoln's Inn Fields
London WC2A 3ED

Jagusch, Stephen
Allen & Overy
One New Change
London EC4M 9QQ

Kaplan, Charles
Herbert Smith
Exchange House
Primrose Street
London EC2A 2HS

Kaplan, Neil
Member of ICCA
Essex Court Chambers
24 Lincoln's Inn Fields
London WC2A 3ED

Kean, Joseph
Eversheds
Senator House
85 Queen Victoria Street
London EC4V 4JL

Key, Paul
Essex Court Chambers
24 Lincoln's Inn Fields
London WC2A 3EG

King, Ronnie
Ashurst Morris Crisp
Broadwalk House
5 Appold Street
London EC2A 2HA

Knutson, Robert
Corbett & Co
Churcham House
1 Bridgeman Road
Teddington
Middlesex TW11 9AJ

Von Kumberg, Wolf
Northrop Erumman Corporation
16 Charles II Street
London SW1Y 4QU

Lambert, Robert
Clifford Chance LLP
200 Aldersgate Street
London EC1A 4JJ

Landau, Toby
Essex Court Chambers
24 Lincoln's Inn Fields
London WC2A 3EG

Lee, Michael
20 Essex Street
London WC2R 3AL

Lester, Claire
Berwin Leighton Paisner
Bouverie House
154 Fleet Street
London EC4A 2JD

Lew, Julian D.M.
Herbert Smith
Exchange House
Primrose Street
London EC2A 2HS

Littman, Mark
Advisory Member of ICCA
Littman Chambers
12 Gray's Inn Square
London WC1R 5JP

Majeed, Nudrat B.
45 Connaught Square, Flat 3
London W2 2HL

Maloney, Tim
Eversheds
Senator House
85 Queen Victoria Street
London EC4V 4JL

Marriott, Arthur
Member of ICCA
Debevoise & Plimpton
Tower 42
Old Broad Street
London EC2N 1HQ

Marsh, Richard
Taylor, Joynson, Garrett
Carmelite House
50 Victoria Embankment
London EC4Y ODX

Maton, Anthony
KLegal
1-2 Dorset Rise
London EC4Y 8AE

May, Madeleine
Martindale-Hubbell
Holden House
57 Rathbone Place
London W1T 1LD

Melnyk, Tanya
Masons
30 Aylesbury Street
London EC1R OER

Merrett, John
ICC
14-15 Belgrave Square
London SW1 8PS

Miles, Wendy
Wilmer Cutler & Pickering
4 Carlton Gardens
Pall Mall
London SW1A 5AA

Mohtashami, Reza
Freshfields Bruckhaus Deringer
65 Fleet Street
London EC4Y 1HS

Moorhead, Martin
Martin Moorhead Consulting
Holyrood House, 2nd Floor
11-13 Swan Street
West Malling ME19 6TU Kent

Morgan, Simon
Simmons & Simmons
Citypoint
1 Ropemaker Street
London EC2Y 9SS

Moser, Michael
Freshfields Bruckhaus Deringer

65 Fleet Street
London EC4Y 1HS

Mulcahy, Carol
Berwin Leighton Paisner
Bouverie House
154 Fleet Street
London EC4A 2JD

Mustill, Michael
Essex Court Chambers
24 Lincoln's Inn Fields
London WC2A 3EG

Nairn, Karyl
Simmons & Simmons
Citypoint
One Ropemaker Street
London EC2Y 9SS

Newburg, Andre
Cleary Gottlieb Steen & Hamilton
18 Cleveland Square
London W2 6DG

Newmark, Christopher
Baker & McKenzie
100 New Bridge Street
London EC4V 6JA

Nowinski, Richard
Richards Butler
15 St. Botolph Street
London EC3A 7EE

Oakley-White, Olivier
Allen & Overy
One New Change
London EC4M 9QQ

O'Keeffe, David
University College London
4-6 Endsleigh Gardens
London WC1H 0EG

Oxnard, Paul
Hammond Suddards Edge
7 Devonshire Square
Cutlers Gardens
London EC2M 4YH

Partasides, Constantine
Freshfields Bruckhaus Deringer
65 Fleet Street
London EC4Y 1HS

Perry, Graham
Buckingham House
Stanmore
Middlesex HA7 4EB

Pope, Polly
Debevoise & Plimpton
Tower 42
Old Broad Street
London EC2N 1HQ

Rawding, Nigel
Freshfields Bruckhaus Deringer
65 Fleet Street
London EC4Y 1HS

Reed, Lucy
Freshfields Bruckhaus Deringer
65 Fleet Street
London EC4Y 1HS

Reid, Greg
Linklaters & Alliance
1 Silk Street
London EC2Y 8HQ

Ruff, Deborah
Debevoise & Plimpton
Tower 42
Old Broad Street
London EC2N 1HQ

Runeland, Per
Kilpatrick Stockton
68 Pall Mall
London SW1Y 5ES

Ruttley, Philippe
Clyde & Co
51 Eastcheap
London EC3M 1JP

Saunders, Matthew
DLA
3 Noble Street
London EC2V 7EE

Sellers, David
Eversheds
Senator House
85 Queen Victoria Street
London EC4V 4JL

Shackleton, Stewart
Baker & McKenzie
100 New Bridge Street
London EC4V 6JA

Sheppard, Audley
Clifford Chance LLP
200 Aldersgate Street
London EC1A 4JJ

Shore, Larry
Herbert Smith
Exchange House
Primrose Street
London EC2A 2HS

Sims, John H.M.
Common Farm
The Common
Leiston
Suffolk IP16 4UN

Singh, Kuldip
5 Paper Buildings
Temple
London EC4Y 7HB

Spence, Malcolm
2/3 Gray's Inn Square
London WC1R 5JH

Starr, Toby
Starr Legal
64 Queen Street
London EC4

Staughton, Christopher
20 Essex Street
London WC2R 3AL

Stebbings, Simon
Freshfields Bruckhaus Deringer
65 Fleet Street
London EC4Y 1HS

Style, Christopher
Linklaters & Alliance
One Silk Street
London EC2Y 8HQ

Tackaberry, John
Arbitration Chambers
22 Willes Road
London NW5 3DS

Trittmann, Rolf
Freshfields Bruckhaus Deringer
65 Fleet Street
London EC4Y 1HS

Turner, James
4 Essex Court
Temple
London EC4Y 9AJ

Turner, Peter
Freshfields Bruckhaus Deringer
65 Fleet Street
London EC4Y 1HS

Valner, Nick
Eversheds
Senator House
85 Queen Victoria Street
London EC4V 4JL

Veeder, Van Vechten
Essex Court Chambers
24 Lincoln's Inn Fields
London WC2A 3EG

Vigrass, Christopher
Ashurst Morris Crisp
Broadwalk House
5 Appold Street
London EC2A 2HA

Volterra, Robert
Herbert Smith
Exchange House
Primrose Street
London EC2A 2HS

Winstanley, Adrian
The International Dispute Resolution Centre
8 Breams Building
Chancery Lane
London EC4A 1HP

Wyld, David
David Wyld & Co
58 Vestry Court
Monck Street
London SW1P 2BW

York, Stephen
Vinson & Elkins
Citypoint 33rd Floor
1 Ropemaker Street
London EC2Y 9UE

Zaiwalla, Sarosh
Zaiwalla & Co
47/48 Chancery Lane
London WC2

United States

Aksen, Gerald
Thelen Reid & Priest LLP
40 West 52nd Street
New York, NY 10019

Alford, Roger
Pepperdine University School of Law
24255 Pacific Coast Highway
Malibu, CA 90263

Arkin, Harry L.
Arkin & Associates
1660 Lincoln Street, Suite 2230
Denver, CO 80264

Baker, Mark
Fulbright & Jaworski LLP
1301 McKinney Street, Suite 5100
Houston, TX 77010-3095

Bishop, Raymond Doak
King & Spalding
1100 Louisiana, Suite 3900
Houston, TX 77002

Bowman, John
Fulbright & Jaworski LLP
1301 McKinney Street
Houston, TX 77010

Cann, Frederic
Allen & O'Halloran LLP
1300 SW Fifth Avenue

Suite 2750
Portland, OR 97201-5617

Carter, James
Sullivan & Cromwell
125 Broad Street
New York, NY 10004-2498

Davis, Platt
Vinson & Elkins LLP
1001 Fannin Street, Suite 2300
Houston, TX 77002

Delman, David
Pepe & Hazard
225 Asylum Street
Hartford, CT 06103

Diamond, Shari
Northwestern University
357 E. Chicago Avenue
Chicago, IL 60657

Dobranski, Christopher
The Ave Maria School of Law
3475 Plymouth Road
Ann Arbor, MI 48105

Donovan, Donald
Member of ICCA
Debevoise & Plimpton
875 Third Avenue
New York, NY 10022

Drahozal, Christopher
University of Kansas
School of Law
Green Hall
1535 W 15th Street
Lawrence, KS 66045-7577

Fantechi, Massimo
Law Offices Massimo Fantechi PC
730 Fifth Avenue
New York, NY 10019

Friedman, Mark
Debevoise & Plimpton
875 Third Avenue
New York, NY 10022

Garfinkel, Barry
Skadden Arps Slate Meagher & Flom LLP

Four Times Square
New York, NY 10036-6522

Goldstein, Marc J.
Proskauer Rose LLP
1585 Broadway
New York, NY 10026

Goodman, Ronald
White & Case
601 13th Street NW
Washington DC 2005-3807

Green, Allen B.
Howrey Simon Arnold & White
1299 Pennsylvania Ave NW
Washington DC 20004

Hanessian, Grant
Baker & McKenzie
805 Third Avenue
New York, NY 10022

Holtzmann, Howard M.
Honorary Vice President of ICCA
630 Fifth Avenue, Suite 2000
New York, NY 10111

Huckstep, Lee
The Halliburton Company
4100 Clinton Drive
Building #1 Room 539
Houston, TX 77020

Kerr, John
Simpson Thacher & Bartlett
425 Lexington Avenue
New York, NY 10017-3954

Loftis, James
Vinson & Elkins LLP
1001 Fannin Street, Suite 2300
Houston, TX 77002-6760

Logerwell, Don
2832 43rd Avenue W
Seattle, WA 98199-2424

McGee, William
Travel Agent Arbiter Inc.
5820 Trinity Parkway, Suite 170
Centreville, VA 20120

Molineaux, Charles
8201 Greensboro Drive, Suite 1000
McLean, VA 22102

Naimark, Richard
Global Centre for Dispute
Resolution Research
335 Madison Avenue
New York, NY 10017

O'Brien, Eileen
Stoll Keenon & Park
300 West Vine Street, Suite 2100
Lexington, KY 40507

O'Toole, Austin
509 Nineteenth Street
Galveston, TX 77550

Paparella, Christopher
Nixon Peabody LLP
437 Madison Avenue
New York, NY 10022

Park, William W.
Boston University Law Faculty
765 Commonwealth Avenue
Boston, MA 02215

Presby, J. Thomas
Deloitte & Touche
1633 Broadway
New York, NY 10019

Raeber, Michael
King & Spalding
191 Peachtree Street
Atlanta, GA 30303

Rivkin, David
Debevoise & Plimpton
875 Third Avenue
New York, NY 10022

Russell, William
King & Spalding
1100 Louisiana #4000
Houston, TX 77002-5213

Samberg, Gilbert
Torys
237 Park Avenue
New York, NY 10017

Schwebel, Stephen M.
1917 23rd Street NW
Washington D.C. 20008

Sentner, Robert
Nixon Peabody LLP
437 Madison Avenue
New York, NY 10022

Sheppard, Ben
Vinson & Elkins LLP
1001 Fannin Street
Houston, TX 77002-6760

Slate, William K. II
American Arbitration Association
335 Madison Avenue
New York, NY 10017-4605

Smit, Hans
Columbia University
435 W. 116th Street
New York, NY 10027

Tincopa, Lourdes
1933 N. Hicks Road 210
Palatine, IL 60074

Tytell, Peter
Forensic Research
116 Fulton Street, Suite 2W
New York, NY 10038-2712

Wagoner, David
International Arbitration Chambers
1420 Fifth Avenue, 22nd Floor
Seattle, WA 98101

Uzbekistan

Zinoveva, Yelena
Almalyk GMK
53 Amira Temura Street
Almalyz

INTERNATIONAL COUNCIL FOR
COMMERCIAL ARBITRATION (ICCA)

Correspondence address:
Mr. Ulf Franke
Secretary General ICCA
c/o Arbitration Institute of the
Stockholm Chamber of Commerce
Jakobs Torg 3
PO Box 16050, S-10321 Stockholm
Sweden
Phone: (46-8) 555-100-50
Telefax: (46-8) 566-31-650
E-mail: arbitration@chamber.se

LIST OF OFFICERS AND MEMBERS

June 2003

OFFICERS

Honorary Presidents

THE HON. GIORGIO BERNINI (Bologna, Italy)
Professor, University of Bologna, Chair of Arbitration and International Commercial Law; President, Association for the Teaching and Study of Arbitration (AISA); Member, Executive Committee, Italian Arbitration Association; Advocate, Studio Bernini & Associati, Bologna-Rome

MR. FALI S. NARIMAN (New Delhi, India)

President, Bar Association of India; Honorary Member, International Commission of Jurists; Past President, Law Association for Asia and the Pacific (LAWASIA); Member, Court of the LCIA; Vice Chairman, International Court of Arbitration of the International Chamber of Commerce (ICC); Co-Chair, Human Rights Institute of the International Bar Association (IBA); Senior Advocate, Supreme Court of India

PROF. PIETER SANDERS (Schiedam, The Netherlands)

Honorary President, Netherlands Arbitration Institute; Professor Emeritus, Faculty of Law, Erasmus University of Rotterdam

President

DR. GEROLD HERRMANN (Vienna, Austria)

Former Secretary, United Nations Commission on International Trade Law (UNCITRAL); Member, Presiding Council of the International Arbitral Centre of the Austrian Federal Economic Chamber, Vienna; Honorary Professor, University of Vienna; President, LCIA; Fellow and Director, International Entry Course, The Chartered Institute of Arbitrators; International Dispute Resolver

Honorary Vice Presidents

JUDGE HOWARD M. HOLTZMANN (New York, USA)

Honorary Chairman of the Board, American Arbitration Association (AAA); Substitute Judge, Iran-United States Claims Tribunal, The Hague

PROF. SERGEI LEBEDEV (Moscow, Russian Federation)

President, Maritime Arbitration Commission; Member of the Presidium, International Commercial Arbitration Court of the Russian Federation Chamber of Commerce and Industry; Head, Private International and Civil Law Department, Moscow Institute of International Relations

DDR. WERNER MELIS (Vienna, Austria)

Chairman, International Arbitral Centre of the Austrian Federal Economic Chamber, Vienna; Former Vice President, LCIA

MS. TINUADE OYEKUNLE (Lagos, Nigeria)
Member, Association of Arbitrators of Nigeria; Fellow, The Chartered Institute of Arbitrators, London; Member, Arbitration Committee of the Lagos Chamber of Commerce; Correspondent Member, The Chartered Institute of Arbitrators, London; Member, Nigerian Branch of the Chartered Institute of Arbitrators; Barrister and Solicitor of the Supreme Court of Nigeria, Arbitrator and Notary Public

Vice Presidents

MR. DONALD FRANCIS DONOVAN (New York, USA)
Chair, U.S. National Committee International Chamber of Commerce (ICC), International Court of Arbitration; Member, Advisory Board, Institute for Transnational Arbitration; Executive Council, American Society of International Law; Board of Directors, Lawyers Committee for Human Rights

MR. MICHAEL HWANG, SC (Singapore)
Vice Chair, Committee D, International Bar Association; Member, Permanent Court of Arbitration; Former Acting High Court Judge, Singapore; Fellow, Chartered Institute of Arbitrators; Fellow, Singapore Institute of Arbitrators; Former Visiting Professor, National University of Singapore; Advocate and Solicitor, Singapore; Partner, Allen & Gledhill, Singapore

PROF. DR. IVÁN SZÁSZ (Budapest, Hungary)
Professor of Law, University of Economic Sciences, Budapest; Member, Presidential Council of the Arbitration Court and Honorary President, Legal Commission at the Hungarian Chamber of Commerce; Past Ambassador of Hungary to the European Communities; Member, International Court of Arbitration of the International Chamber of Commerce (ICC); Attorney-at-law, Squire Sanders & Dempsey

Secretary General

MR. ULF FRANKE (Stockholm, Sweden)
Secretary General, Arbitration Institute of the Stockholm Chamber of Commerce; President, International Federation of Commercial Arbitration Institutions (IFCAI)

MEMBERS

MR. CECIL ABRAHAM (Kuala Lumpur, Malaysia)
Fellow, Chartered Institute of Arbitrators; Fellow, Malaysian Institute of Arbitrators; Member, LCIA; Past President, Inter-Pacific Bar Association; Partner, Shearn Delamore & Co.

MR. GUILLERMO AGUILAR-ALVAREZ (Mexico D.F., Mexico)
Past General Counsel, International Court of Arbitration of the International Chamber of Commerce (ICC); Principal Legal Counsel for the Government of Mexico for the Negotiation and Implementation of NAFTA; Partner, Serra & Associates International (SAI)

DR. HUSSAIN M. AL-BAHARNA (Manama, Bahrain)
Former Minister of Legal Affairs, Bahrain; Member, Arbitration Board of the Bahrain Centre for International Commercial Arbitration; Member of the UN International Law Commission, Geneva; Practising Advocate, Court of Cassation, Bahrain; Barrister-at-law of Lincoln's Inn, London

PROF. DR. ALBERT JAN VAN DEN BERG (The Netherlands)
General Editor, ICCA (*Yearbook Commercial Arbitration* and *ICCA Congress Series*); Vice President, Netherlands Arbitration Institute; Professor of Arbitration Law, Erasmus University, Rotterdam; Attorney, Rottterdam and Brussels

DR. PIERO BERNARDINI (Rome, Italy)
Professor of Arbitration Law, LUISS University, Rome; Director, Italian Arbitration Association; Vice President, International Court of Arbitration of the International Chamber of Commerce (ICC); Member, LCIA

PROF. DR. KARL-HEINZ BÖCKSTIEGEL (Bergisch-Gladbach, Germany)
Professor Emeritus of International Business Law, University of Cologne; Chairman, German Institution of Arbitration (DIS); Past President, LCIA; Past President, Iran-United States Claims Tribunal, The Hague

DR. ROBERT BRINER (Geneva, Switzerland)
Chairman, International Court of Arbitration of the International Chamber of Commerce (ICC); Past President, Iran-United States Claims Tribunal, The Hague

PROF. DR. NAEL G. BUNNI (Dublin, Ireland)
Former President, The Chartered Institute of Arbitrators; Board Member, LCIA; Visiting Professor in Construction Law & Contract Administration, Trinity College, Dublin; Chartered Engineer and Chartered Registered Arbitrator

PROF. BERNARDO M. CREMADES (Madrid, Spain)
Professor, Faculty of Law, Madrid University; Lawyer

M^E YVES DERAINS (Paris, France)
Past Secretary General, International Court of Arbitration of the International Chamber of Commerce (ICC); Member of the Paris Bar

PROF. AHMED S. EL-KOSHERI (Cairo, Egypt)
Professor of International Economic Law and President, International Uni-versity for African Development (Alexandria); Member, *l'Institut de Droit International*; Partner, Kosheri, Rashed & Riad Law Firm

DR.DR. OTTOARNDT GLOSSNER (Kronberg, Germany)
Past Chairman, International Chamber of Commerce (ICC) Commission on International Arbitration; Honorary President, German Institution of Arbitration (DIS) Cologne/Berlin; Attorney-at-law

MR. MICHAEL F. HOELLERING (New York, USA)
Former General Counsel, American Arbitration Association (AAA); Former President, International Federation of Commercial Arbitration Institutions (IFCAI)

PROF. J. MARTIN H. HUNTER, SC (London, United Kingdom)
Professor of International Dispute Resolution, Nottingham Law School; Member, LCIA; Honorary Dean of Postgraduate Studies, T.M.C. Asser Instituut, The Hague; Barrister

MR. NEIL KAPLAN, QC (London, England)
Former Judge, High Court, Hong Kong; Chairman, Hong Kong International Arbitration Centre; Honorary Professor, City University of Hong Kong; Former President, The Chartered Institute of Arbitrators

MS. GABRIELLE KAUFMAN-KOHLER (Geneva, Switzerland)
Professor, Private International Law and International Dispute Resolution, Geneva University Law School; President, Swiss Arbitration Association (ASA); Attorney, Partner, Schellenberg Wittmer

PROF. ALEXANDER S. KOMAROV (Moscow, Russian Federation)
International Chamber of Commerce (ICC) Russian National Committee, Arbitration Commission, Chairman; Professor, Russian Academy of Foreign Trade; President, International Commercial Arbitration Court at the Russian Federation Chamber of Commerce and Industry

PROF. DR. PIERRE LALIVE (Geneva, Switzerland)
Honorary President, Swiss Arbitration Association (ASA); Professor Emeritus, Geneva University; Honorary Chairman, Institute of International Business Law and Practice (ICC); Member (Former President), *l'Institut de Droit International*; Attorney-at-law, Lalive & Partners, Geneva

THE HON. MARC LALONDE (Montreal, Canada)
Ad-hoc Judge, International Court of Justice; Former Minister of Justice and Attorney General; Former Minister of Energy, Mines and Resources; Former Minister of Finance; President, LCIA North American Users Committee; Senior Counsel, Stikeman, Elliott

MR. ARTHUR MARRIOTT, QC (London, United Kingdom)
Board Member, LCIA; Board Member, Hong Kong International Arbitration Centre; Solicitor

M^E CARLOS NEHRING NETTO (São Paulo, Brazil)
Former Member, International Court of Arbitration of the International Chamber of Commerce (ICC); Member, LCIA

MR. JAN PAULSSON (Paris, France)
General Editor, ICCA (*International Handbook on Commercial Arbitration*); Vice President, LCIA; Judge, World Bank Administrative Tribunal; General Editor, *Arbitration International*

THE HON. ANDREW JOHN ROGERS, QC (Sydney, Australia)
Former Chief Judge, Commercial Division, Supreme Court of New South Wales; Chairman, National Dispute Centre, Sydney; Adjunct Professor, University of Technology, Sydney

PROF. DR. HEINZ STROHBACH (Berlin, Germany)
Board Member, German Institution of Arbitration (DIS), Cologne/Berlin; Vice President, Federation on the Promotion of Arbitration, Berlin; President, Berlin Court of Arbitration

PROF. YASUHEI TANIGUCHI (Tokyo, Japan)
Professor Emeritus, Kyoto University; Past President, Japan Association of Civil Procedure; Special advisor to the Japan Commercial Arbitration Association (JCAA); Member of Appellate Body of the World Trade Organization (WTO); Of Counsel, Matsuo & Kosugi

THE HON. S. AMOS WAKO (Nairobi, Kenya)
Attorney General, Republic of Kenya; Former Chairman, Arbitration Tribunal, Kenya Chamber of Commerce and Industry; Vice President, LCIA – Africa Region; Arbitrator, Vienna Convention on Law of Treaties, Centre for Settlement of International Disputes; Former Chairman, Law Society of Kenya; Member, International Advisory Committee of WIPO Centre for Settlement of Disputes; Former Member, International Commission of Jurists; Former Deputy Secretary-General, International Bar Association (IBA)

MR. WANG SHENG CHANG (Beijing, People's Republic of China)
Vice Chairman, China International Economic and Trade Arbitration Commission (CIETAC); Director, The Legal Affairs Department of the China Council for the Promotion of International Trade (CCPIT); Professor of Law, University of International Economics and Business, Beijing

Advisory Members

MR. ROBERT COULSON (Connecticut, USA)
Former President, American Arbitration Association (AAA)

PROF. DR. RADOMIR DJUROVIČ (Belgrade, Yugoslavia)
Former President, Arbitration Court of Yugoslavia; Professor of International Commercial Law, Belgrade University

DR. MAURO FERRANTE (Rome, Italy)
Secretary General, Italian Arbitration Association; Managing Director, ICC-Italy

MR. MARK LITTMAN, QC (London, United Kingdom)
Barrister

DR. ALAIN PLANTEY (Paris, France)
Former Member of the *Conseil d'État de France*; Member and Former President, *Institut de France*; Member and Former President, Academy of Moral and Political Sciences (*Institut de France*); Former Ambassador of France; Former Professor of Law, University of Paris I; Honorary President, International Court of Arbitration of the International Chamber of Commerce (ICC); Member, ICAS (CIO, Lausanne)

PROF. DR. JOSÉ LUIS SIQUEIROS (Mexico City, Mexico)
Past President, Mexican Academy of International Commercial Arbitration; Past President, Inter-American Bar Association; Past Chairman, Inter-American Juridical Committee (OAS)

DR. HABIL. TADEUSZ SZURSKI (Warsaw, Poland)
Past President, Court of Arbitration at the Polish Chamber of Commerce; Vice President, Polish Arbitration Association; Member, Polish Bar Society; Member of the Scientific Council of the Institute of International Law, Warsaw University; Legal Consultant to the Management of Elektrim SA, Warsaw

PROF. HOUZHI TANG (Beijing, People's Republic of China)
Vice Chairman, China International Economic and Trade Arbitration Com-mission (CIETAC); Vice Chairman, CCPIT/CCOIC Beijing Conciliation Centre; Professor, Law School of the People's University of China; Visiting Professor, Amoy University School of Law; Arbitration Adviser, UN International Trade Centre; Fellow and Chartered Arbitrator, The Chartered Institute of Arbitrators; Member, LCIA; Honorary Professor, Hong Kong City University School of Law; Vice President, International Federation of Commercial Arbitration Institutions (IFCAI)